THE SOUL OF A NATION

The soul of a nation: constitution-making in South Africa

Hassen Ebrahim

Cape Town / OXFORD UNIVERSITY PRESS / 1998

.

Oxford University Press

Great Clarendon Street, Oxford OX2 6DP, United Kingdom

offices in
Oxford, New York
Athens, Auckland, Bangkok, Bogotá, Buenos Aires, Calcutta, Cape Town
Chennai, Dar es Salaam, Delhi, Florence, Hong Kong, Istanbul, Karachi
Kuala Lumpur, Madrid, Melbourne, Mexico City, Mumbai, Nairobi, Paris
São Paulo, Singapore, Taipei, Tokyo, Toronto, Warsaw

and associated companies in
Berlin, Ibadan

Oxford is a registered trade mark of Oxford University Press

The soul of a nation: constitution-making in South Africa

ISBN 0 19 571505 5

INDEXER: Jeanne Cope
EDITOR: Arthur Attwell
DESIGNER: Mark Standley

Published by Oxford University Press Southern Africa,
PO Box 12119, N1 City, 7463, Cape Town, South Africa

Set in Dante by PG&A, Cape Town
Printed and bound by ABC Book Printers,
Kinghall Avenue, Epping Industria II

To Ruby and Yusuf, who have been more than patient with me. Your selfless love and devotion have inspired and sustained me through the most difficult times. This book is my assurance to you that I remain committed to helping make this country a better place for us to live in. You are indeed very special people.

And to the memory of Oliver Tambo, Yusuf Akhalwaya, and Prakash Napier. The transition in this country bears testimony to the great leadership and wisdom of Oliver Tambo. Yusuf Akhalwaya and Prakash Napier sacrificed their lives to help bring about the miracle that is today's South Africa. Their courage, strength, and commitment to justice will remain a standard against which I will measure myself.

Contents

Part Two: Schedule of Documents

Acknowledgements

THE AUTHOR AND PUBLISHERS wish to thank Subash Jeram and the Constitutional Assembly for all photographs (except nos. 1, 2, 3, and 41, taken by the author, and no.45); David Goldblatt, the photographer for illus. 45, copyright for which resides with the state; Paul Davids and Katherine McKenzie for help with research; the South African Communist Party for permission to reproduce 'Our Annual Conference' from the *South African Worker*, January 1929; the National Archives of South Africa for confirmation of the text of the Treaty of Vereeniging, 31 May 1902; Lesley Hart at the Manuscripts and Archives Department of the University of Cape Town for her help confirming the text of Albert J. Luthuli's letter to J. G. Strijdom, 28 May 1957; and the Jagger Library of the University of Cape Town for permission to use W. P. Schreiner's notes on the South Africa Act dated 28 July 1909 (BC 112: W. P. Schreiner Papers, Jagger Library, UCT) on the cover and page 1 of this volume.

Foreword by Arthur Chaskalson

THE SOUL OF A NATION is being published at a time when South Africa is a country very different from what it was before the constitution-making process it describes. We tend to have short memories, and in our pervasive concern for the problems of the present, to forget where we have come from and how much has been achieved in a comparatively short time.

We need to think back no more then ten years to the South Africa of 1988, a country isolated from most of the world, racked with conflict, ruled by decree under a state of emergency, with thousands detained in prison under emergency regulations or serving sentences for politically motivated offences. We see also a severely damaged economy, a negative growth rate, political strikes, mass stay aways, and pessimism concerning the future.

We avoided the catastrophe that had been prophesied by so many people inside and outside of South Africa. In the place of a political order based on rigid control through arbitrary and oppressive laws, we now have a constitutional state in which fundamental rights and freedoms are guaranteed by a justiciable bill of rights. In the place of institutionalized racial discrimination we now have a democratic society committed to equality and human dignity. We are no longer isolated from the rest of the world; instead, we are held out as an example to others and heads of state from all parts of the world make formal visits to our country to acknowledge this, and to restore links broken under apartheid.

Hassen Ebrahim's account of the making of South Africa's Constitution is an important and faithful record of what happened during the six years of negotiations that culminated in the adoption of the South African Constitution of 1996.

There were three stages in the constitution-making process. The first was the pre-negotiation phase during which preliminary contacts were made between the ANC, then a banned organization, and the National Party government. Mr Nelson Mandela, still a prisoner serving a life sentence, initiated these secret discussions. Following the unbanning of the ANC in February 1990, and Mr Mandela's release from prison shortly after that, formal meetings took place between delegations from the ANC and the National Party which set the stage for the constitutional negotiations that followed.

The second stage involved formal negotiations to which all political groupings with significant support were invited. These began in December 1991 and lasted for approximately two years. They resulted in agreement on the terms of an interim Constitution under which a democratic order would be established for the first time in South Africa's history. The Constitution came into force in April 1994; it was an interim Constitution because it made provision for an elected Constitutional Assembly to draw up a new Constitution in accordance with thirty-four constitutional principles agreed upon by the negotiators.

The third and final stage was the debate in the Constitutional Assembly itself, the drafting of a Constitution to replace the interim Constitution, and the proceedings for the confirmation of that Constitution by the Constitutional Court.

Hassen Ebrahim explains why a two-phase process of constitution-making was necessary. He identifies the obstacles that had to be overcome, the breakdowns and difficulties which occurred during the negotiations, and the positions of the various parties as consensus slowly evolved. He is well placed to tell us about these events. He was the secretary of the ANC's negotiating committee during the second stage of the process during which the interim Constitution was adopted. He then became the Executive Director of the Constitutional Assembly, where he had an important role in coordinating the work of the Assembly and in the process leading up to the two confirmation hearings by the Constitutional Court.

The commitment to engage in negotiations was the result of a crucial decision taken by the political leaders in the country who accepted that South Africa's best hope lay neither in oppression nor war but in a commitment to reconciliation and the reconstruction of our society. This is reflected in the resolution on national unity and reconciliation set out in the interim Constitution:

> This Constitution provides a historic bridge between the past of a deeply divided society characterised by strife, conflict, untold suffering and injustice, and a future founded on the recognition of human rights, democracy and peaceful co-existence and development opportunities for all South Africans, irrespective of colour, race, class, belief or sex.
>
> The pursuit of national unity, the well being of all South African citizens and peace require reconciliation between the people of South Africa and the reconstruction of society.
>
> The adoption of this Constitution lays the secure foundation for the people of South Africa to transcend the divisions and strife of the past, which generated gross violations of human rights, the transgression of humanitarian principles in violent conflicts and a legacy of hatred, fear, guilt and revenge.
>
> These can now be addressed on the basis that there is a need for understanding but not for vengeance, a need for reparation but not for retaliation, a need for ubuntu but not for victimisation.
>
> In order to advance such reconciliation and reconstruction, amnesty shall be granted in respect of acts, omissions and offences associated with political objectives and committed in the course of conflicts of the past. ...
>
> With this new Constitution and these commitments we, the people of South Africa, open a new chapter in the history of our country.

The foundations of the bridge to a new society were to be democracy, human rights, peaceful co-existence, and development opportunities for all. In the light of our history there were formidable obstacles to the pursuit of each of these goals; to pursue them simultaneously was going to be extraordinarily difficult.

The agreement to adopt the Constitution was welcomed by the great majority of the population. It was followed by a surge of optimism which swept the country when the new constitutional order came into force in April 1994. The euphoria was understandable, there was indeed cause for optimism, but the realities of life and conditions in our country should have served as a warning of problems that lay ahead.

The present mood of the country does not reflect what has been achieved; instead it is dominated by concerns and anxieties relating to the problems of the day. It is natural that we should be concerned about the problems that affect us as individuals; but they need to be seen in their proper perspective. The past hangs over us and has had a profound effect on the environment in which we live. It is seen most obviously in the disparities of wealth and skills between those who benefited from colonial rule and apartheid and those who did not. There are still millions of people without adequate housing, health facilities, and proper education, without access to clean water and with limited employment opportunities. These realities of our society are sobering, but in the light of our history they should surprise no one. The process of transformation was always going to be difficult.

Transformation takes time, resources are scarce and competition for those that are available leads to conflict and tension. In building for the future we need to recapture the energy, the idealism, and the commitment to establishing a new and better society which fuelled the long struggle against injustice in our country, but which in the scramble for a share of scarce resources is now in danger of being lost. That energy and that idealism were present during the constitutional negotiations and enabled our political leaders to find solutions to seemingly intractable problems. Hassen Ebrahim's book, which takes us back to those days, reminds us of that commitment and idealism. It is a timely reminder: we can draw upon it to find solutions to the problems of transformation, and to build a country in which we can all live in dignity, freedom, and equality.

JUSTICE ARTHUR CHASKALSON
PRESIDENT OF THE CONSTITUTIONAL COURT

Foreword by Cyril Ramaphosa

⌊FEW EXPERIENCES could easily match sharing my fortieth birthday with the adoption of South Africa's interim constitution on 17 November 1993. However, witnessing the adoption of the final constitution on 11 October 1996 matched it and more, for at that moment I and all South Africans shared in the birth of a new country.

The collective relief of those in the negotiating chamber on that day, of South Africans throughout the country, and of observers world-wide owed its intensity to the gruelling, frustrating, and yet thrilling trajectory begun tens, perhaps hundreds of years ago, when people in southern Africa first talked about how they were going to live together. From the late 1980s to 1996 that process finally took flight in the ways Hassen Ebrahim describes here: at first in secret, in prison cells and abroad, later in advertised bilaterals, and later still at public hearings and in formal chambers of elected representatives. It was a trajectory that always moved towards South Africans in an ever-widening funnel of interests, rather than abstracting away from them in high-flown political debate.

In turn, parties' leaders and negotiators began to live every day in the public eye of the media, and to become increasingly accountable to that environment like no political leaders in South Africa had before them. At times it seemed that negotiators were less their human selves than the sum of images cast in news reports. The media's coverage, therefore, is the manifestation of negotiations in the public sphere. This was an important part of our responsibilities as negotiators: to be clear and unequivocal, and thus understood when we appeared in print. Ebrahim's notes provide a thorough catalogue of that process, which forms a crucial part of the record of our constitution's development.

There was always the fear, of course, that the manifestation of political leaders in print and film would make them larger than life, and that our attention to the difficult, less glamorous lives of many South Africans would suffer as a result. There may not be a way to know where our attention was most focused in the end, and to what extent our regard for the individual lives our work would influence was shaped by the very process defining that regard on paper. However, we do know now that negotiations teach their participants humanity and mutual respect more than any other form of transformative politics. THE SOUL OF A NATION will remind South Africans and the world of that for years to come.

Ebrahim is honest to the experience of mapping out our new country's basic law: it is tiring and it is full of conflict; it is also a route to a nation's self-realization, and an incomparably exciting process. In the many different ways we as South Africans have taken and will take our lives since its drafting, the constitution will ensure that we remain free, that our rights remain secure, and that our leaders remain accountable. We will also hope that our journey has made the same possible for others.

CYRIL RAMAPHOSA
CHAIRPERSON OF THE
CONSTITUTIONAL ASSEMBLY
1994–1996

Preface

SOUTH AFRICA'S first democratic constitution came into force on 4 February 1997. This was the last in a series of events that irrevocably set the country on the road to peace and democracy.

My association with the process of negotiating the constitution started in December 1991. The years that followed until the promulgation of the constitution were the best years of my life. This book is my attempt to honour this experience. There is no need to romanticise about it. It was gruelling, frustrating, difficult and extremely hard work. It was, however, also exhilarating. It was an experience that placed us at the cutting edge of change in the country.

Much will be written about the great political actors in this grand theatre of negotiations. This is necessary. However, there is also some need to mention the many that worked tirelessly behind the scenes to bring about this great success. It is therefore my duty to honour and pay tribute to them.

The administration of the Constitutional Assembly bonded around one objective – the adoption of the first democratically mandated constitution. The passion with which members of the administration carried out this mission ensured that the political mandate of the Constitutional Assembly was effectively executed. The recording of this history is therefore a celebration of the selfless energy provided by all in the administration.

HASSEN EBRAHIM

PART ONE

Constitution-making
in South Africa

I Introduction

ON 10 DECEMBER 1996, the signatures on the country's new and final Constitution fixed a milestone beside the road of South African history, and marked the way for a new democratic order. The Constitution was also the birth certificate of the South African nation, a text adopted by an overwhelming 85 per cent of the Constitutional Assembly.[1] → p. 263

This Constitution is one of the most advanced in the world, establishing a constitutional democracy in which a finely crafted Bill of Rights enjoys pride of place. It divides government into national, provincial, and local spheres.[2] In order to avoid the tensions and conflict inherent in this separation, a principle of co-operative governance was adopted, which obliges each sphere of government to co-operate for the greater good of the entire country.[3] The Constitution makes provision for an independent and impartial judicial system including a powerful Constitutional Court. An entire chapter is devoted to the establishment of state institutions designed to support a constitutional democracy, and a representative, open, and accountable government is guaranteed. It also obliges the civil service to be broadly representative and to conduct itself in a transparent and accountable manner. In addition, all institutions of government must adhere to strict financial and accounting procedures.

In short, the Constitution establishes a system of government that allows South Africa to become one of the world's leading democracies. This Constitution is the icon of South Africa's miracle, for it is the product of negotiations between political parties that were at war with each other not long before. It is also a political agreement between mandated leaders about what the most basic law in the land should be.[4]

In a sense, the Constitution represents a discovery of nationhood because it reflects the soul of the nation.

A journey through the history of this negotiation reveals a uniquely South African characteristic: an obsession with consultation. South Africans tend to be suspicious of any process about which they have not been consulted, and as a result, the process tends to be as important as the substance of agreements. More time and energy was spent on negotiating the process of arriving at the final Constitution than on negotiating the substance of it. The most vigorous opposition, disruptions, and disturbances took place in support of demands relating to the *process* of drafting the Constitution, and were manifest even in high levels of political violence during the negotiations.

The experience of constitution-making revealed another South African characteristic: the determination not to succumb in times of adversity. Despite their difficult circumstances, negotiators succeeded in finalizing one of the most advanced constitutions in the world with the greatest possible public participation. These negotiations also witnessed some of the finest leadership in South African history; for when political violence and civil strife seemed to threaten the prospect of peace and democracy most, parties were able to prove the prophets of doom wrong.

2 Historical background

THE NEW CONSTITUTION was negotiated between May 1994 and October 1996 in the country's first democratically elected convention, the Constitutional Assembly. However, the demand for a democratic constitutional dispensation was not new, and was in fact as old as South Africa itself. The Constitution was not a product solely of negotiation in the Constitutional Assembly. Experiences in other parts of the world played a role in its development, and many of its provisions are the realization of years of struggle and are imbued with historical significance.

The history of this constitutional development spans nine decades between two major milestones, both peace treaties that ended conflict and gave birth to new constitutional orders. The first was the Treaty of Vereeniging of 31 May 1902, which ended the Anglo-Boer War and laid the basis for the adoption of South Africa's first constitution. This

---

The vagaries of race continue to beset discussions of South African, and indeed international, politics and society. The myriad terms and associations linguistic communities have invented for racial classification leave very few windows through which to look on and speak about the world without committing some or other grave discursive misapprehension. This is a good thing, if only because it keeps us questioning our own points of view. It also means that, until we find news ways of speaking about different-looking people or until we stop talking about the differences altogether, we have to make hard decisions about the terms we are going to use to denote race when we write South African history. In this book, therefore, feeling not a little fettered by their histories and the complex responses they engender, I will use terms we have learned from our long-categorized and stratified understandings of 'race' in South Africa: black, or African, coloured, white, and Indian, among a few others that may become necessary in places. We may not like the characters' names, but we still have to tell the story.

constitution was drafted in an unrepresentative convention. The second was the 1993 interim constitution, which has also been described as a peace treaty that ended conflict. Like the previous peace treaty, it laid the basis for a new constitution, only this time it was to be drafted in a democratically elected convention, the Constitutional Assembly.

The birth of South Africa

The Anglo-Boer War, which began in 1899, resulted in the unification of four independent territories into the Union of South Africa. During this war, many African people associated themselves with the British in the hope of improving their lot.

According to André Odendaal, a prominent historian at the University of the Western Cape, 'in stating the reasons for their surrender in the discussions that preceded the Treaty of Vereeniging in May 1902, the Afrikaner leaders gave as a third reason the fact that "the Kaffir Tribes" inside and outside the Republics had almost all been armed and were fighting against them. ... A fortnight before the Republican surrender, General Botha had declared, "The Kaffir question is becoming daily more serious"'.[1]

The Africans were mistaken, however, for at least 37 472 African people were incarcerated alongside Afrikaners in British concentration camps. The British seemed to have much in common with the Afrikaners: in the Treaty of Vereeniging, clause 8 simply stated, 'The question of granting the Franchise to natives will not be decided until after the introduction of [Afrikaner] self-government'. The repeated pleas by African leaders to the British not to compromise the few pitiful rights they had in the Cape were ignored.

On 12 October 1908, exactly nine years after the outbreak of the Anglo-Boer War in 1899, a National Convention of white representatives from the four colonies assembled in Durban. Whites, who were until then at war with each other, united to form a government that excluded the African majority. Two major debates were to dominate the deliberations of these constitution makers: the 'Native question', and the choice between a federal and a unitary dispensation.

The latter debate cut across the racial divide. For the Afrikaner-ruled republics, a federation would mean that they could maintain their independence, and would not have to succumb to the liberalism of the Cape. The question was also vociferously debated in African newspapers and within African organizations.[2] At the first meeting of the South African Native Congress held in August 1907, the members resolved:

> That this Conference of the coloured people and natives of the Cape Colony assembly at Queenstown is of the opinion that in the event of the adoption of any form of closer union of the South African colonies:
> (a) Federation is preferable to unification.
> (b) That form of federation should be adopted in which the Federal Parliament exercises such powers only as are specifically given to it in the federal constitution.
> (c) The Cape Franchise should be the basis of federal franchise.
> (d) The basis of representation of the Federal Parliament should be the voters' list.
> (e) The present so-called native territories (Swaziland, Basutoland and British Bechuanaland) should be regarded as outside Federal territory and under the protection of the Imperial government represented by the High Commissioner for such native territories, unless or until provision shall be made for the representation of such territories in the Federal Parliament by members elected on the same basis as in colonies forming the federation.[3]

While African people were not represented in the negotiation of the constitution, they were not prevented from petitioning the convention drafting it. The fear of losing what rights they did hold agitated many African people and boosted support for the few organizations that represented their interests. Upon the convergence of such interests,

African organizations consulted with each other to find ways of influencing the convention. This, in part, laid the basis for a single national organization. In its submission to the convention, the Natal Native Congress declared:

> We Natives of Natal, though loyal subjects of the Crown and sharing the burden of taxation, are labouring under serious disabilities by being excluded from free access to the Franchise, and having no efficient means of making our wants known to Parliament and no say in matters regarding our most vital interests such as taxation and other things. We humbly beg, with regard to our future government, for some degree of representation in the Legislature. This would go far to remove all causes of complaint and make the Natives a more contented and devoted people under His Majesty's gracious rule. ... Any scheme for the Closer Union of the Colonies under the British Crown should include a provision that representation should be accorded fairly to all sections of the community, without distinction of colour, and that in Natal, as a precedent to any union with the other Colonies of South Africa, the native population should first be placed in the fair position Natives hold in the Cape Colony.[4]

The report of the National Convention, the draft South Africa Act, was released on 9 February 1909. Anticipating the negative approach of the constitution makers, the Orange River Colony Native Congress prepared for the first joint convention of Africans from the whole of South Africa, with the aim of formulating and publicizing its views on the union.[5]

The draft South Africa Act was endorsed by the four colonial Parliaments and referred back to the National Convention at the beginning of May that year. However, not all parliamentarians supported it. In a debate in the Cape Parliament, W. P. Schreiner, who was also a supporter of equal rights, made an impassioned plea for non-racialism under the slogan, 'Union with honour':

The rights of the coloured people should not be bartered away from any benefit which the Europeans should get. Union with honour before all things. There was something pathetic in it that they should take the rights of others away, and make them a matter of bargaining, and say, 'If you do not give them up there will be no Union. . . .' He would stand out of Union rather than give up his trust in the matter. Federation, Unification etc. were questions of detail; but the question stood out as an absolutely essential one. . . . Union without honour . . . was the greatest danger any nation could incur.[6]

After approval the draft constitution was submitted to Britain for assent by the Imperial Parliament, and African people saw this as a further opportunity to ensure that their interests were consulted. A delegation of leaders, including Schreiner, went to London and presented a petition to the House of Commons:

The Bill now before the Parliament of Great Britain and Ireland for the purpose of enacting a Constitution to unite the self-governing British Colonies of South Africa into a legislative union under the Crown would for the first time in the history of the legislation of that Parliament by virtue of the phrase 'of European descent' . . . create a political discrimination against non-European subjects of His Majesty, and thus introduce for the first time since the establishment of representative institutions in the year 1852 into the Colony of the Cape of Good Hope a colour line in respect of political rights and privileges.

Your Petitioners are deeply disappointed at the non-extension of political and civil rights and privileges to the coloured people and the natives in the Transvaal and the Orange River Colony.

Your Petitioners feel aggrieved that solely on account of differences in race or colour it is contemplated by the proposed Constitution to deprive the coloured and native inhabitants of the colony of the Cape of Good Hope of their existing political rights and privileges. Your Petitioners fear that the franchise rights of the coloured people and the natives of the Cape Colony are not adequately protected under the provisions of the proposed Constitution, but are indeed threatened by the provisions of Clause 35.

Your Petitioners apprehend that by the racial discrimination proposed in the aforesaid Bill as regards the qualification of members of the Union Parliament, the prejudice already existing in the Transvaal, the Orange River Colony and Natal, will be accentuated and increased; that the status of the coloured people and natives will be lower, and that an injustice will be done to those who are the majority of the people in British South Africa, who have in the past shown their unswerving loyalty to the Crown, their attachment to British institutions, their submission to the laws of the land, and their capacity for exercising full civil and political rights.[7]

While the principle of the union was supported, the petitioners argued that 'the only practical and efficient means whereby fair and just administration and legislation can be attained, peace, harmony and contentment secured, is by granting equal political rights to qualified men irrespective of race, colour, or creed'. Despite these protestations and petitions, the bill in the British House of Commons was duly passed on 19 August 1909.

It was however only on 31 May 1910, however, eight years after the Treaty of Vereeniging, that the Union of South Africa was inaugurated. The constitution provided for an all-powerful government consisting only of white men, even removing the minimal voting rights which black people had previously held.

The new dispensation was seminal in the development of South Africa's constitutional history. Quite aside from being the first constitution, it gave rise to two parallel streams of constitutional thought that would dominate the country's political and social history. One stream of thought developed within the framework of the established status quo, while the other was shaped by the struggle of the majority for a system free of discrimination.

This constitution allowed the government to quickly introduce a series of legislative measures, including the infamous 1913 Land Act, effectively to dispossess and disenfranchise African people. The response of the African people was to unite under a single body that would pursue their interests. One of the pioneers in this regard was Pixley Ka Isaka Seme, a lawyer trained in Britain, who immediately set about the establishment of a 'Native Union'. He called for a congress that would get 'all the dark races of this subcontinent to come together, once or twice a year, in order to review the past and reject therein all those things which have retarded our progress'. He made a significant appeal for the unity of the African people: 'The demon of racialism, the aberrations of the Xhosa-Fingo feud, the animosity that exists between the Zulus and the T[s]ongas, between Basothos and every native, must be buried up and forgotten; it has shed among us sufficient blood. We are one people. These divisions, these jealousies are the cause of all our woes and all our backwardness and ignorance today'.[8]

The call made by Seme was answered with the formation of the African National Congress (ANC) on 8 January 1912. The birth of the ANC provided the African majority with a united leadership that articulated their plight and led their resistance, but more importantly, it provided African people with a vision of a better life. Almost invariably the struggles they fought were against a constitutional dispensation that provided the legal basis for their oppression. Accordingly, their vision also included a just and democratic constitutional dispensation.

The rise of nationalism

The Union of South Africa also meant economic cohesion between previously separate and competing economies, affording the British-owned mines greater access to cheaper labour and the ability to transport their goods to harbours for international export. As a result, constitutional and legislative development focused on the restriction of social interaction, and limited the access of African people to skills and the market to such an extent that they became no more than cheap labour. Along with industrialization and the development of the economy came urbanization, greater segregationist laws, and a growing militancy among workers.

This economic boom was soon threatened by a post-war economic crisis, which resulted in great social upheaval. An example of this crisis was the drop in the price of gold from 130 shillings an ounce in 1919 to 95 shillings in 1921. To maintain profitability, the Chamber of Mines decided to reduce its white work force by employing semi-skilled black workers at lower rates of pay, inadvertently fostering conflict between black and white workers.

Politically, the formation of the Union of South Africa made possible the development of nationalism among white and black people alike. The previously separate African tribes were presented with a common authority that sought to disenfranchise them; in other words, they now had one enemy. The Union's new dispensation also paved the way for an economy that was increasingly dependent on a common working class. As a result, this period also saw the rise of the South African Communist Party (SACP), which already had a growing base amongst the white working class. In December 1928 the SACP formulated a new rallying call: 'A South African Native Republic as a stage towards a workers' and peasants' government with full protection and equal rights for all national minorities'.[9]

This was the seed for the concept of majority rule in South Africa, and it provided a basis for the theoretical development of the African nationalism that would develop in the following years. It was based on the following argument:

The overwhelming majority of the population is made up of Negroes and coloured people (about 5 500 000 Negroes and coloured people and about 1 500 000 white people according to the 1921 census). A characteristic feature of the colonial type of the country is the almost complete landlessness of the Negro population: the Negroes hold only one-eighth of the land whilst seven-eighths have been expropriated by the white population. There is no Negro bourgeoisie as a class, apart from individual

Negroes engaged in trading and a thin strata of Negro intellectuals who do not play any essential role in the economic and political life of the country. The Negroes constitute also the majority of the working class: among the workers employed in industry and transport, 420 000 are black and coloured people and 145 000 white; among agricultural labourers 435 000 are black and 50 000 are white.[10]

The social transformation brought about by the replacement of expensive white, particularly Afrikaner labour with cheaper black labour saw the development of a growing number of poor whites. White people demanded further segregation and job reservation laws, and these demands in turn encouraged the development of Afrikaner nationalism. At the same time, the development of an urban African working class allowed for greater unity.

The development of a vision

In August 194 Franklin D. Roosevelt and Winston Churchill signed the Atlantic Charter.[11] This agreement contained eight principles: renunciation of territorial aggression; no territorial changes without consent of the peoples concerned; restoration of sovereign rights and self-government; access to raw materials for all nations; world economic co-operation; freedom from fear and want; freedom of the seas; and the disarmament of aggressors. These principles inspired the emerging African nationalists of South Africa, for it raised the general issue of basic rights and, more particularly, the question of self-determination. Drawing from the Atlantic Charter, the ANC drafted its own 'African Claims', which demanded full citizenship, the right to land, and an end to all discriminatory legislation.[12] This was the first time that the concepts of fundamental rights or self-determination were considered demands.

In 1948 the National Party (NP) came to power, introduced the policy of apartheid, and enacted such notorious laws as the Suppression of Communism Act, the Group Areas Act, the Separate Registration of Voters Act, the Bantu Authorities Act, the pass laws, and the stock limitation laws. Apartheid provoked resistance. In response to these laws, the African, coloured, and Indian people found cause to unite in action, and launched a defiance campaign in 1952. The campaign commenced on 6 April 1952, the 300th anniversary of the arrival of Jan van Riebeeck, a leader of the first Dutch settlers in South Africa.

On 26 June 1955 the Congress of the People took place, a meeting to which all political parties were invited. After nation-wide consultation, several thousand delegates met in Johannesburg to draft the Freedom Charter, which was in effect the first draft of a new constitution for South Africa.[13] The political movement of the oppressed majority had finally matured, graduating from a simple opposition to a movement with leadership and solutions. This charter, particularly its opening paragraph, sketched a vision of what the country's political landscape ought to be, a vision that was to become deeply etched in the thinking of several generations of political leaders. The inspiration provided by the Charter can be seen clearly in the drafting of the final Constitution.[14] Its opening paragraph states:

We, the People of South Africa, declare for all our country and the world to know: that South Africa belongs to all who live in it, black and white, and that no government can justly claim authority unless it is based on the will of all the people; that our people have been robbed of their birthright to land, liberty and peace by a form of government founded on injustice and inequality; that our country will never be prosperous or free until all our people live in brotherhood, enjoying equal rights and opportunities; that only a democratic state, based on the will of all the people, can secure to all their birthright without distinction of colour, race, sex or belief.

The demand for a national convention

In May 1957 the ANC President-General, Albert Luthuli, made an impassioned appeal for a national convention that would allow representatives from all sections of the population to meet to discuss the conflict and look at solutions.[15] His appeal was ignored.

On 16 December 1960 a Consultative Conference of African Leaders was held in Orlando, Soweto, when forty African leaders met with liberal and progressive whites. This conference rejected the establishment of a republic and made a call to the African leadership to attend an 'all-in conference', with the purpose of demanding a call for a national convention. This convention had to be representative of the people of South Africa, and it had to consider a new political dispensation and individual fundamental rights.

On 25 March 1961 the All-in Conference met and called for the negotiation of a democratic dispensation. Fourteen hundred delegates from all over the country representing 150 different religious, social, cultural, and political bodies gathered. At this conference, Nelson Mandela's call for a national convention of elected representatives to determine a new non-racial democratic constitution for South Africa was adopted. The conference resolved that:

1. WE DECLARE that no constitution or form of government decided without the participation of the African people who form an absolute majority of the population can enjoy moral validity or merit support either within South Africa or beyond its borders.

2. WE DEMAND that a National Convention of elected representatives of all adult men and women on an equal basis irrespective of race, colour, creed or other limitation, be called by the Union government not later than 31 May 1961; that the convention shall have sovereign powers to determine, in any way the majority of the representatives decide, a new non-racial democratic constitution for South Africa.[16] Vol.3

The conference also directed Mandela to draw Prime Minister Hendrik Verwoerd's attention to the resolution. In a letter to the Prime Minister, Mandela referred to the rising tide of unrest in many parts of the country, and stated that 'It was the earnest opinion of Conference that this dangerous situation could be averted only by the calling of a sovereign national convention representative of all South Africans, to draw up a new non-racial and democratic Constitution. Such a convention would discuss our national problems in a sane and sober manner, and would work out solutions which sought to preserve and safeguard the interests of all sections of the population'.[17]

Unfortunately, this call, like Luthuli's, went unheeded. In an attempt to gain further support for the idea, Mandela addressed a further letter to the leader of the parliamentary opposition, Sir de Villiers Graaff:

> We can see no workable alternative to this proposal, except that the Nationalist Government proceeds to enforce a minority decision on all of us, with the certain consequence of still deeper crisis, and a continuing period of strife and disaster ahead. Stated bluntly, the alternatives appear to be these: talk it out, or shoot it out. Outside of the Nationalist Party, most of the important and influential bodies of public opinion have clearly decided to talk it out. The South African Indian Congress, the only substantial Indian community organisation, has welcomed and endorsed the call for a National Convention. So, too have the Coloured people, through the Coloured Convention movement which has the backing of the main bodies of Coloured opinion. A substantial European body of opinion, represented by both the Progressive and the Liberal Parties, has endorsed our call. Support for a National Convention has come also from the bulk of the English language press, from several national church organisations, and from many others.
>
> But where, Sir, does the United Party stand? We have yet to hear from this most important organisation – the main organisation in fact of anti-Nationalist opinion amongst the European

community. Or from you, its leader. If the country's leading statesmen fail to lead at this moment, then the worst is inevitable. It is time for you, Sir, and your Party, to speak out. Are you for a democratic and peaceable solution to our problems? Are you, therefore, for a National Convention? We in South Africa, and the world outside expect an answer. Silence at this time enables Dr. Verwoerd to lead us onwards towards the brink of disaster.[18]

This appeal also came to nought, and the tension in the country had reached breaking point. A successful national general strike was called with the start of a massive defiance campaign, during which more than 10 000 people were arrested. There were clear signs of frustration on the part of the African nationalists. The change of tone between the letters by Luthuli in 1957 and those of Mandela in 1961 clearly reflect a growing militancy in ANC thinking.[19] On 31 May 1961 the government, after holding a whites-only referendum, declared South Africa a republic.

This marked a decisive break in South Africa's history, for the country was to slide into an armed conflict lasting 30 years. Instead of heeding the advice of the All-in Conference, the government banned the ANC and other organizations, and left them with no legal avenue to pursue their interests. They found they had no option but to resort to armed struggle. The ANC had been transformed from a non-violent African nationalist organization into a revolutionary liberation movement. By 1964, most of the ANC's leaders were jailed and the resistance seemed effectively silenced. However, this silence did not last.[20]

The politics of reform and repression

In June 1976 the government met its fiercest resistance yet from students protesting against the imposition of Afrikaans as a medium of education. Several hundred students were killed in the uprisings that ensued and South Africa became a focus of attention throughout the world as apartheid was condemned internationally. Thousands left the country to join the liberation movements, and the armed struggle gained momentum. The government was obliged to prove some willingness to reform.

Upon coming to power in 1978, Prime Minister (and later President) P. W. Botha began reorganizing the state. One of the significant developments was the creation of a new government department, the Department of Constitutional Development and Planning. This department was mandated to introduce 'reforms' while the security establishment took over the major strategic decision-making responsibilities of the state.[21] This unusual delegation of tasks was given effect through the creation of a multi-tiered, interdepartmental structure, dominated by the military but staffed by civilians, called the National Security Management System (NSMS). The role of the NSMS was to address economic and social problems in local 'hotspots', in a plan designed to win the support of the populace in a given area. The idea was that this would isolate those responsible for 'political unrest' and leave them to the mercy of the state's repressive might.

As part of Botha's reform strategy, the next major constitutional development took place in 1983, in the form of a new Tricameral Parliament and a President's Council. Parliament was made up of three houses: the white House of Assembly, the coloured House of Representatives, and the Indian House of Delegates. Africans were excluded from this dispensation. Differences between the three houses were referred to the President's Council.

Botha's regime was characterized by a dual approach to the growing militancy of the anti-apartheid forces – reform and repression. It was a method informed by Botha's militarized style of government, learnt while in office as Minister of Defence, and drawing on the strategies of the military dictatorships of Latin America.

The NSMS, which was initiated in 1979, and the 1983 constitutional reforms initiated by Chris Heunis, Minister of Constitutional Affairs and Planning, were manifestations of a shift in NP thinking and strategy. While maintaining the apartheid project, the NP had begun to focus more closely on other cleavages that could be exploited within the black community. The reform packages that characterized the

1980s were aimed at creating a group of 'urban insiders', which were a small, privileged African élite who could act as a buffer against the majority of black South Africans.[22]

The reform and repression approach employed by the NP, at its most sophisticated in the form of the NSMS, created a brief respite for the Botha regime, for it was able to quell some of the political turmoil of the mid-eighties, and to illustrate the sophisticated might of the apartheid state. In retrospect, it appears that at this point in South Africa's history an impasse had been reached. The NSMS clearly showed the military might of the South African regime, ruling out the possibility of any successful military victory by the anti-apartheid forces. On the other hand, real tensions were developing within the state itself as securocrats and political reformers began plotting different trajectories for South Africa's future.

The strategy of reform and repression had only limited success. Armed resistance intensified, and by 1984 armed actions had risen to an average of fifty operations per year. In 1985 the ANC first deployed landmines and began to develop a presence in rural areas. The organization declared 1986 the year of the people's army, Umkhonto we Sizwe (MK). As alternative township structures, street committees, and people's courts began functioning in many areas, the state, whose agenda was dominated by insurrectionary politics, was struggling to govern much of the country. The next step for the resistance was 'the transformation of armed propaganda into a people's war'.[23] From 1986 onwards the number of attacks rose to between 250 and 300 per year. It was also during this period that a vigorous debate arose within the liberation movement between those who argued for an 'insurrectionary people's war' and those who wanted a war to force the regime to the negotiating table.[24]

The search for constitutional solutions

It was in this context that the first exploratory discussions began in 1985 between Nelson Mandela and representatives of P. W. Botha's government. It had become apparent to Botha that the crisis in South Africa was reaching unmanageable proportions, and that drastic political changes had to take place. He also realized that constitutional changes would have to include representatives of the black majority. In August 1985 he was confronted with a choice between two broad approaches: he could release political leaders and start a process of genuine negotiation, or he could consult with representatives hand-picked by himself in a process that he could manage, and be reasonably certain of a satisfactory outcome. Botha was not bold enough for negotiation, and chose the latter;[25] he was not yet prepared to cross the Rubicon.[26] However, this arrogance did not last much longer.

The period saw a similar attitude in South Africa's relationship with its neighbours. Until the first quarter of 1988 South Africa carried out a brutal campaign of aggression and destabilization against its southern African counterparts. However, the balance of forces in the region was to be altered by a historic military defeat suffered by the South African Defence Force (SADF) that year at Cuito Caunavale in Angola. The defeat proved that South Africa's military might was not invincible after all. The effect was immediate: 'In the first week of May, South African negotiators travelled to London for the first of several rounds of talks on Angola and Namibia with officials from Angola, Cuba and the United States. These resulted in an agreement over the withdrawal of SADF troops from Angola (completed on 30 August 1988), followed by accords signed in Brazzaville and New York (on 13 and 22 December respectively) providing for Namibia to begin its transition to independence in accordance with United Nations Security Council Resolution 435 of 1978 on 1 April 1989'.[27]

Botha now had further incentives to seek solutions to the crisis. On 21 April 1988 he outlined a new constitutional framework for the country based on a federal or confederal structure that would enable black people to be co-opted into the political process as far as the cabinet.[28] The proposal included: the creation of black regional bodies representing black people outside the homelands; the appointment of a prime minister; that 'recognizable' black leaders be co-opted as cabinet members; the establishment of a national council referred to as the

'Great Indaba' ('indaba' is Zulu for a gathering or council); and the downgrading of the President's Council to a part-time body. Part of the responsibility of the 'Indaba' would be to negotiate a new constitution for consideration by the white Parliament.

The demand for a negotiated settlement

Two overriding principles shaped Botha's proposals: the first was the NP's determination to retain political control, and the second, to continue the separation of races.[29] Whites would continue to control all decision-making structures, which were essentially undemocratic. The result was that the proposals were roundly condemned.[30] Until this stage, the demands made by the anti-apartheid movement had been for the release of political prisoners, free political activity, the unbanning of political organizations, and a universal franchise. What changed was the reintroduction of a demand first made in March 1960 for the negotiation of a new constitutional dispensation with the true representatives of the people.

The government's constitutional proposals took shape during June and July 1988 when a package of several bills was introduced.[31] The primary purpose of the reforms brought about by these laws was to strengthen the hand of 'moderate' black people and pave the way for their involvement in the constitution-making process.[32] Black 'moderates' had a great deal to gain by these proposals, for it provided them with unprecedented powers over townships. The lifting of restrictions imposed by the Group Areas Act would appease a significant number of moderate coloured and Indian people, and it was hoped that the changes brought about by these reforms would also make it possible for moderate black leaders to participate in the proposed national council. The objective of this council would be to produce a constitution that would win the hearts and minds of the majority.

But this was not to be, for a constitutional crisis developed when the Houses of Representatives and Delegates, in a move that amounted to filibustering, refused to allow debate on the Group Areas Act.[33] The government's response was to change the rules of Parliament and force the legislation through, raising a storm of protest. Botha failed to obtain the support of even moderate black leaders.

At the same time, political parties both inside and outside the country were revising their views on a constitution for the country. After two years' work, the ANC published the main provisions of its constitutional vision, which included the establishment of a democratic state that guaranteed rights and freedoms on the one hand, and promoted affirmative action on the other.

The constitutional vision of the Progressive Federal Party (PFP) was also being reviewed. Its policy proposed a government based on a geographic federation with universal franchise, but with various checks and balances to prevent majority rule including a bill of rights and a minority veto over cabinet decisions. The PFP also saw the constitutional dispensation negotiated at a national convention.[34]

In August 1988 the spotlight fell on Mandela when he was hospitalized with tuberculosis at Tygerberg Hospital, and speculation about the release of political prisoners and the unbanning of the ANC intensified. In the meantime, a power struggle was taking place within the NP: Botha's ill health provided an opportunity for the party to look to new leadership in the figure of F. W. de Klerk. Soon after taking over, De Klerk committed himself to seeking a new constitution that would offer 'full participation' to all South Africans in a new federal constitutional dispensation.[35] Its goals would be to eliminate the domination of any one group by another; the maintenance of community life in a non-discriminatory manner; a strong economy based on free enterprise and competition; social and economic upliftment for those communities suffering backlogs; and the firm maintenance of law and order. In this regard, he recognized the need for inclusive negotiation among the leaders of the different parties. However, De Klerk remained implacably opposed to a one-person-one-vote system, which he argued would lead to domination by the majority.

The Minister of Constitutional Development and Planning, Chris Heunis, voiced similar sentiments as the white electorate prepared to

1989

go to the polls on 6 September of that year.[36] This election provided De Klerk's government with a mandate to proceed with the new constitutional proposals;[37] it was also to be the last whites-only general election. The demand for constitutional negotiation was developing a momentum of its own. Contemporary events in Eastern Europe around the 'collapse' of communism were also relevant: the world seemed to be going through a process of tremendous and far-reaching change, and South Africa was an integral part of it.

To prepare for the forthcoming elections, the NP on 29 June 1989 published its five-year plan. There was a deliberate lack of detail in its provisions. It confined itself to general statements that pointed to various reforms, such as a bill of rights which allowed for group rights; the engagement of 'recognised leaders of all groups' to negotiate a new dispensation; a review of the functions and powers of the head of state; the promotion of 'self determination regarding own affairs', along with joint decision-making on 'general affairs', by means of the division and devolution of power in a non-discriminatory manner; and a vote for black people within five years. Despite the lack of detail, the policies of the NP were beginning to look more like those of the Democratic Party (DP), the recently remade and renamed PFP. Most importantly, the NP had started to question many of its own earlier beliefs.

Black leaders rejected the plan, insisting that apartheid be scrapped altogether to create a climate conducive to negotiation.[38] The plan also received attention in the British media, and they too were disappointed.[39] According to an editorial in the *Star*, 'The Nationalist government is chasing a train that has already left the station. Where it intends to be five years from now is where it should have been a decade ago'. However, the positive aspect was that 'The plan envisages negotiation with black South Africans and it offers black people a vote at national level within five years. This is an encouraging shift, especially following years of oppressive apartheid and erosion of the rule of law'.[40]

By this time, influential sectors in society, including business, religious bodies, youth organizations, and academics were holding consultations with the ANC in various African countries in defiance of

South African law. These meetings considered issues such as violence, sanctions, constitutional models, the economy, and the role of whites in the transformation and future of South Africa, issues that the South African public was debating and wanted leadership on. The NP lacked the boldness or confidence required to provide such leadership, and hesitated in breaking with its apartheid past and its obsession with group rights.

Nonetheless, the 1989 election was a resounding success for De Klerk, one which he interpreted as a mandate for reform. In the second week of September De Klerk felt confident enough to allow a protest march by 30 000 people on the city hall in Cape Town, led by Archbishop Desmond Tutu and Alan Boesak, a cleric and prominent leader in the United Democratic Front. This marked the relaxation of restrictions on protest action, and 'petty apartheid' legislation was no longer stringently enforced.

In another development, the Department of Constitutional Development and Planning was streamlined under the leadership of Gerrit Viljoen to deal specifically with the process of negotiation.[41] The department began looking at various constitutional models, and all major government speeches now spoke of a 'new South Africa'. The continued state of emergency, incarceration of political prisoners, and ban on a number of political parties, however, remained obstacles in the way of negotiation. There was a determination to effect certain changes, and for these De Klerk had the public support of Dr Zach de Beer, the leader of the Democratic Party.[42]

The beginning of October 1989 saw the government's international allies intensify the pressure for change. British Prime Minister Margaret Thatcher looked to the South African government to provide her with sufficient grounds to stave off demands made by Commonwealth leaders for tougher sanctions. In the United States, the Assistant Secretary of State, Herman Cohen, set out state policy options on South Africa, which included demands that the South African government unban political parties, lift the state of emergency, allow for the return of exiles, remove all discriminatory legislation, and begin negotiating with credible black leaders on a new constitutional order by June 1990.[43] Internally, even the Inkatha Freedom Party (IFP) refused to negotiate until these obstacles were removed.[44] Weeks later, the government unconditionally released several senior political prisoners.

One of the difficulties the government faced was recognizing the ANC as a major negotiating partner. Hence, the government's chief negotiator, Gerrit Viljoen, mooted the idea of an election among black people outside the homelands to choose their negotiating leaders,[45] a proposal which the Mass Democratic Movement (MDM) and other major organizations immediately rejected.[46] Walter Sisulu, one of the ANC leaders released in October 1989, denounced the government's plan to lift the state of emergency and to repeal the Separate Amenities Act as not enough to start a process of genuine negotiation. According to him, in order to create a basis for discussions the government had to release political prisoners, unban organizations like the ANC, withdraw troops from the townships, and scrap all undemocratic laws. He described Gerrit Viljoen's plans to hold elections to identify black leaders as ridiculous,[47] and even the homeland leaders were opposed to this idea.[48]

On 10 November 1989 a high-powered delegation of business leaders from the Associated Chambers of Commerce and Industry (ASSOCOM) met with De Klerk to urge him to speed up the process of constitutional reform.[49] The accumulated pressure of South Africa's political crisis, right-wing resistance, economic concerns, the changing political situation in Eastern Europe, and the international community led De Klerk to the inescapable conclusion that clinging to power would only lead to a bloody conflict. Thus, in November 1989, he called for an accord among all peoples of the country that would offer full political rights to everyone. He argued that nowhere in the world had a minority been able to cling to power without facing a revolution.[50] The demand for the creation of a climate conducive to negotiation could not be refused: there was simply no other option open to the government.

The pressure on De Klerk did not let up. By early December critics in the United States were still not convinced that the changes were sufficient, and regarded them as merely cosmetic.[51] De Klerk sought to lower the expectations made of his government and asked for greater latitude, arguing that his government was different from that of his predecessor, and that, only a few months in power, he needed more time to effect change.[52]

To add to the woes of the South African government, the United Nations (UN) General Assembly was to hold a special session from 12 to 14 December 1989 to consider a declaration on apartheid and its destructive consequences for southern Africa. The twelve leaders of the European Community (EC) also met in Strasbourg, and after a two-day summit issued a declaration adopting economic measures to ban the promotion of tourism to South Africa and the import of certain South African goods. While De Klerk's commitment to reform was recognized, it was stated that 'these measures, however, are still insufficient with respect to the immense task posed by the dismantling of apartheid'.[53]

In response to the mounting pressure, De Klerk and his cabinet held a special work session on 4 and 5 December 1989. Some of the matters considered included the release of Mandela and other prisoners, the unbanning of political organizations, constitutional proposals, and the announcement De Klerk was to make at the opening of the new parliamentary session on 2 February 1990.[54] After this meeting the Minister of Constitutional Development and Planning, Gerrit Viljoen, declared that group rights were no longer a non-negotiable demand of the government in constitutional negotiation. This was one of the most significant policy shifts in NP thinking.[55]

The momentum generated by the demand for constitutional negotiation was further intensified by the Conference for a Democratic Future that started its work on 8 December 1989. The conference, organized by the Mass Democratic Movement (MDM), was attended by more than 6 000 delegates from throughout the country representing 2 000 organizations.[56] Even eleven affiliates of the National Congress of Trade Unions (NACTU), an Africanist union federation, defied its central committee and attended the conference. Parties and leaders from various homelands were also present.

Speaking at the conference's opening session, Walter Sisulu invited De Klerk to attend its deliberations and urged the government to abandon the ideas of a 'Great Indaba' and a 'black election'. He confirmed the commitment of the United Democratic Front (UDF), MDM, and civil society to the demands set out in the Harare Declaration, and called on the government to create the necessary climate for negotiation to take place. The conference adopted a resolution and recommitted delegates to intensify the pressure on the government to commit itself to genuine negotiation.[57] A call was also made to the international community to maintain the pressure already mounted on the South African government.

3

Exploring the feasibility of negotiation

BY 1985 THE STRUGGLE for democracy in South Africa had intensified, and the country found itself on the brink of a potentially devastating civil war. The conflict threatened the very fabric of society, for the economy was in shock and the country was isolated by the international community. While the liberation movements were not in a position to defeat the government by armed force, the government was also not able to continue governing as it had been.[1] It was a stalemate, in effect, and change was inevitable.

However, negotiation does not take place merely because political conditions make it a viable alternative, and this was especially so in the South African situation. The contending parties were not only ideological opponents, but were at war with one another. Why should the government listen to calls for negotiation? After all, they had the military means to stay in power. Furthermore, years of negative perceptions of one another did not make it easier for the parties to negotiate.

Experience has shown that in addition to these conditions it is also necessary for contending parties to realize that negotiation is the *only* viable option. Moreover, there must also be a catalyst to initiate this process. South Africa had a unique catalyst to the process of negotiation in Nelson Mandela, speaking from his prison cell. The key to unlock peace in South Africa came from within the very depths of apartheid's dungeons. In many other countries the international community played this role, as it did in Angola, Namibia, Zimbabwe, and Mozambique. In fact, the vision contained in the ANC's Harare Declaration in 1989 included a prominent role for the international community. The Pan Africanist Congress (PAC) supported a prominent role for the international community as well. South Africa was also unique, therefore, in that the international community played no direct role in the process.[2]

Ironically, Mandela's imprisonment also gave parties the opportunity to explore the feasibility of negotiation, for prison conditions provided the secrecy required in the event that the exercise misfired.

Realizing the option of negotiation

There is little consensus about when negotiations began and who initiated them.[3] Did it start with the 1990 speech in Parliament by F. W. de Klerk? With the first meeting of the Convention for a Democratic South Africa (CODESA I) in December 1991? Or in 1985 when Mandela initiated discussions with P. W. Botha's government? It is generally accepted that the latter view is most accurate.

At a meeting in Nassau in October 1985, the British Commonwealth discussed a proposal for further international sanctions against South Africa. Only Margaret Thatcher opposed them. As a compromise, a delegation composed of 'eminent persons' was sent to South Africa, to investigate whether sanctions would be helpful in bringing an end to apartheid. The delegation came to be referred to as the 'Eminent Persons Group' (EPG). The EPG sought discussions with key role-players, but on the day that the delegation was to meet with cabinet ministers, the South African Defence Force launched an attack on the ANC in Botswana, Zambia, and Zimbabwe, under the direct orders of P. W. Botha.

Reaction to this naked act of aggression was immediate. The EPG left the country in disgust and the ANC called on its supporters to render the country ungovernable. The ensuing resistance was followed by even greater repression than before, and in turn the Botha government came under tremendous pressure from the international community. All in all, the government was finding it more and more difficult to govern.

In the same year Mandela wrote to the government expressing his concerns about developments and asking for a meeting. Kobie Coetsee, the Minister of Justice, responded positively, and a meeting between the two took place in November 1985 in a hospital room in the Volks Hospital in Cape Town.[4] The meeting was a success and the government wanted to hear more.

Mandela was transferred after his hospitalization to a single cell at Pollsmoor Prison, which afforded government negotiators direct access to Mandela as an individual. Kobie Coetsee, Neil Barnard, S. S. van der Merwe, and the Commissioner of Prisons represented the government in the meetings that followed.[5] These discussions were no more than exploratory talks to explore the feasibility of negotiation. Mandela made it clear that he regarded the ANC to be under the leadership of Oliver Tambo, who was in exile, but the government became confident that Mandela was the person it could do business with. However, it was not so sure about the ANC itself. Its next step would be to organize clandestine exchanges with the ANC in exile.[6]

It was important for Mandela to win the confidence of the government, for in his view it had to believe that it could negotiate with the ANC. For this reason he wrote again to President P. W. Botha and tried to convince him that the ANC 'were not wild-eyed terrorists, but reasonable men'. In his memorandum, Mandela stated, 'I am disturbed as many other South Africans no doubt are, by the spectre of a South Africa split into two hostile camps – blacks on one side . . . and whites on the other, slaughtering one another. . . . Majority rule and internal peace are like two sides of a single coin, and white South Africa simply has to accept that there will never be peace and stability in this country until the principle is fully applied'.[7]

At the end of the letter, Mandela offered a very rough framework for negotiation: 'Two political issues will have to be addressed; firstly, the demand for majority rule in a unitary state; secondly, the concern of white South Africa over this demand, as well as the insistence of whites on structural guarantees that majority rule will not mean domination of the white minority by blacks. The most crucial tasks which will face the government and the ANC will be to reconcile these two positions'.

Mandela was successful in his mission, and the discussions he started with Coetsee continued in as many as forty-seven meetings. These discussions were of fundamental importance, for they allowed both the government and Mandela to realize that the option of negotiation was not only real, but that it was a valid strategy through which both parties could realize their respective objectives.

For the ANC, armed struggle was a tactic rather than a strategy, and since its inception the organization had tirelessly demanded an opportunity to discuss the future of the country with the government. So for the ANC it was not too difficult to accept the value of negotiation. Of primary importance among its leaders was Oliver Tambo, a long-time associate and partner of Mandela. Both leaders were cut from the same political cloth.

There were also powerful indicators of the kind of change that was sweeping the subcontinent, such as social, political, and economic developments within the southern African region, changes in the Soviet Union, and the rising tide of international pressure for reform in South Africa. Tambo, an ingenious strategist, lost no time in recognizing this, and initiated widespread debate within the leadership of the ANC to consider the option of negotiation.[8] Hence, in 1988, for the first time since it was banned the ANC formally considered the option of a negotiated settlement.

It was different for the NP, for discussion with the genuine leadership of the black majority had been a taboo of which it had no experience. The leaders of the majority were perceived as too radical, and the only black people the government ever spoke to were those regarded as 'moderates'.

The first meeting between Mandela and the Botha government took place at a leadership level. This was followed by meetings between functionaries (at least on the side of the government), which became a trend throughout negotiation. Meetings at leadership level dealt essentially with principles rather than substance, while functionaries attended to the latter. Representatives from the intelligence and security establishment invariably became involved during the initial stages of negotiation. Another characteristic of these meetings was the veil of secrecy that surrounded them, for very few leaders on either side were made aware of what was happening. Considering the context within which these talks took place, it is understandable that neither side wanted anything to jeopardize them. Similarly, there was also no guarantee of the outcome of the discussions, so both sides felt it necessary to ensure that the talks did not appear as a sign of weakness. As for Mandela, he did not even inform his closest colleagues in prison about these discussions, and was intent on presenting them with a fait accompli.[9]

While both sides were keen to commence negotiations, the politics of the government made this difficult. The government was uncomfortable negotiating with the ANC before it renounced violence or severed its relationship with the Communist Party, which the ANC refused to do. There were also several other obstacles in the way of negotiation. Senior negotiators and decision-makers from the liberation movements were either in prison or in exile, wanted by the security forces of the country. There was a barrage of security legislation in place that would have made it impossible for negotiation to take place without the negotiators courting arrest or harm. The most graphic illustration of this is in the only statement released by Mandela while he was still in prison:

> What freedom am I being offered while the organisation of the people remains banned? What freedom am I being offered when I may be arrested on a pass offence? What freedom am I being offered to live my life as a family with my dear wife who remains in banishment in Brandfort? What freedom am I being offered when I must ask for permission to live in an urban area? . . . What freedom am I being offered when my very South African citizenship is not respected?
>
> Only free men can negotiate. Prisoners cannot enter into contracts.[10]

It was therefore necessary to create the conditions conducive for negotiation to take place, and this too had to be negotiated. It meant identifying the obstacles and negotiating their removal before substantive negotiation could take place; hence, the idea of 'talks about talks'.

A commitment to negotiation

The second half of 1989 proved to be an important period in the history of the negotiations. In early July 1989 the exploratory discussions held between the government and Mandela resulted in a meeting with P. W. Botha that took place only because Botha was convinced that a nego-tiated settlement was feasible, or he would not have risked such a meeting.[11] However, Botha resigned a month later to be succeeded by F. W. de Klerk.

By this time Operation Vula was active: senior ANC operatives were infiltrating the country to establish a political and military presence, and to facilitate efficient and direct lines of communication between Mandela and Tambo. The ANC was spurred on by Mandela's initia-tives, and under Tambo's leadership it sought to prepare itself for negotiation by successfully lobbying African governments in 1989 to adopt the Harare Declaration, a document drafted by the Organization of African Unity (OAU).[12] Tambo was keen to seize the initiative in preparing for negotiation, for he was aware that unless the ANC did this, the international community would happily play this role. To lose this initiative would have meant losing the ability to determine the agenda of the process, which was what had happened in Zimbabwe and Namibia. Tambo's efforts were ingenious, for at the time many did not fully realize the importance of the Harare Declaration, when in fact it proved to be prophetic.

The declaration contained the first real vision of a transition to democracy. It set out a basis for negotiation to take place and spoke of a climate conducive to such negotiation. Such a climate, it was argued, could be created by the unconditional release of political prisoners and detainees, the lifting of bans on restricted organizations, the removal of troops from the townships, the ending of the state of emergency, the repeal of repressive legislation, and the cessation of political trials and executions. Once this climate existed, the representatives of all parties could sit down to negotiate a new constitutional dispensation, which would have to be based on universally agreed constitutional principles.

According to the declaration, the process of negotiation had to take account of several priorities. The process had to commence with initial discussions designed to achieve a suspension of hostilities, which would then facilitate agreement on basic constitutional principles to underpin the new dispensation. The parties could then define the forum that would draft the new constitution; the participation of the international community could be taken into account here. An interim government could be formed which was to supervise the drafting and adoption of the new constitution and govern the country in the interim period. Once the new constitution was adopted, all armed hostilities would be formally terminated. For its part, the international community would then lift sanctions and South Africa would qualify for membership of the Organization of African Unity.

The United Nations also discussed the Harare Declaration, which must have made an impact on the government. The change from earlier NP strategy was evident in the immediate action taken after the assumption of office by De Klerk, for where Botha dithered, De Klerk was prepared to cross the Rubicon. The request by Mandela for the release of political prisoners was accepted, and in October 1989 the first group of political prisoners was unconditionally released.[13] This was the first tangible result of Mandela's endeavours and he was clearly gaining the confidence of the government.

Mandela met the new incumbent on 13 December of that year to discuss the question of the creation by the government of a climate conducive to negotiation.[14] During this period, Mandela lived in a prison warden's house at Victor Verster Prison, where he had unlimited access to anyone he wanted to see, including the recently released political prisoners. This was important for him, for it allowed him to ensure that his efforts conformed to the thinking of both the ANC in exile and the anti-apartheid structures within the country.

The meetings between Mandela and the two leaders of the National Party and the release of the political prisoners served as an important indication of the change of heart in government. There was a growing realization that negotiation was a feasible option. However, there was still no agreement on the process of negotiation, for De Klerk ruled out the possibility of forming a transitional government or an elected constituent assembly.[15]

The meeting between Mandela and De Klerk was fortuitous for another reason: it took place while the United Nations was debating a resolution that mirrored the Harare Declaration. The government publicly reported the meeting with Mandela, and the office of US President George Bush consequently applauded De Klerk's efforts, stating that 'the commencement of dialogue between the South African government and credible representatives of the black majority was the most important first step in the process of change'.[16] Sir Crispin Tickell, Britain's UN representative, adopted a similar approach. Therefore, the meeting provided the major powers in the UN with an excuse to water down the impact of the resolution. They could argue that by its patience with the De Klerk government the international community would retain its influence over South Africa.

The momentum gathers

For De Klerk, his first hundred days in office, until 28 December 1989, produced major changes. The significance of these changes lay not so much in what they achieved but in the action they triggered. But De Klerk's next hundred days in office produced events that were even more dramatic. South Africa teetered precariously on the verge of constitutional negotiation that would transform the country into a non-racial democracy. Never before did South Africa end a year, let alone a decade, with so much expectation as it did in the December of 1989. The opening paragraphs of the *Sunday Times* editorial of 14 January 1990 described the mood succinctly and profoundly. Appropriately entitled 'Enter Mandela: now let the show begin', it read:

The stage is set. All the main players are in position except for one towering figure waiting in the wings. When Nelson Mandela takes his rightful place on the South African political stage, an entrance that now seems certain within weeks rather than months, the curtain will rise.

What happens next is the unwritten script of South Africa's future. It will be an ad lib creation, beset by countless disputes and setbacks, haunted by many ghosts from the past. But there is a mood of optimism, a climate of hope, among both the players and the audience, which should engender sufficient common purpose and goodwill to produce a reasonably happy ending.

President F. W. de Klerk, as the man who will release Mr Mandela, has the initiative. He is fully aware of the accelerating momentum of the reform process he has skilfully directed for the past six months. Having gone this far, one must assume he is prepared to fulfil the expectations his Government has created. President de Klerk can no longer fudge on key issues such as the removal of Group Areas.

The release of Nelson Mandela, and the concomitant unbanning of the ANC and lifting of the state of emergency are opening gambits. Ahead lies the politically intricate and emotive task of dismantling the apartheid structure, and establishing a platform for negotiation.

It would be unrealistic to expect all this to happen in one shattering reformist sweep. The release of Mr Mandela will be the beginning of a long series of quid pro quos.

With these high expectations came increased fear among white South Africans, and frantic attempts were made in response to ensure that the process of reform slowed down.[17] There was a great deal of speculation in the media on 17 January 1990 about how negotiation would take place. To many it was still an area of doubt and concern.

Nonetheless, the government resolutely continued its preparations for negotiation. The Minister of Constitutional Development and Planning, Gerrit Viljoen, responded to the Harare Declaration at the end of January 1990, arguing that the negotiations should be both inclusive and comprehensive.[18] A chairperson or panel of chairpersons would have to be neutral and designated by the negotiating conference. Two fundamental issues required some compromise: these were first, the demand for majority rule in a unitary state, and second, structural guarantees for the protection of minorities. Significantly, both of these issues were raised in the document Mandela prepared for his meeting with Botha in July 1989.

At the opening of Parliament on 2 February 1990, F. W. de Klerk made a dramatic speech in which he announced the unbanning of liberation movements, the release of political prisoners, and a series of measures intended to address obstacles to the process of negotiation.[19] This unlocked a chain of events that changed the course of the history of South Africa. By positively responding to a number of the demands made in the Harare Declaration, De Klerk signalled his commitment to negotiate. It also established his bona fides because he went further than any other minority party leader had ever been prepared to go before.[20]

Preparations for the first formal talks

The measures put in place by De Klerk went some way to creating conditions for negotiation to take place.[21] Mandela was released the week following this speech, and the view of the media was that substantive negotiation on a new constitutional dispensation could now commence. The ANC hastily convened its National Executive Committee (NEC) to consider its response,[22] confirming that a delegation would meet De Klerk in what was to be the first meeting between the ANC's exiled leaders and a South African head of state. The ANC made it clear, however, that this did not signal the start of substantive negotiations, since it was prepared to enter into such negotiations only after the preconditions set out in the Harare Declaration had been met. According to Mandela, 'everyone who takes part in negotiation must be properly mandated and the only way of giving authority to the people who will sit at the negotiating table is through democratic elections'.[23]

The government was keen to ensure that the ANC renounced violence in exchange for lifting the state of emergency. In addition, it would release only those prisoners jailed solely because the organization to which they belonged was banned. The implications of complying with the ANC's demand to the letter, they warned, would be unwelcome; for instance, it would mean the release of convicted right-wing murderer Barend Strydom, the end of the Harms Commission investigation into police and army hit squads, as well as the release of ANC cadres convicted of murder.[24] This presented the first major problem. To avoid the impasse, it was agreed that the category of political prisoners to be released be precisely defined.[25] The response of the right wing was to convene their largest political gatherings since the creation of the republic to protest against these developments.

It was only at the end of March 1990 that an agreement to hold formal discussions was reached. These discussions were scheduled to take place on 11 April, and ANC members Jacob Zuma, Matthews Phosa, and Penuel Maduna were secretly allowed to enter the country from exile to prepare for them.[26] Together with Curnick Ndlovu, Ahmed Kathrada, and other ANC members, a steering committee that included government representatives was formed to prepare for the meeting, which was held under a veil of secrecy. The steering committee dealt with the details of possible agreements that would clear the remaining obstacles in the way of negotiation. Some of the issues that required immediate attention related to the definition of the term 'political prisoners' and the basis for granting indemnities to returning exiles.

The position adopted by the NP at the time was that any negotiated constitution would have to be approved first by the white electorate.[27] The negotiations would only then include other organizations and parties. However, only those who committed themselves to peaceful solutions would be able to take part. Leaders working within the system should have seats 'reserved' for them at the negotiating table; it would also have to be determined who had substantial enough support to participate. A neutral chairperson could be appointed, though no international intervention would be sought.[28]

Setting trends

The preparations for this meeting provided an early glimpse of trends that were to follow. In the first instance, it was recognized that the NP and the ANC were not the only role-players in settling the South African conflict, and the outcome of the negotiations would also depend on the alliances that each major role-player was able to develop. Secondly, the process of negotiations would not continue uninterrupted, for political violence flared up regularly to set the process back.

In preparation for the meeting, De Klerk arranged to meet with the chief ministers of the six non-independent homelands and the three chairpersons of the Ministers' Councils.[29] This was a significant development, for one of the major political role-players was now competing to win the confidence of smaller parties.[30] In fact, both the ANC and the NP recognized that various political formations would be role-players in negotiation.[31] According to Mandela, the ANC consulted with other black political organizations in a drive for a 'unity of the oppressed'.[32]

The government was developing two important themes. Firstly, it intended to ensure that it had allies in the negotiation process.[33] As a result of this, the ANC feared that the NP wanted to 'pack' the negotiating line-up. Secondly, it wanted to seize the initiative by immediately dealing with substantive constitutional negotiation.[34]

On 1 April 1990 the ANC suspended all negotiation with the government in protest against the shooting of unarmed demonstrators in Sebokeng only seven days after the thirtieth anniversary of the Sharpeville massacre. The shooting resulted in the loss of sixteen lives, and was the third time in as many weeks that the police or army had killed demonstrators.[35] The stop-start nature of negotiations was to become a pattern, but, as would happen time and again, Mandela and De Klerk agreed to meet to bring negotiations back on track. Their meeting was successful and a formal meeting was rescheduled for 2 May. Mandela was satisfied with De Klerk's assurance that the Sebokeng incident would be investigated, possibly even by a judicial inquiry.[36]

A group of the most senior ANC leaders arrived in South Africa on 27 April 1990, exactly four years short of the first democratic election the country was to experience. They included Joe Slovo (General Secretary of the South African Communist Party), Joe Modise (commander of Umkhonto we Sizwe), Alfred Nzo (Secretary-General of the ANC), Ruth Mompati (ANC National Executive Committee member), and Thabo Mbeki (ANC Department of International Affairs).

The arrival of these negotiators in the country symbolized the changes taking place. Slovo occupied a special place as a bogeyman of the old white politics. He was a communist, a military strategist, and an influential leader in the ANC, and for nearly thirty years had been branded apartheid's 'public enemy number one'.[37] Casually dressed and wearing the red socks that would become part of his dress code, he expressed the emotion he felt on returning to South Africa through the 'front door', after having had to leave it many years before through the 'back door'. As for Joe Modise, he had left the country with a mission to destroy apartheid through armed struggle, and was now returning to the country to sit down and talk to his former adversaries to create a new South Africa.

4 Removing the obstacles

THE YEARS 1990 AND 1991 were as important as they were eventful. The agreements recorded during this period ensured that obstacles in the way of substantive negotiation were removed. The Groote Schuur Minute, the D. F. Malan Accord, and the Pretoria Minute were the first formal agreements signed between the government and the ANC, and set in place measures designed to establish an environment conducive to negotiation.

Considering the heightened conflict and increasing tension, the parties' supporters viewed any compromise with much suspicion. There was little tangible change in people's lives. Most white people watched this period with growing concern and trepidation as property prices plummeted and hundreds emigrated. There was constant talk of 'selling out' on all sides: even the PAC denounced the scheduled meetings. According to the PAC, 'slaves have nothing to gain from negotiating with their masters. . . . We do not need reform. We need a complete overhaul of the entire economic and political system'.[1] The Azanian People's Organization (AZAPO) also stood impatiently in line to dole out its own condemnation of the talks: according to Strini Moodley, 'the De Klerk regime has succeeded in tying up the ANC in the perennial structures designed to delay the struggle, and to water down solutions to our problems in this country'.[2] The right wing was growing in support and militancy, and even P. W. Botha, the NP leader responsible for the first contact with Mandela, publicly renounced the talks as 'unacceptable'.[3] Even ANC members questioned the agreement to halt armed activities because they were suspicious of the government's motives in granting indemnities.[4] It was hardly surprising, therefore, that these early discussions were extremely tense. Most participants were uncertain about the eventual outcome of negotiation, and generally there was a great deal of mistrust among them.[5]

The quality and foresight of the leadership in both negotiating parties during this period were most crucial. Were it not for their political maturity and shared commitment to a negotiated settlement, it would not have been possible to steer the country through the stormy waters they encountered.

The Groote Schuur Minute

THE AGREEMENT

The first formal meeting between the ANC and the government began on 2 May 1990 at Groote Schuur in Cape Town, and lasted three days.[6]

The first day of the meeting dealt with a general exposition by each party on the obstacles to negotiation, several of which were identified.[7] These included security legislation, the return of exiles, the presence of troops in the townships, political prisoners, the state of emergency, the adherence to armed struggle, and the need to end violence. The discussions were characterized by openness on both sides. A commitment to making the maximum effort at finding common ground to eliminate tension, and the desire to make a success of the meeting were equally evident in both parties. By the second day, delegates were asking why these talks had not taken place years ago. According to Thabo Mbeki, within minutes of sitting down, 'everyone understood that there was nobody there with horns'.[8]

The meeting produced an agreement, hailed as a major breakthrough, that came to be known as the Groote Schuur Minute.[9] More than 400 journalists and diplomatic personnel attended the historic international news conference announcing the agreement. The Minute consisted of several major points: the ANC committed itself to reviewing its policy of armed struggle; a joint working group was formed to work on a definition of 'political offences', the release of prisoners, and the granting of immunity; and the government re-iterated its intention to review security laws, lift the state of emergency, and enable exiles to return to the country.[10] This working group, the first of many, was instructed to table a report by 21 May 1990. In the meantime, some offences were to receive immediate attention by the government, including leaving the country without a valid travel document and any offence relating to previously prohibited organizations. In addition, temporary indemnities for the ANC's National Executive Committee and other members were to be processed and issued urgently.

THE SIGNIFICANCE OF THE AGREEMENT

The Groote Schuur Minute showed that problems which were previously perceived to be intractable really could be amicably resolved. Within three days a remarkable rapport had been established between parties in an experience described as 'cathartic'. The government delegation learnt about the frustrations of being banned and why the ANC was forced to take up arms, while the ANC learnt about the economic implications of sanctions. Both sides realized that they had to rethink some of their previous assumptions.[11]

The excitement of many South Africans was reflected vividly in the media. A *Sunday Times* editorial entitled 'The hopeful spirit of Groote Schuur' asked:

Who but incurable bigots or escapist clingers to apartheid myths could fail to be moved by the television images? The youngish, imperturbably calm and sure-footed State President, and the tall, dignified and articulate black leader sitting side by side, making history together.

True, there was much on which they still differed. True, grinding months of hard talk lie ahead. True, many anxious or angry people still need persuading that there is a peaceful way out of our crisis.

But the signs were evident as much in the body language as in

their calm, measured speech. Two South Africans. Two generations and from separate poles of the political spectrum, had begun
to discover each other as humans. More, there was dawning
recognition that our future lies in the same diversity which, by
making victory impossible for any party, makes compromise
inescapable for all parties.[12]

The *Sunday Star* editorial entitled 'Road to normality is irreversible'
stated, 'Bearing in mind that this week's contact between the
Government and the African National Congress was not about
constitutional negotiation, but a means to that end, the historic accord
reached by the two sides is the most promising political development in
our country yet'.[13]

The *Sowetan* editorial commented that 'Last week's breakthrough
talks between the ANC and the Government have shown it is possible
for even the fiercest antagonists to sit down and discuss their
problems'.[14]

The editorial of *New Nation* was no less excited and confirmed that:

The talks this week should hopefully see some of the obstacles to
negotiation removed and, for the first time this century, the
prospects of peace for our people have never been so encouraging.

In spite of the great hope the talks have given the majority of
our people, there are those who have tried to trivialise the event.
These represent that cynical fringe that has a vested interest in
continued apartheid rule. They also represent those whose
claimed leadership may in the not too distant future be put to the
test and found wanting.[15]

The *Sunday Tribune* editorial was appropriately entitled 'Now there is
hope', and stated, 'Today, all South Africans who yearn for the chance to
live in peace – and to work for enduring prosperity and a better quality of
life for all – will have good reason to feel on top of the world'.[16]

The meeting had been delayed by two months because of the

violence gripping the country and the failure of the government to arrest it. When it eventually took place, the Groote Schuur Minute was a watershed in the negotiation process for a number of reasons. It was the first formal meeting between the two sides, and both delegations consisted of senior leaders. While the meeting took place behind closed doors, it was a matter of public knowledge that the meeting would and did take place. The meeting also concluded the first formal agreement of its kind and was the first public commitment by both sides to continue with the talks. A common feature in later talks, working groups were established to attend to detail.

Beyond the Groote Schuur Minute

Before the ink had time to dry on the Groote Schuur Minute, two important developments emerged. Firstly, the government secured the passage of the Indemnity Bill through Parliament on 7 May 1990. The aim was to grant permanent indemnity to people who, in the process of conflict and in the pursuance of a cause, may have committed a political offence. However, the extent of the application of the law was to depend on the definition of a 'political offence'. The only opposition to the bill came from the Conservative Party (CP).[17] On 19 May the government indemnified 38 ANC leaders for a period of six months.[18] Secondly, the progress in the working group established by the Groote Schuur Minute was better than had been anticipated, and there was even hope that the timetable for future talks might be accelerated.[19] However, there were still several outstanding issues to be dealt with, including amnesty for the estimated 22 000 exiled ANC personnel, the lifting of the state of emergency, and a review of security and repressive legislation.[20] The report by the joint working group was tabled on time.[21] But it became increasingly evident that the breakthrough had generated expectations that were not immediately realizable. In view of the successful talks, the media and the public, locally and inter-nationally, expected that the parties would immediately proceed into negotiation of a new constitutional dispensation. There was now pressure on parties to maintain the momentum gathered by the agreement, but this did not take place for at least another ten weeks. Despite timeous tabling of the working group report, nothing happened, and both sides alledged the other was dragging its heels. Ken Owen, a prominent liberal editor, may have been right when he suggested that the euphoria had been overdone.[22] On the other hand, considering the nature of the agreement, there was every reason to be euphoric, and every reason to put pressure on the parties. Once it was recognized that change was possible through negotiation, why should the parties not get on with the job? Their apparent inaction only served to generate further doubt and uncertainty, and it was a feeling that would well up often over the next few years of negotiation.

One of the reasons for the delay was that both Mandela and De Klerk separately visited a number of countries to mobilize support for their political positions.[23] Various new developments meant that frequent delays became a general characteristic of the negotiation process. However, it is not unusual for political negotiations to be protracted; they are never smooth, and almost always take place in spurts rather than continua.

Mistrust between the parties

Despite the agreement at Groote Schuur, both parties were fresh from their trenches after waging war for over thirty years, and mutual suspicions and mistrust remained. Each party, for example, remained uncertain as to whether support for the process of negotiation extended to the other's security forces. The most difficult aspect of their mistrust stemmed from the personalities involved, so that it was often perception more than fact that led to the mistrust. By the same token, parties used the excuse of mistrust as an effective negotiating tactic.

During this period several developments deepened this mistrust, the main one being that violence continued unabated. At the same time as the report on the definition of a 'political offence' was tabled, at least twelve residents of Thabong, a township south-east of Johannesburg, were killed by police, shortly after similar killings in the township of Welkom and in Natal.[24] Speaking in Zimbabwe, Mandela claimed that 'while the Government is talking about peace and negotiation, it continues to wage war against us and against neighbouring states'. He also condemned the continuing violence, adding that it was not clear whether the government was actually unable to control its armed forces or whether the violence was a deliberate ploy.[25]

Another aspect of mistrust was a fear of communism. Barely two days after the Groote Schuur Minute, journalists such as Ken Owen studied the composition of the ANC delegation to consider how many of them were communists.[26] Some weeks later, Owen pursued this theme in greater detail, arguing that, 'We know very little else about the SACP, and still less about its role within the ANC. We can see the horse, but the rider is wrapped in mendacity and deceit. Mbeki says we have no future without trust, and he is right: it is time for the SACP to come out of the shadow'.[27]

This mistrust extended to the fear of majority rule.[28] A week after the first formal talks, Nigel Cunningham, a member of the DP, argued in the *Sunday Tribune* that:

> Society is made up of minorities. Democracy is concerned with the protection of the rights and liberty of those minorities. Majority Rule, on the other hand, may deny the rights and liberty of individuals and of the minority groups to which they belong. It is based on the premise that the individual and the minority have no rights and liberties, other than those determined by the majority. There is a danger that all minorities are subordinated to the will of one majority of society, thereby replacing individual choice and liberty with mob rule.[29]

Public debate

Vigorous public debate arose on four crucial questions: whether an interim government was necessary to oversee an election before the drafting of a constitution; whether the new constitution should be drafted by a constituent assembly (should this be after an election or before?); whether sanctions should continue; and whether or not group rights had a place in the constitution. These debates clearly identified the battle lines in future talks.

There were three competing scenarios. The perspective of the National Party had not evolved since the views put forward by P. W. Botha in 1988, in terms of which the present government would remain intact while a 'Great Indaba' (a concept drawn from the KwaZulu Indaba experience) representing the different parties would negotiate a new constitution. This constitution would then be passed by the white-dominated Parliament and brought into effect. This proposal was criticized for its lack of representativeness. The government's response to the criticism was that an election could be held among African people only to verify the representativeness of the negotiators; as for whites, coloureds, and Indians, they had already elected their representatives. The PAC's position was that a new constitutional dispensation could be drafted only in a constituent assembly, but this proposal lacked substantial ideas on the nature of the process leading to the constituent assembly.

The view of the ANC was contained in the Harare Declaration. Thabo Mbeki elaborated the party's ideas further, explaining the framework within which the ANC envisaged constitutional change.[30] The first step was to remove obstacles to negotiation, towards which the Groote Schuur Minute was a start. The second step would be to determine who would be at the negotiating table. The ANC preferred the Namibian process, where the new constitution was drafted only after an election: 'That would stop all the debates about who is bigger, and who is genuinely represented'. The third step would be to agree on the supervision of elections, for the government could not be both referee and player in the same game. The fourth step would be the establishment of an interim government that enjoyed the confidence of all political groups. Another aspect was the question of who would direct the South African Broadcasting Corporation (SABC): 'It is a public corporation, not the property of the NP. It is a very powerful voice. We need to have confidence in their impartiality. They must be able to operate with no pressure from either side'.[31]

International pressures

The support of the international community was important to both the ANC and the NP. Various reforms were instituted by the South African government to shape international opinion, and to this end Minister Gerrit Viljoen confirmed a significant policy shift by the NP. He said that the government did not regard the concept of group rights as non-negotiable, arguing that the protection of minorities was not a principle but rather an element to be considered in the nation-building process.[32] 'Petty apartheid' and other discriminatory laws such as the Separate Amenities Act were to be scrapped. There was also a change of policy in the public service.[33] The Own Affairs ministries, National Education and Agriculture, were consolidated into a single administration, and the government abandoned its policy of 'independent homelands'.[34] Quite apart from the reform they represented, these measures were cost-efficient and made financial sense.[35] They also assisted De Klerk in presenting the case of the government to the European nations that he visited.[36]

De Klerk's visits were successful, for several countries were willing to consider lifting embargoes and restrictions to trade. In his international tour, however, Mandela urged countries to maintain sanctions until there was positive proof that the process of transformation was irreversible. Apartheid was still intact, there were still political prisoners, and the violence continued unabated. Moreover, there was also growing evidence of security force complicity in what came to be called 'third force' violence. Mandela argued that the government had not made sufficient changes to warrant the lifting of sanctions, summing up his argument by pointing out that 'twenty-seven years ago I could not vote. Twenty-seven years later I still cannot vote'.[37]

Public pressure

Public pressure had an enormous impact on the conduct of both negotiating parties, as was the case throughout the process. Upon the announcement of the breakthrough at Groote Schuur, Harold Pakendorf warned in a sobering article:

> Both need to show progress, both need the talks to develop into negotiation – and for the same basic reasons. For the National Party and the ANC know that they are not the only actors on the political stage, that there are others waiting to take over their positions instead of joining the process which has now begun. For the NP it is the Conservative Party and those to its right. For the ANC, it is the Pan Africanist Congress.
>
> The CP walked out of Parliament in protest at what it saw as a sell-out by the NP. The PAC publicly called the ANC sell-outs for talking at Groote Schuur. The oppressors and terrorists have overnight begun to represent the centre of South African politics.[38]

The difficulty the NP found itself in became apparent when P. W. Botha publicly repudiated the Groote Schuur Minute and the talks, revealing that he had not renewed his membership of the NP and that he differed substantially with De Klerk on the path he had forged. De Klerk responded by arguing that his approach was a continuation of that laid down by Botha.[39] The Afrikaner Weerstandsbeweging (AWB) leader, Eugene Terre'Blanche, put his *boere* (Afrikaner farmers) army on display for the benefit of the local and international media.[40] By all accounts they were proficient, well trained, and duly inspired by their leader and a patriotic duty to defend the *volk* (the people) and their land against a black take-over.

Considering such opposition evoked by De Klerk's reforms, it took great courage and leadership to stick to them. This opposition became clearer in a by-election that took place in Umlazi, Natal, a predominantly English-speaking constituency of lower-middle-class NP supporters. The NP majority dropped from 3 000 to only 547 in a year, representing a 27 per cent shift in the vote to the CP.[41] De Klerk maintained that the mandate he had obtained in the 6 September 1989 elections was sufficient, and that he did not require further approval by the electorate for his reform programme.[42]

The ANC also had to deal with the mixed reactions engendered by the Groote Schuur Minute by allaying the fears of its supporters that it was selling out on its objectives of liberation, majority rule, and democracy.[43] The *Sowetan*, on 17 May 1990, argued that negotiation is not a good strategy for liberation: 'Any oppressed people who were fighting for liberation had to bargain with the oppressor from a position of strength – a position which could only be achieved if fundamental liberatory programmes were embarked upon by black people'.

Preparations for constitutional negotiation

The preparations carried out by each of the parties after Groote Schuur clearly showed the seriousness with which they approached the process. The ANC's Constitutional Committee, headed by Zola Skweyiya, convened in South Africa for the first time on 11 June 1990.[44] *p. 276* This committee was assigned to carry out detailed research into the development of the ANC's negotiating positions on a new constitutional dispensation. The National Party, for its part, had the benefit of the Department of Constitutional Development and Planning, which was specifically streamlined to prepare for the negotiation. By mid-June 1990 several cabinet members had produced an important charter of bottom-line principles for a new society, intended as a precondition for all parties intending to participate in the negotiation. It was put to the test in a meeting between government and homeland leaders on 18 June 1990. The meeting agreed that:

> the common interests, aspirations and needs of all South Africans could be expressed in the following six principles:
> - There should be efficient government and administration at national, regional and local levels at all times, before and

during the process of negotiating a new constitutional dispensation.

- There should be economic growth and development to create jobs for our people, to fight poverty and to ensure business and investment confidence in our country and the Southern African region.
- Intimidation and political and other violence should cease, not only for the sake of reconciliation but also because a new, peaceful, just and prosperous South Africa cannot be attained through violence and destructive and unjust methods.
- Peaceful protest as a political method should be used sparingly and responsibly because of its disruptive and emotive effects.
- For any new constitutional dispensation eventually to be approved and supported by the majority of South Africans, all political entities and interests committed to peaceful solutions and having a proven base of support should be involved in negotiating a new constitution.
- The real negotiation for a new constitution should be the highest priority, and should start as soon as possible.[45]

The purpose of this agreement was to put pressure on the ANC to abandon some of its policies.

The obstacles to negotiation

On 25 June 1990, European Community (EC) leaders met at a summit in Dublin and agreed not to ease any of the pressure the EC had previously put in place.[46]

Both the ANC and the NP were agreed that it was necessary to create a climate conducive to negotiation. The Harare Declaration listed five conditions to create such a climate. By the end of June, forty-eight more political prisoners were released, organizations were unbanned, the state of emergency was lifted in all areas but Natal, there was a moratorium on all executions, and a joint working group was formed to deal with the definition of political offences affecting political prisoners, and returning exiles requiring indemnity.[47]

For De Klerk, South Africa was irrevocably on the road to far-reaching constitutional change. Sanctions and armed struggle were therefore inimical to a negotiated settlement. However, according to Roelf Meyer, the NP was not ready to remove the remaining obstacles identified in the Harare Declaration until the ANC committed itself to abandoning its policy of armed struggle.[48] Mandela argued otherwise: both sanctions and the ANC's policy on armed struggle were weapons of change that had to remain in place until change was irreversible. Armed struggle, for example, could be ended only by a mutually binding cease-fire agreement.

The ANC, for its part, complained that the government failed to deal with the paramilitary right wing and was unwilling to deal with the lack of discipline in the police force.[49] The ANC described the Harms Commission of Inquiry into politically motivated crimes as 'toothless'. The government, it claimed, also failed to dismantle the Civil Co-operation Bureau (CCB), which was a military intelligence front carrying out 'dirty tricks' against opponents of the government.[50] As confirmation of the bona fides of the ANC, the commander of Umkhonto we Sizwe, Joe Modise, promised to agree to a cessation of hostilities if the obstacles in the way of negotiation were removed.[51]

By the end of June 1990, however, the tide of media opinion had begun to turn against the ANC, and it was accused of delaying the negotiations unnecessarily. Because the ANC did not timeously respond to these concerns, it was assumed that the ANC could offer no credible reason for the delay.[52] Finally, on 10 July, a meeting of the joint working group took place and agreed to a revised report containing recommendations to be made to their principals.[53]

The Pretoria Minute

DEALING WITH THE OBSTACLES

In the meantime, bilateral discussions continued around the shape of future negotiations and key constitutional issues.[54] At the beginning of July 1990 Mandela's statements reflected greater optimism, and for him, the prospects for dismantling apartheid were better now than ever before.[55] There were also other signs that the ANC was prepared to review its stand on several matters including sanctions and armed struggle.

The ANC's review of sanctions was informed by the reluctance of the international community to maintain heavy sanctions and the negative impact they made in the media. According to Mandela, the ANC was 'even more concerned than government' about sanctions because they were destroying the economy and blacks were the first to suffer through the loss of jobs.[56] However, this debate was a red herring. As pointed out by former leader of the opposition, F. van Zyl Slabbert,

> the most dangerous illusion created by the sanctions debate is that when De Klerk and Mandela agree to end the call for sanctions, untold millions of investment capital will pour into SA. Nothing of the kind will happen. If the process of transition does not lead to confidence no turnabout on the sanctions debate will have any effect whatsoever. It is far more important to persuade investors of the viability of the society that will result from transition than to score debating points in the campaign for or against sanctions.[57]

The real issue was not so much the economic impact of sanctions but their symbolism. The question of armed struggle was more difficult, for it was a symbol of hope of liberation to the majority in the country. Yet it was, by the same token, evident to the ANC that liberation would not come from the 'barrel of the gun'. For the government, however, the concept of a 'mutual cessation of hostilities' posed real problems.[58]

Aside from the lack of clear meaning in the phrase, the government interpreted this demand to mean that the ANC wanted the security forces hamstrung. Related to this was the question of legislation that made armed acts unlawful. The government mooted a 'cut-off date' for purposes of indemnification, which was convenient as the date could also be applied to the return of exiles and the release of political prisoners. There was still some hesitation, however, in allowing exiles to return and in releasing prisoners while the ANC maintained its policy of armed struggle. It was during this period that the ANC began to recognize that it was not possible for the government to address all the obstacles identified in the Harare Declaration, and that it needed to review its position.

The first indications of such a review came from the ANC's educational publication entitled *The Road to Peace* early in July 1990. In its evaluation of progress, it recognized that

> In the present situation, it seems that we need to consider some of these questions afresh or in greater depth. Do all our preconditions need to be met before there can be negotiation? Must all apartheid laws be scrapped before the democratic forces can negotiate with the forces of apartheid?
>
> We need to be more precise and examine which preconditions need to be met immediately to ensure participation of authentic leaders acting with a mandate from organisations in an atmosphere where consultation is possible. What is suggested here, is a shift in the way we tackle preconditions. In no way do we abandon our demand for the total abolition of apartheid laws. ... We cannot conduct a struggle in some pure form where one tactic serves us all the time, or where we use only one weapon. We must change if the struggle needs it. What we need now is to reorient ourselves towards the questions of negotiation.[59]

The agitation of the ANC was obvious, never more so than during Mandela's international tour, when his concerns were apparent in the changing tone of his statements. In the last few weeks of this tour he was more optimistic and reconciliatory, and promised to meet De Klerk within '48 hours' of his return to the country.[60]

The NP was also agitated, aware that ongoing public parrying was damaging to themselves and to the process. The urgency of the encounter between the two leaders injected an air of immediacy into the negotiations and served to restore some of the momentum lost in the weeks past. They agreed to a further round of formal talks on 6 August 1990.

There was also concern about the effect of the delay on the planning of the process of negotiation. It was necessary to have a new constitutional dispensation by no later than 1994, because in that year the mandate of the De Klerk government expired, and it was obliged to call an election in 1995. According to Roelf Meyer, 'we would have to have some resolutions before then. . . . We can't foresee another election in South Africa to elect a parliament and a new executive without blacks participating in that as well'.[61]

The idea developed by the NP over the preceding months was for a two-chamber parliament, a concept much like that of the 'Great Indaba'. In terms of the proposal, the upper house (senate) would consist of representatives elected by 'cultural groups'. By giving the upper house significant powers, positions adopted in parliament would not adversely affect any particular group. This was the NP's response to the fear of a black majority, while the ANC, though it remained opposed to a minority veto, was not averse to rights for minorities.[62]

The concept of an interim government was also elaborated upon. The ANC insisted that a new constitutional dispensation had to be drafted by an elected constituent assembly after the installation of an interim government, the scenario proposed in the Harare Declaration. However, what the ANC did not elaborate on was the constitutional dispensation under which such an interim government would operate. For the NP, its opposition was based on the fear of a constitutional hiatus during the interim period.[63] The DP and the Labour Party[64] shared the NP's opposition to an election for a constituent assembly and an interim government.[65] This argument was not valid, however, because there could be no constitutional hiatus until the prevailing constitution was repealed or replaced. Nevertheless, the issue was that if the country continued to have parliamentary sovereignty, an interim government over which the NP had no control could effect legislation that might not be in its interests. What concerned the NP was the lack of a guaranteed protection of its interests during the tenure of an interim government. Naturally, the party was also concerned about the impression that would be caused by the installation of a government in which it would have no control.

In the meantime, the ANC was preparing a massive campaign to mobilize public support in favour of its demand for an interim government and constituent assembly.[66] The government feared mass action, and did everything possible to persuade the ANC to desist from such tactics; but during November 1990 the powerful Pretoria-Witwatersrand-Vereeniging (PWV) region of the ANC launched such a campaign, demanding the release of all political prisoners and the return of exiles, as well as the suspension of political trials, before the end of the year. It also demanded the establishment of an interim government and the reincorporation of Bophuthatswana into South Africa. In a further show of strength, the ANC held large marches in several major centres.[67] The response of the government was to question the ANC's commitment to peace.[68]

OVERCOMING THE OBSTACLES

On the eve of the scheduled 6 August meeting between the ANC and the government, news broke of the arrest of the leadership and a number of operatives of Operation Vula, among them Mac Maharaj, a member of the ANC's NEC since 1985 and the operation's commander.[69] Ronnie Kasrils, Maharaj's deputy, was on the run.[70] It has been noted above that Operation Vula was an ANC operation planned after the ANC's Kabwe Conference in 1985, and that it aimed at relocating some of its most senior leadership inside South Africa. Hence Maharaj, an NEC member, and Kasrils and Siphiwe Nyanda, both senior members of the ANC, had been deployed inside the country by 1988.[71] The operation had been treated with such sensitivity that not even the

NEC was aware of it; it was directly accountable only to Oliver Tambo and, in his absence, Alfred Nzo, the ANC's Secretary-General.

There was immediate speculation that there would be either a split in the ranks of the ANC or a plot to overthrow the government by force.[72] The ANC denied this and demanded the release of Maharaj.[73] But the organization had been tardy in its response to the arrests, and this gave rise to allegations based on significant negative media speculation and coverage. Despite the media hype, both parties agreed not to allow anything to jeopardize the scheduled meeting,[74] despite demands by the right wing that the meeting be called off.[75] The ANC announced its team as comprising Nelson Mandela, Alfred Nzo, Thabo Mbeki, Joe Slovo, and Joe Modise, and the government's delegation included De Klerk, Gerrit Viljoen, Kobie Coetsee, Adriaan Vlok, and Pik Botha.[76] Since Operation Vula had been labelled a communist 'insurrectionary plot', De Klerk again unsuccessfully called upon Mandela to exclude Slovo from the delegation.[77]

Despite these events, there was increasing hope and speculation that the 6 August meeting would produce another major breakthrough.[78] However, the troubled experience did highlight two points, namely the commitment of both parties to negotiation, and the recognition that the situation in the country was extremely dynamic and volatile. It was therefore necessary to allow the process of negotiation to continue post-haste.[79] The *Business Day* editorial of 6 August 1990 said:

> The air of fragility that surrounded the Groote Schuur meeting of the ANC and the National Party has dissipated, thanks in part to the testing events of the past fortnight during which the 'Red scare' did its worst, and failed to derail the process. Nelson Mandela and the ANC are committed, beyond much doubt, to a search for peace; President de Klerk and his Cabinet have staked their political future on the same purpose.
>
> Precarious hope has given way to confidence; the odds favour continuing negotiation rather than breakdown.

THE AGREEMENT TO REMOVE OBSTACLES

On 6 August 1990 the government and the ANC met at the Presidensie in Pretoria[80] for talks that started at 9a.m. and continued for a marathon thirteen hours.[81] This meeting gave birth to the Pretoria Minute,[82] an agreement that all the obstacles identified by the ANC as obstructing negotiations would be removed or addressed.[83]

Both parties accepted the amended report of the joint working group. Moreover, the ANC announced its decision to suspend its armed actions 'In the interest of moving as speedily as possible towards a negotiated peaceful political settlement and in the context of the agreements reached'.[84] Target dates were set for the phased release of political prisoners to start on 1 September 1990, and for the granting of indemnities as of 1 October 1990.[85] A working group was established and instructed to draw up a plan for the release of ANC political prisoners and the granting of indemnity to exiles.[86] The working group was also authorized to appoint a body of local experts to assist it in its task. This process was to be completed by the end of the year.

In addition, the government undertook to lift the state of emergency in Natal as soon as possible and to review the Internal Security Act.[87] Both parties committed themselves to steps aimed at normalizing and stabilizing the situation 'in line with the spirit of mutual trust obtaining between the leaders involved'. Finally, they agreed that 'against this background, the way is now open to proceed towards negotiation on a new constitution'.

OPPOSITION TO THE AGREEMENT

The Pretoria Minute also recognized the need to include other political parties in the process of negotiation. With this in mind, the government invited the PAC on 17 August 1990 to hold similar talks. The PAC rejected this invitation,[88] in spite of the fact that the PAC would not be able to derive any benefits from the Pretoria Minute as its terms only affected the ANC.[89] AZAPO was also invited and also responded with a rejection.[90]

The international community was unanimous in applauding the outcome of the talks,[91] as were the South African business and religious communities. The Conservative Party, on the other hand, rejected the agreement; in his respose to the Pretoria Minute, Dr Ferdi Hartzenberg called on whites to 'resist the moves of the government and to fight for our liberation'.[92] Similarly, the PAC and AZAPO recorded their unequivocal rejection of the agreement reached.[93] There was also a considerable amount of disquiet within ANC ranks, especially from its youth.[94] To ease matters, the ANC asked senior leaders to explain the agreement to its supporters throughout the country,[95] and to this end a report was also placed in several newspapers.[96]

The Inkatha Freedom Party (IFP) and its leader, Mangosuthu Buthelezi, welcomed the ANC's announcement of the suspension of its armed action and the Pretoria Minute. However, Buthelezi threatened that the violence would not end until there was agreement between himself and Mandela, for it seemed that the IFP leader felt slighted by the fact that he was not respected as a role-player and invited to these meetings.[97] This theme would surface throughout the process and poison the relationship between the two leaders.

On 16 September the IFP's Central Committee resolved to urge De Klerk to hold an urgent conference for all those who hoped to sit around the negotiating table.[98] At the same time it called on the OAU and the UN to demand that Mandela meet with Buthelezi to deal with the question of violence. However, when Mandela first requested a meeting with Buthelezi, it was rejected.[99]

THE ESCALATION OF POLITICAL VIOLENCE

The ANC's NEC met in October 1990 to discuss the escalation of violence, and resolved that a meeting be called with the IFP.[100] This time Buthelezi welcomed the invitation. It was to be the first face-to-face encounter between the two since Mandela's release from prison. Meanwhile, Buthelezi met with Dr Andries Treurnicht, leader of the CP, early in November 1990 to exchange views on negotiation.[101] At the meeting, Buthelezi again vented his anger at being 'marginalized' by the ANC, stating that it was necessary to take ethnic and group realities into account in a new South Africa.

As these parties manoeuvred, violence was escalating to frightening proportions. Ironically, just as the Pretoria Minute was being nego-tiated, twelve people were killed in a clash between supporters of the ANC and IFP in Kagiso, a township west of Johannesburg.[102] This followed battles the previous month between the same parties in Sebokeng, south of Johannesburg, in which at least twenty-two people died. The conflict that had resulted in the loss of 3 000 in Natal in the previous three years was now spreading to the PWV (Pretoria / Witwatersrand / Vereeniging) region. According to the South African Institute of Race Relations, deaths as a result of political violence increased to 3 699 during 1990, up from 1 403 deaths the year before. Roughly half of the victims in 1990 came from Natal.[103] A related problem was the growing evidence of a 'dirty tricks' campaign waged by the security forces and their involvement in the violence. Allegations were also made that the security forces were not doing enough to curb the violence.[104]

At the end of August the parties announced the names of their members on the Pretoria Minute joint working group that would consider the question of a cessation of hostilities.[105] The ANC delegates included Joe Modise, Thabo Mbeki, Jacob Zuma, Joe Nhlanhla, and Pallo Jordan, as well as Chris Hani, included in the team despite the fact that the government refused to renew his indemnity.[106] The govern-ment's delegates were Adriaan Vlok, Roelf Meyer, General B. J. Beukes of the Security Police, Johan Geyser of the Department of Justice, Dr H. P. Fourie of the Department of Foreign Affairs, and Maritz Spaar-water of the National Intelligence Service.

At the beginning of September 1990 the mood in the country was buoyant, for it was becoming evident that negotiating the transfor-mation of South Africa could succeed. Mandela confirmed that 'the next stage of the talks between the government and the ANC should be concerned with the question of identifying the people who are going to be entrusted with the task of drawing up a new constitution'.[107] The excitement was short-lived, however, as the escalation of violence again began to threaten the negotiation process.[108] Mandela argued that the government had the capacity to put an end to the violence and should be held responsible for this failure, while it was also alleged that the government was waging war and talking about peace at the same time.[109] The dreaded 'Operation Fist' was intended to prevent intimidation and deal with the political conflict, but the result was a continuation of repression that made it difficult to carry out free political activity. Even under this cloud Mandela refused to abandon the negotiations, arguing that this would only serve to play into the hands of those responsible for 'third force' violence.[110]

The ANC believed that the situation was serious enough to warrant a further summit with the government, but the government disagreed.[111] It was during this period that another form of potentially violent resistance was beginning to emerge in the form of the right wing. After the government announced its plans to reform or repeal the Land Act, the CP confirmed that it had plans for a resistance campaign.[112] To this extent, there was added criticism from black people that the government was not acting even-handedly.[113]

DEVELOPING CONSTITUTIONAL PROPOSALS

In a separate development, the National Party announced that its membership was open to all races, a decision that was welcomed by many. De Klerk was confident enough to confirm that 'South Africa will never go back to the pattern of racism and apartheid'.[114] The development of the NP's constitutional proposals was also at an advanced stage as the Broederbond prepared its constitutional model.[115]

The proposal included a multi-party cabinet with rotating chairpersons; a ceremonial head of state; and two chambers of parliament including a one-person-one-vote house of representatives and a senate with ten members elected by each region and ten members elected by each group (defined non-racially). There would be ten regions, each with a democratic regional government and its own constitution. The dispensation would also include a bill of rights. An important development in government thinking was the move away from the system of provincial and homeland governments to one comprising strong regional governments.[116] According to De Klerk, expanded powers of local and regional government would prevent any single group from monopolizing power at central government level. Such a devolution of power would play an important role in protecting minorities.[117] In November 1990 the National Party considered abandoning its ideas of parliamentary sovereignty[118] and the protection of racial or ethnic minorities.[119] With regard to the concept of minorities, Gerrit Viljoen stated that 'The minorities will, of course, have to differ in two respects from the existing groups in South African society in order to gain credence. In the first place, they must not be based on race or colour, and in the second place the definition must allow freedom of association. The rights and values the government wants to have protected for minority groups are moreover not special privileges for a particular minority group alone, but rights and values that must be available to the nation as a whole'.[120]

The crisis in local government and the government's demand for strong regional power forced the debate around a regional dispensation to the centre stage. Viljoen argued that the most likely scenario was for 'development regions' to replace provinces, where each of these units would have a large measure of fiscal autonomy and its own tax base.[121] This idea was rejected by the ANC, which in turn proposed a strong central government, while recognizing the need for decentralization of power. According to Zola Skweyiya, the head of the ANC's legal and constitutional department, 'There is a general feeling that although central government must have some control over the issues that are vital to the conduct of government, national, regional and local authorities must be given some leverage on exercising a choice among competing priorities'.[122]

Skweyiya went on to criticize the proposals as an attempt to entrench white privilege while appearing to concede some powers to black communities. This the NP hoped to achieve by ensuring that the future South Africa would be a capitalist state in which class would balance race in a system of checks and balances. The proposals embraced a weak parliament, a constitution that institutionalized privatized apartheid and maintained inequalities, the entrenchment of powerful economic privileges, and a judiciary to defend this arrangement.

It was on this subject that the government met again with the leaders of all homeland governments, including Buthelezi.[123] The meeting gave rise to speculation that the NP could go into an electoral alliance with other 'moderates', as the Democratic Turnhalle Alliance had done in Namibia. During this period, De Klerk also hinted at a possible alliance with the DP,[124] announcing that, 'our aim is a winning alliance. I believe absolutely that it is attainable'.[125]

Late in October the Human Sciences Research Council (HSRC) released a study arguing that a new constitution would only enjoy legitimacy among the majority if drafted by an elected constituent assembly, and cautioning against any 'quick fix' solutions.[126]

IMPLEMENTATION OF THE PRETORIA MINUTE

Within two months of the Pretoria Minute, the progress made seemed to be rendered virtually meaningless.[127] The joint monitoring group established to track the ANC's suspension of armed action could not even arrive at a definition of 'armed struggle'. Moreover, the report was delayed until November because the government refused to indemnify Chris Hani.[128] When it was finally released, the report was met with some relief. It recorded progress, especially on the sensitive issues of ANC arms caches, military recruitment, and an enforcement of the suspension of armed actions.[129]

Despite the report, however, controversy around the implications of the agreement to suspend armed actions remained.[130] The government insisted that such a suspension include the surrender of arms caches, an end to the recruitment of new MK members, and the abolition of 'mass action'. The ANC disputed this, insisting that the government first disband covert security force units. The ANC also objected to the NP's linking the release of political prisoners and indemnity of exiles to the armed struggle in order to force further concessions from the ANC.

Furthermore, only forty-five prisoners were released between August and September, and a further twenty-seven a few weeks later, just before De Klerk was to undertake yet another tour of European nations.[131] The delay in releasing political prisoners also resulted in disturbances within the prisons as many prisoners went on hunger strike to apply further pressure.[132] There was no movement on the return of exiles either, since the ANC was unhappy with the amount of detail required on the questionnaire provided by the government for those requiring indemnity.[133]

To help the process along, the United Nations High Commission for Refugees (UNHCR) offered to assist in the repatriation of some 20 000 refugees.[134] At a meeting between Mandela and De Klerk it was agreed that the cut-off date for indemnity be fixed as the date of the meeting: 8 October 1990.[135] This came after agreement on the report by the joint working group on this question was reached. In addition, the joint working group agreed on 1 November 1990 that the indemnities offered affected members of all groups, and not only the ANC.[136]

At another level, the dreaded Reservation of Separate Amenities Act was repealed on 15 October 1990, thus removing the legal basis for 'petty apartheid'.[137] During November De Klerk reshuffled his cabinet in a bid to clear the decks for negotiation, a process that he would repeat later on. [138] In the case of Minister Gerrit Viljoen, while he shed responsibility for one department, he had an additional Deputy-Minister, Tertius Delport, appointed to assist Roelf Meyer. Both government negotiators were to play an increasingly important part in the negotiation effort.

During this period the country also witnessed an intensification of political conflict at the level of local government, as people demanded the resignation of local government councillors and 'bantustan [homeland] regimes'.[139] At the same time, there was a mushrooming of 'organs of people's rule' such as street and village committees. Local authorities in black areas were rendered incapable of governing.

A financial crisis was developing in local government as well, since more than half of the local authorities in the Transvaal, a total of forty-seven, were in the throes of rent and utilities boycotts. The councils faced a total debt of more than R1 billion to the Transvaal Provincial Administration. Eskom, the parastatal responsible for power supply, was taking legal action against seventeen councils that owed R23 million for electricity. Another ten councils were facing similar action. Cut-offs of electricity and water led to unrest and mass action, and a troubled government had to ask itself whether it was still effectively in control.

As the country moved towards a new constitutional dispensation, business and labour began to assert their right to influence the negotiations, adamant that the drafting of the new constitution should not be the task of politicians and lawyers only.[140] The general upheaval and the government's perception of mass action as obstacles to negotiation were cause for a further meeting between Mandela and De Klerk on 27 November 1990.[141] The concern precipitated by the crisis was evident in the editorials of major Sunday newspapers.[142] The meeting confirmed that negotiation was still on track and that progress depended on the outcome of the reports of the joint working groups.[143]

It was against this background that De Klerk's cabinet went into a 'bosberaad', or retreat, to plan its priorities for the approaching parliamentary session.[144] They decided to establish a negotiating team for the NP separate from that of the government.[145] Immediately after the bosberaad, Mandela and De Klerk met several times to consider a wide range of issues, including the ongoing violence and the current dispute with regard to the interpretation of paragraph 3 of the Pretoria Minute, which dealt with armed struggle and armed action.[146] The dispute related to continued recruitment and training by Umkhonto we Sizwe.

Between 14 and 16 December 1990 the ANC held a National Consultative Conference at NASREC near Soweto.[147] This conference called for the establishment of defence units and threatened to suspend participation in the negotiation process if all outstanding obstacles were not removed by 30 April 1991, which was the date agreed to in the Pretoria Minute for the removal of obstacles to negotiation.[148] Delegates were suspicious of the bilateral discussions taking place, and criticized the leadership for not consulting the membership or reporting to them, highlighting the level of mistrust and suspicion that existed even within the party. While the conference mandated the leadership to continue with the talks, its main resolutions set the ANC on a course of mass action aimed at applying further pressure on government.[149]

On 18 December, the government gazetted legislation that allowed for most exiles to return to South Africa. This went a long way to satisfying one of the remaining obstacles to negotiation.[150] In view of the threatened mass action, De Klerk felt moved to bring forward his annual Christmas message and provide a state-of-the-nation address.[151] In a hard-hitting broadcast, he challenged the ANC to choose between supporting peaceful negotiation and reverting to the old order of confrontation and conflict.[152]

The end of 1990 was a disappointing anti-climax to a year filled with great hope and expectation. Some of the most momentous changes in the history of the country had taken place, but the spectre of violence had begun to show its ugly face in the guise of the 'third force'. Furthermore, little was being done to bring about peace, and the people of South Africa were left in a state of great uncertainty.

The D. F. Malan Accord

PAVING THE WAY TO MULTI-PARTY NEGOTIATIONS

The new year began on a more positive note. Every year on 8 January the ANC released on its birthday a policy statement of the challenges facing the organization and its constituencies. In its 1991 statement, it proposed an all-party conference on constitutional negotiation that would include the IFP and the CP.[153] This conference would have three tasks: to set out broad constitutional principles, to determine the composition of the body that would draft the constitution, and to establish an interim government to oversee the process of transition.[154] While the government, the DP, and the IFP welcomed the idea, the PAC, AZAPO, and the CP remained opposed.[155] It was also agreed that the first meeting between Mandela and Buthelezi would take place on 29 January.[156]

The meeting was a success and a joint declaration was released calling on supporters of both parties to desist from vilification of other organizations or their leaders. The declaration also called on people not to 'coerce or intimidate anyone in the pursuit of their organisation's strategies and programmes'.[157] A mechanism to monitor violations of the agreement was settled, and it was resolved that the two leaders would jointly tour the violence-torn areas. Further meetings between the leaders were also agreed to, and the meeting was hailed as an important breakthrough for peace.[158] However, violence continued to escalate without reprieve. A further meeting between the two leaders took place on 31 March 1991 to discuss the problem, in which they agreed to discuss the question of violence jointly with De Klerk.[159] This meeting sought to deal with the establishment of peace committee structures throughout the country.

On the first anniversary of his 2 February 1990 speech, De Klerk was keen to be seen taking the initiative, especially after the ANC's call for an all-party congress. In his opening speech to Parliament he announced the total scrapping of major discriminatory laws, including the Population Registration Act, the Group Areas Act,[160] and the Land Act.[161] Apartheid was given its official death warrant: De Klerk expected these laws to be repealed by June 1991.[162] The requirements for the lifting of the ban on trade by the European Community had now been met, and he accordingly wasted no time in challenging these countries to 'translate basic feelings into real deeds'.[163]

What De Klerk did not explain was that the repeal of the Population Registration Act did not mean that there was a common voters' roll, for the three separate racially-based voters' rolls remained, and the change only affected new citizens.[164] Notwithstanding this indiscretion, the move was a positive development. The NP had argued previously that the Population Registration Act would only be repealed as part of the negotiation for a new constitution, so now it was no longer a bargaining chip. On the other hand, although this was a perfect opportunity for De Klerk to remove all the outstanding obstacles to negotiation, he failed to provide for a general amnesty and amend security legislation.

THE AGREEMENT

In another breakthrough, an agreement was brokered on the meaning of the 'suspension of armed action and related activities'. The agreement was confirmed at D. F. Malan Airport in Cape Town on 12 February 1991 and thus came to be known as the D. F. Malan Accord.[165] The accord effectively removed most obstacles in the way of a multiparty conference. In terms of the agreement, the ANC undertook not to carry out armed attacks or infiltrate South Africa with men or weapons. Recruitment of cadres for military training inside the country would also cease. There would be no statements inciting violence, threats of armed action, or the creation of underground structures.[166] There was no agreement, however, on the surrender of ANC weapons, the identification of arms caches, the demobilization of cadres, or the establishment of self-defence units.[167] It was further agreed that membership of Umkhonto we Sizwe would not be unlawful, individual weapons would be licensed, and the right to peaceful demonstrations would be maintained.

With regard to indemnities, two former judges (Justices Solomon and Leon) and an Appeal Court judge (Justice Steyn) were appointed to chair committees to determine whether awaiting-trial prisoners and exiles should be granted individual indemnity.[168] On 12 March there was a further breakthrough, when it was agreed that ANC members who had undergone military training automatically qualified for indemnity.[169] In March 1991, thirty-three political prisoners were released after being granted unconditional indemnity,[170] these releases bringing the number of political prisoners released to 310.[171] At the same time, the National Co-ordinating Committee for Repatriation (NCCR) was facilitating the return of a number of exiles.[172] Another positive development was the lifting of the ban on outdoor political meetings.[173] This ban had been in force for the last fifteen years and was a source of much contention and frustration. Its removal greatly assisted the move towards free political activity.

However, many in the ANC were suspicious of the agreement, believing that the negotiation was a trap from which the ANC would not be able to recover. However, the ANC leadership remained confident about the negotiations.[174] The agreement also led to relations between the PAC and the ANC being further soured: the PAC denounced the agreement and asked the ANC to review its decision to participate in the all-party conference. The PAC's Benny Alexander asserted, 'in the absence of the ballot, the bullet cannot be abandoned'.[175]

Meanwhile, De Klerk met with leaders of the homelands, including Rev. Allan Hendrickse, Dr J. N. Reddy, and Mangosuthu Buthelezi, late in February 1991.[176] They supported the need for the multi-party conference. Speaking to leaders of the Venda government a month later, De Klerk argued that the agreement to hold the multi-party conference opened the door for the reincorporation of the TBVC states (Transkei, Bophuthatswana, Venda, and Ciskei) into South Africa, and would allow their participation in such a conference.[177]

5

Preparing to negotiate

IT TOOK NEARLY TWO YEARS of formal talks to remove the obstacles in the path of multi-party negotiations. However, it was not until nearly ten months after these agreements were reached that such negotiations actually started. Nonetheless, multi-party negotiations were finally a reality. The major stakeholders began preparations on their negotiating positions and positioned themselves for an outcome that would suit them best. In doing this, the parties faced some of their most difficult challenges.

One of their immediate difficulties was honouring the agreements founded on the Groote Schuur and Pretoria Minutes and the D. F. Malan Accord. The effect of these agreements was to create the necessary conditions for multi-party negotiations to take place. Unfortunately, however, the country was now in the grip of the spectre of 'third force' violence, a factor that presented parties, and particularly their political leaders, with their most serious test yet. In dealing with the problem of violence, the parties would learn an important lesson in political negotiation, that the government cannot be both player and impartial referee at the same time.

Against all odds

By April 1991 the process of negotiation was under threat once more, and as before, the cause of the problem was the unrelenting spiral of violence. De Klerk made it his explanation for the delay in commencing multi-party negotiations.[1] The ANC did not accept this, and on 5 April 1991 issued De Klerk with an ultimatum.

This ultimatum came in the form of an open letter, demanding that the Ministers of Defence, Magnus Malan, and Law and Order, Adriaan Vlok, be removed. The ultimatum also required the government to meet these demands by no later than 9 May, failing which the organization threatened to suspend all constitutional talks.[2] The ANC also made specific demands regarding the security forces,[3] and called for the removal of all officers directly involved with the CCB and other hit squads, and the dismantling and disarming of all special counterinsurgency units including the CCB, Koevoet, and Askaris.[4]

The ANC argued that the government had to accept responsibility for the violence, and questioned the government's failure to bring it to an end, since, in the ANC's view, it had the capacity to do so.[5] The ANC also argued that there was evidence of the state's complicity in the violence, and the IFP was accused of playing a role as well. In explaining the ultimatum to diplomats, Mandela confirmed that what the ANC was really looking for was an act of good faith by the government, as there was a growing perception in the ANC that the government was dragging its heels.[6]

The response of the IFP was equally harsh as Buthelezi angrily threatened to opt out of the negotiations and raised the spectre of civil war.[7] The effect of the exchange served to inflame national debate. The government attacked the ANC ultimatum and accused the organization of shifting the goalposts and derailing the negotiation process.[8]

On 12 April 1991 the ANC unveiled its proposed constitutional principles in a discussion document, which to some extent had the effect of shifting public focus away from the prospect of a total breakdown.[9] It was also a display of serious intent and commitment to the negotiations.[10] The discussion document called for a unitary, nonracial, and democratic state with a bill of rights. There would be an elected president as head of state and a prime minister as head of the cabinet. The judiciary would be independent, and would have the ability to set aside laws that were unconstitutional; in this way, the constitution's sovereignty would be protected. The document also envisaged a two-house parliament composed of a national assembly and a senate elected by way of proportional representation. The document finally called for comment and debate by all. The most striking aspect of these proposals was their similarity to those of the NP. While there remained major differences in approach, it became clear that there was a convergence developing between the two perspectives. This provided a basis for further negotiation.[11]

The government also produced new proposals on both process and substantive matters. While it still rejected the idea of an interim government, it accepted the need for some transitional arrangement to give extra-parliamentary formations a voice in the legislature and executive.[12] In making this concession, the government's chief negotiator, Gerrit Viljoen, insisted that the government would at all times retain ultimate authority throughout the transition and that it had no intention of abdicating power.[13] According to Viljoen, government objected to a surrender of its power and authority to the interim structure,[14] a view supported by the leader of the DP, Zach de Beer.[15] Viljoen made it clear that:

> The continuous, complex and most responsible business of governing a nation remains the task of the National Party government until such time as the proposed changes have taken place. The same applies to the present constitution and its institutions. The Government will continue to govern and the National Party will negotiate. ... The lawful institutions of government and administration, set up according to the valid constitution and laws of the land, will continue to provide sound government and administration. ... But there are four possibilities of acceptable transitional arrangements.
>
> Firstly, the mooted negotiating forum might itself acquire the stature and capacity to influence the legislative, executive and administrative processes directly and with great authority – but its primary task will remain the achievement of consensus on a new constitution.
>
> Secondly, an informal, influential leadership corps could emerge during negotiation, which might even develop into a formal structure.

Thirdly, the Cabinet could be expanded, with the approval of the negotiating forum, to include a relatively broad spectrum of competent South Africans.

Fourthly, multi-party working groups specialising in various fields of government could emerge and provide guidance in the transitional period to the established Government institution.[16]

On the question of power-sharing and minority rights, Viljoen said:

There is no possibility of its [the government's] simply disappearing from the political stage and handing over to one or other potentate or group with no experience of what the governance of a sophisticated country involves. South Africa is not a colony that is now becoming independent; it has been constitutionally emancipated for decades. A system in which the arithmetic majority is effectively given all political power for a period is unacceptable and unworkable. There must be a balance between one person, one vote, and the effective protection of minorities.

There could be a head of state and a head of government, elected by each house, or the Swiss model could be followed, providing for a collective multiparty college with a rotating chairman.

The government's strategy was one that would allow it to emerge from negotiation with as much of its power intact as possible. Ironically, it insisted that a new government did not need the structural power that the National Party had itself relied on for more than four decades. While the government's views accorded with those of the ANC on most issues, the major differences lay in the treatment of minorities. Viljoen continued:

As an instrument of minority protection, consideration should be given to a central legislature comprising two Houses. In this way a balance will be achieved between universal voting rights and majority power in the one House, and minority rights protection through special representation and decision-making power for minorities in the other House, a multi-party compilation of the legislative authority (or Cabinet) and a spreading of the powers that are concentrated in the office of the President.

There should be a chamber of minorities in which special voting procedures and raised majority requirements could operate in decision-making over sensitive, fundamental issues. Structures of self-determination by individual communities must serve as a fundamental building block of minority protection. Where a local community can identify itself on non-racial grounds and through voluntary association, it must, if it so chooses, be allowed to establish its own community structure. This structure would deal with community matters, including aspects of education, welfare, surroundings and culture. Such structures must be able to generate their own funds. . . . Powers should be devolved to regions as far as possible.

Towards the end of April 1991, President F. W. de Klerk carried out one of his most successful international visits to Europe, and returned confident with the praise he received. However, he was also aware that he was returning to one of the most serious crises to threaten the process, for the deadline set by the ANC ultimatum was drawing near, and there were still disagreements, accusations, and counter-accusations over the release of political prisoners.[17]

One of the more serious obstacles to negotiation remained the dreaded Internal Security Act, but on 2 May 1991 De Klerk confirmed that it was to be drastically amended.[18] However, he was keen to address the ANC's demands in a way that would not appear a sign of weakness. A week later De Klerk held separate discussions with Buthelezi and Mandela in the hope that it would be possible to hold a summit on violence. In this way, De Klerk could show that he was seriously addressing the question of violence.[19] However, despite broad agreement that a summit on the question was necessary, it was not to be: on 18 May the ANC announced that it was pulling out of constitutional talks with the government and out of the summit, because the ANC opposed the peace conference's being called by

President F. W. de Klerk; as Joe Slovo explained: 'implicit in it is the inference that the state is an impartial body standing above the violence and is calling all those connected with it plus a broader section of the community to discuss it. We dismiss the implication'.[20]

The editorial in the *Star* on 22 May 1991 pointed out that De Klerk had made a basic negotiating mistake:

> It is this: in the lead-up to negotiation – especially between suspicious parties – process is everything. How the protagonists are lured to the negotiating table is as important as what happens when they get there. Judged by that yardstick, De Klerk made two elementary negotiating errors.
>
> He called the conference unilaterally and without consultation. And he virtually declared himself the referee, though clearly, in the eyes of other parties, he is a participant, even an 'accused'. It was an invitation to breakdown.

The ANC called for a two-day general strike, mass protests, a consumer boycott, and a day of fasting, in solidarity with political prisoners,[21] but did not sever all its contact with the government and continued to take part in the joint working groups on prisoner releases, repatriation of exiles, and the suspension of hostilities. On 20 May De Klerk and King Goodwill Zwelithini agreed to measures prohibiting the carrying of dangerous weapons in public places.[22] The only exception to this rule was for weapons carried for strictly 'cultural' purposes. This was a significant breakthrough towards peace.

On 31 May 1991 white South Africa celebrated its 30th anniversary as a republic. In marking this day, De Klerk made an impassioned plea in support of constitutional change, acknowledging that had it not been for the violence, the country would be well on the road to negotiating its future.[23] Early in June, the twelve members of the European Community gave the South African government a tough warning to end the political violence in the country,[24] the strongly worded reprimand coming in a démarche, a diplomatic protest. To be even-handed, the IFP and the ANC were also sent the message.

It was also at this time that statutory apartheid was finally scrapped,[25] in compliance with a commitment made by De Klerk to the international community, and paving the way for the lifting of sanctions and embargoes by several countries, including the United States. In June, the ANC held its first legal National Congress to elect and hand its new leadership the organization's mandate on negotiation. The congress also elected Cyril Ramaphosa as the new Secretary-General of the ANC.

The Inkathagate scandal

Just as the dust from the storm caused by the ANC ultimatum had settled, there was another controversy. Documentary evidence came to light of covert funding by the government of Inkatha and the arming and training of its membership in offensive actions against the ANC, in a series of revelations that came to be known as the 'Inkathagate' scandal. There were also further revelations about the SADF's involvement in 'death squads' and the ongoing violence, which served as proof that the government was talking peace and waging war at the same time. De Klerk's personal credibility was even called into question, and he was faced with his worst crisis since taking over from P. W. Botha.

While Buthelezi denied any knowledge of the payments, Adriaan Vlok admitted that they had taken place. The revelations took their toll on the financial markets.[26] Even the Bush administration in the United States demanded that the government take all necessary steps to restore the 'integrity of the negotiating process'.[27] These revelations served to add credence to two of the ANC's demands: for the removal of Magnus Malan and Adriaan Vlok from the cabinet, and for an interim government. There was now no doubt that the government could not be a referee and a player, nor could it be solely responsible for managing the transition.

South Africans, however, were to learn that there is nothing better to focus the minds of negotiators, and often speed up the process of negotiation, than a crisis.[28] This was a lesson and an experience that would be repeated on several occasions throughout South Africa's lengthy process of negotiation.

Interestingly, not even the ANC called for the resignation of De Klerk, which might have been the case in any other country.[29] At the end of July, De Klerk responded to the crisis, justifying the covert programmes on the basis that they had been implemented while the ANC was still banned. He promised greater control of state funds and explained the steps he had taken to ensure the impartiality of the security forces. He also confirmed that the government had no desire to be both player and referee. On the question of an interim government, he endorsed the need for transitional measures to overcome this problem.

Vlok was shifted to the post of Correctional Services and Malan to that of Forestry. This was also a useful opportunity for De Klerk to reshuffle his cabinet to prepare effectively for negotiation.[30] De Klerk announced:

Today, I wish to commit myself once again to transitional arrangements which will ensure in a constitutionally accountable manner that the government is unable to misuse its position of power to the detriment of its discussion partners in a negotiating process. I have an open mind on alternative methods. However, any steps in this connection have to result from negotiation. As far as I am concerned, they may be the first item on the agenda of a multiparty congress.[31]

The response of the ANC was swift. Its National Executive Committee met in an extraordinary session to review the situation, identified the crisis facing the De Klerk government, and surmised that it was at its weakest. The ANC wished to capitalize on this weakness and speed up the process of consultation towards the formation of a patriotic front, while it was also imperative to move quickly towards an all-party congress and extract as many compromises from the government as was possible.[32] To this end, the ANC shifted its focus from the obstacles identified in the Harare Declaration and the demands contained in its April ultimatum to the issue at hand.[33]

For the ANC, the revelations moved the issue of an interim government to the top of the agenda, while it was also recognized that control over the security forces was crucial to safeguard the transition. A means had to be found to ensure that the security forces would not pose any threat. This assessment took into account the 'significant degree of consensus' reached in bilateral discussions over the previous two months. According to Ramaphosa, 'We are more convinced than ever that the De Klerk government is the obstacle that stands between us and the resolution of SA's problems. We still want obstacles removed but the best possible way is the removal of the government itself'.[34]

According to Slovo, there were no real obstacles to the ANC's participation in an all-party congress: 'We will be faced with obstacles until the end of time. Subject to consultation with our allies, we are clearly prepared to move towards an all-party conference and that all-party conference must discuss the creation of an interim government'.

Mandela welcomed the changes De Klerk had made to his cabinet. He felt that the ANC and the government were moving closer to each other, and said:

> We are happy if the government is optimistic about the all-party conference, because despite all the problems that have arisen, we still feel that negotiation is the correct solution for South Africa. But we are not going to go into negotiation blindly. The government must carry out its responsibility and it must agree to a mechanism which will ensure that we'll not have a similar scandal to the Inkathagate scandal. And the only mechanism we see which will give this assurance is the immediate installation of an interim government. That is the only mechanism which can be adopted to ensure that we can now proceed confidently with negotiation. . . .
>
> De Klerk is responding to our demands. He may not have met those demands to the full, but we must take into account that he has taken some action. He has removed these two Ministers from

the portfolios they had. That is what we asked them to do. It may well be that the fact that they are now in charge of minor port-folios is a matter which we may not like to take any further.

There is no reason why the government should not accept the idea of an interim government. We are already moving close to the government on this question. De Klerk has said he is prepared to discuss interim arrangements along the lines of a government which embraces the major parties in the negotiating process. We are not satisfied with that. We want him to go further. The idea of an interim government with sovereign powers over all the organs of government and not co-opting certain individuals is our demand. We are not prepared to be co-opted into the existing structures of government. We want a transfer of power from this government to an interim government. That is the only way we can solve the problems that have been raised by the Inkatha scandal.[35]

In the meantime, the PAC deputy leader, Dikgang Moseneke, confirmed the PAC's willingness to engage in a 'pre-constituent assembly conference'.[36] After several months of horse-trading with the UNHCR and the NCCR the government finally agreed on 16 August 1991 to grant a general amnesty to all exiles, paving the way for their return home, in an agreement that opened the way for the UNHCR to set up its first offices in South Africa.[37] The UN described this agree-ment as a 'ringing endorsement' of the reforms taking place in the country.[38]

Negotiating positions on substantive matters

Meanwhile, in preparation for holding a special Federal Congress on 4 September, the NP appointed Stoffel van der Merwe to the newly created post of Secretary-General to streamline the party's negotiating effort.[39] It also produced a discussion document containing its constitutional proposals, but these proposals were effectively no more than a refinement of P. W. Botha's 1988 constitutional proposals. At the same time, the DP also made public its constitutional proposals.[40]

For the first time the constitutional proposals of the ANC (published on 12 April 1991), the NP, and the DP (both on 29 August 1991) were laid out side by side. This was an important moment in the history of South African constitutional development. Historically, it marks a shift in political conflict from competing forces to competing constitutional visions. The dominant terrain of struggle between previously warring parties was now clearly located in the arena of constitutional debate, and the period of 'talks about talks' had come to an end. On the whole, the five obstacles identified in the Harare Declaration had been removed, and a climate in which multi-party negotiation could begin had been achieved. The negotiation thus far was between the ANC and the NP, but both the form and the content of negotiation were to change dramatically, for they would now appear within a multi-party framework. While there was substantial debate as to what ought to be negotiated, in essence the issue remained one of levelling the playing field between parties contending for political power and constitutional perspectives.

The National Party's constitutional proposals

The National Party's proposals relied on a unitary state, though with strong federal characteristics.[41] The NP also maintained three branches of government: an executive, a legislature, and a judiciary. A multi-party executive college that would consist of between three and five members of the strongest parties in the first house of parliament, and making its decisions by consensus, should head the state. These parties together should command a majority of the representatives in this house. The chair of the executive college would operate on a rotational basis. A multi-party cabinet appointed by consensus by the executive college would implement its policy.[42] However, the proposal did not include a view on the future of the TBVC independent homelands.

There would be two houses of parliament. The power of the majority in the first house would be limited by the requirement of an increased majority on some 'sensitive' matters, for which the agreement of the second house would be needed. The second, smaller, house would be the seat of power for minorities, and would represent the proposed nine regions. Each party that achieved more than a specified minimum support level in elections for the legislature in that region would have equal seats for that region. While the first house would pass ordinary laws by a simple majority, the second house would have to approve all legislation amending the constitution, affecting regions or minorities, or initiating laws affecting the specific interests of minorities and regions. Elections for the first house would be by proportional representation, which did not, however, rule out the possibility of some parallel constituency representation. (The proposals cited the German example to support this argument. In terms of this example, only half the seats in the legislature are chosen according to a winner-takes-all system in single-member constituencies.) The NP also supported the argument that the constitution be the supreme law and sovereign, and allowed for a court to set aside laws that were inconsistent with the constitution.

Each of the nine regions would have a legislature. A mixture of direct elections on the basis of proportional representation in constituencies and possibly indirect election would choose the members of the legislatures from representatives of local authorities. Each region would also have an executive committee, which would operate on a similar basis to that of the national executive. The regional and local authorities would enjoy real autonomous powers and would have their own tax bases, while there would be a justiciable bill of rights. In addition, the Auditor-General, Public Service Commission, and Reserve Bank would have greater autonomy, while an independent and objective ombudsman would be appointed.[43]

The ANC's constitutional proposals

The African National Congress envisaged a united, democratic, non-racial, and non-sexist country including the TBVC independent homelands, with a strong central government. As in the NP proposals, there would be three branches of government: an executive, a legislature, and a judiciary. The president would be the head of the executive and head of state, but the proposal was unclear about the election of the president. A prime minister, who would act in consultation with the president, would head the cabinet, with the president appointing both the prime minister and the cabinet.

The ANC's proposal also allowed for two houses of parliament. The first would be a national assembly elected by proportional representation and universal suffrage; primary legislative power would be vested in this house. The second house would be a senate, also elected by universal suffrage, but on a different electoral system allowing for regional but not ethnic representation. The senate, as guardian of the constitution, would refer constitutional disputes to the appropriate courts, and have the power of review. It would be able, where appropriate, to delay legislation from the national assembly but not to veto it. There would be an independent electoral commission that would supervise elections, and there could be both national and regional electoral lists, with regions given, for example, half the available seats. Despite the possibility of having two lists, voters would cast only one vote.

A constitutional court appointed by the president, possibly on the recommendation of a judicial service commission, would be responsible for the interpretation of the constitution. The constitution could be amended only if either two-thirds of the national assembly or two-thirds of voters in a national referendum supported it. The constitution would be supreme, and there would be a justiciable bill of rights and freedoms, including economic rights. A human rights commission would investigate violations and a public service commission would oversee recruitment, promotion, and dismissal, and would implement an affirmative action programme in the public service, while an independent ombudsman would investigate complaints against the public service.

Regions would be based on the distribution of the population, the availability of economic resources, and urban/rural balances. Central government would control external relations, defence and security, general economic fiscal and tax policy, national policy frameworks, and resources for social upliftment and the removal of historical imbalances in society.

Negotiating positions: matters of process

While there may have been a substantial convergence in the two constitutional proposals, there remained two fundamental areas of conflict: the emphasis on minorities, and the extent of the devolution of power. Unfortunately, the excitement generated by the apparent convergence in thinking masked crucial areas of disagreement.

The first related to the development of the NP's ideas. The NP's 1991 proposals still attempted to provide constitutionally entrenched guarantees to the white minority; it did, however, seriously grapple with moving the emphasis from race to class and cultural minorities. Furthermore, the latest proposals made a fundamental leap in favour of constitutional supremacy and a bill of rights, a development that represented a major development in NP thinking and brought the NP's constitutional proposals in line with those of the DP.[44] From this point onwards, there was little fundamental difference in the proposals between the two parties.

The second crucial area of disagreement related, as it had so often before, to the process leading to a new constitutional order. The remaining issue was who would manage the transition period, and how, which was arguably the most pressing political imperative in the country at the end of 1991.[45] There were four proposals: an interim government (ANC), a transitional authority (PAC/AZAPO), a transitional government (DP), and transitional arrangements (NP). Each of these proposals would lead to different results. The position of the IFP was a little more curious, since it offered no competing proposal. The IFP's Walter Felgate merely stated, 'We reject entirely the concept that a multiparty conference or all-party congress is being convened in order to establish an interim government'. The IFP insisted that only a multi-party conference could arrive at an agreement that there should be an interim arrangement. [46]

National Party proposals on transitional mechanisms

The NP proposal allowed for political organizations to influence government decisions by advising it in a fashion similar to that of the President's Council, or the 'Great Indaba' that had been proposed by P. W. Botha in 1988. Such an arrangement would operate within the prevailing constitutional framework. The envisaged multi-party structure could also involve various working groups on specific problem areas, with the effect of creating some form of power-sharing. The government would remain ostensibly in control. The overall objective of the NP would be to allow for broader participation in the transition process.

PAC and AZAPO proposals on transitional mechanisms

The PAC and AZAPO envisaged a transitional authority that would have its participants approved by the liberation movements. These participants would comprise credible and neutral people who were mostly South Africans, but would exclude the government. International bodies would have to endorse the composition of the transitional authority. Such a structure would not take any joint responsibility for public administration and would not implement any apartheid law, though a primary function would be to oversee the security forces. It would have a strictly-defined and limited mandate. The structure would remain in existence for a specified period of time only and would invite international monitors for the elections. The overall objective of the PAC and AZAPO was to secure free and fair elections for a constituent assembly.

Democratic Party proposals on transitional mechanisms

The DP proposed a transitional government that would have its composition decided by the multi-party conference. It would consist of a 'council of leaders' to advise the state president, and oversee state expenditure, the security forces, and public broadcasting. It would also provide for participating local structures, supervise the reintegration of homelands, appoint specialist commissions to resolve particular issues, and broaden the representativeness of the judiciary, the public service, and the armed forces. As in the NP proposals, multi-party committees would advise cabinet ministers on the abolition of certain aspects of the constitution and implement an interim bill of rights. The overall objective would be to secure even-handed preparation for the elections.

ANC proposals on transitional mechanisms

The ANC proposed the establishment of an interim government which would represent only the major players. These would have equal power, and the interim government would be the supreme legal authority. This would necessitate a transfer of power. The interim government would also control the security forces, the public service, and public broadcasting, and would design the electoral process of a constituent assembly. It would be in existence for a specified period of time only, during which it would devise and implement an interim bill of rights. Finally, it would also be the responsibility of the interim government to remove obstacles to negotiation and supervise the transition. The overall objective of the ANC proposal was to secure a swift transfer to majority rule.

There were several points of general agreement. Except for the IFP, it was settled that an interim authority would be in place while the constitution was negotiated. There was also tacit agreement that the NP could not be both referee and player at the same time. Such an interim authority would last for as short a period as possible.[47]

The differences, however, were more substantial. There were three essential questions that had to be addressed: the constitutional framework within which the interim authority would operate (a concern of the NP); whether it was necessary for such an interim authority to be elected at all (a DP proposal); and what authority such an interim authority should have – whether it should act as a government with effective authority, or only have limited responsibility (NP, PAC, and AZAPO positions). These were the issues that were to dominate the negotiation agenda during the next phase of multi-party negotiation.

The National Peace Accord

August 1991 saw significant progress in dealing with the question of violence, in an initiative led by the Consultative Business Movement (CBM), an organization representing a section of business and church leaders. The 'National Peace Initiative' resulted in the signing of the first ever multi-party agreement, the National Peace Accord, on 14 September 1991.[48] This breakthrough paved the way for bilateral meetings between the ANC and the NP to consider the convening of the all-party congress.[49] The editorial in the *Sunday Star* on 22 September 1991 summed up the situation as follows:

> South Africa is up to its neck in committees, working groups, Minutes and Accords, all aimed at preparing the way for one thing – the start of real negotiation over the sharing of political power.
>
> That, in itself, is remarkable – and two years ago, when F. W. de Klerk took over as President, the events of today were unthinkable. In the past two weeks we have taken two important steps on the road to democracy: last Saturday's Peace Accord and this week's declaration by leaders of the Government, the ANC and Inkatha that these three major players are ready for 'real' negotiation as soon as possible.
>
> South Africa desperately needs these negotiations. Each

wasted day brings more unnecessary violence, more senseless killings and immeasurable hardship to hundreds of thousands of innocent and helpless people. Until the negotiations get under way and there are signs that they are likely to succeed, the world will stand back; and although there may be some investment, the massive capital inflow we need will be withheld. Until the world regains its confidence in South Africa our economy will continue to stagnate and the vicious cycle of unemployment-poverty-crime-violence and more unemployment will continue. The more this happens, the harder negotiation will become as an embittered people begin to lose faith in their leaders.[50]

On 25 September 1991 the PAC and AZAPO agreed to join the ANC at the all-party congress and to push for the formation of a patriotic front. According to Mac Maharaj, there was consensus regarding the agenda of the patriotic front conference: 'In particular this means that the three organisations arrived at consensus with regard to the All-Party congress or the pre-constituent assembly conference. Consensus was arrived at with regard to the modalities of transition, the agenda (for the congress or conference), which would include the items: interim government or transitional authority, modalities for constituting a constituent assembly and principles that would underpin a constitution'.[51]

Preparing for multi-party negotiations

By the end of September 1991 there was already an informal agreement that the all-party congress be held in November. The agreed agenda items were the formation of an interim government or transitional arrangement; the principles of SA's new constitution; the modalities of setting up or electing a constituent assembly or negotiating forum; and the role of the international community with special regard to sanctions.[52] It was during this period that the government became embroiled in another conflict, this time with the labour movement,

and the Congress of South African Trade Unions (COSATU) in particular, over the introduction of value-added tax (VAT). COSATU
opposed the introduction of this tax because it would affect the poor
most. The issue reinforced the demand that the NP should not manage
the transition alone.[53] The public debate that ensued became more
acrimonious after the ANC's Secretary-General suggested that the
ANC would consider reneging on international loans made to South
Africa. For his part, Mandela argued that the ANC would also consider
nationalization of some industries, a suggestion which caused much
consternation.[54] This led the leader of the DP, Zach de Beer, to call
upon the ANC and the NP to share power and co-operate for a period
of up to five years 'to get the economy moving again'.[55]

6

Defining the agenda

IT HAD TAKEN NEARLY TWO YEARS of talks almost exclusively between the ANC and the NP to address the obstacles preventing multi-party negotiations. The path to multilateral negotiation was now open. The only remaining issue was to agree what exactly the parties would be negotiating.

The importance of this phase was the commitment to the process of negotiation displayed by each party; by jointly defining the objectives of the negotiation, each party had a stake in the process itself. But this was not enough, for it was also necessary for each party to have some confidence about the outcome of these negotiations. This led to the formation of two alliances, each revolving around major contending parties.

The Patriotic Front

Between 25 and 27 October 1991 more than 400 delegates representing some ninety-two organizations converged in Durban to launch the Patriotic Front, a loose alliance of those parties which had held an anti-apartheid position. It also included some black political structures that had previously collaborated with the NP government.

The decisions of this inaugural conference took the form of a declaration, comprising a joint programme for a negotiated transfer of power. The Patriotic Front's point of departure was that an interim government was a necessary element in this transfer of power, as the government, it was argued, did not qualify to oversee the process of democratizing South Africa. The interim government should at the

① RANGING FROM ANC, PAC, AZAPO, DP, NIC, TIC
  TO: HOMELAND PARTIES
  INDEPENDENT [EX-HOMELAND]
  RELIGIOUS & OTHER STRUCTURES OF CIVIL
  SOCIETY THAT HAD ALIGNED
  SELVES WITH ANTI-AP. MOVEMENT

DP members
attended as observers.

very least control the security forces, the electoral process, state media, and defined areas of the budget and finance, and should secure international participation. The Patriotic Front confirmed a key tenet of the Harare Declaration, that only a constituent assembly, elected on a one-person-one-vote basis in a united South Africa, could draft and adopt a democratic constitution.

Delegates committed themselves to convene an all-party congress as soon as it was possible. In addition, they determined the conduct of Patriotic Front members attending such an all-party congress: on issues that enjoyed support by all members, they would act in accordance with the principles of 'unity in action' and 'unity of purpose', but where there was no consensus, each member would act independently.

To build on the success of the Patriotic Front conference, the ANC consulted those who had a stake in the process of multi-party negotiation. Meetings were held separately with the PAC, AZAPO, the DP, homeland leaders, Mass Democratic Movement organizations, religious leaders, and the NP.[3] From these consultations it was agreed that negotiations be scheduled for 29 and 30 November 1991. These consultations also defined the agenda for such a gathering, including a climate for free political participation, general constitutional principles, the constitution-making body, an interim government, the future of the TBVC states, the role of the international community, if any, and relevant time-frames.

The period leading up to the Convention for a Democratic South Africa (CODESA) provided an important preview of the negotiations that were to follow. It was effectively a rehearsal of an experience that would be repeated several times before the adoption of the final Constitution. The process, particularly the public debate, generated a momentum and pressure of its own that went beyond the control of those who had initiated it. Multi-party negotiations require an engine, or a driving force, and this was found in the bilateral exchanges between the main players. However, political negotiation cannot be abstracted from the human actors involved, and because it is easier to negotiate those areas in which agreement is likely, the more difficult issues were dealt with last, usually in the last moments before settling the final agreement. Agreements are only ever concluded once the detail has been settled, and, as experience often showed, the trouble lay in the detail.

The significance of the Patriotic Front

The establishment of the Patriotic Front had an enormous impact on the negotiations, because it changed the shape of the negotiating table and the political balance of forces in favour of the ANC. Its demand in favour of an interim government and a constituent assembly became unassailable.

The government was obliged to concede the need for joint control over the transition, and the NP was prepared to consider amending the constitution to make this possible.[4] However, if the amendments required were fundamental, the NP insisted on a referendum to confirm public support.[5] According to Gerrit Viljoen, these amendments had to be negotiated. He argued that 'It could be that we negotiate and come to a conclusion that there must be a more authoritative body, and that will involve changes to the constitution. We have not rejected transitional arrangements involving a change in the constitution – provided it has been the result of negotiation. These changes would have to be introduced in a legal and proper way and not simply by way of a suspension of the constitution or abdication of power'.[6] In this regard, the government repeated again and again that a constitutional hiatus should not be allowed.

The formation of the Patriotic Front raised another problem for the government, that of the balance of forces around the negotiating table, for now the government feared that the Patriotic Front would seize the initiative in negotiations.[7] This was the first time since the NP had embarked upon the path of a negotiated solution that it was confronted with the difficult reality that it may have to relinquish the power it had enjoyed for over forty years.

By the end of October 1991 the ANC and the NP were debating which parties had to be invited to the all-party congress. The broad agreement was that all parties represented in Parliament, including those in control of homeland governments and independent territories, should attend. Regarding extra-parliamentary structures, the ANC, the PAC, AZAPO, the SACP, and the Indian Congresses had to be invited.

At the beginning of November 1991 the NP mooted the possibility of an 'interim constitution' that ensured a 'government of national unity' lasting for up to 10 years.[8] This was an interesting solution that would satisfy the demands of all parties, but the proposal also revealed a fear that dominated NP thinking in forthcoming negotiations. A democratically elected constituent assembly might have denied the NP the ability to secure constitutionally entrenched guarantees to safeguard its interests. An interim government of national unity lasting for at least 10 years would secure a role for the NP as well.[9] This was one of several options it considered.[10]

An alternative was to consider the prospect of a referendum to confirm the agreements reached in multi-party talks and to postpone the election, as required in terms of the existing constitution, to 1995.[11] The Patriotic Front, on the other hand, wanted to draft the constitution within six months and the interim government to last for not more than eighteen months.

An aspect of the multi-party talks discussed between the ANC and NP was the treatment of constitutional principles. While both the ANC and the PAC argued that multi-party talks should only negotiate broad, internationally accepted principles of democracy, the NP insisted on greater detail.[12] This important debate continued for the next eighteen months. For the NP it was necessary to secure guarantees should it not enjoy sufficient influence in a democratically elected constituent assembly. While the NP tentatively accepted the possibility of an interim government and an elected constituent assembly, the battle was not lost, for it was still possible for the party to achieve the objectives it had set for itself. In the meantime, the form of the multi-party talks, their membership, and the question as to who was to convene and chair the meetings continued to be controversial.

To prepare for these negotiations the NP met its allies on

5 November 1991.[13] At this meeting, Gerrit Viljoen was mandated to negotiate on their behalf with the ANC.[14] A striking feature of this meeting was the presence of black leaders and the mandate given to the government. Ironically, except for Buthelezi, some of these very leaders were founding members of the Patriotic Front.[15]

Preparations for CODESA

On 13 November 1991 the first multi-party constitutional talks were scheduled for 29 and 30 November at the World Trade Centre in Kempton Park, Johannesburg.[16] This forum was called the 'Convention for a Democratic South Africa' (CODESA). A steering committee and full-time secretariat dealt with preparations for the convention. It was resolved that the meeting be convened by the Chief Justice Mr Justice Michael Corbett and two religious leaders, Johan Heyns of the Dutch Reformed Church, and Stanley Mogoba of the Methodist Church of Southern Africa.[17]

Meanwhile, there was a surprise shift in DP policy. On 15 November the DP's National Congress voted in favour of a proposal put forward by Colin Eglin supporting an elected constitutional conference to draft the new constitution.[18] He argued in favour of a four phase approach: a multi-party conference phase, a constitutional conference phase (drafting the constitution), a referendum phase (a mandate from the people), and an election phase (implementation of the new constitution).[19]

The steering committee entrusted with planning for the talks encountered a number of problems that threatened them, one being the insistence by the IFP that only it, the National Party, and the ANC be responsible for managing the process of negotiation.[20] This matter was resolved only after a meeting between Viljoen and Inkatha's national chairperson, Frank Mdlalose, at which they resolved to include representatives of each of the twenty-two parties attending the multi-party talks.[21]

The PAC also had an opportunity to raise its concerns. Its National

Conference decided that the multi-party talks had to be held outside of the country under an independent convener such as the United Nations, the Commonwealth, or the Organization of African Unity, and threatened to withdraw if this demand was not met.[22] At the end of November, the PAC accused the ANC and the NP of reaching secret agreements and consequently violating the spirit of the Patriotic Front.[23] Once again the question of mistrust emerged, creating suspicions about the bona fides of the negotiating partners.

Agreement eluded the parties until 20 November 1991 when the government, the ANC, and Inkatha jointly announced that the talks had been rescheduled to 20 and 21 December.[24] However, Inkatha remained opposed to the two clerics, Stanley Mogoba and Johan Heyns, serving as conveners with the Chief Justice, preferring the Chief Justice to convene this meeting on his own.

Except for the _Herstigte Nasionale Party_ (HNP) and AZAPO, all parties invited responded positively.[25] Part of the agreement in the steering committee was that the government would attend as a separate delegation from that of the NP.[26] The government's confidence allowed it to announce that a referendum would be held in 1992 should sufficient progress be recorded in the talks.[27]

CODESA I

The agreed agenda for the CODESA plenary[28] consisted of general constitutional principles, a constitution-making body, or process, transitional arrangements or interim government, the future of the TBVC territories, and the role of the international community. A novel approach was the decision-making mechanism agreed to. The standing rules prescribed that where consensus failed, a principle of 'sufficient consensus' would be applied[29] ⇒ ♭·3 ⊙3 ✳

Ten minutes before the end of the steering committee meeting, the PAC repeated its concern that all decisions were subject to bilateral agreements made between the National Party and the ANC.[30] It felt sufficiently aggrieved to walk out of the talks. Despite a joint communiqué by the leaders of Angola, Botswana, Mozambique, Namibia, Tanzania, Zambia, and Zimbabwe urging the PAC to remain, the organization stubbornly refused.[31] However, despite the acrimonious note on which the PAC left, the meeting was a success, and all the objectives set for the meeting were met. The *Weekly Mail* of 29 November 1991 stated, 'Today we celebrate. After almost two year's of waiting, representatives of 20 former and current enemies will sit around a table at the All party Conference to forge a path to democracy in South Africa'.

The *Sunday Times* of 1 December 1991 stated in its editorial: 'When the formal process of drafting a new constitution for South Africa began on Friday the worst, in a sense, was already behind it. The fact that the major parties, with only one important exception, could be brought to the table in an atmosphere of reasonable amity was success enough'.

According to the editorial in the *Sunday Tribune* on 1 December, 'There can be no turning back. Nearly all the parties at the exploratory talks which ended in Johannesburg yesterday committed themselves firmly to constitutional negotiation. For that South Africans can heave a collective sigh of relief'.

The next objective was the establishment of an interim government. For the NP, CODESA was an informal interim government capable of transformation into a formal executive body.[32] In terms of the NP's proposals, a referendum would be required to support any major constitutional change.[33] The ANC argued that the form of interim government it envisaged did not require major constitutional change. The course, it was hoped, would be for the form, powers, and responsibilities of an interim government to be settled at the first meeting of CODESA before being put to Parliament.[34] However, details of these proposals were never spelt out clearly and remained vague for a long time.

Meanwhile, the IFP fired the first of many warning shots by serving notice of its demand that the KwaZulu government, the Zulu monarch, and the IFP be allowed to attend CODESA as three separate delegations.[35] At the same time, the IFP also released its first draft constitutional proposals. According to Buthelezi, the proposals would be 'capable of adaptation to either the unitary or federal structure of government'. The proposals envisaged a division of executive power between the state president and a prime minister who would head a cabinet. On the subject of the legislature, Inkatha proposed a lower house 'elected by universal adult suffrage by means of proportional representation'. The prime minister, chosen from the majority party of a coalition in the lower house, would appoint the cabinet. A second house 'should represent the regions or states as well as any special interests which it is felt should be represented in the legislature'. Laws would require a majority in both houses and assent by the president. On the question of security forces, Inkatha was in favour of 'impartial, professional services owing allegiance to the constitution only'. The 'National Police' should be responsible to the prime minister. At the end of November the steering committee established three working groups to prepare for the plenary, focusing on CODESA's statement of intent and founding charter, the organization of CODESA, and the broad process of negotiation.[36]

see p. 304

By the second week of December, hopes for a successful start to the negotiation were raised with the announcement of the presence of high level national and international observers.[37] Both the ANC and the NP had by this time also produced their draft proposals of the declaration of intent, which was becoming a source of some controversy. The last paragraph of the ANC's draft of the declaration of intent stated, 'WE AGREE that Codesa will establish an implementing mechanism (which shall include the government) whose task it will be to determine the procedures and draft the texts of all legislation and executive and administrative acts necessary to give effect to the decisions of Codesa'.[38]

Until now, the NP had relied on the influence a multi-party structure could exert over the government. But in view of the proposals emerging, they were unwilling to accept a clause effectively giving CODESA the power to draft legislation to be rubber-stamped by Parliament.[39] Mandela warned that progress in the talks depended on the decisions of CODESA having the force of law, since the ANC feared that without such a guarantee the talks would be reduced to no more than a 'talk-shop'.[40] The government, however, was unwilling to compromise the sovereignty of Parliament. As an option, NP Secretary-General, Stoffel van der Merwe, argued that this would not be the case if the decisions of CODESA were also made with the express acquiescence of the NP. The ANC rejected this as it would constitute a veto for the NP.[41] The matter was finally resolved in a late-night bilateral meeting between the ANC and the NP on 18 December, where the government agreed that CODESA would draft the legislation needed to give effect to convention decisions.[42] *see p 304* The government undertook to do everything in its power to have decisions of CODESA implemented.[43]

However, the steering committee faced further problems. On 19 December Inkatha confirmed that Buthelezi, as a Zulu leader, was withdrawing from CODESA because the Zulu King, Goodwill Zwelithini, had not been invited to participate. Inkatha did agree, however, that it would still attend as a party.

The right wing too felt threatened by developments.[44] The AWB even warned that it would 'prepare for war' if the government failed to consider its demand for a boerestaat.[45] The only party represented in Parliament that did not attend was the Conservative Party. The leader of the CP, Andries Treurnicht, argued that the demise of the Soviet Union confirmed that nationalism was indeed the strongest historical trend of the present era.[46] He went on to say, 'The CP wishes to warn those striving for an undivided South Africa – an artificial unitary state like the Soviet Union – to come to their senses in time and to recognise the right of peoples to self-determination and freedom'.[47] *p. 305*

It is not surprising, therefore, that Mandela found it necessary to reassure white people that majority rule was not a threat, and to argue that the ANC was ready to make radical compromises to ensure that.[48] This, he proposed, could be done by guaranteeing a block of white seats in the post-apartheid parliament for a limited period, even though this would mean perpetuating a separate white voters' roll, as in the settlement hammered out at Zimbabwe's Lancaster House constitutional negotiations.[49] Alternatively, the various political parties could enter into an agreement to have a 'government of national unity' for a

This was rejected by NP

given period after the first post-apartheid election, again ensuring that all race groups were represented. Such a compromise however was still subject to the fact that the ANC was not prepared to compromise on the principle of majority rule. Mandela also denounced De Klerk's new proposals for ten years of interim government as a 'trap'.[50]

The first plenary session of CODESA took place on 20 and 21 December 1991.[51] The Chief Justice and Justices Ismail Mohamed[52] and Piet Schabort chaired the meeting, which was attended by nineteen organizations and political parties.[53] Five remarkable statements characterized the first plenary. The first was the speech by Dawie de Villiers, speaking for the NP, in which he expressed 'deep regret' and officially apologized for the policy of apartheid. He said, 'It was not the intention to deprive other people of their rights and to contribute to their misery – but eventually it led to just that'.[54]

The second statement was the compromise suggested by De Klerk when he signalled his government's agreement to an elected constituent assembly provided that it would also act as an interim government.[55] This marked another significant shift in NP policy. The third remarkable feature of CODESA I arose at the end of De Klerk's intervention. By agreement with the ANC, De Klerk was to speak last, and he used this opportunity to lash out at the ANC for not terminating the armed struggle and thereby breaking the undertakings of the Pretoria Minute and the D. F. Malan Accord. Mandela responded using the angriest language to pass publicly between the two leaders, and lambasted De Klerk on the conduct of his government.[56] This extraordinary exchange between the leaders provided a unique window to the tensions and the mistrust that existed between the parties during the process of negotiation.[57] It was also one of its clearest expressions of democracy in action.

The fourth outstanding feature of this historic meeting was the Declaration of Intent.[58] The Declaration was and remains an exceptionally important and historic document.[59] It was not only the first political agreement that was arrived at democratically and made a break from the racially divided past, but it also firmly committed all parties to the basic principles of genuine, non-racial, multi-party democracy where the constitution is supreme and regular elections are guaranteed. In the South African context the statement was revolutionary, and represented, in a sense, the 'preamble' to the first democratic constitution.[60] All parties except the IFP and the governments of Ciskei and Bophuthatswana signed the declaration. The IFP felt that the reference to an 'undivided' South Africa in the declaration ruled out the option of a federal dispensation. However, both the IFP and Ciskei did sign the declaration later on, after an amendment was secured confirming that the offending term ('undivided') did not commit CODESA to a unitary state. As for Bophuthatswana, its leader, Lucas Mangope, argued that CODESA could not enter into any agreements affecting its territory without the formal agreement of the government of Bophuthatswana.[61]

The fifth remarkable statement came in an address by parliamentary veteran Helen Suzman. She demanded that a greater role be given to women to prevent accusations of gender discrimination. In an address that embarrassed most delegations, she argued: 'Here we are in this great hall at a momentous time, and I can't believe my eyes and ears when I see the number of women in the room. As with racism, so with sexism – you can enact legislation, but despite this, racism and gender discrimination exists. When I look around, there are maybe ten out of 228 delegates who are women. Codesa, as a way forward, must include more women'.[62] (Her censure induced immediate positive reaction from the participating parties, who from then on made a welcome effort to ensure gender representivity.)

The first plenary established five working groups and a Management Committee, and resolved that the second plenary session of CODESA would take place in March 1992. The first working group considered the creation of a climate for free political participation and the role of the international community.[63] The second working group was mandated to explore constitutional principles and the constitution-making body. The third working group dealt with an interim government. The fourth working group was to debate the future of the homelands, and the fifth working group was to deal with time-frames.

Each party was entitled to two delegates and two advisers in each working group. However, the Management Committee consisted of one delegate and one adviser from each party. In all, CODESA involved more than 400 negotiators representing nineteen parties, administrations, organizations, and governments. Each working group had a steering committee that attended to the agenda and the programme of work. Also, each working group tabled its reports through its steering committee and was directly accountable to the Management Committee. Agreements concluded were then tabled at the CODESA plenary for approval and ratification.[64]

To assist the Management Committee in its work, a Daily Management Committee and a secretariat were established.[65] The secretariat, consisting of Fanie van der Merwe[66] and Mac Maharaj,[67] was responsible for the implementation of the decisions of the Management Committee. Murphy Morobe[68] headed the CODESA administration, and Dr Theuns Eloff assisted him.[69] The administration was staffed by civil servants seconded by the Department of Constitutional Development and the Consultative Business Movement.

The Structure of CODESA I

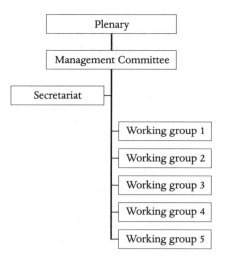

One of the first issues that the Management Committee had to deal with was the question of representation at CODESA. The Management Committee had to consider applications by traditional leaders and a host of at least twenty other structures and organizations for membership.[70] One such application came from Kwazulu's King Goodwill Zwelithini. De Klerk supported his right to attend and participate, but the position of the ANC was that this application should be considered in the same way as that of the other traditional leaders.[71] The Management Committee agreed to establish a subcommittee to consider the merits of traditional leaders being represented.[72]

The importance of the first plenary meeting of CODESA cannot be over-emphasized, for it represented the first formal multilateral meeting to negotiate a settlement of the conflict in South Africa. The meeting generated a great deal of confidence and enthusiasm, reflected in the behaviour of the parties and in the views expressed by economists and editorials in the media.[73] The editorial in the *Financial Times* of 3 January 1991, entitled 'Progress in South Africa', said:

> South Africa starts the new year on a hopeful note. Progress in constitutional talks, coupled with tentative moves towards an interim government, represents the most important step in the country's transition to democracy since the release of Mr Nelson Mandela, the African National Congress (ANC) leader, nearly two years ago.
>
> The agreement on a set of constitutional principles, endorsed by delegates attending the inaugural session of the Convention for a Democratic South Africa (Codesa), is in itself encouraging. While the principles adopted are taken for granted in western democracies, they represent a revolutionary change for South Africa, incorporating as they do commitments to an adult franchise and a multi-party system, a bill of rights and an independent judiciary.

7

Defining the process

CODESA'S FIRST plenary session boosted the chances of a speedy resolution to South Africa's conflict and of substantive negotiation towards democracy. By now, almost all political role-players and commentators had been convinced that negotiation would yield the best outcome. Unfortunately, this confidence was not bearing out in the country's economy. Inflation, an ongoing recession, increasing unemployment, and evidence of corruption all conspired against an early economic recovery. To make matters worse, government expenditure had increased by 18 per cent and the budget deficit was growing, putting the NP government under even greater pressure.[1]

Nonetheless, the government refused to allow this to dampen its spirits. In January 1992 De Klerk restructured Constitutional Development Services and upgraded it to a full state department.[2] He also appointed the head of the National Intelligence Service (NIS), Neil Barnard, to the new post of head of Constitutional Development Services.[3] Tertius Delport was appointed Deputy-Minister of Constitutional Development and Planning and the chief government spokesperson at CODESA, where he went on to play in increasingly important role as a government negotiator.[4] He would also be central to a controversy that brought about a deadlock at CODESA later on.

The ANC too felt it necessary to build on the success of CODESA, and planned a campaign in January 1992 to force the government to yield to the establishment of an interim government within six months and to a constituent assembly before the end of the year.[5] The organization argued that CODESA's success rendered the continued existence of the Tricameral Parliament irrelevant.

The five working groups began their discussions on 20 January

1992.[6] For the sake of efficiency and effectiveness, working groups sat for two days every week, and Parliament during the remaining three days.[7]

CODESA soon effectively replaced Parliament as the most important site of political activity.[8] One of its most extraordinary aspects was the range and seniority of the politicians it brought together, for it was not unusual to find government ministers, former leaders of the armed struggle, and Tricameral politicians swapping jokes over drinks or at a meal between working group meetings.

When Parliament reconvened on the second anniversary of De Klerk's historic 2 February speech, he was at pains to convince its members that CODESA had not replaced it. He argued that Parliament remained an important institution of authority and was needed to translate agreements reached at CODESA into legislation. However, he knew that the only significant legislation Parliament would be enacting could effectively render the legislators jobless.

The way in which CODESA arrived at its decisions set an important precedent, for it represented a significant departure from the way in which Parliament had operated before. Regrettably, even though the public was invited to make submissions on constitutional proposals, CODESA made little attempt to either educate the public about its work or to solicit seriously the views of important interest groups that otherwise may have made useful contributions.[9] Nonetheless, the invitation did elicit responses from many quarters, including the media.[10]

CODESA's progress led to a realignment of political forces and a general review of old strategies, a process that applied equally to the right wing. For the Conservative Party, not all its leaders supported the boycott of CODESA, thus bringing to the surface some of the tension already existing within the party.[11] In early January there were already signs of a possible split, for some of the CP's leaders felt that it was important for the party to play a role in negotiations in order to pursue its objectives.[12]

In an attempt to appease the right wing, the working group dealing with constitutional principles agreed to discuss the principle of self-determination and its application in the South African situation.[13] It was hoped, albeit in vain, that this would allay the concerns of the right wing and allow them to join the negotiations.

The NP was undergoing a review of its own strategies and policies as well. For this reason, its think-tank met late in March to consider what form of political alignment would ensure that the NP won sufficient support at a non-racial election.[14] The plan was to form a new centrist party, and in early April 1992 De Klerk visited a number of black, coloured, and Indian communities to win support for the party.[15] In other words, the party was conducting an election campaign and negotiating at the same time. In establishing itself as the major opposition to the ANC, the NP had to show to its constituency that it would not give in too easily to ANC demands, which presented a serious problem for the NP's negotiating strategy.

Separately, the DP was also considering these and similar issues. Since the DP was concerned with the defection of several of its leaders to the ANC, it was not surprising when DP MP Mike Tarr suggested that the party consider an alignment with the NP against the ANC.[16]

The 17 March all-white referendum

On 24 January 1992 De Klerk publicly recommitted the government to a referendum to confirm the support of the white electorate.[17] Later, on 20 February, he reported that this referendum would go ahead on 17 March as an answer to arguments by the CP that the NP did not represent white people. De Klerk was confident enough to promise that if he lost, he would dissolve the NP government and force an election.[18] The ANC was opposed to the referendum, but it did support the decision of the Management Committee to call on whites to take part in the referendum and to vote 'yes'.[19] Parties resolved on 3 March that the likely dates for CODESA II were 9 to 16 April 1992.[20] With these agreements came the realization that the establishment of a non-racial transitional executive council was possible, a likelihood that was celebrated in the media.[21] However, the working groups were experiencing a sudden halt in progress, and by 9 March the Management Committee had to postpone the plenary beyond April 1992.[22]

1992   The referendum on 17 March proved to be an overwhelming victory for the NP, and its success confirmed that the majority of white people were in favour of a negotiated settlement. This had the effect of obliging all white political parties to re-examine and reposition themselves in the wider political terrain. For any political party to be able to compete effectively in a democracy, it would have to appeal to the black majority.

Even though it was meant to be a confirmation of work already done, the referendum did have an impact on the NP's approach in the negotiations:

> 'Coetsee's role changed noticeably after the referendum', says one WG1 [Working Group 1] participant. 'It was as if he had decided that government could not either get the decisions it wanted in the group, or scupper it. It was probably the size of the "yes" vote that did it. Had the result been narrower, we would probably have made more progress.' Asmal agrees: 'The referendum sent inappropriate signals to government. A week before, they were trying to resolve issues at Codesa. Thereafter, there was a perceptible change in attitude'.[23]

In two important developments, a Gender Advisory Committee was established at the beginning of April to advise the Management Committee on the gender implications of the terms of reference and agreements of the working committees;[24] and on 27 April a special subcommittee of the Management Committee recommended that traditional leaders be allowed special, but not equal, representation in the negotiations, accorded through four provincial delegations.

Levelling the playing field

Working Group 1 had to deal with all matters relating to the creation of a climate conducive to free and fair elections. A list of laws that stood in the way of a level electoral playing field was drawn up by Lawyers for Human Rights, and each item was considered for removal by the working group.[25]

The continued existence of Umkhonto we Sizwe (MK) once again fuelled a row that threatened to stall the process.[26] Gerrit Viljoen and Roelf Meyer warned that any political settlement depended on the ANC abandoning its armed struggle.[27] Moreover, De Klerk warned that the NP would refuse to enter any transitional arrangement, including an interim government or joint control of the security forces, as long as the ANC retained an armed wing.[28] The NP argued that Umkhonto we Sizwe was a 'private army' that should be disbanded and its arms handed over to the security forces. The ANC refused, insisting that MK would only be disbanded once an interim government had been installed. The row was generating a great deal of tension: Mandela threatened mass action, and COSATU, for its part, threatened unprecedented general strikes if the installation of an interim government did not take place by June.[29]

Meanwhile, the ANC and the NP continued to disagree on the need to restructure the South African Broadcasting Corporation (SABC) and its management.[30] According to Kobie Coetsee, the NP did not regard this as a practical or necessary step towards providing neutral broadcasting. The ANC, on the other hand, felt that it was essential to level the playing field through such restructuring, as the present form of the SABC did not lend the confidence required for this purpose. On 30 March the NP finally relented, and agreed to the reorganization of the SABC.[31]

At the end of March the NP had returned from its referendum triumphant and in an aggressive mood. It was now prepared to dig in its heels against the ANC's demands for the speedy installation of an interim government, which encouraged speculation that CODESA's second plenary session was likely to be delayed.[32] *MARCH '92*

Controversy over MK continued unabated, despite the attention focused on the SABC. The NP linked the existence of MK to the delayed installation of an interim government. For although the government did not appear to regard MK as a security threat, it did regard the issue as politically important, especially so because of the public row between De Klerk and Mandela on the matter. The NP also related the existence of MK to the continuing violence, and to this extent threatened to veto agreement on a transitional constitution until political violence had been 'solved decisively'. The NP was keen to force the ANC to take some responsibility for ending the violence, which was a new precondition. To show its seriousness, the NP withheld its agreement to a code of conduct for the SADF for more than six months after the National Peace Accord had been signed.[33]

To add to the negotiators' difficulties, John Hall of the National Peace Accord confirmed that violence was continuing unabated countrywide.[34] The installation of the National Peace Accord had not had the desired effect, and the violence was becoming serious enough to threaten the negotiations.[35]

Working Group 1 was accordingly asked to investigate ways of improving the situation. At the working group, Hernus Kriel tabled a document that berated the ANC for not committing itself to peaceful negotiations.[36] The document was an ill-fitting attempt to absolve the government of any responsibility for violence and to downplay the public outcry against the Trust Feed case, in which a police captain, Brian Mitchell, had been sentenced to death for orchestrating the murder of eleven people at Trust Feed in Natal. It was suggested at the time that Kriel had tabled the document at that time only to scupper the agreements that CODESA II was about to ratify.

In the final report of Working Group 1 to CODESA II, while all parties recommitted themselves to the National Peace Accord, they recommended that it should be revamped.[37] They also argued that the successful implementation of the accord was fundamental to the creation of a climate for free political activity.[38]

Interim government

Working Group 3 dealt with interim government, and was therefore regarded by many as the most important working group.[39]

The end of January 1992 saw a fundamental shift in NP policy. It proposed the formation of an elected interim government and a non-racial parliament with an all-party cabinet. According to the NP Secretary-General, Stoffel van der Merwe, such an interim government would also replace CODESA and would be responsible for the negotiation of the final constitution. He went on to say:

> One would then have a representative government within which the negotiations can take place. In other words – the necessity for Codesa to continue to exist would actually fall away. Parliament would then be an elected body which could act as a Constituent Assembly. This transitional government could discuss the future permanent constitution.
>
> Then, depending on what was negotiated beforehand or depending on the circumstances at the time, I would say it would be wise if such a transitional government would submit the final constitution again to a referendum, and then one would have an election on a permanent basis.[40]

Some leaders within the NP were critical of this apparent change of heart and complained that the NP was succumbing to the ANC's demands, reflecting new tensions within the NP.[41] During the same period, Thabo Mbeki was asked whether the ANC had developed its vision of an interim government. He replied:

> No, we are still very much in the process of discussion. Our national executive committee will meet later this week to deal with this question. But there are important elements to what the ANC has said so far.
>
> We're saying that an interim government should be in place for no more than eighteen months. Whatever detailed arrangements we enter into, it would have to deal with both executive and legislative elements. Clearly, there, you are not talking of a continuing tricameral parliament as a legislative authority. Codesa will have to come up with proposals on who the legislator should be as well as on the executive authority.

When we talk of an interim government of national unity, we visualise both the legislative and executive authorities being broadly representative of the various political forces in South Africa. The constitutional principles agreed at Codesa would be the political mandate of the interim government because everyone would have agreed that this is the kind of South Africa that we want to see in future. And therefore, even in the interim period, you would be governing the country in the direction of those principles. Therefore, the principles agreed at Codesa would have to override any element in the present constitution which is contrary to them. That is not too bad a framework from which to begin planning the detail.[42]

Gerrit Viljoen explained the similarities and differences between the approaches of the NP and the ANC in this way:

Firstly, the Government accepts it will imply a meaningful change bringing about a change in rather than suspension or abolition of the constitution. Secondly, the shift would involve not only the executive, the government, but also the legislature, namely parliament. Thirdly, the existing constitution would apply the method of introducing such a transitional government with a transitional constitution: that means it will have to be brought about by a decision made by the present parliament.

The Government is providing an alternative . . . to the concepts of constituent assembly and an interim government, as defined by the ANC. We believe that a transitional government . . . would be an acceptable forum to argue and negotiate a better alternative to a constituent assembly. While a constituent assembly as generally defined is supposed to be elected on a one-man-one-vote majoritarian basis – where the majority, once elected, will simply finalise the constitution – the approach of the Government is to ensure proper representation of minorities in decision-making.[43]

Discussions between the two parties continued for several weeks.[44]

The NP pursued the notion of a coalition government, proposing a guaranteed minority representation in a second house of Parliament and a collegiate presidency. The ANC rejected the idea of a constitutionally guaranteed representation of the minority. However, ANC Secretary-General, Cyril Ramaphosa, confirmed that the ANC was not averse to a voluntary coalition even if the ANC won the majority of votes. Mbeki elaborated:

> we are opposed to the proposal which the NP is making in regard to this matter: that such a coalition government should be constitutionally entrenched. It must be a political decision. A consequence of constitutionally compelling a coalition is that you write into that arrangement veto powers for the small parties. To ensure that minority parties are effectively part of government, decisions would have to be by consensus in a cabinet. This is giving veto powers to minority parties. We can't accept that.[45]

The NP had been particularly astute in proposing an elected interim government. Since the ANC previously considered only the appointment of one, rather than its election, it found the proposal hard to reject.[46] The proposal also featured an interim constitution, as the intention of the NP, explained by Tertius Delport, was to secure agreement on a 'complete constitution, although imperfect'. This, it was hoped, would undermine the need for the ANC's demand for a constituent assembly. Even if a constituent assembly was established, it would do no more than amend the negotiated constitution. Until now, the ANC had never considered the need to negotiate a complete constitution in the period prior to the election of a constituent assembly.

This narrowed the differences between the ANC and the NP to three major areas: the NP's proposal for a collegiate presidency; the continuation of the interim government for a period of up to ten years; and the constitutional protection of minorities which would in effect constitute a minority veto.

The IFP tabled its proposals on an interim government in early

FEB. 1992 */IFP/*

February. The proposals served to reveal its anxieties: like the NP, the IFP feared a 'constitutional leap in the dark'. It proposed 'A transitional government of reconciliation – broader based than Codesa is at present – constituted under the State President and responsible to Parliament under the existing Constitution, amended as to certain unentrenched clauses to make this legally possible. This government would encompass generally recognised political parties and organisations, the portfolios of Cabinet responsibility to be allocated in an equitable manner and in accordance with recommendations and selection structures agreed upon by such parties and organisations'.[47]

The ANC proposed a two-stage interim government. In the first stage, it would 'level the playing field', and culminate in the election of a constituent assembly. In the second stage, a final constitution would be drafted. The interim government though would continue until after the adoption of the final constitution. The first phase would commence with agreement in CODESA on all issues leading to the establishment of a powerful interim government council, consisting of all participants in CODESA and possibly including other parties as well. The interim government would oversee two independent, non-partisan commissions, four multi-party committees, and the activities of the Tricameral Parliament, the cabinet (which would continue as it was), and all homeland governments.[48]

The ANC envisaged an election for a 300 to 400 seat constituent assembly not more than six months after CODESA had reached agreement on the process. Parties that received 5 per cent or more of the vote would take seats on a proportional basis. The assembly would draft the new constitution within six to nine months of being constituted, and a two-thirds majority would have to take decisions on the constitution. This body would also act as an interim legislature, since the Tricameral Parliament would fall away once the assembly became operational. A multi-party interim cabinet would then be appointed.

The ANC also proposed to include what it referred to as 'sunset clauses' in a new constitution.[49] This concept had been applied successfully at the Lancaster House talks in the Zimbabwe settlement. A sunset clause would be introduced principally to provide white people with some reassurance, and would lapse after a period of time. Examples of these sunset clauses included entrenched seats for whites and regulations inhibiting the complete overhaul of the public service.[50] The ANC's proposal for the second stage of an elected interim government accorded with the views of the government and was close to those of both the DP and the IFP.[51]

This convergence introduced a concern that CODESA was moving too fast, and indeed it was. The government had not yet finalized its constitutional proposals and was therefore not in a position to negotiate constitutional guarantees that would protect the interests of its constituency or the National Party.[52] The IFP was equally unhappy at the thought of an early election. The comment in the *Weekly Mail* summed up the debate:

> Cautious liberal voices are calling for constitutional negotiations to be slowed down and for the Convention for a Democratic South Africa (Codesa) to offer stronger resistance to the call for swift movement to an interim government. 'Slam brakes on that constitutional bulldozer', the *Sunday Times* proclaimed on the weekend arguing that CODESA is in a 'mad rush' to an interim government, 'even if it means leaving until later the task of establishing democratic safeguards'.
>
> How ironic that such voices suddenly find themselves arguing for a prolongation of National Party rule. How absurd to argue that democracy is best served by slowing down the destruction of a minority, racist government. How contradictory, too, that these are the same voices that so frequently lament the long-term economic costs of this period of uncertainty.[53]

The NP proposed the appointment of a series of 'transitional councils' for areas of government 'requiring special attention' during the preparatory phase of a transitional government.[54] The proposals also laid down a framework for the second phase of the transitional government. Each of the transitional councils would consist of six members designated by the CODESA Management Committee and appointed by the President. There would be a maximum of 30 council members, requiring some individuals to serve on more than one council. All councils sitting together would constitute a joint transitional council and operate on the basis of consensus.

The ANC rejected these proposals. The basic objectives of the first phase of interim government were to level the political playing field and ensure free and fair elections, and Mbeki argued that the proposed councils would not achieve this. In terms of the government's formulation, all decisions required full consensus, which meant that council decisions would be few and far between. The NP's proposed terms of reference for the councils also specified that the councils would debate actions the government should take in the future, and so excluded immediate hands-on control. The ANC also opposed the requirement of a regionally based senate. Ultimately, the question of the reincorporation of the TBVC states had also not been resolved.[55]

The proposal did reflect some important developments: for example, it allowed the NP to bring its ideas in line with the ANC's proposed two-phased transitional process. But they had highlighted the differences between the ANC and the NP. The ANC did not want an interim government contaminated with the responsibilities of an apartheid government. By taking some of the responsibility for government the ANC would also become accountable, which would allow the government to escape some of its own responsibilities. This was an attractive prospect for the NP, particularly if it occurred just before an election. Instead, the ANC's vision of an interim government was one in which the power to control was shared without the attendant responsibilities of governance.

The IFP also opposed the NP's proposals. According to Buthelezi, the ANC had to disband its military wing, the King and the KwaZulu government had to be afforded delegation status at CODESA, and KwaZulu had to be consulted on the work of the transitional councils. Agreement would also depend on how the question of self-governing territories was resolved.[56]

The proposals revealed a dilemma facing the government. As Mac Maharaj pointed out, the NP faced the difficulty of changing its focus from 'the negotiation mode to the election mode'.[57] The NP had just come out of a successful referendum, which had allowed it to consolidate its support base, stronger than before. The NP had a head-start over the other parties and was now continuing to electioneer.

On 6 April 1992 CODESA was beginning to flounder, and a critical point had been reached. For the third successive week parties failed to reach a compromise on the first stage of the political transition.[58] While both the ANC and the NP agreed that the first phase of the transition should end in an election, agreement on the actual powers of the executive eluded the negotiators. The ANC proposed that an eight-person interim government council be appointed, the Tricameral Parliament merge into one chamber, and the council approve draft legislation before its being submitted to parliament and again before its being signed by the president. TBVC legislation should also be subject to the same approval. While executive authority would be vested in the president, he or she would only exercise such authority with the approval of the council. The council would have overall responsibility for all departments. In the event of a deadlock, the council should take its decisions by a two-thirds majority. Proclamations issued by the council should have the same force as an Act of Parliament.

The responding submission from the government proposed the establishment of 'preparatory' or 'transitional' councils that would have no more than advisory powers. The government argued that the ANC's proposals would result in two governments governing the country at the same time. Until it was constitutionally or legally possible, a proper interim government could only be established after an election, since the government was not prepared to relinquish any power until it was voted out.

To break the deadlock, a Technical Committee of 11 members was established on 7 April.[59] At the same time, bilateral meetings between the ANC and the NP were stepped up to find ways to bridge the divide.[60] Jacob Zuma and Valli Moosa attended these meetings for the ANC, and Roelf Meyer and Tertius Delport for the NP. The Technical Committee recommended that a transitional executive council representing all CODESA parties be established for the primary purpose of levelling the political playing field.[61] Several six-member subcouncils dealing with defence and law and order, regional and local government, and finance would back up the council. In addition, there should be independent election and media commissions. However, the critical question of the council's relation to the existing executive was not defined. The committee was also not able to recommend whether the council should take decisions by total consensus, as proposed by government, or by 'sufficient consensus'.

May '92

In a surprise move on 11 May, the IFP confirmed its support for an elected constitution-making body.[62] And before the day was over, in another positive development Working Group 3 reported agreement on all issues that it had been assigned and accordingly produced its final report for ratification by CODESA II.[63] Agreements were reached on all aspects of the structure of the transitional executive council. It would operate alongside, and in some instances oversee, government.[64] The activities of the structure were circumscribed by the requirement that it function only to level the political playing field before the installation of a new, elected interim government.

The importance of the agreement was its resolution of the decision-making process in the transitional executive council. It was agreed that the transitional executive council would take decisions by consensus, and failing which, by a majority of 80 per cent of the nineteen members. It was further agreed that all security forces should be placed under the joint control of an interim government and that the electronic media be regulated by an independent body.[65]

A constitution-making body

Working Group 2 was mandated to propose a constitution-making body and the constitutional principles to be applied in the final constitution. Progress was chalked up easily, and early agreement was reached on the principle that a new South Africa would be non-racial, democratic, and non-sexist. It also produced initial agreements on other constitutional principles.

It was not surprising that in February 1992 the ANC argued that sufficient progress had been made, constituting a major breakthrough. It seemed possible to complete CODESA's work within the next six weeks. The government, however, did not share this optimism.[66]

On 18 February 1992 the ANC confirmed its agreement to CODESA's prescribing the status of regional government under a new constitution.[67] In March it was agreed that 'a new constitution should provide for effective democratic participation of minority political parties consistent with democracy'. The qualification was that the principle did not imply simple majoritarianism or minority veto powers.[68] It was also at this time that the ANC's Constitutional Committee released a discussion document entitled *Ten Proposed Regions for a United South Africa*, outlining the organization's thinking on the importance of a decentralized system of government.[69]

Another issue that was gaining prominence was the future of the public service. De Klerk argued in support of job and pension security for public servants during his referendum campaign.[70] At the same time, Mandela too went out of his way to reassure white public servants that their future under a non-racial government was safe.[71] Mandela was aware of the fears among whites, and he promised that no official would lose out financially while the public service was being democratized.

For white South Africa, the referendum was their moment of truth, but for the NP, it represented the transition. *Business Day* observed that: 'Agreement on transitional government was always going to be a critical point in the negotiation process. Almost by definition, it is the point at which the NP, which has ruled SA alone for the last 44 years, hands over a share of that power to others'.[72]

It was difficult for the NP to take a leap into the unknown and accept formal power-sharing in the initial interim phase, especially after the referendum.

Just as seemingly intractable differences were beginning to cast a depressing shadow of gloom over the World Trade Centre, 30 March saw a dramatic turn of events. It was agreed that CODESA II would be convened on 15 and 16 May to bind parties to substantive agreements on an interim government and elections for a constitution-making body.[73] The dates set by the Management Committee were designed to put pressure on the parties to conclude their agreements.

On the same day, the NP government tabled proposals on a constitution-making body consisting of an elected bicameral transitional parliament acting under the transitional constitution. It was this transitional parliament that would also be responsible for drafting the new constitution. The principle divide between the ANC and the NP remained the ANC's objection to a regionally based senate with a veto over the decisions of the elected national assembly.

On 31 March the Management Committee recommended an addendum be attached to the Declaration of Intent adopted at CODESA I. According to the chairperson of the Management Committee, Pravin Gordhan, 'There was general consensus that the declaration leaves the question of a unitary or federal system of government open'.[74] This was the very reason the IFP refused to sign the Declaration of Intent at CODESA I.

On the same day the ANC proposed a 400 member constituent assembly to draw up a constitution within a four-month period.[75] The ANC argued that all South Africans over the age of 18, including those in the TBVC states, should be entitled to vote. Should the constituent assembly not be able to complete its work within the time-frame, it should dissolve and new elections be held, which would prevent any party from unreasonably delaying the process of writing the new constitution. A two-thirds majority should arrive at decisions in the assembly.

The NP responded by arguing that it urgently wanted an interim government of national unity in place. However, such a government and the final constitution had to be based on power-sharing to achieve stability and economic growth.[76] Any deviation from this model would oblige the NP to seek a renewed mandate in a referendum of white voters. Regarding the TBVC states, the NP argued that it could not force reincorporation, as they were independent. The strongest criticism of the ANC proposals came from Tertius Delport. His complaint was that:

In practice, their proposals would mean that legislative authority would be vested in a Constituent Assembly, which would not be subject to any constitutional constraints. What would the consequences of this be when it comes to the acceptance of a new constitution? ... The constitutional vacuum in which the Constituent Assembly would function, would make it possible for the majority to disregard minority wishes. The majority, therefore, would not have to consider proposals by the minority and would function as an authoritarian regime without the need for any agreement, at any time, on a new constitution.

Whereas legislative authority would be vested in this body, nothing in fact would stop the Assembly from passing a law perpetuating its own life span. The body would, in other words, have the power to consolidate its own position in an authoritarian manner. The government cannot but conclude that the ANC proposals lay the foundation for an absolute usurpation of power and authoritarian government.[77]

Despite general confidence in the process, a range of factors seemed to conspire and militate against the possibility of a successful outcome at the plenary. Judging from the statements made by each party, it appeared as if they had almost expected the plenary to fail, and were already beginning to lay the blame on each other.

On 14 April the ANC accused the government of 'intransigence'.[78] According to Valli Moosa, the success of CODESA II depended on agreements being reached on a 'shopping list' of ten items. These items included the establishment of an elected constitution-making body, the decisions of which could not be vetoed by any other body; mechanisms to ensure that elections would be free and fair; a general amnesty for exiles and political prisoners (as opposed to the temporary indemnity granted to exiles so far) as part of the creation of an appropriate climate for the installation of democracy; the scrapping of all legislation impeding free political activity; the passage of a general law guaranteeing basic civil rights to all during the transition; assurances that the security forces would not interfere with free political activity (this included joint multi-party control); a moratorium on unilateral restructuring in the socio-economic, foreign relations, security, and political spheres; impartial control of state-owned media; overall arrangements for the initial phase of an interim government; and the restoration of South African citizenship to the approximately 10 million citizens of the TBVC states to enable them to participate fully in the political process.[79]

The anxiety of the negotiators was not unfounded, for the concern that agreements on the outstanding issues would not be finalized seemed more and more well-founded. The editorial in the *Star* on 22 April rightly pointed out:

> The second plenary session of CODESA – or Codesa II – is less than three weeks away. Unlike Codesa I, Codesa II will be more than a ceremonial occasion marking a formal commitment by the contracting parties to negotiate a settlement.
>
> When the 19 parties convene for Codesa II on May 15 and 16, South Africans will want to hear more than platitudes. They will want to know what progress has been made since Codesa I met last December. The success or failure of Codesa's working committees – set up to resolve differences and chart the path ahead – will be judged by the agreements they hammer out.[80]

On 26 April the ANC proposed the creation of an independent constitutional panel to ensure that the constitutional principles agreed at CODESA would be enshrined in the final constitution.[81] This was an adaptation of a suggestion originally made by the DP as an attempt to satisfy the demand by Inkatha that the constitution be finalized before a new government came into being.

On 28 April 1992, Working Group 2 produced a far more promising report that many regarded as a breakthrough.[82] It was proposed that CODESA decide on general constitutional principles and agree to an interim constitution which would provide for a single-chambered, directly elected constitution-making body. This body would also act as an interim legislature. Regional power formed an important part of the proposal: decisions on matters relating to regional structures would require a special majority of the regional representatives and a special majority of all the delegates in the national assembly.

The NP was more than satisfied with this and temporarily shelved its own plans in favour of these proposals.[83] Its strategy was to try to flesh out the interim constitution proposals to such an extent that the constitution-making body would only have to amend them. The expectation was that CODESA II would establish another working group to draft the interim constitution and be confirmed by a CODESA III.[84] On May 4 a special task group of CODESA unanimously recommended that the TBVC states be reincorporated after testing the will of their citizens: casting their votes in the elections would be considered an adequate test.[85] This too was hailed as a major breakthrough.

However, by 8 May, a week short of the scheduled plenary, prospects for agreement again began to look bleak. The ANC and NP were in a deadlock on the composition of the constitution-making body and the power of a transitional executive appointed by CODESA.[86] Bilateral discussions between the NP and the ANC failed to breach the divide. The ANC insisted that the constitution-making body should be a single chamber body, while the NP was adamant that the option of a second chamber should be kept open. The NP argued that the second house would be where minorities would exercise their power to check the influence of the majority in the first house. This dispute related to the majority required for the adoption of the final constitution. The NP wanted to pitch this percentage higher than that which it believed the ANC could obtain, so that the minority parties would effectively hold a veto over ANC decisions. The debate was whether a two-thirds or a three-quarter majority should be required to adopt the new constitution. The negotiators could also not agree on whether the powers of regional and local government should be entrenched in an interim constitution.

Despite the deadlock, both the NP and the ANC were confident that the first phase of the interim government could be in place by August 1992.[87] On 13 May agreement was reached on the question of regionalism and a two-chambered interim legislature cum constitution-making body. In effect, all adults would have two votes, one for a regional representative, and one for a national representative.[88] This clause was to be entrenched, and those drafting a new constitution would have no alternative but to include it in a new constitution. There was still no agreement, however, on the composition of the legislature.

Tertius Delport was adamant that the issue was not about percentages but about how the constitution would be drafted. The NP insisted on a higher majority as a quid pro quo for softening its demand that the second chamber – a senate – had veto powers over the national assembly.[89] For the ANC, the resolution of percentages was an essential part of a package of agreements that would otherwise be jeopardized. The ANC compromised on a number of issues in an attempt to secure agreement, including agreement that there would be two ballot papers reflecting a national and a regional vote; that the legislature (which would also operate as a constitution-making body) would sit in two chambers, the assembly and the senate; and that the bill of rights could only be amended by a 75 per cent majority.

On 14 May 1992, a day before the CODESA II plenary, the ANC found it necessary to call a meeting of the Patriotic Front and structures of the Mass Democratic Movement, to report on developments and consult on the resolution of the dispute.[90] Eighty-five political and religious organizations, unions, student organizations, and international and diplomatic observers attended the meeting, which resolved that the ANC throw down the gauntlet and force the government to concede. The demands were a one-person-one-vote election on the basis of proportional representation; a two-thirds majority for the drafting of a constitution which could not be vetoed; and the immediate institution of an interim government with executive powers.

Later on that same day Tertius Delport tabled a new proposal.[91] The NP was prepared to accept that the final constitution be adopted by a two-thirds majority, provided that a 75 per cent majority be required for the bill of rights; the principle of restructuring of government at local and regional level; and the principle of multi-party democracy which would include the effective protection of minorities.[92] In addition, those provisions affecting regional government would be subject to a special majority of regional representatives. This the ANC refused to accept.

Apart from these issues, it was still necessary for CODESA II to agree on the road ahead. For this purpose, the Management Committee convened at 4 p.m. on 14 May.[93] It was reported that while Working Groups 1, 3, and 5 had successfully completed their assignments, Working Group 2 remained deadlocked. It was resolved that only those agreements reached would be tabled for adoption at the plenary, and in addition that no amendments to agreements would be entertained at the plenary. The Management Committee was also to seek a mandate from the plenary to establish a structure to take the outstanding tasks forward.[94]

CODESA II

In the build-up to the plenary, negotiators were upbeat and remained cautiously confident. This period was both hectic and dramatic. The media played their part too as deadlock-breakthrough-deadlock messages caused confusion and anxiety among the public. Considering the spiralling violence and general political tension, a great deal of hope was invested in the proceedings unfolding in the gigantic shed-turned-negotiating-chamber called the World Trade Centre. The country and the world was focused on this plenary; but knowledge of this did not make it any easier for negotiators who were experiencing something akin to battle fatigue. Should the parties successfully break the deadlock, South Africa would be taking one giant leap forward towards democracy and peace.

To get to the World Trade Centre on the morning of 15 May it was *1992* necessary to run a gauntlet of demonstrators representing people who were either disenchanted with the process or making one demand or another. When the day started off for those who did manage to get some rest, the atmosphere in the World Trade Centre was already thick with tension and anticipation. Negotiators and staff were filled with a mixture of excitement and panic. While the administrative staff were engaged in a frenzied rush of preparation for the start of the country's most important political convention, journalists jostled for the best seats available and television cameras and photographers competed for the best angles. As for the negotiators, they scuttled nervously between caucuses and meetings to find ways to avert a potential national crisis.

The plenary was opened with a prayer, and the difficult task of chairing the meeting was left to Justices Ismail Mohamed and Piet Schabort. The morning session started at 10 a.m., an hour later than scheduled, only to be adjourned for a further five hours to allow Working Group 2 to seek a last minute compromise.

At this meeting, the NP insisted that a 70 per cent majority take decisions in a constituent assembly. In addition, issues relating to the bill of rights, regions, and the structure of government would require a 75 per cent majority. The ANC proposed a 66.7 per cent, or two-thirds, majority on all constitutional issues. However, after consulting other members of the Patriotic Front, the ANC compromised and argued for a 70 per cent majority for all decisions relating to the constitution and 75 per cent for the bill of rights, if the NP agreed that the senate be democratically elected and not appointed.[95] The ANC also demanded that a referendum be catered for as a deadlock-breaking mechanism or if the constitution were not completed within a limited time-frame. This was not a mandated compromise, as the ANC's national executive was the only structure that could have authorized it. The compromise was a gamble based on the certainty that the NP would reject it, while it also served to show that the NP's primary intention was to build in a veto power. The gamble was worth the risk for the ANC, as the NP rejected the compromise.

It was on this negative note that the formal proceedings finally got under way at about 4 p.m. The IFP did sign the amended Declaration of Intent, but Zulu traditional leaders protesting against the exclusion of KwaZulu and demanding the full participation of the Zulu King handed in a petition to the meeting, and the Bophuthatswana government insisted that it could not be part of any interim government or elections in

South Africa, notwithstanding its commitment to continuing negotiations.[96] From this point onwards, the meeting quickly deteriorated into a verbal brawl. The NP accused the ANC of being intransigent and wanting to draft the final constitution on its own. In its turn, the ANC accused the NP government of bad faith and wanting to ensure that the special majorities it insisted upon would not allow the final constitution to be adopted. This would mean that the interim constitution would remain in place forever.

The deadlock brought to the fore a continuing mistrust, a factor which De Klerk confirmed in his contribution to the debate.[97] It was at this point that the DP's Colin Eglin made a valiant effort to save the day. After lambasting both the ANC and the NP for allowing the dispute to spill onto the conference floor, he made an appeal to the two parties' leaders to intervene. He said, 'I don't believe the differences are so great that the De Klerks and Mandelas can't solve them'.[98] The meeting was then adjourned.

Despite the fact that CODESA II did not ratify any agreements, the adjournment provided the relief that could not have come a moment too soon. The adjournment also provided a useful opportunity for Mandela and De Klerk to meet.

In view of the public row on the first day of CODESA II, the Management Committee met at 10:30 a.m. on 16 May to consider the way forward. It found that while CODESA II failed to live up to expectations, the process of negotiation itself was not in jeopardy. Accordingly, the Management Committee confirmed that it 'is extremely conscious of the fact that the participants in Codesa entered the negotiations process in the belief that it can take our country to a stable order. We have a responsibility to approach our task in such a manner that the confidence of the participants, and our people, in the negotiations process is reinforced'.

It was against this background that the mandate the Management Committee sought and obtained from the plenary was to be 'authorised to exercise such authority, as is necessary, to ensure that the objectives of the Declaration of Intent are attained; including the power to implement any agreement reached by Working Group 1 and also any other agreement falling within its mandate without summoning a plenary session of Codesa. That it also be given the power to increase the representation of individual parties / administrations / organisations on the Management Committee'.[99]

Parties appeared more conciliatory on the second day of the plenary, almost as if they were ashamed of their public tantrums on the previous day. Even Mandela referred to CODESA as a family and said he would look back on CODESA II with fondness. The plenary finally agreed that the meeting adjourn to allow parties to refer the matter to their principals. The Management Committee was instructed to convene another plenary session to adopt agreements entered into later. However, the scheduling of such a plenary had to take into account that the current session of Parliament was scheduled to go into recess on 28 June.

The Daily Management Committee decided that all agreements had to be classified in terms of what was required. They would require elaboration, preparation, and implementation or referral to the transitional executive council when this was established.[100] It was also accepted that the agreements dealing with a climate for free political activity, in particular the future of the SABC and the question of political intimidation, had to be implemented with immediate effect.

The failure of CODESA II produced invaluable lessons, the main one being that process or procedural issues are sometimes as important as substantive matters. The dispute producing the deadlock manifested itself around the percentage required for the adoption of the constitution. While this was a procedural issue, it was nevertheless important enough to block substantive constitutional formulations from being approved in the final constitution. Political negotiations are rarely products of piecemeal agreements, and agreements are usually reached in terms of a package of proposals. Moreover, an agreement is never in place until the detail has been finalized. The idea is that while a party may not achieve every objective, the package of achievements must be such that the party is generally satisfied.

The ANC feared that it would be falling into a trap of living perpetually under the interim constitution only because the adoption of the final constitution was continuously vetoed. For the NP, however, an effective veto would mean that the party would maintain its relevance as a political force. As we have seen, there is nothing like a crisis to focus the minds of negotiators on the crucial issues at hand, and this manifested itself in two respects. Firstly, crises obliged parties that played a role in the Tricameral Parliament and the homelands to decide where their allegiances lay. Secondly, they obliged the NP to confirm clearly what its bottom-line was: that the NP would not concede to a settlement that did not guarantee it some political authority and power in the future. It insisted on a veto and therefore on its role in an interim government for a substantial period of time.[101] Furthermore, the NP insisted that the principle of enforced power-sharing be enshrined in the final constitution. Evidently, its political strength in negotiating the interim constitution would be greater than when the final constitution was drafted.

8

Negotiating an
end to the deadlock

THE DEADLOCK was not about principle, but about political power: the power to determine the final constitutional dispensation. It also served to fuel the intense mistrust already festering among parties, and to bring to the fore long-held perceptions and suspicions. Rumours and speculation about the reasons for the deadlock abounded, in the media especially. On 20 May the ANC alleged that someone had tapped its CODESA office telephones.[1] A professional company appointed by the Management Committee verified the allegation, but the culprits were never caught.[2]

Meanwhile, on 25 May 1992 the ANC and the NP met to find solutions to the deadlock.[3] A day later the ANC, after consulting its constitutional structures, formally withdrew the compromise proposal it had tabled in the closing moments of CODESA II.[4] This was followed by a National Policy Conference the ANC held between 28 and 31 May 1992, which confirmed the agreements reached at CODESA and provided guidelines for its vision of the process.[5] The ANC also decided to embark on a mass action campaign to put pressure on the NP to accept its demands.[6]

A general criticism of CODESA was its lack of transparency. According to Joe Slovo, 'We are perceived as a mysterious cabal . . . we would like to believe the future of all our people is being discussed. They have a right to know more about how we are going about this process'.[7] It was suggested that all CODESA talks take place in full view of the media.[8] The Management Committee meeting of 15 June confirmed that the negotiations should be more accessible to the press, and agreed to set guidelines for this to take place.

This Management Committee meeting also reflected on the lack of progress in the plenary. Morale was low, and the meeting could not even agree on the size and composition of the new Daily Management Committee.[9] There was equally no progress in the meetings between the ANC and the NP.[10] At the same time, Buthelezi threatened that the exclusion of the King and KwaZulu administration from the CODESA process could lead to violence.[11]

The exchange of memoranda

On the morning of 17 June 1992 more than forty residents of Boipatong were massacred in a systematic attack. The incident sent shock waves throughout the country. The ANC's NEC held an emergency meeting to discuss the implications of the massacre. While it reaffirmed its commitment in principle to negotiation, it decided to break off all talks, both bilaterally with the government and multilaterally in CODESA. The ANC also issued fourteen demands to the government, accusing it of complicity in the violence.[12] In its press statement, the ANC stated:

> It [the NP government] pursues a strategy which embraces negotiations, together with systematic covert actions, including murder, involving its security forces and surrogates. ... The Boipatong massacre is one of the most chilling instances of the consequences of the actions of the De Klerk regime. ... The ANC reaffirms its commitment to a negotiated resolution of the conflict in our country which would bring about democracy, peace and justice. The refusal of the regime to accept such a settlement compelled the NEC to review the current negotiations process.
> The ANC has no option but to break off bilateral and CODESA negotiations. The NEC will be keeping the situation under continuous review. The response and practical steps taken by the De Klerk regime to these demands will play a critical role in determining the direction and speed with which bona fide negotiations can take place.[13]

There was an immediate outcry from the business and international community, and on 28 June senior business leaders from the South African Chamber of Business (SACOB) launched a major intervention.[14] The leadership of the European Community also urged all parties to return to the negotiating table, while the chairperson of the OAU and the UN Secretary-General made similar calls. In the meantime, the Management Committee cancelled its meeting scheduled for 29 June 1992 due to the breakdown in negotiations.[15]

What followed was an exchange of memoranda between Mandela and De Klerk detailing their reasons for the breakdown and blaming each other for the violence.[16] In an effort to get the ANC back to the negotiating table, De Klerk significantly softened the NP's demands for minority protection, even dropping its demand to give minority parties an increased representation in the senate.[17] The NP now proposed that each region should have equal representation and seats be allocated to each region in proportion to party support. The NP also dropped its demand that the structure of regions be changed only with a 75 per cent majority. It further proposed that there be a general election should the constitution not be completed within three years. (The ANC was demanding it be six months.)

While these proposals did not entirely meet with the ANC's demands, they provided some basis on which to find agreement. Despite this, Mandela refused to meet De Klerk.[18] The ANC welcomed the proposal but complained that it did not go far enough.[19] In particular, the ANC demanded that the NP abandon any form of minority veto, and accused De Klerk of ignoring the gravity of the ANC's demands.[20]

On 15 July 1992 the ANC and its allies, the SACP and COSATU, declared the month of August a month of 'rolling mass action'. Several hundred thousand people engaged in various forms of mass action throughout the country, and more than 90 per cent of the workforce heeded a national general strike. This was the biggest form of mass mobilization seen in the country since the 1950s, effectively creating a referendum of the black majority in which people 'voted with their feet'. The campaign was an overwhelming success for the ANC, serving to mobilize black people around its demands, particularly for an interim government, which once again became the centre of political and popular debate in the country.

The NP government, for its part, met with the governments of Bophuthatswana and Ciskei, the IFP, the Solidarity Party, the National People's Party, the Ximoko Progressive Party, and the Dikwankwetla Party on 27 July 1992 to discuss ways of getting negotiations back on track.[21] Early in August, Buthelezi began voicing disquiet about the NP's attempts to get talks with the ANC going again, a move he saw as a softening approach towards the ANC. What seemed to bother Buthelezi was the possible exclusion of the IFP from such talks.[22] He threatened to pull out of all future multi-party talks if this was the case. In a partial attempt to appease the IFP, on 20 August the NP met with both the IFP and the DP. They agreed that CODESA should resume in September even if the ANC were not there. De Klerk argued that while this was not a 'go it alone' strategy, multi-party talks had to continue.[23]

In view of the international community's concerns about the situation, the United Nations Security Council held a special session on 2 August 1992 to deal with the question of violence in South Africa. The UN adopted special resolution 765 calling for a special representative of the Secretary-General, Cyrus Vance, to visit South Africa and report back. Later that month, the UN Monitoring Committee under the leadership of Vance arrived in South Africa to monitor the mass action campaign.

One of the first meetings Vance held in South Africa was with Pik Botha, Minister of Foreign Affairs. Vance voiced the UN's concern over the continued incarceration of political prisoners, urging Botha to expedite their release. Botha responded by linking this to the question of a general amnesty, insisting that the ANC first abandon its policy on armed struggle and address the question of MK arms caches and ANC underground units. In his report to the UN Secretary-General, Vance was critical of most institutions of state, but his harshest criticism was reserved for the security forces, which he believed did not have the credibility or legitimacy to assist in the transformation of South Africa. However, he did praise the Goldstone Commission and structures of the National Peace Accord. This intervention by Vance and the United Nations was important, as it seemed to favour joint control over the security forces during the transition.

The 'channel bilateral'

The ANC's National Working Committee, at its meeting of 31 August *1992* 1992, agreed to establish a channel of communication between the ANC and the government, with the purpose of maintaining some form of dialogue with the NP. The ANC mandated Cyril Ramaphosa to maintain this channel, while the NP's representative was Roelf Meyer. In their first formal meeting on 2 September, the government indicated that it wanted to discuss its responses to ANC demands in greater detail.

What followed was a series of exchanges to explore ways and means to take the process of negotiations forward in meetings commonly referred to as the 'channel bilateral'.[24] The meetings were tense but soon showed promise. Three kinds of issues were addressed: political and constitutional issues, including an interim government, the constituent assembly, constitutional principles, and issues of political concern such as dangerous weapons and mass action;[25] political prisoners;[26] and problematic hostels.[27]

The first breakthrough came with the NP's agreement that the constituent assembly be bound only by general constitutional principles, be subject to a set time-frame, and have adequate deadlock-breaking mechanisms. On 3 September the ANC published a discussion document containing comprehensive amendments to the South African Constitution. The purpose of the amendments was to facilitate the establishment of an interim government and a constituent assembly. These proposed amendments were referred to as the 'Transition to Democracy Act'.

The proposal suggested the replacement of the legislature with a single 400-member national assembly elected by proportional representation. This body would also operate as a constituent assembly. A simple majority from amongst its members would elect the president, and a multi-party cabinet would take decisions by a two-thirds majority. All parties with more than 5 per cent support would have a place in the assembly, and there would be a bill of rights. Decisions on the constitution would require a two-thirds majority, and deadlock-breaking mechanisms were proposed to facilitate decision-making. In this regard, unless parties adopted the constitution within nine months, provision was made for fresh elections to be called. The second constituent assembly would then have a further six months to complete its tasks. The constitution would have to conform to constitutional principles previously negotiated, and a seven-member panel of constitutional experts would assist in the adjudication of disputes.

In the meantime, the NP prepared to reconvene Parliament in a special sitting for the purpose of passing legislation on the agreements reached at CODESA.[28] Unfortunately, early on 29 September several ANC demonstrators protesting in Bisho against the homeland of Ciskei were killed and a large number wounded. This served both to heighten tension and to move the reincorporation of homelands up on the agenda.[29] The tragedy also underscored the demands for visible measures to curb the violence and for joint control over the security forces during the period of transition. There was now urgent pressure on all parties to speed up the process of negotiation. De Klerk's response to the massacre was to call an urgent summit with Mandela.

Mandela, for his part, confirmed that the ANC was eager to restart negotiation in order to 'save the country from disaster'. For this to happen, the government had to honour its previous commitments to the ANC and the UN envoy Cyrus Vance on the issues of hostels, political prisoners, and dangerous weapons. The ANC had shown its willingness to facilitate the process towards a negotiated settlement, and consequently Mandela made an impassioned plea to the government to meet the ANC's concerns, and promised to respond likewise.[30] According to Mandela, the proposed summit was urgent.

This, together with the deteriorating security climate, served to place De Klerk under tremendous pressure. To add to the government's woes, the recently appointed Minister of Finance, Derek Keys, confirmed that the country's economy was in dire straits.[31] The country urgently needed to restore investor confidence, and negotiating a speedy resolution to the conflict would help make that happen.

It was against this background that negotiations to break the deadlock continued with greater vigour. Once again, were it not for the maturity of the negotiators, it would not have been possible to make the breakthroughs required. However, just as it seemed as if complete agreement was in the offing, a row broke out within the NP leadership. Kobie Coetsee linked the agreement on the release of political prisoners to a general amnesty, a proposal which the ANC rejected.[32] The NP was forced to settle the matter within its ranks before the negotiations could proceed.[33]

The row was an important indicator of the tension developing within the NP. While it was the first publicly known dispute within the NP regarding the negotiations, it was the second display of the anxiety behind it. The first arose from the submission of a document by Hernus Kriel to Working Group 1 of CODESA. It was becoming evident that there was a body of thought within the leadership of the NP that felt that the party should assume a much more aggressive approach in its negotiations. These tensions soon became a common feature of the negotiation process.

Quite apart from this, the question of political prisoners proved more difficult to resolve than all the other issues in contention. The NP government felt they could not release people they regarded as 'terrorists' without also releasing convicted white right-wingers. The ANC, on the other hand, felt that the victory of a breakthrough would be rather hollow if its supporters continued to languish in jail.

During the last seventy-two hours before the agreement was signed, the dispute around the release of political prisoners centred on three individuals, namely Robert McBride, Mzondeleli Nondula, and Mthetheleli Mncube. All three had been convicted of murder, sentenced to death, and granted a reprieve. The government believed that the release of these prisoners would be unconstitutional, since the

President did not have the necessary powers without empowering legislation. Accordingly, these releases could take place only after Parliament reconvened and passed appropriate legislation.[34]

p. 319

The Record of Understanding

Late on the night of 24 September 1992 both the ANC's National Working Committee and the NP cabinet met with their negotiators to confirm the agreement produced by the 'channel bilateral'. In the ANC's meeting, while the entire extended National Working Committee accepted the agreement, Mandela stunned the leadership of the ANC by disagreeing. He insisted that the three prisoners in question (McBride, Nondula, and Mncube) be released forthwith. For him, the value of all the organization's achievements would be rendered meaningless if the ANC were not able to secure their release. What astonished even the most militant leaders present was the stubbornness of the ANC's President.

Mandela obtained the permission of the National Working Committee to adjourn its meeting to discuss the matter with De Klerk telephonically. Mandela told De Klerk that unless he released the three there would be no summit. De Klerk was taken aback by this demand and promised to give him an answer as soon as he had consulted his cabinet. Mandela had thrown down the gauntlet and challenged De Klerk like never before; the NP leader had to take an immediate decision on an extremely sensitive issue. To add to the tension, it was not only De Klerk who felt challenged; a number of the most senior ANC leaders were just as worried. Despite their attempts to convince Mandela that the agreement was acceptable, he remained adamant. Twenty minutes later De Klerk returned the call acceding to Mandela's demand.

On 26 September 1992 a summit took place between Mandela and De Klerk at which they signed the Record of Understanding.[35] This agreement addressed major deadlock areas and laid the basis for the resumption of multi-party negotiations. Regarding political prisoners, they resolved that 150 prisoners convicted of political offences committed prior to 8 October 1990 be released immediately and a further 250 prisoners be released by 15 November 1992. They also agreed that the public display of dangerous weapons be banned, the Goldstone Commission's recommendations implemented, and various hostels fenced. The agreement represented yet another milestone in the process of negotiations, which De Klerk cogently described in his speech to the Natal NP congress: 'The Government's attitude is that for the sake of reconciliation we want to close the book of the past. We stand here at the cross-roads in our history. We need to turn our back on the past, we need to clean the slate. . . . We need to create an atmosphere conducive to negotiation. . . . We need to start afresh. My hope is that this will be seen as a deed ensuring that we do not remain locked in the disputes of the past. I hope this will be recognised as a deed done to unlock the future'.[36] The Record of Understanding represented a historic turning point, for it established an agreed course of events and constitutional principles, and also confirmed the process of negotiation as set out in the Harare Declaration.

Right-wing reaction

The agreement also proved to be politically costly for the NP and ruptured its already volatile relationship with Inkatha.[37] Despite strenuous efforts by the government, it failed to placate Buthelezi, and relations remained strained for a long time afterwards.[38]

On 6 October 1992 Buthelezi, Ciskei military leader Oupa Gqozo, Bophuthatswana's Lucas Mangope, the CP, its breakaway faction, the Afrikaner Volksunie (AVU), and the Afrikaner Freedom Foundation met in a Conference for Concerned South Africans to respond to the Record of Understanding.[39] The conference demanded that MK be disbanded and that the Record of Understanding be scrapped. This conference gave birth to the Concerned South Africans Group (COSAG). The remarkable aspect of COSAG was that it was the first formal alliance in South Africa between black and white right-wing

1993

organizations uniting around a common rejection of the Record of Understanding and fear of an ANC majority government.

On 9 January 1993 the NP met COSAG and agreed that a conference be called to plan the resumption of multilateral negotiations.[40] COSAG was opposed to both an interim government and the drafting of the final constitution by an elected constituent assembly. It was even opposed to the title 'CODESA'.[41] An important issue for consideration was the status of agreements previously reached at CODESA. The position of the IFP was that the multi-party conference should re-evaluate all agreements, including the Peace Accord, and the process of negotiations. Those parties who did not participate in CODESA should be able to confirm or reject it as they wished.[42]

Buthelezi's attitude and approach did not enamour the United Nations or its Secretary-General, Boutros Boutros Ghali.[43] Furthermore, various attempts made by Boutros Ghali to communicate with Buthelezi were in vain.[44] The isolationist and confrontationist approach adopted by Inkatha intensified in December 1992, when the KwaZulu Legislature provocatively approved a draft constitution that it envisaged as the first step to federal autonomy.[45] Buthelezi was effectively threatening secession.[46]

The ANC's 'Strategic Perspectives'

In October 1992, after the signing of the Record of Understanding, the ANC's most senior leaders met in a *lekgotla* ('a gathering') to plan and develop a comprehensive strategy for the process that lay ahead.[47] An important debate at this meeting focused on the compromises that the ANC may have to make to produce a negotiated settlement. Once again, the question of 'sunset clauses' was considered, a concept previously floated by Mandela in late December 1991 and again considered by the ANC's National Working Committee in February 1992.

The ANC rose from this meeting to consult various role-players, including the Patriotic Front, civil society, and business leaders.[48] It wanted to get all its allies on board before the formal process of negotiation resumed. To finalize its positions, the ANC's NEC met on 23 November 1992 and endorsed the formal resumption of negotiations.[49] Gerrit Viljoen and various other NP policy makers openly supported this move.

At this meeting of the NEC, the ANC also adopted a position paper prepared by Joe Slovo entitled 'Strategic perspectives'.[50] This document had as much a strategic impact on the ANC's negotiating strategy as the Harare Declaration, for it represented a further development of the ANC's ideas on the process of negotiation. The document assessed the political balance of forces and provided a perspective on the transformation of South Africa.

The paper argued that a peaceful political settlement had always been the first option of the liberation movement. It was only when the prospect of any peaceful settlement vanished that the ANC adopted armed struggle and the idea of a revolutionary seizure of power. The strategic perspective of the ANC was the attainment of majority rule, which would proceed in various phases. The pursuit of the objectives in each phase, the document cautioned, should not result in defeats later on. Five phases were identified: the establishment of a transitional executive council; the election of a constituent assembly; the establishment of an interim government of national unity; the drafting and adoption of the new constitution; the phasing in of the new constitution; and the period of consolidation of the new democracy.

The fundamental goal of the national liberation struggle was the transfer of power to the 'people'. In pursuing the policy of negotiation, 'Strategic Perspectives' suggested that unless the liberation movement had the strength and support of the masses it would not be able to achieve its goals at the negotiating table. It was important to ensure that the compromises made did not undermine the new democracy.

The demand for an interim government of national unity was won. This was fundamentally different, however, from the NP's approach to power-sharing, which meant no more than the entrenchment of veto powers for minority parties. Stability during the period of transition to full democracy was crucial, and in this regard, the security forces and the civil service were most important. Accordingly, it was necessary to address the question of job security and retrenchment packages for civil servants as part of a negotiated settlement. The document predicted that while the final negotiated settlement would take the form of multilateral agreements, the ANC and NP would occupy a central position.

Pressure to resume multi-party negotiations

In the meantime, there were several other issues brewing which served to increase pressure for an early resumption of multi-party negotiations and the establishment of an interim government. One of these issues was the ongoing violence plaguing the Natal area. In this regard, the chairperson of the National Peace Accord, John Hall, made various attempts supported by senior business leaders to secure another summit between Mandela and Buthelezi.[51] Then a row broke out when the NP transferred large tracts of land to the self-governing territories.[52] According to the ANC, there was no logic to this when discussions were in progress for the reincorporation of all homelands into South Africa. It concluded that the NP government was providing favours to regionally based political parties in return for their support during the negotiations.[53] Related to this was the publication of the De Meyer Commission's report, which revealed corruption on a huge scale in the Department of Education and Training and the Lebowa government and excessive spending in KwaNdebele.[54] And soon afterwards the Goldstone Commission, in its report of 16 November 1992, confirmed the existence of a 'third force' that operated under cover of military intelligence in fomenting violence.

These controversies placed De Klerk in an awkward predicament and under unbearable pressure. The editorial in *Business Day* on 19 November 1992 said:

It is a measure of South Africa's desperation that a way has to be found for unhooking President de Klerk and his Cabinet colleagues from the scandals of corruption, dirty tricks and lack of credibility. De Klerk and his colleagues might be floundering, but if we are to have any hope of negotiating a settlement of our problems, De Klerk has to be able to deliver his constituency when heads have to be counted.

The national predicament has not gone unnoticed by the ANC's leadership. But it has to heed the opinions of its supporters who may not have as pragmatic an understanding of the realities of political power. Forgiveness or letting bygones be bygones is possible, but only if De Klerk and his government can credibly convince their interlocutors that they have no hidden agendas, that they are not party to any more destabilization tricks and that they are determined to halt undemocratic activities by the state.

Preparations for the resumption of multi-party negotiations

To prepare for the resumption of negotiations, the ANC and the NP held a 'bosberaad' between 2 and 5 December 1992. The venue, a ~~DEC. '92~~ nature reserve in the north-west of the country called D'Nyala, was ideal. The meeting dealt with the status of bilateral discussions, multilateral negotiations, time-frames, elections, the independent media commission, interim government, the constitution-making body, the transitional executive council, free political activity, violence, and unilateral restructuring.[55] In this regard, they drafted various formulations for submission to their respective principals for approval.[56] They also accepted that agreements entered into were binding on them alone.

The purpose of this bilateral and the several meetings that followed was to avoid substantial differences between the two major role-players. While this meeting did not conclude any substantive agreements, the real success of the meeting lay in the fact that it allowed the negotiators to strike up a personal rapport with each other. This proved invaluable in allowing them to work with each other through difficult negotiations. In the two years that the ANC was unbanned, this bosberaad was the first opportunity that these negotiators had to interact with each other at a social level and to get to know each other as people rather than as opponents.

News of the December bosberaad only angered the IFP further.[57] But the IFP was not alone, for the impression of a near cosy relationship between the ANC and the NP also appeared to produce new fault lines within the NP leadership.[58] The international community monitored these negotiations closely, and there was considerable concern about the continued isolation of Inkatha. Attempts were made to persuade Buthelezi to take a more positive approach. Exercising quiet diplomacy, the United States joined Britain and other European Community states in pressing Buthelezi to lead Inkatha back into the multi-party process.

On the international front, two developments were to make an impact on this process. In the United States, Bill Clinton became President, and according to an official of the new US administration, 'he [Buthelezi] has been left in little doubt that, with a new administration soon to take over in Washington, he won't be able to count on the sort of sympathetic hearing he has relied upon in the past'.[59] The British relinquished their presidency of the European Community – another loss of support that Buthelezi had relied on previously. The EC nonetheless pressed Buthelezi to realize the importance of not finding himself isolated when multi-party talks resumed.

The beginning of January 1993 proved to be a good start for the process of negotiations. Early in January the NP met with COSAG to discuss further the resumption of multi-party negotiations and share views on the question of a future regional dispensation.[60] In a surprisingly positive move, the COSAG alliance decided on 10 January to throw in its lot and agreed to the resumption of multi-party talks.[61] Following this meeting there was an extensive bilateral meeting between the NP and Inkatha on 18 January, which helped to bring about a convergence in their perspectives on a regional dispensation.[62] The meeting was however acrimonious, and deadlocked when Inkatha complained about the 'connivance' of the NP with the ANC.[63] The two parties nevertheless managed to patch up their differences before the month was over.[64]

The meetings that followed looked at the resumption of negotiations, which spurred the ANC on to develop its election campaign.[65] Even the government was preparing for the election as the Minister of Home Affairs, Louis Pienaar, confirmed the identification of about 7 000 sites as possible polling stations at which approximately 21 million voters could cast their votes.[66]

A series of further meetings between the ANC and the NP followed between 20 January and 4 February 1993,[67] with the objective of resolving as many of the outstanding issues between them as possible. These meetings proved fruitful and represented a convergence of thinking, placing the ANC and NP in a good position to jointly drive the negotiations forward. The discussions were assisted by a marked shift at the beginning of February 1993 in the NP's conception of power-sharing, signified by the NP's giving up its idea of a collegiate presidency. This meant agreement on one head of state under which a multi-party cabinet would serve.[68] The term for the government of national unity, representing all parties with more than 5 per cent of the vote, would be at least five years.[69] There would also be no need to hold another election or referendum once the final constitution was adopted. Furthermore, the NP abandoned its demand that the multi-party negotiations should determine the powers, functions, and boundaries of regions, which meant that the constitution-making body would be bound only by the agreed constitutional principles. There was also agreement on the establishment of an independent electoral commission, agreement on the process of appointing an SABC board by 31 March, and resolution that the TBVC states be reincorporated.

9 Negotiating the transition

AT THE BEGINNING OF FEBRUARY 1993 it became apparent that most role-players had realized the urgent need for the resumption of multi-party negotiation. However, the question was, where did one start? The ANC and the NP wanted to build on the agreements arrived at in CODESA and to consolidate their bilateral agreements multilaterally. In particular, they were keen to secure multilateral agreement that an elected body draft the final constitution. *Concerned South Africans Group*

Inkatha and COSAG, on the other hand, called for a planning conference to determine both the prospective form of the state and the negotiation process itself.[1] Inkatha was confident that such a conference would choose a federal state and merely instruct the technocrats to draft the final constitution. COSAG was opposed to the final constitution's being drafted by an elected constituent assembly, believing that the constitution had to be multilaterally negotiated and tested in a referendum.

Another point of difference was the name of the conference itself, since COSAG was opposed to the continued existence of CODESA or a process bearing that name. To ensure a more inclusive process of negotiation, the parties agreed to accommodate these views, and renamed the conference the Negotiation Planning Conference.

In February 1993, on the basis of a report to the ANC's NEC on progress made in various bilateral meetings, the ANC adopted a resolution on negotiation and national reconstruction that called for a speedy resumption of multilateral negotiations.[2] The resolution also provided a detailed mandate regarding an interim government of national unity, proposing an interim government that would last up until the adoption of the new constitution. The government of national

FEB 1993

unity would then continue in the same form to phase in the new constitution, but would not exist for more than five years after the election of the constituent assembly.

In discussions with the NP, the date for the conference was set for 4 March 1993. The agenda proposed discussion on the assessment of the current situation and the resumption of multilateral negotiations. Furthermore, the conference would be convened on the basis of each party inviting one other. A panel of chairpersons was selected from parties represented, and it was agreed that three delegates from each party or organization would attend. The principle of inclusivity meant that all the parties that had participated in CODESA were invited, including the PAC, AZAPO, the CP, the AVU, the AWB, and the HNP. Regarding the media, the ANC proposed that the conference be completely open, but the NP disagreed. (This was the beginning of greater transparency: the compromise decision reached meant that the media was barred only from bilaterals and Planning Committee meetings.)

On 2 and 3 March the ANC and the NP met again. According to Cyril Ramaphosa, the ANC wanted agreement in as many areas as possible 'so that when we get to the multiparty table the negotiation will be much smoother and there will be less chance of deadlocks developing'.[3] One of the areas in which agreement was sought was the power of the president in a government of national unity.[4] The NP had retreated from its original demand for a collegiate presidency and now argued for a rotating prime minister with a president as a ceremonial head of state, but the matter remained contentious.

The multi-party negotiating process

On 4 and 5 March 1993 the Negotiation Planning Conference convened at the World Trade Centre. The conference adopted a resolution calling for the resumption of negotiation, and also resolved that a new negotiating forum – the Multi-party Negotiating Process (MPNP) – be established to meet first on 1 and 2 April 1993.[5] Establishing a new process was convenient: not only were parties able to restructure the negotiating forum into a much more efficient organization, they were also able to accommodate the objections of the right wing to CODESA.[6]

The Patriotic Front, including representatives of the Mass Democratic Movement, met shortly thereafter to develop a common perspective on the way forward. A surprising development at this meeting was the agreement to establish an electoral alliance under the banner of the ANC. For several regionally based political entities as well as the Labour Party this move represented a clear political alliance and an end to the dithering and political vacillation witnessed since 1990. The PAC and AZAPO refused to attend this meeting.

The first meeting of the MPNP took place on 1 April 1993, when twenty-six participants, including the PAC, the CP, and the AVU, met.[7] The meeting was a success, so much so that participants managed to complete a two-day programme in one day.[8] This meeting identified the issues requiring attention and the structures necessary.[9]

The structure of the Multi-party Negotiating Process

The structure of the MPNP was more efficient than CODESA because instead of negotiating issues in different working groups, a Negotiating Council became the effective negotiating forum. This council reported to the Negotiating Forum, which had the responsibility of finalizing agreements. The need for the Negotiating Forum soon fell away after it delegated its powers to the Negotiating Council. Accordingly, all agreements negotiated were then ratified by the plenary.

Another innovation was the establishment of Technical Committees consisting of non-party political experts, a facility not present at CODESA. Instead of orally presenting their views in the Negotiating Council, parties made written submissions that were then considered by the Technical Committees. This was a major improvement because the reports from these committees included formulations that took everyone's views into account, and the committees could act as compromise-

MPNP Structures

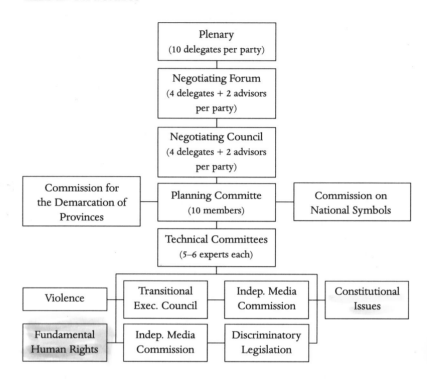

seeking and deadlock-breaking mechanisms.[10] Where CODESA relied on a Management Committee as its day-to-day directing authority, the MPNP established its Planning Committee to the same effect.[11] Also, with the same purpose as CODESA's political secretariat, the MPNP had a subcommittee to the Planning Committee. Here the services of Mac Maharaj and S. S. van der Merwe as key strategists in the process were crucial. This subcommittee also had a third member, Ben Ngubane of the IFP.[12]

To attend to matters of a specialized nature, the council established two commissions which were non-partisan and were to deal with the demarcation of regions and with national symbols.

Commitment to find solutions

Just as the parties prepared to go into the final round of negotiations, disaster struck. On 10 April 1993 Chris Hani, one of the most popular ANC leaders in the country, was assassinated, and the country was plunged into one of its bleakest hours.[13] The commitment of the participants, especially the ANC, was severely tested. The anger of the South African people and the associated violent backlash made political and economic prospects appear bleak. A national strike resulted in 90 per cent worker absence, further deepening the economic crisis, and even the Reserve Bank governor, Chris Stals, expressed concern. Business confidence was at an all-time low, and it was feared that further mass action would accelerate the flight of capital, putting greater pressure on the reserves.[14]

An appeal for calm by Mandela and other ANC leaders greatly assisted in averting a national crisis. The leadership of the Tripartite Alliance (the ANC, the SACP and COSATU) believed that the assassination posed a threat to the negotiation process and efforts to bring about peace.[15] The alliance accordingly resolved to speed up the process and seek an early announcement of an election date, the immediate establishment of the Transitional Executive Council (TEC), and multi-party control over all armed forces.

Hani's assassination and its aftermath demonstrated several important aspects of South Africa's political dynamism.[16] The response of all political parties – particularly the ANC, its tripartite allies, and the youth – reflected the political maturity of the leadership in the country across the political spectrum, and also clearly expressed the commitment of this leadership to negotiation and the desire for peace. However, at the same time, the anger of the black majority and its youth in particular portrayed the tenuous and fragile nature of a society in transition. What also became evident was that the De Klerk government was not solely in control of the process of transition, as the government helplessly witnessed events unfold while the country relied on Mandela and the ANC to provide leadership and to restore calm.[17]

The assassination affected the agenda for negotiation as well. The only responsible way for negotiators to respond was to instill a new sense of urgency into the process. Roelf Meyer was astute enough to understand this responsibility, arguing that 'time is running out. . . . The situation is unstable and the economy is under great threat. That is why we have to move quickly to keep to the time-frames of the transition schedule and get a settlement'.[18] It was now more critical then ever that the tangible fruits of conciliatory negotiations be made visible. This translated into two immediate measures – agreement on a date for the first non-racial democratic election, and the establishment of the Transitional Executive Council.[19]

At this time, the NP sought to separate the establishment of the TEC from the other aspects of the transition. It proposed that the TEC be formed immediately while negotiating the other aspects of the transition, but the ANC rejected this as a trap. The ANC feared that it would be bound to the TEC without making any progress on other issues, and once again insisted on a 'package deal' that included all aspects of the transition.

In another ominous development during this precarious period, General 'Tienie' Groenewald, a retired chief director of military intelligence in the SADF, together with several former military leaders including General Constand Viljoen, formed the 'Committee of Generals', the purpose of which was to support Afrikaner right-wing demands for self-determination. General Groenewald warned of a right-wing secession backed by an army of 500 000 white national army personnel, and outlined the objectives of the Committee of Generals as the unity of the fragmented right wing.[20] The objective was to maximize pressure for a volkstaat at the negotiating table and to bolster the strength of COSAG in multi-party negotiations.[21]

Support for this committee was manifested at a meeting of 7 000 right-wing farmers in Potchefstroom, where the NP had been routed by the Conservative Party in a recent by-election.[22] Angered at the number of farmers killed in the area recently, the meeting adamantly refused to be governed by the ANC. Even the militant white Mineworkers' Union gave its unqualified support.[23] Despite the denial of political ambitions, the Committee of Generals formed themselves *APRIL 1993* into a political party, the Afrikaner Volksfront (AVF), and soon became far more successful than other right-wing parties in uniting Afrikaners.

The MPNP's Planning Committee first met on 22 April to prepare a report on all agreements reached at CODESA, and to ensure that the essence and value of the previous negotiation were not lost.[24] The Negotiating Council met on 30 April and resolved to establish six Technical Committees.[25] Each committee consisted of six experts – none of whom were representatives of any political organization or party. The Negotiating Council meeting on 7 May adopted a further Declaration of Intent by sufficient consensus, the primary thrust of which was to call for an election date that was not later than April 1994.[26]

To ensure that the COSAG alliance remained at the negotiating table, the ANC offered a significant concession, proposing a constitutional principle that structured government at national, regional, and local levels. Each level of government would be democratically elected with appropriate legislative and executive powers and functions, which would be entrenched in the constitution. There were two important aspects to the proposal. Firstly, the ANC agreed to accord regions significant legislative and executive powers which would be entrenched in the interim constitution. Secondly, the proposal effectively cast regional powers in stone, denying the constituent assembly the power to change them. The power of the national government to override a region's powers was restricted to matters that were not allocated in the constitution to the regional level of government exclusively.

The month of May saw significant progress. Despite the compromise offered by the ANC, De Klerk remained insistent that he would not tolerate or accede to a constitution-making provision for majority rule.[27] After more than two years of formal negotiation, the debate between the concept of 'power-sharing' and a 'government of national unity' crisply brought to the fore – for the first time – the bottom-line for the NP. De Klerk insisted that the NP continue to play a central role in a coalition government lasting well into the next century, for he did not want to negotiate the NP out of political power. *2 MAY 1993*

This demand went beyond the understanding reached with the ANC that a five-year government of national unity be formed after the country's first multiracial elections. For the ANC, its starting point was majority rule, but it also believed that it was necessary to build and establish national unity and reconciliation during the transition, particularly so in view of the polarized past and the need to develop one national identity. The principle of national unity, therefore, went beyond the compromise of merely accommodating the NP in the interim government.[28]

A date for the election

Parties were under pressure to produce tangible and positive results from the process.[29] Senior business leaders under the aegis of the Consultative Business Movement met with the ANC, the NP, and the COSAG group, demanding a swift settlement confirming the election date while also keeping all parties on board.[30] Shortly afterwards, the organized labour movement led by COSATU applied further pressure. COSATU's general secretary, Jay Naidoo, complained that they were losing patience with the political parties' failure to deliver. He went on to say, 'It is not just COSATU which is putting the World Trade Centre on trial. The entire South African nation and international community are all waiting to see what agreement will be reached on the setting of an election date, installation of the transitional executive council and joint control of security forces'.[31]

COSATU had reason to be worried, for structures such as the National Economic Forum and National Manpower Commission that were set in place to facilitate South Africa's reconstruction were 'paralysed because of the lack of political progress'.[32]

The Negotiating Council meeting on 1 June 1993 finally agreed that sufficient progress had been made to enable it to set 27 April 1994 as the date for South Africa's first ever non-racial elections.[33] Accordingly, the council instructed the Technical Committee on Constitutional Matters to draft a transitional constitution that enabled the drafting and adoption of the democratic constitution by an elected constituent assembly. This was a significant point in the history of negotiation. The editorial in the *Sunday Times* on 6 June 1994 commented:

> The act of setting a date for national elections, however hedged about with qualifications, has carried South Africa into the final stretch of its journey from racial oligarchy to mass democracy. This is the outcome so feared by whites that they ruined their country and made themselves outcasts from humanity to avoid it. The end of three-and-a-half centuries of struggle to dominate the sub-continent is in sight. It may be advanced from April 27 1994, but it cannot be delayed: any effort to do so must trigger national and international consequences of devastating proportions.

On 15 June 1993 the entire COSAG grouping staged a walkout, only to return to the next meeting of the Negotiating Council.[34] The IFP tabled a resolution calling on the council not to consider any of the constitutional principles recommended by the Technical Committee, further calling on the council to consider proposals for a federal constitution drafted by the Technical Committee and adopted by the MPNP. In support of the resolution, the IFP and the KwaZulu government threatened that should the resolution be rejected they would not have any part in any further decisions of the council. They further threatened to disrupt the rest of the proceedings or withdraw from the process altogether. However, the Negotiating Council rejected the resolution in a vote in which every party except the PAC, who abstained, took part.

Parties were given until 15 June 1993 to secure greater consensus for any opposition to the resolution supporting 27 April 1994 as the election date. The IFP and all the COSAG parties promptly walked out. The Planning Committee then reconfirmed the recommendations made by the Technical Committee, which did not expressly or by implication exclude the constituent assembly from deciding whether the form of state should be federal or unitary. This satisfied the COSAG group, and the Negotiating Council resolution was accordingly confirmed.[35] A further resolution on 22 June called for the establishment of an independent media commission and an independent electoral commission.

The commitment and seriousness of parties were to be tested once again in dramatic fashion. At the end of June, several hundred armed white right-wingers stormed the World Trade Centre and invaded the negotiating chamber. Several people were injured and a great deal of property was damaged. Following this event, on 2 July 1993, the IFP, the KwaZulu government delegation, and the Conservative Party walked out of the negotiation process, the main reason given being the date set for the elections. The support key negotiating role-players enjoyed did not deter them from seeking ways to placate the COSAG group, however, and they were sincere in their intention to ensure that each step forward received the unanimous support of all.[36]

The process of negotiation was now at a cross-roads. With the pressure for results mounting on all parties, the key role-players had to decide whether they should stall the process to coax the recalcitrant parties back. The Negotiating Council agreed to continue, and on the same day went on to adopt twenty-six of the final thirty-four constitutional principles that were to serve as the building blocks of the final constitution. The NP met with Inkatha shortly thereafter, but despite a significant degree of convergence between their constitutional perspectives, it was not enough to get the IFP to return.[37]

Regions

The Negotiating Council established the Commission on the Delimitation and/or Demarcation of Regions on 28 May 1993.[38] The commission's mandate was to make recommendations on the boundaries of regions that would be relevant to both the electoral process and the structures of the constitution.

Until July 1993 commentators focused on the debate between a federal and unitary state in a rather abstract fashion, but this changed when the Commission on Demarcation and/or Delimitation of Regions started its work. The submissions made by parties revealed a remarkable level of convergence: for one, the ANC favoured eight regions and the NP seven.[39] It was common cause among parties that these regions had to be economically viable entities and not based on ethnic differences only. No party argued for an exclusively centralized system of governance, not even the ANC. A common point of departure in several proposals was the Development Bank of South Africa's definition of 'economic' or 'developmental' regions.

In performing its tasks, the commission had to consider the constitutional principles and criteria recommended by the Negotiating Council and the oral and written representations made by the public and interest groups.[40] On 2 August 1993 it tabled its report, in which it recommended nine regions.[41]

The first draft of the interim constitution was published on 26 July 1993 after giving parties five days to study it. Both the ANC's National Working Committee and the NP cabinet held separate caucuses to discuss the draft.[42] A characteristic of this draft, and every subsequent draft, was that no party was satisfied with every aspect of it. However, it always had something that did appeal to each party.

A constitution-making body

The Technical Committee recommended the establishment of a constitution-making body made up of the joint sitting of a national assembly and a senate.[43] A national assembly would be made up of 400 representatives, with 200 elected on a national list and 200 on a regional list.[44] A senate would be made up of ten representatives from each of the regions and indirectly elected from the regional legislatures. The Technical Committee also proposed the establishment of a constitutional court, one of the important functions of which would be to ensure that the draft constitutional text conformed to the agreed constitutional principles. The constitution was to be the supreme law.

The draft also proposed the establishment of a commission on regional government, which could make recommendations to the constitution-making body on the finalization of the number and boundaries of the various regions and the powers, functions, and duties of those regional structures. In terms of the draft, the elected constitution-making body was sovereign and entitled to draft and adopt a new constitution subject only to the agreed constitutional principles. The constitution had to be adopted within two years and by a two-thirds majority, and deadlock-breaking mechanisms were considered to ensure that the adoption took place.

Regarding legislation, the draft recommended that laws be introduced in either the national assembly or the senate, and would need the support of at least the majority of the total number of the members in both houses. In addition, decisions on legislation affecting the exercise of powers or functions allocated to a particular region needed a majority of the senators of that particular region. Both the national and regional legislatures would be elected at the same time. The executive of a region would consist of ten members each. A regional legislature could, if it deemed it necessary, adopt a constitution for that region by a two-thirds majority. Such a regional constitution could not be inconsistent with the national constitution or the constitutional principles, and should meet the approval of the constitution-making body. While much of a draft constitution had been completed, there were still a number of issues that remained outstanding, which were subject to further political agreements.

Transitional measures

On 27 July 1993 the Technical Committee dealing with the Transitional Executive Council (TEC) produced its report in the form of a draft bill. The bill defined the objective of the council as the promotion of and preparation for a transition to a democratic order in South Africa, and to achieve this, there had to exist a climate for free political participation, conducive to the holding of free and fair elections. Each government, party, or organization represented in the Multi-Party Negotiation Process that committed itself to the objects of the council, undertook to implement its decisions, and renounced violence could be a participant. This commitment entitled such a party to one representative member on the council.

The council had substantial power, including access to all information and records, to achieve its objectives. Decisions in the council were by consensus, but should no consensus be possible, a majority vote of 80 per cent would be necessary. There was also provision for the establishment of subcouncils for regional and local government, law and order, defence, finance, foreign affairs, and the status of women.

Each subcouncil could have six members, and no party could have more than one representative on a particular subcouncil. Of these subcouncils, those dealing with security had even more authority. The subcouncil on law and order could establish a national inspectorate to investigate and monitor all policing agencies, and could also establish a national independent complaint mechanism under civilian control. To perform its duties, the subcouncil could obtain any information or crime intelligence reports and establish a committee of experts to monitor police action. Even the minister could only declare a state of emergency or an unrest area in consultation with the subcouncil.

The subcouncil on defence had similar powers. It could apply a code of conduct for the members of all military forces, and could also oversee the planning, preparation, and training of a future defence force. However, its key responsibility was to ensure that no military activity had any negative impact on the creation of conditions for free and fair elections. In effect, it took responsibility for a national peacekeeping force made up of the armed forces of different parties.

The multi-party talks were making real progress. The parties agreed to a date for the proposed elections, published the first draft of the interim constitution, and produced a bill for the establishment of the transitional executive authority. This was the most positive development to come out of the negotiation during 1993.

However, these developments also distressed the COSAG alliance, and Constand Viljoen urged Afrikaners to repudiate the negotiations.[45] Viljoen, nevertheless, still held out great hope for the future. The right wing objected to the agreement by government to delegate its responsibility to the transitional executive authority. According to

Tienie Groenewald, this delegation meant that the government had lost its authority to govern.[46] Groenewald therefore regarded the adoption of the Transitional Executive Council Bill as a declaration of war.[47] Ironically, the PAC, generally regarded as a left-wing extremist party, joined the right wing in their opposition to the TEC.[48]

As far as Inkatha was concerned, Mandela complained that despite several meetings held with Buthelezi, he had failed to persuade him to return to the talks. Nonetheless, Mandela was adamant that 'no spoiler is going to hamper this process'.[49] Later in September De Klerk also tried unsuccessfully to convince the Inkatha leader to rejoin.[50] The intractable position held by Inkatha and the 'war-talk' of members of the COSAG alliance led many observers to predict a civil war, but in spite of this, both the ANC and the NP government remained committed to the process. Their efforts were not in vain: at the beginning of October 1993 Inkatha's Central Committee resolved to prepare for the April elections.[51]

The Negotiating Council proceeded with its efforts despite the absence of the COSAG alliance, and it made good progress. Early in September it passed the final draft of the Transitional Executive Council (TEC) bill as well as bills for the establishment of an Independent Electoral Commission (IEC), Independent Media Commission (IMC), and the Independent Broadcasting Commission (IBC). The delegations of the Bophuthatswana and Ciskei governments maintained their seats in the Negotiating Council, though they both opposed these agreements. The four bills were tabled for debate in Parliament on 16 September and were passed into law by 23 September 1993.[52]

The Transitional Executive Council was set to function in tandem with the NP cabinet, and in certain areas of government enjoyed an effective veto. From this point onwards, the NP lost its sole authority as the governing party.

During September the Negotiating Council came closer to defining the powers, functions, and decision-making processes of an interim cabinet and the president.[53] It agreed that the president would be the executive head of state and would be directly elected by parliament. The outstanding issue was the appointment of the deputy-president or prime minister and ministers, where the ability of minority parties in the cabinet to assert dissenting views was at stake.

Right-wing reaction

At the beginning of October the COSAG alliance was set to fragment. _Oct.' 93_ When the alliance met at its first anniversary and took stock of its situation, several parties complained about Inkatha, arguing that Inkatha tried to manipulate the group as a battering ram against the ANC and the government. The fact that a number of the partners were engaging in some form of talks with the ANC or the NP also made Buthelezi want to scupper the group and form another type of alliance, since his view of COSAG was that 'maybe it has outlived its usefulness'.[54] On 7 October the Ciskei and Bophuthatswana delegations gave in to pressure from Inkatha and walked out of the Negotiating Council as Inkatha made a similar announcement.

The Freedom Alliance was born out of the ashes of COSAG, and consisted of Inkatha, Bophuthatswana, Ciskei, the CP, and the Afrikaner Volksfront.[55] The Freedom Alliance, like COSAG, united around Inkatha's complaint that the most important decisions were really taken by the ANC and the NP. In short, Inkatha did not feel that it enjoyed respect as the third large role-player.

The Freedom Alliance claimed to represent two homeland governments: all Zulu-speaking people, and the Afrikaner community, which made it the second strongest political force in the country. It believed that it would be able to wrest greater concessions from the ANC than from the NP.[56] The Freedom Alliance was flawed, however, because it was a political Frankenstein, made up of parts that simply did not fit and were potentially at odds with one another. Except for the IFP, the other Freedom Alliance partners did not favour a federal dispensation, but rather aspired towards confederalism. When the Negotiating Council learnt of the Freedom Alliance, it suspended discussion on key constitutional matters until the Alliance had made its agenda known.[57]

The Freedom Alliance made an impact on the thinking of the NP, because after a meeting with the leaders of the Alliance, De Klerk proposed that a referendum be held to break the impasse.[58] The NP floated this idea unsuccessfully for several weeks. At its Federal Congress on 13 October, the NP's key focus was to find ways and means to ensure that a majority government would not enjoy unfettered rule, particularly after the five-year government of national unity.[59] According to Roelf Meyer, there were several critical outstanding issues, namely the functioning of the government of national unity, deadlock-breaking mechanisms in the constitution-making body, greater regional powers, and the constitutional court.[60]

Regarding the government of national unity, there were essentially three areas of dispute: the majority required to arrive at decisions, what the powers of the deputy-president would be, and who would represent the largest minority party in cabinet. The priority for the ANC was to allow the government to rule effectively, while the NP insisted on some form of loaded majority and significant powers for the deputy-president.

The distribution of powers between the national and regional governments was another difficult debate. While the ANC was not averse to regions being given substantial powers, it argued that these should not become an impediment to national reconstruction. The NP and the DP argued for greater powers for the regions with the national government dealing with only those exclusively national powers such as defence, foreign policy, and finance. Furthermore, the ANC wanted the constitution-making body to finally determine the regional boundaries, an idea which the other parties opposed. Fortunately, however, on the question of deadlock-breaking mechanisms there appeared to be little difference between the parties.

On 25 October 1993 the ANC met the leaders of the Freedom Alliance in a bid to secure their support for the interim constitution that was now nearing completion. The talks broke down on the critical question of the final constitution being drafted by an elected body, since the Freedom Alliance insisted that the final constitution be negotiated before elections. In addition, the Alliance wanted a negotiation of the final constitution between three blocs – the ANC, the NP, and itself, in an attempt to subvert the process unfolding at the World

Oct.
1993

Trade Centre. In this regard, it proposed a summit between the leadership of these three formations, but the ANC refused, and the discussions with the Freedom Alliance failed.

The fundamental question facing the ANC and the NP was whether they were prepared to finalize the interim constitution without the participation of an important political bloc. According to Ramaphosa, 'the process should be all inclusive but no party, including government and the ANC, should be in a position to block the process or hold it to ransom. There is a lot at stake and the respective parties must take that into account'.[61]

The stance adopted by the Freedom Alliance clearly bothered the ANC and the NP, and on 26 October Mandela met De Klerk in an attempt to find ways of securing the participation of the alliance. Both leaders publicly confirmed that the course of the constitutional dispensation, and in particular the two-stage transition, was unchangeable. However, De Klerk still sought Mandela's approval, albeit in vain, for a dispensation giving regions greater autonomy as he hoped that this would entice the Freedom Alliance back to the negotiating table.

At the same time, the Freedom Alliance gathered in Ulundi, the capital of KwaZulu and the site of Inkatha's power, to discuss its strategy. It called on 'opinion-makers and men and women of stature in South Africa to support our call for urgent talks between national leaders'.[62] It also called for the recognition of the political realignment that had taken place in the country since the formation of the Alliance, arguing that this realignment had resulted in the emergence of three dominant power blocs. It was the hope of the Alliance that such a summit between the leaders of the three blocs would pre-empt the scheduled multi-party plenary that was to ratify the agreements.

Finalizing the interim constitution

Between 25 and 28 October 1993 the ANC and the NP met to finalize the interim constitution. The purpose of the meeting was to flesh out their bottom-line demands prior to the resolution of the interim constitution. This bilateral then produced a number of agreements that were jointly tabled with the Technical Committee on Constitutional Issues.

The first major agreement related to the government of national unity. The bilateral proposal offered every party with more than 20 per cent of the electoral support the right to choose a deputy-president, which meant that there would be two deputy-presidents.[63] The agreement also obliged the president to consult with the deputy-presidents on matters of government policy and cabinet business.

There was further agreement that the cabinet would consist of no more than twenty-seven members, and that each party enjoying more than 5 per cent of total support would be entitled to a proportionate number of seats. The agreement recorded that 'the Cabinet would take decisions by consensus but where this is not possible, it will decide by an increased majority to be determined. In this regard there may be a differentiation between financial and state security matters and other matters'.[64]

The ANC finally won its argument, and the ruling party would be given sufficient authority to govern effectively. Conversely, the NP abandoned its arguments in favour of a veto over cabinet decisions. So, at best, the NP won no more than the right to be consulted, though decisions would have to be taken with a higher majority.

The compromise lay in the powers of provinces, where the ANC shifted its position to accommodate the federalist demands of both the NP and Inkatha. Regions had increased powers that guaranteed them a fixed percentage of revenues collected nationally, and in addition were able to levy taxes in terms of national legislation. Provinces were also given wide concurrent legislative powers, and local government was strengthened as well. Local governments obtained autonomy with 'adequate powers to make by-laws not inconsistent with law at national or provincial levels'. In this regard, the purpose of the agreement contained in the Local Government Transition Act was to regulate the restructuring of local government. This was a particularly sensitive agreement, since it affected all white local government structures.

While the proposals did not address all the outstanding issues, the agreements went a long way to accommodate the views of Inkatha. The NP was delighted with the deal struck with the ANC, and De Klerk defended the agreements insisting that nothing should be allowed to interfere with them. He was confident that South Africa would be a federal republic, and Mandela, for his part, responded by challenging proponents of federalism to 'tell us what more powers you want'. Nevertheless, De Klerk was still fearful that further violence could erupt if parties proceeded without the Freedom Alliance, though he realized that 'it [right-wing opposition] will be a picnic compared to the violence that will erupt if elections on April 27 are postponed'.[65]

Both Inkatha and the Freedom Alliance remained unimpressed, and steadfastly refused to discuss the proposals until the negotiation process was reorganized on their terms at a summit of select leaders. Despite this hard line, Rowan Cronjé, chairperson of the Freedom Alliance, admitted of the agreement: 'It's better than what we had, but our approach is different. It moves forward, but not far enough'.[66] In a final attempt to accommodate the Freedom Alliance, the plenary was postponed to 12 November, and the NP scheduled a three-day meeting with the Alliance starting on 2 November. At the same time the NP also arranged to talk to the PAC in a bid to secure its agreement. However, the meeting with the Freedom Alliance was not successful.

The NP cabinet met on 6 November 1993 to review its progress. It resolved to adopt the interim constitution despite the absence of the Freedom Alliance.[67] At this time, Joe Slovo found it necessary to address an open letter to General Constand Viljoen, one of the more reasonable leaders in the Freedom Alliance. In his letter, published in *Business Day,* Slovo argued that the Afrikaners remained an integral part of South Africa. In an impassioned plea, Slovo said:

> Looking at the history of negotiation from CODESA I onwards, the ANC has travelled an enormous distance in the quest for a settlement. In contrast, your camp has hardly moved an inch. We are at the point, General, where there can be no turning back.
> Coming from me, your ears may be jarred when I say that the

dispensation that we are moving towards is in the deepest interest of your people as well as every other community. The biggest threat to genuine Afrikaner aspirations comes not from us, but from those who hanker after a past that can be no more. You can make it possible for all of us to share a new history.[68]

The 'six-pack' agreement

Meanwhile, work to resolve several outstanding issues at the World Trade Centre continued at a feverish pace. These were settled at bilateral level between the ANC and the NP. It was necessary to settle agreements by the middle of November so that they could be passed into law before the year-end by a special session of Parliament. Any delay would place the establishment of the TEC, the Independent Electoral Commission (IEC), and the preparations necessary for the elections by 27 April 1994 in jeopardy. The rush meant little rest: while parties were negotiating outstanding issues, technical experts were drafting proposals and the administration preparing for the plenary. The atmosphere at the World Trade Centre was electric. The negotiators were weary but restless. Experts were nervous and drafters frantic, and keeping it all moving, exhausted, anxious staff worked incessantly behind the scenes.

On 7 November there was a further breakthrough, and the NP heaved a sigh of relief. It had persistently campaigned for security of tenure to be given to the public and security services, and the ANC finally relented.[69] This agreement did not rule out affirmative action or the restructuring of the public service, however. On 10 November there was another dramatic development. The emotive question of language had long meant the NP and Afrikaners in general feared the overshadowing of Afrikaans as one of two major languages. The compromise found was to cater for eleven official languages without diminishing the status of Afrikaans.

There were now only four major issues outstanding: a deadlock-breaking mechanism, the decision-making majority in cabinet, the appointment of judges, and the final aspects of local government. Late on the night of Tuesday 16 November, Mandela met with De Klerk to resolve these issues in what was probably the most important bilateral of the negotiations.[70] During this crucial meeting Mandela persuaded De Klerk to shift from insistence on a minority veto and an enforced coalition to voluntary co-rule. More importantly, the outcome showed that De Klerk had come to accept that he would have to rely on the ANC's commitment to national unity.

In the four-hour meeting the two leaders, assisted by their chief negotiators Ramaphosa and Meyer, agreed in principle on all the outstanding issues in a compromise agreement that came to be known as the 'six-pack' deal. In terms of the deal, the NP agreed to decisions being taken by a simple majority in the cabinet. The formulation specified that 'Cabinet shall function in a manner which gives consideration to the consensus-seeking spirit underlying the concept of a government of national unity as well as the need for effective government'. The ANC in return compromised on the deadlock-breaking mechanisms for the adoption of the final constitution, agreeing that if a referendum failed, the new constitutional assembly would only be able to adopt the final constitution by a 60 per cent majority.

The ANC also agreed that the amendment of the boundaries, powers, and functions of provinces would require an additional majority of two-thirds of the senate. The ANC conceded that provinces be allowed to adopt their own constitutions provided that these were consistent with the final constitution and the constitutional principles agreed to. The Freedom Alliance, and Inkatha in particular, had fought hard for these assurances, and it was hoped that by making these concessions it would be easier for the Freedom Alliance to return to the process.

A major row erupted around the appointment of the constitutional court judges when the DP complained that the proposal agreed to between the ANC and the NP would politicize the constitutional court. The DP insisted that the appointment of judges involve the judiciary and legal profession by offering them greater latitude in the appointment procedures. The opposing arguments suggested that neither the judiciary nor the legal profession were representative of the country's population, since their members were overwhelmingly male and white.

In a concession to the DP, the ANC agreed that six constitutional court judges be appointed from among ten nominated by the Judicial Services Commission; the Chief Justice would then appoint another four. The president of the country would appoint the president of the constitutional court in consultation with the cabinet. The DP approved of this arrangement.[72]

Regarding local government, the ANC made a further concession by agreeing to guarantee the white minority a substantial share of power.[73] In terms of the agreement, local government elections were to be held within two years and guaranteed whites at least a 30 per cent share of the seats on each council. The deal was aimed at rural towns in which the majority of residents were black. As for the relative wealth of white local authorities as opposed to impoverished black areas, the compromise gave whites an effective veto by requiring a two-thirds majority for decisions on budgets.

In concluding this last bilateral, the two leaders agreed to go ahead without the Freedom Alliance's participation. The door was left open, however, for the Alliance to return at a later stage.

An agreed text

The final agreement on the text of the interim constitution was to come in the early hours of the morning of 18 November 1993. The leaders of all the participating political parties signed the agreement bringing into effect the single most dramatic political and constitutional change ever experienced in South Africa. The agreement reached was more than a legal contract: it set the basis for a new constitutional order. It was in effect a peace treaty that sought to relegate conflict and civil strife, which had become a way of life for South Africans, to the status of a shameful blemish on South Africa's history, and marked the beginning of the democratic era.

In a fitting tribute to the importance of the event, and as witness to the exemplary leadership displayed by both De Klerk and Mandela, each made an impassioned plea for national unity and tolerance. Political leaders also immediately seized the initiative to convince investors of the value of the new constitutional dispensation. The message was clear: the country had a constitution that it could 'bank' on.[74] The international community responded well, and US President Bill Clinton, in his State of the Union Address, pledged support to South Africa during its transition.[75] Offers of financial assistance and aid poured in.[76] The business community and organized workers declared 1 January 'peace day' and planned to celebrate it by distributing nearly R10 million worth of T-shirts emblazoned with the logo of the national peace effort.[77] p. 330

The opinion column in the *Sunday Times* on 21 November 1993 captured the moment, saying:

We, the people of South Africa, have wrought a miracle. We have accomplished what few people anywhere in the world thought we could do: we have freed ourselves, and made a democracy, and we have done so without war or revolution.

The interim constitution is not perfect. No constitution is perfect, and our constitution needs still to be infused with the spirit of democracy. We need to learn again the habits of free men and women, which we have lost. We have work to do, and wounds to heal, and problems to solve; our greatest labours lie ahead of us, not behind.

The document passed by the plenary was not a complete text, however. The plenary accordingly instructed the Negotiating Council to complete the outstanding technical issues and refer the document to Parliament for its formal passage into law. The constitution was to come into force on 27 April 1994. Ten minutes after the plenary adopted the text it also passed the electoral law in the form of a bill. Support for the constitution and the bill was not unanimous, though, for the PAC lodged its official reservations about the power-sharing component of the government of national unity, while the AVU objected to the text on the basis that it did not make provision for a system of self-determination.

17 November 1993 was also Cyril Ramaphosa's fortieth birthday, so the agreement on the text was especially momentous for him, and the occasion added excitement to the celebrations that started immediately after the agreements had been concluded in the plenary. Meyer and Ramaphosa, both pioneers, master negotiators, and leaders, who had carefully guided the process through some of its most traumatic times, came to dance away the remaining hours of that morning content in the knowledge that their job had been well done.

Addressing right-wing concerns

While the country rejoiced at the adoption of the interim constitution, not everybody felt satisfied. Speculation was rife that many senior NP members were displeased. But when the NP caucus met on 22 November, De Klerk threw down the gauntlet and demanded the party's endorsement of the compromises effected. No serious objections were raised.[78] There was also intense speculation that many senior Inkatha leaders were equally unhappy about the party's non-participation. Buthelezi saw this as a criticism of his leadership, and threatened to resign as leader if Inkatha's special conference decided to contest the April elections.[79]

While the constitution represented a peace treaty to most South Africans, the white right wing saw it as a declaration of war. General Constand Viljoen called on all supporters of the Afrikaner Volksfront to undergo military training and prepare to defend themselves.[80] Likewise, the black right wing, represented by Inkatha, pledged to meet the new constitution with 'determined resistance'. Despite this war of words, both the ANC and the NP persisted in their efforts, especially with two important components of the Freedom Alliance, the AVF and Inkatha.[81] On 19 November the ANC met the AVF in a meeting that established a joint working committee to explore areas of possible convergence. It was an effort that would pay off well.[82]

The ANC's negotiations with the Freedom Alliance were conditional upon the Alliance first committing itself to the interim constitution, the TEC, and the outcome of the April elections.[83] The response of the Alliance was to raise preconditions of its own, namely non-interference in the TBVC states and self-governing territories, a two-ballot voting system that would separately take into account the votes cast in the TBVC states, and constitutional leeway for Afrikaner self-determination.[84] By 20 December it became evident that the attempt to bring the Freedom Alliance on board was bound to fail.

The debates in Parliament were already at an advanced stage and there was little opportunity for any amendment.[85] However, all was not lost, and on 20 December the ANC announced that it was to enter into a strategic agreement with the Afrikaner Volksfront.[86] There were just two immediate obstacles to signing this agreement: on the one hand, the NP government was not willing to compromise, while on the other hand, the AVF did not want to give the impression of a rift in the Freedom Alliance.[87]

On 22 December the debate on the interim constitution in the last white Parliament completed its course. The Department of Constitutional Affairs and Planning initiated a campaign to promote the new constitution that would cost approximately R19.2 million. This campaign included advertisements in a variety of media and the distribution of booklets on the constitution.[88] And as further confirmation of South Africa's burgeoning democracy, the Independent Electoral Commission (IEC) and Independent Media Commission (IMC) were established in January 1994.

On 10 January 1994 Brigadier Oupa Gqozo confirmed that the Ciskei would join the Transitional Executive Council, a step that flew in the face of the position adopted by the Freedom Alliance.[89] There was also a significant amount of anger brewing among conservative Afrikaners, and Constand Viljoen was booed by right-wingers at a rally of 20 000 Afrikaners when he called for a non-violent way to achieve a volkstaat.[90] There was an evident rise in tension accompanied by an increase in politically motivated violence, and fears of ethnically based strife and confrontation were expressed by many.[91] The deadline for parties to register for the elections had been set as 10 February 1994, but since no agreement with the Freedom Alliance materialized, the date for the registration of parties was extended.[92] At the same time, however, Inkatha opposed the April elections, and Buthelezi warned his political opponents that an Inkatha boycott of the elections would lead to further bloodshed. He also called for the establishment of self-defence units, saying, 'It is impossible for me to lie to you and reassure you that the IFP opposition to fighting the elections under the present constitution will not bring casualties and even death. . . . If we do not defend our people, no one else will. We must defend our communities with all our might. We must defend and fight back. We must resist the African National Congress and their communist surrogates'.[93]

The ANC called an emergency meeting of its national executive to discuss the rising tensions. A concerned Nelson Mandela argued that 'we must treat the threat of civil war seriously'.[94] In an attempt to seize the high ground, the ANC unveiled a package of concessions aimed at securing the Freedom Alliance's role in the election without demanding its commitment to taking part.[95] De Klerk supported the proposal, and his party argued that 'What is clear now is that we must go to Parliament whether we have an inclusive deal or not. We must be seen to have made a real effort to accommodate the Freedom Alliance'.[96]

The ANC's package of concessions included a constitutional principle on self-determination; mechanisms considering the feasibility of a volkstaat; acceptance of the demand for two ballot papers (national and provincial); a provision enabling provinces to draft their own constitutions and raise taxes; a principle ensuring that the final constitution did not 'substantially diminish' provincial powers; and the granting to provincial legislatures the authority to decide the names of their provinces, with Natal renamed KwaZulu/Natal.[97] The proposals failed to impress the IFP, however, despite the fact, according to Colin Eglin, that they were 'very close to the amendments that Inkatha itself put on the order paper when parliament was debating the Interim Constitution Bill'.[98]

Preparing for the elections

On 21 January 1994 the ANC announced its electoral list, which was voted in by the organization's branches and provincial structures.[99] The threat to boycott the April elections by the Freedom Alliance, and more particularly by Inkatha, was viewed with much concern by the international community. An urgent fax was sent to Buthelezi by the 140 delegates of the joint assembly of the European Parliament and the African/Caribbean/Pacific countries, urging him to take part in the elections.

The ANC and the NP were also concerned. On 21 February the Negotiating Council reconvened, and the ANC and the NP proposed constitutional amendments to draw the Freedom Alliance back into the process.[100] All mention of concurrent powers was removed and provinces were granted powers which would prevail over those of national government in all areas within their competency. This effectively gave provinces exclusive powers over areas within their competency, the power of national government to override provinces was limited. The Electoral Act was also amended to extend the date for the registration of political parties from 4 to 9 March.

The return of the right wing

Inkatha remained opposed to the changes, but the ANC did not lose hope. On 1 March 1994 Mandela met Buthelezi to persuade him to change his stance. The ANC accepted the idea of <u>international mediation</u> and Inkatha agreed to register the party provisionally. This quid pro quo represented the beginning of the end of the formal alliance of right-wing political formations. The two parties immediately set about discussions on how such mediation could take place.[101] There was agreement on a set of mediators and their terms of reference. Among these mediators were the former British Foreign Secretary, Lord Carrington, former US Secretary of State, Henry Kissinger, the chairperson of the Venice Commission on federalism, Prof.

Antonio La Pergola, Goldstone Commission assessor, Judge Praful-lanchandra Bhagwati of India, constitutional experts from Germany and Canada, and a black American judge. However, while the mediators assembled in South Africa by 10 April, disagreement on the terms of reference wrecked the initiative before it started. The ANC and the NP insisted that the election date was not negotiable, but Inkatha refused to accept this. Shortly afterwards, agreement was also reached between the ANC and the Freedom Front (FF), a newly-constituted party under the leadership of General Constand Viljoen, on the process in terms of which a volkstaat could be established.[102]

The collapse of the homelands

Meanwhile, civil unrest was spreading throughout the homeland of Bophuthatswana, started by civil servants who were uncertain about the future of their pensions. The homeland's security forces were sympathetic to their cause, and the future of the Mangope government was placed in jeopardy. The white right wing rallied in support of Mangope. In a short while, pictures of the execution of three white militants shocked the world.[103] The TEC concluded that Mangope was no longer in de facto control of the territory and was unable to govern, and accordingly reincorporated the homeland into South Africa. Similar unrest arose in the homeland of Ciskei and it too was reincorporated.

On the basis of a tripartite agreement reached between the ANC, the NP, and the IFP only a few breathtaking days away from 27 April, the IFP agreed to participate in the elections.[104] The Freedom Front also agreed to participate.[105] In the end, all major political stakeholders and parties participated in the elections held on 27 to 29 April 1994. The elections were an overwhelming success, and the prophets of doom were confounded. The elections were completely peaceful. The overwhelming majority of voters came out in their droves to cast their votes, and despite enormous logistical problems and ordinary election squabbles, the IEC was able to find the election substantially free and fair.

10

A framework for negotiating the final constitution

THE GENERAL ELECTION ON 27 APRIL 1994 was the product of negotiated agreements to bring an end to conflict and usher in a new process of negotiation towards the final constitution. When the people of South Africa voted in this election, they voted to provide their newly elected leaders with two separate and distinct mandates: one, to govern a new democratic society, and two, to draft the final constitution.[1] The election produced 490 political leaders at national level: 400 in the National Assembly and 90 in the senate. In terms of section 68 (1) of the interim constitution, a joint sitting of these bodies made up the Constitutional Assembly.[2]

In drafting the final constitution, the Constitutional Assembly had to work within constitutional and political parameters. This presented a real challenge. A clear understanding of these parameters is fundamental to understanding the final Constitution, as they shaped the process as well as determined its content. In the main, the objective of the Constitutional Assembly was to produce a constitution that would be both legitimate and enduring.[3] The legitimacy of the constitution depended on the extent to which the exercise of drafting itself was credible. It was also important that the final text be accepted by all, and in order to be fully legitimate, that it be accessible to all.[4]

Several important constitutional requirements had to be considered: the requirement of a two-thirds majority for the adoption of the text, the text's compliance with the thirty-four constitutional principles, and complete adoption within two years.[5]

Constitutional requirements

Strict time-frames were imposed to provide the assurance that the final constitution would be drafted within a reasonable period of time. To deter parties from unreasonably withholding their support for the new constitutional text, there were elaborate deadlock-breaking measures. The use of constitutional principles was a relatively novel approach, since Namibia provided the only precedent where a set of constitutional principles determined the parameters of a drafted constitution. (On 21 November 1989 Namibia's Constituent Assembly had formally adopted UN resolution 435, which incorporated a set of constitutional principles laid down in 1982 by the Western Contact Group.[6]) In South Africa, however, the Constitutional Court was to test the new constitution against the constitutional principles, unlike Namibia where the principles were merely guidelines.

The interim constitution, therefore, defined itself quite correctly in its closing section as 'a historic bridge between the past of a deeply divided society characterised by strife, conflict, untold suffering and injustice, and a future founded on the recognition of human rights, democracy, and peaceful co-existence and development opportunities for all South Africans, irrespective of colour, race, class, belief or sex'.

The interim constitution was a historic bridge in two senses. It was a bridge between the past and the present, and also between the present and the future: a future governed in terms of the new constitution.[7] The most important elements in the building of that bridge were the constitutional principles.

Schedule 4 of the interim constitution cited the thirty-four constitutional principles.[8] These had arisen from the negotiating process as a compromise between two extremes: the view that CODESA was not a properly mandated forum, and the fear that only the dominant party would draft a constitution of its choice.[9] The principles found a middle road: they were sufficiently precise to guarantee that the constitution-making body did not stray from certain fundamental notions, but not so detailed as to pre-empt the work of that body.[10]

The constitutional principles and their interpretation affected not only the debates in the Constitutional Assembly but also its structure. The six Theme Committees established to facilitate the work of the Constitutional Assembly had terms of reference based on a division of the thirty-four principles. Section 73 (1) of the interim constitution required the Constitutional Assembly to complete its assignment within two years of the first sitting of the National Assembly. At the onset of work in the Constitutional Assembly, some raised concerns that there might not be sufficient time to complete the task. Any extension of the time would have required an amendment to the interim constitution, so the agreement reached was that the assembly should complete its work within the time allocated.[11]

At the start, parties settled a work programme, that envisaged three broad phases.[12] The first phase saw a public participation programme through which the collated views of all role-players were translated into a draft text. The second phase included the publication of the first draft text and a further invitation for public comment. During the third phase the Constitutional Assembly finally negotiated and adopted the constitution.

The process: principles

Fundamental to the process was the principle of inclusivity. The new constitution, it was agreed, had to be the product of an integration of ideas of all major role-players.[13] The Constitutional Assembly defined three categories of role-players. The first category consisted of those political parties represented in the Constitutional Assembly.[14] The second category included political parties outside the Constitutional Assembly together with organized civil society. The third category consisted of individual citizens.

The second principle was accessibility. The Constitutional Assembly invested a great deal of its energy and resources in ensuring that the process was as accessible as possible. This principle suggested that it was not good enough merely to invite submissions, but it was necessary to reach out to and solicit these views deliberately. To this end, an elaborate media campaign was devised to reach as many South Africans as possible.

The third principle was transparency. All meetings of the Constitutional Assembly and its structures were open to the public.[15] Such was the nature of the transparency that one journalist described it as being virtually invisible: there were no scoops, since every journalist had equal access to information. The Constitutional Assembly also established a project to ensure that all its materials, from minutes, reports, and all submissions, were accessible through the internet. This was the first example of such an exercise in the world: never before had a project of this nature been undertaken in full view of the international community.

Political structures

The interim constitution obliged the elected representatives to establish two particular structures for the purposes of drafting and adopting a new constitution, namely the Constitutional Assembly and the Independent Panel of Constitutional Experts.[16] In terms of section 68 of the interim constitution, the Constitutional Assembly consisted of both houses of Parliament – the National Assembly and the Senate – totalling 490 members.

The 490 members of the Constitutional Assembly represented seven political parties proportionally in accordance with the results of the 1994 elections.

The Constitutional Committee was the main negotiating and co-ordinating structure reporting directly to the Constitutional Assembly.[17] It consisted of forty-four members, appointed by parties on a proportional basis.[18] The Constitutional Committee met at first on a weekly basis to receive reports from Theme Committees, but met less frequently after the establishment of the subcommittee. It continued to function, however, as *the* decision-making structure.

Party	No. of members	Leader
African National Congress (ANC)	312	Nelson Mandela
National Party (NP)	99	F. W. de Klerk
Inkatha Freedom Party (IFP)	48	Mangosuthu Buthelezi
Freedom Front (FF)	14	Constand Viljoen
Democratic Party (DP)	10	Tony Leon
Pan Africanist Congress (PAC)	5	Clarence Makwetu
African Christian Democratic Party (ACDP)	2	Kenneth Meshoe

A smaller subcommittee of the Constitutional Committee was established in June 1995 to facilitate negotiations.[19] This subcommittee proved to be extremely effective, and was possibly one of the most important structures because of its size and ability to meet frequently. The subcommittee was not a decision-making structure and reported directly to the Constitutional Committee, which improved the efficiency of the Constitutional Committee. The subcommittee at any one time consisted of about twenty members, and was able to meet more regularly and easily than the Constitutional Committee. It could also meet at the same time as the National Assembly without affecting the quorum of Assembly meetings. A unique feature of the subcommittee was that its membership was dependent on the issue at hand, with the result that the Constitutional Committee could meet less frequently and attend to the reports produced by the subcommittee.

The twelve-member Management Committee met once a week throughout the process.[20] The Management Committee was charged with the day-to-day management of the negotiations and dealt with matters of process rather than substance. One of its responsibilities was to ensure that the Constitutional Assembly worked according to an agreed schedule. Timekeeping, while not as glamorous as the issues of political debate, was an essential ingredient in the Constitutional Assembly's recipe for success. Confronted with the hard reality of a two-year deadline, it was clear that unless structures worked according to plan, the constitution would not be completed by 8 May 1996. It was to the credit of the Management Committee and all players in the process that the Constitutional Assembly met all of its target dates.

To deal effectively with the wide variety of issues in the new constitution, and to ensure the involvement of as many members of the assembly as possible, Theme Committees were established to work on different parts of the constitution. Each Theme Committee consisted of thirty members nominated by political parties in proportion to their representation. However, due to the difference in numbers between the largest and smallest parties, a bias in favour of the smaller parties was agreed. Three chairpersons were elected for each committee by its members to ensure that no single party chaired meetings of the committee. Together with a core group of seven to eight members, the chairpersons were responsible for managing and co-ordinating the work of the Theme Committee.[21] This included developing the agendas of meetings and deciding when meetings were to take place.

The main function of the Theme Committees was to ensure the inclusive nature of the constitution-making process by receiving views and submissions from each of the role-players. In keeping with the policy of the Constitutional Assembly to ensure maximum public participation, members of the public and civil society were invited to send in their submissions. In this regard, it is also important to note that many of these submissions came from ordinary citizens in all official languages. The submissions were translated and processed as reports, which effectively recorded the convergence of ideas and agreements, points of contention, and possible approaches in dealing with the areas of contention. The reports were then debated in the Constitutional Committee. Theme Committees were therefore the Constitutional Assembly's initial interface with the public.

A Technical Committee consisting of specialists and experts in particular fields supported each Theme Committee, and some Theme Committees were assigned additional technical advisers to deal with specialized matters.[22] Theme Committees started work in September 1994 and had a target date of 30 June 1995 for the completion of their assignments.

By 13 February 1995, a mere six weeks after the annual December recess, the first reports were ready. Theme Committees completed most of their work by the end of June as planned, and tabled their final reports, accompanied by draft constitutional texts, in September 1995. Theme Committee 1 dealt with the character of the democratic state.[23] It was mandated to discuss:

- the preamble to the constitution; and matters dealing with the establishment of a single sovereign state, common citizenship, democracy, and equality (Constitutional Principle I);
- the supremacy of the constitution, binding on all organs of state (Constitutional Principle IV);
- matters dealing with representative government, regular elections, suffrage, and proportional representation (Constitutional Principle VIII);
- matters dealing with freedom of information and accountable administration (Constitutional Principle IX);
- the name and description of the state and symbols;
- citizenship and franchise; and
- matters dealing with the separation of powers (Constitutional Principle VI).[24]

Theme Committee 2 dealt with the structure of government.[25] It was mandated to discuss:

- matters dealing with the separation of powers (Constitutional Principle VI);
- adherence to formal legislative procedures by legislative organs (Constitutional Principle X);

- participation of minority parties in the legislative process in a manner consistent with democracy (Constitutional Principle XIV);
- amendments to the constitution requiring special procedures involving special majorities (Constitutional Principle XV);
- structure of government at national, provincial, and local levels (Constitutional Principle XVI);
- democratic representation at every level of government, without derogating from the role of chieftainship (Constitutional Principle XVII);
- the National Assembly, Senate, and Parliament in general;
- the electoral system;
- matters dealing with the constitutional status and role of traditional leadership (Constitutional Principles XIII);
- traditional leaders; and
- the executive.[26]

Theme Committee 3 dealt with the relationship between levels of government.[27] It was mandated to discuss with regard to Constitutional Principles XVI, XVII, and XXIV:

- the nature and status of the provincial system and local government;
- national and provincial executive and legislative competencies;
- intergovernmental relations;
- local government; and
- financial and fiscal relations.[28]

Theme Committee 4 dealt with fundamental rights.[29] The mandate and work of the Committee was guided by Constitutional Principle II, which states: 'Everyone shall enjoy all universally accepted fundamental rights, freedoms and civil liberties, which shall be provided for and protected by entrenched and justiciable provisions in the Constitution, which shall be drafted after having given due consideration to *inter alia* the fundamental rights contained in Chapter Three of the Constitution'.[30]

A workshop on human rights and international law was held in April 1995, organized jointly by the Constitutional Assembly, Parliament, and the Raoul Wallenberg Institute from Sweden. Members also attended workshops on gender, pornography, abortion, and freedom of expression organized by various organizations such as the University of the Western Cape Community Law Centre, the Institute for Multi-party Democracy, and the Freedom of Expression Institute.

Members of Theme Committee 4 also attended a number of national sector public hearings. These involved children's rights, labour, women, religion, traditional authorities, youth, business, land, and socio-economic rights.

Theme Committee 5 dealt with the judiciary and legal systems.[31] With regard to Constitutional Principles VII and XIII, the Committee considered:

- the structure of the court system;
- the relationship between the different levels of courts;
- the composition and appointment of judicial officers;
- access to courts including lay participation;
- traditional courts and customary law;
- legal education and the legal profession;
- transitional arrangements;
- correctional services;
- international law and interpretation; and
- Attorneys-General.[32]

Theme Committee 6 dealt with specialized structures of government.[33] Given the expanse of its work, the Theme Committee decided to establish four Sub-Theme Committees for the sake of convenience and expediency:

- Sub-Theme Committee 6.1 dealt with public administration (Constitutional Principles XXIX, XXX);
- Sub-Theme Committee 6.2 dealt with financial institutions and public enterprises (Constitutional Principle XXIX);
- Sub-Theme Committee 6.3 dealt with transformation and monitoring (Constitutional Principle XXIX); and

- Sub-Theme Committee 6.4 dealt with the security services (Constitutional Principle XXXI).

The Theme Committee also resolved for the sake of the smaller parties to allow each party to nominate additional members to serve in the Sub-Theme Committees. The Theme Committee itself held eight meetings.

Sub-Theme Committee 6.1 dealt with public administration and the Electoral Commission.[34] Sub-Theme Committee 6.2 dealt with the Auditor-General, the Reserve Bank, the Financial and Fiscal Commission, and general financial matters.[35] Sub-Theme Committee 6.3 dealt with the Public Protector, Human Rights Commission, Commission for Gender Equality, and land rights.[36] Sub-Theme Committee 6.4 dealt with the security services and worked in the following areas: police, defence, intelligence, and correctional services.[37]

Other structures

The Constitutional Assembly established an Independent Panel of Constitutional Experts in terms of section 72 of the interim constitution.[38] Its primary role was conflict resolution, and it aimed to avoid deadlocks or potential deadlocks between parties. The interim constitution was amended to allow the Constitutional Assembly to refer to the panel on or after 8 May 1996 if the need arose.

The other function of the panel was to advise the Constitutional Assembly through the chairperson on any matter to do with the functions of the Constitutional Assembly. In November 1996 the panel undertook a trip to Europe to attend workshops in Britain and Germany to exchange ideas with international experts on technical issues in the new constitution.[39]

A Commission on Provincial Government was also established, in accordance with section 163 of the interim constitution. Its main task was to bring about the establishment of provincial government in terms of the new arrangements outlined in the constitution. This commission also had the important function of advising the Constitutional Assembly on provisions in the new constitution on boundaries, structures, powers, functions, and transitional measures for the provinces. Members of the commission regularly attended meetings of Constitutional Assembly structures. The final report and recommendations from the commission were received in February 1996 in response to the working draft of the new constitution published in November 1995.

The Volkstaat Council was set up in terms of chapter 11A of the interim constitution to enable proponents of the idea of a volkstaat to pursue the establishment of a volkstaat constitutionally. The council had the task of gathering information and reporting to the Constitutional Assembly and the Commission on Provincial Government. Its final report was tabled in January 1996.[40]

1

Joe Slovo (left) and Mac Maharaj (right) working on the interim constitution during a bilateral between the African National Congress and the National Party, 17–18 November 1993. Both Slovo and Maharaj would go on to become Ministers of Parliament after South Africa's first democratic elections in April 1994.

2

Joe Slovo of the South African Communist Party takes a break during an important meeting to prepare for the Multi-Party Negotiations Process (MPNP). This preparatory meeting took place in the offices of the Department of Constitutional Development, 120 Plein Street, Cape Town.

3 (ABOVE)
Cyril Ramaphosa, Brigitte
Mabandla, and Thabo Mbeki, senior
negotiators for the African National
Congress, caucus during a break at
the bilateral between the African
National Congress and the National
Party, 17–18 November 1993.

4 (MIDDLE RIGHT), **5** (RIGHT)
Chairperson of the Constitutional
Assembly Cyril Ramaphosa and deputy
chairperson Leon Wessels meet in
mind (4) and in spirit (5).

6 (TOP)
William Hofmeyr of the African National Congress and Noël Taft, the managing secretary of Theme Committee 5 on the judiciary and legal systems.

7 (ABOVE)
Sam Shilowa (left) raises the concerns of South African trade unions at a workshop on labour issues. On the far right is Ebrahim Patel, a leading negotiator for the Congress of South African Trade Unions (COSATU).

8 (RIGHT)
Premier of Mpumalanga Mathews Phosa and Minister Valli Moosa in discussion between sessions.

9
Colin Eglin, a negotiator
for the Democratic Party.

10
Sheila Camerer, a negotiator for the National Party.

11
Colin Eglin (left) and Dene Smuts (right), both for the Democratic Party, watch the debate unfold during negotiations.

12

William Hofmeyr (left), and Naledi Pandor (right)
of the African National Congress.

13

Pravin Gordhan and Melanie Verwoerd, negotiators for the
African National Congress. Melanie Verwoerd is married to
the grandson of former South African statesman for the
National Party, Hendrik Verwoerd.

14 (TOP)
Kevin Nkoane, an education expert for the African National Congress, makes a point to Roelf Meyer of the National Party.

15 (ABOVE)
Negotiators from different sides of the political spectrum made an effort to talk among themselves to solve differences. Here General Constand Viljoen (left), the leader of the Freedom Front, is in close consultation with Douglas Gibson (right) of the Democratic Party.

16

General Constand Viljoen (centre) of the Freedom Front meets informally with members of the Congress of South African Trade Unions (COSATU) during consultations with public stakeholders on the lockout clause. In front from left to right: Neil Coleman, Ebrahim Patel, Sam Shilowa, Constand Viljoen, John Gomomo (President of COSATU), and Roelf Meyer of the National Party.

17

18

19

20

17, 18, 19, 20
A diverse range of people attended the public meetings on the constitution as part of the Constitutional Assembly's public participation programme. These meetings were widely advertised and always well attended.

21

Public interest in the constitution-making process arose in every part of
South Africa. Like those shown at this meeting, people were prepared
to go to great lengths to find out about the process and to participate.

22

In order to actively address concerns about women's rights in the new South Africa, particular workshops, such as the one at which this picture was taken, were dedicated to that purpose. The workshops also helped to emphasize the way in which the status of women in South Africa concerns all South Africans in every sector of society.

23

Speaker of Parliament Frene Ginwala takes some time to meet scholars visiting the Assembly venue.

24
Chairperson of the
Constitutional Assem-
bly Cyril Ramaphosa
meets with Christian
groups demonstrating
for the importance of
acknowledging religion
and God in the consti-
ution.

25
Sam Shilowa, leader of the Congress of South African Trade
Unions (COSATU), greets those gathered at a demonstration
by COSATU over the strike and lockout clauses in the draft
constitution.

26

L. M. Mti of the African National Congress
takes live calls from the public on the
constitution-making process.

27

Senior members of the Constitutional Assembly presented the
public meetings on the drafting process. Here Gora Ebrahim
leads such a meeting, with Louisa Zondo assisting him.

28

The Constitutional Assembly used South African National Defence
Force (SANDF) Dakotas to reach outlying areas for public meetings.
The Assembly was especially eager to involve those in rural areas, and
the Dakotas offered a relatively inexpensive way to do so. Here Assembly
members are about to board a Dakota to Mhluzi, 12 June 1995.

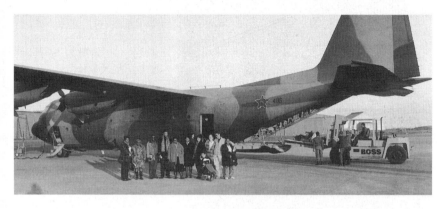

29

Members of the Constitutional Assembly on their way to
public meetings on the constitution in a South African
National Defence Force Dakota.

30
The Constitutional Assembly's public meetings, which were held in all parts of South Africa, were advertised widely, and sometimes unexpectedly innovatively. The public meetings were always well attended.

31 (BELOW)
Roelf Meyer finds ways to speak to the public about the drafting process.

32

Cyril Ramaphosa on-line after the launch of the Constitutional Assembly's Internet website. The Constitutional Assembly was the first branch of government to realize the importance of such a site. On Ramaphosa's left is Julian Hofman of the Law Faculty at the University of Cape Town, who helped set up the site.

33

Submissions poured in until the very last minute. Here, on the last day for the public submissions to the Constitutional Assembly, two animal rights groups (left), a Rastafarian lobby group (far end), and human rights organization Amnesty International (right) make their submissions.

34

Towards the end of the negotiations, meetings went on into the night. Here leading negotiators work out transitional arrangements. It is 3 a.m., and despite their expressions, everyone's patience is being tested to the utmost.

35

Hassen Ebrahim (left), Cyril Ramaphosa (centre), and Leon Wessels (right). It is 3 a.m., the process has deadlocked, and negotiators are almost certain that there will be no constitution, when Cyril Ramaphosa reads aloud a spoof proposal drafted in jest. This human side of the negotiators often smoothed their most difficult and intractable discussions.

36

This private discussion between Cyril Ramaphosa of the African National Congress and Roelf Meyer of the National Party took place as part of the Channel Bilateral, an agreement designed to maximize communication between the two parties. Such discussions often solved deadlocks and serious problems in formal negotiations.

37

Leon Wessels watches negotiators doing overtime. The time is 3.33 a.m.

38
Dullah Omar, a leading negotiator for the African National
Congress, at the last meeting of the Constitutional Committee.

39

Eventually the tremendous pressure began to take its toll. In the early hours of the morning negotiators took advantage of every break to get some rest. Patricia de Lille (below) is lucky enough to find a couch. Louisa Zondo (above right) stops right where she is.

40

The staff of the Constitutional Assembly were constantly under tremendous pressure. Here a number of staff members take part in a stress-management workshop.

41

S. S. (Fanie) van der Merwe, along with Mac Maharaj, was a key part of the Constitutional Assembly's administration. As director general of the Prisons Department he had been involved in negotiations with Nelson Mandela as far back as 1987.

42 (TOP)
The technical refinement team at work. This was where the constitution was literally drafted, where the actual words came together.

43 (BOTTOM)
The translators were a crucial part of the process of writing South Africa's new constitution. They worked day and night to the very end of the process to ensure that the constitution could be read in all of the country's eleven official languages.

44

Halton Cheadle (left), Sandy Liebenberg (centre),
and Ignatius Rautenbach (right) fulfilled vital roles
as technical advisors on the bill of rights.

45

The Constitutional Assembly gathered on the steps
of the Senate building, Cape Town.

46
The unveiling of the Constitutional Assembly
mural, Plein Street, Cape Town.

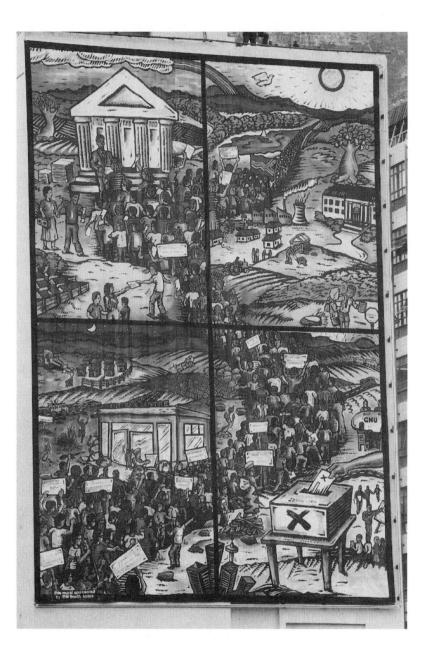

47

Christo Brand, a key staff member in the printing department of the
Constitutional Assembly, checking the printing of the bill that will
propose the new constitution. During the late eighties Brand had been
a warden at Pollsmoor Prison where he had come to know Nelson
Mandela, and Mandela to know him and his family.

48

Leon Wessels and Cyril Ramaphosa shake hands
after the adoption of the final constitution on 11
October 1996.

49

The members of the Constitutional Assembly applaud the adoption of the final constitution. President Nelson Mandela is in the front on the right.

50
President Nelson Mandela speaks at the formal
celebration of the new, final constitution.

II

Negotiating the final constitution

THE ADOPTION of the final Constitution concluded some of the most successful negotiations in recent constitutional and political history. The most striking and encouraging feature of this event was the degree of consensus achieved, especially since one of the strongest influences on the process had always been the need to achieve the greatest possible consensus.

The level of consensus achieved during this process becomes even more impressive when considered against the background of the relative strength of the different negotiating partners. The voting strength of individual parties was as follows: ANC, 312 members (63.7 per cent); NP, 99 members (20.2 per cent); IFP, 48 members (9.8 per cent); FF, 14 members (2.8 per cent); DP, 10 members (2 per cent); PAC, 5 members (1 per cent); and ACDP, 2 members (0.4 per cent). The interim constitution required that a two-thirds majority adopt the final constitutional text. While the ANC did not have sufficient votes to adopt the constitution on its numbers alone, its relative strength did weigh heavily on its negotiating partners. In the end though, achieving consensus between the parties proved to be more important.

There were a number of factors responsible for the successful negotiation and adoption of the final constitution. Some of these factors relate to the willingness of the majority party to compromise to gain wider support for given formulations. Furthermore, the political will of major role-players allowed them to complete the process timeously. The political maturity and the quality of the leadership in the Management Committee were also a great advantage. The personal chemistry and camaraderie that developed between negotiators laid the foundation for future co-operation as well, and the dynamism of the chairperson also made a valuable contribution. The suitability of the political structures and the degree of flexibility in the structural process greatly facilitated negotiations, and the brilliance of the technical and expert advice was indispensable. Finally, the energy and enthusiasm of those involved in administrative and logistical support ensured an environment conducive to successful negotiations.[1]

Collating the 'wish list'

In order to identify those areas on which submissions were necessary, the negotiators agreed on agendas for each Theme Committee. Once areas had been identified and agreed upon, advertisements were placed in all major newspapers inviting submissions, and a number of workshops and consultations with affected sectors were organized to facilitate the process of public participation. All submissions were collated and processed for consideration by experts in the Technical Committees, who prepared reports based on these submissions for consideration by Theme Committees.

The invitation to make submissions elicited a 'wish list' of issues. This sparked off an important debate: what issues should be dealt with in the constitution and which issues were matters for legislation? There was a natural inclination, especially by smaller political parties and lobby groups, to seek to secure particular interests by including them in the constitution. To a large extent, this was also the way in which the broader public responded.[2]

The reports produced by Theme Committees could not reflect the full spectrum of the submissions,[3] but generally contained the major trends, whether they demonstrated consensus or considerable differences of opinion. Often, these reports were supported by a set of draft formulations. This resulted in a further difficulty, for giving effect to the political reports developed by Theme Committees invariably begged the question: how much detail should a formulation include? In the report on the Independent Electoral Commission, the final report from the Theme Committee clearly distinguished those issues for inclusion in the final text from those that should best be incorporated in national legislation. However, not all Theme Committee agreements on their report and draft formulations were this congenial.

At the request of the chairperson, the Panel of Constitutional Experts drafted a document on the criteria that should be applied when considering issues for inclusion in the constitution. The document was tabled at a meeting of the Constitutional Committee in May 1995:

> 5.1 When it is debated whether a particular institution or right should be included in the Constitution, some questions which follow from the above criteria could serve as guidelines:
>
> > i) Does the implementation of democracy and the constitutional state, based on the values recognised in the Constitution, require its inclusion (either as an institutional necessity, or in view of the country's history and needs)?
> >
> > ii) Is it necessary for effective and democratic government?
> >
> > iii) Is it necessary in order to address a vital constitutional agreement reflected in a Constitutional Principle?
> >
> > iv) Would it be conducive to an integrated approach, in other words is it not sufficiently dealt with or likely to be dealt with elsewhere in the Constitution?[4]

The debates in Theme Committees were repeated in the Constitutional Committee, often without any progress. Part of the difficulty was that the political representatives debating issues in the Theme Committees were often the same people dealing with these matters in the Constitutional Committee. The fact that the Constitutional Committee consisted of forty-four members did not help, for it was often too big a structure to negotiate matters effectively. In addition, members who had not had the benefit of the debates in Theme Committees participated in matters in which they did not have sufficient expertise.[5] Where there were differences of opinion, compromises had to be found, but clearly parties were not ready to make the necessary compromises.[6]

The solution found in the establishment of sub-committees provides a vivid illustration of the flexible approach that the Constitutional Assembly adopted. The establishment of subcommittees proved to be invaluable, for it was easier to find solutions in smaller structures.[7]

Producing a working draft

According to the work programme, the first working draft had to be published and the comments processed by the end of 1995, but this was not possible, for the Constitutional Assembly had to adjourn to allow political parties to participate in local government elections on October 1995.[8]

The success of the public participation programme and the overwhelming number of submissions made led to increased concern, especially among structures of civil society, as to whether their views would be seriously considered. This concern generated a pressure that was to remain with the Constitutional Assembly to the end of the negotiating process, and it was in this context that the administration proposed a comprehensive process of public comment and participation subsequent to the publication of the working draft.[9]

After some debate, the Management Committee resolved that a working draft be published by 15 November to allow for public comment. This would make it possible to produce the first draft of the final text by the end of February and to adhere to the agreed time-frame by adopting the constitution on 8 May 1996.[10] The Management Committee further resolved to establish a team of experts, including law advisers, language experts, and the Panel of Experts, to begin the work of preparing a working draft, which was to serve as a report on how the Constitutional Assembly had addressed the submissions made. The format of the draft was to draw attention to areas that remained contentious or were outstanding.

On 19 September 1995 a consolidated working draft containing draft formulations on a vast majority of issues was produced. This draft took into account legal and linguistic consistency and coherence as well as ensuring that the text was in plain and accessible language.[11] Accordingly, on 12 October 1995 the first edition of the *Refined Working Draft* was produced for discussion at the Constitutional Committee meeting of 19 October.[12] At last the stage was set. This draft provided the first glimpse of what the final text might look like and what the areas of contention were. More importantly, the draft reflected the treatment of the views of different role-players, including the public and civil society. The importance of the draft was that it clearly set out the agenda for further negotiation.

In a sense, therefore, the meeting of the Constitutional Committee on 19 and 20 October was the first at which serious negotiations on the final text took place. Political parties were now, after a year of meeting to consider different views and submissions, sufficiently primed and ready to plunge into closing negotiations. The enthusiasm and seriousness of the negotiators were clearly visible from the vast number of issues addressed and agreements reached. One kind of issue that produced much debate arose from the use of particular words or a selection of words that politicians believed most appropriately reflected their agreements.[13] Politicians, especially those with a legal background or knowledge, often rebelled against the use of plain language in drafting.[14] p 345

One of the greatest advances made in this working draft was in its plain language. This was the first time that constitutional issues were formulated in this way. Despite the initial hesitation amongst negotiators, they accepted the idea and got used to the style.

Because a number of matters were still outstanding, it was agreed that publication of the draft be delayed, and a further meeting of the Constitutional Committee be scheduled to seek greater agreement before publication.[15] The drafters had to provide a further edition incorporating new agreements, which they were obliged to complete by 30 October 1995 for discussion on 9 and 10 November.[16] It was a task that proved to be extremely demanding and difficult. However, this kind of pressure became a trend that continued until the eve of the adoption of the text.[17] New formulations were always required within an unreasonable amount of time.

The launch of the publication, however, proved to be an overwhelming success. More than 4.5 million copies of the draft constitution were distributed in tabloid form throughout the country. Meanwhile, guided by the discussions of the Constitutional Committee and after further research,[18] the drafters prepared a third edition of the working draft on 18 December.[19] Revised drafts were produced at regular intervals to reflect the latest agreements.

Composing an agreed text

SLOW PROGRESS

The closing date for submissions was 20 February 1996. Considering the fact that the publication of the draft had taken place immediately after the local government elections and before the festive period, this exercise was a huge success. The public response to the working draft was overwhelming as 1 438 submissions and 248 504 petitions poured in.[20]

In the meantime, the subcommittee continued after the Christmas recess to make progress on outstanding issues.[21] By agreement, Parliament reorganized its schedule to provide negotiators with additional time to concentrate on completing their tasks.[22] But even this was not enough, and a mild sense of panic began to set in amongst negotiators. In an attempt by parties to find agreement, a series of bilateral and multilateral meetings was held behind closed doors. While bilateral meetings were privately arranged between the parties themselves, multilateral meetings between parties were facilitated by the Constitutional Assembly's administration. That these meetings were held behind closed doors did not augur well with members of civil society or the media.[23] These were nevertheless important meetings as they allowed parties to make compromises gracefully without appearing in the media to have betrayed their constituencies.

They also allowed for very frank discussions without negotiators having to make statements purely for the benefit of the media.

The major issues requiring resolution related to the bill of rights, the council of provinces, national and provincial competencies, courts and the administration of justice, and local government. The Management Committee meeting on 15 February 1996 identified sixty-eight individual issues outstanding. A later survey on 14 March reflected five issues on which there was deadlock: the death penalty, lockout clauses, education, the appointment of judges, and the Attorney-General; fifty-four further issues of contention in respect of which political decisions were necessary, and twenty-five matters that required technical attention.

The fourth edition of the working draft was completed by 20 March 1996. This edition also contained a detailed study and survey of all the submissions made in response to the publication of earlier drafts.[24] The survey included endnotes intended to facilitate consideration of the public submissions. Technical experts and the Independent Panel of Experts processed these submissions and produced reports for consideration by negotiators.

During March 1996 it became clear that it would be extremely difficult to adopt the constitution timeously. One of the options explored by the Management Committee was to consider ways in which they could avail themselves of the deadlock-breaking mechanism offered in section 73 (3) of the interim constitution. In terms of this section, should it not be possible to adopt the text by the requisite majority, a text passed by a majority of members of the Constitutional Assembly could be referred to the Independent Panel of Experts, which had a period of thirty days within which to develop formulations that would find favour with parties, and have the text adopted with the necessary majorities.

THE ARNISTON MULTILATERAL

There were two options open to the negotiators: they could either pass a text by simple majority by 8 April 1996, or amend the interim constitution to make provision for a similar deadlock-breaking mechanism to come into effect after 8 May 1996. After much discussion, it was agreed to opt for the latter approach.[25] However, parties recognized that they would still have to expedite their negotiations. And in any event, all parties were keen to have a final constitution adopted within the shortest possible time, as there were many other issues of government and governance that required their attention.

The negotiators accepted a proposal mooted by the administration to hold a multilateral in an isolated area over several days. This would allow parties, with the benefit of experts being present, to hold intensive negotiations without the disruptions occasioned by remaining in close proximity to their work environments. The multilateral was held in Arniston between 1 and 3 April 1996 at Die Herberg, a venue with both the facilities and the isolation required for effective talks.[26]

This meeting proved extremely successful, and most of the outstanding issues were resolved.[27] An excited Cyril Ramaphosa stated, 'It defies logic, all parties are happy with their scores – it's a win-win situation for everybody'. A similar statement was made by the NP's Roelf Meyer, who said, 'The outstanding items have been reduced to only a few'.[28] The only issues that remained in contention were the death penalty, education, and lockout procedures. Formulations on the preamble and local government were still in the process of completion and were also outstanding. For the first time since May 1994, negotiators began to see the light at the end of the tunnel. However, this was not the end of the process.

As it turned out, these issues of deadlock proved to be serious enough to throw into question the adoption of the final constitution by general consensus. What was most extraordinary was that none of the major political debates that had raged between parties for several years, namely, the question of the government of national unity, the senate, and national and provincial competencies, were among these issues. Yet the NP and DP felt strongly enough about them to consider voting against the entire constitution. Parties reported the progress recorded at Arniston to the Constitutional Committee on 4 April. The

Easter recess period that followed provided the technical refinement team with an opportunity to produce the fifth edition of the working draft for 15 April.

IDENTIFYING THE ISSUES OF CONTENTION

Together with the fifth edition of the constitution's working draft, a draft of the transitional arrangements was produced for the first time.[29] While in reality little progress seemed to have been made, the second week of April was probably one of the most important periods for the negotiations, underlined by the fact that the formal process of adoption was to begin on 22 April. During this week all parties had to take stock of the fruits of their negotiation and to consider whether they were able to support the end product or not.

This week also saw the process of negotiation intensify, and the period following this week saw a great deal of pressure mount on Parliament. Despite a full legislative programme, it was agreed that the work of the Constitutional Assembly would take priority.[30] Between Tuesday 16 April and Friday 19 April the Constitutional Committee met intermittently amid a hectic series of bilateral, multilateral, and subcommittee meetings.[31] Party caucuses and meetings of the policy-making structures were regularly convened to renew or obtain fresh mandates. Generally, meetings took place at all hours, even stretching late into the night. During this week the so-called 'channel bilateral' was resumed as well.

There was also a great deal of lobbying by interest groups, particularly by business and labour. Over 15 and 16 April, representatives of the South African Chamber of Business, Business South Africa, Die Afrikaanse Handelsinstituut, the Chamber of Mines, the South Africa Foundation, the Free Market Foundation, the South African Property Owners' Association, and the South African Agricultural Union held extensive discussions with different parties on the proposed property clause.[32] The business community expressed concern, arguing against replacing the property clause in the interim constitution with what it believed to be a weaker protection of property rights.[33] The NP and the

DP supported the business community, but the ANC insisted on a clause that allowed for land reform and payment of compensation on the basis of clearly set out criteria. The ANC was prepared to go to a deadlock on this matter.[34]

On the side of labour, COSATU held similar discussions concerning the lockout clause.[35] On 16 April, thousands of chemical workers country-wide marched in support of their demand for a rejection of the lockout clause and presented a memorandum to this effect to the chairperson of the Constitutional Assembly, Cyril Ramaphosa.[36] Thousands of workers belonging to the National Education Health and Allied Workers Union also marched the next day with a similar demand.[37] Consultations were held with the Congress of Traditional Leaders on 18 April as well, regarding the concerns of traditional leaders about their authority and customary law.[38] The traditional leaders insisted on representation at all levels of government and that customary law not be subject to the rights laid out in the bill of rights. They demanded furthermore that a ministry responsible for traditional affairs be established, and that any legislation rejected by a council of traditional leaders should only be passed by a 60 per cent majority of Parliament. They also demanded that traditional authorities should be the primary structures of local government.[39]

In a marathon meeting of the Constitutional Committee that started at 8 p.m. on 18 April and ended at 5:47 p.m. the next day, the basic text of the constitution bill was agreed upon. This meeting heralded some of the most dramatic breakthroughs in all the negotiations.[40] One of those agreements came about in the early hours of the morning of 19 April, and was reached primarily between the ANC, the Freedom Front, and the NP.[41] They agreed that the new constitution feature a commission to promote and protect the rights of cultural, religious, and language groups. This was vitally important to bringing the right-wing constituency on board, and the move was supported unanimously by all parties.[42] Constand Viljoen was so excited about the agreement that he was visibly emotional when it was announced.[43] The commission, it was agreed, would be listed among the other institutions supporting constitutional democracy, with the aim of promoting respect for the cultural, religious, and language rights of communities, and the promotion, development, and attainment of humanity, peace, friendship, and tolerance among these communities on the basis of equality and free association. In addition, a clause would be included reflecting the principle of collective rights for cultural, religious, and linguistic communities to give effect to Constitutional Principle XXXIV.[44]

Another major agreement emerged during the early hours of that morning on the preamble.[45] The preamble to the constitution had been an issue that parties avoided until the very last, simply because drafting it reflected the often conflicting emotions of those involved. Surprisingly enough, the matter was settled with little of the drama that had preceded other difficult agreements. The text was simply discussed in a bilateral between Blade Nzimande for the ANC and Boy Geldenhuys for the NP, and was presented to the Constitutional Committee.

However, the agreements produced by this meeting did not resolve all outstanding issues, for the major areas of difference between the parties after the Arniston accord still remained. Among the issues outstanding were the lockout clause, the property clause, the death penalty, the appointment of judges, the Attorney-General, language, local government, the question of proportional representation, and the bar against members of parliament crossing the floor. Nevertheless, a great deal of progress had been made. The text was now polished and politically refined with formulations on all agreed matters, and it was therefore in a form acceptable for tabling as a bill.

There was a perception that parties would not vote against the constitution, since they considered the text and the outstanding issues as a 'package deal'.[46] Roelf Meyer of the NP had stated this as his position immediately after the Arniston multilateral.[47] The media reacted to the developments in different ways. Cyril Madlala of the *Sunday Times* saw it as 'the controversial fruit of a long night's bargaining'.[48] John McLennan of the *Sunday Tribune* saw it as 'a matter of fine tuning', explaining that 'all parties might not like all of it, but that's to be expected with something which came about through give and take'.[49] The editorial of *Rapport* entitled 'Deurbraak' ('Breakthrough') reflected qualified excitement.[50]

The draft constitution was published in bill form on Monday 22 April, incorporating all the agreements achieved as at Friday 19 April. The drafters were provided with no more than thirty-six hours to draft the text, proofread, and prepare the document for printing. This week also saw negotiators more upbeat, for the progress made during the last week of negotiations was reason enough for many of the negotiators to be confident that the constitution would be complete by the due date.[51] However, the differences between parties sharpened. COSATU planned to call a massive national strike for 30 April in support of its demand to exclude any provision for a lockout. The ANC supported the call,[52] but as with most national strikes, the business community and all opposition parties slammed the move.[53]

DEADLOCKS

The draft constitution was tabled in the Constitutional Assembly on Tuesday 23 April 1996. The historic process of drawing up a constitution entered its final lap with a plenary debate lasting two days.[54] In tabling the draft, Ramaphosa paid tribute to those who had died since the beginning of colonialism in South Africa. The country, he said, had come a long way since 1909, when the first Union constitution was passed in the House of Commons in the United Kingdom. He pointed out that the new, final constitution would serve as a healing balm and would ensure that what had happened in the past did not occur again. In effect, it would be the birth certificate of the South African nation.

For his part, Deputy-President Thabo Mbeki argued that the new constitution would mean that 'the immense sacrifices of so many people for freedom were not in vain', pointing out that the draft was not an ANC constitution but a 'South African Constitution'. While no single party was expected to be happy with all the provisions of the constitution, no democrat should feel it necessary to vote against the bill, Mbeki urged.[55] All other parties in their opening addresses welcomed the tabling of the draft and indicated in general the amendments they intended to file.

In this five-hour debate, while the ANC concentrated on the bill of

BUT:

rights, the NP and DP indicated their unhappiness with key clauses relating to the economy. The NP leader, F. W. de Klerk, warned of the 'negative consequences' if trade union and property rights were tampered with.[56] The NP and the Freedom Front focused on the question of minorities. The DP's chief negotiator Colin Eglin warned: 'If properly managed, [South Africa's] cultural diversity could be the glue that welds our communities together. But, if badly managed, cultural diversity could be the gunpowder that blows our nation and our democracy apart'.[57] During this debate the PAC, the DP, and the ACDP indicated that should the draft not be amended to take their separate concerns into account, they would consider voting against it.[58]

In terms of an agreement on the procedure to be followed, the proposals for amendments had to be tabled by parties on 23 April. It became clear from bilateral discussions between the parties that some of their differences might be intractable, and the possibility of adopting the constitution with the necessary support was for the first time placed seriously in doubt. There were various exchanges between the ANC and the NP in a bid to bridge their differences, and to this end, key negotiators from the ANC and the NP including Mandela and De Klerk met and agreed that a further bilateral involving both leaders should be held.[59]

The pressure generated by the impasse intensified with the looming threat of the COSATU strike.[60] The first stage of the adoption procedure lasted two days in a plenary session of the full Constitutional Assembly. The second stage was the committee process, which, it was agreed, would be dealt with in the Constitutional Committee. The object of the exercise during this stage was to consider proposals for amendment of the bill made by the various parties and to seek agreement.

The first meeting of this Constitutional Committee took place on 25 April 1996. Placed before the meeting were 298 proposed amendments to the bill tabled by the various parties.[61] The ANC and the NP arrived at agreements reflected in twenty-eight amendments that were jointly tabled. The ANC tabled seventy-six further amendments, the NP ninety, the DP sixty-nine, the PAC seven, the ACDP twenty-three, and the Freedom Front five. In the main, the amendments were of a technical nature while others were no more than a restatement of well-known party positions that had been addressed in the previous two years.[62] At the opening of this meeting it was agreed that debate should take place in various subcommittees: the bill of rights and state institutions supporting constitutional democracy; founding provisions, co-operative government, parliament, the president and the executive, local government, competencies, provinces, and traditional leaders; courts and the administration of justice; security services; finance; and general provisions and transitional arrangements.[63] Unfortunately, even the subcommittees did not make much progress, and the parties remained deadlocked.

Roelf Meyer, speaking at a media briefing after the NP's weekly caucus, identified one aspect of the collective rights issues on which parties were deadlocked: whether the constitution should allow for state-aided, monolingual schools. He defined this as being 'very sensitive' to the interests of the NP: 'From our perspective, and that of our constituency, there is a strong feeling that schools should be entitled to instruction in only one medium if the situation allows that to be the case. Where a school has students that all speak a specific language, a school should not be forced to cater for other languages of a dual or parallel nature'.[64] However, despite the deadlock, senior negotiators remained confident that they could bridge the divide.

An important series of deadlock-breaking meetings took place on Sunday 28 April, when Mandela met with De Klerk at Mandela's Mhlamba Npofu official residence in Pretoria.[65] Within ten hours three further delegations arrived for discussions.

Overshadowing these talks was the feared national strike on 30 April and the fact that the rand was at an all-time low. Mandela's day started with De Klerk and NP negotiators at 9 a.m., and a while later Sam Shilowa and other COSATU leaders arrived to discuss their opposition to the lockout clause. The last delegation consisted of some of the country's leading business figures, whose aim it was to deal with both the lockout issue and the property clause. These meetings produced significant agreements in principle on some issues, and settled broad formulations on the lockout clause and clauses relating to education and official languages.[66] The only point on which parties still remained deadlocked was the property clause. In reporting on the tentative agreements, the chairperson of the Constitutional Assembly stated that he was now '1000% sure of adopting the constitution on May 8'.[67] In spite of these advances, COSATU remained adamant that the strike would go ahead.

The intensification of the process of negotiation was beginning to take its toll. After 15 April negotiators found themselves involved in a hectic round of bilaterals, subcommittees, extensive consultations, and continuous reporting to policy-making bodies of their parties. The announcements made by Ramaphosa and Meyer that tentative agreements had been reached over the previous weekend did not help matters, since despite the announcement, no report on the agreements was provided, and the agreements were just too broad and tentative.

The negotiators' difficulties manifested themselves in two forms. Negotiators were already showing signs of physical strain and stress at the long hours of concentrated debate. In this regard, the smaller parties were subjected to a further impediment, as they did not have sufficient members to field in the various subcommittees or to engage other parties in lobbying support. Therefore, they often found themselves led by agreements between the ANC and the NP.[68] Since the Freedom Front was becoming increasingly irritated, Constand Viljoen urged the two parties to report on the outcome of their meetings without delay, a request which Colin Eglin of the DP supported. However, while on the one hand it was necessary to arrive at agreements multilaterally, the deadlocks were essentially between the two bigger parties. Unless it was possible to bridge the divide between these two parties, it would not be possible to make compromises that would satisfy all the parties.

The Constitutional Committee considered every proposal for amendments to the bill, without formal tabling or motivating as would be required with other law-making. This is an example of ways the Constitutional Assembly broke with formal legislative procedures and traditions. The Constitutional Committee continued to be the main negotiating forum, so that negotiators from smaller parties would have a better opportunity to argue the merits of their positions than they would have had in the plenary.

Nonetheless, on 29 April, to expedite matters the Constitutional Committee broke up into subcommittees. Its meeting then reconvened at 8 p.m. to take reports and consider progress made, but by midnight there was still no resolution to the deadlock, and the Constitutional Committee had to hold yet another unscheduled meeting the next day. This next day proved to be more eventful. The committee dealt with several important issues including provincial powers, the preamble, language, and the property clause. At a media briefing that morning Pravin Gordhan, a senior negotiator from the ANC, made a dramatic announcement. The ANC proposed a new package of provincial powers that included a host of exclusive competencies.[69] For several months the ANC had debated within its structures the question of greater powers for provinces, and the proposal was made in the context of the development of the principle of co-operative government. These ideas finally matured when chapter 3 of the working draft on co-operative government was agreed upon multilaterally.

Only in the last week of April 1996, and a few days short of adoption, did the ANC's National Working Committee finally approve the package. Ironically, by this time the ANC had already been able to assert itself and obtain agreement with the NP on a package of lesser powers for the provinces.[70] It was therefore under no particular political pressure to accede to wider provincial powers. Despite this, the ANC suspected that since wider powers lacked adherence to the constitutional principles, the Constitutional Court might not certify the constitution. The ghost of the constitutional principles that were the subject of a compromise negotiated by the ANC two years previously had come back to haunt the organization's negotiators. With the new package, provinces were further empowered by being assigned both exclusive and concurrent legislative powers. The package also created new certainty and effective powers for local government. It was also during these debates that an important constitutional shift took place, by which national, provincial, and local government came to be viewed as equally important 'spheres' rather than 'tiers' of government. Accordingly, while each of the three spheres of government had been endowed with tremendous powers to govern effectively, no sphere was free from the overriding principle of co-operative government.

It was hoped that this package would entice the IFP, which had boycotted the process since April 1995, to return and be part of the adoption. According to the overly confident Gordhan, 'Once the IFP looks at this, they will regret not having been part of this process. There is now no reason for the IFP to stay out. They must be there on May 8. In terms of this package, international mediation pales into insignificance'.[71] In keeping with the IFP track record in the negotiation, in a general condemnation of the entire constitutional text they also dismissed this package as unacceptable, arguing that the provinces would end up with even less power than they had in the interim constitution.[72]

On 30 April the formulation of the preamble was finalized. The only outstanding debate in this regard was the recognition of God in the preamble. The compromise was to include the words 'may God protect our people' at the end. The Freedom Front and the NP successfully motivated a further amendment: the words 'respect those who have worked to build and develop our country' were inserted after the sentence ending 'honour those who suffered for justice and freedom in our land'. Needless to say, these amendments were not sufficient for the ACDP, who insisted on the words 'in humble submission to God'. In this regard, a submission that weighed heavily on the minds of some negotiators came from Prof. M. H. Prozesky, of the Department of Religious Studies at the University of Natal, who argued that inclusion of the word 'God' discriminated against non-theists, and that such an inclusion was contrary to the principle of equality in the bill of rights.[73]

There was also agreement on the language and property clauses.[74] Negotiators agreed that the eleven official languages must enjoy parity of esteem and be treated equitably. However, it also allowed national, provincial, and local governments to choose a minimum of two languages for practical communication. On the property clause, agreement in principle required that the formulation still be drafted.

By the end of the day, parties were still not able to complete the outstanding matters, which meant that the meeting would have to reconvene on 1 May 1996. It was agreed that the bilateral would continue that morning and the Constitutional Committee would reconvene at 2 p.m.: the constitution-making process was now effectively into overtime. The delay in finalizing the text was beginning to cause significant problems for the administration and drafters.[75] The administration, who had hoped that the adopted text would be presented to the Constitutional Assembly in all eleven official languages for adoption, would also be disappointed on this score. Language experts were recruited from different parts of the country to carry out the translations, but their effort was completely frustrated by continuous amendments. In any event, the adopted text still had to be certified, and it would not have been cost-effective to print different drafts of a text that still had to be certified in all eleven languages.

The tension reached fever pitch. While the spirits of negotiators in the previous week had been buoyed by the agreements reached, they were now less confident of adopting the constitution in time.[76] There was simply not enough time to complete the drafting work or fulfill the logistical implications for the adoption programme, and moreover, there was still no agreement in sight on deadlocked issues, as parties still clung stubbornly to their positions. The Constitutional Committee meeting on 1 May continued until 5:17 a.m. the next day without much success. The deadlock on the lockout, property, and education clauses remained. DEATH PENALTY?

The demand by the NP for the entrenchment of single-medium (monolingual) education was unpalatable to the ANC. The frustration of negotiators was now clearly visible, and parties resorted to attacking each other's positions in the media to justify their own. The ANC complained that it could make no further concessions, and together with the PAC accused the NP of racist attempts to entrench white privilege at the expense of redressing the wrongs of apartheid. Roelf

Meyer, on the side of the NP, accused the ANC of being dictated to by forces outside the constitution-writing process. In the thick of these debates, the realization had dawned on parties that they would have to find solutions and compromises in the next few hours. Unless they could do so, the Constitutional Committee was obliged to take a firm decision on whether the constitution could be adopted on 8 May.

On the morning of 2 May the chairperson, Cyril Ramaphosa, for the first time in the process of constitution-making, dropped his guard and expressed concern: 'We are now in the danger zone. If we take a wrong turn in the next twenty-four hours, we could do something we could regret for many months, possibly a number of years'. According to him, the entire transformation process was now in jeopardy. He feared the Constitutional Assembly would have to resort to deadlock-breaking mechanisms, including a referendum. 'If we ever go down that route, there are a number of implications for our country, economy, race relations, reconciliation. All sorts of things will start to become undone, the centre may not hold.' He appealed to parties not to stick to their old positions and become arrogant: 'This is the time to think about South Africa, this country, and about our people. The route we may enter within twenty-four hours, if we do not reach agreement, may well be a route that could spell disaster. I don't want to believe we sat here for two years wasting our time, to go for a referendum'.[77] The process of multi-party constitution-writing was in jeopardy.

It was in the midst of this looming crisis that one of the lighter moments in the process took place at 3 a.m. that morning. When the Constitutional Committee had reconvened to take reports on developments arising from bilateral discussions and subcommittee meetings, and members were taking their seats, the chairperson began reading out a document: 'We must start with Chapter One, Founding Provisions. This constitution is the constitution of SA and constitutes constitutionalism. The constitution is applicable to the extent that it applies to all those to whom it is applicable. It furthermore binds all who are bound by it. The rights in the constitution are limited only to the extent that they are limitable, subject to reasonable limitations imposed by national legislation'. He continued in this vein but was unable to keep a straight face when reading: 'In a spirit of decency and propriety, all organs, including organs of state, must remain in their own functional areas, and not encroach on the functional areas and spheres of influence pertaining to other organs'. The spoof was greeted by hoots of laughter from negotiators when they realized what was going on.[78] It was theatre such as this that so perfectly illustrated that the negotiators never lost their humanity or sense of humour, even in the most difficult and daunting circumstances.

BREAKING THE DEADLOCK

After a short break, the participants agreed to reconvene at 11 a.m. to deal with the outstanding issues. Despite the gloom and the possibility of failure to adopt the constitution on 8 May with the required majority, negotiators never lost their confidence and maintained their faith in the process. Hence, they instructed the technical refinement team to continue amending the draft text to reflect the latest political agreements on refinement of the formulations. Furthermore, preparations went ahead to finalize the text for publication and for the adoption programme. In this regard, the negotiators also accepted a request by the executive director that the refined text incorporating all agreements be presented to representatives of all political parties on Saturday, which would ensure that the text presented on adoption day accurately reflected all political agreements.[79]

Not surprisingly, the Constitutional Committee only managed to reconvene at 9:35 p.m. (ten hours later than scheduled) on 3 May, allowing bilateral discussions and subcommittees time to complete their tasks. This meeting dealt with various reports on outstanding issues.[80] The first report on the education clause in the bill of rights was tabled by Blade Nzimande, the ANC's chief negotiator on education and the preamble. Nzimande reported that the ANC had tried to meet all the parties concerned but had been unable to come to a common understanding. Agreement had thus eluded the negotiators. In view of this, he proposed a clause which he argued be included in the amended bill that was placed before the Constitutional Assembly for adoption.

He explained that the ANC felt that the clause showed the extent to which it wished to build a united country and yet recognized linguistic diversity in the context of education.

The NP believed that the constitution should allow for the alternative of single-medium institutions as a right. However, the NP wished to give further consideration to the proposed wording of the section. Dene Smuts, for the DP, opposed the formulation as it meant that independent schools would have to function at their own expense. The Freedom Front also opposed it. Richard Sizani of the PAC felt that the ANC had gone a long way in meeting the concerns of those parties who wanted education in their own language, and therefore supported the amendment. The proposal was held in temporary abeyance, until further work could be done on it. The effect of this debate was to mark a turning point in the negotiation process, for it was the first time the ANC asserted its role as the majority party. The ANC was prepared to risk a deadlock even if this meant that a referendum and ultimately an election would have to be held.

Naledi Pandor, a senior ANC negotiator on the bill of rights, reported on the clause allowing for 'Cultural rights and Self-determination'. The only difference between the parties here was whether the right had to be framed in the positive or the negative. Again, the view of the ANC, that it be negative, prevailed, supported only by the PAC.[81]

There was further positive development regarding the property clause when Baleka Mbete-Kgositsile of the ANC tabled an amended formulation for inclusion in the bill. She argued that it was the preference of the ANC not to have property protected by a provision in the constitution at all. The ANC's constituency included those who did not have property at all, and its goal was to ensure that poverty and landlessness would be addressed in the new dispensation: the ANC agreed that there should be no absolute right to property. Sheila Camerer of the NP confirmed that there had previously been agreement between the parties on the principles that should govern the clause: that while land reform should be addressed, security of tenure should also be guaranteed to an extent that was acceptable to those who did hold property. This should also open the way to those without property to acquire a similar security of tenure in the future. The negotiators agreed on the proposal. Camerer further added that the ANC had gone out of its way to meet the concerns of the constituencies the NP represented, and the NP appreciated the patience, spirit, and positive approach of its fellow negotiators. Even though the DP did not support the proposal tabled by the ANC, the meeting agreed that the clause as proposed by the ANC be included in the bill as it stood.

On the lockout clause, Dullah Omar of the ANC tabled a proposal to remove it from the bill of rights and include it under the interpretations clause as a new subsection that ensured that the right given to employers in the provisions of the Labour Relations Act of 1995 would not be rendered unconstitutional. Omar realized that the proposal would not entirely satisfy business or the union movement, but that the ANC had tried to come up with a proposal that would find acceptance. It was important to ensure that stability in the country was always maintained and that industrial peace was not threatened. The ANC wanted to ensure that the relationship between employers and employees was properly regulated by law, and that it was through the process of collective bargaining that problems and disputes be resolved. Only the PAC supported the proposal, while the NP and the Freedom Front reserved their positions. The proposal was accordingly settled and included in the amended bill.

Sam de Beer of the NP reported on the developments finalizing the transitional arrangements that were agreed to by all parties. The only outstanding point related to a proposal by the NP to provide a special dispensation affecting the powers and functions of governing bodies in existing educational institutions.[82] This was a compromise made by the ANC in finalizing the interim constitution that the NP and the Freedom Front argued be retained in the transitional arrangements of the final constitution. However, the proposal failed.

The appointment mechanisms for state institutions supporting constitutional democracy had long been a sticking point. In view of the ANC's majority in Parliament, smaller parties regarded the normal requirement of a simple majority in making these appointments as insufficient, for it would mean that the ANC could make its decision without reference to the views of other parties. On the other hand, it was the view of the ANC that the majority required should not be such that smaller parties effectively held a veto, which had been one of the causes of the deadlock that arose in June 1992 when CODESA II collapsed. Here again, there was no agreement and the ANC preference prevailed. The formulation on the appointment of judicial officers was settled in the same way. At this point the Constitutional Committee meeting adjourned at 12:30 a.m. on Saturday 4 May. The technical refinement team drafted the amended bill for consideration by representatives of political parties later that morning, and the process was successfully completed by late that Saturday evening. The agreements of the parties on the formulations made it possible to finalize the draft, and have it proofread and ready for printing on the next day.

The prospect of a stalemate was daunting. The Sunday newspapers unanimously voiced concern. 'Let the miracle continue' urged the *Sunday Tribune* on 5 May. The editorial continued:

Although the final deadlines are over, all is not yet lost. Past experience has shown that deadliness are merely guidelines and a breakthrough could happen at any time before Wednesday's crucial vote. All the parties should do their utmost to ensure the constitution by which the people of this country will have to live gets as wide an acceptance as possible. . . . The pity of it all is not so much those areas of the proposed constitution that are sticking points, but that after two years there are still issues so contentious that they could bring the whole constitutional process to a halt. The country has already enjoyed many miracles of compromise between people who, not long ago, were sworn enemies. That spirit of solidarity with the entire country, rather than with sectional interests, needs to continue for some time to come if this country is to soar into the future on the wings of a people unified in their differences by their love of the country and the trust in their fellows.

The *Sunday Times* of the same date was not confident, and seemed to think it likely that the text would not be adopted timeously.[83] *City Press*, in its editorial, spoke of the constitution as 'the final seal on our freedom'. It stated:

> This week support, prayers and sheer old-fashioned staying power were the bouquets we threw at the feet of men and women writing our country's new constitution. The work has been hard. Almost back-breaking. ... But they have one consolation: the harder their work, the more glorious will be their triumph. This will be *the* victory for the new South Africa: the rainbow nation millions of our people desperately want to see become a reality in our time. Our people of all colours have fought long and hard for this rainbow nation. Hence we are hopeful that our constitution writers will make the deadline. ... We believe our country cannot afford a referendum should the Constitutional Assembly not deliver a new constitution.

Rapport, however, adopted a different attitude. Like the editorial of the *Citizen* the next day, it expressed clear support for the positions espoused by F. W. de Klerk and the NP and urged them to stand their ground. However, the editorial in *Business Day* on 6 May ignored the threat of a referendum and attacked the image of the constitutional text as a 'people's document'.

In the meantime, the ANC and the NP continued to meet on the mornings of Sunday and Monday, led by the Deputy-Presidents Thabo Mbeki and F. W. de Klerk.[84] To assist NP negotiators in their quest for a mandate to find a solution, the NP's Federal Council executive met on Monday morning to evaluate the crisis.[85] After this meeting, F. W. de Klerk said that his party would keep talking to the ANC on the unresolved issues. The NP was considering alternate wording for the education clause, and the NP executive and its caucus would meet again to evaluate the progress made. Later that day, De Klerk also confirmed that 'a few other matters have cropped up in the process of finishing off the constitution which are also receiving attention'.[86] At a special meeting of the ANC caucus that also met early in the morning, the negotiating positions adopted by its negotiators were endorsed. One of the issues considered was whether the ANC would opt for a different formulation should the text not be adopted.[87] As for the DP and the Freedom Front, neither had decided yet how they would vote.

PREPARING FOR ADOPTION

When the Management Committee met at 8:15 a.m. on Monday morning it dealt with matters of process leading to adoption.[88] Even at this meeting, senior negotiators ignored the possibility of the failure to adopt. The issue at hand was to find ways in which the rules accommodated further amendment of the text when, not if, agreement took place. The state of play in terms of the rules required that the text not supported by all parties be put to the vote, but the rules did not make provision to process amendments at such a late hour. Since the final text was not finalized, in terms of the rules, it would be impossible to adopt an agreed text by consensus. Yet again, the Constitutional Assembly refused to be bound by the dogma of convention, and the matter was resolved by a resolution put to the Constitutional Assembly proposing that matters be referred to the Constitutional Committee to effect the required amendments.

Later on Monday 6 May, the Constitutional Assembly sat in plenary to debate the amended bill. This irreversibly set in motion a process that would oblige parties to either adopt the text or allow the deadlock-breaking mechanisms to come into effect. At the beginning of the proceedings, a resolution was passed allowing a further amendment of the bill. The ANC's Valli Moosa was the first speaker in the second reading.[89] He defined the final constitution as a tool to build the nation and a statement to the world that never again would the country have apartheid as a policy. He was at pains to point out that the final constitution had many commendable features including the founding provisions that confirmed that South Africa was a united democratic state founded on human dignity. Amendment of these provisions was only possible by a 75 per cent majority. Another feature was that local government, which had always been treated as a 'stepchild' of national and provincial government, was now a fully-fledged sphere of government.

Pieter Mulder of the Freedom Front confirmed that the negotiations were made difficult by the need to make compromises to ensure the success of the talks. While the Freedom Front had not succeeded in achieving everything it wanted, the test was whether, through its participation, the party had succeeded in bringing Afrikaners closer to their 'ideals'. He was convinced that the great risks the Freedom Front had taken did achieve this. Colin Eglin, chief negotiator for the DP, said that his party believed the constitution went a long way to creating governance that was representative, democratic, and accountable. However, the DP favoured a smaller National Assembly and cabinet and hoped that the constituency feature would be brought back for the next general election.[90]

While the Constitutional Assembly continued to meet in plenary, bilateral meetings primarily between the ANC and the NP continued until the early hours of Tuesday morning without any success. The meetings of Monday 6 May, therefore, did not produce anything material.

The plenary session of the Constitutional Assembly continued on Tuesday 7 May, as did the bilateral meetings. As the plenary sat, another meeting was taking place in a different part of the parliamentary premises, where the IFP was holding a workshop detailing its differences with the proposed new constitution.[91] Mario Ambrosini, an IFP adviser, delivered a paper which was a thinly disguised motivation for the IFP's continued boycott of the final proceedings for the adoption of the constitution. The paper condemned the bill as an attempt to establish a unitary state under the guise of a devolution of powers to provinces. The party denounced the last minute package of powers for provinces and local government tabled by the ANC and accepted by the Constitutional Committee: 'On its introduction, this Bill has been described by Constitutional Assembly Chairman Cyril Ramaphosa as the birth certificate of a new nation, while on a more attentive analysis it is the advanced death certificate of pluralism, federalism, and freedom of a country which, constitutionally speaking, is committing suicide by instalments'.

At 8 a.m. on Tuesday 7 May the NP's Federal Council executive had another opportunity to review the various formulations and consider whether it would give its support upon adoption. At 10 a.m. the Constitutional Assembly reconvened for its second day of debate but adjourned by noon to allow for possible new amendments and to allow the Constitutional Committee to meet. However, the bilateral meetings continued and made it impossible to convene the Constitutional Committee. The Constitutional Assembly finally decided to resume its debate at 5:30 p.m., as the delay meant that the Assembly would only complete its debate very late that evening. The Constitutional Committee finally convened nearly ten hours after it was scheduled to meet, but even then it was interrupted by adjournments on several occasions to allow parties to caucus on different positions. By this time negotiators, who had been through weeks of extremely difficult negotiations over exhausting hours, started becoming irritable. However, for most, including the army of journalists who faithfully witnessed and experienced the trauma and excitement of the process, there was a sense of expectation. For the faithful staff of both the administration and Parliament, it was no different to the experience of an expectant parent waiting to see a newborn after long and difficult labour.

When the members of the Constitutional Committee assembled at 10:45 p.m., an incredible air of excitement ran through the room. By this time, many of the members of the Constitutional Assembly who were attending the plenary debate had squeezed into the old assembly chamber to hear the outcome of the bilateral discussions. Blade Nzimande of the ANC was first to report on the education clause, which had been worked on further. He said it was appropriate that as South Africa drew closer to the twentieth anniversary of the 16 June 1976 uprisings, he was able to present a clause that would 'once and for all close the chapter on apartheid education in this country'.[92] He reported that parties had reached an understanding on the education clause. In terms of the agreement, section 29 (2) was amended to read:

Everyone has the right to receive education in the official language or languages of their choice in public educational institutions where that education is reasonably practicable. In order to ensure the effective access to, and implementation of, this right, the state must consider all reasonable educational alternatives, including single medium institutions, taking into account:

(a) equity;

(b) practicability; and

(c) the need to redress the results of past racially discriminatory laws and practices.

In conclusion, Nzimande confirmed that the amendment accommodated most concerns. It posed single-medium institutions as one of the alternatives to be considered by the state in securing the right to be taught in one's home language or the language of one's choice. The NP confirmed the agreement, the PAC reserved its position, and the Freedom Front recorded its objection. The DP was not happy, for agreement with the formulation represented one compromise too many, and it was prepared to make its last stand. Should it fail in this bid, the DP was prepared to vote against the entire text. In support of its complaint, Dene Smuts argued that the degree of independence enjoyed by independent schools be retained. She appealed for a formulation in terms of which the state could not discriminate in giving a basic grant or funding to any school founded on any basic principle or idea.[93] Ms Smuts accordingly proposed the amendment of section 29 by adding the following sentence as subsection (4): 'This provision does not preclude state subsidies for independent educational institutions'. The amendment was accepted.

These compromise amendments were in effect largely responsible for the support of the parties concerned of the entire constitutional text. The next issue was the lockout clause, and William Hofmeyr of the ANC proposed an amendment that came in two parts. The first part involved the insertion of a new section as section 241 into the chapter on general provisions under the title Labour Relations Act (LRA), 1995:

(1)   A provision of the Labour Relations Act, 1995 (Act No. 66 of 1995) remains valid, notwithstanding the provisions of the Constitution, until the provision is amended or repealed.

(2)   A Bill to amend or repeal a provision of the Labour Relations Act may be introduced in Parliament only after consultation with national federations of trade unions, and employer organisations.

(3)   The consultation referred to in subsection (2), including the identification of the federations to be consulted, must be in accordance with an Act of Parliament.

The second part of the amendment involved the deletion of the provision for the lockout in the bill of rights. He confirmed, however, that there was still no full agreement on the matter. To most parties, while they did not agree with the formulation, their opposition to the amendment was not sufficient to warrant voting against the entire constitution. The formulation proposed was an attempt to meet the interests of both business and labour to a certain extent, and it meant that while there would be no right to a lockout in the constitution, it would not exclude legislation dealing with it.

Senator Ray Radue of the NP said the party had consistently held the view that there must be an equitable balance between the rights of employers and employees, especially in the bill of rights. While it was not the best solution, the rights recorded in the LRA were the result of intensive negotiations, and were acceptable to business, labour, and the government. Those labour relations could now only be changed through a consultative process regulated by an Act of Parliament. The NP therefore recorded its strongest protest at the diminution of the employer's right to collective bargaining required by Constitutional Principle XVIII and included in the interim constitution. However, he said that this would not prevent the NP from supporting the constitution.

Tony Leon, leader of the DP, complained that the clause represented an outright victory for COSATU. Whatever attitude and response his party took on the constitution on 8 May, he wanted to record this formally so that there could be no accusations of bad faith after the event. He also gave notice that the DP intended to lodge its objection to the certification of the constitution, on the grounds of Constitutional Principle XVIII which recognizes and protects the rights of employers to engage in collective bargaining. It was the view of the DP's Senior Counsels that effect should be given to the requirements of recognition by including in the constitution the right of employers to collective bargaining. However, this would not satisfy the further requirement that the right to collective bargaining be protected. Having given to trade unions the right to strike, there was a fundamental imbalance and, in the view of the DP, a constitutional problem with this clause. Richard Sizani, senior negotiator for the PAC, confirmed its support for the amendment. The chairperson accordingly confirmed the proposed amendment to section 241.

Regarding the property clause, the ANC's Dullah Omar reported agreement that subsection (8) be amended to read: 'No provision of this section may impede the state from taking legislative and other measures to achieve land, water and related reform, in order to address the results of past racial discrimination, provided that any departure from the provisions of this section is in accordance with the provisions of section 36(1)'.

The issue being addressed, he said, was mainly that of land, something for which thousands of people had made sacrifices. Since 1910, and indeed before, millions of people had suffered, for those deprived of the right to vote found that the denial of political rights was used to drive people off the land. Thus, one finds that those who were disenfranchised were also the people who were landless and without property. There would be no peace, therefore, if the issue of land and property was not satisfactorily addressed. The ANC believed that it could not allow the illegitimate practices of the past to be legitimized through the process of writing the new constitution. The property clause now proposed, he said, addressed the concerns of those who owned property, ensuring that there would be no arbitrary deprivation of property and dealing with the issue of expropriation in a way that was consistent with standards throughout the democratic world. The

ANC believed that all of South Africa's people must have security in every respect. However, that security must be ensured once the legacy of the past had been addressed. This proposed clause, while providing protection for all property owners, addressed the needs and aspirations of the majority of the people. Finally, he stated, the provision was still subject to the limitations clause and that this was a standard to which the ANC aspired, for the ANC did not believe that it should do things that were not in accordance with the values of an open and democratic society.

According to Sheila Camerer of the NP, making the amendment subject to the provisions of the limitations clause changed the picture as far as her party was concerned. While this proposal might not represent a 'first prize', the ANC's initial position had been that there should be no property clause, so in this sense the ANC had definitely improved its position. In conclusion, she explained that a satisfactory compromise had been reached between the need for land reform and the security of the interests and rights of property owners.

Dene Smuts of the DP complained that it would be an unwise and unjust Constitutional Assembly that attempted to freeze the property relations as they stood in South Africa, which was not the DP's wish or intention. However, at the same time, the most problematic area of the section had always been subsection (8), which the DP considered to be a 'Trojan horse'. In addition, the DP believed that this was not an appropriate property clause for South Africa. The property clause had to enshrine eligibility to all property: the same eligibility that was denied to most South Africans in the past.

Richard Sizani for the PAC conceded that this clause was an improvement on the interim constitution. However, the promise that subsection (8) had held out for the PAC was that of overriding subsection (3) in the area of land reform and equitable access to natural resources. The new clause promised water, which the PAC had never believed was a commodity that could be owned by an individual. Ultimately, however, he said, land barons and the mining magnates would retain the mineral wealth of the country. He asked whether this national question could ever be resolved on a democratic basis: this latest move, of removing equitable access to natural resources had, he said, reaffirmed the PAC's position that one could not balance these difficult issues. The view of the PAC therefore remained that there should be no property clause in the constitution. Despite the objections, however, the amendment was confirmed.

It was at this late hour that the NP veteran, Alex van Breda, raised a new matter, that of pensions. He argued that even though members of Parliament had been in office for two years and the monthly deductions for pension payments had been made, proper pension arrangements were still outstanding. The NP unsuccessfully attempted to secure constitutional guarantees for these pensions. The NP further wished to retain section 189 of the interim constitution that provided for special pensions, and also wished to retain section 246 of the interim constitution, which could be construed as the protection of pensions for former political officer bearers. The issue of pensions, he said, was an oversight and was not intended as a 'trade-off' as some members of the media were arguing. In the ANC's response, Valli Moosa said that the constitution provided a constitutional order for the country as a whole, and these negotiations were not an opportunity that negotiators should use to grant themselves privileges as individuals. It would lower the status of the constitution if parties, as drafters of the constitution, inserted a provision that was clearly aimed at self-interest rather than the interests of the people as a whole. Therefore, the proposal failed.

The Constitutional Committee then proceeded to agree to a series of amendments dealing with the seat of Parliament, the rights of an arrested person, the definition of 'organs of state', and the commencement of the constitution. The meeting ended at 12:30 p.m., with Kader Asmal paying special tribute to the chairperson and deputy-chairperson for their contribution to the success of the Constitutional Committee. The process of constitution-making in South Africa was unique, and those who had studied constitution-making since the Second World War would know that no other country had followed such a process. The success of the process, he said, was largely due to the role the chairperson had played, and the support the deputy-chairperson had given to the chairperson. Asmal then went on to pay tribute to the support staff in the administration who had often had to work through the night and had provided the Constitutional Committee with quality documentation. This, and the speed with which they had delivered documents, showed that 'a new body cannot only do things right, but can do them well'.

The Constitutional Committee then adjourned at 11:30 p.m. to allow members of the Constitutional Assembly to return and complete the debate. The finalization of outstanding issues and confirmation of sufficient support for the adoption of the constitution several hours later undoubtedly affected the rest of the debates, and the excitement of the negotiators was reflected in the final speeches they made. After agreeing to cut short the proceedings, the Constitutional Assembly went on to adopt the resolution containing amendments that reflected the latest agreements. Around 11 a.m., some ten hours later, the Constitution was adopted.

12   Certification of the final constitution

WITHIN TWENTY-FOUR HOURS of adoption, the executive director of the Constitutional Assembly began receiving calls from the Constitutional Court enquiring how soon the text of the Constitution would be lodged with the Court for its consideration. The Court was intent on dealing with the certification expeditiously. It was also concerned about the enormous caseload it had and wanted to ensure that the process of testing the adopted text was dealt with in the same open manner as the drafting.

The test of compliance with the agreed constitutional principles was an important part of the process of arriving at a final constitutional text. It was as important to the ANC, who had proposed it in the Harare Declaration, as it was to the NP and other minority political parties. These principles offered all parties a guarantee that the final Constitution would be based on principles with which they could identify. This test before the Constitutional Court allowed the negotiating parties, especially those with minority support, to buy into a process of arriving at a final constitutional dispensation and to make a break with the conflict of the past. To provide further assurance, the Constitutional Court was to be the only and final arbiter as to the compliance of the text with the agreed constitutional principles.

Constitutional democracy at work

The Court was in a rather difficult position. The constitutional principles agreed to were essentially political agreements between parties bringing an end to conflict. To make matters worse, a fair number of the thirty-four principles could be interpreted in various ways. Still, the Court had to use these principles to test the constitutional text; and then too, against the background that the text was adopted by an overwhelming majority.[1]

To the credit of the Court, the approach adopted in the directions issued by the Judge President assured that the process of certification was open and transparent:

> The President of the Court, considering it to be in the national interest to deal with the matter as thoroughly yet expeditiously as possible, determined that both written and oral representations would be received and fixed 1 July 1996 as the date for the commencement of oral argument. On Monday 13 May 1996 he issued detailed directions, including a timetable, for its disposal.
>
> The directions included provision for written argument on behalf of the Constitutional Assembly to be lodged with the Court and invited the political parties represented in the Constitutional Assembly that wished to submit oral argument to notify the Court and to lodge their written grounds of objection. Although there was no legal provision for anyone else to make representations, because of the importance and unique nature of the matter, the directions also invited any other body or person wishing to object to the certification of the text to submit a written objection.
>
> The directions required objectors to specify their grounds of objection and to indicate the Constitutional Principles allegedly contravened by the text. The Court, through the good offices of the Constitutional Assembly, also published notices (in all official languages) inviting objections and explaining the procedure to be followed by prospective objectors. Each written objection was studied and, if it raised an issue germane to the certification exercise which had not yet been raised, detailed written argument was invited.[2]

These procedures met with significant success. Five political parties tabled objections to the certification: the ACDP, the DP, the IFP (which was joined by the KwaZulu/Natal Province), the NP, and the Conservative Party. The report of the Court as contained in its judgment is as follows:

> Objections were also lodged by or on behalf of a further 84 private parties. The political parties and the Constitutional Assembly as well as 27 of the other bodies or persons were afforded a right of audience.[3] In deciding whom to invite to present oral argument, we were guided by the nature, novelty, cogency and importance of the points raised in the written submissions. Interest groups and individuals propounding a particular contention were permitted to submit argument jointly notwithstanding the absence of a formal link between them. The underlying principle was to hear the widest possible spectrum of potentially relevant views. . . .
>
> Hearings commenced on Monday 1 July 1996 and continued until Thursday 11 July 1996. Individual objectors were heard in person; otherwise representation was permitted through persons ordinarily entitled to appear before the Court or through a duly authorised member of the organisation concerned. . . . In the process all relevant issues were fully canvassed in argument.[4]

The Court delivered its judgment on 6 September 1996. The judges found that the text adopted on 8 May 1996 did not comply with the constitutional principles in eight respects. Notwithstanding this, the judgment concluded with two observations: 'The first is to reiterate that the Constitutional Assembly has drafted a constitutional text which complies with the overwhelming majority of the requirements of the Constitutional Principles. The second is that the instances of non-compliance which we have listed . . . although singly and collectively important, should present no significant obstacle to the formulation of a text which complies fully with those requirements'.[5]

Amending the text

The judgment did not spark any controversy; instead, it was hailed as a victory for constitutional democracy. None of the shortcomings in the text were regarded as fatal. The judgment did not give rise to a crisis and neither did it negate in any way the fruits of the previous two years of negotiation. Ironically, the return of the text presented the Constitutional Assembly with some unique opportunities, the main one being that it was now possible to make another attempt at bringing the IFP back on board, which was a distinct possibility. One of the more serious flaws in the adopted text was the finding that the powers of the provinces were substantially reduced compared to those in the interim constitution.

The return of the text also allowed the drafters a chance to improve the text. The process of drafting during the last fourteen days before 8 May had been extremely difficult because the text was being continuously amended. A constitutional text, like any other legal draft, is a cohesive document, and changes effected in one part of the text invariably affected another. This is particularly so in the use of particular words for legal and linguistic consistency.[6] Within forty-eight hours of the judgment two independent legal opinions analysed it and identified the amendments necessary to cure the defects in the constitutional text. The Management Committee met on 12 September to consider the judgment and decide on a way forward.[7]

A representative of the IFP, Peter Smith, who was assisted by Walter Felgate, attended this meeting. Smith insisted that their presence in the meeting did not mean that they had reviewed their decision to boycott the process, and that they were there as no more than observers. Smith explained that the IFP was to review its position at a meeting of their National Council that was to be held on 21 and 22 September. Considering a possible return to the process, the IFP felt it could not afford to ignore developments in the Constitutional Assembly.[8] Because parties believed that this was an opportunity for the IFP to end its boycott, they agreed to the request made by the IFP that negotiations only take place from 25 September.

The first issue that required the attention of the committee was the question of time-frames. Both the Freedom Front and the IFP repeated their previous positions that no deadline be set for obtaining certification, for they felt that the exercise was far too important to rush. The general view that prevailed was that it was important to ensure that the Constitution be certified before January 1997. Should this not happen, it would not be possible to establish the National Council of Provinces or implement any other aspects of the Constitution in 1997.[9] There was a sense among members that it was necessary to finalize the Constitution as soon as possible, and by so doing allow members of the assembly to redirect their time more profitably to the crucial demands of governance and transformation.

The Management Committee also considered whether the Constitutional Assembly should entertain issues for negotiation that fell outside those flaws identified by the Constitutional Court. This was an important question, as the amended text had to be lodged by 7 October if the Court was to consider certification and give its judgment before the end of 1996.[10] The Committee concluded that these negotiations should focus solely on those amendments that were necessary to secure certification. The Committee was also required to consider the process of effecting the amendments, which could only be done with a proper mandate from a full sitting of the Constitutional Assembly that was scheduled for 20 September. It was agreed that the Constitutional Committee be convened to negotiate the amendments and table its report with the Assembly for adoption at its earliest possible convenience. In this regard, the Management Committee proposed the formation of two subcommittees, each of which had to be supported with technical assistance. When work began in the subcommittees on 25 September two sets of draft formulations were tabled. The first provided suggested amendments to address the defects identified in the judgment of the Constitutional Court, while the second proposed a technical refinement of the text, adding value to it but not effecting any substantive changes.[11] This proved to be a very useful time-saving device.

The first subcommittee was chaired by Mavivi Myakayaka-Manzini and dealt with the Bill of Rights, the Public Protector, the Auditor-General, and public administration. The second subcommittee was chaired by Pravin Gordhan and dealt with provincial powers and local government. Those clauses immunizing the Labour Relations Act and Truth and Reconciliation Commission and militating against certification were addressed by mere deletion.[12] Regarding the Public Protector and Auditor-General, the Constitutional Court stated that, for them to be truly independent, measures more stringent than an ordinary majority were required to remove the two office-bearers.[13] The Court required a higher majority of two thirds.

The Constitutional Court had no complaint with only one national Public Service Commission, as opposed to provincial commissions as afforded in the interim constitution. However, it did feel that the powers and functions of the commission had to be detailed without compromising provincial autonomy in the appointment and staffing of provincial administration.[14] The remedy here involved the virtual redrafting of section 196 with detailed provision for the powers and function of the Public Service Commission. Section 197 was also amended to clearly give provincial governments the power to recruit, appoint, promote, transfer, and dismiss members of the public service in their administrations.

While the Court did not object to the state of emergency clause, it did recommend that a clear distinction be drawn between derogable and non-derogable rights in a more thoughtful and rational way.[15] Section 37(5) was therefore improved and accordingly amended. On the question of collective bargaining, the Court complained that the right of individual employers to collective bargaining had to be secured.[16] This was addressed by an amendment of section 23(5) which read: 'Every trade union, employers' organisation and employer has the right to engage in collective bargaining. National legislation may be enacted to regulate collective bargaining. To the extent that the legislation may limit a right in this Chapter, the limitation must comply with section 36(1)'.[17]

The complaint of the Constitutional Court with regard to the constitutional amendment procedures was that these should require special procedures in addition to a special majority. The Court suggested that this be done by way of involving both houses in the amendment procedure, giving proper notice periods, and by allowing extra time for reflection on the amendments proposed.[18] In addition, the Court insisted that the Bill of Rights also be entrenched. Amendment to it should require greater majorities than ordinary amendments, or even the involvement of both houses.[19] Because of the clear guidance given by the Court, amendment of these offending provisions did not prove difficult to achieve.

Of all the provisions that failed the test of compliance, it was with the area of provincial powers that the Court was most concerned. There were several respects in which provincial powers were affected, the most important of these being the ability of the National Assembly to override provincial legislation that came at the expense of the powers of a province. This was with regard to the appointment of provincial police commissioners, weaker provincial powers on local government, and the inability of provinces to determine the payment of traditional leaders.[20] Regarding the National Council of Provinces, the Court insisted that the collective powers of provinces had to be enhanced. This was in relation to the National Assembly's ability to override an objection by the council, and the participation of the Council in the election or impeachment of the President. The council should also have the right to refer bills to the Constitutional Court.[21]

The Court also found that the powers of a province relating to policing were diminished, affecting the ability of a province to issue directions to provincial commissioners, to approve or veto these commissioners' appointments, and to institute legal proceedings against them.[22] The powers of a province in respect of the Public Service Commission and its ability to influence the role played by traditional leaders were also reduced.[23] The Court concluded that the powers of provinces were substantially less than and inferior to the powers they had enjoyed previously under the interim constitution, and that this was in violation of the constitutional principles. Once again, because of the clear guidance found in the Court's lucid judgment, it became immediately apparent what amendments ought to be made.

In addressing the failure to obtain certification, there were only three areas in the text that required complete redrafting as opposed to mere amendment. These were the sections dealing with the police, local government, and the public administration. Of these sections, the negotiation of the provincial powers on policing and local government proved to be the most difficult.

The primary issue regarding the policing provisions was the ability of the province to control the appointment and thus secure the loyalty of the provincial police commissioner. The Western Cape, where the NP had won a majority in the elections, championed the cause of greater powers for the provinces on policing. In particular the Premier, Hernus Kriel, was insistent on negotiating greater powers on behalf of the NP. This reflected the new relationship between the ANC and the NP since the NP's decision to leave the government of national unity and become an opposition party. More particularly, it also reflected the power relationship within the NP and the resurgence of its right-wing faction. Ironically, there was strong support for Kriel's position on this matter from within some of the provinces under ANC control.

It eventually became clear that Kriel's aggression had more to do with asserting his role within the NP than securing greater provincial powers. In terms of the agreement, the determination of national policing policy is arrived at only after consulting provincial governments and taking into account provincial policing needs and priorities as determined by the provincial executives. In addition, provision was made for different policies in respect of the different provinces after taking into account their needs and priorities. Regarding political control of the police, while the President would appoint the national commissioner, the national commissioner would only appoint provincial commissioners with the concurrence of the provincial executive. Only in the case of disagreement would the national minister mediate between the parties. Provinces were also entitled to institute proceedings for the removal, transfer, or dismissal of a provincial commissioner if their executive were to lose confidence in such an appointee.

The provisions on local government proved equally problematic.

Constitutional Principle XXIV required a framework for local government in the text, which had to identify the different categories of local government a province could establish, and make provision for appropriate fiscal powers and functions for each of the categories. Furthermore, it had to convey an overall structural design within which local government structures were to function, and indicate how local government executives were to be appointed. Such a structural design had to include how decisions were to be taken and the formal legislative procedures involved.[24] In this regard, it was also necessary to remove the power of a local government to excise taxes.[25]

Negotiating the amendment of the local government provisions also proved difficult. There was a considerable amount of criticism of this section of the Court's judgment, for many felt that the Court did not fully understand the conceptualization of the new structures of local government. In its interpretation of the constitutional principles the Court insisted on a level of detail that required crystal ball gazing into one of the most important aspects of government. The difficulty was that local government was in the process of transition and evolution. New structures had to be established where none existed before and old structures that existed had to be radically transformed. It was therefore not only difficult to provide detail, but such detail could become an impediment in the course of implementation. The issue also led to the reopening of very difficult debates which negotiators were keen to avoid.

Nevertheless, the negotiations on this subject proved to be useful in that the agreed text was a vast improvement on the old text, and did away with the vagueness that had existed before. The new text clearly distinguished three categories of local government structures and set out the internal procedures within which they should function. It was also fortuitous in offering an opportunity to amend the transitional measures on the establishment of new structures by taking into account budgetary realities. The problem was that the new Constitution was planned to come into effect immediately before the budget votes. The budget of the country would already be determined and it would be impossible to accommodate the establishment of the new institutions financially. In addition, the Local Government Transition Act was settled on a multi-party basis as part of the negotiated transition. This act basically allowed for structures that afforded traditional leaders ex officio status. More particularly, it was necessary to ensure that the amended text on local government retained the prevailing structures until April 1999. This was of particular relevance to the IFP, as it directly affected its constituency.

The IFP was still never certain as to whether it was in or out of the process. Members of the IFP attended a number of meetings and participated in bilateral and multilateral discussions with the ANC and other parties. They also insisted that meetings renegotiate matters long settled which did not offend any constitutional principle; these requests were rejected though, for to accede to them would have taken the process back to the beginning again by allowing parties to question every agreement. Thus, shortly before the completion of the amendment exercise, the IFP for the last time abruptly withdrew its participation.

The subcommittees tabled their reports with the Constitutional Committee and the amendments were approved for adoption. The Constitutional Assembly met at its last sitting on 11 October to pass the amended text. Once again, the IFP failed to attend and lost its opportunity to either abstain from voting or oppose the resolution. The amended text was passed with the same overwhelming majority as on 8 May.

Certification of the Constitution

The revised text was tabled before the Constitutional Court as soon as it was passed. The Court was required to examine afresh whether the text complied with the constitutional principles, which is what sections 73A(1), (2), and (3) read with section 71(2) of the interim constitution dictated.[26] Nevertheless, the Court could not ignore what had gone before. In particular the judges had to approach the present certification exercise in the context of their previous judgment on the matter, for the Constitutional Assembly had been obliged to take these into account in drafting the amended text. Upon receipt of the request for certification the Court issued directions similar to those given for the previous certification proceedings.[27] The Court also directed the Constitutional Assembly to publish the directions of the Court as widely as possible and to make copies of the amended text freely available. The Court subsequently issued further directions indicating a schedule for hearings, to commence on 18 November 1996.

Although the two certification exercises were essentially the same, there was one significant difference.[28] While any objector could raise any issue, whether previously considered or not, the proponent of such a contention had a formidable task.[29] The previous certification exercise had been conducted in the light of very extensive written and oral submissions emanating from the broad spectrum of South African society.[30] Because of the thoroughness of the process, the Court found it unlikely that an issue of importance had been overlooked.

The Court went on to further state that:

By like token it is possible that we erred in our analysis of an objection and wrongly concluded that the provision of the text to which it was directed complied with the CP's [constitutional principles]. Many of the questions raised at the time were difficult and we have no claim to infallibility. Nevertheless we cannot vacillate. The sound jurisprudential basis for the policy that a court should adhere to its previous decisions unless they are shown to be clearly wrong is no less valid here than is generally the case. Indeed, having regard to the need for finality in the certification process[31] and in view of the virtually identical composition of the Court that considered the questions barely three months ago, that policy is all the more desirable here.

Furthermore the procedure prescribed by s73A of the interim constitution clearly contemplates interaction between the Constitutional Assembly and this Court in relation to the amendment of a constitutional text found not to comply with the CP's. Subsection 73A(1) obliges the Court to give the Constitutional Assembly 'the reasons for its finding' of non-compliance, while the succeeding subsection requires the Constitutional Assembly to pass an amended text 'taking into account the reasons of the Constitutional Court'. We accordingly tried to make plain in the CJ [court's judgment] precisely in what respects – and why – we found that the text failed to measure up to the CP's. And it was probably also the reason why the amended text bears every sign that the Constitutional Assembly took the CJ as the blueprint for amending the text.

NOTE

Only two of the political parties represented in the Constitutional Assembly, the Democratic Party and the Inkatha Freedom Party, lodged written submissions objecting to certification. The NP formally announced that it did not intend objecting to certification of the amended text. The province of KwaZulu/Natal and eighteen private individuals and interest groups also lodged written submissions, while the Constitutional Assembly in turn filed written submissions in support of certification. The DP, the IFP, KwaZulu/Natal, and the Constitutional Assembly presented oral arguments at the hearing, which continued for some two and a half days. Although their respective written submissions were not co-extensive, the IFP made common cause with KwaZulu/Natal.

A crucial difference in approach between the two exercises in certification was that in the last attempt the Constitutional Assembly was not asked to explain why the text should be certified. Instead, there was an implicit presumption that the text should be certified. The assembly therefore only had to answer the arguments of those who felt that it should not be certified. The Constitutional Court delivered its judgment on 4 December 1996. In certifying the amended text of the Constitution, the Court stated in conclusion:

NOTE

> In the CJ this Court held that '[s]een in the context of the totality of provincial power' the powers of the provinces in the text taken as a whole were substantially less than or substantially inferior to the powers vested in them under the interim Constitution.[32] This would

not have been the conclusion were it not for the provisions of text 146(2) and (4) which tilted the balance against the provinces.[33]

We are satisfied that:

(a) The amendments to the text contained in the amended text 146(2) and (4) effectively restore the balance referred to in the preceding paragraph.

(b) The amendments to provincial police powers contained in the amended text 205-8 increase the powers of the provinces in respect of police services compared with those accorded to the provinces in terms of the text.

(c) The provisions of the amended text in regard to the Public Service Commission do not materially affect the balancing process.

(d) The combined effect of the changes made in the amended text is such as to produce a conclusion different to that at which we arrived in respect of the text. In particular those relating to provincial police powers and to the terms of the override contained in the amended text 146 have played a material role in this change of assessment.

(e) In the result, the powers and functions of the provinces in terms of the amended text are still less than or inferior to those accorded to the provinces in terms of the interim Constitution, but not substantially so.[34]

The signing ceremony

While the signing of the Constitution into law was primarily an executive act, it was thought that the Constitutional Assembly's administration was best placed to deal with the planning of it. Conceptually, the event had to be dignified and solemn as opposed to celebratory, for the President was to sign into law a constitution, not just any ordinary law, a constitution that was democratically arrived at in the most effective public participation process in the country and in pursuance of a mandate given by the electorate when they voted in April 1994.

There were two aspects to the signing: the date and the venue, both of which, it was argued, had to have some historical significance. For the date, the choices were 10 December, International Human Rights Day, or 12 February, the date of Mandela's release. Since Parliament was scheduled to open on 7 February, it was not possible for the ceremony to take place later, and the date of 10 December was accordingly decided upon. Regarding the venue, it was argued that the ceremony had to take place outside of traditional government precincts and among the people: in other words, the event should be taken to the people and not vice versa. To this extent, the Constitutional Assembly favoured rural and disadvantaged communities, and it was in this context that the choice of Sharpeville, in Vereeniging, was logical and symbolically perfect.[35] It was in Vereeniging on 31 May 1902 that the Treaty of Vereeniging between the Boers and British had been signed. This treaty had brought to an end a bitter anti-imperialist war and had allowed South Africa to be united as one sovereign territory from four independent states. It had paved the way for the first constitutional dispensation; and the eighth clause of this treaty effectively sealed the fate of the black majority in that it ensured that black people remained disenfranchised.

In much the same way as the Treaty of Vereeniging laid the basis for the first constitutional dispensation, the interim constitution, also regarded as a peace treaty, laid the basis for the final Constitution. Since this history began in Vereeniging, it certainly displayed the full circle of constitutional history by ending there as well. It is in this sense that the two treaties appear as bookends to a history that starts in division and conflict and ends in reconciliation. In more recent history, Vereeniging was an area that witnessed much political conflict and strife, gaining international notoriety after the Sharpeville massacre on 16 June 1960. In 1996 Sharpeville was one of the most economically depressed regions in the country with a sprawling informal settlement and high unemployment; the Vereeniging area, of which Sharpeville is a part, also remained a largely right-wing stronghold.

The decision to hold the event in Sharpeville on 10 December was only approved in mid-November. Since the Constitution had not been certified by then, it would have been disrespectful to the Constitutional Court to plan publicly for the signing ceremony to take place before certification. Accordingly, arrangements for a programme to mark International Human Rights Day were made, and in the event that the Constitution was certified, it would also be signed then. It was therefore only on 4 December when the certification took place that the planning for the signing ceremony was made public.

The image and message for the day, in addition to marking International Human Rights Day, was the delivery on a mandate given by the electorate in 1994. Thus, it was the responsibility of the chairperson of the Constitutional Assembly to deliver a report on the mandate given and then to present the Constitution to the President for his signature. After extensive planning within extremely tight time-frames the event was a tremendous success. Today, Sharpeville and Vereeniging will not be known only for the sad history that they engendered for so long, but more importantly for the signing of South Africa's new and final Constitution.

13

The public participation process

IT IS THEREFORE IMPORTANT that as we put our vision to the country, we should do so directly, knowing that people out there want to be part of the process and will be responding, because in the end the drafting of the constitution must not be the preserve of the 490 members of this Assembly. It must be a constitution which they feel they own, a constitution that they know and feel belongs to them. We must therefore draft a constitution that will be fully legitimate, a constitution that will represent the aspirations of our people.

M. C. Ramaphosa, chairperson, Constitutional Assembly, 24 January 1995.[1]

The people of South Africa must be involved. They must be consulted in an organised fashion, on specific issues in order for the new law to be sensitive to and shaped by their realities, and for it to address these realities.

Ms B. Mbete-Kgositsile, MP, African National Congress, Constitutional Assembly, 15 August 1994.

Our priority is to ensure that the process is not confined to these walls. We need to ensure that the communities along the Limpopo Valley also have their views heard in this Chamber and in our committee rooms. The final draft must reflect the views of our people in the villages, informal settlements, hostels, factories, towns and cities.

O. C. Chabane, MP, African National Congress, Constitutional Assembly, 24 January 1995.

An important difference between this exercise and the negotiation at the World Trade centre is that all the proceedings of the Constitutional Assembly are open to the public. Submissions have been invited – and two million received! Information on the Constitutional Assembly is available on the Internet. And you have solicited the views of ordinary citizens in hundreds of meetings around the country. Whilst proceedings may at times appear cumbersome, they have given real meaning to the phrase 'participatory democracy'.

Chief Emeka Anyaoku, Commonwealth Secretary-General, address to International Round Table on Democratic Constitutional Development, 17 July 1995.

The stated sentiments of key role-players and influential observers such as these shaped the spirit of the public participation process. As the process manifested itself in the public sphere, in newspapers, on television and radio, and even in casual conversation, these kinds of affirming, cautionary and guiding statements maintained a high level of public interest and political accountability in negotiations. Emeka Anyaoku's words, especially, are a fitting tribute to the Constitutional Assembly's programmes for comprehensive public participation. By all accounts the Assembly's efforts were a resounding success that presented many valuable lessons for government and democracy in South Africa because, even though the elected Constitutional Assembly did have a legitimate mandate in terms of which it was entitled to draft the final constitution, it knew that this was not all it needed.

One of the stated objectives of the Constitutional Assembly was that the process of constitution-making had to be transparent, open, and credible.[2] Moreover, the final constitution required an enduring quality and had to enjoy the support of all South Africans irrespective of ideological differences.[3] Born out of a history of political conflict and mistrust, the credibility of the final constitution was an important aim, and as such it depended on a process of constitution-making through which people could claim ownership of the constitution. It was also necessary to placate the fears and concerns of minorities and yet find favour with the majority. In short, the constitutional foundations of democracy had to be placed beyond question, which made it essential to embark upon a programme of public participation. The South African people not only had to feel a part of the process, but the content of the final constitution itself had to be representative of their views. In addition, the process had to be seen to be transparent and open.

The programme developed was daring and difficult. The odds were stacked against its successful implementation, for there was no precedent for such public participation anywhere in the world. The directorate, whose responsibility it was to establish an administration for the Constitutional Assembly, was only appointed in August 1994, three months after the process of negotiation and consultation should have begun, and it was not until the second quarter of 1995 that the full complement of staff was in place. The time available for the project was short, and budgetary constraints meant that funds were never sufficient.[4]

The challenge was to find ways to enter into effective dialogue and consultation with a population of more than 40 million people. South Africa had a large rural population, most of whom were illiterate and did not have access to print or electronic media. Moreover, South Africa had never had a culture of constitutionalism, or human rights for that matter, which accordingly made it difficult to enter into consultation with communities that did not recognize the importance of a constitution. Thus, without the necessary empowerment, consultation would have been hollow and without meaning.

The timing of the exercise made it even more difficult. The process of drafting the constitution followed closely after South Africa's 'liberation' election. Therefore, the programme of public participation had to compete for public attention with the process of transformation. In particular, the programme had to take place during two local government elections, the Masakhane campaign, the Reconstruction and Development Programme (RDP), and various other government programmes.[5] It was also very difficult to make clear in the minds of ordinary members of the public the difference between this process and the growing demand on government for delivery on basic services and election promises. Besides, constitutional debates are often abstract and not likely to attract the interest or attention of a population expecting to be delivered from the evils of apartheid.

Despite these odds, the public participation programme stands out as a monumental exercise, remaining second in effect and extent only to the April 1994 elections. The overwhelming success of the exercise has made it an international point of reference. By empowering civil society to participate in the constitution-making process, the Constitutional Assembly was able to add a new dimension to the concept of democracy in South Africa; that is, a participatory democracy. This set a tough precedent for government and provided a window to what a participatory democracy could achieve.

Creating awareness

The need for a public participation programme was addressed in three ways: community liaison, media liaison, and advertising. This move broke with the convention set in the public service, where departments saw no need for anything more than media liaison for communication with the public. Government saw no need for interaction, dialogue, or consultation with the public it was established to serve, and this allowed for communication in one direction only: from the departments to the public. There was no formal mechanism through which departments of government could be informed of the public's views.

The function of community liaison was to initiate face to face interactive programmes between members of the Constitutional Assembly and the broader public. To ensure effective communication, a Media Department was established, which involved the use of print, radio, and television as well as a national advertising campaign.[6] The primary objectives of the media strategy for the Constitutional Assembly were to inform, educate, stimulate public interest, and create a forum for public participation. An important consideration in implementing the strategy was the optimum use of existing channels of mass communication, effective media liaison, and a national advertising campaign, supplemented by the production of in-house media. A major objective of this strategy was to reach disadvantaged rural communities. Furthermore, it was not sufficient merely to be transparent and, accordingly, the strategy was to actively disseminate information and carry out constitutional education.

The media campaign was launched on 15 January 1995 just before work in the Constitutional Assembly began. Its aim was to raise public awareness about the constitution-making process, encourage individuals and interest groups to make submissions, and publicize constitutional public meetings. The primary message was that an important process was unfolding, and that the outcome of this process would affect the lives of all South Africans, including those of future generations. Every South African was provided with a unique opportunity to take part in it. The specific messages carried in the many advertisements were, 'You've made your mark, now have your say', and 'It's your right to decide your constitutional rights'. Advertisements were run on television, radio, in local newspapers, and on outdoor billboards.[7]

The Community Agency for Social Enquiry (CASE) and Roots Marketing were commissioned by the Constitutional Assembly to undertake a national survey. The purpose of the survey was to assess the penetration and impact of this media campaign and to ascertain public attitudes to key constitutional issues.[8] The results revealed that the Constitutional Assembly media campaign reached 65 per cent of all adult South Africans in the three months between 15 January and 19 April 1995 since it started work. However, the survey also revealed that the public were clearly sceptical about the seriousness of the Constitutional Assembly in calling for their involvement, and about the treatment their submissions would receive. The credibility of the process was obviously an issue that needed some attention. Levels of knowledge about the constitution were fairly high, but a sizable proportion of the population still needed education about the nature and function of a constitution. They also needed information about the Constitutional Assembly and the constitution-making process. Nevertheless, these were still encouraging results.

The success of the strategy was also seen in the number of submissions made: nearly 1.7 million were received. The bulk of these were petitions, however, rather than submissions. The petitions dealt with a wide variety of issues, among them animal rights, abortion, pornography, the death penalty, and the seat of Parliament. Of the submissions received, just over 11 000 were substantive. These were often wide-ranging 'wish lists' that arrived at an early stage in the process when political parties were still developing their thinking on many issues. In whatever form, these submissions were a reflection of the views of a large number of people and could hardly be ignored.

Engaging the public

The Constitutional Assembly's media campaign also advertised the constitutional public meetings that were held. These served two functions: the political actors in the Assembly were able to report on their activities, and the public were invited to voice their views on various issues addressed in negotiation. Each submission was then recorded and transcribed for consideration by the political structures established by the Constitutional Assembly.

Most of these meetings were held with rural and disadvantaged communities, largely because people in these areas did not have access to media to follow the process. Furthermore, they were not equipped to contribute on issues without assistance, so it was necessary to ensure that the programme had an educational orientation. To this end, the Constitutional Education Programme was developed.

This project involved participatory workshops, and worked to consult with local structures of civil society to prepare for each public meeting. Between February and August 1995, twenty-six public meetings were organized in all nine provinces, and more than 200 members of the Constitutional Assembly became involved in them. It was calculated that 20 549 people attended workshops, and 717 organizations participated.

For most people, this was the first occasion on which they were able to directly interact with their elected representatives. More importantly, it was the first time in South Africa that public meetings were held involving politicians, who were previously at war with each other, talking jointly to the people. The public meetings held were extremely successful: discussions were lively, ideas original, and the exchange of views appreciated.[9] These meetings also served to highlight the point that constitutions are about basic values affecting society and should be understood by even the least educated. It was a humbling experience to realize that constitutional debates and issues are not only the domain of the intellectual elite, but that they belong to everyone.

Besides the public meetings held, there was a National Sector Public Hearing Programme. This emerged out of a need for Theme Committees to consult and engage those structures of civil society with an interest in a particular debate; for instance, the different rights in the bill of rights, the judiciary, security services, and institutions supporting constitutional democracy and public administration. The preparation for these hearings was handled by a partnership between the Constitutional Assembly and structures of civil society.[10] This was a deliberate part of the strategy, for it avoided the possible accusation of partiality, and also ensured the greatest possible representativeness at the hearings, and an agenda that was acceptable to all.[11]

The majority of hearings took place within the four weeks between 8 May and 4 June 1995. Given the limited time that the Constitutional Assembly had to develop and implement this programme, it was to its credit that 596 organizations were consulted. In addition, Theme Committees hosted many seminars and workshops when expert opinion and further debate was required on particular issues. Many of these workshops included international experts. The programme of public participation during this period proved extremely successful.[12]

Several other communication tools were used with much success. These included a newsletter, television and radio programmes – all bearing the title *Constitutional Talk* – a telephone talk-line, and an Internet home page.

The television programmes were launched on 24 April and continued till 10 October 1995, in total twenty-five programmes on two SABC channels. The 1996 series of (twelve) programmes was launched on 18 February and continued until 12 May. The format of the programmes allowed representatives from structures of civil society to engage a multi-party panel of Constitutional Assembly members in debate on important issues. Some of the topics for the programmes included the bill of rights, separation of powers, the national anthem and flag, freedom of expression, traditional authorities, and the death penalty.

Radio was an even more effective delivery mechanism, because it could reach more people in both rural and urban areas. In collaboration with the SABC's Educational Directorate, a weekly constitutional education radio talk show was launched on 1 October 1995, comprising hour-long programmes that were broadcast on eight SABC radio stations in eight languages. Constitutional experts appeared as studio guests. These programmes reached over 10 million South Africans each week.

The Constitutional Assembly's official newsletter, *Constitutional Talk*, was produced to provide information to members of the public, by presenting material in a detailed and educative manner. It was usually an eight-page publication produced fortnightly and distributed to 160 000 people. Of this number, 100 000 copies were distributed nationally through taxi ranks and another 60 000 sent to subscribers.[13] This newsletter generated a substantial following by those who were keen to follow the process of constitution-making.

To extend the level of education and information, new communication vehicles such as the telephonic *Constitutional Talk-line* were used.[14] The talk-line enabled people with access to a telephone to get an up-to-date briefing on political discussions. Callers were also able to leave messages requesting information, or to record their comments and submissions. This service was available in English, Afrikaans, Tswana, Xhosa, and Zulu, and over 10 000 people made use of it.[15]

The Constitutional Assembly was one of the first constitutionally established institutions to use the Internet home page. This project was established in conjunction with the University of Cape Town, which assumed responsibility for maintaining it. The home page consisted of a database of all information, including minutes, drafts, opinions, and submissions of the Constitutional Assembly. This too was overwhelmingly successful.[16]

THE REFINED WORKING DRAFT

The *Refined Working Draft* was a complete set of formulations required by a constitution, produced at the end of the work of the Theme Committees. It was a novel approach to what was effectively a first draft of a bill. It provided alternative options to contentious formulations and supporting notes explaining formulations, and was effectively a progress report on the negotiation of the final constitution. It also clearly reflected the way in which the ideas and submissions made were addressed. The distribution of the *Refined Working Draft* took place on 22 November 1995, and over five million copies in user-friendly, tabloid form were distributed throughout the country.[17]

The production of the *Refined Working Draft* required a different level of consultation and public participation. A supporting media campaign was launched with the publication of the *Refined Working Draft* in November 1995, and ran through the period of public debate to 20 February 1996. In this campaign, the public was invited to make further submissions. However, on this occasion the public was asked to comment specifically on the provisions of the *Refined Working Draft*, and the submissions that followed were accordingly much more focused.

While it was necessary to consult with all interested parties during the first phase in producing the *Refined Working Draft*, the second phase required consultations specific to the issues under debate and in contention. To assist in the education process, material about constitutions and the constitution-making process, including posters, copies of the *Constitutional Talk* newsletter, and a booklet entitled *You and Building the New Constitution* were produced. The Constitutional Assembly also produced a pamphlet entitled *Constitutions, Democracy and a Summary of the Working Draft*, in all official languages.

The Constitutional Assembly received 250 000 submissions in the second phase, and again the vast bulk of these were petitions. The petitions dealt with much the same kind of issues as they did in the first phase: the death penalty, sexual orientation, and animal rights in particular. There was much scepticism, however, about the seriousness of the Constitutional Assembly's invitation to the public for written submissions, a scepticism which was also expressed in some of the submissions received. While the Constitutional Assembly was praised for involving the public, some of those who made submissions did wonder whether the politicians would take them seriously.

Once the areas of contention had been identified, negotiations were able to begin. After including the views contained in the submissions, a further edition of the *Refined Working Draft* was produced. This edition recorded where the submissions came from and the formulations that were affected accordingly, as well as reports by the experts who had processed the submissions. A copy of this draft was sent to each person or party that had made a submission.[18]

Finalizing the text

A seven-week campaign in various media was designed to focus on various socio-economic and political issues. The advertising messages for 1996 were 'Securing your freedom. Securing your rights. The new Constitution' and 'One law for one nation. The new Constitution'. These issues were used to highlight the importance and meaning of the new Constitution to South African people.[19]

It was only after the Easter recess of 1996 that the issues of potential deadlock crystallized. To facilitate agreement, parties held various bilateral and multilateral meetings behind closed doors, which did not augur well with the media or civil society. Moreover, consultations with affected interest groups were limited to those areas of deadlock only, and when these consultations did take place, they were carried out with very little time to plan or prepare. With the benefit of an excellent database the organization of these consultations did not prove too difficult, but this did not mean that there were no problems.

The Constitutional Assembly had prided itself throughout on an excellent relationship with the structures of civil society. However, several structures saw themselves outside the process, particularly when political parties found it necessary to hold closed bilateral or multilateral meetings. The complaint was that even if consultations did take place, the agreements reached between the elected representatives in the Constitutional Assembly still had to be open to comment by these structures.[20] Some sectors that lobbied for particular views that were not taken up in agreements became disenchanted with the process itself. Fortunately, this discontent did not reflect the views of the public or the majority of the structures of civil society.

Owning the constitution

In keeping with the principle of accessibility, the final project carried out by the Constitutional Assembly was the distribution of seven million copies of the Constitution in all eleven official languages. The distribution took place in the week of 17-21 March 1997, which was dubbed 'National Constitution Week'. While intended as a mechanism to distribute the Constitution, National Constitution Week also aimed to create the impetus that would ensure that the Constitution became a reference point for all South Africans as the foundation of their democracy. It also had to create a sense of ownership and engender respect for the new Constitution.

A distribution strategy was designed to ensure that the new Constitution was accessible to all South Africans, particularly the historically disadvantaged sectors of society. Four million copies were distributed to secondary schools in the appropriate language of instruction. Two million copies were available at post offices country-wide enabling members of the public to pick up a copy in any of the official languages, while 500 000 copies were distributed to all members of the South African Police Service and South African National Defence Force as well as all members of the Department of Correctional Services and prisoners, in their language preference. A further 500 000 were distributed through structures of civil society.

Each copy of the Constitution was distributed with an illustrated guide in the same language. This guide highlighted key aspects of the Constitution and made many of the legal concepts contained in the Constitution more accessible. Other publications produced included one million copies of a human rights comic, which was distributed to all schools and adult literacy organizations. A teacher's aid to introduce the Constitution to students was also provided to all secondary schools. In addition, tape aids and Braille versions of the Constitution and guide were available for visually impaired members of the community.

To ensure that the distribution of the Constitution made a lasting impact, a campaign was planned to draw on all sectors of society. This took place during National Constitution Week, beginning in the week of 17 March 1997 and culminating on 21 March 1997, South Africa's national Human Rights Day. The idea was to ensure that elected representatives at the national, provincial, and local levels were seen by their constituencies to be 'delivering' the new Constitution.

14 Epilogue: lessons from the negotiating table

THE NEW CONSTITUTION is a celebration of the creativity of the South African people, for few, if any, other countries have been as successful in negotiating a political settlement. This is especially true when one considers the fact that it was a negotiation between parties that held diametrically opposed ideological views.

This negotiation also went on to produce a constitutional framework within which previously warring parties could co-exist to form a vibrant democracy. From the smouldering ashes of a divided society, the basis for a new nation and a new South Africa was produced, which is why this Constitution is referred to as the birth certificate of a nation. The success of the negotiations lay in both the agreed constitutional provisions as well as the process adopted. It was an experience that offers many lessons for other negotiations.

This experience revealed the determination of South Africans not to succumb in times of adversity. When political violence and civil strife most threatened the prospect of peace and democracy, parties were able to strike agreements that proved the prophets of doom wrong, so that, despite the adversity, it was possible to finalize one of the most advanced constitutions in the world with the greatest possible public participation.

To each party the negotiations were as much about constitutional change as pursuing the interests of its constituency. On the other hand, fundamental to the success of the process was its inclusiveness, which clothed the Constitution with the legitimacy it needed as supreme law. Accordingly, the process was designed to give parties the confidence that they could achieve their objectives through negotiation, and that their success was not entirely dependent on their voting strength. Everyone knew that the Constitution could not be drafted unilaterally by the elected majority. Furthermore, the new dispensation provided reassurance by making the Constitutional Court the final arbiter in certifying that the text complied with agreed constitutional principles. Were it not for these mechanisms, it would not have been possible to secure the different parties' commitment to the process of negotiation.

To produce a 'win-win' formula, it was important to recognize and respect the diversity of the interests involved. The point is that while not all parties supported each of the provisions, the rejection of certain unacceptable provisions was not sufficient to warrant the rejection of the entire Constitution. Hence, the Freedom Front chose to abstain from voting rather than oppose its adoption. Differences that were previously responsible for blood-letting became an asset, and differing political, social, cultural, and religious interests were allowed to co-exist. This diversity made the Constitution the vibrant document it is, for it bears the imprint of all parties and the interests of the constituencies they represent.

The method of negotiation used contributed to its success. For instance, in the vigorous public debate on the virtues of federalism as opposed to a unitary state, negotiators began by asking themselves what the qualities were of the state they desired, and this redefined the parameters of the debate and helped to resolve the seemingly intractable question of the distribution of powers between different levels of government. The end product allows for strong provincial and local government without a weak national government. While not all parties were completely satisfied with this, they were not dissatisfied to the extent that they opted out of the whole agreement.

As a whole, the Constitution was drafted by first negotiating areas of potential agreement. What followed was an attempt to bring expression to the interests of individual parties, which gave parties the confidence to buy into the Constitution as a whole. There are several examples of this in both the interim and the final constitutions. The interim constitution established a Volkstaat Council and a principle permitting the notion of self-determination, a compromise that convinced right-wingers to vote in 1994 and pursue their interests within the framework of the Constitution. In addition, a provision establishing the Commission for the Promotion and Protection of Cultural and Religious Communities found its way into the final Constitution. The result was that the legitimacy of the final Constitution was beyond right-wing contest. Similar compromises were reached on the clauses dealing with property, language, education, and minority parties. However, the accommodation of minority interests did not come at the expense of the majority.

Furthermore, several creative mechanisms balanced the interests of the majority with those of the minority and thus facilitated agreement. Set time-frames and a deadlock-breaking mechanism ensured that the final Constitution was timeously completed. A further mechanism *JUDGES* ensured that the majority party would not be able to appoint all judges without referring to the smaller parties. Were it not for mechanisms such as these, it would not have been possible to resolve the conflicts of the past or draft a constitution for the future.

The lessons learnt from the process of constitutional negotiation obviously cannot be applied dogmatically to any other situation. However, if considered carefully, they may, for instance, benefit those engaged in the resolution of conflict between labour and capital at an industry level. Without being too presumptuous, there may be room for employers and employees within an industry to go beyond merely negotiating the relationship or conflict between them. As with political negotiations, it may even be possible to negotiate a framework within which parties associated with an industry may be able to co-exist without ignoring their fundamental or inherent differences. It may also be possible to secure improved productivity levels and a vibrant economy, without compromising either the workers' struggle for better conditions or the employers' quest for higher profits.

The human side of negotiating

The process of negotiations is often discussed using abstract accounts of complex constitutional issues, and it is consequently easy to forget about the actors responsible for producing this miracle in South

African history. It is only when one considers the state of civil conflict, the deep mistrust that existed, and the abstract constitutional ideas that had to be dealt with, that it is possible to discover that the political leaders responsible for negotiating the new constitutional dispensation were extraordinary human beings.

Far-reaching personal and political mistrust existed between political leaders to start with. The early talks about talks between the ANC and the NP government were generally carried out by those with a background in the intelligence services, right until formal negotiations began in 1991. The theory was that people with an intelligence background would know the people on the 'other side' best. However, it was not too long before the actors realized that the negotiators from 'the other side' were not evil or intractable. With the advent of the bosberaad in December 1992 negotiators got to spend time with each other informally over several days, which helped tremendously in allowing them to discover the people they were negotiating with. One of the highlights of the bosberaad at D'Nyala was a late night performance by Pik Botha in the boma (rough enclosure) around a fire, berating the NP for wanting to hold on to power for too long and the ANC for wanting too much power too soon. Then there were Jacob Zuma's endless tales from Zulu folklore, the hysterical jokes of Hernus Kriel, Joe Slovo's cracks about socialists, his ability to sing the Internationale in various languages, and his early morning swim with Leon Wessels and Sam de Beer. This shared time did a great deal to remove the scales of prejudice from the participants' eyes, for they recognized that they all had common fears and aspirations.

Of course, this did not mean that they spared each other during their debates. It is hard to forget Mandela's fiery attack on De Klerk at CODESA I. During the closing moments of the negotiation of the Record of Understanding, Cyril Ramaphosa and Roelf Meyer exchanged such harsh words that the entire agreement hung in the balance. Such differences were not only between parties either, for there were several clashes between negotiators from within the same party. But these moments were always the cue for a tea break, and it was during these breaks that discussions were usually put back on track.

Over time negotiators began to learn to separate their political differences from their growing respect for each other as people. They learnt how to laugh together and at each other. They joked about the time an angry Kobie Coetsee wanted to find Mac Maharaj and Fanie van der Merwe and got their names confused by referring to them as 'Fac and Manie'. They joked about Kader Asmal's use of words such as 'lugubrious' and 'lacunae' in debate, and they joked about the conservatism of Kobie Coetsee and the debating style of Zola Skweyiya.

Quite aside from their political differences, which were substantial, it was with this mutual respect that the negotiations graduated from the World Trade Centre to the Constitutional Assembly. The difference was that after the 1994 elections all negotiators espoused a common nationalism. At the end of meetings a special place was reserved for wishing our rugby and soccer teams well in their international matches, and negotiators rejoiced together at the success of our teams when they won and were saddened by defeats. Often, meetings only started after some discussion about the performance of our sporting teams, and then proceeded only with repeated interruptions for the latest scores.

During their darkest moments, when negotiations seemed to falter and deadlock loomed, negotiators never failed to find something to make light of the moment. On several occasions technical advisers drafted spoof clauses with witty puns on phrases like 'organs of state', at about three in the morning.

Despite the difficult nature of the negotiations, particularly when deadlock loomed, Cyril Ramaphosa's masterful chairing of meetings ensured that negotiators never lost their good humour. His personality, charm, and wit enabled him to deal with difficult and unhappy people from all parties. He was able to command the respect of all and able to steer the process through very difficult waters. More importantly, no matter how tired negotiators were after two years spent negotiating and no matter how difficult the issues at hand, they never failed in their respect for one another.

Special mention must also be made of the trust and mutual respect that developed between Cyril Ramaphosa and Roelf Meyer. They created a relationship of trust that buoyed the process through some of its most dire moments. It was a relationship which developed into the official 'channel' between the ANC and the NP. The same could be said of the relationship between Mac Maharaj and S. S. 'Fanie' van der Merwe at the secretariat.

The negotiations succeeded not simply out of compromise, but because individuals from opposing ends of the political spectrum were able to trust one another. Were it not for their political maturity, it would not have been possible for them to guide the conflict-ridden country through its stormiest waters. To have succeeded at this task was a great feat in itself, but to have done so with the humanity that they did can only make South Africans proud of the leadership they elected to draft the final Constitution.

Reflecting the soul of the nation

The final Constitution is the birth certificate of a new nation – yet the issues it deals with are not new. It is the single most important document in the lives of South Africa's people – yet it is not perfect or free of controversy. It is a triumph over adversity – yet it cautions not to be boastful and repeat the mistakes of the past. Indeed, the new Constitution does represent the growing soul of a new nation. The Constitution was negotiated over a period of two years, but the ideas it contains are as old as South Africa itself. The Constitution was negotiated mainly by seven political parties, but while it is the product of an agreement between political parties it also represents the interests of the majority of South Africans.

The vigorous debate on the question of a unitary or federal state, for instance, was not new. Ironically, this debate took place at the first National Convention South Africa held to draft a new constitution in 1909. Then, the idea of unification won the day over federation. Coming a full circle, this debate was finally resolved in the final Constitution with a dispensation allowing for strong provincial governments without weakening national government.

Evidence of the fears and aspirations of various sectors in society abounds in the Constitution. Some of these relate to the different forms of discrimination people had experienced, the need for affirmative action, the importance of equality, the desire for self-determination, the importance of effective checks and balances, the need to ensure political control over the security forces, and the need for accountability and transparency and respect for cultural diversity.

Of particular significance is the recognition of the role of civil society and the protection granted to individuals and cultural and religious communities. An entire chapter of the Constitution has been dedicated to institutions supporting constitutional democracy. These institutions include the Human Rights and Gender Equality Commissions, the Public Protector, the Auditor-General, and the Commission for the Promotion and Protection of Cultural and Religious Communities. A strong Constitutional Court also protects the interests of the individual and communities.

However, the vibrancy of different interests and ideas can best be seen in the Bill of Rights. The interests of the ANC and the PAC and their constituencies in the reconstruction and transformation of society are clearly reflected in the catalogue of socio-economic rights. The DP's traditional stance on individual rights, such as freedom of expression, is also present. The PAC's principled positions on fundamental rights and the rights of those detained and arrested also have a special place. The interests of the NP were secured by tempering the clauses on property, labour relations, education, and culture. What is perhaps of importance is the influence of civil society, especially religious, human rights, business, labour, and women's groupings, on the various clauses.

What is also striking about these provisions is the emphasis on public participation in legislative processes, which was a lesson learnt from the very process of drafting the new Constitution and the success of its public participation campaign. Finally, there is a significant international influence evident in the Constitution. This was in part a response to South Africa's long years of isolation, but in the main was an attempt to ensure that the Constitution was comparable with the most advanced constitutions of the world. The Bill of Rights was influenced by the most recent developments and is therefore one of the most advanced in the world.

The German constitution was also influential, particularly regarding the principle of co-operative governance. This principle, which is based on a strong provincial dispensation, ensures that all levels of government co-operate with each other for the greater good of the country as a whole. The role and status of the civil services internationally were also thoroughly researched before formulations were finalized.

Senior negotiators from all parties visited a number of different countries in a bid to study different models. Similarly, leading international experts in a number of fields were invited to make presentations. This experience ensured that the Constitution was not only comparable with the best in the world, but could become a point of reference in constitutional debates internationally.

A vision of a better future

The constitution of a country is a sacred document, for it represents the values and aspirations of a nation. The South African Constitution represents the end of an era and the dawn of a new chapter, one that contains a vision of a better future. Until 1994, South Africa's Parliament was sovereign, which meant that Parliament was entitled to pass virtually any law it wished. This changed only when the new dispensation became a constitutional democracy.

The Constitution is the supreme law of the land, the yardstick by which all other laws are judged and tested. It sets out the rules by which government is obliged to run and how it is accountable to the ordinary people who elect it. Any citizen who is aggrieved by any law or any aspect of the conduct of government is entitled to seek the assistance of the Constitutional Court in calling government to order.

Sadly, soon after the first democratic elections the country experienced a devastating tyranny of rampant, violent crime. Armed villains appeared to continue their trade in death and misery with such contempt that citizens felt obliged to take the law into their own hands. The electorate demanded action by the government and its security forces.

The victory of democracy over apartheid and the establishment of a new government and advanced Constitution appeared hollow, for the police appeared to be hamstrung by a Constitution that demanded rights for alleged criminals too. The rising chorus of voices in society demanding the reimposition of the death penalty – and a corresponding change to the Constitution or the judgment of the Constitutional Court – reached a deafening crescendo.

However, it is up to government to be visibly successful in combating crime in all the ways it can under the Constitution: in effective policing, in efficient and impartial judicial systems, in secure correctional facilities, and in raising the standards of living of its citizens. If it falls short in this regard, it is important to resist the easy temptation of looking to amend the Constitution for solutions, for such change would deprive the Constitution of the very respect that it requires to thrive. It is often a difficult reality that the Constitution grants the same rights to all. The Constitution cannot afford to discriminate. Unless it accepts the equality, universality, and indivisibility of rights, how can society truly differ from its state under apartheid?

The final Constitution is one of the most advanced in the world, with a bill of rights second to none. As such, it enables South Africans to create and enjoy one of the most vibrant democracies in the world; but, like any other law, the Constitution is only as good as its citizens allow it to be. The Constitution does no more than set out rights, the rules by which government is run, the structures of such a government, and the parameters within which laws can be made and government conducted. No matter how dynamic any law may be, unless the government is able to implement and enforce that law it will lose its value. Similarly, no matter how wonderful the Constitution may be, unless it is respected by all – government and citizens alike – it will not be of much value. Laws do not make a better society, people do. Law can only be of assistance in empowering people to achieve their aspirations.

While a law depends primarily on government to implement and enforce it, the Constitution requires everyone's undivided respect. Democracy thrives on the existence of different ideological, religious, or cultural values. No matter what these differences may be, it is crucial that the people of South Africa unite around a common respect for the Constitution. This does not in the least suggest that the Constitution is perfect, for it is not, and the assumption that it could be is naive. There may well arise a need for improvement and a need to incorporate new values and new rights. In fact, these developments will depend on the vibrancy and éclat of the democracy it helps establish in ensuring the accountability and respectability of government. The Constitution provides the necessary instruments to ensure that the elected government remains answerable to the electorate.

That electorate's involvement is a sobering yet exciting part of the history of the Constitution. For the first time in South Africa, ordinary people began to realize that they had the ability to influence laws and the government. There was a ground swell of interest among citizens in matters which were previously the exclusive preserve of those in government. In other words, the country grasped that old principle of democracy: a government of the people, by the people, for the people. This is the fundamental ingredient required to ensure that the vision of a better South Africa – which is what the Constitution represents – becomes a reality.

Despite these hard won, sturdy old principles of democracy, it would be foolhardy to become complacent. The Constitution like any organism requires constant nourishment, which can only come from the respect of every one of its citizens. It is vital that they always be vigilant, to ensure that the values contained in the Constitution are upheld. In this regard, the roles of the judiciary, civil society, and the electorate are pivotal, for unless they carry out their responsibilities scrupulously, the very essence of democracy will be quickly eroded. This need imposes an added obligation on both government and civil society, that of the continuous education of the public. Ordinary citizens need to be empowered to understand what their rights are and how to access those institutions capable of providing redress to legitimate grievances. For this reason, it is necessary to continue to build on the success of the Constitutional Assembly and the programmes that it put into place. In the final analysis, we must always remember that the Constitution was drafted for the benefit of all the people of South Africa.

Notes

Chapter 1 Introduction

1 The African National Congress (ANC), National Party (NP), Democratic Party (DP), and the Pan Africanist Congress (PAC) voted for the adoption of the Constitution. The ten members of the Freedom Front (FF) abstained, and the African Christian Democratic Party (ACDP) voted against with its two members. It should also be noted that the Inkatha Freedom Party (IFP) remained outside the process and did not vote.

2 The term 'sphere' was used deliberately to avoid one sphere being regarded as more important than another.

3 This principle was borrowed from German constitutional jurisprudence, upon which several other European countries also rely.

4 The term 'basic law' has been used in Germany, among other European countries, and gained currency in the months prior to its adoption in South Africa as a way of describing the Constitution. 'Basic law' is a useful term in that it explains conceptually what a constitution is.

Chapter 2 Historical background

1 André Odendaal, *Vukani Bantu! The Beginnings of Black Protest Politics in South Africa to 1912* (Cape Town: David Philip, 1984), p. 36.

2 *Izwi labantu*, 16 July 1907. For further references to federation in the newspapers around this time, see *Izwi*, 7 May 1907, 21 May 1907, 28 May 1907, 25 June 1907, and 30 July 1907. See also Odendaal, p. 95.

3 Odendaal, p. 100. At the heart of this debate lay the concern that

the benefits acquired in the Cape by virtue of its more liberal government should not be lost.

4   Odendaal, p. 142.

5   The call for this convention was made publicly on the same day as the release of the report. The South African Native Convention then met in Bloemfontein on 24 March 1909. It was a seminal event in the history of African political activity in South Africa, for it was the first occasion on which African political leaders and the fledgling political associations began co-operation. This meeting was a major step towards the formation of a permanent national African political organization.

6   Quoted in Odendaal, pp. 191–192.

7   W. P. Schreiner papers (UCT) BC 112, file 11 (7.24): Appendix to *Fourth Report on Public Petitions: the Petition of the undersigned representatives of the Coloured and Native British subjects resident in the British Dominions in South Africa to the House of Commons, W. P. Schreiner, A. Abdurahman, J. Tengo Jabavu, etc.* See also Odendaal, p. 224.

8   Richard Rive and Tim Couzens, *Seme: the founder of the ANC* (Johannesburg: Skotaville, 1991) pp. 9–10. See also Peter Walshe, *The Rise of African Nationalism in South Africa* (Berkeley: University of California, 1971), p. 33. This was not the first attempt to establish unity among different African tribes. The colonization of South Africa resulted in several attempts by Dingaan and Shaka, amongst other leaders, to bring this about, all with limited success.

9   The 'Native Republic' thesis was developed after the Communist International discussed the situation in South Africa at its sixth congress. The concept was developed further by the South African Communist Party. See a copy of the annual report of the party dated 31 January 1929, dealing with the 'Native Republic' thesis in the Schedule of Documents (Document 4). Its programme issued on 1 January 1929 clearly reflects how the adoption of this thesis translated into actual demands. A copy of this document is included in the Schedule of Documents (Document 5).

10   Extract from a resolution on 'The South Africa Question' adopted by the executive committee of the Communist International following the Sixth Comintern Congress. A copy of this document is included in the Schedule of Documents (Document 3).

11   The Atlantic Charter was an Anglo-American statement of common principles issued on 14 August 1941 by United States President, Franklin D. Roosevelt, and British Prime Minister, Winston Churchill. They had conferred for four days (9–12 August) aboard the U.S.S. *Augusta* off Newfoundland. Although the United States had not yet entered World War II, the statement became an unofficial manifesto of American and British aims in war and peace. The charter's principles were endorsed by 26 allies in the United Nations Declaration signed in Washington D.C. on 1 January 1942.

12   A copy of the document, with a useful preface and notes by the President-General of the ANC, is included in the Schedule of Documents (Document 6).

13   A copy of the Freedom Charter is included in the Schedule of Documents (Document 7).

14   Some of the concepts promoted in the Charter, which reads more like a bill of rights than a constitution, included non-racialism, non-sexism, equality, affirmative action, and representative government. All of these ideas are expressed in the final Constitution.

15   A copy of Luthuli's letter dated 28 May 1957 is included in the Schedule of Documents (Document 8).

16   Karis, T. and Carter, G. M., *From Protest to Challenge – a documentary history of African politics in South Africa 1882–1964, Vol. 3, Challenge and Violence 1953–1964* (Stanford, California: Hoover Institute Press, 1977).

17   A copy of Mandela's letter dated 20 April 1961 is included in the Schedule of Documents (Document 9).

18   A copy of Mandela's letter dated 23 May 1961 is included in the Schedule of Documents (Document 10).

19 A copy of Mandela's second letter to Verwoerd dated 26 June 1961 is included in the Schedule of Documents (Document 11).

20 The ANC's 'Guidelines on Strategy and Tactics', which was produced at the organization's National Conference in Morogoro, Tanzania, in 1969 provides a clear explanation of the revolutionary armed strategy the ANC was to pursue. (See the Schedule of Documents, Document 20.)

21 Mark Swilling and Mark Phillips, 'State power in the 1980s from "total strategy" to "counter-revolutionary warfare" in Jacklyn Cock and Laurie Nathan (eds.), *War and Society* (Cape Town: David Philip, 1989), p. 144.

22 Cock and Nathan (eds.), p. 139. This was the aim that informed both the Riekert and Wiehan Commissions and the 1983 constitution.

23 The Bethal trial of ANC underground activists exposed the elaborate plans the ANC had developed for its revolutionary warfare. See also Glen Moss, 'MK and the armed struggle' in *Work in Progress* no. 52, March 1988, p. 3.

24 See Tom Lodge, 'Peoples war or negotiation? African National Congress strategies in the 1980's' in G. Moss and I. Obery (eds.), *South African Review* no. 5 (Johannesburg: Ravan, 1989), p. 42.

25 There was some debate during this time as to whether the state was prepared to enter negotiations or not. See the debate between Mark Swilling in *Work in Progress* no. 50 (October 1987) and Ivor Sarakinsky in *Work in Progress* no. 52 (March 1988).

26 See P. W. Botha's Rubicon speech, made to the NP congress on 15 August 1985. In the days before P. W. Botha was due to deliver the speech, the media increased expectations that he would announce a break with apartheid, and take an irrevocable, 'Rubicon' step towards democracy. The expectation was fuelled by strategic leaks made by the then Minister of Foreign Affairs, Pik Botha. However, when P. W. Botha did give his speech it showed no move towards greater freedoms, but instead a renewed clampdown on the liberation movements. It later emerged that Pik Botha had in fact written a speech for P. W. Botha that did

announce the breaks with apartheid everyone was expecting, but that P. W. Botha had rejected the speech at the last minute.

27 See Robert Davies, 'South African regional policy before and after Cuito Cuanavale' in G. Moss and I. Obery (eds.) *South African Review* no. 5, p. 155.

28 *Business Day,* 'PW outlines future of SA constitution', 22 April 1988.

29 *Business Day,* 'The new shape of government', 4 May 1988.

30 *Sowetan,* 'Leaders hit out at PW's plan', 22 April 1988; *Business Day,* 'Constitution plan criticised', 25 April 1988.

31 Among these were the Promotion of Constitutional Development Act, the Extension of Political Participation Bill, the Group Areas Amendment Bill, the Free Settlement Areas Bill, and the Local Government Affairs in Free Settlement Areas Bill.

32 *Weekly Mail,* 'The 9 bills which may change SA', 22 July 1988.

33 *Star,* 'Crisis may force PW into early election', 23 August 1988; *Business Day,* 'ANC plans the future in a draft constitution', 6 May 1988.

34 *Sunday Star,* 'PFP updates its constitutional policy', 1 May 1988.

35 *Citizen,* 'De Klerk pledges new constitution', 26 April 1989.

36 His ideas were unveiled in his budget vote speech on 5 May 1989. *City Press,* 'Heunis unveils new plan', 7 May 1989.

37 *Citizen,* 'NP announces its five year plan', 29 June 1989.

38 *Star,* 'Scrap apartheid, say black leaders', 30 June 1989.

39 *Citizen,* 'Britain disappointed by Nat plan say papers', 1 July 1989.

40 *Star,* editorial, 'Obsolete before birth', 29 June 1989.

41 *Business Day,* 19 September 1989. Gerrit Viljoen was a leader of the Broederbond and the government's chief ideologue, negotiator, and spokesperson on constitutional matters. He was one of the most influential people in the shaping of the development of government and National Party strategy.

42 *Citizen,* 'Zach backs some of FW's aims', 2 October 1989.

43 *Star,* 'Deadline for big changes June – US', 4 October 1989.

44 *Citizen,* 'Inkatha has hopes for reform', 7 October 1989.

45 *Star,* 'Government considering election for blacks', 23 October 1989.

46   *Star*, 'Blacks reject government's "racist" election plan',
     30 October 1989.

47   *Business Day*, 'FW has not yet gone far enough', 16 November
     1989.

48   *Star*, 'Blacks opposing the government's election plan',
     13 November 1989.

49   The importance of a bill of rights, of the removal of discrimina-
     tory legislation, and of meeting with credible black leaders was
     emphasized at this meeting. The delegation also argued that the
     business community had a stake in ensuring that a new consti-
     tutional dispensation produced a stable economy. *Star*,
     'ASSOCOM to press FW for bill of rights', 9 November 1989;
     Business Day, 'FW told business can help create negotiation
     climate', 13 November 1989.

50   *Citizen*, 'Clinging to power means revolution – FW tells PC',
     17 November 1989.

51   *Business Day*, 'FW's critics seek evidence of reform',
     5 December 1989.

52   He made these appeals in an interview with the *Washington
     Post*. See also the *Citizen*, editorial, 'Unrealistic', 29 November
     1989.

53   *Star*, 'SA is not moving fast enough – EC', 11 December 1989.

54   *Star*, 'Cabinet in indaba on new reforms', 4 December 1989.

55   *Star*, 'Group Areas is negotiable, says Viljoen', 8 December 1989.

56   The MDM was a loose alliance of anti-apartheid organizations
     that came into being when the United Democratic Front was
     banned and unable to operate legally.

57   A copy of the resolution is contained in the Schedule of Docu-
     ments (Document 14).

Chapter 3 Exploring the feasibility of negotiation

1   The analysis of the balance of forces in the ANC's 'Guidelines on
    strategy and tactics' (Schedule of Documents, Document 20) is

helpful in understanding the views of the liberation movement during this period.

2 This unique absence also influenced the different parties' perspectives with regard to the question of international mediation as mooted by the IFP.

3 *Business Day*, 'Talks about talks', 14 December 1989.

4 Mandela had been admitted to hospital for surgery to an enlarged prostate. See Alistair Sparks, *Tomorrow is Another Country* (Johannesburg: Struik, 1994), p. 21.

5 Neil Barnard was the head of the National Intelligence Service. S. S. van der Merwe was a government adviser, and previously Director-General in the Department of Justice.

6 According to the accounts of various role-players, it appears that this was the vital role that Neil Barnard played in the process. To satisfy the government's concern about the ANC in exile, Barnard was able to organize the clandestine exchanges as a result of his role as apartheid's spy boss.

7 Nelson Mandela, *Long Walk to Freedom*, (Boston: Little, Brown, 1994) pp. 476.

8 It has been said that when Botha was due to make his 'Rubicon' speech, an anxious Oliver Tambo journeyed to the Zambian broadcast centre to see the speech televised live. His concern was that if Botha was astute enough to allow for genuine change the ANC would not have been ready to meet the demands of the new political environment.

9 See Sparks, p. 26.

10 On 31 January 1985, in a debate in Parliament, President P. W. Botha publicly offered to release Mandela if he were to unconditionally reject violence as a political instrument. Mandela responded in a statement read out by his daughter at a rally to celebrate Desmond Tutu's being awarded the Nobel Peace Prize.

11 A copy of the document prepared by Nelson Mandela before meeting with P. W. Botha on 5 July 1989 is included in the Schedule of Documents (Document 12). Since there are no

minutes or record of this meeting, the notes Mandela prepared are the best indication of the issues he intended to raise.

12 Excerpts from the Harare Declaration are included in the Schedule of Documents (Document 13). Drafted soon after Namibia gained independence from South Africa through negotiation, the Declaration marked the recognition by African leaders that negotiation was a viable option for achieving change. As such, it determined to a large extent the ANC's approach to the transition.

It was in the process of lobbying African governments in support of the Declaration that Oliver Tambo suffered a stroke from which he never recovered. Stories of the energy that Tambo invested in this lobby indicate the great intensity with which he worked.

13 On 10 October 1989 President de Klerk announced that Walter Sisulu, Raymond Mhlaba, Ahmed Kathrada, Andrew Mhlangeni, Elias Motsoaledi, Jeff Masemola, Wilton Mkwayi, and Oscar Mpetha were released.

14 To marshal his thoughts, Mandela prepared 'A Document to Create a Climate of Understanding' which he handed to De Klerk. A copy of this document is included in the Schedule of Documents (Document 15). Once again, this document provides some indication of the issues that were discussed at this meeting.

15 *Citizen*, 'No black-white transition govt – FW', 27 November 1989.

16 *Business Day,* 'Bush applauds meeting', 14 December 1989.

17 *Citizen*, 'HNP tells FW to slow reform', 16 January 1990.

18 *Star*, 'Viljoen sets out govt's thinking on negotiation', 29 January 1990.

19 A copy of the speech is included in the Schedule of Documents (Document 16).

20 One of the important measures was the granting of temporary indemnity to ANC negotiators who were in exile, allowing them to enter the country without fear of arrest.

21 Some of the demands made by the government on the ANC were,

in addition to renouncing violence, that the ANC break its relationship with the SACP and abandon its call for majority rule. Needless to say, these demands were not acceded to. See Mandela, pp. 468–469.

22 This meeting took place in Lusaka on 14–16 February 1990.

23 *Star*, 'ANC to send team for talks with FW', 17 February 1990. This was regarded as a major breakthrough welcomed by both the NP and DP.

24 Strydom was an extreme right-wing militant who fired on innocent black pedestrians in the centre of Pretoria on a busy weekday afternoon. A number of his victims were killed in the attack.

25 *Sunday Star*, 'Great hurdle blocking the road to talks', 25 February 1990.

26 *Star*, 'Govt and ANC to pave way for talks', 23 March 1990.

27 By this time the government had identified its team of negotiators for the first formal discussions. The delegation consisted of nine leaders under President F. W. de Klerk. The other members of this delegation were the Minister for Constitutional Development and Planning, Gerrit Viljoen; Minister of Foreign Affairs, Pik Botha; Minister of Mineral and Energy Affairs and Public Enterprises, Dawie de Villiers; Minister of Justice, Kobie Coetsee; Minister of Finance, Barend du Plessis; Minister of Law and Order, Adriaan Vlok; Minister of Education and Development Aid, Stoffel van der Merwe; and Deputy-Minister of Constitutional Development and Planning, Roelf Meyer.

28 *Star*, 'Govt names 9-man team for pre-negotiation talks', 29 March 1990.

29 These were Kobie Coetsee (House of Assembly), Dr J. N. Reddy (House of Delegates), and Rev. Allan Hendrickse (House of Representatives). However, the scheduled meeting was a failure as more than four of the six chief ministers failed to attend the meeting. De Klerk blamed this on Mandela whom he accused of interference. *Citizen*, 'FW slams interference', 6 April 1990.

30 Already in December 1990, Hudson Ntsanwisi, Chief Minister of Gazankulu and leader of the Ximoko Progressive Party (XPP),

indicated his plans to go to the negotiating table with an independent agenda and not in an alliance with any other party. The XPP would decide on each issue whether to ally itself with one party or another. *Star*, 'Veteran homeland leader will play it cool', 5 December 1990.

31   The humiliation these smaller parties faced came from both sides of the political spectrum. To the white minority government they were second class and their views always subject to those of the white 'majority'; while to those who had always opposed apartheid, these parties were 'sell-outs' and collaborationists negating the efforts of the majority and legitimizing the minority.

32   *Business Day*, 'ANC consulting others in unity drive – Mandela', 26 November 1990

33   Even at the NP Federal Congress held in Bloemfontein on 4 September, De Klerk predicted that the NP and its allies would form the majority in a future government. He told the congress that since the party had thrown open its doors to all races it had 'dramatically' increased its support base. *Business Day*, 'NP will be in majority', 5 September 1991.

34   The ANC's team of 11 negotiators included Mandela, Beyers Naude, Joe Slovo, Walter Sisulu, Alfred Nzo, Archie Gumede, Cheryl Carolus, Ruth Mompati, Joe Modise, Ahmed Kathrada, and Thabo Mbeki. While the NP delegation included only white Afrikaner males older than 50 years (except for Roelf Meyer), the ANC delegation reflected to a far greater degree the gender and racial balance of South Africa's people. Henceforth, all parties became increasingly sensitive about the composition of their negotiating teams.

35   *Sunday Star*, 'Reason talks are off', 1 April 1990.

36   De Klerk appointed Judge Richard Goldstone to look into this shooting. The judge's report criticized police conduct and training, and Judge Goldstone developed a reputation as an independent thinker who carried out his assignments meticulously.

37   *Business Day*, 'Rally told of bid to keep out SACP boss', 30 April 1990. The NP would remain uneasy about Slovo for several years.

Mandela was asked by the NP to exclude him from the ANC delegation as it would be unacceptable for the government to be seen to be negotiating with a communist. This request was refused.

Chapter 4 Removing the obstacles

1 *Business Day*, 'PAC denounces ANC's meeting with government', 30 April 1990.
2 *Citizen*, 'AZAPO condemns the talks as delaying the struggle', 7 May 1990.
3 *Star*, editorial, 'Up a peak – on a roller-coaster', 7 May 1990.
4 It was this scepticism that the ANC must have had in mind when it drafted a detailed document for the benefit of its membership in February 1991 on its strategy and tactics. It was important for the ANC to explain that it had not abandoned its objective of ensuring majority rule. The document sought to identify the balance of forces and to characterize the nature of the state and interpret its intentions. It concluded by identifying the tasks that lay ahead.
5 At the end of April, just before the talks were to begin, a leaflet appeared in public under the name of the ANC calling on blacks to kill whites, coloureds, and Indians. This seemed to be the work of sinister forces bent on disrupting the talks. *Business Day*, 'Rally told of bid to keep out SACP boss', 30 April 1990.
6 Groote Schuur had become the official residence of the former prime ministers in Cape Town. This grand residence was built by Sir Herbert Baker for Cecil Rhodes, and Rhodes's fine collection of books, art works, and antiques remains intact. Priceless Flemish tapestries and antique oils and prints adorned the rich wood-panelled walls of the house, and created a particularly colonial ambience and an ironic setting for such a historic meeting. The meeting was in the dining room around a long rectangular table.
7 *Business Day*, 'Immediate agreement on talks agenda', 3 May 1990.

8   *Business Day*, 'Gov't, ANC signal talks are on track', 4 May 1990.

9   A copy of the agreement is included in the Schedule of Documents (Document 17).

10 *Citizen*, 'Breakthrough at CT talks', 5 May 1990.

11 *Star*, 'They want to meet again!', 5 May 1990.

12 *Sunday Times*, editorial, 6 May 1990.

13 *Sunday Star*, editorial, 6 May 1990.

14 *Sowetan*, editorial, 7 May 1990.

15 *New Nation*, editorial, 4 May 1990.

16 *Sunday Tribune*, editorial, 6 May 1990.

17 *Business Day*, 'Indemnity bill also covers those who attacked banned organisations', 8 May 1990.

18 *Sunday Times*, 'ANC welcomes indemnity moves', 20 May 1990.

19 *Sunday Times*, 'Talks may be speeded up', 13 May 1990.

20 *Sunday Times*, 'Big talks hurdle cleared', 20 May 1990.

21 *Sowetan*, 'Zuma is confident about talks', 22 May 1990.

22 *Business Day*, 'Noses flat against the window, we try to share the sun', 7 May 1990.

23 The media did not take this into account. Due to the euphoria and media hype, the only factor that remained important to them was that the parties had agreed to meet on 21 May but did not. Accordingly, the media read something sinister into this.

24 *Sunday Star*, 'Negotiation back on track', 27 May 1990.

25 *Sowetan*, 'Mandela hits at "war" by SA', 22 May 1990.

26 *Business Day*, 'Noses flat against the window, we try to share the sun', 7 May 1990.

27 *Business Day*, 'In this time of trust and mendacity, let's come into the open', 28 May 1990; also 4 June 1990, 11 June 1990, and his article, 'It's time to shed the world's last communist party', 23 July 1990.

28 The 'mistrust' of majorities was a common argument which in many respects became a mistrust of the ANC, which many perceived to be the most likely majority party after an election. In part, the mistrust of the ANC also lay in the fact that there were many communists in influential positions in the ANC.

29 *Sunday Tribune*, 'Minority rights or majority rule? The choice for a new South Africa', 13 May 1990. This theme was pursued by Ken Owen in his article in the *Business Day* of 21 May 1990 entitled 'Cry out against the tyranny of the majority'. In an interesting twist in the debate, *Business Day* also argued on 8 May 1990 that 'blacks, too, are fearful of the reality of majority rule'. Related to this theme was the new-found emphasis and demand in the media for a bill of rights.

30 These views were expressed at the Cape Town Press Club on 3 May 1990. *Financial Mail*, 'New constitution – ANC's outline', 11 May 1990.

31 *Star*, 'New constitution: ANC wants an elected assembly', 4 May 1990.

32 *Business Day*, 'Minority protection could be temporary', 10 May 1990.

33 The chairperson of the Commission for Administration, Piet van der Merwe, stated that there were no longer any barriers in the way of black advancement, other than qualification, degree of experience, and suitability, which applied to all job-seekers. The racial composition of the civil service as at July 1990 was 41% white, 38% black, 17% Coloured, and 4% Indian. This, however, obscured the fact that the vast majority of black civil servants were employed in menial jobs. In the editorial of the *Cape Times* of 18 July 1990 the idea of some form of affirmative action with regard to the employment of black people was already mooted.

34 *Sunday Star*, 'Change phased in "softener"', 20 May 1990.

35 *Sowetan*, editorial, 'Cost is the real motive', 21 May 1990.

36 *Sunday Star*, editorial, 'The emergency is our Achilles heel', 20 May 1990.

37 *Star*, 'ANC talks of a possible "truce"', 21 May 1990.

38 *Sunday Times*, 'ANC joins the NP in a vortex of change', 6 May 1990.

39 *Citizen*, 'FW hits back at PW', 8 May 1990.

40 *Citizen*, editorial, 14 May 1990.

41 *Star*, editorial, 'The nettle De Klerk must now grasp', 8 June 1990.

42 *Citizen*, editorial, 'Fair test', 21 June 1990.

43 *Sowetan*, 'Clearing the air on talks', 15 May 1990.

44 *Sowetan*, 'ANC talks on constitution', 12 June 1990. Participants at this meeting were Prof. Kader Asmal, Prof. Fink Haysom, Z. N. Jobodwana, Brigitte Mabandla, Nat Masemola, Bulelani Ngcuka, Dullah Omar, Prof. Albie Sachs, and Louis Skweyiya SC. It is worth noting that some of these individuals went on to play a prominent role in the country's transition. Kader Asmal and Dullah Omar became ministers in the first elected government of national unity. Bridgette Mabandla became a deputy-minister, Fink Haysom was the President's legal adviser, Albie Sachs became a judge in the Constitutional Court, and Bulelani Ngcuka became the first deputy-chairperson of the National Council of Provinces.

45 This meeting assisted De Klerk in consolidating possibly the first alliance or front assembled for the constitutional negotiations. Present at the meeting were De Klerk, Pik Botha, Gerrit Viljoen, Kobie Coetsee, Barend du Plessis, Adriaan Vlok, Stoffel van der Merwe, Hernus Kriel, and Roelf Meyer. The other leaders present were Nelson Ramodike (Lebowa), Dr Hudson Ntsanwisi (Gazankulu), Mangosuthu Buthelezi (KwaZulu), Enos Mabusa (KaNgwane), S. J. Mahlangu (KwaNdebele), Rev. Allan Hendrickse (House of Representatives), and Dr J. N. Reddy (House of Delegates). *Citizen*, 'Priority for new constitutional talks', 19 June 1990.

46 *Star*, 'FW feels time for games is over but ANC says the ball is still in his court', 16 June 1990; *Daily Mail*, editorial, 'Just what do you mean Mrs T?', 28 June 1990.

47 On the question of indemnity, De Klerk accepted the report tabled by the joint working group. The ANC, it was claimed by the NP, was delaying the matter, but this was not the case. On 14 June 1990 the ANC responded to the working group by providing various 'amendments, suggestions and amplifications'. *Daily Mail*, 'ANC says it has amended Groote Schuur Report', 10 July 1990.

48 Roelf Meyer was to inherit from Gerrit Viljoen the post of

Minister of Constitutional Development and Planning and became the government's chief negotiator and spokesperson on constitutional matters. A pragmatist and brilliant negotiator, he was responsible for steering the government through some of the stormiest experiences of the negotiation process. *Business Day*, 'Meyer wants pledge on peace', 3 July 1990.

49 *Business Day*, 'ANC hands UN team a list of obstacles to talks', 19 June 1990.

50 *Citizen*, 'Sisulu: free discussion prevented', 19 June 1990.

51 *Business Day*, 'ANC might initiate a cease-fire', 14 May 1990.

52 *Natal Mercury*, editorial, 'Scrape the barrel', 20 June 1990; *Sunday Times*, editorial, 'Foot-draggers', 24 June 1990; *Sunday Star*, 'ANC delays irritating govt', 24 June 1990; *Business Day*, 'Top ANC men deny they're dragging their heels on talks',
25 June 1990. When the matter was attended to later, the ANC accused the government of acting unilaterally in prematurely announcing its acceptance of the report. It was agreed at the outset that the report would first be tabled with each of the principals and dealt with privately until agreement was reached. Evidently, the ANC's media liaison did not have the capacity to attend effectively to issues such as this.

53 *Citizen*, 'ANC-gov't group is defining "political offences"', 11 July 1990.

54 *Sunday Star*, 'Nats and ANC narrow the gap', 1 July 1990.

55 There was some speculation in this regard that a possible agreement was in the offing relating to a government of national unity that included the ANC, an end to sanctions, and an end to armed struggle. The significance of this speculation lies in the fact that this was the first appearance of the concept of a 'government of national unity'. *Star*, 'Time is right, says Mandela', 6 July 1990.

56 *Business Day*, 'ANC and govt to meet on sanctions later this month', 3 July 1990.

57 These views were reflected in his article in *Business Day*, 28 June 1990.

58 *Sunday Star*, 'First steps to a cease-fire', 15 July 1990. What made it

more difficult for the government were statements issued by Chris Hani. Speaking in Transkei late in June 1990, he confirmed that the ANC continued training and deploying its military cadres, which raised a great deal of controversy and added to the debate on the bona fides of the ANC. *Star*, '"Seize power" warning slated', 20 July 1990; *Citizen*, 'FW to take up Hani speech', 20 July 1990.

59   This was the first in a series of booklets and papers produced by the ANC's Department of Political Education.

60   It was very evident that Mandela was monitoring the situation in the country throughout his international tour. Mandela was praised for taking this initiative in the editorial in the *City Press* on 22 July 1990. See also the *Star*, 'Mandela FW meet 2 days after touchdown', 21 July 1990.

61   *Sowetan*, 'Plans for blacks to share power', 2 July 1990.

62   The fear of majorities was not merely confined to the majority of African people, but also the majority of the ANC itself. A survey conducted by Market Research Africa, published in the *Star* of 23 July 1990, provided firm statistical evidence of the popularity of ANC support among Africans. Nearly 50% of blacks outside the KwaZulu/Natal area between the ages of 16 and 24 supported the ANC, against a mere 10% for the PAC, and a minute 2% for Inkatha.

63   *Business Day*, 'FW in TV pledge to never allow SA to descend into anarchy', 28 June 1990.

64   At its annual congress in Cape Town in December 1990, the Labour Party also opposed sanctions and agreed that the future of South Africa would be determined by alliances formed. It asked the leadership to investigate the possibility of alliances with other parties. *Sunday Star*, 'Labour rejects assembly, wants all to be in talks', 30 December 1990.

65   *Business Day*, 'DP rejects idea of interim government', 3 July 1990.

66   *Business Day*, 'Move to push for constituent body', 4 July 1990.

67   *Sowetan*, editorial, 6 December 1990; *Business Day*, 'Tight control at ANC's city marches', 7 December 1990.

68   *Business Day*, 'ANC commitment to peace questioned',
      21 November 1990.
69   Mac Maharaj was a stalwart of the ANC, and was jailed as one of
      the ANC's first soldiers in the early 1960s. On his release in the
      mid-70s he became one of the most senior leaders responsible for
      building the ANC's underground presence in the country. He was
      elected to the ANC's NEC in 1985 and would become the first
      Minister of Transport in the government of national unity in 1994.
70   Kasrils was to become the Deputy-Minister of Defence in the
      government of national unity in 1994.
71   Siphiwe Nyanda would go on to become one of the most senior
      commanders in the South African National Defence Force after
      1994.
72   *Star*, editorial, 'Histrionic but unhelpful', 24 July 1990.
73   *Star*, 'There was no plot', 25 July 1990.
74   *Sunday Times*, editorial, 'This plot must be unthickened', 29 July
      1990; *Citizen*, editorial, 'Plot sequel', 28 July 1990. According to
      the *Star* (1 August 1990), a very cordial meeting took place
      between Mandela and De Klerk at the end of July 1990 to address
      the question of the arrests and to ensure that the forthcoming
      talks were not jeopardized. It was also reported in the *Business Day*
      of 2 August 1990 ('Talks are on and Joe Slovo will be there') that it
      was Mandela who requested the meeting. He confirmed that 'In
      my discussion with the President today I reiterated the total
      commitment of the ANC, Umkhonto we Sizwe and the SACP to
      the Groote Schuur Minute. I also made an undertaking that I
      personally, together with the NEC, will do whatever we can to
      ensure that steps are taken to guarantee strict adherence to the
      Groote Schuur Minute'.
75   *Citizen*, 'Dr. T: cancel talks', 31 July 1990.
76   *Business Day*, 'Gov't and ANC confident that obstacles to talks will
      be swept away', 26 July 1990.
77   *Business Day*, 'Get rid of Slovo, insists De Klerk', 27 July 1990;
      Sunday Times, 'ANC stands by Red Joe', 29 July 1990.
78   The *Sunday Times* of 5 August 1990 was clearly optimistic about

the outcome of the meeting and speculated that 'the 30 year war between the ANC and the Government could effectively be over by tomorrow night'. See also *Business Day*, 'Breakthrough at meeting expected', 3 August 1990.

79   *Sunday Times*, editorial, 'Across the real Rubicon at last?', 5 August 1990. The editor said: 'The peace talks at the Presidensie tomorrow come not a moment too soon. The costs of delayed negotiation are apparent everywhere – confusion, heightened expectations and the unleashing of a hundred private agendas. Yet it is to the boundless credit of both sides that the talks are going ahead despite the tumult caused by "Red plots", arms caches and the detention of senior ANC people'.

80   The Presidensie was the residence of the Prime Minister for many years. It was an old building, filled with outstanding antiques and had an air of authority about it. It was to be the venue of many important bilaterals and meetings during the process of negotiation.

81   Incredibly long meetings at awkward times became the hallmark of the negotiations.

82   A copy of the agreement is included in the Schedule of Documents (Document 18).

83   *Business Day*, 'ANC suspends armed struggle', 7 August 1990.

84   See the Pretoria Minute (Schedule of Documents, Document 18), section 3. At the press conference after the meeting, Mandela explained that the suspension of armed struggle meant that there would be no infiltration of men or arms into South Africa, nor any other activity related to military action.

85   It was reported in the *Daily Mail* of 14 August 1990 that the 'Future of political trials hangs in the balance after Pretoria pact'. One such trial was that of the 'Delmas Three' in which twelve Pretoria activists were charged, among other charges, with conspiring with each other and the ANC to commit murder, attempted murder, and terrorism, and being in possession of illegal arms and ammunition.

86   An important qualification to this aspect of the agreement was

that the indemnity, return of exiles, and release of prisoners applied only to ANC members. This meant that the benefit of this agreement did not cover the PAC, which was encouraged, therefore, to enter into a similar agreement.

87 This notorious law was designed to give the state widespread powers of search, arrest, and detention without trial. Many South Africans suffered as a result of the powers this law gave to the state. According to the editorial in the *Citizen* on 13 August 1990, about 151 members of the ANC had been detained under this act since its unbanning on 2 February 1990.

88 *Business Day*, 'Gov't invites PAC to talks', 31 August 1990.

89 The restriction of these benefits to members of the ANC was removed and made applicable to all on 1 November 1990 in terms of an agreement arrived at in the joint working group. However, the government still refused to grant indemnity to fourteen exiled PAC leaders to enable them to attend the organization's National Conference, because they refused to 'subscribe to the principles of peaceful solutions and developments in SA'. See *Business Day*, 'Indemnity refused for PAC leaders', 20 November 1990. The government finally backed down on this on 3 December 1990 and issued the leaders with temporary indemnity. See *Business Day*, 'Gov't backs down on PAC indemnity', 4 December 1990.

90 *Business Day*, 'Gov't invites AZAPO to talks', 17 September 1990.

91 However, both the Dutch and US governments confirmed that the lifting of sanctions was only likely once 'real progress in negotiation' had been made. *Business Day*, 'Wide acclaim for SA peace accord', 8 August 1990.

92 The *Citizen* in its editorial of 7 August 1990 argued that, in view of the CP response, the rift in Afrikanerdom had been widened.

93 *Business Day*, 'CP, PAC criticise outcome of talks', 8 August 1990. The PAC maintained this position at its National Conference held near Soweto in December 1990. See *Business Day*, 'PAC unlikely to budge on negotiating stance', 5 December 1990.

94 The South African Youth Congress in the Western Cape produced a lengthy document condemning the decision of the

ANC to suspend armed actions and called for the establishment of a 'militia'. *Sunday Star*, 'ANC dispute over talks', 18 November 1990.

95 *Sowetan*, 'ANC to explain all to its supporters', 9 August 1990.

96 See the *Weekly Mail* of 10 August 1990.

97 *Business Day*, editorial, 'The Buthelezi factor', 21 August 1990. The editor argued that 'It would not seem to be stretching the point to assume that Buthelezi is seeking, further, an honourable place at the negotiating table'.

98 *Citizen*, 'Hold negotiation indaba now; Inkatha', 17 September 1990. The IFP further warned the United States of disastrous consequences if it continued a funding bias in favour of the ANC, in response to an allocation of seven million dollars to the ANC for its relocation to South Africa and participation in the negotiation process. It also complained of the 'bi-polar' nature of negotiation involving only the ANC and the NP government.

99 The apparent reason for Buthelezi turning down this meeting was that he was being invited in his personal capacity and not as the President of the IFP. He saw himself at the same level as Mandela, a national leader and not a homeland leader. *Business Day*, editorial, 'Little victory', 3 October 1990.

100 *Business Day*, 'Buthelezi and Mandela set to meet soon', 23 October 1990.

101 *Citizen*, 'ANC attacked by Buthelezi', 3 November 1990.

102 *The Economist*, 'The struggle ends, the struggle continues', 11 August 1990.

103 South African Institute of Race Relations, *Race relations survey 1991/1992* (Johannesburg: SAIRR, 1992), pp. 485–486. A joint call for peace was made by King Goodwill Zwelithini and the Transkei Paramount Chief Tutor Ndamase in Thokoza on the East Rand and at Jabulani in Soweto. The King chided Mandela for not meeting with Buthelezi to bring the violence to an end.

104 According to F. van Zyl Slabbert, the unresolved status of South Africa's security apparatus was the major obstacle in the way of normalizing and democratizing the society. Nothing could be

achieved at the negotiating table if there was suspicion of 'dirty tricks' campaigns. See *Business Day*, 'Security apparatus status could wreck talks, says Slabbert', 31 August 1990. Slabbert went on to plead for a South African equivalent of UNTAG, the United Nations' Transitional Assistance Group, to maintain law and order while political organizations negotiated a new constitution. He proposed that such a force could be made up jointly of members of the SADF, the police force, and Umkhonto we Sizwe. *Business Day*, 'Transitional group must maintain stability – call', 24 September 1990.

105   *Weekly Mail*, 'Hani to head cease-fire talks', 31 August 1990.

106   There was significant controversy surrounding the fact that the government refused to provide the necessary indemnities to Chris Hani, Mac Maharaj, and Ronnie Kasrils after the Vula arrests were made. Chris Hani had also incurred the wrath of the government because of statements he made relating to the armed struggle. He had argued that what had been suspended were armed actions and not armed struggle, and that all MK cadres should accordingly 'remain in their trenches'.

107   *Daily Mail*, 'It's time to draw up new constitution – Mandela', 4 September 1990.

108   According to the *Citizen* of 12 September 1990, a meeting between Mandela and De Klerk took place to consider the question of violence. This meeting followed a detailed memorandum submitted by the ANC, to which there had been no response. According to Mandela, quoted in the *Citizen* on 17 September 1990, 'the government could not conduct negotiation and wage war against the people at the same time'. This statement also led to a war of words in which both Gerrit Viljoen and Magnus Malan attacked Mandela for his 'unsubstantiated remarks', at the same time questioning his commitment to the negotiation process. *Citizen*, 'Mandela honeymoon over', 17 September 1990.

109   While Mandela stopped short of personally implicating De Klerk in the violence, he stated that the National Intelligence Service,

the CCB, and Military Intelligence, with groups such as Koevoet (a counter-insurgency military unit that cut its teeth in the campaign against the South-West African People's Organization (SWAPO) prior to Namibian independence) and Askaris (former ANC guerrillas now working for the South African Police (SAP)), were behind the carnage. In this regard, Mandela was to give affidavits to De Klerk on 8 October 1990 supporting this claim. *Sunday Star*, 'Mandela names the third force', 7 October 1990.

110 *Business Day*, 'ANC will not abandon talks – Mandela', 18 September 1990. Despite Mandela's attitude, the ANC's National Executive Committee was to meet to review the situation in the country. 'If we find there is no will on the part of the government to take emphatic steps to stop this violence then we will have to take a decision that will reverse almost everything that was done since May this year. . . . If the government does not carry out its duties we will have to consider ways and means of defending our people against these criminal attacks . . . then we will have no alternative but to concede to the demands of our people for arms. We are reluctant to do this because we are committed to the idea of peace. But we will not stand by and see our people mown down like dogs. We will have to defend them.' *Citizen*, 'ANC may quit talks: Mandela', 18 September 1990.

111 *Business Day*, 'ANC seeks summit meeting with gov't', 27 September 1990.

112 *Business Day*, 'CP tells of secret resistance plans', 18 October 1990.

113 *Sowetan*, 'The gov't must take on the right-wing', 18 October 1990.

114 *Business Day*, 'Referendum to test constitution – FW', 6 September 1990.

115 The Broederbond was a secretive Afrikaner organization that developed the NP's policies and strategies for power. *Sunday Star*, 'Nat document details non-racial constitution', 9 September 1990.

116 *Business Day*, 'New regional gov't plan is outlined', 5 October 1990.

117 This position followed a study by the Urban Foundation and the

Private Sector Council that urged the government to admit the failure of its decentralization policies and to develop an entirely new non-racial approach to development planning on a regional basis. According to the study, this failure cost the country more than one billion rand per year. *Star*, 'Decentralisation drive has failed', 11 September 1990; *Business Day*, 'Regional incentives put the wrong jobs in the wrong places', 12 September 1990.

118 *Citizen*, 'Sovereignty of parliament must go', 14 November 1990.

119 The NP's consideration must be seen against the background that there was a perception that De Klerk, more than the NP, held significant credibility among all sections of the South African people. *Star*, 'Why winner take all won't do', 1 November 1990.

120 *Citizen*, 'Viljoen spells out minorities' protection', 21 November 1990.

121 *Business Day*, 'Gerrit Viljoen tells how borders will fade away', 23 March 1991.

122 *Business Day*, 'ANC debating decentralisation', 28 November 1990.

123 *Citizen*, 'FW, black leaders agree on regional government', 1 December 1990.

124 *Business Day*, 'FW hints at closer links with DP', 6 November 1990.

125 *Citizen*, 'NP can forge "winning alliance", claims FW', 14 November 1990.

126 Bertus de Villiers proposed a step-by-step approach to drafting a new constitution and phasing in the transfer of power to a newly elected government. His proposal included an initial meeting between the leaders of existing political groups to reach a consensus on broad issues, such as the levels of government and a universal franchise; agreement on a 'statement of intent' and a timetable for the implementation of the new constitution; target dates for elections to the various levels of government; the formation of a 'government of national reconciliation' to govern the country in the transition phase (not necessarily an interim government); the start of 'mini-national conventions' on local and regional levels to determine the structure of those bodies; and elections for a constituent assembly to draft the final

constitution. *Sunday Times*, 'Why a "quick fix" plan will fail', 28 October 1990.

127   *Financial Mail*, 'Negotiation peace on hold', 5 October 1990.

128   *Business Day*, 'Report on suspension of armed struggle is delayed', 25 October 1990.

129   *Business Day*, 'Working group report ready', 15 November 1990.

130   *Sunday Star*, 'Dispute over talks', 18 November 1990.

131   *Business Day*, 'Dutch gov't pledges support to strive for normal relations with SA', 24 October 1990.

132   Prisoners often complained that they were not consulted or kept informed and were becoming increasingly restless. One of the disputes with the government which remained unresolved until late in the process was the number of political prisoners and the definition of such a prisoner. *Financial Mail*, 'Negotiation exile glacier', 16 November 1990.

133   The estimated 100 000 exiles were classified into seven categories: ordinary members of the liberation movements; trained soldiers; conscientious objectors; defectors from the liberation movements; prisoners held by the ANC; members of non-aligned organizations; and individuals who left South Africa for other reasons.

134   This was at an estimated cost of R30.4 million. The figure was based on the cost of repatriating Namibian refugees, which had stood at US $600 (at the time approximately R1 600) per person. The figure for repatriation provided by the ANC was R270 million. This was based on a figure that included the cost of permanent accommodation, and not merely tents as proposed by the United Nations. *Business Day*, 'UN body could help return 20 000 exiles', 23 October 1990. These figures were revised several times. In March 1991 the UNHCR assessed the cost of repatriating exiles to be in the region of US $40 million (at the time approximately R120 million). *Business Day*, 'UNHCR puts cost of repatriation at $40m', 25 March 1991.

135   *Business Day*, 'Gov't stops the clock for indemnity', 9 October 1990.

136 *Business Day*, 'Indemnity to be available to all groups', 2 November 1990.

137 *Sunday Star*, 'Separate Amenities Act finally bites the dust', 14 October 1990.

138 According to the *Business Day* editorial of 13 November 1990, 'the reshuffle was probably prompted more than anything else by the fact that the negotiation process is delicate and difficult; even in the preparatory stages, it has taken up an increasing part of the time of the Ministers most closely involved. Those with heavy administrative loads are having them lightened'. Effectively what happened was that ministers who were directly involved in the negotiation process had new deputies appointed to assist them. The cabinet was also increased from eighteen to twenty members.

139 More than 237 of the seats in the Transvaal's 82 councils were vacant, while between 1984 and 1990 the homes of 120 councillors were attacked and more than 20 councillors murdered. *Citizen*, editorial, 'Both ways', 13 November 1990.

140 *Business Day*, 'Business is a key party to a social contract for SA', 6 November 1990; *Weekly Mail*, 'A union call goes out: we want our seats', 16 November 1990.

141 *Star*, 'Mass action will be on the agenda', 23 November 1990; 'ANC, gov't draw battle lines' and 'Mandela will demand interim government', 24 November 1990; *Sunday Times*, 'Plan for talks leapfrog', 25 November 1990.

142 The *Sunday Times* editorial of 25 November 1990 called for a mutual need for mutual trust. It argued that 'President F W de Klerk and Nelson Mandela are due to meet next week in an atmosphere of recrimination and mounting suspicion which, for the first time since February, casts serious doubt on the viability of negotiation. It is time to reconsider the underlying realities'. The editorial of the *Sunday Star* of the same day claimed that 'President F W de Klerk's greatest success so far has been to win local and international credibility that South African heads of government have not enjoyed for decades. But he should not take

this achievement for granted. There are warning signals that a new scepticism is beginning to tarnish the well-deserved respect his remarkable reforms have achieved'.

143 *Business Day*, 'No agreement on mass action, but gov't and ANC will meet again', 28 November 1990. There was some unhappiness that the leaders did not say more about their discussions, since uncertainty was responsible for much of the tension in the country. Accordingly, the editorial in the *Business Day* of 29 November 1990 called for greater openness of discussions. A similar call was made in the editorial of the *Citizen* of 30 November 1990. However, the *Sunday Star* ('Mandela, FW move too much too soon', 2 December 1990) argued that the fact that not much was achieved from this meeting was proof that the negotiation process was faltering because it was moving too fast too quickly without taking the supporters of either side along. In its editorial, the *Sunday Star* was extremely critical of this non-disclosure and called for greater transparency.

144 The term 'bosberaad' is a South African term meaning 'bush retreat'. Bosberaads became a common feature of the process of negotiation, and played a useful role as mechanisms for ensuring focused discussions under cover of privacy and general isolation.

   Among the issues De Klerk's cabinet discussed were the constitutional proposals of the NP; breaking the log-jam in negotiation; the collapse of black local authorities; the government's response to mass action and the instability in the country; and the options the NP had in terms of possible alliance partners. *Business Day*, 'Gov't bush summit today', 6 December 1990.

145 *Citizen*, 'NP to have separate negotiation team', 10 December 1990.

146 *Business Day*, 'FW, Mandela hold frequent talks on violence', 10 December 1990.

147 NASREC is the venue for the annual Easter Trade Show, and is situated close to Soweto. *Business Day*, 'April 30 is our talks deadline says ANC', 17 December 1990.

148   A copy of the resolution from the consultative conference is included in the Schedule of Documents (Document 21).

149   The European Community in the meantime agreed to lift the ban on new investments in South Africa and to remove other sanctions once apartheid legislation had been scrapped. As it was pointed out in the *Business Day* editorial of 17 December 1990, the ANC was clearly out of step with the rest of the world on the question of sanctions.

150   *Business Day*, 'Gov't opens door to most exiles', 19 December 1990.

151   *Business Day*, 'De Klerk to address the nation tonight', 18 December 1990.

152   *Business Day*, 'Mass action is unacceptable, says De Klerk', 19 December 1990.

153   *Business Day*, 'ANC to grab initiative on government's all party conference idea', 7 January 1991.

154   *Business Day*, 'Gov't thumbs up to ANC's plans for talks', 9 January 1991.

155   The PAC insisted that, before negotiating on the mechanisms of a constituent assembly, all pillars of apartheid should be removed, all security legislation 'inimical to free speech and human rights' scrapped, all political prisoners released unconditionally, and exiles permitted to return without hindrance or application for indemnity. The ANC agreed to hold a meeting with the PAC to discuss the matter further. *Business Day*, 'PAC rejects all-party indaba', 25 January 1991; *Business Day*, 'AZAPO dismisses ANC demand for interim gov't', 29 January 1991.

156   This was to be their first face-to-face meeting since the late 1950s when Buthelezi was a stalwart of the ANC.

157   *Business Day*, 'Inkatha and ANC agree to stop fighting', 30 January 1991.

158   See the *Sowetan*, editorial, 30 January 1991; *Citizen*, editorial, 31 January 1991; and *Beeld*, editorial, 31 January 1991.

159   Unfortunately, this proposal saw the beginning of speculation on the concept of a 'troika' which would also deal with constitutional issues. It was argued that the value of a troika was that it would be

representative of almost 90% of the population. *Business Day*, 'Gov't covets wider role for proposed troika', 2 April 1991.

160   During the year 1990 there were, according to the Department of Welfare and Housing, 1 546 cases of people contravening the Group Areas Act. *Citizen*, 'Group Areas permits still required', 21 February 1991.

161   *Citizen*, editorial, 'Bombshell', 2 February 1991; *Star*, editorial, 2 February 1991.

162   *Business Day*, 'FW tells IOC June is apartheid deadline', 26 March 1991.

163   *Business Day*, 'Multiparty talks might be held soon', 18 February 1991.

164   *Citizen*, 'No change to voters' rolls yet – Viljoen', 4 February 1991.

165   The D. F. Malan Accord took an earlier partial agreement of the joint working group further. For details of this partial agreement, see *Business Day*, 'Breakthrough over armed struggle', 22 January 1991. A copy of the D. F. Malan Accord is included in the Schedule of Documents (Document 19). The agreement was subject to ratification by the two principals. *Business Day*, 'FW and Mandela thrash out an agreement',
13 February 1991.

166   *Sunday Times*, 'Government-ANC deal smooths the road ahead', 17 February 1991

167   *Business Day*, 'The Mandela and De Klerk act works again', 14 February 1991.

168   As at 14 February 1991 only one individual indemnity had been granted. In terms of the government regulations, exiles were only granted indemnity in two categories of offences, namely membership of a previously banned organization and leaving the country illegally. *Business Day*, 'Judges head hearings into exiles' indemnity', 15 February 1991.

169   This did not cover cadres who had committed any act of sabotage as they would still be required to seek indemnity in respect of that particular offence. *Business Day*, 'Gov't, ANC strike indemnity deal', 13 March 1991.

170   Included among these prisoners were Jenny Schreiner, Carl
        Niehaus – sentenced in 1983 to fifteen years for treason – and Piet
        'Skiet' Rudolph, the white right-winger. See *Business Day*, 'Piet
        Skiet and 33 prisoners to be set free', 19 March 1991. Both
        Schreiner and Niehaus were to become MPs for the ANC, elected
        on 27 April 1994. Piet 'Skiet' was to face charges that included the
        stealing of arms and ammunition from South African Air Force
        headquarters and the planting of several bombs, including ones at
        Melrose house (a children's shelter) in Pretoria, the NP offices in
        Pretoria and Roodepoort, and at the *Beeld* newspaper offices in
        Johannesburg. The release of Piet 'Skiet' Rudolph was an
        important move by government to show that it was even-handed
        in the way in which it treated the question of indemnity and the
        release of political prisoners. It was also important to appease the
        right wing, who were becoming increasingly violent.

171   These releases took place against a background of growing
        discontent among political prisoners who often went on hunger
        strike or questioned the ANC's agreements. Generally, this was a
        period of uncertainty which understandably affected political
        prisoners most. A major difficulty brewing was the question of
        how to deal with prisoners on death row. This served to place a
        great deal of pressure on both the ANC and the government
        which often only served to make the process of negotiation that
        much more difficult. *Business Day*, 'Prisoners becoming impatient
        for freedom', 20 March 1991. At the same time, concerns were
        already being expressed by members of the public about the
        possible release of prisoners such as Barend Strydom and Robert
        McBride, whose actions had resulted in a loss of life. This was an
        emotional matter which took a long time to be finally resolved.
        The concerns voiced by the public were clearly evident in a
        number of editorials. See the editorials of 20 March 1991 in
        Business Day, 'Left and Right'; *Citizen*, 'Freed'; *Beeld*, 'Tweede
        kans'; and the *Star*, 'Wiping the slate clean'.

172   This was not an easy process and was fraught with complications.

There were often recriminations and complaints made by the exiles, the NCCR, and the government about one another.

173   This ban was already being relaxed towards the end of 1989, a few months before the release of Mandela. The government made an important concession by switching the initiative from organizers of gatherings to the authorities. The very act of having to seek approval angered people as it often left them hamstrung by the red tape involved. *Star*, 'Into the open', 25 March 1991.

174   The ANC produced a document entitled 'Guidelines on Strategy and Tactics' which was designed to offer to its members an analysis of the reasoning behind its decisions. A copy of the document is included in the Schedule of Documents (Document 20).

175   *Business Day*, 'ANC, PAC relations sour after agreement', 19 February 1991.

176   The last meeting of this forum had taken place in November 1990. This was the first meeting at which it was agreed to establish a joint working group to plan details relating to the proposed conference. See the *Citizen*, 'Gov't to discuss multi-party conference', 27 February 1991.

177   *Citizen*, 'TBVC states can rejoin SA – FW', 27 March 1991.

Chapter 5 Preparing to negotiate

1   *Citizen*, 'Unrest has delayed negotiation on new SA: De Klerk', 1 June 1991.

2   *Star*, 'Fire Vlok, Malan – ANC', 6 April 1991. Most major newspapers warned that the position adopted by the ANC was incorrect. The media were generally unsympathetic and almost unanimously critical of the ANC ultimatum. *Star*, editorial, 'Ill-conceived ultimatum', 6 April 1991; *Sunday Times*, editorial, 'It's buffoonery, or it's madness', 7 April 1991; *Sunday Star*, 'Era of confrontation looms in SA', 7 April 1991; *Sunday Tribune*, 'Damaging ultimatum', 7 April 1991; *City Press*, editorial, 'It's

time to take out the peace pipe again', 7 April 1991; *Sowetan*, editorial, 'Peace is the priority', 8 April 1991; *Citizen*, editorial, 'Bloody cheek', 8 April 1991; *Business Day*, editorial, 'Self delusion', 8 April 1991. In July when the Inkathagate scandal broke, the same newspapers suddenly found it acceptable to reshuffle the cabinet and move Adriaan Vlok and Magnus Malan.

3 Also included in the list of demands were the immediate suspension of all police officers implicated in various shootings; that satisfactory assurances be given that security forces would use civilized methods of crowd control; the introduction of legislation to prevent the carrying of weapons, including traditional weapons, at public gatherings; the phasing out of hostels; and an independent commission of inquiry to investigate complaints of misconduct by the security forces. The open letter containing the ultimatum was reproduced in full in the *Star* of 9 April 1991.

4 The Askaris were a specialized counter-insurgency unit used effectively against the South-West Africa People's Organization (SWAPO) in the Namibian struggle. The unit was made up of Namibians, Angolans, and South Africans and gained a particular reputation for its viciousness and aggression.

5 So-called 'black-on-black' violence began in 1994. This was when the country witnessed the development of a new form of violence: clearly politically motivated violence essentially carried out by black people against other black people. In part, this started between those who collaborated with the regime in its reform measures and those who resisted it (predominantly members of the UDF). Later on, however, violence against anti-apartheid activists was apparently carried out by gangsters who acted in collaboration with the police. It would only be revealed in the proceedings of the Truth and Reconciliation Commission some years later that gangs were used by the police as part of their efforts to deal with anti-apartheid resistance.

6 Mandela also met with a variety of structures of civil society, as well as the UDF and the PAC, to explain the ANC's position. The

UDF and the PAC supported the ANC's demands. See *Business Day*, 'ANC may do deal over its ultimatum', 10 April 1991.

7 *Business Day*, 'Temperature rises', 9 April 1991.

8 *Business Day*, 'Buthelezi and Vlok lash out at the ANC', 9 April 1991.

9 *Citizen*, 'Constitution: ANC sets out tentative plan', 13 April 1991.

10 The ANC as a movement and as a 'broad church' of differing political views united people in their opposition to apartheid. As a movement, rather than a political party, its strength lay in the fact that it consulted with all sectors of society in the development of its policies.

11 The publication of the ANC proposals and the invitation to make comments were generally welcomed by the media.

12 The earlier meeting with regional leaders and the rejection of the idea of an elected constitutional assembly took place after a petition, signed by more than 200 000 people, was submitted to the government by the ANC and the Congress of South African Trade Unions (COSATU). The petition demanded an interim government and an elected constituent assembly. *Business Day*, 'Gov't says no to assembly', 27 March 1991.

13 What the government had in mind was to establish a formal council of leaders involved in the negotiation process to exert influence on a transitional government. This was stated by Gerrit Viljoen in the House of Delegates when he rejected a motion calling for the dissolution of the three Ministers' Councils and their replacement with a consultative cabinet. *Star*, 'Negotiators could influence gov't', 28 February 1991.

14 *Business Day*, 'Viljoen lists transition options', 4 April 1991.

15 De Beer argued that an elected constituent assembly could result in a majority or coalition riding roughshod over the minorities and imposing a constitution which placed no limitations on majority power. *Business Day*, 'Write constitution by consensus – De Beer', 19 March 1991.

16 *Star*, 'Viljoen's blueprint for new SA', 22 May 1991.

17 The disagreement was over fifty prisoners sentenced for necklace

murders and 150 jailed members of Umkhonto we Sizwe, while the category of 4 000 unrest-related prisoners was another area of disagreement. (See *Business Day*, 'Deadline nears amid dispute on prisoners', 29 April 1991.) According to De Klerk, the release of prisoners were very much on track and it was the ANC that was dragging its heels in not submitting the necessary applications timeously. (See the *Star*, 'ANC is dragging its feet, says FW', 1 May 1991.) However, in terms of a further remission of sentence announced by Minister Coetsee, it was agreed that at least 1 000 prisoners classified by the Human Rights Commission as political prisoners were due for release during May 1991. (*Business Day*, '1000 prisoners await release', 3 May 1991.)

18 Both European and American governments often cited this act as one of the reasons for maintaining pressure on South Africa. This move, therefore, not only satisfied the ANC's demand as one of its obstacles to negotiation, but also paved the way to the lifting of sanctions. *Business Day*, 'Big changes in security law promised', 3 May 1991.

19 *Business Day*, 'Gov't, ANC reach broad consensus', 10 May 1991.

20 *Sunday Times*, 'ANC snubs FW peace appeal', 19 May 1991.

21 *Sunday Times*, 'ANC snubs FW peace appeal', 19 May 1991.

22 *Business Day*, 'Royal nod for spear ban in unrest areas', 21 May 1991.

23 *Citizen*, 'Unrest has delayed negotiation on new SA: De Klerk', 1 June 1991.

24 *Sunday Times* 'Europe fires a shot across SA bows', 9 June 1991.

25 The eight discriminatory acts related to the constitution were the Child Care Act, the Coloured Persons Education Act, the Indians Education Act, the Indians Advanced Technical Education Act, the Social Pensions Act, the General Pensions Act, the Referendums Act, and the Local Government Bodies Franchise Act. See the *Financial Mail*, 'Parliament end of the beginning', 14 June 1991; and *Business Day*, 'Apartheid is now history, FW declares', 18 June 1991.

26 *Financial Mail*, 'A question of trust', 2 August 1991.

27 *Business Day*, 'Washington tells FW to come clean', 23 July 1991. This scandal was reminiscent of the information scandal in the 1970s, in which the government was involved with the funding of a newspaper, the *Citizen*, to promote its views. Connie Mulder, the Minister of Information, was made to take the rap and was fired from the cabinet.

28 This dictum became almost a mantra that would be recited by Leon Wessels during some of the most difficult times in negotiating the final Constitution.

29 *Financial Times*, 'Moment of truth for apartheid reformer', 27 July 1991.

30 *Sunday Times*, editorial, 'Clearing the decks', 4 August 1991.

31 *Citizen*, 'Negotiation process won't be stopped', 31 July 1991. By all accounts, De Klerk was praised for the way in which he dealt with the crisis.

32 *Sunday Star*, 'Conference goes on, Viljoen', 4 August 1991.

33 *Business Day*, 'Inkathagate – a shot in the arm for flagging talks', 5 August 1991.

34 *Business Day*, 'ANC says it is ready for all-party talks', 2 August 1991; *Citizen*, 'ANC makes interim gov't top demand', 2 August 1991.

35 *Business Day*, 'ANC and gov't moving closer on interim administration, says Mandela', 8 August 1991; *Citizen*, 'Must be interim gov't – Mandela', 8 August 1991.

36 *Business Day*, 'ANC and gov't moving closer on interim administration, says Mandela', 8 August 1991.

37 *Business Day*, 'Gov't agrees to amnesty for all exiles', 16 August 1991; *Star*, 'UN agency set to assist exiles in SA', 17 August 1991.

38 *Business Day*, 'UN deal on exiles endorses reform in SA', 19 August 1991.

39 *Business Day*, 'Special NP congress to prepare for negotiation', 22 August 1991.

40 This took place on 29 August 1991. *Business Day*, 'DP puts forward constitutional proposals', 30 August 1991.

41 *Star*, 'Two visions of the new South Africa', 30 August 1991.

42 Speaking to the Federal Congress in Bloemfontein, President F. W. de Klerk believed that the power he had as President hampered co-operation in SA. He therefore proposed a system of collective presidency. *Business Day*, 'President holds too much power, says FW', 5 September 1991.

43 In response to the NP proposals, the DP said the proposals included almost everything the DP and its predecessors had called for over the past 20 years, with the exception of the five-member presidential council. *Business Day* 'New constitutional plans under fire', 5 September 1991.

44 The *Business Day* of 6 September 1991 published an article entitled 'Nat proposals are designed to sway many constituencies'. This article suggested that 'the old adage that politicians do not look for solutions but merely for ways to stay in power could correctly be applied to President F. W. de Klerk and the NP, despite his altruistic words and the party's special federal congress in Bloemfontein'. The *Sunday Star* of 8 September 1991 in an article entitled 'A constitution – or just a con?' had this to say: 'A cunning formula to maintain white minority rule under the veneer of a one-person-one-vote non-racial democracy? A slippery slope towards inevitable black majority rule? A reasonable plan for a full democratic participation by all South Africans without discrimination and domination? These are some of the widely differing assessments of the National Party's constitutional proposals, which will be argued nationally and internationally for months and perhaps years ahead'.

45 In the article, 'How the major players see things', in the *Star* of 6 September 1991, Shaun Johnson and Peter Fabricius identified the different views of parties on the question of managing the transition.

46 *Star*, 'Constitutional malaise', 6 September 1991.

47 The position of the NP on this point changed dramatically during the negotiations that were to follow.

48 The National Peace Accord also provided for a code of conduct for all security forces in an attempt to depoliticize them and

make them more accountable. This provided some comfort to those alleging that the security forces were involved in the violence.

49 The ANC, government, and Inkatha confirmed that, after the signing of the National Peace Accord, there were no further obstacles to the start of constitutional negotiation. Dr Gerrit Viljoen said, 'I can say we have succeeded in picking up the thread. There is already a degree of informal understanding on the agenda, logistics, chairmanship and participants at the conference'. *Business Day,* 'Gov't, ANC and Inkatha give the green light to multiparty talks', 20 September 1991.

50 In the meantime, there was already speculation in the media as to the relative strength of each of the parties. According to the *Financial Mail* of 27 September 1991, the ANC would become the majority party, with the NP and the DP following. However, a Gallup-Markinor political poll found that nearly half the urban black population could be classified as 'potential' NP voters: 6% said they would 'definitely' vote NP in an election, 22 % said 'perhaps', and 18% said that they 'feel quite good' about the ruling party even if they would not vote for it. (Nearly 60% of the black population was urban.) The major player was the ANC, supported by 68% of urban blacks. Only 3% of Africans polled rejected the ANC completely, with another 3% being 'personally' against it.

The opposite applied to whites polled: 42% completely rejected the ANC, 26% were 'personally' against it, and 19% had no feelings about it. Only 11% of whites felt 'quite good' about the ANC, though they would not vote for it. A mere 2% 'perhaps would', but no whites in the survey said they would definitely vote ANC. With regard to the IFP, the survey showed that it had more support among whites polled (4%) than among urban blacks (2%), who seemed more repelled by the IFP (completely rejected by 52%) than by the Conservative Party (48%). Another 16% were 'personally against' the IFP, even if they thought it was of benefit to others. Only 3% of urban blacks said they would definitely, or perhaps, vote for the IFP in an election. In contrast, just over 30% of whites felt 'quite good' about the IFP with an additional 15% 'perhaps' voting for it and 4% 'definitely'. Among whites, 42% said they would definitely vote NP and 20% 'perhaps'. The CP had 16% 'definite' votes and 9% 'perhaps'.

51   The meeting was led by Mandela, Clarence Makwetu, President of the PAC, and AZAPO President Pendalani Nefolovhodwe. This opened the way to the holding of the first Patriotic Front meeting in October 1991. *Business Day*, 'PAC, AZAPO agree to join all-party talks', 26 September 1991.

52   *Business Day*, 'Multiparty talks on track', 27 September 1991.

53   *Sunday Times*, 'It's war over who runs SA', 6 October 1991.

54   *Business Day*, 'Quarrels set back talks', 11 October 1991.

55   *Business Day*, 'Zach urges ANC, NP to share power', 9 October 1991.

Chapter 6 Defining the agenda

1   The organizations that attended ranged from political structures such as the ANC, the PAC, AZAPO, the DP, the Natal Indian Congress (NIC), and the Transvaal Indian Congress (TIC), to parties representing the different homelands and independent territories. Religious and other structures of civil society that had aligned themselves with the anti-apartheid movement also attended. Members of the Democratic Party attended the conference as observers.

2   *Citizen*, 'PF talks favour interim gov't', 26 September 1991. The parties still had to agree on the extent of the power that such an interim government should have. While the ANC argued that an interim government should have the maximum possible power, the PAC opted for a more restricted form of transitional authority. In this regard, delegates were warned of the consequences of the interim government's assuming sovereign authority: it would

mean that the crises generated by the apartheid government of the past would haunt the interim government. It would also generate expectations among the country's people which could not be met.

3   These consultations took place between 2 and 12 November 1991.

4   *Business Day*, 'Gov't willing to amend the constitution', 29 October 1991.

5   The explanation given for this was that the need for a referendum was in terms of the undertaking given by De Klerk to the white electorate during the last election in 1988.

6   *Business Day*, 'Gov't willing to amend the constitution', 29 October 1991.

7   *Star*, 'Will their fingers form a fist?', 1 November 1991.

8   *Sunday Times*, 'Nat bid for coalition rule', 3 November 1991.

9   The *Finance Week* of 7 November 1991 in an article entitled 'Expert opinion' had this to say about the NP proposals: 'Finally robbed of the long-cosseted idea of racial separateness, State President F. W. De Klerk's National Party took refuge in a commendable pragmatism. But this increasingly went hand-in-hand with the belief that the De Klerk government is indispensable to the future, even if leading a "DTA-type" alliance with others. It became obvious that De Klerk sought to manage change his way. Having botched things so badly, the government – instead of allowing the early election of a government representing the broad mass of people, which is what democracy is about – is clinging to power. Considering the past 43 years, it is one of the most breathtaking attempts at self-perpetuation in history'.

10   *Finance Week*, 'NP options pan out', 7 November 1991.

11   A Referendums Amendment Bill deleting the requirement of race classification was prepared by the government for this purpose. *Citizen*, 'Votes for all in referendum', 13 November 1991. This idea was vigorously opposed by the Conservative Party. *Business Day*, 'Treurnicht slams Referendum Bill', 14 November 1991;

Business Day, 'Nats debate forum to draft constitution',
15 November 1991.

12 *Sunday Times,* 'Nat bid for coalition rule', 3 November 1991.

13 *Citizen,* 'Gov't discusses multi-party talks', 5 November 1991.
This was its eighth consultative meeting with members of the
Ministers' Councils of Parliament, the governments of self-
governing territories, and the Administrators of the provinces.
Present at the meeting were Viljoen and other members of De
Klerk's cabinet, Buthelezi, Gazankulu leader Hudson Ntsanwisi,
Lebowa's Nelson Ramodike, KaNgwane's M. C. Zitha, the
Labour Party's Allan Hendrickse, and the Solidarity Party's J. N.
Reddy. While QwaQwa leader T. K. Mopeli and KwaNdebele
leader Prince S. J. Mahlangu were unable to attend, their
governments were represented as well.

14 *Business Day,* 'Inkatha gives gov't mandate on talks',
6 November 1991.

15 The irony lies in the fact that the Patriotic Front did reach
agreement on the nature and agenda of the multi-party talks.
There was very evidently still some doubt in the minds of these
leaders as to whether they should align themselves with the
Patriotic Front or the government. According to the *Star* editorial
entitled 'Open options' on 11 November 1991, 'They are judi-
ciously keeping their options open'.

16 *Business Day,* 'Stage is set for start of all-party talks',
14 November 1991. There was some controversy around the fact
that it was Mandela that made the announcement first. Viljoen
complained that it appeared as if it were the ANC that was
unilaterally calling the meeting. With regard to the venue, the
World Trade Centre, the NP initially insisted that it take place in
one of the government facilities. This was controversial and not
acceptable to the ANC who felt that such a venue would not
convey the proper image that the negotiation ought to be associated with, so as a compromise, the World Trade Centre was
agreed to. This proved to be convenient as it was located in close
proximity to Johannesburg International Airport and allowed

delegates from throughout the country to easily travel to the venue. Additionally, there were also a number of hotels in close proximity which proved to be a bonus during later negotiation. The negotiators' choice of this venue proved to be good business for its owners as it acquired a status that made it a much-sought-after venue.

17   The agenda would include: the creation of a political climate for stability by reducing violence; an interim government or transitional arrangements; constitution-making mechanisms such as a constituent assembly; the reincorporation of the TBVC states into SA; and the role of the international community and sanctions in particular.

Stanley Mogoba would go on to succeed Clarence Makwetu as leader of the PAC in 1997. Johan Heyns was assassinated at his home in 1994, allegedly by right-wing elements. The assassination would have a profound effect on a range of South African people and organizations, especially in that it suggested a festering, hidden malice existed towards the transition among some individuals.

18   In what was described as one of Eglin's best political speeches, he won the debate despite opposition from Tony Leon, Douglas Gibson, and Roger Hulley, who argued that the DP was too small to win a place in an elected constitutional conference. *Star*, 'DP in crucial shift on constitution', 16 November 1991.

19   *Sunday Star*, 'DP vision of the way forward for new SA', 24 November 1991.

20   *Business Day*, 'Inkatha move sets back all-party talks', 15 November 1991. Unfortunately, this would become a pattern throughout the negotiations that followed.

21   *Business Day*, 'Agreement on talks steering committee', 20 November 1991.

22   *Sowetan*, 'PAC insists on talking at neutral place', 20 November 1991.

23   The allegations related to a briefing which ANC Director of International Affairs, Thabo Mbeki, gave to African ambassadors.

The claim was that Mbeki confirmed a secret deal with the NP about an interim government, constituent assembly, and sanctions. The PAC produced a copy of the minutes documenting this. In response, the ANC alleged that no minutes were kept of the relevant meeting, and that there was some mischief at play.

24 *Business Day*, 'Key players set date for negotiation', 22 November 1991.

25 *City Press*, editorial, 'AZAPO should return to talks', 24 November 1991.

26 *Business Day*, 'Separate gov't, NP delegates at talks', 26 November 1991. While this gave the government added weight in the talks should it be necessary to arrive at a decision, it was thought best only because it was necessary to bind the NP and the government separately in the agreements, especially when it came to implementation.

27 *Business Day*, 'Government seeks 1992 referendum', 25 November 1991.

28 The terms 'CODESA I' and 'CODESA II' denote the first and second plenary sessions.

29 This proved to be a most controversial yet very useful concept. It described those instances where there was no general consensus, but enough agreement from a sufficient number of parties to enable the process to continue. There was still some debate as to how decisions were to be arrived at. Since parties were not mandated by an electorate and the process was designed to be as inclusive as possible – no matter how small a party may have been – it was agreed in principle that no decision would be taken on any matter unless the government and the ANC, at the very least, were in agreement. Nonetheless, it was agreed implicitly that no agreement by the ANC and the government alone would be enough for a decision to be taken. This was a matter about which the IFP felt so aggrieved that they were willing to challenge a decision arrived at during the negotiation in court. The Supreme Court ruled against its claim that all decisions arrived at on the basis of 'sufficient consensus' be invalidated.

30   *Star*, 'PAC rocks the talks boat', 30 November 1991.

31   *Citizen*, 'Front-line 7 urge PAC to join Codesa', 30 March 1992.

32   *Business Day*, 'Codesa set to be informal interim gov't', 2 December 1991.

33   *Financial Times*, 'ANC may join interim government next year', 25 November 1991.

34   *Business Day*, 'Gov't plots strategy for change', 4 December 1991.

35   *Business Day*, 'Include KwaZulu in talks', 9 December 1991.

36   *Business Day*, 'Task groups make progress', 10 December 1991.

37   The Commonwealth announced a six-member observer team, including former British Foreign Secretary Sir Geoffrey Howe and former Zimbabwian President, Rev. Canaan Banana. It also included two other former foreign ministers, Malaysia's Tan Sri Ghazali Shafie and India's Shri Dinesh Singh, the former Australian Governor-General Sir Ninian Stephen, and Telford George, former Chief Justice of the Bahamas. President de Klerk was to lead the government delegation with Pik Botha, Gerrit Viljoen, Kobie Coetsee, Barend du Plessis, Piet Marais, Tertius Delport, Sam de Beer, Dr Rina Venter, Leon Wessels, Abe Williams, and Fanie van der Merwe. The National Party's delegation was led by Dawie de Villiers, George Bartlett, Roelf Meyer, and Hernus Kriel. *Business Day*, 'Top-level teams named for Codesa', 13 December 1991.

38   The *Sunday Times* of 15 December 1991 in an article entitled 'We, the people' reproduced the entire texts of the NP and ANC proposals.

39   *Business Day*, 'PAC refuses to take part in negotiation', 17 December 1991.

40   *Business Day*, 'Gov't, ANC locked in talks to decide on status of Codesa decision', 18 December 1991.

41   *Business Day*, 'PAC refuses to take part in negotiation', 17 December 1991.

42   The leaders present at this bilateral were Thabo Mbeki, Jacob Zuma, Cyril Ramaphosa, Joe Slovo, and Valli Moosa for the ANC. For the NP, present were Gerrit Viljoen, Roelf Meyer, Tertius

Delport, Dawie de Villiers, and Barend du Plessis. See the *Sunday Times*, 'With the best of intentions', 22 December 1991. According to this article, the ANC's National Working Committee was not happy with this resolution and insisted that the declaration should read that the decisions of CODESA have 'legal' effect. The matter was apparently left to be resolved between Mandela and De Klerk. De Klerk appeared to have convinced Mandela that the clause in the declaration should not be changed – a decision about which the ANC's working committee was not happy.

43 *Business Day*, 'Codesa given go-ahead to draw up laws', 20 December 1991.

44 *Citizen*, '5 right-wing groups say no to Codesa', 13 December 1991.

45 *Business Day*, 'AWB war threat over boerestaat', 10 December 1991. 'Boerestaat' is an Afrikaans term referring to an independent white republic.

46 The question of the right-wing threat should be considered against the turmoil which the Soviet Union was experiencing. The rise of nationalism in the Soviet Union during this period was always referred to by the right wing in support of their arguments for self-determination. *Citizen*, editorial, 'Parallels', 28 December 1991.

47 The CP found itself associated with the IFP, who were also disgruntled about the King and the KwaZulu administration not being allowed delegates to CODESA. The IFP also promoted the concept of self-determination. Accordingly, a second meeting in January 1992 was scheduled between Buthelezi and Treurnicht, and their relationship was later to develop into a formal alliance.

48 *Sunday Tribune*, 'Mandela warns of "trap" and reassures whites', 29 December 1991.

49 Ironically, this call was rejected by the NP. *Business Day*, 'NP rejects Mandela's white block', 28 January 1992.

50 *Business Day*, 'ANC pledges to entrench white seats', 30 December 1991.

51 These meetings, and all subsequent multilateral negotiation until

agreement on the interim constitution was reached, took place at the World Trade Centre in Kempton Park. Hence, these negotiations are often referred to as the 'Kempton Park talks' or 'World Trade Centre talks'.

52 Ismail Mohamed was the country's first black judge and had acquired a tremendous amount of respect within the legal fraternity for his legal skills. As an advocate, he gained an excellent reputation in several appearances for the defence in political trials. He was also noted for his most eloquent speeches at the opening and closing of CODESA. Mohamed was subsequently appointed Deputy-President of the first Constitutional Court and later as the country's first black Chief Justice.

53 The parties attending were the ANC, the NP, the South African government, the PAC, the IFP, the Labour Party, the Inyandza National Movement (KaNgwane), the Transvaal and Natal Indian Congresses (one delegation), Venda government, Bophuthatswana government, the United People's Front (Lebowa), the Solidarity Party, the DP, the National People's Party, Ciskei government, the Dikwankwetla Party (QwaQwa), the Intando Yesizwe Party (KwaNdebele), the Ximoko Progressive Party (Gazankulu), and the SACP.

54 *Star*, "'We're sorry for apartheid" NP apologises as Codesa paves way for new SA', 21 December 1991.

55 *Star*, 'FW's Codesa bombshell', 21 December 1991.

56 What made Mandela more angry was that the government had negotiated for De Klerk to be the last speaker. De Klerk was accused of abusing this privilege by attacking the ANC in public, especially when he did not even forewarn Mandela in their telephone conversation the previous evening. *Star*, 'Fiery first round as leaders clash over MK', 21 December 1991.

57 The leaders' exchange was not a piece of 'unscripted theatre' as suggested in Steven Friedman (ed.), *The Long Journey* (Johannesburg: Ravan, 1993, p. 24), but was a real reflection of what negotiations are about. The editorial in the *Star* on 21 December captured the significance of the exchange when it

noted that 'the extraordinary public battle at Codesa between Nelson Mandela and F. W. De Klerk had visibly shocked all those in attendance. In shattering the atmosphere of bonhomie that had been created, it marked the start of "real" negotiation'.

58   A copy of the Declaration of Intent is included in the Schedule of Documents (Document 22).

59   Friedman (p. 25) suggests that 'the centrepiece of Codesa I was the signing of a Declaration of Intent, consisting largely of vague statements of goodwill and designed primarily to avoid possibilities for disagreement'. Such an interpretation of the declaration is unfortunate, as it ignores the historical significance of the agreement.

60   See the *Star*, 'Planning a new nation', 21 December 1991.

61   What troubled Lucas Mangope and the other homeland leaders was the fact that they would not win support for their opposition to reincorporation in a referendum.

62   Suzman was supported by speakers from the IFP, the NP, the ANC, and the SACP. The largest high-level female representation was found in the Transvaal and Natal Indian Congress delegation, which included seven women delegates. This speech made an impact on the composition of future delegations to multi-party talks. See the *Sunday Times*, 'Don't leave women out, says Suzman', 22 December 1991.

63   These issues dealt with in the working groups were among the requirements set out in the Harare Declaration.

64   Considering the structure of this forum for multilateral negotiation, there are several factors that become relevant when considering the format of later multilateral negotiation. These were: the absence of technical structures to provide legal and constitutional advice to the meeting; each party's having to include its own technical experts in its delegation of advisers; the negotiation in the working groups was cumbersome because of the large number of delegates involved; all negotiation was held behind closed doors and the only views entertained were those of the parties participating.

65   The Daily Management Committee was elected on 13 January 1992. The elected members were Zach de Beer (DP), Pravin Gordhan (Natal Indian Congress), Peter Hendrickse (Labour Party), Frank Madlalose (IFP), Roelf Meyer (NP), Selby Rapinga (Inyandza), Zamindlela Titus (Transkei), and Jacob Zuma (ANC).

66   S. S. van der Merwe (or 'Fanie') was the Director-General of Constitutional Development Services. He was later replaced by Neil Barnard. Van der Merwe and Barnard were the government officials that had met secretly with Mandela before his release. Fanie van der Merwe later became a constitutional adviser in the Department of Constitutional Development and Planning. As a civil servant he made an invaluable contribution to the negotiations, especially at the bilateral level.

67   Maharaj was a member of the ANC NEC, and was previously also commander of Operation Vula. Mac and Fanie became a formidable team that worked tirelessly to ensure that the multiparty talks were a success.

68   Morobe was a prominent leader in the United Democratic Front (UDF) and the manager of a private company. He was seconded to CODESA for purposes of managing the process.

69   Eloff was seconded to the process by the Consultative Business Movement (CBM).

70   Parties were allowed to become members of CODESA if they had 'proven support'. See *Business Day*, 'Codesa open to "outside" ideas', 15 January 1992.

71   *Sowetan*, 'FW supports Zulu king for Codesa', 13 January 1992.

72   The subcommittee was made up of Madlalose and one representative each from QwaQwa, Lebowa, and KwaNdebele.

73   The ANC NEC's traditional 8 January statement for 1992 set out clear time-frames for the process. It set a target date for elections as 1992. This statement also set out the basic principles underpinning the ANC's approach to negotiation.

Under cover of prevailing confidence and enthusiasm the NP government called the last, though controversial, all-white referendum to seek a general mandate for its positions in negotiation. The NP received overwhelming support in this referendum.

Economists suggested that the readmission of South Africa to the world business scene and its improving political stability should result in a move towards a sustainable annual growth rate of 5%. See the *Sunday Star*, '5% growth rate come-on for US investors', 12 January 1992. Simon Brand, of the former Development Bank of Southern Africa, was also confident about the economic future of the country. See *Business Day*, 'Brand is optimistic about SA's political and economic future', 13 January 1992.

Chapter 7 Defining the process

1 Details of these economic problems were related to Parliament by Barend du Plessis' budget vote on 17 February 1992. The *Sunday Times* in its editorial on 19 January 1992 urged De Klerk to act immediately. It complained that 'no sane South African wants to bring down President de Klerk at this juncture of history, but the time has surely come to warn him – and his party – that the failure to establish control over the corrupt, profligate state machine created by his predecessor is impoverishing the nation. It is undermining the Reserve Bank's fight against inflation, and so extending the recession. Thus it greatly compounds all his problems, from unemployment and crime to the rise of the right-wing, and he is running out of time'.

2 De Klerk had also ordered an investigation into the feasibility of proportional representation as an electoral system. *Business Day*, 'FW seeks inquiry into polling system', 24 January 1992.

3 Neil Barnard was appointed by former Prime Minister P. W. Botha to head the NIS in 1980. Barnard was the longest-serving Director-General in the public service. He previously headed the University of the Orange Free State's Department of Political Science, and was one of the first government members to start

talking clandestinely to the ANC. See *Business Day*, 'Spy chief to head constitutional services', 22 January 1992. Barnard held the position of Director-General of the department until late in 1996 when he left to take up an appointment at the same level in the Western Cape.

4   Tertius Delport had studied at the University of Stellenbosch with the likes of Minister of Public Enterprises, Dr Dawie de Villiers, where he was the President of the Students' Union and national Vice-President of the Afrikaanse Studentebond. He rose very quickly in the ranks of the NP and became the Deputy-Minister of Provincial Affairs in May 1990, and six months later was appointed Deputy-Minister of Constitutional Development and Planning. After the 1994 election, he became an NP MEC in the Eastern Cape provincial government. On his position at CODESA, see the *Star*, 'Codesa's new spokesman takes the floor', 7 February 1992.

5   This was part of the campaign for a 'People's parliament'. See the *Star*, 'ANC, SACP issue interim gov't deadline', 23 January 1992; *Citizen*, 'ANC demands interim gov't within 6 months', 25 January 1992.

6   Each party had two delegates, making thirty-eight delegates per working group and nearly two hundred representatives in total. See the *Star*, 'Real political horsetrading begins', 20 January 1992.

7   See the *Star*, 'Plotting the brave new SA', 4 April 1992; and the *Citizen*, 'Parliament to sit 3 days a week', 22 January 1992.

8   *Business Day*, editorial, 'Short time', 23 January 1992.

9   *Citizen*, 'Codesa to call for submissions on new constitution', 5 February 1992. The CODESA secretariat published a letter stating that 'only bona fide political parties, organisations and administrations should have full participant status. At the same time, the organisers of Codesa wish to encourage the greatest possible participation by interest groups from all walks of life. Provision has been made for all interest groups to make submissions to the five working groups'. See also *Business Day*, letters, 7 February 1992.

10 *Star*, 'Get editors involved in Codesa', 31 March 1992. The call pronounced in this article's title was to have a sequel in the negotiations on the final constitution.

11 The CP Hoofraad, the party's highest executive authority, met on 27 March 1992 to thrash out the party's stand on taking part in CODESA. CP officials were divided on whether or not to enter into the negotiations, which only served to strengthen the hand of MP Koos van der Merwe, who argued in favour of negotiating. Van der Merwe later resigned his post to join the IFP and went on still later to be elected to the National Assembly on the IFP ticket. See *Business Day*, 'CP to thrash out party stand on Codesa', 27 March 1992.

12 *Citizen*, 'CP may split cover Codesa – claim', 23 December 1991; *Sunday Times*, 'Meeting averts CP split', 29 March 1992.

13 *Business Day*, 'Codesa in new bid to woo right-wing', 7 February 1992.

14 *Star*, 'White politics at cross-roads', 28 March 1992.

15 *Business Day*, 'NP, ANC prepare for election battle', 13 April 1992.

16 One of the effects of the referendum's result would be the NP and the DP's preparation for a future election 'against' the ANC. *Citizen*, 'First non-racial poll next year?', 8 April 1992.

17 *Star*, 'Referendum: gov't faces a bruising', 25 January 1992.

18 *Business Day*, 'FW stakes future on vote for reform', 21 February 1992.

19 *Business Day*, 'Support for talks is vital – Codesa', 26 February 1992.

20 *Business Day*, 'Likely dates for Codesa II mooted', 4 March 1992.

21 *Sunday Star*,' editorial, 'When slow is the quickest', 8 March 1992; *City Press*, editorial, 'Let Codesa select cabinet members', 8 March 1992.

22 *Star*, 'Lack of progress holds up next plenary', 10 March 1993; *Sunday Times*, 'Brakes on Codesa II', 29 March 1992.

23 Steven Friedman (ed.), *The Long Journey* (Johannesburg: Ravan, 1993), p. 40.

24 *Citizen*, 'Gender committee meets', 11 April 1992.

25 The list of laws included the Prohibition of Foreign Financing of Political Parties Act; the Secret Services Account Act; the Intimidation Amendment Act; the Disclosure of Foreign Funding Act; the Demonstration in or near Court Buildings Act; the Affected Organizations Act; the Gathering and Demonstrations Act; the Admission of Persons to the Republic Act; section 205 of the Criminal Procedure Act (which compelled journalists to identify their sources); and section 29 of the Internal Security Act (detention without trial). See *Business Day*, 'Codesa to review nine laws', 19 February 1992.

26 *Citizen*, 'Don't let dispute about MK delay Codesa: Zach', 23 March 1992.

27 Speaking at CODESA the next day, Roelf Meyer stated that he had never threatened to suspend CODESA II if MK was not disbanded, but had emphasized the government's principles. The matter was nevertheless being dealt with bilaterally and both Meyer and Ramaphosa were confident that the matter would be resolved. See *Business Day*, 'MK agreement close, says ANC', 24 March 1992.

28 *Sunday Star*, 'Bite the MK bullet, Nats warn ANC', 1 March 1992.

29 *Sowetan*, 'Codesa to resume its work today', 23 March 1992.

30 *Citizen*, 'Kobie: no need to restructure SABC', 25 March 1992.

31 This submission was made on 30 March 1992.

32 *Sunday Times*, 'Brakes on Codesa II', 29 March 1992; *Sunday Star*, 'Codesa talks set to stumble', 29 March 1992. Speculation in the *Sunday Star* of 29 March ('Behind Codesa's doors the contenders concentrate on consensus') was that 'At the start all parties concentrated on bridging the gaps which separated them and did so with a fair amount of success. Now they have to resolve these areas of dispute before they can move ahead. The next major public accomplishment was to have been Codesa II when interim government arrangements were to have been announced. But some of the unfinished business which was left in abeyance to get the process running properly has already caused postponements. Now it is not expected until May'.

33 *Sunday Star*, 'Codesa talks set to stumble', 29 March 1992.

34 *Sowetan*, 'Violence: Codesa to intervene', 10 April 1992.

35 *Sunday Star*, 'Sword of Damocles hangs over Codesa II', 12 April 1992.

36 *Citizen*, 'ANC hits back at Kriel's allegations', 6 May 1992.

37 Final report of Working Group 1 to CODESA II, 13 May 1992.

38 See the *Citizen*, 'Peace accord to be revamped', 13 May 1992.

39 'In a sense, the entire process is hostage to the deliberations in this Working Group'. *Star*, 'Timing the transition', 6 February 1992.

40 *Citizen*, 'Plan for interim parliament', 28 January 1992.

41 *Business Day*, 'Government changes tack on ANC demands for transitional rule', 29 January 1992. There were already early indications that a split had emerged within the NP, because some felt that it would be impossible to negotiate an acceptable form of regional government that year and that there would be a diversion from the original NP proposals. Also see the *Sunday Times*, 'Split emerges in Nat camp', 2 February 1992. Later developments point clearly to a rift beginning to develop within the ranks of the NP. The question was to remain the same throughout – should the NP negotiate itself out of power?

42 *Finance Week*, 'Mbeki speaks out', 23 January 1992.

43 *Star*, 'Near and yet so far apart in thinking', 29 January 1992.

44 *Finance Week*, 'Quiet moves to coalition', 20 February 1992.

45 *Finance Week*, 'Mbeki speaks out', 23 January 1992.

46 *Finance Week*, 'Transition unfolds', 6 February 1992.

47 *Star*, 'IFP proposal put to Codesa', 6 February 1992.

48 The two commissions would include an electoral commission, in which the international community would participate, and a media commission. The four multi-party committees would focus on security, the budget, foreign relations, and local government.

49 This and the ANC's vision for the transition had been discussed in mid-February 1992 at the meeting of its National Working Committee and placed before its national executive a week later for approval. These issues were not discussed in detail and no concrete decision had been taken.

50 The Lancaster House agreement had provided white people with an entrenched number of seats in Parliament. An example of protection for civil servants is an agreement in Ghana made soon after independence, in terms of which no major change could take place with regard to the civil service for a specified period of time. See the *Financial Mail*, 'The transition', 28 February 1992.

51 *Business Day*, 'ANC presents its proposals for transition', 25 February 1992.

52 This position must also be seen against the background of the by-election defeat the NP had suffered not long before in Potchefstroom at the hands of the CP. The government used this as a strong bargaining chip at CODESA to press participants and especially the ANC for more room in which to manoeuvre. *Sunday Star*, 'NP will turn Potch defeat to advantage', 16 February 1992.

53 *Weekly Mail*, 'Liberalism – or just fear', 14 February 1992.

54 *Business Day*, 'Gov't tables proposals for interim rule', 24 March 1992. The areas which would fall within such an interim rule would be, in terms of the NP government's proposal, elections, regional government, local government, government finance, law and order, defence, and possibly education, housing, health, and international relations.

55 The ANC argued that the only way to deal with the TBVC states and self-governing territories was to cut off their government subsidies and so force them to co-operate. The government, however, was not yet ready to take such a drastic step, especially with political role-players that were potential allies.

56 *Business Day*, 'New Inkatha threat to pull out of talks', 25 March 1992.

57 *Business Day*, 'ANC spells out demands for Codesa', 15 April 1992.

58 *Business Day*, 'Codesa parties at a deadlock on transition', 7 April 1992; *Citizen*, 'Gov't, ANC differ on 1st interim stage', 7 April 1992.

59 *Business Day*, 'Progress on interim executive', 8 April 1992. The Technical Committee was chaired by Ken Andrew of the DP. The

election of members such as Andrew on the committee was an effective means of ensuring that the smaller parties were given a say in the process.

60 *Sunday Times*, 'Secret bid to clear impasse', 12 April 1992.

61 *Business Day*, 'Codesa plan for interim super cabinet', 28 April 1992.

62 *Sowetan*, 'IFP backs down on constitution', 11 May 1992.

63 Final report of Working Group 3 to CODESA II, 13 May 1992.

64 *Business Day*, 'Codesa talks make headway', 12 May 1992.

65 *Business Day*, 'Codesa agrees on joint control of security forces by interim gov't', 13 May 1992.

66 *Business Day*, 'Codesa not near breakthrough – gov't', 12 February 1992.

67 *Business Day*, 'ANC set to make concession to federalism', 18 February 1992.

68 *Weekly Mail*, 'Codesa briefs', 14 March 1992.

69 *New Nation*, 'Unity in diversity', 6 March 1992.

70 *Sunday Times*, 'FW: this is my bottom line', 8 March 1992.

71 *Business Day*, 'Jobs are safe, Mandela tells public service', 10 March 1992.

72 *Business Day*, 'NP takes a deep breath before leap into the unknown', 16 April 1992.

73 Minutes of the Management Committee, 30 March 1992. See also *Business Day*, 'May date set for Codesa agreement on interim rule and elections', 31 March 1992.

74 *Business Day*, 'Request for clarity on unitary state', 1 April 1992.

75 *Business Day*, 'ANC calls for 400 member assembly', 1 April 1992. The proposal was based on the understanding that there were 20 million eligible voters. Each seat in the assembly would therefore be supported by at least 50 000 voters. The proposal that the final constitution be negotiated within four months was no more than a negotiating position designed to force the NP into agreeing to some form of mechanism that would ensure that the new constitution could not be blocked.

76 *Business Day*, 'NP insists on power sharing', 2 April 1992.

77 *Citizen*, 'Risk of authoritarian gov't in ANC proposals', 4 April 1992.

78 The ANC's Negotiations Commission also had an opportunity to take stock of the progress made and to consider what its prospects were for CODESA II. The Commission identified two possibilities. Either CODESA II agreed on a package of substantive agreements which unmistakeably constituted a move towards a democratic order, or the plenary would simply record progress and identify blockages. The Commission suggested in an internal memorandum that there should be no agreement that CODESA II be postponed. Instead, CODESA II should be used to set out ANC views clearly and to isolate the government for its failure to measure up to its public commitment to a democratic order. See *Business Day*, 'ANC spells out demands for Codesa', 15 April 1992.

79 In this regard, the ANC was prepared to entertain the possibility of an interim arrangement of dual citizenship.

80 This point of view was echoed by Dr Alex Boraine, the executive director of the Institute for a Democratic South Africa (IDASA), in an interview with *New Nation* published on 24 April 1992. Boraine argued that CODESA II dare not fail because of the enormous expectations from the public who were anxious to see positive changes taking place.

81 *Business Day*, 'Independent panel on constitution proposed', 27 April 1992.

82 *Business Day*, 'Accord fuels hope for new constitution', 29 April 1992.

83 *Business Day*, 'Interim gov't plan is put on ice for Codesa', 30 April 1992.

84 *Business Day*, 'On the brink of a big bang', 30 April 1992; *Sunday Star*, 'Gov't/ANC almost there', 3 May 1992.

85 *Business Day*, 'Codesa settles TBVC issue', 6 May 1992.

86 *Star*, 'Codesa II prospects dim after key talks deadlock', 9 May 1992.

87 *Business Day*, 'Push to clear final hurdle at Codesa', 14 May 1992.

88 *Business Day*, 'Push to clear final hurdle at Codesa', 14 May 1992.

89 *Star*, 'Agonisingly close', 14 May 1992.

90 *Business Day*, 'ANC, gov't on collision course as Codesa II opens', 15 May 1992.

91 *Business Day*, 'Cloud over Codesa II as talks stall', 15 May 1992.

92 *Citizen*, 'Pik states gov't package', 15 May 1992.

93 Minutes of the Management Committee, 14 May 1992.

94 This suggests that the Management Committee itself had come to accept the shortcomings of the structure and size of the working groups as negotiating bodies.

95 *Business Day*, 'Air of acrimony and dissent prevails', 18 May 1992.

96 *Citizen*, various articles, 16 May 1992.

97 *Business Day*, 'Frustrations spark personal attacks', 18 May 1992.

98 *Star*, 'Mandela and FW step in', 16 May 1992.

99 Minutes of the Management Committee, 16 May 1992.

100 Minutes of the Daily Management Committee, 19 May 1992.

101 *Business Day*, 'Constitution will dominate next phase', 18 May 1992.

Chapter 8 Negotiating an end to the deadlock

1 Minutes of the Management Committee, 25 May 1992. This complaint was raised at the Management Committee where it was agreed that a professional company should be engaged to verify the allegations and give advice on preventative measures. *Star*, 'ANC telephones lines at Codesa tapped', 21 May 1992.

2 Minutes of the Management Committee, 1 June 1992.

3 *Business Day*, 'Govt and ANC try to mend relations', 26 May 1992.

4 The compromise proposal put forward by the ANC proved to be most controversial and was widely criticized. In their defence, the negotiators had argued that the compromise proposal was possible precisely because they were confident that it would be rejected by the NP government.

5 *Business Day*, 'Codesa accords on track – gov't', 4 June 1992.

6 *Citizen*, 'Mandela: ANC regrets impact on economy', 13 June 1992. The NP also complained about the effect of mass action in the Management Committee meeting on 15 June 1992.

7 *Citizen*, 'Open all Codesa talks to journalists: Slovo', 2 June 1992.

8 Minutes of the Management Committee, 1 June 1992.

9 Minutes of the Management Committee, 25 May and 1 June 1992.

10 *Business Day*, 'Codesa grinds to a halt on main issues', 16 June 1992.

11 *Star*, 'A case of blackmail', 18 June 1992.

12 ANC NEC press statement of 21 June 1992; *Star*, 'Angry ANC threatens to pull out of Codesa', 22 June 1992; *Business Day*, 'ANC suspends talks at Codesa', 24 June 1992.

13 A copy of the statement is included in the Schedule of Documents (Document 23: Annexure A).

14 *Business Day*, 'Business acts to help end talks crisis', 29 June 1992.

15 This breakdown proved very expensive – the cost of running CODESA for each month, excluding air transport and per diems offered to negotiators, was R400 000. The Department of Constitutional Development paid R43 000 in salaries, R100 000 for equipment rental, and R250 000 for office and parking rental. *Star*, 'Codesa logjam costs taxpayer a fortune', 16 July 1992.

16 Mandela's memorandum dated 26 June 1992 (Document 23 in the Schedule of Documents) set out the decision of the NEC of the ANC and detailed the fourteen demands made on the regime. De Klerk's reply, dated 2 July 1992 (Document 24), while it did not address the demands, denied government complicity in the violence and refused to commit the government to the principle of majority rule. Nevertheless, the government disbanded Battalion 31, Battalion 32, and Koevoet, referred the future of hostels to the Goldstone Commission, issued a proclamation banning dangerous weapons, and agreed to international monitoring of the violence.

17 *Star*, 'Gov't softens its interim demands', 3 July 1992.

18 *Star*, 'SA on collision course', 5 July 1992.

19 *New Nation*, editorial, 'Gov't's decision does not go far enough', 17 July 1992.

20 *Business Day*, 'ANC pours cold water on new govt plan', 27 July 1992.

21 *Citizen*, 'Gov't, Codesa allies meet', 28 July 1992.

22 Buthelezi described the possible bilateral relations between the NP and the ANC as a 'threat to democracy'. *Financial Times*, 'Buthelezi hints at pull out', 11 August 1992.

23 *Citizen*, 'Codesa parties to meet without ANC', 21 August 1992.

24 During the finalization of the negotiation of the final constitution, there were further bilaterals between the ANC and the NP headed by Ramaphosa and Meyer respectively which were also referred to as the 'channel meetings'.

25 The ANC's delegation was led by Ramaphosa and supported by Joe Slovo, Jacob Zuma, Mac Maharaj, and Valli Moosa. The NP's delegation was led by Roelf Meyer and supported by Leon Wessels, Sam de Beer, Dawie de Villiers, Fanie van der Merwe, and Neil Barnard.

26 The negotiators were Penuel Maduna and Mathews Phosa for the ANC, and General Willemse for the Department of Prisons.

27 The negotiators were Hassen Ebrahim and Billy Cobbett for the ANC, and Leon Wessels and Gert Myburgh for the NP.

28 *City Press*, 'FW plans law for unity gov't', 13 September 1992.

29 *Business Day*, 'Bisho tragedy will harden attitudes on negotiations', 9 September 1992.

30 *Star*, 'Mandela's olive branch', 15 September 1992.

31 *Business Day*, 'Mandela calls for help on peace summit', 16 September 1992.

32 *Sunday Times*, 'Kobie wrecks summit deal', 20 September 1992.

33 *Business Day*, 'De Klerk, Meyer in damage control talks', 21 September 1992.

34 At the same time, the police confirmed that they were investigating seventeen of the most senior ANC leaders, including Oliver Tambo, Chris Hani, and Joe Slovo, for various alleged crimes.

35 A copy of the agreement is included in the Schedule of Documents (Document 27).

36 *Star*, 'SA wakes up to a fresh beginning', 26 September 1992.

37 *Business Day*, 'Inkatha out of talks with government', 28
    September 1992.
38 *Business Day*, 'Buthelezi rejects overtures', 29 September 1992.
39 *Business Day*, 'Homeland leaders want Codesa scrapped',
    7 October 1992.
40 *Sunday Tribune*, 'Kick-start for Codesa', 10 January 1993.
41 *Business Day*, 'Treurnicht rejects Codesa III', 12 January 1993.
42 *Business Day*, 'Shift in Inkatha strategy on Codesa', 14 January
    1993; *Citizen*, 'Buthelezi repeats call for review conference',
    29 October 1992.
43 *Business Day*, 'UN leader criticises Buthelezi', 18 November 1992.
44 Apparently, Buthelezi even refused to answer the Secretary-
    General's calls.
45 *Citizen*, 'KwaZulu approves federal system', 1 December 1992.
46 *Financial Times*, 'Buthelezi threatens to form new state',
    2 December 1992.
47 This meeting was held at a reserve, Aloe Ridge, north-east of
    Johannesburg.
48 The ANC met with the Tripartite Alliance (formed by the ANC,
    SACP, and COSATU) on 28 October 1992, the Patriotic Front on
    29 October, the DP on 6 November, business leaders on 13
    November, the Bophutatswana government on
    16 November, and the AVU on 19 November 1992.
49 At this meeting, the ANC also considered the mandate to be given
    to its negotiators. A document containing its proposed nego-
    tiating positions was also settled, a copy of which is contained in
    the Schedule of Documents (Document 28). *Star*, 'Codesa still
    best forum for settlement – Mandela', 30 November 1992.
50 A copy of the document is included in the Schedule of Documents
    (Document 28).
51 *Business Day*, 'New bid for ANC, Inkatha to meet', 3 November
    1992; and on the support of business, see *Business Day*, 'Interim
    rule needed – Relly', 3 November 1992.
52 *Citizen*, 'ANC wants transfers of public land frozen', 4 November
    1992.

53 *Business Day*, editorial, 'Buying friends', 5 November 1992.
54 *Business Day* and *Sowetan*, editorials, 16 November 1992.
55 ANC *Negotiation Bulletin* no. 19, 10 December 1992.
56 *Citizen*, 'Codesa will be restructured', 5 December 1992.
57 *Star*, 'ANC-govt deal angers IFP', 12 December 1992.
58 It was suggested that a conservative faction formed in the NP – including Justice Minister Kobie Coetsee, Law and Order Minister Hernus Kriel, Local Government Minister Tertius Delport, and Natal leader George Bartlett – was more inclined to develop a relationship with Inkatha as an ally against the ANC. On the other side in the NP were Constitutional Development Minister Roelf Meyer, Manpower Minister Leon Wessels, Cape leader Dawie de Villiers, and Foreign Minister Pik Botha, who argued that the success of the negotiations process lay in the ability of the NP to effectively engage the ANC. While publicly the only evidence of this rift was the odd statement made by NP MPs such as George Bartlett and Jurie Mentz, the reality of the rift became obvious in the bilaterals. Tertius Delport was largely responsible for the deadlock in Working Group 2 at CODESA II, while Kobie Coetsee worked hard to wreck the Record of Understanding. Later, Hernus Kriel would make a valiant effort in the bilaterals during January on the question of security. See the *Sunday Times*, 'Strains show in cabinet', 12 December 1992.
59 *Weekly Mail* 'US nudges Buthelezi to join negotiations', 8 January 1993.
60 *Star*, 'Negotiations '93 kick off', 9 January 1993.
61 *Citizen*, 'CP men did not exceed mandate – Dr T', 11 January 1993.
62 *Citizen*, 'Federalism: govt is close to IFP, says min.', 18 January 1993.
63 *Business Day*, 'Inkatha talks with govt end in stalemate', 20 January 1993.
64 *Sowetan*, 'IFP, NP make up', 28 January 1993.
65 *Business Day*, 'ANC's election campaign shifts into first gear', 21 January 1993.

66 *Citizen*, 'Sites for polling stations identified', 12 February 1993.
67 The January meetings took place at the Presidensie in Pretoria and the February meetings at the Denel missile test range at Arniston in the Western Cape.
68 *Sunday Times*, 'U-turn as NP backs single leader for SA', 7 February 1993.
69 *Star*, 'Govt, ANC reach deal on future', 13 February 1993.

Chapter 9 Negotiating the transition

1 *Star*, 'Scenarios differ as democracy's dawn beckons', 27 February 1993.
2 The National Executive Committee of the ANC met in full plenary session from 16 to 18 February 1993 in Soweto, Johannesburg. ANC *Negotiation Bulletin* no. 21, February 1993.
3 *Business Day*, 'Meeting tackles differences', 2 March 1993.
4 *Citizen*, 'ANC, govt can't decide on president's powers', 29 March 1993.
5 A copy of the resolutions adopted is included in the Schedule of Documents (Document 29).
6 This was the subject of several consultations between members of the Patriotic Front. Some in the Patriotic Front felt that the crisis in the country obliged political leaders to find an urgent resolution. It was therefore necessary, they believed, to proceed within the CODESA format and not pander to the views of the right wing.
7 The political parties and their representatives were: African National Congress: M. C. Ramaphosa (B. Masekela, J. Zuma), T. Mbeki, M. Maharaj, M. Manzini; Afrikaner Volksunie: C. D. de Jager (C. Viljoen, C. Pienaar, R. de Ville), M. J. Mentz, A. S. Beyers, A. Lombard; Bophuthatswana government: R. Cronje, R. Mangope, B. E. Keikelame, S. G. Mothibe; Cape traditional leaders: M. Nonkonyana, G. D. Gwadiso, G. S. K. Nota, Jongilanga (initials not given), S. M. Burns-Ncmashe, S. Sigcau; Ciskei

government: M. B. Webb, I. J. Smuts, R. M. Ngcofe, F. M. Faku, W. M. Zantsi, V. T. Gqiba; Democratic Party: C. W. Eglin, A. L. K. Jordaan, K. M. Andrew, M. Finnemore, D. Smuts, M. Moriarty, M. Rajab; Dikwankwetla Party: T. J. Mohapi, S. P. Matla, O. M. Moji, Prof. Wessels (initials not given), J. S. S. Phatang; Inkatha Freedom Party: F. T. Mdlalose, M. F. Cassim, V. J. Matthews, M. G. R. Oriani-Ambrosini, S. Felgate, F. X. Gasa; Intando Yesizwe Party: N. J. Mahlangu, N. A. P. Laka, V. N. Mtsweni; Inyandza National Movement: S. S. Ripinga, M. M. S. Gininda, N. F. S. Baloi, E. N. Ginindza; Conservative Party: T. Langley, F. Hartzenberg, P. Mulder, F. J. Le Roux; Kwazulu government: B. S. Ngubane, M. Jiyane, S. H. Gumede, D. R. B. Madide, H. Ngubane; Labour Party: I. M. Richards, E. Samuels, L. Landers, D. Lockey/T. Abrahams, P. A. C. Hendrickse, Y. Bassier/P. Lategan; Natal/Transvaal Indian Congress: P. J. Gordhan, K. Mayet, C. Saloojee, F. Cachalia, H. Wardi; National Party: D. J. de Villiers, O. van Zyl, L. Wessels, P. Coetzer, J. Rabie, E. Ngcobondwane; National People's Party: A. Rajbansi, B. P. Jaglal, S. Ismail, A. Hurbans, M. Govender, A. Rambarran; Orange Free State traditional leaders: R. H. Mopeli, R. Ramasiea, M. B. Mota, E. T. Phoofolo, M. A. Molefe; Pan Africanist Congress: B. Alexander, M. Lithero, W. Seriti, E. Mothopeng, D. Desai, J. Serdile; Solidarity Party: J. N. Reddy, C. Pillay, Y. Moolla, S. Razak, N. Singh; South African Communist Party: J. Slovo, E. Pahad, T. Mtintso, Z. Kota, S. Shilowa; South African government: R. P. Meyer, S. J. Schoeman, H. J. Kriel, L. D. Barnard, J. T. Delport, A. Routier; Transkei government: H. B. Holomisa, M. Titus, Z. Titus, J. T. Madiba, N. Jajula, M. Mpahlwa; Transvaal traditional leaders: N. M. Malekane, W. Mabunda, M. A. Netshimbupfe, M. E. Mabena, M. M. Khumalo, J. Kekana; United People's Front: M. J. Mahlangu, M. E. Mapheto, R. J. Dombo, A. Tshabalala, S. J. Maake, M. I. Moroamoche; Venda government: S. E. Moeti, M. P. Nthabalala, M. Ligege, N. E. Mulaudzi, K. B. Magwaba, A. Masehela; Ximoko Progressive Party: E. E. Ngobeni, K. R. Myakayaka, J. C. Ackron, T. B. Shibambu, P. T. Shilubane.

8   Copies of the resolutions adopted are included in the Schedule of
    Documents (Documents 30 and 31).

9   The structures established to support this new phase of nego-
    tiation were: the plenary (ten persons per party), a Negotiating
    Council (two delegates and two advisers per party), a Planning
    Committee (which operated in the same format as the Manage-
    ment Committee of CODESA) with a subcommittee (consisting
    of S. S. van der Merwe of the NP, Mac Maharaj of the ANC, and
    Ben Ngubane of the IFP), and Technical Committees of experts.
    The Planning Committee received reports from the Technical
    Committees and prepared resolutions for consideration by the
    Negotiating Council. The two major improvements on the
    format of negotiation at CODESA were that the negotiation in the
    Negotiating Council was now open to the media, and that the
    process had the benefit of technical experts.

10 These committees would later also become especially valuable in
    isolating, and prioritizing, among a range of problematic areas,
    the most crucial and intractable deadlock issues, such as educa-
    tion and language rights.

11 The members of the Planning Committee were B. Alexander, C.
    W. Eglin, P. J. Gordhan, C. Kruger, R. P. Meyer, M. C. Ramaphosa,
    S. Sigcau, J. Slovo, and Z. Titus. The committee was chaired by
    one of its members on a rotating basis.

12 The inclusion of Ben Ngubane allowed the IFP to be and feel a
    part of the entire process. Ngubane was noted for his congenial
    style and proved to be helpful. He subsequently became the
    Minister of Arts and Culture in the government of national unity,
    and later the IFP chairperson and Premier of the province of
    KwaZulu/Natal.

13 Chris Hani, at the time of his assassination, was the Secretary-
    General of the SACP and a member of the ANC's NEC. He was
    also one of South Africa's most popular leaders among the youth.
    Chris Hani was shot in cold blood in front of his daughter at his
    house. A man closely linked to right-wing elements was arrested
    for the murder several hours later.

14 *Sunday Times*, 'Economy set for a nose-dive', 18 April 1993.

15 ANC *Negotiation Bulletin* no. 24, April 1993.

16 *Business Day*, 'Negotiation under pressure', 16 April 1993.

17 *Sunday Star*, 'Govt stares at the abyss', 18 April 1993.

18 *Business Day*, 'Pressure on to pick up pace', 23 April 1993.

19 *Business Day*, 'Focus on transitional council', 19 April 1993.

20 *Star*, 'Ex-general warns of secession', 5 May 1993.

21 *Star*, 'Marching to Afrikanerland', 6 May 1993.

22 *Business Day*, 'Right-wing threatens to strike back', 7 May 1993.

23 *Citizen*, 'Mineworkers back Front', 11 May 1993.

24 The reason for the delay in starting this meeting was to allow the ANC to attend to matters following the assassination of Chris Hani earlier that month. This meeting also dealt with the name of the process but without successful resolution. See the minutes of the Planning Committee, 22 April 1993.

25 The Technical Committees were asked to submit initial reports to the Planning Committee on 14 May for tabling in the Negotiating Council on 18 May 1993. The idea was that once the reports were approved by the Council, the Council would then table the reports with the Negotiating Forum for approval. See the minutes of the Negotiating Council, 30 April 1993.

26 The Ciskei government and the CP opposed the motion and the AVU give it qualified support. See the minutes of the Negotiating Council, 7 May 1993. The declaration noted the urgent need to inspire the broad public's confidence in the negotiating process and of the ability of parties to peacefully resolve problems, offer the people of South Africa a clear vision of the major milestones in the negotiating and transition process, and to create conditions which would eliminate violence in South Africa. Recognizing the need for democratic elections, the parties committed themselves to reach agreements on binding constitutional principles, the constitutional framework, and the constitution-making process in terms of which elections would be held. They further agreed to ensure that the negotiating process moved forward sufficiently over the next four weeks, at which stage the exact date for an

election could be set that should be not later than the end of April 1994.

27 *Financial Times*, 'De Klerk resists black majority rule', 26 May 1993.

28 A later submission of the NP's draft of the constitution would take this debate a step further. See the *Weekly Mail*, 'Pretoria takes a hard line', 4 June 1993.

29 At a meeting of the Tripartite Alliance on 22 April 1993 it was resolved to demand that there be an immediate announcement of an election date; the transitional executive council should be installed as a matter of urgency; and all armed formations should be placed under immediate joint multi-party control. In addition, the ANC called for the process of multi-party negotiation to be speeded up.

30 *Sunday Times*, 'Big business in push for election date', 30 May 1993.

31 *Business Day*, 'Cosatu plans push for settlement', 4 June 1993.

32 These structures were multilaterally negotiated and established for the purpose of advancing the economic situation in South Africa. It would appear that the government representatives in these structures deliberately stalled on important discussions, a manoeuvre which seemed to go hand in hand with situations in which there was little political progress.

33 Minutes of the Negotiating Council, 1 June 1993.

34 ANC *Negotiation Bulletin* no. 29.

35 Minutes of the Negotiating Council, 15 June 1993.

36 *Star*, editorial, 'No time left to waste on the spoilers', 3 July 1993.

37 *Business Day*, 'Govt, Inkatha's constitutional aims similar, says Meyer', 16 July 1993.

38 The commission was made up of fifteen members, and was chaired by Prof. Bax Nomvete.

39 *Business Day*, 'Govt, ANC unveil similar proposals for new-look regional borders', 7 July 1993. The original ANC position was that the question of regions should only be dealt with in the consti-tuent assembly. In this regard, they proposed that the boundaries

of the bantustans and self-governing territories be removed and the country revert to four provinces as originally agreed to in the 1910 constitution. However, influential experts within the ANC such as Thozamile Botha were also convinced of the merit of the proposal put forward by the Development Bank of South Africa. This proposal recommended the division of the country into a number of provinces that would constitute 'developmental regions' with focused economic concerns. The decision to have nine provinces was based in large part on the ideas put forward by the Development Bank.

40　The commission received and considered 304 written submissions and heard eighty oral presentations at various centres around the country, but still voiced its concern at the inadequacy of local community involvement in the process. This was due to a number of factors, including the limited time allowed, the lack of capacity to respond, either orally or in written form, and the limited number of people and organizations that the notification of the commission's brief was able to reach.

41　Minutes of the Planning Committee and Negotiating Council, 2 August 1993. The commission was instructed by the Negotiating Council to take into account historical boundaries, infrastructure, administrative considerations, the necessity of limiting financial and other costs, the need to minimize inconvenience or the dislocation of services, demographic considerations, economic viability, development potential, and cultural and language realities. There were three overarching national concerns pertaining to the formation and demarcation of regions which the commission considered important. These were the need to fashion a democratic culture by bringing government closer to the people, the need to create an environment that was conducive to economic growth and development, and the need to build one nation through the acknowledgement of diversity and the reduction of conflict.

42　*Business Day*, 'Row looms today over interim constitution which pleases no one', 26 July 1993.

43   The first report of the Technical Committee (dated 13 May 1993)
     sought to do no more than analyse the constitutional issues
     raised. Its second report (dated 19 May) presented its approach on
     these issues. It was only in its third report (dated 27 May) that the
     committee warmed up to the issues and presented the first
     glimpses of substantive constitutional matters.

44   The first formulations in this regard appeared in the eighth
     Technical Committee report dated 26 July 1993. These formu-
     lations were then improved and part of five chapters was set out in
     the ninth report dated 10 August 1993.

45   *Citizen*, 'Reject talks, prepare to defend yourselves – Viljoen',
     20 August 1993.

46   *Business Day*, 'Govt has lost right to rule, says General', 20 August
     1993.

47   *Business Day*, 'Viljoen still full of hope for the future', 9 September
     1993.

48   *Business Day*, 'Transitional gov't rejected by PAC, CP',
     21 September 1993.

49   *Business Day*, 'Buthelezi cannot hold SA to ransom',
     9 September 1993.

50   *Star*, editorial, 18 September 1993.

51   *Business Day*, 'Inkatha takes heart from secret meetings and
     prepares for elections', 4 October 1993.

52   *Business Day*, 'Transitional gov't bill tabled in parliament',
     17 September 1993.

53   *Business Day*, 'Form of interim gov't begins to shape up'
     15 September 1993.

54   *Business Day*, 'Cracks in Cosag threaten existence', 5 October
     1993.

55   *Business Day*, 'Bophuthatswana, Ciskei quit talks and join new
     right-wing Alliance', 8 October 1993.

56   *Citizen*, 'Strategy of Alliance', 8 October 1993.

57   Some members of the Negotiating Council were unhappy about
     tolerating any delays. They believed that the intention of the
     Freedom Alliance was to prevent the plenary sitting of the multi-

party process from taking place. *Business Day,* 'Crucial talks on hold until new Alliance states its case', 11 October 1993.

58   *Business Day,* 'FW proposes referendum to break impasse', 12 October 1993.

59   *Business Day,* 'NP congress seeks ways to restrict majority gov't', 13 October 1993.

60   *Sunday Times,* 'Unfinished business', 24 October 1993.

61   *Business Day,* 'ANC talks with Freedom Alliance stall', 26 October 1993.

62   *Business Day,* 'Mandela, FW in bid to end talks impasse', 27 October 1993.

63   See the bilateral agreement between the South African government and the ANC tabled with the MPNP as document no. 1/3/2/5/191 dated 28 October 1993.

64   See par. 11 of MPNP document no. 1/3/2/5/191 dated 28 October 1993.

65   *Sunday Times,* 'It's eyeball to eyeball', 31 October 1993.

66   *Business Day* 'Some progress made with Freedom Alliance', 5 November 1993.

67   *Sunday Times,* 'De Klerk decides to push ahead without Alliance', 7 November 1993. Apparently, this decision was not made lightly or without resistance from within the cabinet. Several members of the NP cabinet wanted a closer relationship with Inkatha in particular. *Business Day,* 'Freedom Alliance showing signs of strain', 12 November 1993.

68   *Business Day,* 10 November 1993.

69   *Business Day,* 'Govt and ANC agree on formula to give public servants security', 8 November 1993.

70   *Business Day,* 'D-Day as FW and Mandela clinch deals', 17 November 1993.

71   See the interim constitution, sec. 89(2), Act 200, 1993. See also the *Financial Times,* 'Dawn of the new South Africa', 18 November 1993.

72   *Business Day,* 'New era begins with compromise', 18 November 1993.

73 *Financial Times*, 'ANC and De Klerk in local power-share deal',
17 November 1993.

74 *Sunday Times*, 'A constitution we can bank on', 21 November
1993.

75 *Business Day*, 'US considers ways to support a new SA',
27 January 1994.

76 *Business Day*, 'World salutes "historic" pact on constitution',
19 November 1993.

77 This did not necessarily mean that all in the business community
supported the interim constitution. Leon Louw of the Free
Market Foundation called it an 'authoritarian and undemocratic'
constitution. Referring to the bill of rights, he stated that it was a
'weasel constitution'. *Sunday Times*, 'Business fettered by a flawed
constitution', 23 January 1994.

78 *Business Day*, 'NP backs De Klerk on new constitution',
23 November 1993.

79 *Business Day*, 'CP threats as gov't tries to woo Alliance',
23 November 1993.

80 *Business Day*, 'Volksfront supporters must now do military training, says Viljoen', 18 November 1993.

81 *Star*, 'Alliance inclusion: hopes fade', 20 November 1993.

82 *Star*, 'ANC, AVF reach working agreement', 20 November 1993.

83 *Business Day*, 'Alliance concerns over ANC's preconditions',
10 December 1993.

84 *Business Day*, 'Alliance demands disappoint govt', 15 December
1993.

85 *Business Day*, 'Freedom Alliance talks fail', 21 December 1993.

86 *Business Day*, 'Volksfront set to sign pact with ANC',
21 December 1993.

87 *Business Day*, 'Volksfront does about-turn on pact',
22 December 1993.

88 *Business Day*, 'Govt to spend R21m on new constitution drive', 29
December 1993.

89 *Star*, 'Ciskei to join TEC, says Gqozo', 11 January 1994. Talks
with the Alliance broke down again in early February. *Business*

Day, 'Freedom Alliance pulls out of negotiation', 9 February 1994.

90 *Sunday Times*, 'Viljoen sparks fury by talking peace', 30 January 1994.

91 *Star*, 'Boycott: the risks show', 15 February 1994.

92 *Sunday Times*, 'ANC says it is not against extension', 13 February 1994.

93 *Financial Times*, 'Inkatha joins with right-wing to boycott elections', 14 February 1994.

94 *Financial Times*, 'Mandela moves to accommodate South African right-wing', 17 February 1994.

95 *Business Day*, 'ANC unveils concessions to Alliance', 17 February 1994.

96 *Business Day*, 'Plan to call special session of parliament', 16 February 1994.

97 These six principles were extended by the proposal to make allowance for the establishment of a twenty-member 'volkstaat council' to cater for demands for an Afrikaner homeland. The council would have the authority to gather, process, and make available information regarding proposed boundaries, powers, and functions, and legislative, executive, and other structures of such a volkstaat, its proposed relationship with government at national and provincial level, and any other matter directly relevant to the establishment of a volkstaat. *Business Day*, 'Govt, ANC propose volkstaat council', 21 February 1994.

98 *Business Day*, 'Mandela, De Klerk still hopeful that election boycott can be averted', 18 February 1994.

99 *Star*, 'The shape of things to come', 22 January 1994.

100 *Business Day*, 'New regional concession to woo Alliance', 22 February 1994.

101 *Business Day*, 'Sides "find each other" in first mediation talks', 9 March 1994.

102 *Business Day*, 'Negotiators set to sign volkstaat deal', 25 March 1994.

103 The drama of this period was graphically shown in media reports,

photographs, and television broadcasts showing soldiers of the AWB being killed as they retreated from the area. Lucas Mangope, in his last moments of rule, called upon his allies in COSAG to defend his government. Right-wingers rallied to his call, and in the ensuing conflict, forces allied to General Constand Viljoen were forced to retreat in the face of South African troops.

104   This agreement became a source of much controversy. In terms of the agreement, certain changes were effected to the constitutional principles and it was resolved that there would be international mediation between the NP, the ANC, and the IFP on a number of issues. Because the international mediation never materialized, the IFP saw it as grounds on which to withdraw from the negotiations on the final constitution in the Constitutional Assembly.

105   In this agreement, a Volkstaat Council was established in terms of the constitution to enable Afrikaners promoting the idea of self-determination to pursue their ambitions within a constitutional framework. This agreement was seminal in that it ensured that a right-wing backlash to the process of transition never materialized.

Chapter 10   A framework for negotiating the final constitution

1   These were not compatible tasks and a political leader's engagement in one of them was often to the detriment of the other. The major problem was one of available time. While on the one hand, political leaders were expected to establish a new, democratic dispensation, for which there was neither precedent nor experience, on the other they were expected to engage in extended negotiations with many different role-players to draft the final constitution.

2   See chapter five of the interim constitution, which deals with the adoption of the new constitution.

3   See Constitutional Assembly resolution of Monday 31 October

1994, no. 4 sec. 11.1. The question of the durability of the constitution was also affected by the technical and legal integrity of the text. The text had to display foresight and wisdom, for while it had to provide necessary protection, it had to avoid suffocating government or making good governance difficult. The success of the final text of the constitution would not be judged by how well it served the country in the immediate future, but by how well it served the country in the distant future. Generations to come had to appreciate the value of the constitution as much as the present.

4 The principle of accessibility relates to both the question of plain language as well as the ability of ordinary citizens to obtain physical copies of the actual text. The argument was that the constitution had to be drafted in a way in which the ordinary citizen affected by it should be able to read and understand it.

5 See Schedule 4 of the interim constitution.

6 Marinus Wiechers, 'Namibia: The 1982 constitutional principles and their legal significance' in the *South African Yearbook of International Law* 1, 1990.

7 *Executive Council of the Western Cape Legislature and Others v President of the Republic of South Africa and Others*, 1995 (4) SA 877 (CC) at 895D-G per Chaskalson P.

8 The constitutional principles are included in the Schedule of Documents (Document 35).

9 This was the argument put forward by the Constitutional Assembly in its submission of the new constitution to the Constitutional Court.

10 For a perspective on the manner in which the constitutional principles came into being, see Prof. Hugh Corder's article, 'Towards a South African constitution' in *Modern Law Review* 57, 1994, p. 491, and particularly pp. 514–517. See also Francois Venter, 'Requirements for a new constitutional text: the imperatives of the Constitutional Principles' in *South African Law Journal* 32, 1995, especially pp. 32–33; Gretchen Carpenter, 'The Republic of South Africa Constitution Act 200 of 1993 – an overview' in *South African Public Law*, 1994, p. 227.

11   Such an amendment would affect sec. 73, and secs. 73 (1) and 73 (9) in particular. While such an amendment would not have been barred in terms of sec. 74 (1), sec. 73 (9) was clearly intended to impose an obligation to complete the new constitution within the required two years, failing which the President was obliged to dissolve Parliament and call for an election.

12   The work programme was agreed to by the Constitutional Committee on 2 December 1994.

13   See Constitutional Assembly resolution of Monday 31 October 1994, no. 4 sec. 11.4.

14   The political parties represented in the Constitutional Assembly were the ANC, the NP, the IFP, the Freedom Front (FF), the DP, the PAC, and the African Christian Democratic Party (ACDP). (The IFP stopped participating in the affairs of the Constitutional Assembly in April 1995. They did continue to play a role in media productions, however, such as *Constitutional Talk* on television, and were provided with copies of all documentation dispatched to the other parties.) Included in this category should be the role of the Commission on Provincial Government and the Volkstaat Council. Both of these structures were given the constitutional right in terms of sec. 164 and sec. 184B respectively to make submissions to the Constitutional Assembly for its consideration.

15   However, there were a large number of bilateral and multilateral meetings that took place in private without the media or public in attendance. These were meetings privately agreed to between the parties. This did cause some controversy, especially with structures of civil society, among others, the Human Rights Commission, the Gender Project, and the South African Council of Churches. This matter is addressed in greater detail further on. It is worth noting that in general the media were accommodating about this arrangement, although they voiced strong objections to being excluded from multilateral meetings.

16   See Chapter 5 and secs. 68–74 of the interim constitution.

17   The members of the Constitutional Committee were: M. C. Ramaphosa (chairperson), L. Wessels (deputy-chairperson), C.

Ackermann, K. M. Andrew (alt.), K. Asmal, M. Bhabha, S. Camerer (alt.), O. C. Chabane, D. Dalling (alt.), S. J. de Beer (alt.), J. H. de Lange, P. de Lille (alt.), D. C. du Toit, C.W. Eglin, A. Fourie, G. J. Fraser-Moleketi, F. N. Ginwala, N. J. Gogotya, P. J. Gordhan, L. M. Green (alt.), P. J. Groenewald (alt.), W. A. Hofmeyr, S. P. Holomisa, J. L. Kgoali, B. Mbete-Kgositsile, T. J. King, L. Landers (alt.), M. G. Ligege, D. Lockey, J. Love, B. S. Mabandla, P. C. Maduna (alt.), M. Maharaj (alt.), M. J. Mahlangu, N. J. Mahlangu, D. W. Makhanya, D. M. Malatsi (alt.), N. N. Mapisa-Nqakula (alt.), P. G. Marais, J. W. Maree (alt.), S. Mdladlana (alt.), K. R. Meshoe, R. P. Meyer, M. V. Moosa, M. W. Moosa (alt.), L. M. Mti (alt.), L. P. H. M. Mtshali, C. P. Mulder, P. W. A. Mulder (alt), Y. L. M. Myakayaka-Manzini, S. Mzimela, B. T. Ngcuka, B. E. Nzimande, D. Omar (alt.), E. G. Pahad, G. N. M. Pandor, J. A. Rabie, R. Rabinowitz, S. S. Ripinga, N. N. Routledge-Madlala (alt.), S. J. Schoeman (alt.), J. Schreiner (alt.), D. P. A. Schutte, S. A. Seaton (alt.), W. M. Serote (alt.), L. Sisulu (alt.), T. V. Sifora, R. K. Sizani, Z. S. T. Skweyiya (alt), P. F. Smith, P. J. Steenkamp (alt), M. E. Surty (alt), R. S. Suttner, L. J. Swanepoel (alt.), I. Vadi (alt.), A. van Breda, F. J. van Deventer, F. J. van Heerden (alt.), and C. L. Viljoen. The Committee's staff were: Margaret Keegan, minutes secretary; and Laetitia Meter, administrative secretary.

18 The reason for the Constitutional Committee's being the main negotiating body was to ensure that the smaller parties, which were not able to field members in Theme Committees all the time, were not unduly prejudiced. It was also for this reason that the key negotiators of each party were located in the Constitutional Committee.

19 The permanent members of the subcommittee were: M. C. Ramaphosa (chairperson), L. Wessels (deputy-chairperson), L. M. Green, K. R. Meshoe (alt.), M. V. Moosa, M. Myakayaka-Manzini, O. C. Chabane, C. W. Eglin, K. Andrew (alt.), C. Mulder, P. Groenewald, R. Meyer, P. G. Marais, S. de Beer (alt.), A. van Breda (alt.), J. Rabie (alt.), T. King (alt.), R. Sizani, and P. de Lille (alt.). Parties also nominated additional members who served on

the subcommittee from time to time to deal with specialized matters. A team of staff members from the Secretariat department of the administration provided back-up to the subcommittee. Lucille Meyer, head of the department, co-ordinated agendas and the production of documentation, while Katharine McKenzie, Margaret Keegan, Susan Rabinowitz, and Thomas Smit minuted meetings of the subcommittee. Laetitia Meter was administrative secretary.

20   The members of the Management Committee were: M. C. Ramaphosa (chairperson), L. Wessels (deputy-chairperson), O. C. Chabane, C. W. Eglin, W. Felgate, B. S. Mabandla (later substituted by M. Myakayaka-Manzini), K. Meshoe, R. Meyer, M. V. Moosa, R. Sizani, A. van Breda, C. Viljoen.

21   The membership of the core groups was also made up in proportions similar to the Theme Committee to prevent any unfair advantage of one party over others.

22   Each Technical Committee consisted of three or four experts. In addition, various ad hoc committees of experts were also appointed to deal with specific subjects dealt with by a Theme Committee. Examples of these are local government, self-determination, and traditional leaders.

23   The chairpersons of Theme Committee 1 were: N. J. Mahlangu (ANC), P. G. Marais (NP), and L. P. H. M. Mtshali (IFP). The members were: A. Ally (alt.), M. S. Booi, M. F. Cassim (alt.), L. Chiba (alt.), M. M. Chikane, L. L. L. Chiwayo (alt.), C. S. Cwele (alt.), P. de Lille (alt.), M. M. Dyani, L. M. Fani (alt.), E. T. Ferreira (alt.), F. Ginwala, A. D. Goosen (alt.), L. M. Green (alt.), D. M. Gumede, N. E. Hangana, A. P. Janse van Rensburg, N. N. Kekana, N. E. K. Kuzwayo (alt.), N. E. Lamani, M. K. Lekgoro, M. C. Mabuza (alt.), S. J. Macozoma, N. T. Majola-Pikoli, A. Marais, K. R. Meshoe, P. G. Mngomezulu, P. Mokaba, J. H. Momberg, E. K. Moorcroft, T. Msane (alt.), M. Msomi, T. T. Mukhuba (alt.), P. W. A. Mulder, B. S. Ncube, C. G. Niehaus, B. J. Nobunga (alt.), B. E. Nzimande, S. S. Ripinga, N. C. Routledge, E. A. Schoeman, S. Seaton, J. Selfe, M. W. Serote (alt.), G. Shope (alt.), N. R. Shope, A.

N. Sisulu, P. Smith, D. M. Streicher, L. Swanepoel, T. J. Tshivase, F. J. van Deventer, M. C. J. van Schalkwyk, I. D. van Zyl, B. H. Vilakazi, C. L. Viljoen, A. J. Williams, and M. K. Zondi. The members of the Technical Committee were: Prof. H. M. Corder, Dr C. J. Heunis, Mr Z. Hussain, and Prof. C. Dlamini. The Theme Committee's staff were: Leola Rammble, managing secretary; Susan Rabinowitz, minutes secretary; and Aziza Parker, administrative secretary.

24   Theme Committee 1 held fifty-six meetings from 19 September 1994 to 11 September 1995 and processed 3 000 submissions. Six orientation workshops were held to facilitate submissions of parties on various issues dealt with by the Theme Committee. Public hearings were held on the seat of government, languages, names and symbols, the secular state, equality and affirmative action, and the character of the state.

25   The chairpersons of Theme Committee 2 were: M. J. Mahlangu (ANC), V. B. Ndlovu (IFP), and J. A. Rabie (NP). The members were: C. Ackerman, K. M. Andrew (alt.), M. J. Badenhorst, G. Bhengu (alt.), A. S. Beyers, B. C. Bester (alt.), B. P. Biyela (alt.), P. Dexter (alt.), N. Diale, G. Q. Doidge, A. G. Ebrahim, C. W. Eglin, J. A. Forster, P. H. Groenewald, S. P. Holomisa, P. A. C. Hendrickse, D. P. S. Jana (alt.), H. P. Lebona (alt.), M. G. Ligege, S. K. Louw, E. Lucas (alt.), R. T. Mabhudafhasi, P. Maduna, J. L. Mahlangu (alt.), I. Mars, F. B. Marshoff, N. L. Mashile (alt.), A. Mlangeni, C. P. Moloto (alt), G. M. Mohlamonyane, P. K. Mothoagae, M. Msomi, L. M. Mti (alt.), C. Mulder, G. M. Mushwana, I. Mutsila, M. J. Mwedamutsu, S. D. Nxumalo, W. A. Odendaal (alt.), D. A. A. Olifant, E. G. H. Pahad, N. E. Phakathi, M. C. Ramusi, B. Ranchod, P. S. Sekgobela, J. Selfe (alt.), B. E. E. Setheema, S. Shabangu, R. K. Sizani (alt.), P. J. Steenkamp, D. P. Taunyane, L. J. Tolo, V. Tyobeka, and C. A. Wyngaard. The members of the Technical Committee were: Prof. D. van Wyk, Dr W. Seriti, Adv. A. M. M. Motimele, Prof. N. Steytler; on traditional leaders: Prof. T. Nhlapo, Ms T. Madonsela, Prof. R. B. Mqeke; on self-determination: Prof. H. M. Corder, Prof. A. W. G. Raath, and

Prof. W. Breytenbach. The staff were: James Nene, managing secretary; Thomas Smit, minutes secretary; and Charmaine Fredericks, administrative secretary.

26   Theme Committee 2 held sixty-one meetings between 19 September 1994 and 11 September 1995 and processed 1 295 submissions. Six orientation workshops were held for Theme Committee members. A public hearing on traditional authorities and customary law was held on 12 and 13 May 1995 in conjunction with Theme Committee 5.

27   The chairpersons of Theme Committee 3 were: K. M. Andrew (DP), P. de Lille (PAC), D. C. du Toit (ANC), and T. J. King (NP). The members were: M. Abraham (alt.), J. T. Albertyn (alt.), M. S. Appelgryn (alt.), M. Bhabha, A. Blaas, Y. I. Carrim, L. D. Chue-nyane (alt.), M. P. Coetzee, P. C. Cronje, Z. A. Dingani (alt.), M. M. Z. Dyani (alt.), C. W. Eglin (alt.), T. S. Farisani (alt.), B. L. Geldenhuys, M. J. Golding (alt.), A. D. Goosen (alt.), P. J. Gordhan, P. J. Gous (alt.), P. J. Groenewald, N. B. Gxowa (alt.), M. J. Khasu (alt.), O. N. Khobe, N. Kondlo (alt.), G. W. Koornhof, Z. A. Kota, N. E. Lamani (alt.), S. J. Leeuw (alt.), H. G. Loots (alt.), L. K. Losabe (alt.), N. I. Mabude (alt.), A. F. Mahlalela, S. J. Mahlangu (alt.), M. S. Maine (alt.), S. M. Malebo (alt.), M. S. Manie, N. N. Mapisa-Nqakula, G. Marais (alt.), J. W. Maree, H. J. Mashamba, V. J. Matthews (alt.), H. W. Mayimele (alt.), E. S. Mchunu (alt.), L. J. Modisenyane, S. J. Mongwaketse (alt.), S. D. Montsitsi, M. V. Moosa (alt.), T. T. Mukhuba (alt.), B. M. Nzimande (alt.), J. B. Peires (alt.), E. D. Peters (alt.), R. Rabinowitz, K. Rajoo (alt.), I. Richards (alt.), P. W. Saaiman (alt.), M. S. Seperepere, E. E. N. Shandu, M. V. Sisulu (alt.), P. F. Smith, M. A. Sulliman (alt.), S. L. Tsenoli (alt.), M. Verwoerd, and M. I. Vilakazi. The members of the Technical Committee were: Prof. D. Basson, Prof. D. Davis, Prof. B. Majola, Prof. F. Venter; on local government: A. Boraine, A. Cornelissen, and B. Moseley. The staff were: Mbasa Mxenge, managing secretary; Sandra Haydon, minutes secretary; and Vanessa Calvert and Beverline Thomas, administrative secretaries.

28   Theme Committee 3 held fifty meetings between 19 September

1994 and 28 August 1995 and processed 471 submissions from political parties, government departments, organizations, and individuals. Eight orientation workshops were held for Theme Committee members. A public hearing on local government was held on 14 August 1995.

29 The chairpersons of Theme Committee 4 were: A. J. Leon (DP), M. M. S. Mdladlana (ANC), and G. B. Myburgh (NP). The members were: K. Asmal, D. Bakker, I. M. Cachalia, S. Camerer, J. Chalmers, M. Coleman, B. O. Dlamini, G. Ebrahim (alt.), S. L. E. Fenyane, T. Gamndana, X. F. Gasa (alt.), D. Govender, P. Govender (alt.), J. L. Kgoali, E. N. Lubidla (alt.), B. S. Mabandla, T. G. G. Mashamba, M. G. Masher (alt.), P. Mathebe, L. R. Mbuyazi (alt.), K. R. Meshoe (alt.), S. B. Mfayela (alt.), M. W. Mfebe (alt.), M. A. Mncwango, I. J. Mohamed (alt.), R. S. Molekane, C. P. Mulder, Y. L. Myakayaka-Manzini, M. A. A. Njobe (alt.), M. I. B. Ntuli, G. N. M. Pandor, M. M. Phenethi (alt.), M. M. Piliso, R. J. Radue, S. M. Rasmeni, B. Ranchod, R. T. Rhoda, E. Saloojee, R. K. Sizani, B. M. Skosana, D. Smuts (alt.), G. Solomon, J. E. Sosibo, M. E. Surty, E. Thabethe, B. Thompson, T. J. Tshivhase, V. M. Thobeka, V. Viljoen, S. C. Vos, C. H. Werth (alt.), and L. M. Xingwana (alt). The members of the Technical Committee were: Prof. H. Cheadle, Prof. J. Dugard, Ms S. Liebenberg, and Prof. I. Rautenbach. The staff were: John Tsalamandris, managing secretary; Zuleiga Adams, minutes secretary; and Pamela Crowley, administrative secretary.

30 Theme Committee 4 held thirty-two meetings from 19 September 1994 to 14 August 1995. This Theme Committee received the bulk of the submissions from the public and had processed 5 634 submissions by 30 June 1995. After the Theme Committee had completed its work, 1 360 further submissions were received. In total, 12 000 petitions were received by the Committee. By the end of the process, Theme Committee 4 had presented 33 reports and explanatory memoranda and a draft bill of rights which was tabled at the subcommittee of the Constitutional Committee on 9 and 10 October 1995.

judiciary & legal systems

31   The chairpersons of Theme Committee 5 were: W. A. Hofmeyr
      (ANC), D. Schutte (NP), and J. van der Merwe (IFP). The
      members were: A. Bruwer (alt.), D. J. Dalling, J. de Lange, R. de
      Ville, A. G. Ebrahim, G. A. Fredericks, S. D. Fisher, E. Gandhi, D.
      H. M. Gibson, R. H. Groenewald, S. P. Grove, D. P. Jana, Z. B.
      Jiyane (alt.), E. E. Jassat, M. J. Khasu, A. J. Leon (alt.), J. W. le Roux
      (alt.), G. L. Mahlangu, P. A. Matthee, V. J. G. Mathews, S. N. N.
      Mdutyana, J. S. Mgidi, S. Mkhatshwa, S. E. Moeti, M. P. E. Mogale
      (alt.), M. W. Moosa, M. L. Mushwana (alt.), M. Mzizi, A. G. V.
      Naidoo (alt.), A. C. Nel, B. Ngcuka, L. Ngwane, T. C. Ntsizi (alt.),
      D. Omar (alt.), R. A. M. Saloojee, L. Singh (alt.), N. Singh (alt.), B.
      P. Sonjica, F. van Heerden. The members of the Technical
      Committee were: P. Benjamin, Judge P. J. J. Olivier, L. Gcabashe,
      and Adv. J. Gauntlett. Staff: Noël Taft, managing secretary; Eunice
      van Eck, minutes secretary; and Beverline Thomas, adminis-
      trative secretary.

32   Theme Committee 5 held thirty-one meetings between
      19 September 1994 and 14 August 1995 and processed 477
      submissions, most of which were received from organized civil
      society. Fourteen public hearings were held with a wide variety of
      role-players between 1 February and 26 July 1995.

33   The chairpersons of Theme Committee 6 were: S. de Beer (NP),
      Ms B. Mbete-Kgositsile (ANC), and P. Powell (IFP). The members
      were: T. G. Alant, A. Balie, H. J. Bekker (alt.), D. Bloem (alt.), M. S.
      Booi (alt.), W. J. Botha (alt.), S. Camerer (alt.), O. C. Chabane
      (alt.), J. Chiole (alt.), R. H. Davies, P. de Lille, P. D. Dexter, M. M.
      Z. Dayni, E. I. Ebrahim (alt.), A. Erwin, F. C. Fankomo, S. L. E.
      Fenyane, N. B. Fihla (alt.), F. X. Gasa, C. Gcina, D. H. M. Gibson
      (alt.), M. E. George, N. J. Gogotya, P. J. Groenewald, L. Hani (alt.),
      M. W. Hlengwa, F. P. Jacobsz, J. A. Jordaan, Q. J. Kgauwe (alt.), T.
      S. Khoza (alt.), L. Louw (alt.), J. Y. Love, I. B. N. Luthuli, J.
      Mabhudafhasi (alt.), S. S. Makana (alt.), H. G. Makgothi , T. J.
      Malan (alt.), D. M. Malatsi, M. Malumise (alt.), G. Marais, J. N.
      Mashimbye (alt.), S. N. N. Mdutyana, Z. W. Mwayi, P. G. Mlambo-
      Ngcuka, P. Moatshe, M. C. Mokitlane, M. L. Mokoena, R. S.

Molekane (alt.), R. S. Mompati, C. H. Motshabi (alt.), M. B.
Mpahlwa (alt.), T. E. Mtintso, L. M. Mti, F. S. Mufamadi, J. Naidoo,
B. Nair, H. M. Neerahoo, M. A. Netshimbupfe, B. S. Ngubane, H.
Ngubane, J. M. Nhlanhla, R. Z. Nogumla (alt.), I. M. Phillips (alt.),
J. Schreiner, M. I. Scott (alt.), J. Selfe, N. Singh, L. Sisulu, Z. S. T.
Skweyiya (alt.), M. Smuts, J. E. Sosibo (alt.), M. E. Tshabalala
(alt.), M. E. Turok (alt.), I. Vadi, J. van Eck (alt.), S. C. Vos, A.
Watson, P. J. Welgemoed, G. G. Woods, T. Yengeni (alt.), and D.
A. Zitha.

34 The chairperson of Sub-Theme Committee 6.1 was: I. Vadi
(ANC). The members were: T. G. Alant, M. S. Booi (alt.), J.
Chiole, S. J. de Beer, P. D. Dexter, F. C. Fankomo, M. George (alt.),
N. J. Gogotya, M. W. Hlengwa, J. A. Jordaan, T. S. Khoza (alt.), J. Y.
Love, D. M. Malatsi, Z. W. Mkwayi, P. G. Mlambo-Ngcuka, M. C.
Mokitlane, H. M. Neerahoo, B. S. Ngubane, N. Singh, Z. S. T.
Skweyiya (alt.), D. Smuts, M. E. Tshabalala (alt.), A. Watson, E. I.
Ebrahim, I. J. Pretorius, and M. R. Sikakane. The members of the
Technical Committee on public administration were: Prof. P. van
der Merwe and Ms L. Nyembe; on the electoral commission: Ms
D. Pillay, Mr A. Tredoux, and Mr P. Harris. The staff were:
Nkateko Nyoka, managing secretary; Saaliegah Zardad, minutes
secretary; and Penny Carelse, administrative secretary. The
Committee held twenty-four meetings between 24 October 1994
and 1 August 1995 and processed 159 submissions. Thirteen
public hearings were held from 25 January to 1 June 1995. The
committee participated in workshops on public administration
with a number of international experts from the United
Kingdom, United States of America, France, Netherlands,
Namibia, Mozambique, and Tanzania. Workshops on the Electoral Commission engaged experts from Kenya and Zambia.

35 The Chairperson of Sub-Theme Committee 6.2 was: R. H. Davies
(ANC). The members were: K. M. Andrew, H. Bekker, W. J.
Botha, J. Chiole, A. Erwin, B. Hogan, F. Jacobsz, W. A. Jordaan, H.
Makgothi, G. Marais, G. Marcus, B. Nair, M. Sisulu, P. Welge-
moed, and G. Woods. The members of the Technical Committee

were: N. Morrison and C. Rustomjee. The staff were: Nkateko
Nyoka, managing secretary; Patricia Fahrenfort, minutes secretary; and Agness Murubata, administrative secretary. The
Committee held twenty-eight meetings from 24 January 1995 to 5
September 1995 and processed 96 submissions. Nine public
hearings and seminars were held, engaging all major stakeholders
in the financial sector.

36 The Chairperson of Sub-Theme Committee 6.3 was: Ms B.
Mbete-Kgositsile (ANC). The members were: A. Balie, W. J.
Botha, S. Camerer, S. L. E. Fenyane, F. X. Gasa, M. George, F.
Jacobsz, L. Louw, B. N. Luthuli, T. J. Malan, S. N. Mdutyana, P.
Moatshe, L. M. Mokoena, E. K. Moorcroft, R. Mompati, M. A.
Netshimbupfe, H. Ngubane, B. H. Ngubane, J. K. Nkadimeng, K.
W. Nqwemesha, J. Sefe, D. Smuts, M. E. Tshabalala, M. Turok, A.
van Wyk, I. D. van Zyl, S. C. Vos, and D. A. Zitha. The members
of the Technical Committee on the Public Protector, Human
Rights Commission, and Commission for Gender Equality were:
Dr C. Albertyn and Prof. R. Erwee; on land rights: Dr A.
Gildenhys, Ms A. Claassens, and Dr F. Njobe. The staff were:
Nkateko Nyoka, managing secretary; Bronwen Levy, minutes
secretary; and Penny Carelse, administrative secretary. The
Committee held twenty-nine meetings between 24 October 1994
and 11 September 1995 and processed 200 submissions. Eight
seminars were held dealing with the Commission for Gender
Equality, the Public Protector, the Human Rights Commission,
and the Commission for Land Restitution. Sub-Theme
Committee 6.3 also attended national sector hearings dealing
with national machinery for the advancement of women and land
rights, as did representatives from over 150 organizations, and
speakers from the Australian Law Reform Commission, Zambia,
the University of Saskatchewan in Canada, and the Maori Land
Court in New Zealand.

37 The Chairperson of Sub-Theme Committee 6.4 was: Ms J.
Schreiner (ANC). The members were: T. G. Alant, M. S. Appelgryn, D. Bloem (alt.), N. Booi (alt.), W. N. Breytenbach, O. C.

Chabane (alt.), J. Chiole (alt.), M. M. Z. Dyani, E. I. Ebrahim (alt.), M. Ellis, N. B. Fihla (alt.), D. Gibson (alt.), N. J. Gogotya, P. J. Groenewald, L. Hani (alt.), J. A. Jordaan, Q. J. Kgauwe (alt.), L. Louw (alt.), J. Mabudafhasi (alt.), S. Makana (alt.), T. J. Malan (alt.), M. Malumise (alt.), J. A. Marais, J. N. Mashimbye (alt.), R. S. Molekane (alt.), C. Motshabi (alt.), M. B. Mpahlwa (alt.), T. E. Mtintso, L. M. Mti, H. M. Neerahoo, J. M. Nhlanhla, R. Nogumla (alt.), I. M. Phillips (alt.), P. Powell, M. I. Scott (alt.), J. Selfe, L. Sisulu, J. Sosibo (alt.), J. van Eck (alt.), J. C. N. Waugh, and T. Yengeni (alt). The members of the Technical Committee were: A. Cachalia and Prof. A Seegers. The staff were: Nkateko Nyoka, managing secretary; Katharine McKenzie, minutes secretary; and Agness Murubata, administrative secretary. The committee held twenty-nine meetings from 24 October 1994 to 8 August 1995 and processed 191 submissions. Five workshops were held dealing with correctional services, security services, police service, defence, and intelligence services. While no public hearings were held, members of the committee did attend constitutional public meetings and national sector hearings hosted by the Constitutional Assembly.

38 The members of the panel were: Prof. M. G. Erasmus, Prof. J. Kruger, M. P. Sedibe-Ncholo, Adv. I. Semenya, Prof. J. van der Westhuizen, and Adv. Z. Yacoob.

39 This trip proved to be a tremendous success. The workshop in Britain was hosted by Prof. Jeffrey Jowel QC and the Commonwealth Secretariat. It was attended by participants from Botswana, India, the United States of America, Germany, Hong Kong, Australia, Canada, and Zimbabwe. The workshops in Germany were hosted by the Frederich Naumann Foundation in Bonn and focused on the German system and its possible relevance for the South African process.

40 The Volkstaat Council produced a further discussion document on self-determination and the working draft of the new constitution, for its presentation to the subcommittee on 27 February 1996.

Chapter 11 Negotiating the final constitution

1   The Constitutional Assembly only called a vote when one was required in terms of the rules or the interim constitution. Otherwise, all matters were decided by consensus. However, whenever a vote was called, the resolution concerned was passed unanimously.

2   These issues included such concerns as the property clause, animal rights, strike and lockout procedures, traditional leaders, and customary and religious personal law.

3   While many views and ideas contained in various submissions were not accepted, great care was taken to ensure that these were carefully recorded and noted in the reports presented to the Constitutional Committee by the Theme Committees.

4   Minutes of the 19th meeting of the Constitutional Committee, 12 May 1995.

5   This is the price that had to be paid for trying to involve as many of the 490 members of the Constitutional Assembly as possible in negotiating a constitutional text.

6   While much ground had been covered by May 1995, Theme Committees had not completed all their reports, and those reports that were prepared were not accompanied by draft formulations. In terms of the work programme all Theme Committee work had to be completed by June 1995, but this was not going to be possible.

7   Minutes of 8 June 1995, par. 4.

8   In a report of the Management Committee on 14 September 1995 it was reported that the only outstanding assignments from Theme Committees were the chapters on the bill of rights, the senate, local government, inter-governmental relations, and financial and fiscal relations. These, it was reported, would be ready by the end of September.

9   See the proposal by the administration dated 30 August in the minutes of the Management Committee, 31 August 1995.

10   Minutes of the Management Committee, 14 September 1995.

11 The team established consisted of Hassen Ebrahim (executive director), Louisa Zondo (deputy-executive director), Gerrit Grove (law adviser), Philip Knight (plain language expert), Prof. Johann van der Westhuizen, and Prof. Christina Murray (both members of the Independent Panel of Constitutional Experts).

12 The title *Refined Working Draft* remained with each successive edition. The term 'refined' was used to indicate that the text was amended not only to include political agreements but also to remain sensitive to legal and linguistic coherence. In this regard, it is important to note that one word could not be allowed to mean different things, nor different words to mean the same thing. Accordingly, agreements reached on formulations affecting one chapter invariably had an impact on other chapters.

13 In this regard, the agreement to draft the constitution in plain language caused much controversy. An example of this is the use of the word 'shall' as opposed to 'must', which was finally agreed to. Many politicians felt on numerous occasions that 'shall' represented a far more forceful obligation than 'must'.

14 The increasing use of plain language was an international but relatively recent phenomenon. South Africa suffered from a dearth of legal drafting skills. This problem was compounded by the fact that the few good drafters available to the state were not well versed in the latest international trends.

15 This decision was not very popular with the administration. Arrangements with printers, newspaper companies for distribution, and advertising were placed in jeopardy by the delay. However, the fears of the administration turned out to be unfounded.

16 See the minutes of the 32nd meeting of the Constitutional Committee, 9 and 10 November 1995.

17 It was discovered somewhat painfully that the new schedule provided very little time within which to complete a very complicated and difficult task. Moreover, it was difficult to draft collectively, and the bigger the team the longer it took to draft. Legal drafting is very much an art form, and each individual has a different way of expressing a view or idea.

18 At the end of November 1995 the Panel of Experts travelled to Europe and held several fruitful exchanges with leading constitutional experts from a number of different countries. This experience fuelled members of the panel with fresh, valuable ideas and influences.

19 This draft was sent by courier to members of the Constitutional Committee during the December recess period.

20 Of the 1 438 of the submissions, 238 (16.5%) were received from structures of civil society. The highest concentration of issues covered related to the bill of rights (56%). This was followed by the founding provisions which enjoyed 15.2% of the submissions, while only 12% of the submissions affected general legislative demands. This reflects well on the public's awareness of constitutional issues.

21 Minutes of the Constitutional Committee, 10 November 1995, par. 17.2.

22 This was a significant concession on the part of Parliament, especially in view of the various budget votes that were due within the first quarter of the year.

23 The Human Rights Committee and several other civil society structures were particularly critical of this.

24 The fourth edition of the text was published in limited quantities, and was distributed to those who had made submissions. In part, this publication was an attempt to prove that the Constitutional Assembly was indeed giving due consideration to the views of the public. The submissions were made part of public record and were clearly reflected in the memoranda of the experts who processed these submissions.

25 The interim constitution was accordingly amended on 29 March 1996.

26 Ironically, Die Herberg belonged to arms manufacturers Denel, and was adjacent to the Overberg test range. It had provided a perfect venue during arms embargoes to accommodate secretly various national and international scientists working on South Africa's missile capacity.

27 The progress recorded here is contained in the minutes of the
38th meeting of the Constitutional Committee on Thursday 18
and Friday 19 April 1996, which received the report from the
Arniston meeting.

28 *Mail & Guardian*, 4 April 1996.

29 *Citizen*, 'Constitution may be in effect in 90 days', 16 April 1996.

30 Drafting work on the fifth edition was only completed at 2 a.m. on
15 April. See the *Cape Times*, 'Constitution will top political
agenda – busy session for parliament', 15 April 1996.

31 *Citizen*, 'Inter-party constitutional talks continue', 18 April 1996.

32 *Citizen*, 'Parties hold talks on property clause', 16 April 1996.

33 *Argus*, 'Land rights must be protected, business groups tell politicians', 17 April 1996.

34 *Business Day*, 'ANC resists property clause concessions', 17 April
1996.

35 *Citizen*, 'Inter-party constitutional talks continue', 18 April 1996.

36 *Business Day*, 'Workers on the march', 17 April 1996.

37 *Citizen*, 'Cyril leads marching Cosatu in viva chant', 18 April 1996.

38 *Die Burger*, 'Kontralesa maak kapsie oor "leë erkenning" in
grondwet', 19 April 1996.

39 *Natal Mercury*, 'All-night bid for consensus', 19 April 1996.

40 *Argus*, 'New SA deal struck', 19 April 1996. Also see the minutes of
the Constitutional Committee, 19 April 1996.

41 Some of the key players in this trilateral were Cyril Ramaphosa,
Valli Moosa, Dr Essop Pahad, Andries Beyers, Constand Viljoen,
and Corné Mulder.

42 *Argus*, 'New watchdog will guard group rights', 19 April 1996.
Also see the minutes of the Constitutional Committee, par. 3, 19
April 1996.

43 *Daily News*, 'Collective rights to be enshrined', 19 April 1996.

44 Minutes of the Constitutional Committee, 19 April 1996, par. 3.2.

45 *Daily News*, 'New preamble to the constitution approved',
19 April 1996.

46 *Daily News*, 'Minority rights deal', 19 April 1996.

47 See Marion Edmunds' article in the *Mail & Guardian*, 4 April 1996.

48 *Sunday Times*, 21 April 1996.

49 *Sunday Tribune*, 21 April 1996.

50 *Rapport*, 21 April 1996.

51 *Citizen*, 'Meyer: NP is happy with constitution', 22 April 1996. See also 'Parties "close to" compromise deals', 22 April 1996.

52 *Argus*, 'ANC supports strike call', 22 April 1996.

53 *Cape Times*, 'Opposition slams ANC's strike stand', 23 April 1996.

54 *Cape Times*, 'Birth certificate of a nation – final lap for SA constitution', 24 April 1996.

55 *Citizen*, 'Constitution means sacrifices not in vain', 24 April 1996.

56 *Star*, 'Key clauses of constitution under attack in assembly debate', 24 April 1996.

57 *Business Day*, 'Mandela, De Klerk in bid to break parties' deadlock on constitution', 24 April 1996.

58 *Argus*, 'Constitution battle ahead', 24 April 1996.

59 *Argus*, 'Negotiators set to talk as constitution faces changes', 25 April 1996; *Sowetan*, 'ANC, NP heads meet to save constitution', 25 April 1996; *Star*, 'Strike may be averted – Ramaphosa', 25 April 1996. Throughout this period the leaders of both parties were continually briefed on developments and took a keen interest in the proceedings.

60 *Citizen*, editorial, 'Call it off', 25 April 1996.

61 Minutes of the Constitutional Committee, 25 April 1996.

62 *Star*, 'Deadline extended as parties remain deadlocked on key constitutional issues', 26 April 1996.

63 Minutes of the Constitutional Committee, 25 April 1996, pars. 2 and 3.

64 *Star*, 'Deadline extended as parties remain deadlocked on key constitutional issues', 26 April 1996.

65 *Cape Times*, 'Constitution accord fails to avert strike', 29 April 1996.

66 Despite fiercely polarized public opinion, a decision on the issue of the death penalty actually passed without incident. Most negotiators realized that the right to life had been enshrined in the Constitutional Principles and interim constitution, and that the

issue had already been resolved there. The NP did argue for a proviso that would enable government to legislate for the reim-position of capital punishment at a later date. However, when push came to shove the issue was not as important for the NP as more intractable deadlock issues such as education and language rights.

67 *Star*, 'National strike goes on despite agreement', 29 April 1996.

68 Constand Viljoen made this complaint at the opening of the Constitutional Committee meeting on 29 April 1996. See the minutes of the Constitutional Committee, 29 April 1996, par. 2.1. Also see the *Sowetan*, 'MP's work round the clock', 30 April 1996.

69 *Citizen*, 'Province power: ANC move', 1 May 1996.

70 The DP's Colin Eglin, however, steadfastly maintained that the agreement did not comply with the constitutional principles. He would eventually prove to be correct.

71 *Daily News*, 'Comprehensive powers to entice IFP back', 1 May 1996.

72 *Citizen*, 'IFP no to plan', 1 May 1996.

73 Prof. M. H. Prozesky objected to the certification of the Constitution as he believed that in mentioning the word 'God' the text failed to comply with the constitutional principles.

74 *Citizen*, 'Agree on language clause', 1 May 1996.

75 The request made by the directorate was for time to complete drafting by the Friday (which was in any event already insuffi-cient), a meeting between the drafters and representatives of all political parties on the Saturday to confirm the veracity of the formulations, and the printing of the amended bill for consid-eration on Monday.

76 *Daily News*, 'Deadline on constitution – three clauses prove stumbling block', 2 May 1996.

77 *Daily News*, 'Warning on constitution deadlock', 2 May 1996. See also the minutes of the Constitutional Committee, 2 May 1996.

78 *Star*, 'Ramaphosa raises a smile as constitutional negotiations plod on', 3 May 1996. See also the minutes of the Constitutional Committee, 2 May 1996.

79 This was also a form of insurance against an attack similar to the one launched by the DP against the administration on the production of the 1st edition of the *Refined Working Draft*. The DP had alleged that a formulation which was not to the satisfaction of the ANC mysteriously disappeared from the draft. The administration saw this as an attack on its integrity. The allegation, which was made by the DP at a press conference, turned out to be unfounded.

80 Minutes of the Constitutional Committee, 3 May 1996.

81 See the final Constitution, sec. 31 (2).

82 A similar clause was included in sec. 247 of the interim constitution.

83 *Sunday Times*, 'Constitution: what happens now?', 5 May 1996.

84 *Star*, 'Constitution countdown', 6 May 1996.

85 *Business Day*, 'NP tensions mount over schools clause', 6 May 1996.

86 *Citizen*, 'Progress at talks', 7 May 1996.

87 *Star*, 'Constitutional deadlock continues amid flurry of talks', 7 May 1996.

88 Minutes of the Management Committee, 6 May 1996.

89 *Citizen*, 'Constitution a tool to build a nation', 7 May 1996.

90 *Citizen*, 'You should have apologised, NP told', 7 May 1996.

91 *Daily News*, 'IFP challenges validity', 7 May 1996.

92 Minutes of the Constitutional Committee, 10 October 1996.

93 Such a formulation can be found in the Indian constitution.

Chapter 12 Certification of the final constitution

1 The approach of the court is evident in its judgment (CCT 23/96, 6 September 1996):

First and foremost it must be emphasised that the Court has a judicial and not a political mandate. Its function is clearly spelt out in Interim Constitution 71(2): to certify whether all the provisions of the New Text comply with the

Constitutional Principles. That is a judicial function, a legal exercise. Admittedly a constitution, by its very nature, deals with the extent, limitations and exercise of political power as also with the relationship between political entities and with the relationship between the state and persons. But this Court has no power, no mandate and no right to express any view on the political choices made by the Constitutional Assembly in drafting the New Text, save to the extent that such choices may be relevant either to compliance or non-compliance with the Constitutional Principles. Subject to that qualification, the wisdom or otherwise of any provision of the New Text is not this Court's business.

2 Judgment of the Constitutional Court, CCT 23/96, 6 September 1996.

3 The written objections and supporting submissions ultimately ran to some 2 500 pages, excluding the extracts from judgments, textbooks, and other publications which were annexed.

4 Judgment of the Constitutional Court, CCT 23/96, 6 September 1996.

5 See par. 31 of Constitutional Court judgment CCT 23/96, 6 September 1996.

6 As pointed out in note 12 to chapter eleven of this book, the general rule in drafting is that one word cannot be used to mean different things. Conversely, different words cannot be used to mean the same thing. These anomalies could have serious and adverse effects when interpreting a text, particularly if such a text becomes the subject of litigation or contest.

7 This was the last meeting attended by the deputy-executive director, Marion Sparg, who went on to take up a position as the chief executive officer of the Vereeniging City Council at the end of September 1996.

8 Minutes of the Management Committee, 12 September 1996.

9 The Constitution envisaged the establishment of a number of institutions including the National Council of Provinces. Because the Council replaced the Senate, it would have been impossible to

implement unless it was done before or after a session of Parliament. To do this at any other time would be too disruptive. Furthermore, the establishment of any institution would have financial implications. Since the financial year ends in March and budgets are usually drawn up a year in advance, any delay would have had enormous implications for the implementation of the Constitution.

10 The court advised that due to the heavy workload it had had during the year, it was to go into recess at the beginning of December. A decision would have to made before then.

11 An opportunity for technical refinement was especially fortunate. As previously experienced with the interim constitution, political agreements were usually finalized at the last moments before adoption. The result was that technical refinement of the language involving legal and linguistic consistency was not always possible. The return of the text therefore allowed the experts an opportunity to propose the necessary amendments, which were finally agreed to on
3 October in a meeting between the legal experts from most parties and chaired by the executive director of the Constitutional Assembly.

12 See pars. 149–150 of Constitutional Court judgment CCT 23/96, 6 September 1996.

13 See pars. 163–165 of Constitutional Court judgment CCT 23/96

14 See pars. 170–177, 275–278, 298, and 390 of Constitutional Court judgment CCT 23/96.

15 See par. 95 of Constitutional Court judgment CCT 23/96.

16 See par. 69 of Constitutional Court judgment CCT 23/96.

17 This was an ingenious formulation. While on the one hand it cured the defect identified by the court by offering the right to collective bargaining to individual employers and therefore the right to lockout, it effectively brought this right within the parameters of national legislation.

18 See pars. 153–156 of judgment CCT 23/96.

19 See par. 158 of judgment CCT 23/96.

20 See pars. 477–481 of judgment CCT 23/96.

21 See pars. 328–333 of judgment CCT 23/96.

22 See pars. 394–400 of judgment CCT 23/96.

23 See par. 403 of judgment CCT 23/96.

24 See pars. 301, 302, and 364 of judgment CCT 23/96.

25 See par. 303 of judgment CCT 23/96.

26 The relevant parts of those subsections read as follows:

(1) If the Constitutional Court finds that a draft of the new constitutional text passed by the Constitutional Assembly ... does not comply with the Constitutional Principles, the Constitutional Court shall refer the draft text back to the Constitutional Assembly together with the reasons for its finding.

(2) The Constitutional Assembly shall ... pass an amended text in accordance with section 73(2) ... taking into account the reasons of the Constitutional Court.

(3) The amended text shall be referred to the Constitutional Court for certification in terms of section 71, whereupon the provisions of subsection (1) and (2) of this section again apply. ...

27 See pars. 22–23 of Constitutional Court judgment CCT 23/96.

28 Chapter II.A of the first judgment (CCT 23/96), more particularly pars. 34–38, 41, and 42 thereof, explain the general approach the Constitutional Court adopted to such comparison.

29 See pars. 5–10 of Constitutional Court judgment CCT 37/96.

30 The procedure adopted by the Constitutional Court to ensure optimal consultation is described in pars. 22–25 of judgment CCT 37/96; the multiplicity and scope of the objections and comments considered appear in Annexure 3 of the judgment.

31 There is a time-frame built into chapter 5 of the interim constitution, and sec. 71(3) thereof provides that the certification of a text is the last word on the matter.

32 Constitutional Court judgment CCT 37/96, par. 479.

33 Constitutional Court judgment CCT 37/96, par. 480.

34 Constitutional Court judgment CCT 37/96.

35   Vereeniging was also the constituency and base of former President F. W. de Klerk.

Chapter 13 The public participation process

1   This and the following three excerpts appear in the Annual Report of the Constitutional Assembly 1996.
2   Constitutional Assembly resolution, 11 October 1995.
3   These objectives did have their critics. In particular, see the editorial of *Business Day* on 13 March 1995 entitled 'Unfocused folly', which argued that 'the entire constitution-making process is flawed by its open-ended nature. The sensible thing would have been to use the interim constitution as a starting point and to amend it as desired. . . . The idea of beginning by asking "the people" to state their wishes would be fine if we were merely compiling a wish list. But we are not. And "the people" will certainly be disappointed when they discover that the final product is, after all, another deal cut between competing political parties. It would be more "transparent" not to have pretended otherwise in the first place'.
4   When the programme was announced, many experts and representatives from the international community scoffed at the idea of drafting a constitution within less than two years, even without any public participation. It was only after the production of the working draft that many warmed up to the process and became more than willing to offer funds to support the programmes.
5   The Reconstruction and Development Programme (RDP) was a government programme and policy drawn up in terms of the policies of the first democratically elected government. The Masakhane Campaign ('masakhane' means 'let's build together') aimed to involve communities in the implementation of the RDP. A number of community projects were put together under the Masakhane umbrella to realize the objectives of the RDP.

6   The members of the Media Department were Enoch Sithole, Tango Lamani, Penny Carelse, Katharine McKenzie, Leonora De Souza, Sibongiseni Hintsho, Sarah Hetherington, and Pat Govender.

7   The import of the message was that because people had made their mark by voting in the 1994 elections, they now had the opportunity to have their say in the type of constitution and democracy they wanted.

8   The survey was designed and analysed by CASE and questionnaires were designed and went into the field on 19 April 1995. Later surveys were conducted throughout the process. The surveys are an interesting guide to many people's attitudes towards the development of a new constitution. The results of the survey appear in an unpublished volume entitled Taking the constitution to the people: evaluating the Constitutional Assembly, compiled by David Everett (CASE, 1997).

9   It was found that within one year of the process of public participation, just less than half (48%) of all adult South Africans felt part of the Constitutional Assembly process, while just over a quarter (28%) did not. In this the Constitutional Assembly maintained the surge of support which attended its launch and which was detected in an earlier evaluation in 1995. It is particularly noteworthy that the positive feeling about the Constitutional Assembly process was expressed nearly evenly across formal metropolitan areas (48%) and formal urban areas (49%), as well as the more disadvantaged areas such as informal residents of both metropolitan and urban areas (43%) and people in rural areas (46%).

The campaign also seemed to catch the attention of the younger generation; in other words, the people who would live most of their lives under the new constitution.

10 Unfortunately, this partnership was not entirely successful. It seems that few organizations in civil society – with the notable exception of the trade union movement – made a concerted attempt to draw their members into meetings or discussions

about the constitution-writing process. Of respondents who belonged to a range of societies, clubs, or organizations, 79% had not been informed about the Constitutional Assembly process by their organization.

11 The result led to the following schedule of hearings:

Sector	Dates	Venue	Structures attending	Partner
Judiciary	27 Feb 1995	UNISA	38 (70 people)	Multi-party Democracy (MPD)
Business	8 May 1995	Parliament	20 (80 people)	
Children's rights	13 May 1995	SRC – Pretoria	30 (120 people)	HSRC
Trad. authorities	12–13 May 1995	Parliament	8 (220 people)	MPD
Religious groups	26 May 1995	World Trade Centre	50 (140 people)	IDASA
Youth	27 May 1995	World Trade Centre	40 (160 people)	IDASA
Labour	3 June 1995	World Trade Centre	20 (140 people)	IDASA
Women	2–4 June 1995	World Trade Centre	85 (170 people)	IDASA
Local Government	14 Aug 1995	Parliament	58 (62 people)	
Socio-economic rights	1 Aug 1995	Parliament	103 (110 people)	
Land rights	1–2 Aug 1995	Parliament	64 (76 people)	

12 The success of the programme was reflected in the following results:
- direct interaction with approximately 117 184 people;
- 807 public events;
- regular liaison with 1 588 structures of civil society;
- 26 constitutional public meetings, which 20 549 people attended and 200 MPs and 717 organizations participated in;
- 13 sectoral events involving 1 508 representatives from 596 organizations;
- the Constitutional Education Programme including 486 workshops and 259 briefings.

13 Occasionally, large numbers of the newsletter were distributed as inserts in various newspapers. These inserts were placed at important points in the constitution-making process.

14 The talk-line used recordings of reports on progress and a facility to record verbal submissions by callers. It was sponsored by the South African telecommunications company, Telkom.

15 While this mechanism would seem to be an effective means of communication, it was used with limited success. There was insufficient time to plan and prepare for it, and the system put into place to update the information and monitor the responses was not very efficient.

16 This project was made possible by a donation from the British High Commissioner. An easily searchable database was on offer, which contained all submissions, minutes, reports, and various editions of the draft formulations. It was used extensively both within and outside South Africa. The statistics give some indication of the extent of the interest in South Africa's constitution-making process. People from 46 countries contacted the Constitutional Assembly via the Internet from 1 January 1996 to 17 April 1996. A total of 6 655 people connected to the Constitutional Assembly home page in the same period, which translated into an average of 107 people per day. The countries which indicated the most interest were the United States, Germany, Canada, and Australia. The most sought-after

information included the various working drafts of the new constitution, the Constitutional Assembly's annual report, press releases, the Constitutional Assembly newsletter *Constitutional Talk*, and briefings on the process.

17   Of these, 2.8 million copies were inserted into newspapers, 1.8 million were distributed directly to the public door to door, 94 700 were distributed in *taxi-net* kiosks at major centres, and the rest were distributed by the administration. The CASE survey took place a couple of months after the *Refined Working Draft* was released. It was found that by then 8% of all South African adults – some two million people – had seen the document, while 5% of the sample – some 1.3 million people – had read some or all of the Constitution.

18   It is interesting to note that in distributing these copies to those who made submissions, many complained that they did not make any submissions and could not understand why they had been identified as such. Upon investigation it became apparent that a number of submissions had been sent under names from the congregation lists of churches. Some school teachers also encouraged school children to make submissions by dictating a submission to them.

19   Research showed that despite the considerable competition for the political attention of South Africans, just less than two-thirds (60%) of all respondents had heard of the Constitutional Assembly. This is roughly equivalent to some 15.2 million adults. Those who had not heard of the Constitutional Assembly were mainly from disadvantaged sectors. Those in rural areas were least likely to have heard of the Constitutional Assembly, as were the elderly. These figures in turn reflected patterns of media access – and non-access – in South Africa.

Equally important was the fact that while 76% of respondents first heard of the Constitutional Assembly via mainstream media, 12% were first informed of it by word of mouth (from a friend, at work, at school, and so on). This suggested that the Constitutional Assembly campaign was able to achieve one of the key goals of a social education media campaign, to generate interpersonal communication and enter popular discourse. An additional 4% of respondents heard about the Constitutional Assembly from political rallies, or civic or church meetings.

In all, the Constitutional Assembly media campaign succeeded in reaching a massive 73% of all adult South Africans, equivalent to some 18.5 million people. The actual figure can be safely assumed to be higher, since media access increases disproportionate to age, and the sample included only those aged 18 and above.

20   In this regard, the views of Prof. Jeremy Sarkin of the Human Rights Committee were relevant. In a letter to the President of the Constitutional Court dated 18 April 1996, Sarkin argued that 'the final stages of the constitution-making process have been characterised by closed political party negotiation (referred to as bi- or multilaterals), and it is in these forums where political agreement on contentious issues has been reached. . . . Thus civil society has been effectively excluded from the last and crucial phases of the process. This is particularly true of more marginalised groups. Moreover, civil society has not been afforded the opportunity to comment on whether the final package complies with the principles which underlie a democratic nation'. Ironically, the Human Rights Committee, despite having filed an objection to the certification of the Constitution, failed to appear at the Constitutional Court to argue its case.

PART TWO

Schedule of Documents

Document I

Peace Treaty of Vereeniging
31 May 1902

THE FOLLOWING NOTICE is hereby published for general information. By order of His Excellency the High Commissioner and Administrator of the Transvaal.

WE Davidson, Acting Secretary to the Transvaal Administration – 3rd June 1902.

ARMY HEADQUARTERS, SOUTH AFRICA

General Lord Kitchener of Khartoum, Command in Chief

AND

His Excellency Lord Milner, High Commissioner, on behalf of the BRITISH GOVERMENT,

AND

Messrs S.W. Burger, F.W. Reitz, Louis Botha, J.H. de la Rey, L.J. Meyer, and J.C. Krogh, acting as the GOVERNMENT of SOUTH AFRICAN REPUBLIC,

AND

Messrs W.J.C. Brebner, C.R. de Wet, J.B.M. Hertzog, and C.H. Olivier, acting as the GOVERNMENT of the ORANGE FREE STATE, on behalf of their respective BURGHERS

Desirous to terminate the present hostilities, agree on the following Articles.

1. The BURGHER Forces in the Field will forthwith lay down their Arms, handing over all Guns, Rifles, and Munitions of War, in their possession or under their control, and desist from any further resistance to the Authority of HIS MAJESTY KING EDWARD VII, whom they recognise as their lawful SOVEREIGN.

   The Manner and details of this surrender will be arranged between Lord Kitchener and Commandant General Botha, Assistant Commandant General de la Rey and Chief Commandant De Wet.

2. Burghers in the field outside the limits of the TRANSVAAL and ORANGE RIVER COLONY, and all Prisoners of War at present outside South Africa, who are burghers, will, on duly declaring their acceptance of the position of subjects of HIS MAJESTY KING EDWARD VII, be gradually brought back to their homes as soon as transport can be provided and their means of subsistence ensured.

3. The BURGHERS so surrendering or so returning will not be deprived of their personal liberty, or their property.

4. No proceedings CIVIL or CRIMINAL will be taken against any of the BURGHERS so surrendering or so returning for any Acts in connection with the prosecution of the War. The benefit of this Clause will not extend to certain Acts contrary to the usage of War which have been notified by the Commander in Chief to the Boer Generals, and which shall be tried by Court Martial immediately after the close of hostilities.

5. The DUTCH language will be taught in Public Schools in the TRANSVAAL and the ORANGE RIVER COLONY where the Parents of the Children desire it, and will be allowed in COURTS of LAW when necessary for the better and more effectual Administration of Justice.

6. The Possession of Rifles will be allowed in the TRANSVAAL and ORANGE RIVER COLONY to persons requiring them for their protection on taking out a licence according to Law.

7. MILITARY ADMINISTRATION in the TRANSVAAL and ORANGE RIVER COLONY will at the earliest possible date be succeeded by CIVIL GOVERNMENT, and, as soon as circumstances permit, Representative Institutions, leading up to self-Government, will be introduced.

8. The question of granting the Franchise to Natives will not be decided until after the introduction of Self-Government.

9. No Special Tax will be imposed on Landed Property in the TRANSVAAL and ORANGE RIVER COLONY to defray the Expenses of the War.

10. As soon as conditions permit, a Commission, on which the local inhabitants will be represented, will be appointed in each District of the TRANSVAAL and ORANGE RIVER COLONY, under the Presidency of a Magistrate or other official, for the purpose of assisting the restoration of the people to their homes and supplying those who, owing to war losses, are unable to provide for themselves, with food, shelter, and the necessary amount of seed, stock, implements etc. indispensable to the resumption of their normal occupations.

His Majesty's Government will place at the disposal of these Commissions a sum of three million pounds sterling for the above purposes, and will allow all notes, issued under Law No. 1 of 1900 of the Government of the SOUTH AFRICAN REPUBLIC, and all receipts, given by the officers in the field of the late Republics or under their orders, to be presented to a JUDICIAL COMMISSION, which will be appointed by the Government, and if such notes and receipts are found by this Commission to have been duly issued in return for valuable consideration they will be received by the first-named Commissions as evidence of War losses suffered by the persons to whom they were originally given. In addition to the above named free grant of three million pounds, His Majesty's Government will be prepared to make advances as loans for the same purpose, free of interest for two years, and afterwards repayable over a period of years with 3 per cent interest. No foreigner or rebel will be entitled to the benefit of this Clause.

Signed at Pretoria this thirty first day of May in the Year of Our Lord One Thousand Nine Hundred and Two.

[Signed]

KITCHENER OF KHARTOUM, MILNER, S W BURGER, F W REITZ, LOUIS BOTHA, J H DE LA REY, L J MEYER, J C KROGH, C R DE WET, J B M HERTZOG, W J C BREBNER, C H OLIVIER

Document 2

British Association for the Advancement of Science
RECEPTION ROOM
UNIVERSITY OF GLASGOW
5 September, 1928
General Secretary
C.P.S.A. [Communist Party of South Africa]

Dear Douglas,

I am at present attending the science congress here, having just returned from the continent.

When I left Moscow the question of the new slogan had not yet been finally disposed of though the Negro Commission (in which the matter was discussed at some length though not as fully as I should have liked) had already delivered its judgement. You will probably have heard of the result of our final appeal by the time this reaches you. I hope to see S.P.B. on his return to England and get acquainted with the final position.

However, as a result of the discussions in Moscow I have come to a number of conclusions with regard to the slogan and with regard to Party policy in general, and I think my views might interest the C.E.C.P.S.A. Hence this letter.

In the first place I think the decision has shown that it is time the

C.P.S.A. put its theoretical house in order. We have been content too long to jog along with a minimum of theory, and I think this is as true of those who supported as of those who opposed the new slogan.

In my opinion we have got to distinguish clearly between the natives as a subject race and the natives as members of the S. African working class. We have got to put forward definite race demands on behalf of the natives, demands which we must fight for in the face of opposition from all sections of whites, even the white workers.

Our trade union work, important as it is, is only a part of our activities. Our slogan on the trade union field is *'workers unite, irrespective of colour'*. But as a general political slogan appealing to the native masses, this is inadequate. I do not say it should not be used as a general political slogan: *it should be used more than ever*. But it is necessary to have an additional slogan or slogans which take account of the position of the natives as a subject race. It is equally necessary to say *'natives unite; unite as black men to free yourselves from slavery'*. The demands of the democratic revolution in Africa (the franchise, abolition of passes, equal land laws, free education, abolition of the indenture system and forced labour, right to ride on the trams, walk on the pavement, use the public libraries, enter the city halls, etc. etc.) are demands of the natives *as natives*. They are demands for things which the white workers already have. On the political field these demands culminate historically in a single final slogan – *national independence*, i.e. complete freedom and independence for the native race, complete political power to the natives. As the natives are not a scattered racial minority like the Jews but a compact majority inhabiting a single country, national independence means quite literally a *native republic*. This is the logic of the position and this we must accept.

But before formulating the slogan for complete national emancipation of the Bantu in its final platform form, it is necessary to take two things into consideration. These are (1) the question of the role of the white workers, as the only skilled section of the proletariat, cannot in any way be ignored. There is an increasing tendency with some comrades – in their more exasperated moments when the actual requirements of the situation have been forgotten for the moment – to say 'let the white workers go hang'. We must remember that we should be patient revolutionists and not lose our heads in this matter. To the extent that the white workers are interested in fighting the boss to that extent they can and must be harnessed to the revolution. We entirely disagree of course with the view formerly held by Danchin (I hope he has long since discarded it) that the white workers are the *main* revolutionary element in S. Africa.

As far as revolutionary expediency is concerned it is obvious that this may easily degenerate into opportunism. Our chief difficulty in Moscow was to convince the comrades that there were genuine tactical reasons against adopting the 'Black Republic' slogan and that our objections were not founded on opportunist deviations. In the present weak condition of the native movement every foothold in the white trade unions, every little bit of white support must be utilised to the fullest extent, in order to maintain the legality of the native movement, to prevent pogroms and the danger of lynching, and to secure the rapid development of a cadre of native Communists. I think it is fairly plain that we cannot afford to go underground at the present time.

The object of the slogan of course is not to please the white workers but to rally the whole of the native masses behind the C.P. This is our main job; everything else is secondary. At the same time there is no reason why we should unnecessarily antagonise the white workers. Such unnecessary antagonising would have disastrous results not only for the inter-racial labour movement but also for the native nationalist movement as such. The slogan should therefore be formulated in such a way as to make the maximum appeal to the racial consciousness of the oppressed Bantu and at the same time provide a weapon for continuing the fight in the trade union movement on the basis of working class unity irrespective of colour.

The amendment which I suggested to the Negro Commission in my opinion meets these requirements as far as it is possible to do so. It was *'an independent workers' and peasants' S. African Republic, with equal rights for all toilers irrespective of colour,* AS A BASIS FOR A NATIVE MAJORITY GOVERNMENT'. Supplemented by immediate demands for an equal franchise throughout the Union, the admission of natives to Parliament, and the abolition of all helot relations, this will be a revolutionary rallying slogan guaranteeing to the C.P. leadership of the racial struggle of the natives. At the same time it will enable us to argue our case in the white trade unions. If we say a 'Black Republic' and they qualify this by saying that there will be autonomy for whites, we cannot but expect to be howled down in the white trade unions; we shall not even be allowed to state our case. At the mention of 'Black Republic' the bricks will begin to fly and our subsequent qualifications will be relegated to the post-mortem examination. It is much more sensible to approach the white workers in these terms: 'You are workers, trade unionists; you are exploited and shot down by the boss; unite to overthrow capitalism; unite with your native fellow workers; demand full equality for *all* workers; the native workers are the majority; YOU must therefore be prepared to *grant* THEM *their* MAJORITY RIGHTS'. This will probably be howled down in many cases, but at least it provides a tactical approach to the subject.

Unfortunately Comrade Petrovsky and the members of the Negro Commission did not trouble to reply to these arguments. They said that the C.P.S.A. had committed Social-Democratic sins of the gravest nature and had to be severely reprimanded. They therefore would allow of no modification in the slogan whatever. They would not even allow a slight editorial change in the wording, because they said any such slight change would be interpreted as a partial victory for the S. African delegation.

I think this is quite a wrong way of approaching the subject.

I have some further remarks to make with regard to certain practical questions, particularly with regard to Com. Harrison's candidature and the forthcoming elections, but I will keep them for a further letter.

Kind regards to all comrades,
Yours fraternally,
E. R. Roux

Document 3

Resolution on 'the South African question' adopted by the Executive Committee of the Communist International following the sixth Comintern congress
1928

SOUTH AFRICA is a British Dominion of the colonial type. The development of relations of capitalist production has led to British imperialism carrying out the economic exploitation of the country with the participation of the white bourgeoisie of South Africa (British and Boer). Of course, this does not alter the general colonial character of the economy of South Africa, since British capital continues to occupy the principal economic positions in the country (banks, mining and industry), and since the South African bourgeoisie is equally interested in the merciless exploitation of the negro population.

In the recent period in South Africa we have witnessed the growth of the manufacturing iron and steel industries, the development of commercial crops (cotton, sugar, cane), and the growth of capitalist relations in agriculture, chiefly in cattle-raising. On the basis of this growth of capitalism there is a growing tendency to expropriate the land from the negroes and from a certain section of the white farming population. The South African bourgeoisie is endeavouring also by legislative means to create a cheap market of labour power and a reserve army.

The overwhelming majority of the population is made up of negroes and coloured people (about 5 500 000 negroes and coloured people and about 1 500 000 white people according to the 1921 census). A characteristic feature of the colonial type of the country is the almost complete landlessness of the negro population: the negroes hold only one-eighth of the land whilst seven-eighths have been expropriated by the white population. There is no negro bourgeoisie as a class, apart from individual negroes engaged in trading and a thin strata of negro intellectuals who do not play any essential role in the economic and political life of the country. The negroes constitute also the majority of the working class: among the workers employed in industry and transport, 420 000 are black and coloured people and 145 000 white; among agricultural labourers 435 000 are black and 50 000 are white. The characteristic feature of the proletarianisation of the native population is the fact that the number of black workers grows faster than the number of white workers. Another characteristic fact is the great difference in the wages and the material conditions of the white and black proletariat in general. Notwithstanding a certain reduction in the living standard of the white workers which has lately taken place, the great disproportion between the wages of the white and black proletariat continues to exist as the characteristic feature of the colonial type of the country.

The political situation

The political situation reflects the economic structure – the semi-colonial character of the country and the profound social contradictions between the black and white population. The native population (except in the Cape province) of the country have no electoral rights, the power of the State has been monopolised by the white bourgeoisie, which has at its disposal the armed white forces. The white bourgeoisie, chiefly the Boers defeated by the arms of British imperialism at the close of the last century, had for a long time carried on a dispute with British capital. But as the process of capitalist development goes on in the country, the interests of the South African bourgeoisie are becoming more and more blended with the interests of British financial and industrial capital, and the white South African bourgeoisie is coming more and more inclined to compromise with British imperialism, forming with the latter a united front for the exploitation of the native population.

The Nationalist Party, which represents the interests of the big farmers and landowners and a section of white (mainly Boer) bourgeoisie and petty-bourgeoisie is winding up its struggle for separation from the Empire and is surrendering before British capitalism (the formula proposed by the leader of this Party, General Hertzog, and carried at the British Imperial Conference). Furthermore, this party is already coming out as the open advocate of the colonial expansion of British capital, carrying on an agitation for the extension of the territory of the Union of South Africa to the north (the annexation of Rhodesia), hoping in this manner to secure a vast fund of cheap native labour power.

Simultaneously with the importation of British capital and British goods, there are imported to South Africa the methods of corrupting the working class. The Labour Party of South Africa, representing the interests of the petty bourgeoisie and of the skilled labour aristocracy, openly carries on an imperialist policy, demoralising the white workers by imbuing them with a white racial ideology. Nevertheless, the influence of this party is being undermined by the steady worsening of the material conditions of the mass of the white workers. At the same time the South African bourgeoisie is endeavouring to attract to its side certain elements of the non-European population, for instance, the 'coloured' population, promising them electoral rights, and also the native leaders, turning them into agents for the exploitation of the negro population. This policy of corruption has already brought about the fact that the leaders of the negro trade union organisations – the Industrial and Commercial Union – having expelled the Communists from the union, are now endeavouring to guide the negro trade union movement into the channel of reformism. The inception of negro reformism, as a result of the corruptionist policy of the white bourgeoisie, a reformism which acts in close alliance with the Amsterdam International, constitutes a characteristic fact of the present political situation.

The united front of the British and South African white bourgeoisie against the toiling negro population, backed by the white and negro reformists, creates for the Communist Party in South Africa an exceptionally complicated but favourable position of being the only political Party in the country which unites the white and black proletariat and the landless black peasantry for the struggle against British imperialism, against the white bourgeoisie and the white and black reformist leaders.

The Communist Party and its tasks

The Executive Committee of the Communist International [ECCI] recognises the successes which the Communist Party of South Africa has recently achieved. This is seen in the growth of the Communist Party, which is now predominantly native in composition. The communist Party has a membership of about 1 750 of whom 1 600 are natives or coloured. The Communist Party has also spread into the country districts of the Transvaal. The Party has waged a fight against the reactionary Native Administration Act. The ECCI also notes the growth of native trade unions under the leadership of the CP, the successful carrying through of a number of strikes and efforts to carry through the amalgamation of the black and white unions.

The present intensified campaigns of the Government against the natives offer the CP an immense field to develop its influence among the workers and peasants, and it is among this section of the South African population that the chief field of activity of the CP must continue to lie in the near future.

(a)   The first task of the Party is to reorganise itself on the shop and street nuclei basis and to put forward a programme of action as a necessary condition for the building up of a mass Communist Party in South Africa.

(b)   The Party must orientate itself chiefly upon the native toiling masses while continuing to work actively among the white workers. The Party leadership must be developed in the same sense. This can only be achieved by bringing the native membership without delay into much more active leadership of the Party both locally and centrally.

(c) While developing and strengthening the fight against all the customs, laws and regulations which discriminate against the native and coloured population in favour of the white population, the CP of South Africa must combine the fight against all anti-native laws with a general political slogan in the fight against British domination, the slogan of an independent native South African republic as a stage towards a workers' and peasants' republic, with full equal rights for all races, black, coloured and white.

(d) South Africa is a black country, the majority of its population is black and so is the majority of the workers and peasants. The bulk of the South African population is the black peasantry, whose land has been expropriated by the white minority. Seven eighths of the land is owned by whites. Hence the national question in South Africa, which is based upon the agrarian question lies at the foundation of the revolution in South Africa. The black peasantry constitutes the basic moving force of the revolution in alliance with and under the leadership of the working class.

(e)   South Africa is dominated politically by the white exploiting class. Despite the conflict of interests between the Dutch bourgeoisie and the English imperialists, the basic characteristic of the political situation in South Africa is the developing united front between the Dutch bourgeoisie and the English imperialists against the native population. No political party in South Africa with the exception of the Communist Party advocates measures that would be of real benefit to the oppressed native population, the ruling political parties never go beyond empty and meaningless Liberal phrases. The CP of SA is the only Party of native and white workers that fights for the complete abolition of race and national exploitation, that can head the revolutionary movement of the black masses for liberation. Consequently, if the CP correctly understands its political tasks it will and must become the leader of the national agrarian revolutionary movement of the native masses.

Unfortunately the CP of SA did not give evidence of sufficient understanding of the revolutionary importance of the mass movements of the native workers and peasants. The CP of SA carried on a correct struggle for unity of the native and white workers in the trade union movement. But at the same time the CP of SA found itself in stubborn opposition to the correct slogan proposed by the Comintern calling for an independent native South African republic as a stage towards a workers' and peasants' republic with full, equal rights for all races.

This opposition shows a lack of understanding of the task of our Party in South Africa relative to the revolutionary struggles of the native masses, which explains partly the still insufficient growth of the political influence of our Party upon the negro masses despite the extremely favourable conditions.

South Africa is a British dominion of a colonial type. The country was seized by violence by foreign exploiters, the land expropriated from the natives, who were met by a policy of extermination in the first stages of colonisation, and conditions of semi-slavery established for the overwhelming majority of the native masses. It is necessary to tell the native masses that in the face of existing political and economic discrimination against the natives and ruthless oppression of them by the white oppressors, the Comintern slogan of a native republic means restoration of the land to the landless and land-poor population.

This slogan does not mean that we ignore or forget about the non-exploiting elements of the white population. On the contrary, the slogan calls for 'full and equal rights for all races'. The white toiling masses must realise that in South Africa they constitute national minorities, and it is their task to support and fight jointly with the native masses against the white bourgeoisie and the British imperialists. The argument against the slogan for a native republic on the ground that it does not protect the whites is objectively nothing else than a cover for the unwillingness to accept the correct principle that South Africa belongs to the native population. Under these conditions it is the task of the Communist Party to influence the embryonic and crystallising national movements among the natives in order to develop these movements into national agrarian revolutionary movements against the white bourgeoisie and British imperialists.

The failure to fulfil this task means separation of the CP of SA from the native population. The CP cannot confine itself to the general slogan of 'Let there be no whites and no blacks'. The CP must understand the revolutionary importance of the national and agrarian questions. Only by a correct understanding of the importance of the national question in South Africa will the CP be able to combat effectively the efforts of the bourgeoisie to divide the white and black workers by playing on race chauvinism, and to transform the embryonic nationalist movement into a revolutionary struggle against the white bourgeoisie and foreign imperialists. In its propaganda among the native masses the CP of SA must emphasise the class differences between the white capitalists and the white workers, the latter also being exploited by the bourgeoisie as wage slaves, although better paid as compared with the natives. The CP must continue to struggle for unity between black and white workers and not confine itself merely to the advocacy of 'co-operation' between the blacks and whites. It must explain to the native masses that the black and white workers are not only allies, but are the leaders of the revolutionary struggle of the native masses against the white bourgeoisie and British imperialism. A correct formulation of this task and intensive propagation of the chief slogan of a native republic will result not in the alienation of the white workers from the CP, not in segregation of the natives, but, on the contrary, in the building up of a solid united front of all toilers against capitalism and imperialism.

In the struggle against the domination of British imperialism in SA and against the white bourgeoisie under the slogans of the agrarian revolution and native republic the CP of SA will undoubtedly meet with the most brutal attacks of the bourgeoisie and the imperialists. This can be no argument for not adopting the slogan of a native republic. On the contrary, the Party must wage a struggle for this slogan preparing all possible means, first and foremost by mobilising the black and white workers, to meet the attacks of the ruling class.

The ECCI, while fully approving of the Party's agitation against the native Bills put forward by the Pact Government, considers that this agitation should be further strengthened and intensified and should be coupled with agitation against all anti-native legislation.

The Party should pay particular attention to the embryonic national organisations among the natives, such as the African National Congress. The Party, while retaining its full independence, should participate in these organisations, should seek to broaden and extend their activity. Our aim should be to transform the ANC into a fighting nationalist revolutionary organisation against the white bourgeoisie and the British imperialists, based upon the trade unions, peasant organisations, etc., developing systematically the leadership of the workers and the CP in this organisation. The Party should seek to weaken the influence of the native chiefs corrupted by the white bourgeoisie over the existing native tribal organisations by developing peasants' organisations and spreading among them the influence of the CP. The development of a national-revolutionary movement of the toilers of South Africa against the white bourgeoisie and British imperialism, constitutes one of the major tasks of the CP of SA.

The Party should immediately work out an agrarian programme applicable to the native agrarian situation. The ECCI considers that the Party was correct in launching at its last Congress the slogan of 'Expropriate the big estates and give them to the landless whites and natives'. But this can only be treated as a general slogan. It is necessary to work out concrete practical demands which indicate that the basic question in the agrarian situation in South Africa is the land hunger of the blacks and that their interest is of prior importance in the solution of the agrarian question. Efforts should be made immediately to develop plans to organise the native peasants into peasant unions and the native agricultural workers into trade unions, while attention to the poor agrarian whites must in no way be minimised.

In the field of trade union work the Party must consider that its main task consists in the organisation of the native workers into trade unions as well as propaganda and work for the setting up of a South African trade union centre embracing black and white workers. The principle that the Party's main orientation must be on the native population applies equally well to the sphere of trade union work. The Party should energetically combat the splitting policy of the Industrial and Commercial Union leaders under the slogan of unity of the whole trade union movement of South Africa. Further, the Party should work out a detailed programme of immediate demands for the native workers. The Communists must participate actively in the trade union organisation of the native workers, pursuing the policy of building up a strong left-wing within these organisations under Communist leadership.

The Party should continue its exposure of the South African Labour Party as primarily an agent of imperialism in the Labour movement.

While concentrating its chief attention on organising the native workers in the trade unions the Communist Party should not neglect the workers in the white trade unions. Its tasks are the organisation of the unorganised workers in the existing trade unions, to intensify the propaganda for reorganisation of the trade union movement on an industrial basis, increased agitation for affiliation of all trade unions to the Trade Union Congress. In all trade union organisations the Party must strive to build up a strong left-wing under Communist leadership.

The Party must energetically combat the influence of the Amsterdam International in the black and white trade union movement, intensifying the propaganda for world trade union unity along the lines of the Profintern (RILU) policy.

In connection with the danger of world war, the present imperialist intervention in China and the threatening war against the USSR the Party must fight by all means against the help given to the military policy of Great Britain which found its expression in the tacit support of the break of the British imperialists with the USSR. The Party should not neglect anti-militarist work.

The ECCI repeats its previous proposal to launch a special paper in the chief native languages as soon as technical difficulties have been overcome. Such a step is of great political importance.

Document 4

THE SEVENTH ANNUAL CONFERENCE of the Communist Party of South Africa, which lasted from Saturday evening, December 29th to Wednesday night, January 2nd, was the finest ever held, although it had been preceded by much serious controversy during the year. There were 30 delegates, 20 black and 10 white. The visitors were guests of the party during the conference, and their daily meetings round the hospitable board of Comrade Mrs Jacobs, who did the catering, contributed not a little to the success of the conference.

Opening greetings

Beginning with a 'social' entertained by talent of a high order from Vereeniging, Potchefstroom and Johannesburg branches, the 'real business' was ushered in next morning by a procession with band and banners from the Party Headquarters to the Inchape Hall where a great throng before entering the building sang the Internationale.

Inside, every seat was occupied by a keenly interested crowd consisting mainly of native workers with a very few from white trade unions, although they had all received invitations. The credential committee reported that a membership of nearly 3 000 was represented by the delegates.

Greetings were read from the British Communist Party, from our former chairman Jimmy Shields (recently arrested for free speech in Greenock, Scotland), from the African National Congress and from sundry trade unions and organisations, white and black, from the Cape to the Zambezi. In turn greetings were sent to Soviet Russia as the workers' 'fatherland', to the class war prisoners of the world and to the workers of Rhodesia and the Congo.

Comrade SP Bunting, opening the proceedings as chairman, spoke on the lines of the introduction to the new Party Programme (see page 3 and 6) and hailed the coming into power of those now contemptuously dubbed 'kitchenboys' by labour Minister Sampson, or the 'Jim Fishes' for whom the chairman of the Labour Party pleaded his detestation as a ground for soliciting votes, whereas Lenin said every cook must become a politician and a ruler. If the masses seemed unripe today that was only the result of just this stunting oppression: once this was removed a rapid ripening would result under Communist leadership.

War danger

Comrade J Gomas (Cape Town) on the WAR DANGER showed how the imperialists were doubling their armaments and using armed force on more fronts than ever, fomenting trouble everywhere, whether in the colonies or against the USSR. The USA having become Britain's great capitalist rival, Americans are now called 'too foreign blooded' as the Germans were called 'Huns' by the British press. Meanwhile their whole system is challenged by the very existence of the USSR. If war comes, it must be made to mean 'disorder at home' leading to socialism. The non-Europeans, who are also being trained for the next war, must thus play their part in the campaign against imperialist war.

An ICU official in the audience recalled the king's personal promise of benefits to African soldiers, which remained unfulfilled.

Political review

The POLITICAL SITUATION was ably reviewed by Comrade DG Wolton, who stressed the growth of colonial liberation movements and the colonial workers' growing unity with the workers of the home countries. Witness the Pan Pacific Secretariat, to which even 'white Australian' labour had affiliated; also the growth of the Anti Imperialist League. The Chamber of Mines was for breaking down the Colour Bar with a view to rationalisation and cheaper labour. Social democracy had captured the ICU and hoped to kill the liberation movement 'by kindness' to a few chosen natives.

In discussion it was urged that the CP could now stand and lead the masses from slavery without the need for white leaders. Union with 'Home' workers was facilitated by the fall of their standard to 'Kaffir level', leading them to support the colonial revolt. The white unemployed here flocked to the CP for bread; when they had got it they disappeared, warned not to associate with 'Reds'. But only the CP offered any salvation to white workers, bywoners, etc.: the alternative sjambok policy of the 'Bourgeoisie' and its 'Scabinet' ministers could lead them nowhere. Native Trade Unions could not really flourish until special oppressions such as passes were removed: hence they must take up politics. Salaaming the bosses in the hope of favours was useless. It was resolved to contest one or more constituencies in the general election.

Trade unionism

Comrade ES Sachs, reporting on the TRADE UNION movement, denounced the Conciliation Act chloroform, which led to the Industrial Councils being preferred above Trade Unions, the latter in some cases surviving only as salary providers for Government controlled officials. The bright feature of TU life is the growth and heroism of our native Unions and their coming together with white unions. If the SAFNTU applied for affiliation to the TUC, it would be well supported. Anyway, the native unions must fight for complete political freedom and equality, and the basic industries must be organised. These unions can exercise great influence in regard to war.

In discussion the dangers were mentioned of party members

absorbed in TU work becoming lost to the party or debarred from doing propaganda in TU's or of black and white TU unity being used to subordinate black militancy to white reaction.

The native republic

The new PARTY PROGRAMME was debated for over a full day. The point that raised most discussions was the 'Native Republic' slogan. The chairman ruled that any motions involving its rejection or modification were out of order under the CI statutes, but welcomed discussions tending to its explanation. In the result it was understood that it implied, by whatever stages, a workers' and peasants' Republic, but with the necessary stress on its overwhelmingly native character; for practically all natives are workers and peasants, and again, probably only a workers' and peasants' victory can achieve such a republic. After further discussion the clause 'Self-determination of the African peoples' was adopted by 11 votes to 4.

Next a new PARTY CONSTITUTION was adopted, providing for delegates of branches on the Central Committee meeting quarterly, with an Executive Bureau meeting weekly in Johannesburg, and otherwise on the lines of the CPGB rules.

Party affairs

Comrade DG Wolton, General Secretary, explained his desire to leave for Britain, urging that his successor should be a non-European, and attacking alleged 'chauvinistic errors' in the party. Discussion was eventually cut short by a general request to him to remain at his post, to which he eventually yielded 'until', as he said, 'a non-European is ready to take my place.'

The most moving and inspiring of all the proceedings was 'Branch Reports'. The unvarnished yet splendid tales of struggle, heroism and sacrifice in the teeth of incredible persecution, intimidation and espionage (even at the hands of other native workers) which made up the story of the country branches especially, including the very live women's branches, brought tears to the eyes of more than one.

At the close a white comrade said: 'I come to this Conference somewhat prejudiced, but the comradeship and success achieved have given me enthusiasm, and I can see how worth while the propaganda among natives is.'

Head-office officials were elected as follows:– Chairman and Treasurer: SP Bunting; Vice-Chairman: ES Sachs; General Secretary and Editor: DG Wolton; Members of Executive Bureau: R Bunting, M Wolton, TW Thibedi, J Nkosie; Organising and Assistant Secretary: A Nzula; Bookkeeper: S Malkinson.

Document 5

Programme of the Communist Party of South Africa adopted at the seventh annual conference of the Party
1 January 1929

Introduction

Most of the world is living under the system of Society called Capitalism. The essence of Capitalism is the ownership of land, mines, factories, machinery and all other means of production by private individuals and financial groups who are thus able to exploit the propertyless workers for their own gain and profit.

The phase of Capitalist colonial expansion known as Imperialism has brought whole nations under its domination and capital, ever seeking cheaper labour, new markets and spheres of investment, has migrated to India, China, Africa etc., where the mass of the people have been robbed of their land and forced to work for a pittance on farms and plantations, in mines and factories.

The struggle between Imperialist powers for domination and control of colonies leads to war on a world-wide scale, and the 1914-1918 war threatens to be eclipsed by a greater conflagration than was ever known.

South Africa is in a period of transition. At first it was a source of raw materials, and also to some extent a market for British manufacturers; and in addition there is a commencement of cultivation of commercial crops and a more highly developed system of agriculture on large scale capitalist lines.

Whilst South Africa continues to be financed mainly by British Capital, American capital too is beginning to penetrate rapidly, thus giving rise to pronounced rivalry between two powers.

In the industrial life of South Africa the native predominates as worker, and the numerical increase of native workers is greater than of white, although measures of repression debar the native·from developing freely into skilled spheres of labour, and prevailing wage rates are on a very low level. A position of domination is exercised by the whites as a whole, but the position of the white workers as sharers in the exploitation of the natives is gradually breaking down with the reduction of their average standard of living.

In addition to the economic exploitation suffered by the natives they have the additional burden of a whole system of race discrimination measures which keep them socially and politically under semi-feudal conditions. This double burden of exploitation carried by the native masses calls for a democratic revolution which will mean the smashing of all feudal relationships and the securing of full citizen rights. To all natives, whether farm labourers, factory workers, chiefs or peasants, this revolution means the abolition of all discrimination against blacks as such, with independence and the opportunity to develop as a national or racial unit. Such a revolution does not by itself mean the final liberation of the broad masses of South Africa. The stage remains to be traversed to the final abolition of exploitation and combination of class by class, of man by man, the final stage of the Social Revolution for the establishment of Socialism under which all men shall be socially, economically and politically free to share alike in the fruits of their joint labour, with equal opportunity and equal access to all the comforts of life.

This can only be accomplished under the leadership of the United Workers and Peasants of town and country.

The overthrow of Imperialist domination and the Capitalist system is the recognised objective of the Communist Parties of the World, united in the Communist International which points to Soviet Russia and the wonderful progress already achieved there as proof that Imperialism and the Capitalist system can be overthrown and that Socialism can be and is being built up.

The tasks of the CPSA

The accelerating intensification of Imperialist exploitation and oppression in recent years, in South Africa no less than in other countries, colonies and semi-colonies, has led to new stages in the development of the revolutionary working class movement, necessitating a certain revision of Communist programmes. The Communist International itself has just issued its new world programme which must be read as the foundation of all local party programmes.

The Communist Party of SA, for its part, has always been an active champion, ever since its origin in 1915, of complete political and industrial equality for the black man, declaring for working class unity irrespective of colour, and for removal of all race oppressions and discriminations, such as pass laws. In recent years it has succeeded in drawing into its ranks an overwhelming majority of native workers and also peasants who are learning to acclaim it as their own party, the party of the masses, giving it already the largest Negro membership of any Communist Party in the world. The work of the party in its turn has come to centre more than ever on native agitation, education and organisation, political and industrial extension of the party's influence wherever possible in native bodies like the African National Congress or ICU; promotion of an assistance to native trade unions, strikes and political demonstrations; and a commencement of mobilisation of the agrarian masses who constitute the great bulk and potentially, owing to land hunger, perhaps the most revolutionary section of the oppressed race; accompanied by strenuous propaganda among the white workers both on their own particular demands and also in favour of labour unity and militancy and one Trade Union centre, as against the estranging and debilitating effects of 'white chauvinism' and reformism.

The native national clause

Moreover, as a weapon in the overthrow of Imperialism i.e. world capitalism in its last phase, and in its principal strongholds, the colonies, the Party devotes special attention to the national cause of the native people as such, not indeed in the sense of a campaign 'to drive the white man into the sea', but in the Leninist sense of underlining the prime importance of supporting movements for complete national liberation of colonial peoples, removing all the political and social disabilities which make up their enslavement, restoring to them lands and liberties taken away from them by foreign conquerors, settlers and financiers, and vindication of their right, as the immense majority and in the truest sense the people of Africa, to equality, emancipation, independence and self-determination, and hence (for freedom here means power) to predominant political power in their own country – on a basis however of equal rights for Europeans and other minorities as 'most favoured nations'.

Class and race emancipation

Is this a departure from the strict class outlook? By no means. 'Labour solidarity' cannot mean ignoring race discrimination or subjection. Moreover, modern capitalism typically treats colonial races, at any rate in Africa, as constituting, en bloc, reservoirs of labour. South African imperialism helotises the whole of the native people as a race as providing a national labour breeding and recruiting ground. Again, unity postulates equality. If we are to achieve real labour unity we must first remove the greatest obstacle to it, viz., the unequal, subjected, enslaved status of the native workers and people. Hence race emancipation and class emancipation tend to coincide. Hence too the conception and realisation of native rule merges into that of the Workers' and Peasants' Republic, non-imperialist, non-capitalist, non-racialist, classless and in effect Socialist.

This policy has become all the more necessary as the result of the markedly increased aggressiveness of the South African ruling class which today flaunts and stresses the racial domination of the whites as against the old Cape nominal equality, deliberately inflaming white chauvinism, suppressing native movements as 'creating hostility between black and white,' attacking the native franchise such as it is and, through General Hertzog's bills, promoting increased native landlessness and proletarianisation – to mention only a few recent turns of the screw.

The non-exploiting whites

As for the white working class and peasantry, they will not for ever be content with a position of tinsel 'aristocracy' whose material advantages are continually dwindling, or with the venal role of mere policeman, watchdog or bully for the master class over the black slaves. Today there is almost as great poverty and hopelessness to be found among large strata of whites as among blacks. 'Poor whites' are already a 'depressed class' and many white proletarians tend to become declassed or excluded as 'redundant' from the working class proper. White labour today, viewed as a racially exclusive section, hangs in mid-air between ruling class and proletariat with no room for it in either; without stability or prospects, heading for degeneration or fascism, a role of either helplessness or treachery in the class struggle. The SA Labour Party is in collapse because it no longer represents the working class centre of gravity in South Africa.

At the same time white workers are beginning to realise the need of joint action with black if they are ever to win in a first class 'forward movement', which clearly implies that if the black is not to scab on the white his demands must be espoused by the white. And after all, the whites are only a small minority of the population and still more of the proletariat.

Hence the Communist Party, which has always been in the forefront of the battles of the white workers in South Africa, claims their support also for its present programme as the only practical one for the overthrow of capitalism and imperialism and attainment of workers' rule in South Africa. In this revolutionary epoch the world labour movement cannot allow itself to be held up in favour of one or another small privileged section; it must march forward for the emancipation of the whole labouring class and subject population of the world, 'subordinating', as the Comintern programme says, 'the temporary, partial, group or national interests of the proletariat to its lasting, common and international interests'.

Accordingly the Communist Party, on behalf of the working class and subject population of South Africa, puts forward the demands set forth below, the struggle for which will lead to the forging of the revolutionary weapons necessary for the attainment of power.

Down with imperialism, British and Afrikaner!

Down with the capitalist class!

Down with the Subjection of race by race!

For equality and majority rule!

For the liberation of the whole world from slavery and exploitation!

WORKERS OF THE WORLD UNITE!

General demands

Complete equality of races in South Africa; abolition and repeal of all laws, regulations, customs and administrative practices tending to support white domination over black, conferring special privileges on Europeans as such, or placing restrictions, disqualifications or disabilities on non-Europeans as such, persecuting or discriminating against them or favouring their segregation, exploitation or treatment as a subject race, including removal of all limitations on their right to own, acquire and occupy land in any part of the Union, or to reside in any town.

The land for the landless, expropriation of the expropriators, restoration of the land of South Africa to the land workers and poor peasants, consisting chiefly of non-Europeans but also including poor whites, bywoners, etc.

Unity of the working class of all races in South Africa in the militant revolutionary struggle, in conjunction with the peasantry, for the overthrow of capitalism and imperialist rule.

Self-determination of the African people, i.e. their complete liberation from imperialist as well as the bourgeois and feudal or semi-feudal rule and oppression, whether 'British' or 'South African', and wresting of power for a Workers' and Peasants' Soviet Republic wholly independent of the British or any other Empire, and comprising all the toiling masses, whether native or otherwise, of the Union and adjacent protectorates, etc., under the leadership of the working class, with the slogan of 'An Independent South African Native Republic as a stage towards the Workers' and Peasants' Republic, guaranteeing protection and complete equality to all national minorities' (such as Europeans): leading to the reconstruction of the country and rehabilitation of its people on a non-Imperialist, Socialist basis.

Internationally: strenuous campaign against the growing danger of Imperialist war, and support by every means of the USSR as the present headquarters of the world revolution against imperialism.

Particular demands

As immediate, interim or partial demands and subject to revision from time to time as the various needs become clarified.

POLITICAL AND SOCIAL

Retention intact of the Cape Native Franchise and extension of the parliamentary, provincial, divisional and municipal franchise to the whole of the adult male and female population of the Union irrespective of colour, on the same purely residential qualification as applies to Europeans in the Northern Provinces, with the right to sit in Parliament and on all other public bodies, to enter the public service and to occupy all ministerial and other public offices.

Total repeal of the pass laws. Abolition of hut and poll taxes, and of all other taxes calculated to drive the taxpayer into the labour market. Poorer workers and peasants to be relieved of taxation altogether.

Repeal of the Native Urban Areas Act. Self government for locations, native townships, etc., pending their abolition.

Repeal of Clause 29 of the Native Administration Act, with

compensation to all who have been sentenced thereunder. Recognition of full rights of free speech, press and assembly.

Abrogation of all special or arbitrary powers (whether of proclamation, regulation or otherwise) conferred by that Act on the Governor-General, and abolition of his Supreme Chieftainship.

Universal free compulsory non-religious primary education for non-Europeans with higher education on the same terms as enjoyed by Europeans.

A National Health Service meeting the needs of the whole native as well as white population.

Abolition of the present system of Government-paid chiefs and revival of the popular authority of the tribe in the form of elected tribal councils.

A Native Citizen Force. The right of non-Europeans to purchase arms.

JUDICIAL

Equal justice for all races in the courts. Non-Europeans to serve on juries.

Establishment of popular tribunals of native justices, especially in native areas and labour districts.

Severe punishment for police bullying of prisoners.

A public defender in every Court for poor accused.

LABOUR

Removal of all restrictions on right of combination and strike irrespective of race. Recognition of all bona-fide working class unions, urban or rural, and no prosecution of same.

Repeal of master and servant act and all other laws criminally penalising failure to work or breach of contract to work or enforcing serf or semi-serf relations.

Abolition of indentured and contract labour, no labourer to be bound for longer than one month.

Abolition of labour compounds.

Abolition of labour recruiting system.

Provision of full facilities for family life of workers in labour districts.

No importation of native labour from outside the Union.

Prohibition of child labour, including all obligation or compulsion of heads of families to supply the services of members of their families.

Repeal of colour bar laws and regulations.

Civilised wages, hours, housing and conditions generally for non-European workers equally with European, including sickness, accident, occupational disease, unemployment and old age insurance, workmen's compensation and pensions.

Equal pay for equal work irrespective of sex or colour.

National provision of work or maintenance for unemployed of all races.

LAND ETC.

Repeal of Natives Land Act.

In view of the extreme land hunger of the native population, immediate provision of vastly increased areas of land for natives.

Expropriation of big estates, large farms and land held by big trusts or companies and all land lying idle, and throwing open of Crown Land, for redistribution among landless squatters, poor peasants and labourers, black and white.

Where tribes or portions of tribes occupy European owned land, this to become the property of the native occupiers.

Mineral wealth of areas set aside for native inhabitants to be developed for their sole benefit.

Rejection of General Hertzog's Land Bill and of all legislative interference with squatting or attempt to drive natives off European lands.

Protection of crops and stock and security of tenure of squatters, labour tenants, etc., on farms, and compensation for improvements made by them.

Abolition of pound charges.

Application of Wage Act to agricultural labour; Wage Board to be empowered to revise agricultural conditions of service of all kinds.

Establishment of large up-to-date scientific model community farms under communal control with proper provisions for housing, schooling and common village life and for expert management in the sole interests of those working thereon.

Promotion of irrigation on a national scale, and conversion of irrigated areas into self administered co-operative farm units.

Increase of agricultural schools and farm demonstrators, encouragement of improved stock breeding, provision of improved seed, fertilisers, implements, fencing, marketing, credit, banking and co-operative facilities, railways and transport services, and promotion of greater and better agricultural and pastoral production generally in native districts and among poor peasants and farmers everywhere.

Tasks of Communist Party

In support of the foregoing the Party's tasks will include:

Formation of factory, mine, works and farm groups or committees and councils of action, and formation of unions and co-operatives of poor natives and white peasants.

Energetic promotion of militant trade union organisations of all unorganised workers, especially non-Europeans, on industrial lines, including farm labourers.

Organisational contact and co-operation between rural and urban workers, between non-European and European workers, and between South African workers and workers of Britain as the imperialist 'home' country, and also of the USSR. Promotion of affiliation with the Red International of Labour Unions.

Strenuous campaign in labour organisations against white 'chauvinism', against all illusions of 'class peace' or 'the classless state' under capitalism, against bourgeois reformism, social democratic confessionalism, corruption and treachery.

Document 6

Africans' claims in South Africa
16 December 1943

(Including 'The Atlantic Charter from the Standpoint of Africans within the Union of South Africa' and 'Bill of Rights,' adopted by the ANC Annual Conference.)

Preface

In the following pages the reader will find what has been termed '*Bill of Rights*' and '*The Atlantic Charter from the African's Point of View*'. This document was drawn up after due deliberations by a special committee whose names appear at the end of this booklet. Their findings were unanimously adopted by the Annual Conference of the African National Congress at Bloemfontein, on the 16th December, 1943. We realise as anyone else the apparent inappropriateness and vagueness of the expressions when adopted by us. We have, however, adapted them to our own conditions as they give us, the most dynamic way of directing the attention of our Government in the Union of South Africa, the European population of our country to the African position and status in this land of our birth – South Africa – because the Government and the European section alone have the absolute legislative and administrative power and authority over the non-Europeans. We know that the Prime Minister of the Union of South Africa and his delegation to the Peace Conference will represent the interests of the people of our country. We want the Government and the people of South Africa to know the full aspirations of the African peoples so that their point of view will also be presented at the Peace Conference. We want the Government of the United Nations to know and act in the light of our interpretation of the 'Atlantic Charter' to which they are signatories. This is our way of conveying to them our undisputed claim to full citizenship. We desire them to realise once and for all that a just and permanent peace will be possible only if the claims of all classes, colours and races for sharing and for full participation in the educational, political and economic activities are granted and recognised.

Already according to press reports there seem to be differences of opinion as to the applicability of the 'Atlantic Charter' as between the President of the United States of America and the Prime Minister of Great Britain. It would appear that president FD Roosevelt wanted the Atlantic Charter to apply to the whole world while the Prime Minister, Mr Winston Churchill, understood it to be intended for the white people in the occupied countries in Europe.

In South Africa, Africans have no freedom of movement, no freedom of choice of employment, no right of choice of residence and no right of freedom to purchase land or fixed property from anyone and anywhere. Under the guise of segregation, they are subjected to serious educational, political and economic disabilities and discriminations which are the chief causes of their apparent slow progress.

We urge that if fascism and fascist tendencies are to be uprooted from the face of the earth, and to open the way for peace, prosperity and racial good-will, the 'Atlantic Charter' must apply to the whole British Empire, the United States of America and to all the nations of the world and their subject peoples. And we urge that South Africa as a prelude to her participation at the Peace Conference in the final destruction of Nazism and Fascism in Europe must grant the just claims of her non-European peoples to freedom, democracy and human decency, as contained in the following document since charity must begin at home, and if to quote B.B.C. Radio News Reel: 'We Fight for World Democracy'.

The soldiers of all races Europeans, Americans, Asiatic and Africans have won their claim and the claims of their peoples to the four freedoms by having taken part in this war which can be converted into a war for human freedom if the settlement at the Peace Table is based on human justice, fair play and equality of opportunity for all races, colours and classes.

We deliberately set up a committee composed exclusively of Africans in South Africa to deal with this matter so that they can declare without assistance or influence from others, their hopes and despairs. The document that follows is their deliberate and considered conclusion as well as their conviction. Others who believe in justice and fair play for all human beings will support their rightful claims from Africans themselves.

The list of names of the members of the committee who produced this document tells a story, for those who would understand. These fruits of their labours are a legacy, nay a heritage which they will leave behind for future generations to enjoy. For it, and to them, we are all forever indebted.

As African leaders we are not so foolish as to believe that because we have made these declarations that our government will grant us our claims for the mere asking. We realise that for the African this is only a beginning of a long struggle entailing great sacrifices of time, means and even life itself. To the African people the declaration is a challenge to organise and unite themselves under the mass liberation movement, the African National Congress. The struggle is on right now and it must be persistent and insistent. In a mass liberation movement there is no room for divisions or for personal ambitions. The goal is one, namely, freedom for all. It should be the central and only aim or objective of all true African nationals. Divisions and gratification of personal ambitions under the circumstances will be a betrayal of this great cause.

On behalf of my Committee and the African National Congress I call upon chiefs, ministers of religion, teachers, professional men, men and women of all ranks and classes to organise our people, to close ranks and take their place in this mass liberation movement and struggle, expressed in this Bill of Citizenship Rights until freedom, right and justice are won for all races and colours in the honour and glory of the Union of South Africa whose ideals – freedoms, democracy, Christianity and human decency cannot be attained until all races in South Africa participate in them.

I am confident that all men and women of goodwill of all races and nations will see the justice of our cause and stand with us and support us in our struggle.

If you ever feel discouraged in the struggle that must follow remember the wise and encouraging words of the Prime Minister, Field Marshal the Right Honourable JC Smuts who says: 'Do not mind being called agitators. Let them call you any names they like, but get on with the job and see that matters that vitally require attention, Native health, Native food, the treatment of Native children and all those who cognate questions that are basic to the welfare of South Africa are attended to'.

A. B. XUMA
President-General of the African National Congress
Secretary-Organiser Atlantic Charter Committee, South Africa.

The Atlantic Charter and the Africans

1. The Atlantic Charter, agreed upon by the President of the United States and the Prime Minister of Great Britain in their historic meeting of August 14, 1941, and subsequently subscribed to by the other Allied Nations, has aroused widespread interest throughout the world. In all countries this summary of the war aims of the Allied Nations has aroused hopes and fired the imagination of all peoples in regard to the new world order adumbrated in its terms.

2. For us in South Africa particular significance attaches to this document because of its endorsement on more than one occasion by Field-Marshal Smuts, who has announced that the post war world will be based upon the principles enunciated in the Atlantic Charter. The Honourable Deneys Reitz, speaking on behalf of the Natives Representative Council in December, 1942, indicated that the Freedoms vouchsafed to the peoples of the world in the Atlantic Charter were indicated for the African people as well.

3. In view of these pronouncements and the participation of Africans in the war effort of various Allied Unions, and to the fact that the Atlantic Charter has aroused the hopes and inspirations of Africans no less than other peoples, the President-General of the African National Council decided to convene a conference of leaders of African thought to discuss the problems of the Atlantic Charter in its relation to Africa in particular and the place of the African in post-war reconstruction. In other words, the terms of reference of the conference were to be:-

   (a) To study and discuss the problems arising out of the Atlantic Charter in so far as they relate to Africa, and to formulate a comprehensive statement embodying an African Charter, and

   (b) to draw up a Bill of Rights which Africans are demanding as essential to guarantee them a worthy place in the post war world.

4. The President-General accordingly invited various African leaders to become members of the Atlantic Charter Committee which would meet in Bloemfontein on December 13 and 14, 1943 to perform this important national duty, as he saw it. At the same time the President-General called upon those invited to submit memoranda on different aspects of this subject for the subsequent consideration of the whole committee on the dates indicated above.

5. The response to the President-General's invitation as indicated by the number of well prepared and thought provoking statements submitted from different parts of the country was proof that his action was timeous and in line with the thinking of Africans on the vital subject of post war reconstruction.

6. The Committee met at Bloemfontein and deliberated on Monday and Tuesday, December 13 and 14, 1943. The Committee elected Mr Z. K. Matthews as Chairman and Mr L. T. Mtimkulu as Secretary, and a Sub-Committee consisting of Messrs. S. B. Ngcobo, M. L. Kabane and J. M. Nhlapo, with the chairman and secretary as ex officio members, to draft the findings of the

Atlantic Charter Committee. Throughout its deliberations the committee acted under the able guidance of the President-General, Dr. A. B. Xuma.

7. As already indicated above, the work of the committee fell into two parts, viz., (a) the consideration and interpretation of the Atlantic Charter, and (b) the formulation of a Bill of Rights. In dealing with the first part of its work the Committee discussed the articles for the Atlantic Charter one by one and made certain observations under each article.

8. In considering the Charter as a whole, the Committee was confronted with the difficulty of interpreting certain terms and expressions which are somewhat loosely and vaguely used in the Atlantic Charter. Among the terms or words to which this structure applies are 'nations,' 'states,' 'peoples' and 'men'. Whatever meanings the authors had in mind with regard to these terms, the Committee decided that these terms, words or expressions are understood by us to include Africans and other Non-Europeans, because we are convinced that the groups to which we refer demand that they shall not be excluded from the rights and privileges which other groups hope to enjoy in the post-war world.

9. The Committee noted with satisfaction that the twenty-six other nations which subscribed to the Atlantic Charter on January 2, 1942 made it quite clear that the freedoms and liberties which this war was fought for, must be realised by the Allied Powers 'in their own lands as well as other lands'. This is the common cry of all subject races at the present time.

10. The articles of the Atlantic Charter and the observations of the Committee under each were as follows.

The Atlantic Charter

(From the standpoint of Africans within the Union of South Africa.)

FIRST POINT – NO AGGRANDISEMENT

'Their countries seek no aggrandisement, territorial or otherwise'.

In this article there is very important assurance which is intended to exonerate the Allied Nations from the charge of having entered into this war for territorial gains or imperialistic reasons. With that understanding we support the principle contained in this article and hope that the rejection of aggrandisement in the War Aims of the Allied Nations is genuine and well meant. Having regard, however to the possible danger of aggrandisement in the form of the extension of the Mandates System which was instituted after the last Great War, in spite of similar assurances in President Wilson's FOURTEEN POINTS, and also to the possibility of 'annexation' of certain African territories though their economic strangulation under veiled forms of assistance, we have deemed it necessary to make these three reservations.

Firstly, the status and independence of Abyssinia and her right to sovereignty must be safeguarded, and any political and economic assistance she may need must be freely negotiated by her and be in accordance with her freely expressed wishes. Abyssinia should be afforded a corridor into the sea for purposes of trade and direct communication with the outside world.

Secondly, we urge that as a fulfilment of the War Aim of the Allied Nations namely, to liberate territories and peoples under foreign domination, the former Italian colonies in Africa should be granted independence and their security provided for under the future system of World Security.

Thirdly, there are the anxieties of Africans with regard to British Protectorates in Southern Africa. It is well known that the Union of South Africa is negotiating for the incorporation of the three Protectorates of Bechuanaland, Basutoland and Swaziland and that incorporation might be pressed during or after this present war as part of South Africa's price for participation in this war. The schedule to the South Africa Act of 1909 did envisage the transfer, under certain conditions, of the territories to the Union of South Africa, but Africans were not contracting parties to these arrangements and they do not regard the provisions of the schedule as morally and politically binding on them. They would deprecate any action on the part of Great Britain which would bring about the extension of European political control at the expense of their vital interests. Africans, therefore, are definitely opposed to the transfer of the Protectorates to the South African State.

SECOND POINT – NO TERRITORIAL CHANGES

'They desire to see no territorial changes that do not accord with the freely expressed wishes of the peoples concerned'.

This statement is intended to refer to territorial changes which have been brought about in Europe by military aggression. It is clear, however, that territorial changes are also being discussed in regard to other parts of the world. We are mainly concerned with such changes in so far as they related to the African continent, and in this connection mention has to be made to the suggested territorial changes in regard to West Africa, East Africa and Southern Africa under a system of regional regrouping as outlined in the recent speeches and writings of Field Marshal Smuts.

We hope that the mistakes of the past whereby African people and their lands were treated as pawns in the political game of European nations will not be repeated, and we urge that before such changes are effected there must be effective consultation and that the suggested changes must be in accord with the freely expressed wishes of the indigenous inhabitants. Further, where territorial changes have taken place in the past and have not resulted in the political and other advancement of the Africans living in those territories or colonies it would be a mistake to continue to maintain the status quo after the war. The objective of promoting self government for colonial peoples must be actively pursued by powers having such lands under their administrative control, and this objective should also be a matter of international concern more than has been the case in the past.

THIRD POINT – THE RIGHT TO CHOOSE THE FORM OF GOVERNMENT

'They respect the right of all peoples to choose the form of government under which they will live; and they wish to see sovereign rights and self government restored to those who have been forcibly deprived of them'.

The principle of Self Determination made famous by President Wilson is his FOURTEEN POINTS on behalf of small nations has been reaffirmed by this article of the charter. This principle of self determination necessarily raises not only issues relating to the independent existence of small nations besides their more powerful neighbours but those also concerning the political rights and status of minorities and of Africans now held under European tutelage.

In the African continent in particular, European aggression and conquest has resulted in the establishment of Alien governments which, however beneficent they might be in intention or in fact, are not accountable to the indigenous inhabitants. Africans are still very conscious of the loss of their independence, freedom and the right of choosing the form of government under which they will live. It is the inalienable right of all peoples to choose the form of government under which they will live and therefore Africans welcome the belated recognition of this right by the Allied Nations.

We believe that the acid test of this third article of the charter is its application to the African continent. In certain parts of Africa it should be possible to accord Africans sovereign rights and to establish administrations of their own choosing. But in other parts of Africa where there are the peculiar circumstances of a politically entrenched European minority ruling a majority African population the demands of the Africans for full citizenship rights and direct participation in all the councils of the state should be recognised. This is most urgent in the Union of South Africa.

FOURTH POINT – THE OPEN DOOR POLICY IN TRADE AND RAW MATERIALS

'They will endeavour, with due regard for their existing obligations, to further the enjoyment of all states, great and small, victor or vanquished, of access, on equal terms, to the trade and to the raw materials of the world which are needed for their economic prosperity'.

There is envisaged by this article an Open Door Policy in regard to trade and the distribution of the world's resources. Africa has figured prominently in the discussions on the better distribution of the world resources and of free international trade because of her rich raw materials most of which have not as yet been fully tapped. The exploitation that is suggested by the above article, judging by past experiences and present economic evils, raises in our minds considerable misgivings as likely to bring about a continuation of the exploitation of African resources to the detriment of her indigenous inhabitants and the enrichment of foreigners.

We are, however, in agreement with the necessity for the technical and economic utilisation of a country's resources with due regard for the human welfare and the economic improvement of the indigenous inhabitants. The primary obligation of any government is to promote the economic advancement of the peoples under its charge and any obligation, agreement, contract or treaty in conflict with this primary obligation should not be countenanced.

In our view it is essential that any economic assistance that might be rendered to weak and insufficiently developed African States should be of such a nature as will really promote their economic progress.

FIFTH POINT – ECONOMIC COLLABORATION AND IMPROVED LABOUR STANDARDS

'They desire to bring about the fullest collaboration between all nations on the economic field with the object of securing for all improved labour standards, economic advancement and Social Security'.

This article of the charter has reference to the International Labour Office as the machinery by which nations shall collaborate in economic affairs. The Governments of African states have fully participated in the deliberations and exchange of ideas in regard to the promotion of improved living standards and industrial peace. For this reason Africans are vitally interested in the decisions and conventions of the International Labour Office.

But it is regrettable that conventions dealing with the welfare of the African labour – Forced Labour, Migrant or Recruited Labour, Health and Housing, Wage Rates – that have been drawn up at Geneva and accepted by the majority of civilised states have, for selfish reasons, been either rejected or half-heartedly applied by African governments whose protestations at being civilised have been loudest. Thus Africa has not to any large extent felt the beneficent influence of the International Labour Organisation.

Hitherto the International Organisation has been representative mainly of the interests of Governments and the capitalist class. We claim that collaboration between all nations in the economic field must include consideration of the interest of labour as well as of capital, and that all workers, including African workers, must be fully and directly represented in this collaboration. In order to make participation by the workers effective it is essential that their right to collective bargaining should be legally recognised and guaranteed.

We shall understand, 'improved labour standards,' 'economic advancement' and 'social security' as referred to in this article to mean the following –

(a)   the removal of the Colour Bar;
(b)   training in skilled occupations;
(c)   remuneration according to skill;
(d)   a living wage and all other workers' benefits;
(e)   proper and adequate housing for all races and colours.

The policy of economic collaboration is probably more applicable to economic relations between sovereign states rather than to relations with weak and insufficiently developed states or territories. In our view it is essential that any economic assistance that might be rendered to weak and insufficiently developed African territories should be of such a nature as will really promote their economic improvement and not pauperise them.

SIXTH POINT – THE DESTRUCTION OF NAZI TYRANNY

'After the final destruction of the Nazi tyranny, they hope to see established a peace which will afford to all nations the means of dwelling in safety within their own boundaries, and which will afford assurance that all men in all lands may live out their lives in freedom from fear and want'.

Africans are in full agreement with the war aim of destroying Nazi tyranny, but they desire to see all forms of racial domination in all lands, including the Allied countries, completely destroyed. Only in this way, they firmly believe, shall there be established peace which will afford all peoples and races the means of dwelling in safety within their own boundaries, and which will afford the assurance that all men in all lands shall live out their lives in freedom from fear, want and oppression.

SEVENTH POINT – THE FREEDOM OF THE SEAS

'Such a peace should enable all men to traverse the high seas and oceans without hindrance'.

We agree with the principle of the freedom of the seas.

EIGHTH POINT – THE ABANDONMENT OF THE USE OF FORCE

'They believe that all the nations of the world, for realistic as well as spiritual reasons, must come to the abandonment of the use of force. Since no further peace can be maintained if land, sea or air armaments continue to be employed by nations which threaten or may threaten aggression outside of their frontiers, they believe, pending the establishment of a wider and permanent system of general security, that the disarmament of such nations is essential. . . . They will likewise aid and encourage all other practical measures which will lighten for peace-loving peoples the crushing burden of armaments'.

We are in agreement in principle with the idea of the abandoning of the use of force for the settlement of international disputes, but we do not agree with the idea envisaged in this article of the charter concerning the armament of some nations and the disarmament of other nations as this policy is provocative of future wars. As a preliminary, steps must be taken to nationalise the armament industry.

While recognising the necessity for the use of force within a country as part of its policing machinery, we must nevertheless deplore the fact that force, especially in South Africa, is frequently resorted to as a method of suppressing the legitimate ventilation of their grievances by oppressed, unarmed and disarmed sections of the population.

Bill of rights

FULL CITIZENSHIP RIGHTS AND DEMANDS

We, the African people in the Union of South Africa, urgently demand the granting of full citizenship rights such as are enjoyed by all Europeans in South Africa. We demand:-

1. Abolition of political discrimination based on race, such as the Cape 'Native' franchise and the Native Representative Council under Representation of Natives Act, and the extension to all adults, regardless of race, of the right to vote and be elected to parliament, provincial councils and other representative institutions.
2. The right to equal justice in courts of law, including nominations to juries and appointments as judges, magistrates, and other court officials.
3. Freedom of residence and the repeal of laws such as the Natives Act that restrict this freedom.

4. Freedom of movement, and the repeal of the pass laws, Natives Urban Areas Act, Natives Laws Amendment Act and similar legislation.
6. Right of freedom of the press.
7. Recognition of the sanctity or inviolability of the home as a right of every family, and the prohibition of police raids on citizens in their homes for tax or liquor or other purposes.
8. The right to own, buy, hire or lease and occupy land and all other forms of immovable as well as movable property, and the repeal of restrictions on this right in the Native Land Act, the Native Trust and Land Act, the Natives (Urban Areas) Act and the Natives Laws Amendment Act.
9. The right to engage in all forms of lawful occupations, trades and professions, on the same terms and conditions as members of other sections of the population.
10. The right to be appointed to and hold office in the civil service and in all branches of public employment on the same terms and conditions as Europeans.
11. The right of every child to free and compulsory education and of admission to technical schools, universities, and other institutions of higher education.

LAND

We demand the right to an equal share in all the material resources of the country, and we urge:

1. That the present allocation of $12\frac{1}{2}$% of the surface area to 7 000 000 Africans as against $87\frac{1}{4}$% to about 2 000 000 Europeans is unjust and contrary to the interest of South Africa, and therefore demand a fair redistribution of the land as a prerequisite for a just settlement of the land problem.
2. That the right to own, buy, hire or lease and occupy land individually or collectively, both in rural and in urban areas is a fundamental right of citizenship, and therefore demand the repeal of the Native Land Act, the Native Trust and Land Act, the Natives

Laws Amendment Act, and the Natives (Urban Areas) Act in so far as these laws abrogate that right.

3. That African farmers require no less assistance from the State than that which is provided to European farmers, and therefore demand the same Land Bank facilities, State subsidies, and other privileges as are enjoyed by Europeans.

INDUSTRY AND LABOUR

We demand for the Africans –

(1) equal opportunity to engage in any occupation, trade or industry – in order that this objective might be realised to the fullest extent, facilities must be provided for technical and university education of Africans so as to enable them to enter skilled, semi-skilled occupations, professions, government service and other spheres of employment;

(2) equal pay for equal work, as well as equal opportunity for all work and for the unskilled workers in both rural and urban areas such minimum wage as shall enable the workers to live in health, happiness, decency and comfort;

(3) the removal of the Colour Bar in industry, and other occupations;

(4) the statutory recognition of the right of the African worker to collective bargaining under the Industrial Conciliation Act.

(5) that the African worker shall be insured against sickness, unemployment, accidents, old age and for all other physical disabilities arising from the nature of their work; the contributions to such insurance should be borne entirely by the government and the employers;

(6) the extension of all industrial welfare legislation to Africans engaged in Agriculture, Domestic Service and in Public institutions or bodies.

COMMERCE

(1)   We protest very strongly against all practices that impede the obtaining of trading licences by Africans in urban and rural areas, and we equally condemn the confinement of African economic enterprise to segregated areas and localities.

(2)   We demand the recognition of the right of the Africans to freedom of trading.

EDUCATION

(1)   The education of the African is a matter of national importance requiring state effort for its proper realisation. The magnitude of the task places it beyond the limits of the resources of the missionary or private endeavour. The right of the African child to education, like children of other sections must be recognised as a State duty and responsibility,
We therefore, demand that –
(a) the state must provide full facilities for all types of education for African children.
(b) Education of the African must be financed from General Revenue on a per capita basis.
(c) The state must provide enough properly built and equipped schools for all African children of school-going age and institute free compulsory primary education.
(d) The state must provide adequate facilities for Secondary, professional technical and university education.

(2)   We reject the conception that there is any need of a special type of education for Africans as such, and therefore we demand that the African must be given the type of education which will enable him to meet on equal terms with other peoples the conditions of the modern world.

(3)   We demand equal pay for equal educational qualifications and equal grade of work for all teachers irrespective of their race or colour. We also urge that pensions, conditions of service, and

other privileges which are enjoyed by European teachers should be extended to African teachers on equal terms.

(4) We claim that the direction of the educational system of the African must fall more and more largely into the hands of the Africans themselves, and therefore we demand increased and direct representation in all bodies such as Education Advisory Boards, School Committees, Governing Councils, etc., which are responsible for the management and the shaping of policy in African schools, Institutions and Colleges and/or adequate representation in all bodies moulding and directing the country's educational policy.

PUBLIC HEALTH AND MEDICAL SERVICES

1. We regard it as the duty of the state to provide adequate medical and health facilities for the entire population of the country. We deplore and deprecate the fact that the state has not carried out its duty to the African in this regard, and has left this important duty to philanthropic and voluntary agencies. As a result of this gross neglect the general health of the entire African population has deteriorated to an alarming extent. We consider that the factors which contribute to this state of affairs are these: –

    (a) the low economic position of the African which is responsible for the present gross malnutrition, general overcrowding, higher mortality and morbidity rates;

    (b) the shortage of land resulting in the congestion in the reserves and in consequence the bad state of the African's health and the deterioration of his physique;

    (c) the slum conditions in the urban areas;

    (d) neglect of the health and the general education of the Africans;

    (e) neglect of the provision of water supplies, proper sanitary and other conveniences in areas occupied by Africans both in urban and rural areas.

2. To remedy this state of affairs we urge and demand –

(a) a substantial and immediate improvement in the economic position of the African;

(b) a drastic overhauling and reorganisation of the health services of the country with due emphasis on preventive medicine with all that implies in a modern public health sense.

3. We strongly urge the adoption of the following measures to meet the health needs of the African population –

(a) the establishment of free medical and health services for all sections of the population;

(b) the establishment of a system of *School Medical Service* with a full staff of medical practitioners, nurses and other health visitors;

(c) increased hospital and clinic facilities both in the rural and in urban areas;

(d) increased facilities for the training of African doctors, dentists, nurses, sanitary inspectors, health visitors, etc.;

(e) a co-ordinated control finance of health services for the whole Union;

(f) the creation of a proper system of vital statistics for the whole population including Africans;

(g) the appointment of District surgeons in rural areas with a large African population.

DISCRIMINATORY LEGISLATION

1. We, the African people, regard as fundamental to the establishment of a new order in South Africa the abolition of all enactments which discriminate against the African on grounds of race and colour. We condemn and reject the policy of segregation in all aspects of our national life in as much as this policy is designed to keep the African in a state of perpetual tutelage and militates against his normal development.

2. We protest strongly against discourteous harsh and inconsiderate treatment meted out to Africans by officials in all state and other public offices and institutions. Such obnoxious practices are

irreconcilable with Christian, democratic and civilised standards and are contrary to human decency.

We therefore demand the repeal of all colour-bar and/or discriminatory clauses in the Union's Constitution, that is the South Africa 1909 Act.

Document 7

WE, THE PEOPLE OF SOUTH AFRICA, declare for all our country and the world to know: that South Africa belongs to all who live in it, black and white, and that no government can justly claim authority unless it is based on the will of all the people; that our people have been robbed of their birthright to land, liberty and peace by a form of government founded on injustice and inequality; that our country will never be prosperous or free until all our people live in brotherhood, enjoying equal rights and opportunities; that only a democratic state, based on the will of all the people, can secure to all their birthright without distinction of colour, race, sex or belief;

And therefore,

We, the people of South Africa, black and white together equals, countrymen and brothers adopt this Freedom Charter;

And we pledge ourselves to strive together, sparing neither strength nor courage, until the democratic changes here set out have been won.

The people shall govern!

Every man and woman shall have the right to vote for and to stand as a candidate for all bodies which make laws; All people shall be entitled to take part in the administration of the country; The rights of the people shall be the same, regardless of race, colour or sex; All bodies of minority rule, advisory boards, councils and authorities shall be replaced by democratic organs of self-government.

All national groups shall have equal rights!

There shall be equal status in the bodies of state, in the courts and in the schools for all national groups and races; All people shall have equal right to use their own languages, and to develop their own folk culture and customs; All national groups shall be protected by law against insults to their race and national pride; The preaching and practice of national, race or colour discrimination and contempt shall be a punishable crime; All apartheid laws and practices shall be set aside.

The people shall share in the country's wealth!

The national wealth of our country, the heritage of South Africans, shall be restored to the people; The mineral wealth beneath the soil, the Banks and monopoly industry shall be transferred to the ownership of the people as a whole; All other industry and trade shall be controlled to assist the well-being of the people; All people shall have equal rights to trade where they choose, to manufacture and to enter all trades, crafts and professions.

The land shall be shared among those who work it!

Restrictions of land ownership on a racial basis shall be ended, and all the land re-divided amongst those who work it to banish famine and land hunger; The state shall help the peasants with implements, seed, tractors and dams to save the soil and assist the tillers; Freedom of movement shall be guaranteed to all who work on the land; All shall have the right to occupy land wherever they choose; People shall not be robbed of their cattle, and forced labour and farm prisons shall be abolished.

All shall be equal before the law!

No-one shall be imprisoned, deprived or restricted without a fair trial; No-one shall be condemned by the order of any Government official; The courts shall be representative of all the people; Imprisonment shall be only for serious crimes against the people, and shall aim at re-education, not vengeance; The police force and army shall be open to all on an equal basis and shall be the helpers and protectors of the people; All laws which discriminate on grounds of race, colour or belief shall be repealed.

All shall enjoy equal human rights!

The law shall guarantee to all their right to speak, to organise, to meet together, to publish, to preach, to worship and to educate their children; The privacy of the house from police raids shall be protected by law; All shall be free to travel without restriction from countryside to town, from province to province, and from South Africa abroad; Pass Laws, permits and all other laws restricting these freedoms shall be abolished.

There shall be work and security!

All who work shall be free to form trade unions, to elect their officers and to make wage agreements with their employers; The state shall recognise the right and duty of all to work, and to draw full unemployment benefits; Men and women of all races shall receive equal pay for equal work; There shall be a forty-hour working week, a national minimum wage, paid annual leave, and sick leave for all workers, and maternity leave on full pay for all working mothers; Miners, domestic workers, farm workers and civil servants shall have the same rights as all others who work; Child labour, compound labour, the tot system and contract labour shall be abolished.

The doors of learning and of culture shall be opened!

The government shall discover, develop and encourage national talent for the enhancement of our cultural life; All the cultural treasures of mankind shall be open to all, by free exchange of books, ideas and contact with other lands; The aim of education shall be to teach the youth to love their people and their culture, to honour human brotherhood, liberty and peace; Education shall be free, compulsory, universal and equal for all children; Higher education and technical training shall be opened to all by means of state allowances and scholarships awarded on the basis of merit; Adult illiteracy shall be ended by a mass state education plan; Teachers shall have all the rights of other citizens; The colour bar in cultural life, in sport and in education shall be abolished.

There shall be houses, security and comfort!

All people shall have the right to live where they choose, be decently housed, and to bring up their families in comfort and security; Unused housing space to be made available to the people; Rent and prices shall be lowered, food plentiful and no-one shall go hungry; A preventive health scheme shall be run by the state; Free medical care and hospitalisation shall be provided for all, with special care for mothers and young children; Slums shall be demolished, and new suburbs built where all have transport, roads, lighting, playing fields, crèches and social centres; The aged, the orphans, the disabled and the sick shall be cared for by the state; Rest, leisure and recreation shall be the right of all:

Fenced locations and ghettos shall be abolished, and laws which break up families shall be repealed.

There shall be peace and friendship!

South Africa shall be a fully independent state which respects the rights and sovereignty of all nations; South Africa shall strive to maintain world peace and the settlement of all international disputes by negotiation – not war; Peace and friendship amongst all our people shall be secured by upholding the equal rights, opportunities and status of all; The people of the protectorates Basutoland, Bechuanaland and Swaziland shall be free to decide for themselves their own future; The right of all peoples of Africa to independence and self-government shall be recognised, and shall be the basis of close co-operation. Let all people who love their people and their country now say, as we say here:

THESE FREEDOMS WE WILL FIGHT FOR, SIDE BY SIDE, THROUGH-OUT OUR LIVES, UNTIL WE HAVE WON OUR LIBERTY.

Document 8

Letter on the current situation and suggesting a multi-racial convention, from Chief Albert J. Luthuli to Prime Minister J. G. Strijdom
28 May 1957

The Honourable the Prime Minister,
Union of South Africa,
House of Assembly
CAPE TOWN

Honourable Sir,

At a time when in many respects our country is passing through some of the most difficult times in its history, I consider it my duty as leader of the African National Congress, a Union-wide premier political organisation among the African people in the Union of South Africa, to address this letter direct to you as head of the government to apprise you personally of the very grave fears and concern of my people, the Africans, at the situation now existing in the Union, especially anent matters affecting them.

I shall venture to place before you respectfully what I consider to be some of the disturbing features of our situation and suggest steps that could be taken by the Government to meet the position.

I have addressed this letter to you, Sir, and not to any Department for two reasons.

Firstly, because the gravity of our situation requires your direct personal attention and, secondly, because what I shall say fundamentally affects the welfare of the Union of South Africa as a whole since both basically and in practice, the so-called 'Native Affairs' are, not only inextricably interwoven with the true interests of other racial groups, but are a key to a proper understanding and appraisal of South African Affairs and problems for indeed 'ALL SOUTH AFRICAN POLITICS ARE NATIVE AFFAIRS.'

One of the tragic aspects of the political situation in our country today is the increasing deterioration in race relations, especially in Black–White relations. There can be no two viewpoints on this question. Never has there been such an extremely delicate relationship as now exists between the Government of Whites only, of which you are head, and the vast masses of non-European people in general, and the African people in particular. This unfortunate state of affairs has resulted from a number of factors, the basic one being the policy of segregation, especially its more aggressive form, White baaskap and apartheid.

It is in the economic sphere that this disastrous policy of discrimination has affected Africans hardest and most cruelly. It has brought on them an economic plight that has shown itself in the dire poverty of the people both in the urban and in the rural areas. This fact has long been attested to from time to time by economic experts and by findings of Government Commissions. Recently, as a result of the Rand and Pretoria Bus Boycott, the extreme poverty of Africans in urban areas has been acknowledged by even commerce and industry. It is not necessary for one to describe the generally admitted horrifying state of degradation this poverty has brought upon the African people or to refer in any detail to the tragic social consequences such as disease, malnutrition, bad housing, broken families and delinquency among children and youth.

The denial to the African people of the democratic channels of expression and participation in the government of the country has accentuated the stresses and strains to which they are subject. My people have come to view with alarm every new session of Parliament because it has meant the passing of more oppressive discriminatory legislation there. As a result of this annual influx of new legislation there are already in the Statute Books of the Union of South Africa a large number of laws which cause my people tremendous hardship and suffering. The African people view these laws as further weapons of attack on their very existence as a people. For the sake of brevity I shall refer to only a few of such laws in support of my charge. Here are the categories of some of such laws. I cite:

1. THE LAND LAWS which to all intents and purposes deny the African people the right to own land in both the rural and urban areas. In rural areas Africans are tenants in State rural reserves or in privately-owned land. In urban areas they are tenants in municipal lands.

   The land allocated to Africans in rural areas is most inadequate. It will only be 13% of the entire land surface of the Union when all the land promised them in the Native's Land and Trust Act of 1936 shall have been acquired. On account of this inadequacy of land the African people live under extremely congested conditions in rural areas and in the urban areas and find it difficult to make a living above subsistence level from the land. These land laws are in many respects reminiscent of the worst features of the feudal laws of medieval days.

2. THE PASS LAWS, which not only deny the African people freedom of movement, but are enforced in ways that cause the people much unnecessary suffering and humiliation.

   They are definitely an affront to human personality and it is not surprising that their extension to our womenfolk has resulted in Union-wide protests and in the expression of deep indignation by the entire African population. These protests and demonstrations are indicative of a state of unrest and intense tension among the African people.

   Section 10 of the Natives (Urban Areas) Consolidation Act of 1945, as substituted by Section 27 of Act 54 of 1952, places serious and far-reaching restrictions on the right of my people to enter into and remain within an urban area in order to compel them to seek employment on European farms where working conditions are extremely shocking. Acting under this provision local authorities and members of the police force have forcibly removed from their homes and families thousands upon thousands of my people in the interest of the European farming industry.

3. THE MASTER AND SERVANTS ACT, which is designed effectively to limit to unskilled categories the participation of the African people in industry and commerce. This relegates the bulk of African workers to low uneconomic wages. My people note with grave concern the efforts of your Government to destroy the African Trade Union Movement.

The current session of Parliament affords the country no respite from Apartheid legislation. It has before it a large number of measures of far-reaching consequences for the country in general, and the African people in particular. There is the Native Laws Amendment Bill, which is seen by the African people as another measure attacking the civil and religious liberties of the people and aimed at preventing contact on a basis of human dignity and equality between the African people and the rest of our multi-racial population.

The African people are similarly disturbed by other measures now before Parliament such as the bill on Apartheid in University Education, the Apartheid Nursing Bill, the measure to increase indirect taxation of the African people despite their poverty, and a bill intended to prevent the operation of alternative bus services where the boycott weapon has been effectively used by a people who have no other means of seeking redress against an economic injustice.

We are greatly concerned at the policy of Apartheid and the administrative action flowing from it because we honestly believe that these are against the true interest of democracy and freedom. I would like to point out here that the enforcement of the discriminatory apartheid laws brings the African people into unnecessary contact with the police. Unfortunately, the impatient and domineering manner in which the police often do their work among Africans results in unfortunate clashes between the people and the police. The net result is that Africans tend to lose respect for the law and come to look upon the Union of South Africa as a Police State.

What does my Congress stand for?

My Congress is deeply wedded to the ideals of democracy and has at all times emphasised its firm and unshakeable belief in the need for the creation of a society in South Africa based on the upholding of democratic values: values which are today cherished the world over by all civilised peoples.

We believe in a society in which the White and non-white peoples of the Union will work and live in harmony for the common good of our fatherland and share equally in the good things of life which our country offers in abundance. We believe in the brotherhood of man and in the upholding of human respect and dignity. Never has my Congress preached hatred against any racial group in the Union. On the contrary, it has stretched out its hand of friendship to all South Africans of all races, emphasising that there is sufficient room for all in this beautiful country of ours in which we can and must live in peace and friendship. Unfortunately, there are people, among them Ministers of the Crown – Mr. Louw, Mr. Schoeman, Dr. Verwoerd, to mention some – who, according to Press reports, believe that the aims and objects of the African National Congress are to drive the White man out of Southern Africa and set up a 'Native State'. These people charge that the African National Congress is highly subversive and fosters a communistic-tainted African Nationalism or a rabid tyrannical and narrow African Nationalism and intends, in either case, to deprive the White minority in South Africa of their share in the Government of the country.

This is not – and never has been – the policy of my Congress. On the contrary, Congress believes in a common society and holds that citizens of a country, regardless of their race or colour, have the right to full participation in the government and in the control of their future. Anyone who has taken the slightest trouble to study the policy of my Congress and followed its activities should know how baseless and unfounded these fears about Congress are.

Why do we believe in a common society?

Firstly, we believe in a common society because we honestly hold that anything to the contrary unduly works against normal human behaviour, for the gregarious nature of man enables him to flourish to his best in association with others who cherish lofty ideals. 'Not for good or for worse', but for 'good and better things' the African has accepted the higher moral and spiritual values inherent in the fundamental concepts of what, for lack of better terminology, is called 'Western Civilisation'. Apartheid, so far, has revealed itself as an attempt by White South Africa to shunt the African off the tried civilised road by getting him to glorify unduly his tribal past.

Secondly, we believe that the close spiritual and normal contact facilitated by a common society structure in one nation makes it easier to develop friendship and mutual respect and understanding among various groups in a nation; this is especially valuable in a multi-racial nation like ours and these qualities – friendship, mutual respect and understanding, and a common loyalty – are a sine qua non to the building of a truly united nation from a heterogeneous society. In our view, it will not be easy to develop a common loyalty to South Africa when its people by law are kept strictly apart spiritually and socially. Such a state of affairs is likely to give rise to unjustified fears and suspicions which often lead to deadly hatreds among the people and, more often than not, end in industrious antagonism within the nation.

Lastly, we hold the view that the concept of a common society conforms more than does apartheid to the early traditional closer Black–White contact. This undoubtedly, accounts for the relatively rapid way in which Africans, from the days of these early contacts, to their advantage and that of South Africa as a whole, took to and absorbed fairly rapidly Christian teachings and the education that accompanied it.

Strongly holding as we do the views I have just stated, you will appreciate, Sir, with that heartfelt concern, alarm and disappointment we learnt recently from Press reports that the Government intends banning the African National Congress and arresting 2 000 more of its members. I humbly submit that such an action would serve to increase the dangerous gulf that exists between the Government and the African people and, in particular, those African leaders who have knowledge of social and economic forces at work in the modern South Africa of today and the world in general. No loyal South African, White or non-white, should view with equanimity such a situation. It is this loyalty and deep concern for the welfare of the Union that makes me say most emphatically that your Government has no justification whatsoever in banning the African National Congress and making further arrests of its members. I would support my plea by emphasis with all the strength at my command that such actions would be against the true interests of South Africa.

I make no undue claim when I say that my Congress represents the true and fundamental aspirations and views of practically all the African people in the Union, and these aspirations and views are not alien to the best interests of our common country. Rather, it will be found that they conform to the United Nations Charter and the international Declaration of Human Rights.

If it should appear that my Congress pleads strongly and uncompromisingly for the advancement of the African people only, it would not be because it is actuated by a partisan spirit, but rather because the African people are at the lowest rung of the ladder. I am sure that with the same zeal, vigour and devotion it would espouse – and in fact does espouse – the upliftment of other under-privileged peoples regardless of their colour or race.

My people crave for an opportunity to work for a great United South Africa in which they can develop their personalities and capabilities to the fullest with the rest of the country's population in the interest of the country as a whole. No country can prosper when antagonisms divide its people and when, as we Africans see it, Government policy is directly opposed to the legitimate wishes and interests of a great majority of the population.

I might here point out that the African National Congress has always sought to achieve its objectives by using non-violent methods. In its most militant activities it has never used nor attempted to use physical force. It has used non-violent means and ways recognised as legitimate in the civilised world, especially in the case of a people, such as we are, who find themselves denied all effective constitutional means of voicing themselves in the sovereign forum of the country.

I would, for emphasis, reiterate that it is our ardent desire in Congress to see human conduct and relations motivated by an overriding passion for peace and friendship in South Africa and in the world in general and so we would as strongly be opposed to Black domination, or any other kind of domination from whatever source, as we are uncompromisingly opposed to White domination. We regard domination, exploitation and racialism as arch enemies of mankind.

What should be the Government's reply to the views and aspirations of my organisation which I have tried faithfully to present?

In my opinion, the only real answer the Government could give to the stand of my Congress and its inevitable agitation, is for it to make an earnest effort to meet the progressive aspirations of the African people and not to attempt to silence Congress and its leadership by bannings and arrests, for it is the African National Congress and its leadership that is the authentic and responsible voice of the people.

Rather than outlaw the African National Congress or persecute its members and supporters, the Government, in a statesmanlike manner, should reconsider its 'Native policy' with a view to bringing it in conformity with democratic and moral values inherent in any way of life meriting to be described as civilised.

It is the considered view of my Congress that the lack of effective contact and responsible consultation between the Government and the non-European people is at the root of the growing deterioration in race relations and in the relation between the African people and the Government.

Unless healthy contact and purposeful consultation take place at the highest level between the Government and the accredited leaders of the people, misunderstanding and strained relations must grow.

Persistently to ignore the legitimate wishes and interests of the African people and permanently to close the door to consultation with representative organisations enjoying the loyalty of the people, is not the path of statesmanship and can lead only to even more dangerous tensions and chaos in the country.

The Government should earnestly address itself to seeking means and ways of establishing some permanent democratic machinery to enable all citizens to participate intelligently and effectively in the government of the country as is done in all truly democratic states. The existing forms of consultation, such as do exist, are, in my opinion, not only inadequate, but undemocratic: the quarterly meetings of African chiefs, the Bantu Authorities (where these exist) and the Advisory Boards in urban areas; even the so-called Native Representatives in the Senate and in the House of Assembly can be no substitute for truly democratic representation and consultation.

My Congress is convinced that it is today urgently necessary for the Government to devise *new ways* to meet the challenging problems before South Africa. It is eminently in the interest of the country as a whole that this present impasse be broken and the danger to future tensions recognised and averted before it is too late.

It should not be beyond the capacity of statesmen in South Africa – and I would not like to believe that South Africa is bankrupt of statesmanship – to take faith in steps which could inaugurate a new era in interracial co-operation and harmony in our country.

As I have stressed directly and indirectly throughout this letter, no time should be lost in making contact with the leadership of organisations and bodies, among them the African National Congress, representative of organised African opinion, with a view not only to discuss the problems and issues such as I have drawn attention to in this letter, but to consider the advisability and possibility of calling a multiracial convention to seek a solution to our pressing national problems.

In the name of the African National Congress, I am happy to make this approach to you in the hope that our country's future and happiness will triumph over established conventions, procedures and party considerations.

I need hardly to mention that in the event of your Government not acceding to this request, my organisation must continue to fight for the rights of my people.

I am,
Honourable Sir,
Yours respectfully,
A. J. Luthuli
PRESIDENT-GENERAL
AFRICAN NATIONAL CONGRESS

Document 9

First letter from Nelson Mandela to Hendrik Verwoerd
20 April 1961

I AM DIRECTED by the All-In African National Action Council to address your Government in the following terms:

The All-In African National Action Council was established in terms of a resolution adopted at a conference held at Pietermaritzburg on 25 and 26 March 1961. This conference was attended by 1 500 delegates from town and country, representing 145 religious, social, cultural, sporting, and political bodies.

Conference noted that your Government, after receiving a mandate from a section of the European population, decided to proclaim a Republic on 31 May.

It was the firm view of delegates that your Government, which represents only a minority of the population in this country, is not entitled to take such a decision without first seeking the views and obtaining the express consent of the African people. Conference feared that under this proposed Republic your Government, which is already notorious the world over for its obnoxious policies, would continue to make even more savage attacks on the rights and living conditions of the African people.

Conference carefully considered the grave political situation facing the African people today. Delegate after delegate drew attention to the vicious manner in which your Government forced the people of Zeerust, Sekhukhuniland, Pondoland, Nongoma, Tembuland and other areas to accept the unpopular system of Bantu Authorities, and pointed to numerous facts and incidents which indicate the rapid manner in which race relations are deteriorating in this country.

It was the earnest opinion of Conference that this dangerous situation could be averted only by the calling of a sovereign national convention representative of all South Africans, to draw up a new non-racial and democratic Constitution. Such a convention would discuss our national problems in a sane and sober manner, and would work out solutions which sought to preserve and safeguard the interests of all sections of the population.

Conference unanimously decided to call upon your Government to summon such a convention before 31 May.

Conference further decided that unless your Government calls the convention before the above-mentioned date, country-wide demonstrations would be held on the eve of the Republic in protest. Conference also resolved that in addition to the demonstrations, the African people would be called upon to refuse to co-operate with the proposed Republic.

We attach the Resolutions of the Conference for your attention and necessary action.

We now demand that your Government call the convention before 31 May, failing which we propose to adopt the steps indicated in paragraphs 8 and 9 of this letter.

These demonstrations will be conducted in a disciplined and peaceful manner. We are fully aware of the implications of this decision, and the action we propose taking. We have no illusions about the counter-measures your Government might take in this matter. After all, South Africa and the world know that during the last thirteen years your Government has subjected us to merciless and arbitrary rule. Hundreds of our people have been banned and confined to certain areas. Scores have been banished to remote parts of the country, and many arrested and jailed for a multitude of offences. It has become extremely difficult to hold meetings, and freedom of speech has been drastically curtailed. During the last twelve months we have gone through a period of grim dictatorship, during which seventy-five people were killed and hundreds injured while peacefully demonstrating against passes.

Political organisations were declared unlawful, and thousands flung into jail without trial. Your Government can only take these measures to suppress the forthcoming demonstrations, and these measures have failed to stop opposition to the policies of your Government, and we will carry out our duty without flinching.

Resolutions of the All-In African Conference held in Pietermaritzburg – 25–26 March 1961

A grave situation confronts the people of South Africa. The Nationalist Government after holding a fraudulent referendum among only one-fifth of the population, has decided to proclaim a white Republic on May 31st, and the all white Parliament is presently discussing a Constitution. It is clear that to the great disadvantage of the majority of our people such a Republic will continue even more intensively the policies of racial oppression, political persecution and exploitation and the terrorisation of the non-white people which have already earned South Africa the righteous condemnation of the entire world.

In this situation it is imperative that all the African people of this country, irrespective of their political, religious or other affiliations, should unite to speak and act with a single voice.

For this purpose, we have gathered here at this solemn All-In Conference, and on behalf of the entire African nation and with a due sense of the historic responsibility which rests on us. . .

1. WE DECLARE that no Constitution or form of Government decided without the participation of the African people who form an absolute majority of the population can enjoy moral validity or merit support either within South Africa or beyond its borders.

2. WE DEMAND that a National Convention of elected representatives of all adult men and women on an equal basis irrespective of race, colour, creed or other limitation, be called by the Union Government not later than May 31st, 1961; that the Convention shall have sovereign powers to determine, in any way the majority of the representatives decide, a new non-racial democratic Constitution for South Africa.

3. WE RESOLVE that should the minority Government ignore this

demand of the representatives of the united will of the African people –

(a) We undertake to stage country-wide demonstrations on the eve of the proclamation of the Republic in protest against this undemocratic act.

(b) We call on all Africans not to cooperate or collaborate in any way with the proposed South African Republic or any other form of Government which rests on force to perpetuate the tyranny of a minority, and to organise and unite in town and country to carry out constant actions to oppose oppression and win freedom.

(c) We call on the Indian and Coloured communities and all democratic Europeans to join forces with us in opposition to a regime which is bringing disaster to South Africa and to win a society in which all can enjoy freedom and security.

(d) We call on democratic people the world over to refrain from any cooperation or dealings with the South African government, to impose economic and other sanctions against this country and to isolate in every possible way the minority Government whose continued disregard of all human rights and freedoms constitutes a threat to world peace.

4. WE FURTHER DECIDE that in order to implement the above decisions, Conference –

(a) Elects a National Action Council;

(b) Instructs all delegates to return to their respective areas and form local Action Committees.

Document 10

**Letter from Nelson Mandela to Sir de Villiers Graaff,
leader of the United Party
23 May 1961**

Sir de Villiers Graaff,
Leader of the Opposition,
House of Assembly,
CAPE TOWN

Sir,

In one week's time, the Verwoerd Government intends to inaugurate its Republic. It is unnecessary to state that this intention has never been endorsed by the non-white majority of this country. The decision has been taken by little over half of the White community; it is opposed by every articulate group amongst the African, Coloured and Indian communities, who constitute the majority of this country.

The Government's intentions to proceed, under these circumstances, has created conditions bordering on crisis. We have been excluded from the Commonwealth, and condemned 95 to 1 at the United Nations. Our trade is being boycotted, and foreign capital is being withdrawn. The country is becoming an armed camp, the Government preparing for civil war with increasingly heavy police and military apparatus, the non-white population for a general strike and long-term non-co-operation with the Government.

None of us can draw any satisfaction from this developing crisis. We, on our part, in the name of the African people – a majority of South Africans – and on the authority given us by 1 400 elected African representatives at the Pietermaritzburg Conference of 25 and 26 March, have put forward serious proposals for a way out of the crisis. We have called on the Government to convene an elected National Convention of representatives of all races without delay, and to charge that Convention with the task of drawing up a new Constitution for this country which would be acceptable to all racial groups.

We can see no workable alternative to this proposal, except that the Nationalist Government proceeds to enforce a minority decision on all of us, with the certain consequence of still deeper crisis, and a continuing period of strife and disaster ahead. Stated bluntly, the alternatives appear to be these: talk it out, or shoot it out. Outside of the Nationalist Party, most of the important and influential bodies of public opinion have clearly decided to talk it out. The South African Indian Congress, the only substantial Indian community organisation, has welcomed and endorsed the call for a National Convention. So, too have the Coloured people, through the Coloured Convention movement which has the backing of the main bodies of Coloured opinion. A substantial European body of opinion, represented by both the Progressive and the Liberal Parties, has endorsed our call. Support for a National Convention has come also from the bulk of the English language press, from several national church organisations, and from many others.

But where, Sir, does the United Party stand? We have yet to hear from this most important organisation – the main organisation in fact of anti-Nationalist opinion amongst the European community. Or from you, its leader. If the country's leading statesmen fail to lead at this moment, then the worst is inevitable. It is time for you, Sir, and your Party, to speak out. Are you for a democratic and peaceable solution to our problems? Are you, therefore, *for* a National Convention? We in South Africa, and the world outside expect an answer. Silence at this time enables Dr. Verwoerd to lead us onwards towards the brink of disaster.

We realise that aspects of our proposal raise complicated problems. What shall be the basis of representation at the Convention? How shall the representatives be elected? But these are not the issues now at stake. The issue *now* is a simple one. Are all groups to be consulted before a constitutional change is made? Or only the White minority? A decision on this matter cannot be delayed. Once that decision is taken, then all other matters, of how, when and where, can be discussed, and agreement on them can be reached. On our part the door to such discussion has always been open. We have approached you and your Party before, and suggested that matters of difference be discussed. To date we have had no reply. Nevertheless we still hold the door open. But the need *now* is not for debate about differences of detail, but for clarity of principle and purpose. For a National Convention of all races? Or against?

It is still not too late to turn the tide against the Nationalist-created crisis. A call for a National Convention from you now could well be the turning-point in our country's history. It would unite the overwhelming majority of our people, White, Coloured, Indian and African, for a single purpose – round-table talks for a new constitution. It would isolate the Nationalist Government, and reveal for all time that it is a minority Government, clinging tenaciously to power against the popular will, driving recklessly onward to a disaster for itself and us. Your call for a National Convention now would add such strength to the already powerful call for it that the Government would be chary of ignoring it further.

And if they nevertheless ignore the call for a Convention, the inter-racial unity thus cemented by your call would lay the basis for the replacement of this Government of national disaster by one more acceptable to the people, one prepared to follow the democratic path of consulting all the people in order to resolve the crisis.

We urge you strongly to speak out now. It is ten days to 31 May.

Yours faithfully
[Signed] Nelson Mandela
NELSON MANDELA
All-In African National Action Council

Document II

I REFER YOU TO MY LETTER of 20 April 1961, to which you do not have the courtesy to reply or acknowledge receipt. In the letter referred to above I informed you of the resolutions passed by the All-In African National Conference in Pietermaritzburg on 26 March 1961, demanding the calling by your Government before 31 May 1961 of a multi-racial and sovereign National Convention to draw up a new non-racial and democratic Constitution for South Africa.

The Conference Resolution which was attached to my letter indicated that if your Government did not call this Convention by the specific date, country-wide demonstrations would be staged to mark our protest against the White Republic forcibly imposed on us by a minority. The Resolution further indicated that in addition to the demonstrations, the African people would be called upon not to co-operate with the Republican Government, or with any Government based on force.

As your Government did not respond to our demands, the All-In African National Council, which was entrusted by the Conference with the task of implementing its resolutions, called for a General Strike on the 29th, 30th and 31st of last month. As predicted in my letter of 20 April 1961, your Government sought to suppress the strike by force. You rushed a special law in Parliament authorising the detention without trial of people connected with the organisation of the strike. The army was mobilised and European civilians armed. More than ten thousand innocent Africans were arrested under the pass laws and meetings banned throughout the country.

Long before the factory gates were opened on Monday, 29 May 1961, senior police officers and Nationalist South Africans spread a deliberate falsehood and announced that the strike had failed. All these measures failed to break the strike and our people stood up magnificently and gave us solid and substantial support. Factory and office workers, businessmen in town and country, students in university colleges, in the primary and secondary schools, rose to the occasion and recorded in clear terms their opposition to the Republic.

The Government is guilty of self-deception if they say that non-Europeans did not respond to the call. Considerations of honesty demand of your Government to realise that the African people who constitute four-fifths of the country's population are against your Republic. As indicated above, the Pietermaritzburg resolution provided that in addition to the country-wide demonstrations, the African people would refuse to co-operate with the Republic or any form of government based on force.

Failure by your Government to call the Convention makes it imperative for us to launch a full-scale and country-wide campaign for non-co-operation with your Government. There are two alternatives before you. Either you accede to our demands and call a National Convention of all South Africans to draw up a democratic Constitution, which will end the frightful policies of racial oppression pursued by your Government. By pursuing this course and abandoning the repressive and dangerous policies of your Government, you may still save our country from economic dislocation and ruin and from civil strife and bitterness.

Alternatively, you may choose to persist with the present policies which are cruel and dishonest and which are opposed by millions of people here and abroad. For our own part, we wish to make it perfectly clear that we shall never cease to fight against repression and injustice, and we are resuming active opposition against your regime. In taking this decision we must again stress that we have no illusions of the serious implications of our decision.

We know that your Government will once again unleash all its fury and barbarity to persecute the African people. But as the result of the last strike has proved, no power on earth can stop an oppressed people, determined to win their freedom. History punishes those who resort to force and fraud to suppress the claims and legitimate aspirations of the majority of the country's citizens.

Document 12

THE DEEPENING POLITICAL CRISIS in our country has been a matter of grave concern to me for quite some time and I now consider it necessary in the national interest for the African National Congress and the government to meet urgently to negotiate an effective political settlement.

At the outset I must point out that I make this move without consultation with the ANC. I am a loyal and disciplined member of the ANC, my political loyalty is owed primarily, if not exclusively to this organisation and particularly to our Lusaka Headquarters where the official leadership is stationed and from where affairs are directed. In the normal course of events, I would put my views to the organisation first, and if these views were accepted, the organisation would then decide on who were the best qualified members to handle the matter on its behalf and on exactly when to make the move. But in my current circumstances I cannot follow this course, and this is the only reason why I am acting on my own initiative, in the hope that the organisation will, in due course, endorse my action.

I must stress that no prisoner, irrespective of his status or influence, can conduct negotiations of this nature from prison. In our special situation, negotiation on political matters is literally a matter of life and death which requires to be handled by the organisation itself through its appointed representatives.

The step I am taking should, therefore, not be seen as the beginning of actual negotiations between the government and the ANC. My task is a very limited one, and that is to bring the country's two major political bodies to the negotiating table. I must further point out that the question of my release from prison is not an issue, at least at this stage of discussions, and I am certainly not asking to be freed. But I do hope that the government will, as soon as possible, give me the opportunity from my present quarters to sound the views of my colleagues inside and outside the country on this move.

Only if this initiative is formally endorsed by the ANC will it have any significance.

I will touch presently on some of the problems which seem to constitute an obstacle to a meeting between the ANC and the government. But I must emphasise right at this stage that this step is not a response to the call by the government on ANC leaders to declare whether or not they are nationalists and to renounce the South African Communist Party before there can be negotiations: no self-respecting freedom fighter will take orders from the government on how to wage the freedom struggle against that same government and on who his allies in the freedom struggle should be. To obey such instructions would be a violation of the long-standing and fruitful solidarity which distinguishes our liberation movement, and a betrayal of those who have worked so closely and suffered so much with us for almost 70 years.

Far from responding to that call, my intervention is influenced by purely domestic issues, by the civil strife and ruin into which the country is now sliding. I am disturbed, as many other South Africans no doubt are, by the spectre of a South Africa split into two hostile camps – blacks on one side (the term 'blacks' is used in a broad sense to indicate all those who are not whites) and whites on the other, slaughtering one another; by acute tensions which are building up dangerously in practically every sphere of our lives, a situation which, in turn, fore-shadows more violent clashes in the days ahead. This is the crisis that has forced me to act.

I must add that the purpose of this discussion is not only to urge the government to talk to the ANC, but it is also to acquaint you with the views current among blacks, especially those in the Mass Democratic Movement. If I am unable to express those views frankly and freely, you will never know how the majority of South Africans think on the policy and actions of the government; you will never know how to deal with their grievances and demands.

It is perhaps proper to remind you that the media here and abroad has given certain public figures in this country a rather negative image not only in regard to human rights questions, but also in respect of their prescriptive stance when dealing with black leaders generally. The impression is shared not only by the vast majority of blacks but also by a substantial section of the whites. If I had allowed myself to be influenced by this impression, I would not even have thought of making this move.

Nevertheless, I come here with an open mind and the impression I will carry away from this meeting will be determined almost exclusively by the manner in which you respond to my proposal. It is in this spirit that I have undertaken this mission, and I sincerely hope that nothing will be done or said here which will force me to revise my views on this aspect.

I have already indicated that I propose to deal with some of the obstacles to a meeting between the government and the ANC. The government gives several reasons why it will not negotiate with us. However, for purposes of this discussion, I will confine myself to only three main demands set by the government as a precondition for negotiation, namely that the ANC must first renounce violence, break with the SACP and abandon its demand for majority rule.

The position of the ANC on the question of violence is very simple. The organisation has no vested interest in violence. It abhors any action which may cause loss of life, destruction of property and misery to the people. It has worked long and patiently for a South Africa of common values and for an undivided and peaceful non-racial state. But we consider the armed struggle a legitimate form of self-defence against a morally repugnant system of government which will not allow even peaceful form of protest.

It is more than ironical that it should be the government which demands that we should renounce violence. The government knows only too well that there is not a single political organisation in this country, inside and outside parliament, which can ever compare with the ANC in its total commitment to peaceful change. Right from the early days of its history, the organisation diligently sought peaceful solutions and, to that extent, it talked patiently to successive South African governments, a policy we tried to follow in dealing with the present government. Not only did the government ignore our demands for a meeting, instead it took advantage of our commitment to a non-violent struggle and unleashed the most violent form of racial oppression this country has ever seen. It stripped us of all basic human rights, outlawed our organisations and barred all channels of peaceful resistance. It met our just demands with force and, despite the grave problems facing the country, it continues to refuse to talk to us. There can only be one answer to this challenge: violent forms of struggle.

Down the years oppressed people have fought for their birth right by peaceful means, where that was possible, and through force where peaceful channels were closed. The history of this country also confirms this vital lesson. Africans as well as Afrikaners were, at one time or other, compelled to take up arms in defence of their freedom against British imperialism. The fact that both were finally defeated by superior arms, and by the vast resources of that empire, does not negate this lesson. But from what has happened in South Africa during the last 40 years, we must conclude that now that the roles are reversed, and the Afrikaner is no longer a freedom fighter, but is in power, the entire lesson of history must be brushed aside. Not even a disciplined non-violent protest will now be tolerated. To the government a black man has neither a just cause to espouse nor freedom rights to defend. The whites must have the monopoly of political power, and of committing violence against innocent and defenceless people.

That situation was totally unacceptable to us and the formation of Umkhonto we Sizwe was introduced to end that monopoly, and to forcibly bring home to the government that the oppressed people of this country were prepared to stand up and defend themselves.

It is significant to note that throughout the past four decades, and more especially over the last 26 years, the government has met our demands with force only, and has done hardly anything to create a suitable climate for dialogue. On the contrary, the government continues to govern with a heavy hand, and to incite whites against negotiation with the ANC. The publication of the booklet 'Talking with the ANC . . .' which completely distorts the history and policy of the ANC, the extremely offensive language used by government spokesmen against freedom fighters, and the intimidation of whites who want to hear the views of the ANC at first hand, are all part of the government's strategy to wreck meaningful dialogue.

It is perfectly clear on the facts that the refusal of the ANC to renounce violence is not the real problem facing the government. The truth is that the government is not yet ready for negotiation and for the sharing of political power with blacks. It is still committed to white domination and, for that reason, it will only tolerate those blacks who are willing to serve on its apartheid structures. Its policy is to remove from the political scene blacks who refuse to conform, who reject white supremacy and its apartheid structures, and who will insist on equal rights with whites. This is the reason for the government's refusal to talk to us, and for its demand that we disarm ourselves, while it continues to use violence against our people. This is the reason for its massive propaganda campaign to discredit the ANC, and present it to the public as a communist-dominated organisation bent on murder and destruction. In this situation the reaction of the oppressed people is clearly predictable.

White South Africa must accept the plain fact that the ANC will not suspend, to say nothing of abandoning, the armed struggle until the government shows its willingness to surrender the monopoly of political power, and to negotiate directly and in good faith with the acknowledged black leaders. The renunciation of violence by either the government or the ANC should not be a pre-condition to but the result of negotiation. Moreover, by ignoring credible black leaders, and imposing a succession of still-born negotiation structures, the government is not only squandering the country's precious resources, but it is in fact discrediting the negotiations process itself, and prolonging the civil strife. The position of the ANC on the question of violence is, therefore, very clear. A government which used violence against blacks many years before we took up arms, has no right whatsoever to call on us to lay down arms.

I have already pointed out that no self-respecting freedom fighter will allow the government to prescribe who his allies in the freedom struggle should be, and that to obey such instructions would be a betrayal of those who have suffered repression with us for so long. We equally reject the charge that the ANC is dominated by the SACP and we regard the accusation as part of the smearing campaign the government is waging against us. The accusation has, in effect, also been refuted by two totally independent sources. In January 1987 the American State Department published a report on the activities of the SACP in this country which contrasts very sharply with the subjective picture the government has tried to paint against us over the years. The essence of that report is that, although the influence of the SACP on the ANC is strong, it is unlikely that the Party will ever dominate the ANC. The same point is made somewhat differently by Mr Ismail Omar, member of the President's Council, in his book *Reform in Crisis* published in 1988, in which he gives concrete examples of important issues of the day over which the ANC enjoys greater popular support than the SACP. He adds that, despite the many years of combined struggle, the two remain distinct organisations with ideological and policy differences which preclude a merger of identity. These observations go some way towards disproving the accusation. But since the allegation has become the focal point of government propaganda against the ANC, I propose to use this opportunity to give you that correct information, in the hope that this will help you to see the matter in its proper perspective, and to evaluate your strategy afresh.

Co-operation between the ANC and SACP goes back to the early twenties and has always been, and still is, strictly limited to the struggle against racial oppression and for a just society. At no time has the organisation ever adopted or co-operated with communism itself. Apart from the question of co-operation between the two organisations, members of the SACP have always been free to join the ANC. But once they do so, they become fully bound by the policy of the organisation set out in the Freedom Charter. As members of the ANC engaged in the anti-apartheid struggle, their Marxist ideology is not directly relevant. The SACP has throughout the years accepted the leading role of the ANC, a position which is respected by the SACP members who join the ANC.

There is, of course, a firmly established tradition in the ANC in terms of which any attempt is resisted, from whatever quarter, which is intended to undermine co-operation between the two organisations. Even within the ranks of the ANC there have been, at one time or other, people – and some of them were highly respected and influential individuals – who were against this co-operation and who wanted SACP members expelled from the organisation. Those who persisted in these activities were themselves ultimately expelled, or they broke away in despair. In either case their departure ended their political careers, or they formed other political organisations which, in due course, crumbled into splinter groups. No dedicated ANC member will ever heed the call to break with the SACP. We regard such a demand as a purely divisive government strategy. It is in fact a call on us to commit suicide. Which man of honour will ever desert a life-long friend at the instance of a common opponent and still retain a measure of credibility among his people? Which opponent will ever trust such a treacherous freedom fighter? Yet this is what the government is, in effect, asking us to do: to desert our faithful allies. We will not fall into that trap.

The government also accused us of being agents of the Soviet Union. The truth is that the ANC is non-aligned, and we welcome support from the East and the West, from the socialist and capitalist countries. The only difference, as we have explained on countless occasions before, is that the socialist countries supply us with weapons, which the West refuses to give us. We have no intention whatsoever of changing our stand on this question.

The government's exaggerated hostility to the SACP, and its refusal to have any dealings with that party have a hollow ring. Such an attitude is not only out of step with the growing co-operation between the capitalist and socialist countries in different parts of the world, but it is also inconsistent with the policy of the government itself, when dealing with our neighbouring states. Not only has South Africa concluded treaties with the Marxist states of Angola and Mozambique – quite rightly in our opinion – but she also wants to strengthen ties with

Marxist Zimbabwe. The government will certainly find it difficult, if not altogether impossible, to reconcile its readiness to work with foreign Marxists for the peaceful resolution of mutual problems, with its uncompromising refusal to talk to South African Marxists.

The reason for this inconsistency is obvious. As I have already said, the government is still too deeply committed to the principle of white domination and, despite lip-service to reform, it is deadly opposed to the sharing of political power with blacks, and the SACP is merely being used as a smoke screen to retain the monopoly of political power. The smearing campaign against the ANC also helps the government to evade the real issue at stake, namely, the exclusion from political power of the black majority by a white minority, which is the source of all our troubles.

Concerning my own personal position, I have already informed you that I will not respond to the government's demand that ANC members should state whether they are members of the SACP or not. But because much has been said by the media, as well as by government leaders regarding my political beliefs, I propose to use this opportunity to put the record straight. My political beliefs have been explained in the course of several political trials in which I was charged, in the policy documents of the ANC, and in my autobiography *The Struggle is My Life* which I wrote in prison in 1975. I stated in these trials and publications that I did not belong to any organisation apart from the ANC. In my address to the court which sentenced me to life imprisonment in June 1964, I said:

Today I am attracted by the idea of a classless society, an attraction which springs in part from Marxist reading, and, in part, from my admiration of the structure and organisation of early African societies in this country. . . . It is true, as I have already stated, that I have been influenced by Marxist thought. But this is also true of many of the leaders of the new independent states. Such widely different persons as Gandhi, Nehru, Nkrumah and Nasser all acknowledge this fact. We all accept the need for some form of socialism to enable our people to catch up with the advanced countries of the world, and to overcome their legacy of extreme poverty.

My views are still the same. Equally important is the fact that many ANC leaders who are labelled communists by the government, embrace nothing different from these beliefs.

The term 'communist' when used by the government has a totally different meaning from the conventional one. Practically every freedom fighter who receives his military training or education in the socialist countries is to the government a communist. It would appear to be established government policy that, as long as the National Party is in power in this country, there can be no black freedom struggle, and no black freedom fighter. Any black political organisation which, like us, fights for the liberation of its people through armed struggle, must invariably be dominated by the SACP.

This attitude is not only the result of government propaganda, it is a logical consequence of white supremacy. After more than 300 years of racial indoctrination, the country's whites have developed such deep-seated contempt for blacks as to believe that we cannot think for ourselves, that we are incapable of fighting for political rights without incitement by some white agitation. In accusing the ANC of domination by the SACP, and in calling on ANC members to renounce the party, the government is deliberately exploiting that contempt.

The government is equally vehement in condemning the principle of majority rule. The principle is rejected despite the fact that it is a pillar of democratic rule in many countries of the world. It is a principle which is fully accepted in the white politics of this country. Only now that the stark reality has dawned that apartheid has failed, and that blacks will one day have an effective voice in government, are we told by whites here, and their Western friends, that majority rule is a disaster to be avoided at all costs. Majority rule is acceptable to whites as long as it is considered within the context of white politics. If black political aspirations are to be accommodated, then some other formula must be found, provided that that formula does not raise blacks to a position of equality with whites.

Yet majority rule and internal peace are like the two sides of a single coin, and white South Africa simply has to accept that there will never be peace and stability in this country until the principle is fully applied. It is precisely because of its denial that the government has become the enemy of practically every black man. It is that denial that has sparked off the current civil strife.

By insisting on compliance with the above mentioned conditions before there can be talks, the government clearly confirms that it wants no peace in this country but turmoil, no strong and independent ANC, but a weak and servile organisation playing a supportive role to white minority rule, not a non-aligned ANC, but one which is a satellite of the West, and which is ready to serve the interests of capitalism.

No worthy leaders of a freedom movement will ever submit to conditions which are essentially terms of surrender dictated by a victorious commander to a beaten enemy, and which are really intended to weaken the organisation to humiliate its leadership.

The key to the whole situation is a negotiated settlement, and a meeting between the government and the ANC will be the first major step towards lasting peace in the country, better relations with our neighbour states, admission to the Organisation of African Unity, re-admission to the United Nations and other world bodies, to international markets and improved international relations generally. An accord with the ANC, and the introduction of a non-racial society is the only way in which our rich and beautiful country will be saved from the stigma which repels the world.

Two political issues will have to be addressed at such a meeting; firstly, the demand for majority rule in a unitary state, secondly, the concern of white South Africa over this demand, as well as the insistence of whites on structural guarantees that majority rule will not mean domination of the white minority by blacks. The most crucial task which will face the government and the ANC will be to reconcile these two positions. Such reconciliation will be achieved only if both parties are willing to compromise. The organisation will determine precisely how negotiations should be conducted.

It may well be that this should be done at least in two stages. The first, where the organisation and the government will work out together the pre-conditions for a proper climate for negotiations. Up to now both parties have simply been broadcasting their conditions for negotiations without putting them directly to each other. The second stage would be the actual negotiations themselves when the climate is ripe for doing so. Any other approach would entail the danger of an irresolvable stalemate.

Lastly, I must point out that the move I have taken provides you with the opportunity to overcome the current deadlock, and to normalise the country's political situation. I hope you will seize it without delay. I believe that the overwhelming majority of South Africans, black and white, hope to see the ANC and the government working closely together to lay the foundations for a new era in our country, in which racial discrimination and prejudice, coercion and confrontation, death and destruction will be forgotten.

Document 13

**Declaration of the Organization of African Unity (OAU) ad hoc committee on southern Africa on the question of South Africa; Harare, Zimbabwe (The Harare Declaration)
Sections 14–24
21 August 1989**

Statement of principles

14. We believe that a conjuncture of circumstances exists which, if there is a demonstrable readiness on the part of the Pretoria regime to engage in negotiations genuinely and seriously, could create the possibility to end apartheid through negotiations. Such an eventuality would be an expression of the long standing preference of the majority of the people of South Africa to arrive at a political settlement.

15. We would therefore encourage the people of South Africa as part of their overall struggle to get together to negotiate an end to the apartheid system and agree on all the measures that are necessary to transform their country into a non racial democracy. We support the position held by the majority of the people of South Africa that these objectives and not the amendment or reform of the apartheid system should be the aims of the negotiations.

16. We are at one with them that the outcome of such a process should be a new constitutional order based on the following principles among others:

16.1 South Africa shall become a united, democratic and non-racial state.

16.2 All its people shall enjoy common and equal citizenship and nationality regardless of race, colour, sex, or creed.

16.3 All its people have the right to participate in the government and administration of the country on the basis of a universal suffrage, exercised through one person one vote, under a common voters' roll.

16.4   All shall have the right to form and join any political party of their choice provided that this is not in furtherance of racism.

16.5   All shall enjoy universally recognised human rights, freedoms and civil liberties, protected under an entrenched Bill of Rights.

16.6   South Africa shall have a new legal system which shall guarantee equality of all before the law.

16.7   South Africa shall have an independent and non-racial judiciary.

16.8   There shall be created an economic order which shall promote and advance the well being of all South Africa.

16.9   A democratic South Africa shall respect the rights, sovereignty and territorial integrity of all countries and pursue a policy of peace, friendship and mutually beneficial co-operation with all people.

17.   We believe that agreement on the above principles shall constitute the foundation for an internationally acceptable solution which shall enable South Africa to take its rightful place as an equal partner among the African and world community of nations.

Climate for negotiations

18.   Together with the rest of the world we believe that it is essential, before any negotiations can take place, that the necessary climate for negotiations be created. The apartheid regime has the urgent responsibility to respond positively to this universally acclaimed demand and thus create this climate.

19.   Accordingly the present regime should at the very least:

19.1   Release all political prisoners and detainees unconditionally and refrain from imposing any restrictions on them.

19.2   Lift all bans and restrictions on all proscribed and restricted organisations and persons.

19.3   Remove all troops from the townships.

19.4 End the State of Emergency and repeal all legislation, such as and including the Internal Security Act, designed to circumscribe political activity; and

19.5 Cease all political trials and political executions.

20. These measures are necessary to produce the conditions in which free political discussion can take place – an essential condition to ensure that the people themselves participate in the process of remaking their country. The measures listed above should therefore precede negotiations.

Guidelines to the process of negotiation

21. We support the view of the South African liberation movement that upon the creation of this climate, the process of negotiation should commence along the following lines:

21.1 Discussions should take place between the liberation movement and the South African regime to achieve the suspension of hostilities on both sides by agreeing to a mutually binding cease-fire.

21.2 Negotiations should then proceed to establish the basis for the adoption of a new Constitution by agreeing on among others the Principles enunciated above.

21.3 Having agreed on these principles, the parties should then negotiate the necessary mechanism for drawing up the new Constitution.

21.4 The parties shall define and agree on the role to be played by the international community in ensuring a successful transition to democratic order.

21.5 The parties shall agree on the formation of an interim government to supervise the process of the drawing up and adoption of a new Constitution; govern and administer the country, as well as effect the transition to a democratic order including the holding of elections.

21.6 After the adoption of the new Constitution, all armed hostilities will be deemed to have formally terminated.

21.7 For its part, the international community would lift the sanctions that have been imposed against apartheid South Africa.

22. The new South Africa shall qualify for membership of the Organisation of African Unity.

Programme of action

23. In pursuance of the objectives stated in this document, the organisation of African Unity hereby commits itself to:

23.1 Inform governments and inter governmental organisations throughout the world, including the Non-Aligned Movement, the Commonwealth and others of these perspectives, and solicit their support.

23.2 Mandate the OAU Ad-Hoc Committee on Southern Africa, acting as the representative of the OAU and assisted by the Front-line States, to remain seized of the issues of a political resolution of the South Africa question.

23.3 Step up all-round support for the South African liberation movement and campaign in the rest of the world in pursuance of this objective.

23.4 Intensify the campaign for mandatory and comprehensive sanctions against apartheid South Africa; in this regard, immediately mobilise against the rescheduling of Pretoria's foreign debt; work for the imposition of a mandatory oil embargo and the full observance by all countries of the arms embargo.

23.5 Ensure that the African continent does not relax existing measures for the total isolation of apartheid South Africa.

23.6 Continue to monitor the situation in Namibia and extend all necessary support to SWAPO in its struggle for a genuinely independent Namibia.

23.7 Extend such assistance as the Governments of Angola and Mozambique may request in order to secure peace for their peoples; and

23.8 Render all possible assistance to the Front-line States to enable

them to withstand Pretoria's campaign of aggression and destabilisation and enable them to continue to give their all round
support to the people of Namibia and South Africa.

24. We appeal to all people of goodwill throughout the world to
support their Programme of Action as a necessary measure to
secure the earliest liquidation of the apartheid system and the
transformation of South Africa into a united, democratic and non-
racial country.

Document 14

**Resolution by the Conference for a Democratic Future on negotiations and the Constituent Assembly
8 December 1989**

WE, THE 4 600 delegates to this historic Conference for a Democratic Future of the broad anti-apartheid liberation forces:
1. Salute the fighting forces of our people who have conducted armed struggle, in view of the situation in which all peaceful avenues have been closed.

Noting that:
1. Organisations of the people remain banned, restricted and prevented from operating freely and hundreds of key individuals remain restricted.
2. Freedom of assembly, movement, association and speech and free political activity do not exist, thus making consultations with our people difficult, if not impossible.
3. Repression in many forms continues, including detention without trial, political imprisonment, political trials, the state of emergency and suppression of the media.
4. The government totally controls radio and television.
5. All major blocks which constitute and sustain the apartheid system remain intact.

Believing:
1. That there can be no solution in the interests of the oppressed and exploited masses whilst apartheid structures and its laws still exist.
2. That the basis and climate for genuine negotiations do not exist and that De Klerk's proposals for negotiations, supported by the

imperialists, are designed to enmesh our organisations and people in schemes to maintain the status quo.

Realising:
1. Our immediate tasks are to strive for: One person one vote in a united democratic country; lifting of the State of Emergency; unconditional release of all political prisoners; unbanning of all banned organisations.
2. The abolition of all laws which inhibit free speech, press, association and assembly; a living wage; the right to work.
3. That the demand for a Constituent Assembly of the oppressed and exploited is in opposition to all attempts of the regime to divide us in the name of 'power sharing', 'group rights' and negotiated settlement.

Thereby Resolves:
1. To adopt the Harare Declaration on how the conflict in SA could be resolved and the solidarity and support of the Organisation of African Unity and the Frontline states in particular.
2. To call for a Constituent Assembly established on a non-racial basis representing all the people of SA to draw up a New Constitution for our country.
3. To call on our people and organisations to mobilise our forces, to organise and intensify the struggle for the creation of a single non-racial democratic SA with a single parliament and a single universal suffrage.
4. To call on the international community to intensify the isolation of the SA regime and to impose comprehensive and mandatory sanctions.
5. That real democracy be given to the freely elected delegates of the people, united in the Constituent Assembly on the basis of one person one vote in a unitary South Africa.
6. Only the constituent assembly has the right and duty to define a new constitution as well as the form and social content of a new and just society.

Document 15

**'A document to create a climate of understanding';
Nelson Mandela to F. W. de Klerk
12 December 1989**

Mr President,
I hope that Ministers Kobie Coetsee and Gerrit Viljoen have informed you that I deeply appreciate your decision in terms of which eight fellow-prisoners were freed on 15 October 1989, and for advising me of the fact in advance. The release was clearly a major development which rightly evoked praise here and abroad.

In my view it has now become urgent to take other measures to end the present deadlock, and this will certainly be achieved if the government first creates a proper climate for negotiation, followed by a meeting with the ANC. The conflict which is presently draining South Africa's life blood, either in the form of peaceful demonstrations, acts of violence or external pressure, will never be settled until there is an agreement with the ANC. To this end I have spent more than three years urging the Government to negotiate with the ANC. I hope I will not leave this place with empty hands.

The Government insists on the ANC making an honest commitment to peace before it will talk to the organisation. This is the pre-condition we are required to meet before the Government will negotiate with us. It must be made clear at the outset that the ANC will never make such a commitment at the instance of the Government, or any other source for that matter. We would have thought that the history of this country's liberation movement, especially during the last 41 years, would have made that point perfectly clear.

The whole approach of the Government to the question of negotiation with the ANC is totally unacceptable, and requires to be drastically changed. No serious political organisation will ever talk peace when an aggressive war is being waged against it. No proud people will ever obey orders from those who have humiliated and dishonoured them for so long.

Besides, the pre-condition that we should commit ourselves to peace is inconsistent with the statement you made in Nigel shortly before the last general election, in which you appealed to black leaders to come forward to negotiate with the government, and to refrain from setting pre-conditions for such negotiations. It was generally assumed that the appeal was addressed to blacks as a whole and not, as now appears, only to those who work in apartheid structures.

In the light of subsequent Government policy statements, the perception has deepened that the Nigel statement was no more than mere rhetoric. Although the government called on blacks to set no pre-conditions, it considers itself free to do exactly that.

That is the reason why it prescribes to us to make a commitment to peace before we can talk.

The Government ought to be aware that readiness to negotiate is in itself an honest commitment to peace. In this regard, the ANC is far ahead of the Government. It has repeatedly declared its willingness to negotiate, provided a proper climate for such negotiations exists. The organisation has recently published a clear and detailed plan to this effect, which has already been approved by the Frontline States, the Organisation of African Unity, the Non-Aligned Movement and by almost all the members of the Commonwealth of Nations.

Equally relevant is the fact that on many occasions in the past, the ANC has explicitly acknowledged its commitment to peaceful solutions, if channels for doing so are available. As recently as 24 October 1989, the *Star* reported as follows:

> The ANC says it is committed to a peaceful solution in South Africa but accuses the Government of rhetoric. ... At present there is really no serious indication from the Government itself about a peaceful solution to the political crisis. ... Five years ago, President P. W. Botha spoke virtually the same words but nothing happened.

It is history now that the ANC has made impassioned overtures to every single Government of South Africa in vain. Every manoeuvre was met with a negative response, and at times violence.

This and similar other previous statements clearly show that the ANC has an established record of commitment to peace, and that its armed struggle is a purely defensive measure against the violence of the Government. This point was stressed by Mr Oliver Tambo, President of the ANC, during an interview with *Cape Times* editor, Anthony Heard on 4 November 1985, when he said: 'The unfortunate thing is that people tend to be worried about the violence that comes from the oppressed. ... Really, there would be no violence at all if we did not have the violence of the apartheid system'.

There is neither logic nor common sense in asking the ANC to do now what it has consistently done on countless occasions before. It is the Government, not the ANC, that started civil war in this country, and that does not want reconciliation and peace. How does one work for reconciliation and peace? How does one work for reconciliation and peace under a State of Emergency, with black areas under military occupation, when people's organisations are banned, leaders are either in exile, prison or restricted, when the policy of apartheid with its violence is still being enforced, and when no conditions for free political expression exist?

Serious doubts have also been expressed as to whether the Government would be prepared to meet the ANC even when it fully complied with your demand. Political commentators point out that, during the series of discussion you and other Government members held recently with the 'homeland' leaders and their urban counterparts, you avoided meeting the very organisation which, together with the ANC, holds the key to peace in this country. The United Democratic Front and its main affiliates, the Congress of South African Trade Unions, Natal Indian Congress and Transvaal Indian Congress, are all non-violent and peaceful organisations. Why then did the Government ignore them if commitment to peace is the only qualification for participation in negotiations?

In your inaugural address on 20 September 1989, you made an important statement which must have had a formidable impact inside and outside the country. You said: 'There is but one way to peace, to justice for all, that is the way of reconciliation, of together seeking mutually acceptable solutions, of together discussing what the new South Africa should look like, of constitutional negotiation with a view to a permanent understanding'.

The cornerstone of that address was the idea of reconciliation, in which you pleaded for a new spirit and approach. By reconciliation, in this context, was understood the situation where opponents, and even enemies for that matter, would sink their differences and lay down their arms for the purpose of working out a peaceful solution, where the injustices and grievances of the past would be buried and forgotten, and a fresh start made. That is the spirit in which the people of South Africa would like to work together for peace; those are the principles which should guide those who love their country and its people, who want to turn South Africa into a land of hope. In highlighting this theme in your address, you sparked off a groundswell of expectations from far and wide. Many people felt that, at last, the South Africa of their dreams was about to be born.

We understood your appeal for reconciliation and justice for all not to be directed to those blacks who operate apartheid structures. Apart from a few notable exceptions, these blacks are the creation of the National Party and, throughout the years, they have served as its loyal agents in its various strategies to cling to minority rule. Their principal role has been, and still is, to make the struggle for majority rule in a unitary state far more difficult to achieve. For the last three decades, they have been used to defend the NP's policy of group domination – now referred to as group rights – and they have no tradition of militant resistance against racial discrimination. There is thus no conflict to be reconciled between the NP and these people.

The appeal could not have been directed to any of the opposition parties in Parliament either. Although the NP has made positive initiatives here and there, its public image is still tarnished by a cloud of distrust and suspicion, and by an inherent vagueness and indecision as far as the really basic issues are concerned. Many people see no fundamental difference between its policies and those of the Conservative Party. Both are regarded as apartheid parties, the only difference being that one is more blunt than the other in its defence of white privilege.

Although the Democratic Party is the most progressive parliamentary party, and despite the existence of important policy differences between that party and the NP, the relations between the two parties are not so bitter as to justify a call for reconciliation and peace by a head of state. The fairly even relation between the two parties is clearly illustrated by the fact that the DP is not banned, none of its leaders are restricted, imprisoned, driven into exile or executed for purely political offences, as is happening to our people.

The conflict which we believe you wanted to settle was that between the Government, on the one hand, and the ANC and other extra-parliamentary organisations, on the other. It is the activities of these organisations which have turned South Africa into a land of acute tension and fear. It is on this level that the country desperately yearns for reconciliation and justice for all. As pointed out on other occasions, dialogue with the ANC and the mass democratic movement is the only way of stopping violence and bringing peace to the country. It is, therefore, ironical that it is precisely these organisations with whom the Government is not at all prepared to talk.

It is common knowledge that the Government has been sharply criticised, and even condemned, in the past, for squandering precious resources, and for wasting much energy and time discussing with people who can play no significant role in the resolution of the current conflict in the country. Past experience shows that the Government would prefer to make peace with those who accept its policies, rather than those who reject them, with its friends rather than its opponents. It is to be hoped that this time, the Government will not repeat that costly mistake. To continue to ignore this criticism, and to confine consultations on the political crisis almost entirely to those individuals and organisations which help the Government to maintain the status quo, will certainly deepen the distrust and suspicion which impede real progress on negotiations.

In my lengthy discussions with the team of Government officials, I repeatedly urged that negotiation between the ANC and the Government should preferably be in two stages; the first being where the Government and the ANC would together work out the pre-conditions for negotiations. The second stage would consist of the actual negotiations themselves when the climate for doing so was ripe. These were my personal views and not those of the ANC, which sees the problem quite differently. It seems to me that now that I am aware of the attitude of the ANC on the matter, an attitude which is perfectly sound, we should work on the formula indicated by the organisation for the resolution of the present obstacles to negotiation.

The principal source of almost all our problems in this country is undoubtedly the policy of apartheid, which the Government now admits is an unjust system, and from which it claims to be moving away. This means that organisations and people who were banned, restricted, driven into exile, imprisoned or executed for their anti-apartheid activities were unjustly condemned. The very first step on the way to reconciliation is obviously the dismantling of apartheid, and all measures used to enforce it. To talk of reconciliation before this major step is taken is totally unrealistic.

The five year plan of the NP, with its outdated concept of group rights, has aggravated the position almost beyond repair. It is yet another example of the Government's attempt 'to modernise apart-heid without abandoning it'. What the plan means, in effect, is that after resisting racial oppression for so many years, and after making such heavy sacrifices during which countless lives were lost, we should at the height of that heroic struggle, yield to a disguised form of minority rule.

In a nutshell, the plan means that blacks will taste real freedom in the world to come. In this one, whites will go on preaching reconciliation and peace, but continue to hold firmly and defiantly to power and to enforce racial separation, the very issues which have caused so much agony and bitterness in the country. Insistence on such a plan will render meaningless all talk of 'reconciliation and justice for all; of together seeking mutually acceptable solutions, of together discussing

what the new South Africa should look like, of constitutional negotiation with a view to a permanent understanding'.

We equally reject, out of hand, the Government's plan to hold
racially based elections to determine those who should take part in
negotiations. Commentators of different political views consider it
absurd for the Government to advocate essentially racist procedures,
where the overwhelming majority of the population is striving for a
non-racial system of government.

The government argues that our situation is a complex one, and that
a lasting solution will only be found after years of consultation and
planning. We totally reject that view. There is nothing complicated in
replacing minority rule with majority rule, group domination with a
non-racial social order. The position if complicated is complicated
simply because the Government itself is not yet ready to accept the
most obvious solution which the majority demands, and believes that a
racial solution can still be imposed on the country.

The Government claims that the ANC is not the sole representative
of black aspirations in this country; therefore, it (the Government)
cannot be expected to have separate discussion with the organisation. It
can only do so in the presence of other organisations. We reject this
argument as yet another example of the Government's intransigence.
All those who resort to such an argument make themselves wide open
to the charge of using double standards.

It is now public knowledge that the Government has on numerous
occasions held separate discussions with each of the 'homeland'
leaders and with their urban counterparts. For the Government now to
refuse us this privilege would not only be inconsistent with its own
actions, but would seriously undermine the confidence-building
exercises on which we have embarked, compelling all those involved to
seek mutually acceptable solutions under very grave difficulties.
Equally important is the fact that there is a war between the ANC and
the Government, and a cease-fire to end hostilities will have to be
negotiated first, before talks to normalise the situation can begin. Only
Government and the ANC and its allies can take part in such talks, and
no third party would be needed.

I must now refer to a different but related matter, which I hope will receive your urgent attention, that is the release of four fellow-prisoners who were sentenced to life imprisonment by a Natal court in 1978, and who are presently held in Robben Island. They are:

Mr Matthew Meyiwa (66 years)
Mr Elphas Mdlalose (66 years)
Mr Anthony Xaba (56 Years)
Mr John Nene ($\pm$ 56 years)

They were first sentenced in 1964, Mr Mdlalose to 10 years' imprisonment and the rest to eight years. In 1978 they were again convicted and sentenced, this time to life imprisonment. For reasons which were carefully explained to Ministers Gerrit Viljoen and Kobie Coetsee on 10 October 1989, and to the Government team on 16 November 1989, I had expected Messrs Mdlalose and Meyiwa to be freed together with the eight fellow-prisoners mentioned above. I was indeed extremely distressed when the two were not included. Bearing in mind all the surrounding circumstances to the case, the fact that these four persons are not first offenders should be regarded as a mitigating, and not as an aggravating factor.

I would like to believe that my exploratory efforts during the last three years have not been in vain, that I have an important role still to play in helping to bring about a peaceful settlement, that the initiatives you have already taken will soon be followed by other developments on the really fundamental issues that are agitating our people, and that in our life-time our country will rid itself of the pestilence of racialism in all its forms.

In conclusion, Mr President, I should add that, in helping to promote dialogue between the ANC and the Government, I hope to be able to avoid any act which may be interpreted as an attempt on my part to drive a wedge between you and the NP, or to portray you in a manner not consistent with your public image. I trust that you and other members of the Government will fully reciprocate.

Document 16

F. W. de Klerk's speech at the opening of Parliament
2 February 1990

Mr Speaker, Members of Parliament.

THE GENERAL ELECTIONS on September the 6th, 1989, placed our country irrevocably on the road of drastic change. Underlying this is the growing realisation by an increasing number of South Africans that only a negotiated understanding among the representative leaders of the entire population is able to ensure lasting peace.

The alternative is growing violence, tension and conflict. That is unacceptable and in nobody's interest. The well-being of all in this country is linked inextricably to the ability of the leaders to come to terms with one another on a new dispensation. No-one can escape this simple truth.

On its part, the Government will accord the process of negotiation the highest priority. The aim is a totally new and just constitutional dispensation in which every inhabitant will enjoy equal rights, treatment and opportunity in every sphere of endeavour – constitutional, social and economic.

I hope that this new Parliament will play a constructive part in both the prelude to negotiations and the negotiating process itself. I wish to ask all of you who identify yourselves with the broad aim of a new South Africa, and that is the overwhelming majority:

- Let us put petty politics aside when we discuss the future during this Session.
- Help us build a broad consensus about the fundamentals of a new, realistic and democratic dispensation.

- Let us work together on a plan that will rid our country of suspicion and steer it away from domination and radicalism of any kind.

During the term of this new Parliament, we shall have to deal, complimentary to one another, with the normal processes of legislation and day-to-day government, as well as with the process of negotiation and renewal.

Within this framework I wish to deal first with several matters more closely concerned with the normal process of government before I turn specifically to negotiation and related issues.

1 Foreign relations

The Government is aware of the important part the world at large has to play in the realisation of our country's national interests.

Without contact and co-operation with the rest of the world we cannot promote the well-being and security of our citizens. The dynamic developments in international politics have created new opportunities for South Africa as well. Important advances have been made, among other things, in our contacts abroad, especially where these were precluded previously by ideological considerations.

I hope this trend will be encouraged by the important change of climate that is taking place in South Africa

For South Africa, indeed for the whole world, the past year has been one of change and major upheaval. In Eastern Europe and even the Soviet Union itself, political and economic upheaval surged forward in an unstoppable tide. At the same time, Beijing temporarily smothered with brutal violence the yearning of the people of the Chinese mainland for greater freedom.

The year of 1989 will go down in history as the year in which Stalinist Communism expired.

These developments will entail unpredictable consequences for Europe, but they will also be of decisive importance to Africa. The indications are that the countries of Eastern and Central Europe will receive greater attention, while it will decline in the case of Africa.

The collapse, particularly of the economic system in Eastern Europe, also serves as a warning to those who insist on persisting with it in Africa. Those who seek to force this failure of a system on South Africa, should engage in a total revision of their point of view. It should be clear to all that is not the answer here either. The new situation in Eastern Europe also shows that foreign intervention is no recipe for domestic change. It never succeeds, regardless of its ideological motivation. The upheaval in Eastern Europe took place without the involvement of the Big Powers or of the United Nations.

The countries of Southern Africa are faced with a particular challenge: Southern Africa now has an historical opportunity to set aside its conflicts and ideological differences and draw up a joint programme of reconstruction. It should be sufficiently attractive to ensure that the Southern African region obtains adequate investment and loan capital from the industrial countries of the world. Unless the countries of Southern Africa achieve stability and a common approach to economic development rapidly, they will be faced by further decline and ruin.

The Government is prepared to enter into discussions with other Southern African countries with the aim of formulating a realistic development plan. The Government believes that the obstacles in the way of a conference of Southern African states have now been removed sufficiently.

Hostile postures have to be replaced by co-operative ones; confrontation by contact; disengagement by engagement; slogans by deliberate debate.

The season of violence is over. The time for reconstruction and reconciliation has arrived.

Recently there have, indeed, been unusually positive results in South Africa's contacts and relations with other African states. During my visits to their countries I was received cordially, both in private and in public, by Presidents Mobutu, Chissano, Houphouet-Boigny and Kaunda. These leaders expressed their sincere concern about the serious economic problems in our part of the world. They agreed that South Africa could and should play a positive part in regional co-operation and development.

Our positive contribution to the independence process in South West Africa has been recognised internationally. South Africa's good faith and reliability as a negotiator made a significant contribution to the success of the events. This, too, was not unnoticed. Similarly, our efforts to help bring an end to the domestic conflict situations in Mozambique and Angola have received positive acknowledgement.

At present the Government is involved in negotiations concerning our future relations with an independent Namibia and there are no reasons why good relations should not exist between the two countries. Namibia needs South Africa and we are prepared to play a constructive part.

Nearer home I paid fruitful visits to Venda, Transkei and Ciskei and intend visiting Bophuthatswana soon. In recent times there has been an interesting debate about the future relationship of the TBVC countries with South Africa and specifically about whether they should be re-incorporated into our country.

Without rejecting this idea out of hand, it should be borne in mind that it is but one of many possibilities. These countries are constitutionally independent. Any return to South Africa will have to be dealt with, not only by means of legislation in their parliaments, but also through legislation in this Parliament. Naturally this will have to be preceded by talks and agreements.

2 Human rights

Some time ago the Government referred the question of the protection of fundamental human rights to the South African Law Commission. This resulted in the Law Commission's interim working document on individual and minority rights. It elicited substantial public interest.

I am satisfied that every individual and organisation in the country has had ample opportunity to make representations to the Law Commission, express criticism freely and make suggestions. At present, the Law Commission is considering the representations received. A final report is expected in the course of this year.

In view of the exceptional importance of the subject of human rights to our country and all its people, I wish to ask the Law Commission to accord this task high priority.

The whole question of protecting individual and minority rights, which includes collective rights and the rights of national groups, is still under consideration by the Law Commission. Therefore, it would be inappropriate of the Government to express a view on the details now. However, certain matters of principle have emerged fairly clearly and I wish to devote some remarks to them.

The Government accepts the principle of the recognition and protection of the fundamental individual rights which form the constitutional basis of most Western democracies. We acknowledge, too, that the most practical way of protecting those rights is vested in a declaration of rights justiciable by an independent judiciary. However, it is clear that a system for the protection of the rights of individuals, minorities and national entities has to form a well-rounded and balanced whole. South Africa has its own national composition and our constitutional dispensation has to take this into account. The formal recognition of individual rights does not mean that the problems of a heterogeneous population will simply disappear. Any new constitution which disregards this reality will be inappropriate and even harmful.

Naturally, the protection of collective, minority and national rights may not bring about an imbalance in respect of individual rights. It is neither the Government's policy nor its intention that any group – in whichever way it may be defined – shall be favoured above or in relation to any of the others.

The Government is requesting the Law Commission to undertake a further task and report on it. This task is directed at the balanced protection in a future constitution of the human rights of all our citizens, as well as of collective units, associations, minorities and nations. This investigation will also serve the purpose of supporting negotiations towards a new constitution.

The terms of reference also include:

• the identification of the main types and models of democratic constitutions which deserve consideration in the aforementioned context;

- an analysis of the ways in which the relevant rights are protected in every model; and
- possible methods by means of which such constitutions may be made to succeed and be safeguarded in a legitimate manner.

3 The death penalty

The death penalty has been the subject of intensive discussion in recent months. However, the Government has been giving its attention to this extremely sensitive issue for some time. On April the 27th, 1989, the honourable Minister of Justice indicated that there was merit in suggestions for reform in this area. Since 1988 in fact, my predecessor and I have been taking decisions on reprieves which have led, in proportion, to a drastic decline in executions.

We have now reached the position in which we are able to make concrete proposals for reform. After the Chief Justice was consulted, and he in turn had consulted the Bench, and after the Government had noted the opinions of academics and other interested parties, the Government decided on the following broad principles from a variety of available options:

- that reform in this area is indicated;
- that the death penalty should be limited as an option of sentence to extreme cases, and specifically through broadening judicial discretion in the imposition of sentence; and
- that an automatic right of appeal be granted to those under sentence of death.

Should these proposals be adopted, they should have a significant influence on the imposition of death sentences on the one hand, and on the other, should ensure that every case in which a person has been sentenced to death, will come to the attention of the Appellate Division.

The proposals require that everybody currently awaiting execution, be accorded the benefit of the proposed new approach. Therefore, all executions have been suspended and no executions will take place until Parliament has taken a final decision on the new proposals. In the event of the proposals being adopted, the case of every person involved will be dealt with in accordance with the new guidelines. In the meantime, no executions have taken place since November 14th, 1989.

New and uncompleted cases will still be adjudicated in terms of the existing law. Only when the death sentence is imposed, will the new proposals be applied, as in the case of those currently awaiting execution.

The legislation concerned also entails other related principles which will be announced and elucidated in due course by the Minister of Justice. It will now be formulated in consultation with experts and be submitted to Parliament as soon as possible. I wish to urge everybody to join us in dealing with this highly sensitive issue in a responsible manner.

4 Socio-economic aspects

A changed dispensation implies far more than political and constitutional issues. It cannot be pursued successfully in isolation from problems in other spheres of life which demand practical solutions. Poverty, unemployment, housing shortages, inadequate education and training, illiteracy, health needs and numerous other problems still stand in the way of progress and prosperity and an improved quality of life.

The conservation of the physical and human environment is of cardinal importance to the quality of our existence. For this the Government is developing a strategy with the aid of an investigation by the President's Council.

All of these challenges are being dealt with urgently and comprehensively. The capability for this has to be created in an economically accountable manner. Consequently existing strategies and aims are undergoing a comprehensive revision.

From this will emanate important policy announcements in the socio-economic sphere by the responsible Ministers during the course of the session. One matter about which it is possible to make a concrete announcement, is the Separate Amenities Act, 1953. Pursuant to my speech before the President's Council late last year, I announce that this Act will be repealed during this Session of Parliament.

The State cannot possibly deal alone with all of the social advancement our circumstances demand. The community at large, and especially the private sector, also have a major responsibility towards the welfare of our country and its people.

5 The economy

A new South Africa is possible only if it is bolstered by a sound and growing economy, with particular emphasis on the creation of employment. With a view to this, the Government has taken thorough cognisance of the advice contained in numerous reports by a variety of advisory bodies. The central message is that South Africa, too, will have to make certain structural changes to its economy, just as its major trading partners had to do a decade or so ago.

The period of exceptionally high economic growth experienced by the Western world in the sixties, was brought to an end by the oil crisis in 1973. Drastic structural adaptations became inevitable for these countries, especially after the second oil crisis in 1979, when serious imbalances occurred in their economies. After considerable sacrifices, those countries which persevered with their structural adjustment programmes, recovered economically so that lengthy periods of high economic growth and low inflation were possible.

During that particular period, South Africa was protected temporarily by the rising gold price from the necessity of making similar adjustments immediately. In fact, the high gold price even brought prosperity with it for a while. The recovery of the world economy and the decline in the price of gold and other primary products, brought with them unhealthy trends. These included high inflation, a serious weakening in the productivity of capital, stagnation in the economy's ability to generate income and employment opportunities. All of this made a drastic structural adjustment of our economy inevitable.

The Government's basic point of departure is to reduce the role of the public sector in the economy and to give the private sector maximum opportunity for optimal performance. In this process, preference has to be given to allowing the market forces and a sound competitive structure to bring about the necessary adjustments.

Naturally, those who make and implement economic policy have a major responsibility at the same time to promote an environment optimally conducive to investment, job creation and economic growth by means of appropriate and properly co-ordinated fiscal and monetary policy. The Government remains committed to this balanced and practical approach.

By means of restricting capital expenditure in parastatal institutions, privatisation, deregulation and curtailing government expenditure, substantial progress has been made already towards reducing the role of the authorities in the economy. We shall persist with this in a well-considered way.

This does not mean that the State will forsake its indispensable development role, especially in our particular circumstances. On the contrary, it is the precise intention of the Government to concentrate an equitable portion of its capacity on these aims by means of the meticulous determination of priorities.

Following the progress that has been made in other areas of the economy in recent years, it is now opportune to give particular attention to the supply side of the economy.

Fundamental factors which will contribute to the success of this restructuring are:

- the gradual reduction of inflation to levels comparable to those of our principal trading partners;
- the encouragement of personal initiative and savings;
- the subjection of all economic decisions by the authorities to stringent financial measures and discipline;
- rapid progress with the reform of our system of taxation; and
- the encouragement of exports as the impetus for industrialisation and earning foreign exchange.

These and other adjustments, which will require sacrifices, have to be seen as prerequisites for a new period of sustained growth in productive employment in the nineties.

The Government is very much aware of the necessity of proper co-ordination and consistent implementation of its economic policy. For this reason, the establishment of the necessary structures and expertise to ensure this co-ordination is being given preference. This applies both to the various functions within the Government and to the interaction between the authorities and the private sector.

This is obviously not the occasion for me to deal in greater detail with our total economic strategy or with the recent course of the economy.

I shall confine myself to a few specific remarks on one aspect of fiscal policy that has been a source of criticism of the Government for some time, namely State expenditure.

The Government's financial year ends only in two months' time and several other important economic indicators for the 1989 calendar year are still subject to refinements at this stage. Nonetheless, several important trends are becoming increasingly clear. I am grateful to be able to say that we have apparently succeeded to a substantial degree in achieving most of our economic aims in the past year.

In respect of Government expenditure, the budget for the current financial year will be the most accurate in many years. The financial figures will show:

- that Government expenditure is thoroughly under control;
- that our normal financing programme has not exerted any significant upward pressure on rates of interest; and
- that we will close the year with a surplus, even without taking the income from the privatisation of Iscor into account.

Without pre-empting this year's main budget, I wish to emphasise that it is also our intention to co-ordinate fiscal and monetary policy in the coming financial year in a way that will enable us to achieve the ensuing goals – namely:

- that the present downturn will take the form of a soft landing which will help to make adjustments as easy as possible;

- that our economy will consolidate before the next upward phase so that we will be able to grow from a sound base; and
- that we shall persist with the implementation of the required structural adaptations in respect, among other things, of the following: easing the tax burden, especially on individuals; sustained and adequate generation of surpluses on the current account of the balance of payments; and the reconstruction of our gold and foreign exchange reserves.

It is a matter of considerable seriousness to the Government, especially in this particular period of our history, to promote a dynamic economy which will make it possible for increasing numbers of people to be employed and share in rising standards of living.

6 Negotiation

In conclusion, I wish to focus the spotlight on the process of negotiation and related issues. At this stage I am refraining deliberately from discussing the merits of numerous political questions which undoubtedly will be debated during the next few weeks. The focus, now, has to fall on negotiation.

Practically every leader agrees that negotiation is the key to reconciliation, peace and a new and just dispensation. However, numerous excuses for refusing to take part are advanced. Some of the reasons being advanced are valid. Others are merely part of a political chess game. And while the game of chess proceeds, valuable time is being lost.

Against this background I committed the Government during my inauguration to giving active attention to the most important obstacles in the way of negotiation. Today I am able to announce far-reaching decisions in this connection.

I believe that these decisions will shape a new phase in which there will be a movement away from measures which have been seized upon as a justification for confrontation and violence. The emphasis has to move, and will move now, to a debate and discussion of political and economic points of view as part of the process of negotiation.

I wish to urge every political and community leader, in and outside Parliament, to approach the new opportunities which are being created, constructively. There is no time left for advancing all manner of new conditions that will delay the negotiating process.

The steps that have been decided, are the following:

- The prohibition of the African National Congress, the Pan Africanist Congress, the South African Communist Party and a number of subsidiary organisations is being rescinded.
- People serving prison sentence merely because they were members of one of these organisations or because they committed another offence which was merely an offence because a prohibition on one of the organisations was in force, will be identified and released. Prisoners who have been sentenced for other offences such as murder, terrorism or arson are not affected by this.
- The media emergency regulations as well as the education emergency regulations are being abolished in their entirety.
- The security emergency regulations will be amended to still make provision for effective control over visual material pertaining to scenes of unrest.
- The restrictions in terms of the emergency regulations on 33 organisations are being rescinded. The organisations include the following: National Education Crisis Committees, South African National Student's Congress, United Democratic Front, Cosatu, Die Blanke Bevrydingsbeweging van Suid-Afrika.
- The conditions imposed in terms of the security emergency regulations on 374 people on their release, are being rescinded and the regulations which provide for such conditions are being abolished.
- The period of detention in terms of the security emergency regulations will be limited henceforth to six months. Detainees also acquire the right to legal representation and a medical practitioner of their own choosing.

These decisions by the Cabinet are in accordance with the Government's declared intention to normalise the political process in South Africa without jeopardising the maintenance of good order. They were preceded by thorough and unanimous advice by a group of officials which included members of the security community.

Implementation will be immediate and, where necessary, notices will appear in the Government Gazette from tomorrow. The most important facets of the advice the Government received in this connection, are the following:

- The events in the Soviet Union and Eastern Europe, to which I have referred already, weaken the capability of organisations which were previously supported strongly from those quarters.
- The activities of the organisations from which the prohibitions are now being lifted, no longer entail the same degree of threat to internal security which initially necessitated the imposition of the prohibition.
- There have been important shifts of emphasis in the statements and points of view of the most important of the organisations concerned, which indicate a new approach and a preference for peaceful solutions.
- The South African Police is convinced that it is able, in the present circumstances, to combat violence and other crimes perpetrated also by members of these organisations and to bring offenders to justice without the aid of prohibitions on organisations.

About one matter there should be no doubt. The lifting of the prohibition on the said organisations does not signify in the least the approval or condonation of terrorism or crimes of violence committed under the banner or which may be perpetrated in the future. Equally, it should not be interpreted as a deviation from the Government's principles, among other things, against their economic policy and aspects of their constitutional policy. This will be dealt with in debate and negotiation.

At the same time I wish to emphasise that the maintenance of law and order dares not be jeopardised. The Government will not forsake its duty in this connection. Violence from whichever source, will be fought with all available might. Peaceful protest may not become the springboard for lawlessness, violence and intimidation. No democratic country can tolerate that.

Strong emphasis will be placed as well on even more effective law enforcement. Proper provision of manpower and means for the police and all who are involved with the enforcement of the law, will be ensured. In fact, the budget for the coming financial year will already begin to give effect to this.

I wish to thank the members of our security forces and related services for the dedicated service they have rendered the Republic of South Africa. Their dedication makes reform in a stable climate possible.

On the state of emergency I have been advised that an emergency situation, which justifies these special measures which have been retained, still exists. There is still conflict which is manifesting itself mainly in Natal, but as a consequence of the countrywide political power struggle. In addition, there are indications that radicals are still trying to disrupt the possibilities of negotiation by means of mass violence.

It is my intention to terminate the state of emergency completely as soon as circumstances justify it and I request the co-operation of everybody towards this end. Those responsible for unrest and conflict have to bear the blame for the continuing state of emergency. In the mean time, the state of emergency is inhibiting only those who use chaos and disorder as political instruments. Otherwise the rules of the game under the state of emergency are the same for everybody.

Against this background the Government is convinced that the decisions I have announced are justified from the security point of view. However, these decisions are justified from a political point of view as well.

Our country and all its people have been embroiled in conflict, tension and violent struggle for decades. It is time for us to break out of the cycle of violence and break through to peace and reconciliation. The silent majority is yearning for this. The youth deserve it.

With the steps the Government has taken it has proven its good faith and the table is laid for sensible leaders to begin talking about a new dispensation, to reach an understanding by way of dialogue and discussion.

The agenda is open and the overall aims to which we are aspiring should be acceptable to all reasonable South Africans.

Among other things, those aims include a new, democratic constitution; universal franchise; no domination; equality before an independent judiciary; the protection of minorities as well as of individual rights; freedom of religion; a sound economy based on proven economic principles and private enterprise; dynamic programmes directed at better education, health services, housing and social conditions for all.

In this connection Mr Nelson Mandela could play an important part. The Government has noted that he has declared himself to be willing to make a constructive contribution to the peaceful political process in South Africa.

I wish to put it plainly that the Government has taken a firm decision to release Mr Mandela unconditionally. I am serious about bringing this matter to finality without delay. The Government will take a decision soon on the date of his release. Unfortunately, a further short passage of time is unavoidable.

Normally there is a certain passage of time between the decision to release and the actual release because of logistical and administrative requirements. In the case of Mr Mandela there are factors in the way of his immediate release, of which his personal circumstances and safety are not the least. He has not been an ordinary prisoner for quite some time. Because of that, his case requires particular circumspection.

Today's announcements, in particular, go to the heart of what Black leaders – also Mr Mandela – have been advancing over the years as their reason for having resorted to violence. The allegation has been that the Government did not wish to talk to them and that they were deprived of their right to normal political activity by the prohibition of their organisations.

Without conceding that violence has ever been justified, I wish to say today to those who argued in this manner:

- The Government wishes to talk to all leaders who seek peace.
- The unconditional lifting of the prohibition on the said organisations places everybody in a position to pursue politics freely.
- The justification for violence which was always advanced, no longer exists.

These facts place everybody in South Africa before a fait accompli. On the basis of numerous previous statements there is no longer any reasonable excuse for the continuation of violence. The time for talking has arrived and whoever still makes excuses does not really wish to talk.

Therefore, I repeat my invitation with greater conviction than ever:

Walk through the open door, take your place at the negotiating table together with the Government and other leaders who have important power bases inside and outside of Parliament.

Henceforth, everybody's political points of view will be tested against their realism, their workability and their fairness. The time for negotiation has arrived.

To those political leaders who have always resisted violence I say thank you for your principled stands. This includes all the leaders of parliamentary parties, leaders of important organisations and movements, such as Chief Minister Buthelezi, all of the other Chief Ministers and urban community leaders.

Through their participation and discussion they have made an important contribution to this moment in which the process of free political participation is able to be restored. Their places in the negotiating process are assured.

Conclusion

In my inaugural address I said the following:

All reasonable people in this country – by far the majority – anxiously await a message of hope. It is our responsibility as leaders in all spheres to provide that message realistically, with courage and conviction. If we fail in that, the ensuing chaos, the demise of stability and progress, will for ever be held against us.

History has thrust upon the leadership of this country the tremendous responsibility to turn our country away from its present direction of conflict and confrontation. Only we, the leaders of our peoples, can do it.

The eyes of responsible governments across the world are focused on us. The hopes of millions of South Africans are centred around us. The future of Southern Africa depends on us. We dare not falter or fail.

This is where we stand:
- Deeply under the impression of our responsibility.
- Humble in the face of the tremendous challenges ahead.
- Determined to move forward in faith and with conviction.

I ask of Parliament to assist me on the road ahead. There is much to be done.

I call on the international community to re-evaluate its position and to adopt a positive attitude towards the dynamic evolution which is taking place in South Africa.

I pray that the Almighty Lord will guide and sustain us on our course through unchartered waters and will bless your labours and deliberations.

Mr Speaker, Members of Parliament,

I now declare this Second Session of the Ninth Parliament of the Republic of South Africa to be duly opened.

Document 17

The Groote Schuur Minute
4 May 1990

The government and the African National Congress agree on a common commitment towards the resolution of the existing climate of violence and intimidation from whatever quarter as well as a commitment to stability and to a peaceful process of negotiations.

Flowing from this commitment, the following was agreed upon:

1. The establishment of a working group to make recommendations on a definition of political offences in the South African situation; to discuss, in this regard, time scales; and to advise on norms and mechanisms for dealing with the release of political prisoners and the granting of immunity in respect of political offences to those inside and outside South Africa. All persons who may be affected will be considered. The working group will bear in mind experiences in Namibia and elsewhere. The working group will aim to complete its work before 21st May 1990. It is understood that the South African government, in its discretion, may consider other political parties and movement and other relevant bodies. The proceedings of the working group will be confidential. In the meantime the following offences will receive attention immediately:

   (a) The leaving of the country without a valid travel document.

   (b) Any offences related merely to organisations which were previously prohibited.

2. In addition to the arrangements mentioned in paragraph 1, temporary immunity from prosecution of political offences committed before today, will be considered on an urgent basis for

members of the National Executive Committee and selected other members of the ANC from outside the country, to enable them to return and help with the establishment and management of political activities, to assist in bringing violence to an end and to take part in peaceful political negotiations.

3. The government undertakes to review existing security legislation to bring it into line with the new dynamic situation developing in South Africa in order to ensure normal and free political activities.

4. The government reiterates its commitment to work towards the lifting of the state of emergency. In this context, the ANC will exert itself to fulfil the objectives contained in the preamble.

5. Efficient channels of communication between the government and the ANC will be established in order to curb violence and intimidation from whatever quarter effectively.

The government and the ANC agree that the objectives contained in this minute should be achieved as early as possible.

CAPE TOWN,
4th May 1990

Document 18

The government and the ANC have held discussions at the Presidency, Pretoria, today 6 August 1990.

1. The Government and the ANC have again committed themselves to the Groote Schuur Minute.

2. The final report of the Working Group on political offences dated 21 May 1990, as amended, was accepted by both parties. The guidelines to be formulated in terms of the Report will be applied in dealing with members of all organisations, groupings or institutions, governmental or otherwise, who committed offences on the assumption that a particular cause was being served or opposed. The meeting has instructed the Working Group to draw up a plan for the release of ANC-related prisoners and the granting of indemnity to people in a phased manner and to report before the end of August. The following target dates have in the meantime been agreed upon:

   - The body or bodies referred to in paragraph 8.2 of the Report of the Working Group will be constituted by 31 August 1990.
   - The further release of prisoners which can be dealt with administratively will start on 1 September 1990.
   - Indemnity which can be dealt with in categories of persons and not on an individual basis will be granted as from 1 October 1990. This process will be completed not later than the end of 1990.
   - In all cases where the body or bodies to be constituted according to paragraph 8.2 of the Report of the Working

Group will have to consider cases on an individual basis, the process will be expedited as much as possible. It is hoped that this process will be completed within six months, but the latest date envisaged for the completion of the total task in terms of the Report of the Working Group is not later than 30 April 1991.

This programme will be implemented on the basis of the Report of the Working Group.

3. In the interest of moving as speedily as possible towards a negotiated peaceful political settlement and in the context of the agreements reached, the ANC announced that it was now suspending all armed actions with immediate effect. As a result of this, no further armed actions and related activities by the ANC and its military wing Umkhonto we Sizwe will take place. It was agreed that a working group will be established to resolve all outstanding questions arising out of this decision to report by 15 September 1990. Both sides once more committed themselves to do everything in their power to bring about a peaceful solution as quickly as possible.

4. Both delegations expressed serious concern about the general level of violence, intimidation and unrest in the country, especially in Natal. They agreed that in the context of the common search for peace and stability, it was vital that understanding should grow among all sections of the South African population that problems can and should be solved through negotiations. Both parties committed themselves to undertake steps and measures to promote and expedite the normalisation of the situation in line with the spirit of mutual trust obtaining among the leaders involved.

5. With due cognisance of the interest, role and involvement of other parties the delegations consider it necessary that whatever additional mechanisms of communication are needed should be developed at local, regional and national levels. This should enable public grievances to be addressed peacefully and in good time, avoiding conflict.

6. The Government has undertaken to consider the lifting of the State of Emergency in Natal as early as possible in the light of positive consequences that should result from this accord.

7. In view of the new circumstances now emerging there will be an ongoing review of security legislation. The Government will give immediate consideration to repealing all provisions of the Internal Security Act that –

    (a) refer to communism or the furthering thereof;

    (b) provide for a consolidated list;

    (c) provide for a prohibition on the publication of statements or writings of certain persons; and

    (d) provide for an amount to be deposited before a newspaper may be registered.

    The Government will continue reviewing security legislation and its application in order to ensure free political activity and with the view to introducing amended legislation at the next session of Parliament. The Minister of Justice will issue a statement in this regard, inter alia calling for comments and proposals.

8. We are convinced that what we have agreed upon today can become a milestone on the road to true peace and prosperity for our country. In this we do not pretend to be the only parties involved in the process of shaping the new South Africa. We know there are other parties committed to peaceful progress. All of us can henceforth walk that road in consultation and co-operation with each other. We call upon all those who have not yet committed themselves to peaceful negotiations to do so now.

9. Against this background, the way is now open to proceed towards negotiations on a new constitution. Exploratory talks in this regard will be held before the next meeting which will be held soon.

PRETORIA

6 August 1990

Report – Working group established under paragraph 1 of the Groote Schuur Minute

1. On 2, 3 and 4 May 1990, at Groote Schuur in Cape Town, a delegation of the African National Congress met the State President accompanied by Ministers and officials. At the conclusion of the meeting a document, called the Groote Schuur Minute, was adopted. A copy thereof is attached. Paragraph 1 provided for the establishment of a working group. The ANC nominated as its representatives on the working group, Messrs Zuma, Maduna, Nhlanhla, Pahad, Phosa and Ndlovu (its members on the Steering Committee). The Government nominated as its representatives Minister Coetsee, Deputy Minister Meyer and Messrs Van der Merwe, Swanepoel, Louw and Viall, Major General Knipe and Brigadier Kok.

2. The Working Group was charged with –
   - making recommendations on a definition of political offences in the South African situation;
   - discussing, in this regard, time scales; and
   - advising on norms and mechanisms for dealing with the release of political prisoners and the granting of immunity of political offences to those inside and outside South Africa.

3. It is recognised that in terms of the Groote Schuur Minute, the category of persons involved only in offences set out hereunder have already been catered for, for immediate attention:

3.1 The leaving of the country without a valid travel document;

3.2 Any offences related merely to organisations which were previously prohibited (including membership of Umkhonto we Sizwe).

4. Persons in the above category are entitled to be dealt with in terms of the provisions set out in paragraphs 6.2 and 6.3 hereof, as the case may be.

5. The Working Group met on a number of occasions and reports as follows:

DEFINING POLITICAL OFFENCES IN THE SOUTH
AFRICAN SITUATION:

6.1 The following classes of persons, whether inside or outside
South Africa, must be taken into account with regard to pardon
or indemnity for political offences:

(a) Persons already sentenced, including persons serving a
sentence, persons subject to any suspended sentence,
persons awaiting execution of a sentence or where the
case is on appeal or review.

(b) Persons who may be liable to prosecution, or who are
awaiting or undergoing trial.

(c) Persons in detention.

6.2 The power to pardon is vested in the State President by virtue of
section 6 of the Republic of South Africa Constitution Act, 1983
(Act 110 of 1983), and section 69 of the Prisons Act, 1959 (Act 8 of
1959), and will apply to persons already sentenced, i.e. class (a)
above.

6.3 Special power to grant indemnity is required in regard to persons
referred to in class (b) above. The relevant power is contained in
section 2 of the Indemnity Act, 1990. Section 6 of the Criminal
Procedure Act, 1977 provides for the stopping of a prosecution
and may therefore be applied.

6.4 The recommendations contained in this document relate only to
political offences and in no way imply any limitation upon the
general exercise of the powers mentioned in paragraphs 6.2 and
6.3.

6.5 In preparing for the making of 'recommendations on a definition
of political offences in the South African situation', the following
principles and factors were noted (the principles and factors are
largely those applied by Prof. Norgaard in the Namibian situation after study of the jurisprudence and the representations of
the parties concerned and do not purport to be exhaustive):

6.5.1 There is no generally accepted definition of 'political offence' or
'political prisoner' in international law. What is generally

accepted, however, is that principles developed in the field of extradition law are relevant in distinguishing between 'political offence' and 'common crimes'.

6.5.2   The law and practice of states show that there is now a considerable degree of consensus both as to the types of offence which may in principle be classified as political as well as to the sort of factors which should be taken into account in deciding whether an offence is 'political' or not. In particular, the following are aspects of the law and practice of extradition which appear to provide valuable guidance:

(a)   Whether or not an offence is political depends on the facts and circumstances of each individual case. The question is thus approached on a case by case basis.

(b)   Certain offences are recognised as 'purely' political, e.g. treason directed solely against the State and not involving a common or 'ordinary' crime such as murder or assault or the dissemination of subversive literature.

(c)   In certain circumstances a 'common' crime, even a serious one such as murder, may be regarded as a political offence. Here the following are the principal factors which are commonly taken into account by national courts:

  (i)   The motive of the offender – i.e. was it a political motive (e.g. to change the established order) or a personal motive (e.g. to settle a private grudge).

  (ii)   The context in which the offence was committed, especially whether the offence was committed in the course of or as part of a political uprising or disturbance.

  (iii)   The nature of the political objective (e.g. whether to force a change in policy or to overthrow the Government).

  (iv)   The legal and factual nature of the offence, including its gravity (e.g. rape could never be regarded as a political offence).

  (v)   The object of the offence (e.g. whether it was

committed against Government property or personnel or directed primarily against private property
or individuals).

(vi) The relationship between the offence and the political objective being pursued (e.g. the directness or
proximity of the relationship, or the proportionality
between the offence and the objective pursued).

(vii) The question whether the act was committed in the
execution of an order or with the approval of the
organisation, institution or body concerned.

6.6.1 The Working Group endorses the principles and factors set out
in paragraph 6.5.2 and accepts that these will form the basis of
guidelines to meet the South African situation when considering
the grant of pardon or indemnity in respect of political offences.

6.6.2 As stated in the Groote Schuur Minute, it is understood that the
Government may in its discretion consult other political parties
and movements, and other relevant bodies with regard to the
grant of pardon or indemnity in respect of offences relating to
them. For this purpose it shall be free to formulate its own
guidelines which it will apply in dealing with members of such
organisations, grouping or institutions, governmental or otherwise, who committed offences on the assumption that a particular cause was being served or opposed.

Time scales

7.1 Having defined political offences, the norms and the guidelines a
cut-off date will have to be fixed. Pardon and indemnity will only
be considered in respect of political offences committed on or
before that date.

7.2 Bearing in mind the preamble to the Groote Schuur Minute, the
Working Group accepts that the process should proceed as
expeditiously as possible. It is understood that diverse periods for
pardon, indemnity and release will apply to diverse persons,
categories of persons and categories of offences. A mechanism to
provide advice to Government in this regard is necessary.

7.3 It is understood that the Government may, without waiting for the implementation of the process contemplated in this document, proceed to exercise the powers referred to in paragraph 6.2, in terms of existing policy. This may result in substantial results in the very near future in regard to persons referred to in class (a) of paragraph 6.1.

A Mechanism

8.1 The granting of pardon or indemnity in respect of a specific offence or a category of offences, is an executive governmental function. The purpose of devising a mechanism, is to provide the executive with wise advice and to demonstrate that the interests of all parties are being taken into account in as objective a manner as possible.

8.2 It is suggested for this purpose that a body or bodies be constituted, consisting of a convenor with ad hoc appointments from concerned groups when dealing with particular offences (or categories of offences).

8.3 It is recommended that this Working Group be kept active in respect of ANC interests.

Document 19

The D. F. Malan Accord
12 February 1991

Report of the working group under paragraph three of the Pretoria Minute

1. The Working Group was established under paragraph 3 of the Pretoria Minute, which reads as follows:

   In the interest of moving as speedily as possible towards a negotiated peaceful political settlement and in the context of the agreements reached, the ANC announced that it was now suspending all armed actions with immediate effect. As a result of this, no further armed actions and related activities by the ANC and its military wing, Umkhonto we Sizwe will take place. It was agreed that a Working Group will be established to resolve all outstanding questions arising out of this decision to report by 15 September 1990. Both sides once more committed themselves to do everything in their power to bring about a peaceful solution as quickly as possible.

2. Having decided that it would not have been possible to submit a final report by the 15th September 1990, an interim report was brought out on 13 September 1990.
3. Since then a number of meetings have taken place. This report was finalised at a meeting on the 12th of February 1991.
4. With reference to the word 'suspending' as used in paragraph 3 of the Pretoria minute, the Working Group reiterated what was said in paragraph 4 of its Interim Report, namely that suspension

occurred as a step in the process of finding peaceful solutions, with the presumption that the process would lead to the situation where there would be no return to armed action.

5. (a) Under the terms of suspension of 'armed action' and 'related activities' by the ANC, with specific reference also to Umkhonto we Sizwe and its organised military groups and armed cadres, it was agreed that the following will not take place:

(i) Attacks by means of armaments, firearms, explosive or incendiary devices

(ii) Infiltration of men and material

(iii) Creation of underground structures

(iv) Statements inciting violence

(v) Threats of armed action

(vi) Training inside South Africa

(b) The Working Group:

(i) agreed that the democratic process implies and obliges all political parties and movements to participate in this process peacefully and without resort to the use of force;

(ii) therefore accepted the principle that in a democratic society no political party or movement should have a private army;

(iii) noted that the ANC had, in good faith and as a contribution to the process of arriving at a peaceful settlement announced the suspension of all armed actions and related activities, with the presumption that the process would lead to the situation where there would be no return to armed action;

(iv) noted that by virtue of the fact that Umkhonto we Sizwe is no longer an unlawful organisation, membership thereof is not in violation of any of the provisions of paragraph 3 of the Pretoria Minute and the letter and spirit of the Pretoria Minute as a whole;

(v) noted the historical fact that the ANC and Umkhonto

we Sizwe had placed arms and cadres within the
country;

  (vi) agreed that in the context of paragraph 5(b) (ii), (iii)
        and (iv) above, it was vital that control over such
        cadres and arms be exercised to ensure that no armed
        actions or related activities occur;

 (vii) further agreed that in the context of paragraph 5(b) (ii),
        (iii) and (iv) above, a phased process be initiated in
        order to enable these cadres of the ANC to resume
        their normal lives and also facilitate and legalise
        control over the arms and the process to ensure such
        legality will immediately be taken further by the
        Working Group;

(viii) agreed that where applicable, individual weapons
        shall be licensed in terms of existing legislation;

  (ix) further agreed that the security forces take cognisance
        of the suspension of armed action and related activ-
        ities and that the parties hereto will remain in close
        liaison with one another according to the procedure
        prescribed in 6(a) of this document with a view to
        ensuring prompt and efficient reporting, investigation
        and redressing, where applicable, of all allegations of
        unlawful activities or activities contrary to the spirit of
        this agreement, by the security forces.

(c) The Working Group:

   (i) agreed that the population at large has a right to
        express its views through peaceful demonstrations;

  (ii) further agreed that it is urgent and imperative that
        violence and intimidation from whatever quarter
        accompanying mass action should be eliminated;

 (iii) further agreed that peaceful political activities and
        stability must be promoted;

  (iv) further agreed that to this end joint efforts should be
        made to implement the intentions contained in
        paragraphs 5 of the Groote Schuur and the Pretoria

        Minutes to ensure that grievances and conflict-creating situations are timeously addressed.

6. (a) The Working Group agreed that designated members of the ANC would work with government representatives in a Liaison Committee to implement this agreement, and that the existing nominated SAP and ANC liaison officials appointed in accordance with paragraph 5 of the Groote Schuur Minute shall serve as supporting structure of the Liaison Committee.

     (b) It is agreed that this agreement will be implemented forthwith and its objectives attained as speedily as possible.

     (c) It is further agreed that in view of the above the process of attaining the objectives contained in paragraph 2 of the Pretoria Minute will be realised according to the procedures contained in that minute.

7. It is understood that nothing in or omitted from the agreement will be construed as invalidating or suspending the provisions of any law applicable in South Africa.

8. It is recommended that this Working Group be continued to supervise the implementation of this agreement relating to paragraph 3 and the activities of the Liaison Committee and to give attention to further matters that may arise from the implementation of this agreement, such as proposed defence units.

Joint statement by the State President, Mr F. W. de Klerk, and Mr Nelson Mandela, Deputy President of the African National Congress

Delegations led by President F W de Klerk and the Deputy President of the African National Congress, Mr Nelson Mandela, met in Cape Town today.

The problems experienced by the Working Group dealing with paragraph 3 of the Pretoria Minute, were resolved and agreement was reached with regard to the most pertinent points.

It was agreed that there was a need for ongoing consultation with the Working Group. The Cabinet and the National Executive Committee of the ANC will consider the document containing the agreement and when approved a full text will be released immediately.

ISSUED BY THE OFFICE OF THE STATE PRESIDENT CAPE TOWN 12 FEBRUARY 1991

Document 20

Advance to national democracy: guidelines on strategy and tactics of the ANC
February 1991

I. Introduction

1. After 30 years of illegality, the ANC is once more able to operate within South Africa as a legal organisation. This also holds true for our ally, the SACP, which was banned for 40 years, as well as other organisations. Political prisoners are being released and those who had been driven into exile are returning. The ANC has moved back into the country its national Headquarters and leading organs.

2. These developments reflect the deep, all-round crisis afflicting the apartheid system. The South African economy is in a shambles, and the majority of the people refuse to be governed by a regime not based on their will. The apartheid regime and the ruling National Party have been forced to openly admit that the system of white minority domination and exploitation has failed and can no longer be maintained. They have accepted that it is necessary to enter into negotiations with the national liberation movement for the elaboration and adoption of a new constitution.

3. Apartheid stands condemned by the world community of nations as a crime against humanity. The international community is at one in seeking an end to the system of apartheid and the creation of a society based on the will of all the people.

4. All these developments represent a major victory for the forces,

led by the ANC, which have struggled for many decades for the destruction of the system of white minority domination and the transformation of South Africa into a united, democratic and non-racial country. South Africa is entering a phase of transition towards national democracy. The immediate issue on the agenda is the question of political power. To effect the transfer of power into the hands of the people as a whole is the most crucial and immediate challenge facing the national democratic movement.

5. Despite the strategic advances made by the liberation movement, the regime still retains the capacity to implement countermeasures on a whole range of fronts. The white ruling group has entered the negotiations process with its own agenda: a radically reformed system of apartheid which will retain the essentials of white domination of the economic, political and social institutions of our country; its attempts to interpret agreements in a manner that would constitute surrender on the part of the ANC; delays in the implementation of agreements reached; and the systematic use of violence and other repressive measures against the people – all these are part of Pretoria's arsenal to weaken the ANC and its allies and derail the struggle for national liberation.

6. In the words of the OAU (Harare) Declaration, many factors are at play 'which, if there is a demonstrable readiness on the part of the Pretoria regime to engage in negotiations genuinely and sincerely, could create the possibility to end apartheid through negotiations'. Whether or not this process unfolds towards the desired end, depends primarily on the strength of the national democratic movement, the main function of which is the people in political motion.

II. Balance of forces

7. The mid-1970s witnessed the commencement of a process that has led to the passing of the initiative in Southern Africa from the

forces of colonialism and reaction, to those of national liberation and democracy. The defeat of Portuguese colonialism, the fall of the Rhodesian colonial regime and the decolonisation of Namibia have placed the seal of permanence on these changes. The Pretoria regime's campaign of destabilisation and blackmail against neighbouring states has exacted great dislocation and losses in the form of life and property. But it has failed to roll back the frontiers of African liberation. Today, South Africa is the only country in which white domination, rooted in the colonial past, is maintained.

8. The crisis of apartheid colonialism is also the result of concerted campaigns by peoples of the world against this system, and in solidarity with the struggling masses of South Africa. It is these mass-based campaigns which brought pressure to bear on the governments of Western Europe and Northern America to take some practical measures to isolate the apartheid regime. The limited sanctions, the cultural, academic and sports boycott, as well as disinvestment and pressure on financial loans were also influenced by the struggles within South Africa and the un-favourable economic climate resulting, in part, from these struggles. The status of the ANC among the peoples and govern-ments of the world has grown, and it is recognised by friend and foe alike as an alternative power within South Africa.

9. The collapse of a number of governments in Eastern Europe, and the crisis facing the socialist system has somewhat weakened the camp of forces opposed to apartheid. The fact that these coun-tries have been among the closest allies of the ANC and the struggling people of South Africa on its own warrants that the national democratic movement should draw relevant lessons from these experiences. This applies in particular to the question of rooting the anti-apartheid campaign among the mass of the people in all countries of the world. Related to this is the tendency among some governments to relax pressure on the apartheid regime. Such a measure can only have the effect of weakening the national democratic struggle and thus slow down

the process of peaceful transition to a new democratic order in South Africa. At the same time, the liberation movement must creatively utilise the positive developments in the international arena, such as the relaxation of tension among the developed countries, and the enhanced role of the United Nations Organisation.

10. The crisis of apartheid stems, first and foremost, from the objective contradictions rooted within this system. It is due to the system of capitalist exploitation based on colonial racial relations that the South African economy is today experiencing a deep structural crisis. While the system of super-exploitation of the black majority all along fully served the interests of big business and the state, this has become a brake on the development of the economy as a whole. Negative growth rates, low investor confidence, spiralling inflation, shortage of skilled personnel – all these are the fruits of apartheid. The problems of massive unemployment, shortage of housing, high prices and others, resulting from this crisis, cannot be resolved within the ambit of the apartheid system. The state and big business are neither willing to, nor capable of, curing these ills.

11. The struggles of the masses, led by the ANC, are the primary factor which has precipitated the crisis of apartheid.

11.1. The mass revolts of the 1980s were characterised by the following major factors:

- protests around day-to-day issues and united mass action consistently linked to the primary question of national liberation;
- mass uprisings in urban and rural areas challenging apartheid power relations and leading to the emergence of rudimentary organs of people's power;
- progressive merger between mass and armed actions reflected in street battles and barricades and the emergence of popular combat groups;
- emergence of sectoral democratic organisations such as the youth, students', women's and cultural organisations and

civics, and their coalition into a front for national democracy, the UDF;

- the emergence of a broad coalition of anti-apartheid forces on a minimum platform against tyranny and the effects of national oppression; and
- the growth of anti-apartheid forces within the white community, including elements close to the ruling establishment.

11.2. A crucial role in these developments was played by the African National Congress from the underground. This was complemented through the open contacts established with various antiapartheid forces and those elements who did not agree with all our policies but shared the desire to see to the normalisation of the situation on the basis of the eradication of apartheid. Increasingly, the ANC gained acceptance among forces opposed to apartheid as the leader in the struggle and the alternative to the present government.

11.3. The armed struggle waged by Umkhonto we Sizwe contributed immensely to the deepening of the crisis of apartheid. By giving the much-needed cutting edge to the mass uprisings, it helped to weaken the apartheid establishment and to mobilise the masses into militant action. The support armed struggle enjoyed among the oppressed people, and their growing involvement in various forms of armed activity, helped to shape the struggle towards becoming a generalised people's war against the apartheid regime.

11.4. It is a combination of all these factors which deepened the crisis of the ruling class. Faced with a subject population unwilling to be governed in the old way, the Pretoria regime resorted to repression and petty reform, in order to reassert its authority. All these attempts failed to quell popular resistance. This crisis of policy helped to deepen conflict within the white ruling bloc. Confusion and uncertainty within the white community, and desertion by leading ideologues of apartheid further undermined the ideological platform of the ruling group.

12. It is against the backdrop of these developments that the regime has been forced to introduce some changes. These changes constitute a strategic defeat for the apartheid regime and an open admission on its part that all its counter-revolutionary efforts, both inside and outside the country, have failed to suppress and crush the national liberation movement of our country. The strength and invincibility of this movement, the justice of our cause and the adherence of the overwhelming majority of our people to the democratic perspectives represented by our movement are being borne out by history.

13. The regime has completely failed to achieve its central objective of the perpetuation of white minority domination through the use of state terrorism. Its attempts to divide and weaken the oppressed through the balkanisation of the country and the conduct of a campaign of aggression and destabilisation in the sub-continent have not resolved the problems of apartheid. Nor have its earlier attempts to co-opt the oppressed people through the tricameral parliament, town councils and such so-called negotiations fora as the National Council and Great Indaba.

14. The liberation movement has set the stage and defined the agenda of the current phase of struggle. Having taken the initiative to define the terrain within which genuine negotiations should take place, the democratic movement also ensured that its approach enjoys the unanimous formal support of the international community, as reflected in the OAU (Harare) and UN General Assembly Declarations. However, it should be emphasised that the balance of forces which has made the beginning of negotiations possible is not necessarily one which can lead to a genuine resolution of the conflict.

15. While the liberation movement set the arena for the present phase and thus enjoys the strategic initiative, the balance of forces is not a static phenomenon. The regime seeks to minimise the impact of the general crisis of apartheid on itself, and to regain the strategic initiative. In fact, in the months particularly after the August 1990 Pretoria Summit between the ANC and the

government, the regime utilised the terrain of negotiations more effectively than the liberation movement. Combined with the devastating campaign of violence against African communities, this led to situations in which the liberation movement was losing the tactical initiative to the regime. This was compounded by the sense among the people and the international community that the talks and contact with the regime implied a de-escalation of struggle against apartheid. In this regard, 'talks-about-talks' and negotiations must be seen as a terrain of intense struggle.

16. The victories we have scored pose many challenges to the liberation movement. Objectively, we are operating under conditions in which most institutions of apartheid remain intact. The state machinery still possesses the capacity to wreak havoc. Resources of all kinds, including funds and the media, remain in the hands of a white minority establishment. Subjectively, our movement has not been fast enough in establishing its organisational machinery and adapting to the new terrain of struggle. To understand the essence of this terrain, it is necessary to examine the basic issues around which negotiations revolve.

III. Nature of South African society

17. The space won by the liberation movement and the possibility of negotiations do not change the essence of apartheid power relations. The South African regime remains a racist, colonial state, specifically created as a result of the pact concluded between British imperialism and the white settler minority in 1910. In spite of various modifications, its main characteristics remain. Firstly, it is a system of minority rule in which the black majority are by law excluded from the central organs of power. Except for some marginal delegated powers, political power is explicitly the monopoly of the white minority. Further, this system is rooted in the policies, traditions and practices of male domination. Secondly, it is based on the dispossession of the

indigenous peoples of their land and its wealth. The formal repeal of the Land Acts and commercialisation of ownership rights only entrench this act of dispossession. Thirdly, it is a system of labour coercion, based on the deliberate impoverishment of the African people and regulations designed to compel them to avail themselves as sources of cheap labour. Fourthly, it is a system in which access to productive capacity and property, as well as distribution of income, are racially defined, with the real property-owning class drawn exclusively from the white minority.

18. The principal beneficiaries of the system of race domination are the class of monopoly capitalists who control most sectors of the economy. Together, the top six companies account for almost 90% of all shares on the Johannesburg Stock Exchange. Because of the material benefits accruing to the white community as a whole and the ideology of white supremacy, the ruling class has over the years forged an alliance with other classes and strata within this community. The strain that has emerged within this alliance is a reflection of the economic and political crisis of apartheid: primarily, the increasing failure of the system to provide aplenty to the white community and to guarantee them all-round security. Sections of the white community, including forces within big business, have come to accept the need for fundamental change. Others are vowed to fight against this, as shown in the growth of right-wing parties and paramilitary organisations.

19. One of the chief elements in the regime's strategy has been to seek auxiliaries from among the oppressed themselves. The bantustan system was the first comprehensive attempt to create a caste of black junior partners to whom the regime would delegate some powers of social control and repression. Through the tricameral parliament and local government structures the regime has sought to expand the base of collaborators. It is a reflection of the depth of the crisis of the system, that more and more forces from the ranks of the bantustan and other local government functionaries have

abandoned the ship of apartheid and seek to align themselves with the democratic movement. These forces include elements within the civil service, the army and police, and therefore constitute an important loss to the regime.

20. The contradiction between the oppressed black majority and the white oppressor state is the most visible and dominant within South Africa. Conflict within our society derives from the system of oppression and exploitation. This contradiction cannot be resolved by the apartheid state reforming itself. Attempts by the ruling Nationalist Party to change its image and on that basis draw around itself a coalition of forces primarily from the black community are aimed at blunting this contradiction on a platform of modified white domination.

21. The sense of national grievance against oppression and the fight against exploitation constitute the driving force of the national democratic revolution. The liberation movement faces the challenge of harnessing these elements into a mighty force to sweep aside the apartheid state and create a united, non-racial and democratic society. Attempts by the regime and its allies to divert the masses from this reality, and to confine the terrain of debate and contest to areas conveniently defined by the champions of oppression and exploitation must be resisted.

IV. Character and forces of transformation

22. The victories scored by the democratic movement do not change the strategic aims of the struggle. Our central objective remains the transfer of power to the people as a whole, and the use of that power to construct a socio-economic system that will meet the aspirations of all the people of our country. The guidelines outlining the society we wish to build are contained in the Freedom Charter, a document which has become the property of the broad movement for democratic change. The broad perspectives the movement puts forward towards the realisation of these goals are:

22.1. The adoption, through negotiations in an elected Constituent Assembly, of a constitution based on the principle of one-person-one-vote in a united, non-racial, non-sexist and democratic South Africa.

22.2. The guarantee of the fundamental human rights of all South Africans, including their rights to life, liberty, language, culture, religion, freedom of the press and freedom from racial abuse. This will be underpinned by such means as an entrenched Bill of Rights, a multiparty system of government, a representative and independent judiciary and regular elections to all relevant organs of government.

22.3. The restructuring of the economy, as a mixed economy, to ensure that while it achieves high rates of growth, it also meets the fundamental needs of all the people by abolishing poverty and racial inequalities in the distribution of wealth. The economy must enable all the citizens of our country to enjoy a rising standard of living. This will demand of all sectors of the economy – state-owned, private, co-operative and others – to allocate resources and implement policies in keeping with this common national requirement.

23. The main content of the national democratic revolution is the liberation of the black people in general and Africans in parti-cular. The oppressed black masses objectively stand to gain from the victory of this struggle. Among this coalition of national and social forces, the African people are the most adversely affected by the policies of apartheid. Victims of armed conquest and land dispossession, and the chief object of racial policies, they carry the main burden of the edifice of white domination. The regime, in its counter-revolutionary schemes, has targeted the African people to foment divisions and weaken the liberation alliance in its entirety. To defeat these schemes demands a principled, creative and flexible approach on the part of the democratic movement. This demands of the African people that they take the lead in combating any notions of racial or ethnic chauvinism and create the basis for the emergence of a common South

African national identity.

24. The Coloured and Indian people are also victims of national oppression and share with the African people a desire for national emancipation. These oppressed communities are an integral part of the motive forces of the struggle. Over the years, through differential treatment, the white minority regime has sought to attach these communities to itself. The resounding rejection of these schemes by the Coloured and Indian people in struggle, is a fitting rebuff to the regime. Unity of the black people on the basis of unequivocal equality is a vital condition for the success of our struggle.

25. It has always been the view of the ANC that the system of apartheid is to the detriment of the South African people as a whole. The entrenchment of racial hatred and mistrust between black and white, economic dislocation, international isolation, subjection to the warped doctrines of racial superiority, constraints on human freedoms – all these affect the white community as well. The existence of an oppressed and restive majority is also a source of great insecurity; and whites cannot claim to be free and at peace when the rest of their country-men and women are oppressed. The insecurity among sections of the white community is compounded by the fact that the Nationalist Party is increasingly aligning itself with positions of big business to the relative detriment of the lower classes and strata of the white population. The ANC has consistently worked for the unity of all anti-apartheid forces, black and white, for the realisation of a future of democracy, peace and equality. The growth of the movement for democracy within the white community is an indispensable factor in the realisation of the victories scored by the liberation movement and for future advance. It is in the theatre of struggle that the foundation of the South African nation is being forged. As the genuine alternative to the apartheid system, the democratic movement must marry, in splendid combination, the tasks of forging black unity and consolidating the non-racial content of the struggle.

26. Various classes, strata and social groups constitute the coalition of forces struggling for national democracy. Black workers occupy a special place among these forces. As a class subjected to exploitation, and responsible for the creation of the greater part of social wealth, they will be among the chief beneficiaries of fundamental transformation. In the field of organisation and struggle, they have emerged as the leading force. Alongside them have been students, the rural poor, professionals, black business-people, traditional leaders and others. The ANC considers it crucial to organise and mobilise various sectors of the population – women, youth, the religious community, cultural workers and others – into active struggle against apartheid. While these forces occupy varied positions on the economic ladder, this does not subtract from the fact of their oppression as blacks. It is the task of the ANC to unite all these forces, on the basis of their specific grievances and a shared desire to rid our country of apartheid and all forms of inequality into a mighty force for national liberation.

27. These tasks are being carried out in a situation in which new possibilities have emerged for the widest organisation and mobilisation of the forces for fundamental change. Given the legal space conquered in struggle, the ANC must strive to reach out to all our people, black and white. The desire of the over-whelming majority for a peaceful transition, which the ANC is sincerely pursuing, affords the movement ever wider possibi-lities to assert itself as the force representing genuinely national patriotic interests. The movement must at all times exercise maximum creativity and take advantage of new possibilities to unite the people as a whole and speed up the process towards the creation of a just and peaceful dispensation which will be in the interest of all of society.

28. At the same time, new dangers have emerged, with the regime desperately seeking to win over as many people as possible to its camp. By attempting to present itself as a force for change, while weakening the forces of opposition, it hopes to undermine the

liberation struggle and reverse the popular gains achieved at much suffering and sacrifice on the part of the mass of the people. Underpinning the regime's approach is a perspective to impose, by hook or by crook, a constitution which entrenches apartheid in a new and disguised form. Attempts to limit the powers of a new government, and entrenchment of white privilege in property and land ownership and distribution of income, are cunningly designed cloaks under which to perpetuate the system of white minority domination. Their implementation will leave the lot of the black people unchanged. The democratic movement faces the challenge of ensuring that the struggle for fundamental change is not undermined or derailed by means of subterfuge, violence and any other actions by the forces in power.

V. Our approach to the transition

29. The historic period into which we have entered is one of transition from white minority rule to democratic government. As a result of the change in the balance of forces brought about by the national democratic movement and the struggling people as a whole, the possibility has emerged to effect this transition by peaceful means.

29.1. The strategic challenge this period poses is that, as much as the national democratic movement led and continues to lead opposition and resistance to apartheid, it must lead the process of transition to a democratic South Africa. We must not concede such leadership to the very same forces that are responsible for the establishment and perpetuation of the system of apartheid.

29.2. At the same time, the national democratic movement has a responsibility to ensure that the forces of reaction do not reverse the gains it has scored. The irreversibility of these achievements and the peaceful process as a whole, is a function of the strength of the democratic forces, primarily the masses in active struggle, and not the goodwill of those who continue to benefit from the system of apartheid.

29.3. It is in the true interest of the ANC and the masses of our people that transition to a democratic order should take place as soon as possible so as to end the apartheid system without delay. Speed is therefore an essential element in all our efforts to realise this objective. On the other hand, the representatives of apartheid are interested to draw out the process of change to give themselves time to evolve schemes intended to compromise the depth of the process of democratic transformation.

30. Our approach to the process of transition entails in the main:

30.1. The immediate and permanent normalisation of the political situation by an end to all forms of repression and protection of the people from all acts of violence. All hindrances to free political activity, which includes such normal democratic practices as the rights to demonstrate peacefully and to go on strike, must be removed. The process of normalisation includes the release of all political prisoners, ending all political trials, repeal of repressive legislation, the return of exiles and the termination of the practice of detention without trial.

30.2. The establishment of an Interim Government, acceptable to the widest spectrum of the people, to supervise the process of transition from white minority rule to a democratically elected government

30.3. The convening of a Constituent Assembly, elected on the basis of one-person one-vote on a common voters' roll, to draw up a new and democratic constitution for our country

30.4. An end to the campaign of aggression and destabilisation directed against the independent states of our region

30.5. A congress of all parties with a proven constituency should be convened to work out the broad and basic principles to underpin the new constitution as well as to agree on the modalities for the establishment of an Interim Government and a Constituent Assembly.

31. To achieve these objectives requires that the national democratic

movement marshal all anti-apartheid forces, both within the country and abroad, and defeat the schemes of the regime to tailor the transition in a direction suited to the interests of white minority domination. These schemes include attempts by the government to portray itself as the establishment best suited to supervise and direct the transition. At the same time, Pretoria is bent on weakening the national democratic movement by fomenting divisions within the democratic alliance, by attempting to delegitimise popular mass actions, side-lining the national democratic demands of the people by narrowing the terrain of political contest into confines defined by itself and by dividing the most oppressed African masses along ethnic lines.

32. The campaign of violence directed against the black population, which aims at fomenting fear and despondency among the people is also intended to weaken the democratic movement. Under cover of inter-communal conflict, generated primarily by forces within the state machinery, these forces have introduced devastating counter-revolutionary banditry characterised by selective as well as indiscriminate attacks against anti-apartheid forces and African communities in general. While some of the elements involved in this campaign seek to undermine the whole peace process, others aim at debilitating the liberation movement as a negotiating partner. It is crucial that the movement, using a multi-pronged strategy of political and military self-defence, reduces the capacity of the state to act against the people.

VI. Forms of struggle

33. The new situation demands a sober and balanced assessment of our approach to various forms of struggle as well as their inter-relationship. We have, in the past, under a different set of conditions, characterised our struggle as a protracted people's war in which partial and general uprisings would play an

important role. Led by the ANC underground, mass and armed actions were to dovetail and merge in a process leading to seizure of power, in which the armed element would occupy a crucial place. Does this approach still hold?

34. The answer to this question cannot derive solely from a belief in the integrity or otherwise of those in power. Neither can it be seen as a static phenomenon holding out for all time. The most crucial considerations in this regard are:

- the depth of the crisis gripping the apartheid system and the extent to which it compels the regime to act in good faith;
- our capacity to deepen this crisis and ensure that those in power are dissuaded from the temptation or intention to derail the process of peaceful transition;
- the concrete conditions under which we operate, the basic among which is the depth and spread of the atmosphere of free political activity;
- the methods used by the regime and other right-wing forces against the democratic movement and the people in general; and last but not least,
- the line-up of forces within the ruling white establishment, including individuals, parties, organisations and the army and police.

35. The ANC has entered the path of negotiations at our own initiative, and not as a tactic with some hidden agenda. We did so because a negotiated transition to a united, non-racial and democratic South Africa is not only desirable to our movement and people; but it has become possible, at the instance of all-round struggle on a variety of fronts. Negotiations are and should be about the transfer of power to the people as a whole and the democratisation of our society in all spheres of life. They therefore do not constitute a departure from the strategic perspective held by the liberation movement over the years. Rather, they are a result of struggle and a terrain of intense struggle for the final realisation of the strategic objectives of the national democratic revolution.

36. While in the past we pursued the objective of seizure of power, and pledged to enter negotiations if the situation arose, the approach today has definitely changed. We have entered negotiations as a viable mechanism for the transition to a new order, under the new situation, and we pledge to pursue the perspective of seizure of power – armed and/or otherwise – if the situation changes. Given the considerations outlined above, the situation is still fluid. The ANC cannot afford to sacrifice the aspirations of the millions of oppressed South Africans, the people of the region and the world, on the altar of wishful thinking and imagined possibilities. While we prefer a negotiated transition to a new order, it behoves the state and its allies to ensure that this becomes a reality.

37. How then does this affect the role of and balance among the 'internal pillars' of our struggle?

37.1. Central to our approach to the transition and to counter the schemes of defenders of white domination is our reliance on the mass of the oppressed and anti-apartheid forces. In as much as the victories we have scored are a consequence primarily of this approach, and to ensure that what emerges in the end reflects their basic interests, the people must be the engine of the transition and be seen to take active part at all possible levels. This demands the continual strengthening of the ANC and other democratic forces, and mobilising the people to express, defend and advance their point of view through mass action. Negotiations do not mean that the people should be immobilised. Rather, the legitimacy of the process itself and therefore the permanence of its results, will, primarily, derive from the involvement of the people at all levels.

37.2. As part of the struggle to advance the process towards a speedy political settlement, the ANC decided to suspend armed actions. However, the armed struggle has not been terminated. The enemy still has the possibility to re-impose the conditions which necessitated that we resort to this form of struggle. A democratic constitution has not yet been agreed upon, and the regime and other forces in the country continue to maintain their own armed formations. The ANC therefore has a continuing responsibility to maintain its own combat formations, organised in the people's army, Umkhonto we Sizwe. It has the responsibility to ensure people's self-defence at all times.

37.3. Most of the tasks that had to be carried out from the underground can now be conducted openly. But the atmosphere of free political activity has yet to be fully realised, both in general terms and in relation to various parts of the country. Further, possibilities still exist for the reversal of the process of peaceful transition. In this regard, the ANC is duty-bound to maintain such underground structures as present-day conditions and future possibilities demand. The supreme political responsibility for work conducted at all levels rests with the leadership structures of the ANC as defined in its constitution.

VII. Strategic tasks in the transition

38. The fact that we have entered into a period of transition to a democratic South Africa does not mean that the struggle has come to an end. The forces responsible for the establishment of the apartheid system continue to pursue their own objectives which do not originate from any mandate but their own self-seeking interests. A struggle is therefore inevitable between the perspectives represented by these forces and by the democratic movement.

39. The process of negotiations, at all its levels, represents a theatre of intense struggle. In this struggle, we aim to advance the demands of the mass of our people for the fundamental democratic transformation of our country. This form of struggle also requires that the movement should, at all times, keep close contact with the rest of the democratic movement and the people as a whole. The principle and practice of consultation, seeking mandates and reports-back must inform our approach to nego-

tiations, both within the ranks of the democratic movement and in relation to the mass of the people. Those elected to serve in a Constituent Assembly would themselves have been mandated by the people to present a set of demands that would have been canvassed during the election process.

40. The ANC must firmly take the lead in ensuring the earliest adoption and enforcement of a genuinely democratic, non-racial and non-sexist constitution. This is the principal theatre of struggle during the period of transition to a democratic South Africa. It revolves around the central question of the exercise of political power, the decisive element in any revolutionary struggle.

41. The fact of the changes brought about by the struggle does not change the reality that the apartheid structures of government remain in place. These structures, at all levels, from the national to the local, are illegitimate. They represent a continuation of the apartheid system of white minority domination and cannot be expected to act as institutions that would facilitate the transition to a democratic South Africa. The ANC should therefore take all the necessary measures to ensure speedy movement towards the establishment and proper functioning of an Interim Government. At the same time, the liberation movement must resist as well as avoid involvement in dispensations that would in practice entail its co-option into apartheid structures.

42. The achievement and defence of the democratic gains which enable free political activity is also of crucial importance to the struggle. This will ensure that the peace process moves forward as rapidly and as freely as possible towards the earliest adoption of a democratic constitution. The defence of these gains includes actions aimed at preventing the use of violence against the people. The ANC should therefore take all the necessary measures to contain and eliminate such violence and develop the necessary organisational structures for the defence of the people. This should entail a multi-faceted campaign which brings to the fore our strategic political strengths as a liberation movement

which seeks to unite the mass of our people for their own liberation, irrespective of their ethnic, racial and class origins. We must maximise the cost of such acts of banditry to the perpetrators and their allies.

43. The exercise of leadership in the transition also means that the ANC and the rest of the democratic movement must act more than just as a movement of protest. Already, during the mass revolt of the 1980s, the people had started to introduce alternative and popular expressions of government, education, culture, sports and so on. This task becomes even more crucial in the transition, and in a situation in which the balance of forces has shifted in favour of the democratic movement. It entails the building of people's organs from the lowest to the highest possible levels. It also means the clarity and foresight to put forward and implement viable alternatives in all spheres of life.

44. The ANC also faces the challenge of sharpening its strategy and tactics as well as strengthening structures pertaining to negotiations in the narrow sense. This means, first and foremost, ensuring consistent political leadership to our negotiating teams, the mastering, on the part of the movement as a whole, of the art and science of parley, ability to assess and utilise a given balance of forces to our fullest advantage as well as consistency and flexibility at the negotiating table. In order to ensure that we give leadership to the whole process, and not find ourselves responding to initiatives from the other side, we need to deploy such resources as are necessary to the area of negotiations and act with deliberate speed in the formulation of our policies and approaches to various issues.

45. The social forces interested in the democratic transformation of our country are composed of all the oppressed masses, including the majority of those who serve within apartheid state institutions. Also among these social forces are important sections of the white population, including the youth and students, the professional strata and significant sections of the business community. Our organisational work must enable us to reach all

these social forces in their millions, ensure that they understand and support the political perspectives of our movement and draw them into action as a conscious and organised force for the realisation of their aspirations. More attention than before needs to be paid to the organisation and mobilisation of the masses in the rural areas and bantustans, as well as the women and the youth. We must consciously transform into concrete support the sympathy and respect the ANC enjoys among functionaries within apartheid institutions, including the army and police. These forces must be made to feel that they have got a place and a future in the ranks of the anti-apartheid movement.

46. To carry out all the tasks relevant to the entire process of transformation, including the formation of a democratic government, the ANC has to build itself into a strong and well-organised democratic, non-racial and non-sexist mass movement, able to reach all our people throughout the length and breadth of our country. This task is urgent. Its successful accomplishment is decisive for peaceful transition and the victory of the national democratic struggle. The basic task facing the struggle remains the liberation of all our people. The ANC is not a political party, but a liberation movement. It must therefore remain the political home for all individuals interested in and committed to this future, without regard to ideological beliefs that are not in conflict with its basic policy positions and programme. At the same time, the ANC must rapidly develop to master all the methods of political contest that operation under conditions of legality demand. It must deliberately prepare itself for the different challenges of the transition and the future, including work in an Interim Government, elections into a Constituent Assembly and so on. However, this must not be allowed to infringe on the main character of the movement as an organisation of the people, pursuing their aspirations, rather than an elitist cabal. We should also ensure that the ANC and its allies do not behave in such a way that they are seen by the people as formations which they should fear, because of such wrong

methods of work as political intolerance.

47. The ANC has to encourage the formation and strengthening of independent, democratic mass formations of the people, including trade unions, civic associations, youth and women's organisations as well as other organisations representing various strata of our population, such as cultural workers, the intelligentsia, the business community and others. This is to ensure that all sections of the population are organised around the democratic perspective and are able to make their own independent intervention in the process of peaceful transformation of our country. The ANC should maintain a structured relationship with all these formations to ensure joint action in the common effort to bring about a just society. It is, however, in the interest of the ANC and the entire struggle that these formations should maintain their independence and operate on the basis of democratic practices determined by their members.

48. To ensure the widest possible organisation and mobilisation of our people for the achievement of the goal of a united, non-racial and democratic South Africa, the ANC must build and strengthen relations with organisations which share some or all of its policies and perspectives.

48.1. The closest allies of the ANC are the South African Communist Party (SACP) and the Congress of South African Trade Unions (COSATU). This principled and structured alliance, based on a shared commitment to, as well as the strategy and tactics for, the achievement of a united, non-racial and democratic South Africa, should be continually strengthened at national, regional and local levels. Forged in the theatre of struggle, and based on the recognition of the leadership role of the ANC, the tripartite alliance recognises and operates on the basis of the independence of its component parts and is shaped in accordance with the new conditions of legality in which we operate.

48.2. For the purpose of ensuring the fastest movement towards fundamental change, the ANC should work with all forces committed to the basic perspective of a united, democratic and non-racial South Africa in a structured broad patriotic front. This front should act together to effect the transition from white minority domination to democratic rule.

48.3. Furthermore, the ANC must identify and seek co-operation with other political and social formations within the country who, because of their opposition to apartheid, can enter into even limited agreements with the ANC, aimed at facilitating the process of peaceful transition, the dismantling of the apartheid system and the transformation of our country into a non-racial democracy. In the overall, we should ensure that all levels of the movement are well versed in the theory and practice of alliances, and conduct our work in this terrain in such a way that we do not undermine our own base.

49. The international community remains seized with the issue of the abolition of apartheid and the transformation of our country into a non-racial democracy. The ANC must continue its work to ensure that this community sustains its pressure for rapid movement towards the realisation of these goals. The maintenance of such economic sanctions as presently exist, and the all-round isolation of apartheid South Africa, are conditional upon progress in the eradication of the system of apartheid. We must work for the intensification of efforts by the international community to extend political and material support to the ANC, the rest of the democratic movement and the people as a whole, to enable these forces to realise the political and socio-economic objectives which are a necessary component part of the process of change.

VIII. Conclusion

50. South Africa has entered a decisive stage in the struggle for national liberation. The balance of forces both within the country and internationally favours a rapid movement towards the transformation of South Africa into a united, democratic, non-racial and non-sexist country. The strategy and tactics of the

ANC during this period of transition must ensure that this advance is as rapid as possible, leads to genuine democratic change and places the democratic movement in the vanguard of this process. At this critical and historic moment, the unity of the entire democratic movement around common perspectives and a common programme of action is of critical importance.

51. In this regard, the main tasks during the period of transition are:

51.1. A rapid advance towards the transfer of power to the people as a whole, through the adoption of a democratic constitution negotiated by an elected Constituent Assembly.

51.2. The establishment and maintenance of an Interim Government, acceptable to all the people, to supervise the transition to a democratic South Africa.

51.3. The defence of the democratic gains and the defeat of the efforts of the counter-revolutionary forces to take away the political space won through struggle.

51.4. The consolidation of the positions won by the democratic movement in all spheres of life, and its intervention to ensure that the masses increasingly run their own lives and improve their socio-economic conditions.

52. The optimism of the ANC constitutes a challenge to itself and the people in general to realise, sooner rather than later, the dream of millions of South Africans for freedom and democracy. It is primarily the strength of the ANC and its allies, including its ability to lead the people in active struggle, and not the integrity or otherwise of the forces in power, which will guarantee the success of the process of peaceful transition.

THE STRUGGLE CONTINUES!
VICTORY IS CERTAIN!
ALL POWER TO THE PEOPLE!

Document 21

**ANC National Consultative Conference:
resolutions for the coming year
December 1990**

On negotiations and suspension of armed actions

Preamble
Noting that:

1. Negotiation is only one form of struggle towards the transfer of power to the people for the creation of a non-racial, unitary and non-sexist South Africa.
2. Conference supports and endorses the negotiations strategy outlined in the Harare Declaration.
3. The international community has committed itself to supporting the broad principles, procedures and processes laid down in the Harare Declaration, through the relevant resolutions of the Organisation of African Unity, the Non-Aligned Movement and the United Nations.

Further noting that:

4. The regime has not yet removed obstacles contained in the Harare Declaration; namely
   - unconditional release of all political prisoners
   - unconditional return of exiles
   - repeal of all security and repressive legislation
   - termination of all political trials
5. Consequently the regime has failed and/or neglected to create a climate conducive to peaceful negotiation for a new constitution.

6. The current endemic violence creates further obstacles to the creation of a climate conducive to peaceful negotiation.

7. This violence is part of a deliberate attempt by the state and its allies to destabilise the ANC and to sow terror and chaos amongst our people; and believing that whilst the Harare Declaration remains our lodestar, it is not a dogma.

We therefore resolve:

1. To mandate the NEC to proceed with talks about talks and to invest them with discretionary powers, within the stated policies of the organisation, and without any secrecy and confidentiality, in the execution of their tasks with a view to creating a climate conducive to peaceful negotiations.

Further resolve that:

2. In the execution of these tasks the NEC should regularly consult with ANC membership in all regions, on all major issues.

3. Appropriate mechanisms be set up for such consultation and communication with the membership, by the end of 1991.

4. The NEC involves in the negotiation its revolutionary allies.

5. That a comprehensive negotiating team composed of chief negotiators, working groups, researchers be created as a matter of extreme urgency and that such teams include a fair representation of women.

And further resolve that:

6. The NEC serve notice on the regime that unless all the obstacles are removed on or before the 30th of April 1991, the ANC shall consider the suspension of the whole negotiation process. Prior to this date the ANC shall engage in a programme of mass action and all other actions, to achieve our objectives as quickly as possible. In the light of the endemic violence and the slaughter of innocent people by the regime and its allies we:

6.1 Reaffirm our right and duty as a people to defend ourselves with any means at our disposal.

6.2   We hereby serve notice on the regime that unless it ends this carnage, the ANC will find it difficult, if not impossible to adhere to the agreements entered into with the government, especially paragraph 3 of the Pretoria Minute pertaining to armed action and related activities.

Lastly Conference resolves:
1.   To mandate the NEC to take active steps to create people's defence units as a matter of extreme urgency for the defence of our people.

On violence

Noting that:
1.   The current violence sweeping our country is aimed at:
     (a) Undermining and destabilising the growth and consolidation of the ANC and all other democratic forces.
     (b) Ensuring that the government dictates the pace of transition in terms of its own agenda.
     (c) Creating a state of confusion and demoralisation in our own ranks and among our people in an attempt to alienate them from our movement.
2.   The violence is multifaceted and orchestrated through various agencies of the government viz. security forces, councillors, warlords, vigilantes, death squads, askaris and certain bantustan and white right-wing elements.
3.   This violence is part of a counter-revolutionary strategy to maintain white rule in new forms.

And believing that:
1.   The ending of the violence should be at the top of the agenda of the ANC and the entire democratic movement.
2.   There is no contradiction between the Pretoria Minute and our right to self-defence.

This Conference therefore resolves that:

1. Mass campaigns be embarked upon to pressurise the apartheid regime to bring an end to this carnage.
2. Such mass action be waged within the context of our demands for:
   (a) the removal of all obstacles to negotiations as embodied in the Harare Declaration
   (b) the dismantling of the bantustans and all other apartheid structures
   (c) an Interim Government and a Constituent Assembly.
3. The NEC, Regional Executive Committees, and branches to initiate, as a matter of urgency, the building of tight and disciplined defence committees and to ensure that the necessary resources are made available to these structures.
4. MK must play a facilitative role in the defence of our people.
5. Whilst in principle there is no opposition to talks with Inkatha and other surrogates of the regime, such talks must only take place after full consultations with all the regions of the ANC, particularly those immediately affected by the violence.
6. A consultative workshop be convened with our allies, the SACP and Cosatu, together with other democratic formations, as soon as possible to set up a joint programme of action.

On the underground and Umkhonto we Sizwe

We remain committed to the strengthening and growth of our people's army MK and the underground.

We therefore stand resolved:

   (a) to continue with the process of recruitment and training of our forces for the purpose of defending our people against enemy orchestrated violence and to prepare ourselves for a central role in a new army whose tasks will be to defend and uphold democratic values.

(b) that the NEC is directed to ensure that the welfare and future of MK cadres is carefully and fully discussed and catered for.

(c) to build the underground to guarantee that our movement does not suffer any serious set-backs.

(d) that it is a necessity for our movement to maintain and develop a network to carry out appropriate underground work.

(e) that the NEC must demand that the police must explain the disappearances and deaths of a number of our cadres throughout the country in particular the recent disappearance of Comrades Charles Ndaba and Mvuso Tshabalala and the cold-blooded murder of Comrades Welile Saaiman and Vukile Gondiwe.

On sanctions

- Cognisant of the necessity to counteract the growing perception that De Klerk and his government should be rewarded for recent reforms,

- aware that the basic institutions of apartheid are still firmly in place,

- that the South African government continues to use violence and police repression to suppress legitimate political and civic actions,

- alarmed over the orchestrated violence against defenceless citizens, especially in African residential areas, in which elements of the South African security establishment are deeply implicated,

- noting that many of the obstacles to genuine negotiations such as the Internal Security Act and others, remain in the statute books and are still vigorously enforced.

We resolve that the existing package be maintained.

As such the ANC appeals to the EC, US Congress, EFTA and all other international bodies to postpone any consideration of the issue of sanctions against apartheid South Africa until the ANC and all other democratic formations inside our country including trade unions and religious bodies initiate discussion with them on the issues.

On international isolation

We resolve that:

1. The existing sanctions campaign should be maintained.

2. The academic and cultural boycott should be reviewed with the aim of ensuring that it becomes inclusive of the many more institutions that genuinely promote principles of non-racialism, democracy and unity.

3. In the sporting arena, all efforts be made to promote the positions of the democratic sport organisations in regard to the moratorium of international competition; and on sports development programmes.

4. The socio-economic problems facing Black people in housing, education and health be urgently addressed by the government. The provision of these services is the responsibility of the government.

5. The ANC's political task is to mobilise the public in mass campaigns to pressure the authorities to fulfil their tasks.

6. A viable non-governmental organisation should be created to generate necessary economic resources inside the country, including those from the public sector to create project housing, education and health.

7. With regard to investment, we should direct potential investors to such efforts as the 'Viva Project' and which have the specific objectives of 'black empowerment' and redistribution of wealth.

8. We should oppose the lifting of financial sanctions, especially by the IMF, on the grounds that the country is still governed by a white minority regime.

9. We should offer to discuss the issue of trade sanctions with all affected interest groups in the country, including the trade unions, business organisations and the government with a view to addressing apartheid practices within the export sector and tying the easing of trade sanctions to specific commitments to abandon such practices.

10. For the obvious reason that the country is still ruled by a white minority regime, the arms embargo should remain.

11. Equally, the oil embargo should remain. We could relate this to another matter which has now been raised publicly, namely the sale of existing oil reserves, and the use of the money generated to address the socio-economic needs of the majority, under the direction of a properly representative interim government structure. This structure would then have the possibility to negotiate an agreement with foreign suppliers for the replenishment of the stock in a post-apartheid South Africa.

12. Urgent consultations be held with MDM organisations on the question of sanctions.

13. The ANC urgently organise and call an international summit as a follow-up to the Arusha Sanctions Conference to devise and consult on new strategies on sanctions.

14. The Commission considers the formulation of a contingency position on sanctions as tantamount to anticipating defeat on the issue.

15. A campaign against the recruitment of imported labour from Eastern European countries and Asia be immediately undertaken and be included in talks with the South African government.

Document 22

CODESA I – Declaration of Intent
21 December 1991

We, the duly authorised representatives of political parties, political organisations, administrations and the South African Government, coming together at this first meeting of the Convention for a Democratic South Africa, mindful of the awesome responsibility that rests on us at this moment in the history of our country, declare our solemn commitment:

1. to bring about an undivided South Africa with one nation sharing a common citizenship, patriotism and loyalty, pursuing amidst our diversity, freedom, equality and security for all irrespective of race, colour, sex or creed; a country free from apartheid or any other form of discrimination or domination;

2. to work to heal the divisions of the past, to secure the advancement of all, and to establish a free and open society based on democratic values where the dignity, worth and rights of every South African are protected by law;

3. to strive to improve the quality of life of our people through policies that will promote economic growth and human development and ensure equal opportunities and social justice for all South Africans;

4. to create a climate conducive to peaceful constitutional change by eliminating violence, intimidation and destabilisation and by promoting free political participation, discussion and debate;

5. to set in motion the process of drawing up and establishing a constitution that will ensure, inter alia:

    (a) that South Africa will be a united, democratic, non-racial and non-sexist state in which sovereign authority is exercised over the whole of its territory;

    (b) that the Constitution will be the supreme law and that it will be guarded over by an independent, non-racial and impartial judiciary;

    (c) that there will be a multi-party democracy with the right to form and join political parties and with regular elections on the basis of universal adult suffrage on a common voters roll; in general the basic electoral system, shall be that of proportional representation;

    (d) that there shall be a separation of powers between the legislature, executive and judiciary with appropriate checks and balances;

    (e) that the diversity of languages, cultures and religions of the people of South Africa shall be acknowledged;

    (f) that all shall enjoy universally accepted human rights, freedoms and civil liberties including freedom of religion, speech and assembly protected by an entrenched and justiciable Bill of Rights and a legal system that guarantees equality of all before the law.

WE AGREE

1. that the present and future participants shall be entitled to put forward freely to the Convention any proposal consistent with democracy.

2. that CODESA will establish a mechanism whose task it will be, in co-operation with administrations and the South African Government, to draft the texts of all legislation required to give effect to the agreements reached in CODESA.

We, the representatives of political parties, political organisations and administrations, further solemnly commit ourselves to be bound by the agreements of CODESA and in good faith to take all such steps as are within our power and authority to realise implementation.

SIGNED BY:

African National Congress	National Party
Ciskei Government	National People's Party
Democratic Party	Solidarity
Dikwenkwentla Party	South African Communist Party
Inyandza National Movement	Transkei Government
Intando Yesizwe Party	United People's Front
Labour Party South Africa	Venda Government
Natal / Transvaal Indian Congress	Ximoko Progressive Party

We, the South African Government, declare ourselves to be bound by agreements we reach together with other participants in CODESA in accordance with the standing rules and hereby commit ourselves to the implementation thereof within our capacity, powers and authority.

Signed by Mr F. W. de Klerk for the South African Government Nkosi Sikelel' iAfrica. Ons vir jou Suid-Afrika. Morena boloka sechaba sa heso. May the Lord bless our country. Mudzimu Fhatushedza Africa. Hosi katekisa Africa.

Document 23

Memorandum from Nelson Mandela to F. W. de Klerk
26 June 1992

Introduction

1. The Declaration of intent which we adopted at Codesa I
    committed us to the establishment of a 'democratic South Africa'.
    On the basis of this commitment many would have been led to
    believe that it would have been possible to overcome many
    obstacles in the path of realising this goal.

2. Our country is on the brink of disaster. First there is the crisis in
    the negotiation process itself. The central blockage stems from
    the refusal of the NP government to move together with all of us
    in the process of truly democratising South Africa. Secondly, the
    continuing direct and indirect involvement of the NP govern-
    ment, the state security forces and the police in the violence as
    well as your unwillingness to act decisively to bring such violence
    to an end has created an untenable and explosive situation.

3. The NP government persists in portraying the crisis as a creation
    of the ANC. This attitude is unhelpful and extremely dangerous.
    The NP government is placing party political interests above
    national interests by trying to minimise the seriousness of this
    crisis.

4. Attached to this memorandum is the statement of the National
    Executive Committee of the ANC adopted at its emergency
    meeting held on the 24th June, 1992 (marked annexure 'B'). This
    statement explains the basis on which the ANC has decided to
    break off bilateral and Codesa negotiations. It contains a set of
    specific demands addressed to the NP government in connection

with the critical issues around which the negotiation deadlock arises, as well as those relating to the violence ravaging our country. We are of the view that the response and concrete steps by your government to these demands will play a critical role in determining the direction and pace with which bona fide negotiations can take place. For its part the National Executive Committee has resolved to monitor the developing situation on a continuing basis.

In what follows in this memorandum we first address the crisis in the negotiation process, and then proceed to look at the issue of violence.

The negotiations crisis

1. The crisis in the negotiations process arises, primarily, from the fact that the NP government has been pursuing the path of embracing the shell of a democratic South Africa while seeking to ensure that it is not democratic in content.
2. In my letter to you written from prison in 1989 I outlined the kernel of the political problem which the government and the ANC would have to address in order to resolve the SA conflict through negotiations. I stated:

Two political issues will have to be addressed. . . . Firstly, the demand for majority rule in a unitary state; secondly, the concern of white South Africa over this demand, as well as the insistence of whites on structural guarantees that majority rule will not mean domination of the white minority by blacks.
The most crucial task which will face the government and the ANC will be to reconcile these two positions.

In this context I added that:
Majority rule and internal peace are like two sides of a single coin; white South Africa simply has to accept that there will never be

peace and stability in this country until the principle is fully applied.

3. The crux of the deadlock in the negotiations process lies in the failure of the NP government to face up to the need to reconcile these two issues.

4. In the first place, you have chosen to reject internationally accepted democratic principles which define a democracy. You have chosen to equate majority rule, which is the quintessential hallmark of democracy, with black domination.

5. In the second place, you have interpreted 'the concern (and) . . . insistence of whites on structural guarantees that majority rule will not mean domination of the white minority by blacks' to mean establishing a white minority veto (often concealed in intricate formulae).

   Instead of engaging in a constructive exercise of finding ways to address white concerns you continually slide back to white supremacist mechanisms.

6. There can be no movement forward as long as you seek to reconcile the two issues I have outlined through any form of minority veto. Such solutions may well address white concerns, but they are guaranteed to leave majority concerns frustrated. This is a recipe for in-built instability and makes peace unrealisable. For as long as the NP government insists on a minority veto in whatever form, the negotiations deadlock will remain unresolved.

7. The ANC, for its part, has rigorously kept to the need to reconcile the above-mentioned two issues. This is evident in the manner in which we have handled negotiations as well as the way in which we have developed our substantial positions.

8. Thus we advanced the idea that we should formulate and agree on a set of general constitutional principles at Codesa. These principles, which would be binding on the Constituent Assembly, would, to a certain degree, reassure all parties as well as the people of our country, black and white, of a democratic outcome.

9. Along this direction we took on board any suggestions and ideas

as long as they could be accommodated and were consistent with internationally accepted democratic principles. We commit ourselves to one-person-one vote elections on the basis of proportional representation to ensure that every political formation which has any degree of support would have a place in the Constituent Assembly.

10. In our view constitution making should be a unifying and legitimising process which should enjoy overwhelming support. Hence we advocate that the constituent assembly should arrive at decisions by a sixty-six and two-thirds percent majority.

11. In South African regional differences have been fostered by the apartheid system. Irrespective of whether they arise from ethnic factors or vested interests nurtured by the apartheid fragmentation of our country, we sought to accommodate these regional differences. We therefore proposed that the Constituent Assembly should further:

    (a) Be elected by all the people of South Africa, defined as all those whose citizenship could be traced to the boundaries of South Africa as at 1910.

    (b) Be composed of 50% of the delegates elected by means of a national list and 50% elected on the basis of a regional list, both on the basis of proportional representation.

12. Have special procedures for deciding on clauses of the Constitution dealing with regional structures and their powers and duties. That is, the Constituent Assembly as a whole would first decide on such issues by a sixty-six and two-thirds percent majority. In addition such a decision would further require an additional sixty-six and two-thirds percent majority by that half of the delegates to the Constituent Assembly who are elected on the regional list.

13. It is our firm view that the Constituent Assembly be a single chamber body with sovereign powers. The only constraints on it would be:

14. The general constitutional principles agreed upon through the negotiation process.

15. The pre-determined mechanisms to break any deadlock in the Constituent Assembly should it fail to decide on a Constitution within a relatively short time-frame. In our view a short time-frame is essential in order to prevent our country from drifting in uncertainty and instability.

16. The NP government positions have been directed basically at subverting the sovereignty of the Constituent Assembly, subjecting it to the veto of a second house and ensuring that a minority in the Constituent Assembly shall be able to frustrate an overwhelming majority.

17. The NP government's determination to impose a minority veto is also manifest in seeking to make interim government arrangements permanent. Our interim government proposals were fashioned so as to further address minority concerns in a way that would take our country into a democratic order. In our proposals for the transitional period we have further sought to address the concerns of the white people and of minority political parties. You persist in converting these proposals into entrenched constitutional arrangements. This constitutes another effort at destroying the sovereignty of the Constituent Assembly.

The government and violence

1. The negotiations crisis and the issue of violence, particularly with regard to the NP government's involvement in it, are inter-related and impact on each other. Our demands, emanating from the Emergency Session of the National Executive Committee meeting held on the 24th June 1992, are specific and pointed. They relate to the security forces and the police including the use of SADF detachments composed of foreign nationals. They also relate to government's failure to implement agreements made almost a year ago with regard to measures aimed at curbing the violence.

2. The Boipatong massacre on the 17th June, 1992 is but a tragic

culmination of policies and practices followed by the NP
government. In this instance the wilful negligence on the part of
the South African Police in relation to the KwaMadala hostel is
extensively documented. Attached hereto is a letter and
memorandum from Attorneys Nicholis, Cambanis, Koopa-
sammy and Pillay dated the 23rd June, 1992 (marked annexure 'A')
and addressed to Mr Cyril Ramaphosa.* Ministerial defences of
the SAP and your government's failure to act against the
KwaMadala hostel make government collusion an inescapable
conclusion.

3. It is your government which legalised the carrying of dangerous
weapons under the pretext of their being cultural weapons in
1990. The fact that the majority of the deaths and injuries have
been caused by these so-called 'cultural weapons' has not moved
you to restore the ban on carrying them in public on all occasions.
How do we explain the failure of such a formidable force such as
the SAP to arrest people involved in the massacre?

In those few instances where security force personnel and
police, or IFP members have been arrested, how do we explain
the fact that inadequate police investigation is the basis for their
acquittal, laughably light sentences and ridiculously low bail? You
cannot but be aware of the judge's comment when he acquitted
the 7 in the recent Sebokeng trial. How is it possible for you to
ignore the observations of the judge and the evidence of the
investigating officer in the Trust Feed massacre trial which
showed extensive cover up, and the frustrating of investigations
by numerous highly placed officers in the SAP? Recently the
Minister of Police sought to obtain a Supreme Court injunction to
prevent the *Weekly Mail* from publishing a report on the existence
of a highly clandestine police network in the Southern Transvaal
region. The report showed that such covert operation networks
existed in 11 regions into which the Police have divided our
country. Furthermore these covert operation were directed not

---

* *This long annexure has not been included in this volume – H. E.*

against increasing criminal activities as alleged, but against activists and local leaders of the ANC and the democratic movement. Is the effort to obtain an injunction not proof enough that such covert operations are being carried out at the present moment? The evidence shows that either the NP government, even at its top most levels, sanctions such activities or that it is powerless to restrain the very forces it created.

4. At the root of the violence is apartheid and its legacy. All religions recognise that reconciliation requires confession and repentance. I have avoided imposing such requirements in the hope that you and your government would reach that recognition on your own.

5. We believe that your failure to acknowledge and recognise the centrality of apartheid with regard to the issue of violence can no longer be ignored. This is particularly so because the NP government persists in attributing the carnage in the black townships to black political rivalry.

6. In this regard the Second Interim Report of the Goldstone Commission provides a useful point of departure. This report notes that the causes of violence are many and complicated. The report outlines a number of the causes without ordering them in terms of their relative importance. Many of the causes in that report can be categorised in terms of apartheid and its legacy.

7. The Goldstone Commission Report is unequivocal:

The economic, social and political imbalances amongst the people of South Africa. These are the consequences of three centuries of racial discrimination and over 40 years of an extreme form of racial and economic dislocation in consequence of the policy of apartheid. (par 2.3.1. of the Report)

The Report is equally clear on the legacies of apartheid:

A police force and army which, for many decades, have been the instruments of oppression by successive White governments in maintaining a society predicated upon racial discrimination. . . .

For many South Africans, the police and the army are not perceived as fair, objective or friendly institutions. (par 2.3.2.)

A history over some years of State complicity in undercover activities, which include criminal conduct. . . . That and the well documented criminal conduct by individual members of the South African and KwaZulu Police exacerbate the perception of so many South Africans that the Government or its agencies are active parties responsible for the violence. . . . Government has failed to take sufficiently firm steps to prevent criminal conduct by members of the security forces and the police and to ensure that the guilty are promptly and adequately punished. (par 2.3.7)

8. The failure or refusal of the government, which is the sole architect and enforcer of apartheid, to acknowledge that apartheid and its legacy lie at the root of the violence is also inexcusable. You ignore the reality that the security forces and the police are the products of apartheid, have been trained in the ideology of apartheid, deployed in its defence, brutalised by that experience, and nurtured to see the ANC, its allied organisations and black people in general as THE ENEMY. You would have the public believe that such an army and police have undergone a Damascan conversion as a result of your proclaiming that 'apartheid is dead'. Recently the Goldstone Commission recommended that Battalion 32 which is made up of foreign nationals not be deployed in unrest areas. Yet on the 24th of June, 1992 the Chief of the Army, Lt General George Meiring, arrogantly ignored this recommendation by announcing that Battalion 32 will continue to be deployed in Black residential areas.

9. This basic failure by you and your government induces you to perceive the political rivalry between the Inkatha Freedom Party and the ANC as the central cause of the violence. Once more you consciously turn a blind eye to the fact that your government used millions of rands of taxpayer's money to foster such rivalry. The Inkathagate scandal stands as proof of your complicity and bias in

this regard. Your rendering military training to IFP members at a number of bases is also abundant proof of your involvement.

Conclusion

1. None of us can escape the gravity of the crisis facing our country. The point has been reached where your responses will be looked at by us to determine whether you are taking concrete measures to terminate forthwith the involvement of the NP government, the state security forces and the police in the violence. We draw your attention to the demands contained in the statement of the National Executive Committee of the ANC in this regard.
2. Similarly, specific measures are expected of you to make negotiations a bona fide exercise in charting the way to a democratic South Africa, in particular that the future of our country shall be determined by a popularly elected and sovereign Constituent Assembly.

Our demands are the minimum measures required of your government if it is to establish a credible base for resolving the impasse our country has reached.

26th June 1992
Johannesburg

Annexure B

AFRICAN NATIONAL CONGRESS DEPARTMENT OF INFORMATION AND PUBLICITY: STATEMENT OF THE EMERGENCY MEETING OF THE NATIONAL EXECUTIVE COMMITTEE OF THE ANC 23 JUNE 1992

The National Party regime of FW de Klerk has brought our country to the brink of disaster. Riddled with corruption and mismanagement, the regime is determined to block any advance to democracy. It pursues a strategy which embraces negotiations, together with systematic covert actions, including murder, involving its security forces and surrogates. This supervision of political processes to destroy the democratic movement in South Africa led by the ANC cannot be allowed to prevail any longer.

We cannot tolerate a situation where the regime's control of state power allows it the space to deny and cover up its role in fostering and fomenting violence.

The Boipatong massacre is one of the most chilling instances of the consequences of the actions of the FW de Klerk regime. Before the people of South Africa and the bar of international opinion it cannot escape culpability.

What is at issue is more than the crisis of the negotiations process. *The fundamental reason for the deadlock is whether there is to be democratic change, or white minority veto powers.* There is only one way forward. It is a road which must unmistakably and unequivocally lead to the establishment of a democratic South Africa.

To this end it is necessary that the De Klerk regime agrees to:

- The creation of a democratically elected and sovereign Constituent Assembly to draft and adopt a new constitution; and
- The establishment of an Interim Government of National Unity which is the only way all South Africans will recognise that the country shall have moved decisively to end white minority rule.

Demands on the regime

The regime must immediately end its campaign of terror against the people and the democratic movement. *In this regard it must immediately carry out the following measures*:

- Terminate all covert operations including hit squad activity.
- Disarm, disband and confine to barracks all special forces as well as detachments made up of foreign nationals.
- Suspend and prosecute all officers and security force personnel involved in the violence.

- Ensure that all repression in some of the self-governing states, and in the so-called independent states, is ended forthwith.

Our people are compelled to live in a perpetual state of fear – be it in their homes, on their way to work, in trains and taxis, at funerals and vigils, at their places of work and entertainment. This is the stark reality. Between July 1990 and April 1992 there have been 261 attacks on township residents by hostel inmates, which led to 1,207 deaths and 3,697 injuries.

The ANC demands that the regime implements agreements to curbing violence reached with the ANC almost a year ago, in particular:

- The immediate implementation of the programme to phase out the hostels and convert them into family unit accommodation.
- Installation of fences around these establishments.
- Guarding of these hostels by security forces on a permanent basis, monitored by multi-lateral peace structures and the expulsion of those who occupy the hostels illegally.
- Regular searches of hostels with the participation of multi-lateral peace structures.
- Banning the carrying of all dangerous weapons in public on all occasions including so-called cultural weapons.

We insist that the regime agree to:

- The implementation of the universal demand requiring at least the establishment of an International Commission of inquiry into the Boipatong Massacre and all acts of violence as well as international monitoring of the violence.
- Release all political prisoners forthwith.
- Repeal all repressive legislation, including those laws which were so hastily passed during the last days of the recent session of parliament.

Call to the people of South Africa

The crisis caused by the regime constitutes a challenge to all South Africans to unite in a broad movement for democracy, peace and justice now. We all, black and white together, share the responsibility to stop the regime from plunging our country into chaos and anarchy. The ANC shall consult all formations with a view to holding a summit to unite and mobilise our people against continued white minority rule and for democracy. Unity and disciplined struggle remain the surest basis for realising peace and stability.

We call on the entire people of our country, including the business community, to join in observing 29 June as a National Day of Mourning and solidarity with the victims of the Boipatong massacre as the dead are buried.

Appeal to the international community

The National Party regime is acting in contempt of the wishes of the international community for a speedy end to apartheid.

Now, more than ever, the international community is required to compel the De Klerk regime to bring violence to an end and to commit itself to solutions based on internationally accepted democratic principles.

In consultation with sporting bodies, we shall be reviewing the forthcoming international sports engagements involving South Africa.

We appeal to the United Nations Security Council to convene as a matter of urgency to undertake measures which will help stop the violence and reinforce our efforts aimed at bringing about democratic order.

We call on the international community to act in solidarity with our people on the day of the funeral of the victims of the Boipatong massacre, June 29. In particular we appeal to all workers throughout the world not to handle South African carriers and goods on this day.

Negotiations

The ANC reaffirms its commitment to a negotiated resolution of the conflict in our country which would bring about democracy, peace and justice. The refusal of the regime to accept such a settlement compelled the NEC to review the current negotiations process.

The ANC has no option but to break off bilateral and Codesa negotiations. The NEC will be keeping the situation under continuous review. The response and practical steps taken by the De Klerk regime to these demands will play a critical role in determining the direction and speed with which bona fide negotiations can take place.

The decision taken today will be conveyed to the regime by ANC President Nelson Mandela as soon as possible.

Issued by the Department of Information and Publicity,
P.O. Box 61884, Marshalltown 2107

23 June 1992

Document 24

Dear Mr Mandela

I acknowledge receipt of your memorandum dated 26 June 1992. However, an exchange of memoranda is no substitute for face-to-face talks. I was therefore disappointed that you did not accept my invitation to immediate discussions. Every day that is lost will make the resumption of the process more difficult and may lead to the loss of further lives.

Annexures A–F contain observations relevant to issues raised in your memorandum and elaboration on issues dealt with in this letter. There are however a number of fundamental issues which need to be addressed urgently at a meeting between us.

1. Violence

Contrary to the ANC's accusations, the Government has not, and will not plan, conduct, orchestrate or sponsor violence in any form whatsoever against any political organisation or community. The lie that the Government is sponsoring and promoting violence remains a lie no matter how often it is repeated. Where elements in state structures err in this regard, the Government will not hesitate to take appropriate measures. There are prosecutions and convictions on record to prove this.

The second interim report of the Goldstone Commission showed that the causes of violence are numerous and complicated. The fact remains that most political violence occurs between supporters of the

ANC and the IFP. This question must therefore be urgently addressed by the leaders of the ANC and the IFP, and the Government, in view of its responsibility for the maintenance of order. I therefore propose that you, Dr Buthelezi and I meet as soon as possible for this purpose. The agenda for this meeting could be to consider:

- an active full-time monitoring mechanism on the adequacy, efficacy and performance of all the instruments and processes already in place to combat violence and intimidation; and
- the advisability of a joint monitoring body through which the three parties could act to defuse and solve problems that could give rise to violence. The role of the international community in an observer capacity could be considered, especially in relation to this item.

2. The ANC's programme of mass mobilisation

The South African Government acknowledges the right of peaceful demonstration and protest as important civil liberties. However, the ANC Alliance's campaign of mass mobilisation, owing to its nature and aims, poses serious threats to the stability and safety of the whole of South African society, particularly in the current volatile climate.

Furthermore, the use of this kind of mass mobilisation to make and impose demands in the negotiation process is just as unacceptable as the use of violence for this purpose. Our information indicates that the SACP and COSATU have played a dominant role in redirecting the ANC from negotiations to the politics of demands and confrontation which are inherent in mass mobilisation.

Insurrectionist thinking is currently flourishing within the ANC and is being propagated by a cabal with close links to the SACP and COSATU. These elements undermine the attempts of many ANC realists to negotiate in good faith and also induce within the ANC the spirit of radicalism and militancy of the insurrectionist school, which was evident at the SACP's 8th congress in 1991.

The ANC/SACP have been trying to create the impression that they and the South African Government are the only adversaries. This is patently misleading and wrong since there are numerous players on the South African political scene, each with an own identity but opposed to the ANC/SACP policies and methods. The ANC's rhetoric has been radicalised and is now virtually indistinguishable from that of the SACP, and so are the ultimatum and polarisation politics now being conducted. In recent days this rhetoric has degenerated into incitement to violence and hatred at grass-roots level.

The current mobilisation action can unleash forces which the instigators will not be able to control. This will, in turn, make extended government action unavoidable. The programme of mass action, in the prevailing circumstances, will inevitably:

- lead to further violence;
- delay the search for democratic solutions;
- damage the economy, on which all South Africans depend; and
- seriously disrupt social services to the detriment of those in need of medical care, protection, support and education.

The Government does not seek confrontation and has repeatedly stated its belief that negotiations present the only viable option for the solution of our problems. However, it will not hesitate to take all steps necessary to prevent the country from sliding into anarchy. Any change of government must come in a negotiated constitutional manner. The stated ultimate goal of the ANC's mass mobilisation campaign is to overthrow the Government by coercion. This will not be countenanced.

3. The ANC's aborting of the negotiation process

You say that you have withdrawn from the negotiating process because of the Government's involvement in violence and its lack of commitment to genuine democracy in the negotiating process.

Your allegations about Government involvement in violence have already been dealt with.

With regard to your allegations concerning the Government's

commitment to genuine democracy, I should like to refer you to the substantial agreements already reached in the Working Groups of Codesa. The fundamental difference between the approach of the ANC and that of the Government regarding the purpose of negotiation lies, on the one hand, in our commitment to constitutionality and a transitional government as soon as possible; and on the other hand, in the ANC's insistence on an unstructured and immediate transfer of power before a proper Transitional Constitution is negotiated.

Even after Codesa 2, our approach to transitional arrangements was again explained to ANC representatives. Our proposals are in line with universally accepted democratic principles. A summary of our approach can be found in Annexure 'F', and in Annexure 'B' allegations that the Government is clinging to power are conclusively refuted.

Once again, the remaining differences between the ANC, the Government and other political parties on key constitutional questions make multi-party negotiations more – and not less – imperative.

4. ANC 'demands'

In our view what you are presenting as demands are issues that are being tailored by the ANC to support its programme of mass mobilisation and to justify the abortion of the negotiation process. All these issues could have been suitably discussed at the negotiation table and it is imperative that such discussions do take place to remove any misconceptions and misunderstanding. It should be recorded that some of these have already been dealt with by way of agreements, or have been dealt with by governmental measures. Annexure 'E' contains observations in this respect.

However we would like to comment in particular on the hostels and dangerous weapons.

The problems relating to the hostels have been the focus of much concern and attention, but, as you are aware, it is an extremely complex situation and although extensive deliberations and consultations have already taken place, much work remains to be done. This is therefore an issue that we would like to be given particular attention at our proposed meeting.

As regards dangerous weapons, weaponry and explosives measures have been taken and adopted regarding the carrying and possession thereof. These measures will be strictly enforced. Further regulations about the possession and carrying of dangerous weapons are currently under consideration.

The carrying and possession of dangerous weapons should receive attention when we meet, but particular attention must be given to the implementation of measures relating to the illegal possession of fire-arms and explosives, and the introduction of such weapons into the country. The AK47 has become the symbol of criminal and political violence and firearms are the weapons mainly used to kill political opponents and to perpetrate criminal violence. Ways and means must be found to ensure that this problem is resolved and we must discuss this issue when the leaders of the Government, the ANC and the IFP meet. Until integral part of the problem of violence that it can no longer remain solely on a bilateral agenda [sic].

I reiterate the Government's commitment to peaceful negotiations as the only way to bring us to a new democratic constitution as soon as possible. I repeat my proposal that we should meet urgently for fundamental discussions, especially on the abovementioned four issues.

Yours sincerely
F. W. DE KLERK

Annexure A

THE CURRENT INFLUENCE OF MARXISM-LENINISM WITHIN THE ANC

1. Despite initiatives to become more independent, the SACP still has a close relationship with the ANC, which not only enables its members to constantly influence ANC strategy, but creates a climate conducive to radical and militant thinking during a phase in which negotiation and reconciliation should be a priority. In fact, the SACP lends so much support to initiatives to influence and even transform the ANC, that it seems that its independent profile serves only to draw attention away from its primary revolutionary strategising role within the ANC.

2. It is clear that the SACP, COSATU and individuals within the ANC still pursue outdated tactical communist doctrines and objectives. The question arises whether the ANC is not becoming a captive of these forces. The SACP furthermore still regards a socialist system as only a necessary phase towards realising an eventual communist system. It should be obvious that these objectives and the prominent position of their proponents within the ANC cast doubt on the real character of the ANC.

3. There can be no doubt that both the SACP and COSATU were, in their individual and collective capacity, instrumental in a number of recent crucial ANC decisions regarding the negotiation process. These decisions followed intense deliberations between SACP and COSATU members and were clearly the result of specific guidelines drawn up by the SACP/COSATU. The following examples are relevant in this regard:

   - The ANC's decision to implement a programme of mass action in order to force the Government to meet certain bottom lines and/or to transfer power to the ANC.
   - The ANC's attempts to deadlock Codesa.
   - The ANC's decision to suspend negotiations notwithstand-

ing opposition within both the NEC and the so-called
Codesa PF.

4. As South Africa moves towards a new democratic order, the
strategy and policy of various revolutionaries within the ANC
Alliance are increasingly in conflict with internationally accepted
norms. For example, to regard negotiation in principle as a
'terrain of struggle' undermines the essence of the concept itself.
In the final instance it gives rise to concern that the ANC allows
these influences to flourish when these forces are already
committed to extra-parliamentary struggle against the new
dispensation that the ANC is propagating. This extraordinary
approach underlines the fact that revolutionary ethics generally
overrule all other principles, and are therefore incompatible with
democracy.

Annexure B

PERCEPTIONS REGARDING THE NEGOTIATION PROCESS

1. When the process of negotiation was initiated by the Government, it was clearly stated that its aim was to extend democracy to
the whole of the South African nation. It was also made clear that
a fundamental and sincere policy decision had been taken by the
governing National Party, fully endorsed by its supporters and
many others, to remove racial discrimination, to abolish apartheid
and to be instrumental in the establishment of a constitutional
state in the new South Africa in which all citizens would be equal
and justice would reign supreme.

2. This approach will require a restructuring of government and
society on an immense scale. Hardly any sphere of life, any
element of administration or any aspect of politics has been or
will be left untouched by the processes of constitutional change. It
would therefore be irresponsible to advocate less than an orderly,
albeit urgent, *process of transition* from present structures,

administrations, politics and processes to those of a responsibly negotiated new dispensation. That is why, as a first priority, the Codesa negotiation process focused on transitional arrangements whereby those not now represented in government could become involved.

3. The ANC, on the other hand, has been advocating a sudden plunge, virtually without preparation, into simple majoritarianism. The Government responsibly insists upon the replacement of the present dispensation with a fully functional and comprehensive Transitional Constitution providing for proper curbs on the misuse of power during the sensitive period of transition to an eventual constitution. It appears that the ANC wants to avoid proper checks and balances on a 'Constituent Assembly', which, according to a fair construction of the ANC's views, will function in a constitutional void after the destruction of the present dispensation. To accede to such a demand founded on revolutionary thinking would be irresponsible on the part of the Government. The unreasonableness of the ANC in this regard is the real obstacle to progress in constitutional negotiations. Further negotiation on the details of a transitional dispensation with the purpose of extending democracy to all South Africans and to bring social and economic stability to the nation, must be the priority of negotiating parties having the well-being of all South Africans at heart.

4. Given the initiatives that the Government has taken over the past years and the structures created, financed and managed for the purposes of sober negotiation and the restoration of social peace, it is invidious and entirely unconvincing to accuse us of attempting to cling to power in an undemocratic manner. After all, we express our proposals for a transitional dispensation in terms of *power sharing* and fully accept that such political parties as may be capable of demonstrating substantial support in a democratic election, must not merely be present in the decision-making processes, but must also have meaningful influence under a transitional constitution.

5. The progress that was made in the various working groups of Codesa is indeed impressive even in summary. Key elements of agreements which were endorsed by the ANC negotiators as well, include the following:

- 'A climate for free political participation is an essential element of the transitional phase towards and in a democratic South Africa'. (Working Group 1 Report, par 6.1.2.1)
- Political intimidation must be terminated. This means 'any action or set of actions committed by any. . . organisation . . . that is designed by the use or the threat of use of force or violence to disrupt or interfere with the legal rights of an individual, inter alia . . . the right of freedom of movement'. (Working Group 1 Report, par 7.2)
- A reaffirmation of the National Peace Accord. (Working Group 1 Report, par 10)
- 'Political parties and organisations should have fair access to public facilities and venues without discrimination'. (Working Group 1 Report, par 14)
- Codesa should draw up a transitional constitution. (Working Group 2 Steering Committee Proposal of 13 May 1992)
- The Transitional Constitution should provide for a bicameral Parliament elected by universal adult suffrage, proportional representation being the basis for the election of one Chamber: a multi-party executive: the separation of the legislative, executive and judicial powers: a justiciable Charter of Fundamental Rights and the establishment of the boundaries, powers, duties and functions of a regional government structure and its entrenchment in the Transitional Constitution. (Working Group 2 Steering Committee Proposal of 13 May 1992)
- The establishment and detailed structuring of a Transitional Executive Structure for the purposes of preparing the

ground for the institution of a transitional dispensation was fully agreed upon by Working Group 3.

- The principle of and some details concerning the re-incorporation of the TBVC states was agreed upon by Working Group 4.

6. The Government at all times made it clear that it was willing and eager to support and promote progress in the negotiation process, whereas the ANC has lately derailed Codesa 2, reintroduced 'mass action' to a tense and suffering society as a form of 'struggle', and is now making demands in a threatening manner apparently in order to coerce the Government into irresponsible concessions that could not be negotiated with the parties in Codesa.

7. An honest analysis of the events leading to the present impasse makes it clear that the ANC is responsible for obstructing the negotiation process, which was progressing extremely well until shortly before Codesa 2. It would appear that the ANC found shortly before Codesa 2, that such progress did not serve its political purposes, and therefore insisted upon driving Working Group 2 to a point where agreement to its proposals or none at all in the whole of Codesa was demanded. The ANC's perception, it would seem, was that its purpose of an unqualified take-over of power would not be served by the reasonable agreements in Codesa that were ready to be sealed.

8. The Government firmly believes in democracy. We maintain that democracy entails universal adult suffrage and majority decision-making procedures. However, to suggest as the ANC does, that simple majority decision-making is the sole essential feature of modern democracy, is over-extending the notion. A far more fundamental feature of modern democratic states is the extent to which all citizens enjoy meaningful participation and fair representation in government institutions.

9. It is not democratic to attempt to deny meaningful political segments of society access to assemblies tasked with the determination of their future. Furthermore the Government does not

accept the ANC's reduction of South African politics to a battle between Black and White. This reduction ironically exposes the ANC's approach to be founded upon outdated racial considerations.

10. The perception that the road to democracy is simple, is a dangerous one. The approach that mere majoritarianism is sufficient will not bring peace to our land. It is the Government's opinion that participation and representation, and not majority domination, however structured, are the building blocks of a democratic future. In a country whose human wealth lies precisely in the diversity of its population, the exclusion of significant minority political parties from decision-making regarding a matter as fundamental as the terms of a future constitution would be courting disaster.

11. Modern democracy goes beyond the mere identification of the majority: it is equally concerned with the protection of minorities against possible excesses of the majority. Universally acknowledged constitutional mechanisms like bicameralism, regional autonomy (federalism), effective proportional participation in government by all significant parties and enforceable and justiciable fundamental rights entrenched in the constitution, serve precisely the purpose of curbing majority domination. It is significant that the Government has been advocating these and the other elements of the constitutional state, while the ANC was prepared to derail Codesa 2 on the grounds of rejecting such mechanisms of modern democracy which had virtually been agreed upon for the transitional dispensation.

12. A healthy and responsible administration constructed on the basis of the effective representation of all meaningful political parties and providing for their participation in the process of government is surely in the national interest. On the other hand, a constitution in which politically meaningful elements of society had no say, would in all probability lead to political instability of no mean proportion. The ANC seems to be bent on such a disastrous outcome.

Annexure C

THE ANC AS A NEGOTIATING PARTNER

1. The Government believes that a sound foundation for at least a mutually acceptable process was laid at the Groote Schuur and subsequent bilateral agreements which, besides reflecting a clearly identifiable spirit, also contained the following:

   - 'The Government and the ANC agree on a common commitment towards the resolution of the existing climate of violence and intimidation from whatever quarter as well as a commitment to stability and to a peaceful process of negotiations' (Groote Schuur Minute).
   - 'Both parties committed themselves to take steps and measures to normalise and stabilise the situation, within the spirit of mutual confidence that exists between the leaders. . . .' (Pretoria Minute).
   - 'The right of the broad population to make their views known through peaceful demonstrations'.
   - It was further agreed that violence and intimidation, from whatever quarter, that form part of mass action, should be eliminated.
   - Further agreed that peaceful political activities and stability should be promoted (DF Malan Accord).

Despite these agreements and the spirit in which they were concluded, the ANC at regular intervals started using threats and ultimatums as part of its political approach, which from the start had a detrimental and erosive effect on the mutual trust that was beginning to develop. The ANC do have a bad track record in maintaining agreements and can be considered an unreliable negotiating partner.

2. Therefore the decision of the ANC NEC of 24 June 1992, in collaboration with its Alliance partners, to suspend negotiations, is viewed as only the most recent of a range of similar past decisions which further contributed to the creation of negative

perceptions regarding the ANC's approach to negotiations per se and as a process. The perception that has been created includes indications that:

- The ANC is committed to negotiations only to the extent that its own objectives are served.
- The ANC readily enters into agreements but is not committed to supporting the practical implementation of such agreements.
- The ANC is using extremely coercive negotiation tactics, including ultimatums, deadlocks, threats, reneging on agreements, and projecting unrealistic time-frames, etc., almost every time it becomes apparent that genuine compromise on a give-and-take basis is in the offing.

3. The South African Government remains responsible for the maintenance of law and order in South Africa. It is however a truism, conveniently disregarded in the ANC's statements, that to disrupt law and order is simple, but to restore and maintain it with finite resources, is always problematic. Therefore the Government is concerned about the high level of violence in certain parts of our country. The Government regards existing bilateral (Groote Schuur Minute, Pretoria Minute, D F Malan Accord) and multi-lateral (National Peace Accord, Declaration of Intent) agreements as important instruments in preventing and curbing the violence and finding permanent solutions to the problems facing South Africa. The Government endorses the contents of these agreements. Nothing will however be achieved without mutual trust existing between the parties. The ANC and its allies have violated these agreements, the following being examples:

Paragraph 2.4 of the National Peace Accord states as follows:

All political parties and organisations shall respect and give effect to the obligation to refrain from incitement to violence or hatred. In pursuit hereof no language calculated or likely to incite violence or hatred, including that directed against any political party or personality, nor any wilfully false allegation, shall be used at any political meeting, nor shall pamphlets, posters or other written material containing such language be prepared or circulated, either in the name of any party, or anonymously.

In contravention of this agreement numerous inflammatory statements have been made by many ANC leaders, especially in the recent past. Language likely to incite violence and hatred is constantly used. False allegations are made and pamphlets and posters contravening these agreements abound.

For the period November 1991 to June 1992 the ANC was responsible for 186 recorded breaches of the National Peace Accord and the D F Malan Accord.

4. The ANC, by starting planning for mass action even before it became clear that a deadlock might develop at Codesa, reneging on all Working Group agreements on the basis that there was no agreement if all agreements were not accepted, as well as suspending negotiations, cannot but further compound the already negative perceptions surrounding the organisation's approach to negotiations.

5. From these and other decisions and actions by the ANC, in conjunction with its Alliance partners, it can only be deduced that the ANC is indeed negatively viewing negotiations as an 'area of struggle', and even as a battle in the 'struggle' that must be won at all costs. If this is indeed the case, then it is clear that in the ANC's current view of negotiations there is no room for compromise, much less for mutually acceptable agreement.

Annexure D

VIEWS ON THE CURRENT VIOLENCE

1. The South African Government remains responsible for the maintenance of law and order in South Africa. It does, and has been doing, everything possible within its power and within the

existing political climate to address this scourge that has
descended on our country.

2. The Government is however not the only role player in this
    regard. It is the responsibility of every individual, organisation,
    party and leader (whether political or otherwise) to strive for
    stability.

3. The appalling events at Boipatong on 17 June 1992 have once
    again shown that the situation in South Africa is highly volatile
    and accompanied by a vicious spiral of violence and counter-
    violence.

4. The Government wishes to state categorically that, contrary to
    ANC claims, the Government does not plan, conduct, orchestrate
    or sponsor violence in any form whatsoever, against any political
    organisation or community.

5. The time has come for the ANC in particular, but also for other
    political groups, to recognise the fact that policies aimed at
    gaining a monopoly on power in themselves promote violence.

6. The Second Interim Report of the Goldstone Commission of
    Inquiry quite correctly stated that the causes of violence are
    numerous and complex. However the ANC has to date not
    acknowledged its involvement in violence, and as far as the
    Government is aware has consequently taken little constructive
    action to curb violence. As a matter of fact, the ANC is guilty of
    selective quoting from the above report. It never refers to criti-
    cism of the ANC by the Commission but uses the Commission to
    put the blame for violence on other parties. The Government
    takes a serious view of the criticism in the Goldstone Commission
    report, but expects the ANC to do the same.

7. The question may also be asked: to what extent does the ANC's
    non-compliance with the various accords, in particular the
    National Peace Accord, contribute to the web of violence in which
    South Africa is entangled? On the other hand the Government
    regards the existing bilateral and multi-lateral agreements,
    especially the National Peace Accord and the Codesa Declaration
    of Intent, as important instruments for curbing violence and

finding permanent solutions to the problems facing South Africa and its people.

8. The ANC's direct and indirect involvement in the creation of a climate conducive to violence gives rise to the question whether the ANC was ever fully committed to the National Peace Accord, in particular to paragraph 2.4 which reads as follows:

All political parties and organisations shall respect and give effect to the obligation to refrain from incitement to violence or hatred. In pursuit hereof no language calculated or likely to incite violence or hatred, including that directed against any political party or personality, nor any wilfully false allegation, shall be used at any political meeting, nor shall pamphlets, posters or other written material containing such language be prepared or circulated, either in the name of any party, or anonymously.

In this regard the following statements by prominent ANC leaders are highly revealing:

- Mr Harry Gwala admitted that the ANC is fighting a war and that the ANC is killing IFP 'warlords' and their associates (*Natal Witness*, 29 April 1992).
- On 26 April 1992 Mr George Mathusa (Chairman of the ANC in the Western Transvaal) vowed that Bophuthatswana would be made ungovernable through necklace killings and bombs. Addressing people at a funeral service Mr Mathusa said: 'In South Africa we did it through our necklaces and bombs, we can easily repeat it here'. (*Cape Times*, 27 April 1992).
- In *The Citizen* of 23 May 1992 it is reported that Mr Nelson Mandela said in Helsinki that President De Klerk was involved in the violence in which almost 1 000 people in South Africa have been killed this year. Mr Mandela told a news conference that it was a serious responsibility to accuse a Head of State of fuelling the violence and the killing of

innocent people, but that facts indicated that President De Klerk was involved in this.

- In *The Citizen* of 25 May 1992, it was stated that Mr Mandela, in Geneva, likened the violence in South Africa to the killing of Jews in Nazi Germany.
- On 16 June 1992 at the Dan Qeqe Stadium, Zwide, Port Elizabeth, Mr Harry Gwala stated inter alia: 'If the only way to our freedom is through bloodletting, so let it be and if we all perish let that happen'. He said those who believed the time for armed struggle was over were seriously mistaken, ... (*EP Herald*, 17 June 1992).

9. The Government recognises that the ANC's suspension of armed action on 6 August 1990 was taken in the interest of a peaceful transition in South Africa. Unfortunately, this has had no marked effect on violence. Since the suspension of armed action, numerous cases of MK involvement in establishing self-defence units and renegade self-defence units, as well as armed crimes by MK members, have occurred. Numerous ANC arms caches – in violation of the provisions of the DF Malan Accord – still exist. For example 13 MK arms caches have been uncovered since 2 February 1990. Considering the well documented lack of discipline that MK members have demonstrated, both locally and in foreign countries in the past, the Government must inevitably ask whether the ANC still has any control over arms caches and how many of the murder weapons presently being traded to the highest bidder, originate from ANC caches.

10. The Government finds it contradictory that the ANC's answer to violence is the formation of so-called self-defence units, which eventually become uncontrollable, as in the case of Phola Park. It is well known that these self-defence units are themselves major contributors to violence.

11. Another urgent matter is the question of how many incidents of violence can be ascribed to ANC members masquerading as members of the Security Forces. Taking the two recent incidents in this regard into account, the question also arises whether

actions such as these are official ANC policy or reflect a lack of control over ANC members.

12. The ANC owes the people of South Africa an explanation for the extreme forms of violence perpetrated against its own dissenting members in detention camps. Since South Africans were involved and since Codesa (Working Group 1) has interested itself in this issue, all investigations and findings, notably the ANC's own commission's report, should be tabled – preferably at Codesa.

13. The ANC's history of violence, and its murder of innocent civilian men, women and children, its barbaric extra-judicial 'necklace' executions, the torture and murder in its detention camps and its total disregard for the consequences of mass action, remove whatever moral base it may have had to point fingers at others concerning the violence. Most of the perpetrators of the atrocities mentioned are still at large and the dossiers are still open.

14. It is clear, in order to escape their own involvement in violence, that the ANC blames other political parties, the Government and the Security Forces for the violence. What is particularly reprehensible is to blame the State President – the very man who started the negotiation and National Peace Accord processes.

15. There is a clear strategy of discrediting the Security Forces. This statement is made due to the following supporting facts:
   - Complainants in criminal cases are often influenced by the ANC not to co-operate with the SAP.
   - Unfounded allegations are presented as facts to create the perception that the SAP, in particular, is biased and takes part in violent action.

16. In conclusion, the ANC has to account for its direct and indirect involvement in the more than 30 000 incidents of violence since February 1990, and the murder of over 6 000 persons during the same period. Likewise the ANC must also answer the question as to what extent its calls for attacks on Security Force members in the 1980's, and which have never been withdrawn, contributed to the deaths of over 90 members of the SAP in acts of violence since January 1992 alone.

17. When is the ANC going to transform itself from a liberation movement to a conventional political party, and thereby shed its image as a violent organisation?

Annexure E

THE DEMANDS OF THE ANC

1. How the interruption of the negotiation process can be brought to an end, how the demands of the ANC can be dealt with to achieve this end, and how the negotiation process can be structured so as to ensure progress and avoid similar interruptions in future, are matters that should be discussed and deliberated upon at the proposed meeting between the ANC and the Government. What follows are observations about certain aspects of the statement of the ANC on 23 June 1992, and of the Memorandum of 26 June 1992 from Mr Mandela to Mr F W de Klerk.

2. All the information at our disposal points inevitably to the conclusion that factions within the SACP and the ANC were not happy with what was being negotiated at Codesa and that they initiated, before Codesa 2, a strategy to abort the negotiation process by deliberately creating a deadlock and by reverting to the pursuance of their own goals by way of what is euphemistically called mass action, but what is in reality physical confrontational action. This is our perception of what has happened and this is the only interpretation that can be placed on 'demands' backed up by threats to completely destabilise South Africa if these demands are not met. In our view, mass mobilisation and activation with the war-talk presently being built into these can only be described as reckless given the existing climate of violence.

3. A second leg of this strategy is that at the same time the ANC has also been using mass action and confrontational politics to mobilise support when they registered that their support base was dwindling. This has been happening in spite of the ANC's

undemocratic and violent isolation of areas they have taken control of, against all other political parties or viewpoints. They simply do not seem able to adjust to a democratic political process where the people are allowed to listen to the points of view of all the other parties and then to make up their own minds whom they would like to support. We have experienced the violent excluding actions of the ANC and have been informed that these were not isolated incidents but firm policy. Many examples of such 'no go' areas for other political parties can be cited.

4.   Observations on Aspects of the Memorandum:

4.1   Par 1.2 to 1.5 (The Government is blamed for the crisis in the negotiation process and accused of minimising the crisis):

The Government is not trying to minimise the seriousness of the situation. We are convinced that the ANC / SACP tried to engineer a crisis. What other interpretation can be placed on the withdrawal of the ANC from Codesa and from bilateral negotiations? That is how a crisis is created, not how it is solved.

4.2   Par 2 (The Government is accused of ignoring democratic principles and of trying to build a white minority veto into the political process and constitutional structures):

The constitutional negotiation process leading up to the ANC-created deadlock is dealt with in another annexure. What follows are examples of inconsistencies in the Memorandum:

2.5   According to figures of the Development Bank of South Africa approximately 23 million people will be able to vote in 1993 in an election for a constituent assembly / transitional government. Of those only 4 million (17%) will be white voters who will probably be voting for different parties. How can a 70 or 75% majority requirement possibly amount to a white veto?

2.6   Here the deadlock is attributed to the Government's supposed insistence on a minority veto (whatever that may mean); but the ANC itself is proposing a sixty-six per cent majority. There is therefore agreement on the principle that a constitution should not be created by a mere majority but should rather have 'overwhelming' support.

2.10 to 2.13 Here the ANC aligns itself behind the principle that constitution making should be a unifying and legitimising process which should enjoy overwhelming support. This is the guiding principle underlying the Government's approach to the process. This is why the Government wants as many parties and interests as possible to be part of the constitution-making process. The product of the process, the new constitution, must be accepted and supported by all; it should not be a constitution enacted by a majority in a constituent assembly elected on party political issues.

4.3 Par 3 (The Government is blamed for all violence and [read with the NEC statement] accused of pursuing a strategy embracing negotiations together with systematic covert action, including murder, involving security forces and surrogates):

Nothing in this whole paragraph even attempts to support the bizarre and completely unfounded opening sentence of the ANC Statement. The whole paragraph is blatant propaganda rhetoric containing factual inaccuracies and distortions. Thus it is not true that the majority of deaths have been caused by 'cultural weapons'. There is also a distorted description of police investigations, while the ANC itself has been intimidating Boipatong residents from talking to the police. The ANC has also not once fulfilled its obligation under the Peace Accord to assist the police in their investigations when ANC members have been involved in atrocities. Compare this with the numerous instances when the criminal acts by security force members were investigated, prosecuted and punished. Apartheid is blamed for the current violence, while the ANC's history of political intolerance and violence and atrocities against mainly black political opponents over more than a decade is ignored. The difference is that the Government has rid itself and the country of apartheid but the ANC has not been able to adjust to democratic political competition.

4.4 Par 3.3 (The Government is blamed for legalising the carrying of dangerous weapons)

In terms of the National Peace accord the parties agreed that no weapons or firearms may be possessed, carried or displayed by members of the general public attending any political gathering, procession or meeting. The Government has subsequently honoured its obligation in terms of the National Peace Accord by issuing the relevant proclamations after consultation with political parties, i.e. the ANC and IFP. On 28 February 1992 a prohibition was issued in terms of Section 2(2) of the Dangerous Weapons Act, 1968, prohibiting any persons attending or participating in a political gathering at any public place to be in possession of any dangerous weapon which clearly includes traditional weapons.

Other steps taken by the Government are as follows:

- On 19 March 1992 a further prohibition was issued in terms of the Dangerous Weapons Act, 1968, prohibiting a person from being in possession of any dangerous weapon at any property of the South African Rail Commuter Corporation Limited. Objects, including so-called traditional weapons, which are to be regarded as dangerous weapons, are explicitly listed.
- Various prohibitions concerning dangerous weapons were issued under the Unrest Regulations in terms of the Public Safety Act, 1953. Provision was also made for an additional substantial prohibition with regard to spears.
- The Government is presently preparing draft regulations in terms of which the possession and carrying of all dangerous weapons at any public place may be absolutely banned. As the need may arise these regulations will be implemented in areas declared to be unrest areas.

5. The demands

In preparation for the discussion of the demands, the following observations are made and need to be dealt with in such discussions:

- The Government will do whatever it can, without departing from its principles and ideals, to get negotiations, both bilateral and in Codesa, on track again.
- Fourteen issues have been identified:

Re the issues of a constituent assembly and an interim government of national unity. In Codesa complete agreement was reached on the broad structure of transitional arrangements, including a transitional executive council, an independent electoral commission and a constitution-making body within the framework of an elected transitional government. The Government has therefore already agreed in Codesa together with the other parties, to that which is now demanded. What the Government was not prepared to agree to was an appointed, as opposed to an elected, interim government. If there are any misunderstandings on these issues, the Government would like to discuss these when we meet.

Re the issues of covert operations, special forces, prosecution of Security Force personnel and repression in Self-governing States. These demands are introduced with a general demand that the 'regime must immediately end its campaign of terror against the people and the democratic movement'. This is a demand that cannot be met simply because there is no such campaign of terror: and the ANC knows this. The Government is however agreeable to discussing once again the specific issues mentioned, but will also want to discuss the ANC's own contribution to political and other violence and to explore ways and means of bringing that to an end.

Re the issues concerning hostels. The Government is concerned about the hostel situation and has therefore approved a comprehensive hostel strategy. The aim of this strategy is to create humane living conditions for the hostel dwellers by means of upgrading the hostels or converting them into family units. The upgrading/conversion will however be based on consensus reached after negotiation between the hostel dwellers, surrounding town residents, the owners and all other concerned parties such as political groupings, civic organisations, trade unions, employers etc. A peaceful resolution of the issue is therefore not possible without consensus amongst the parties directly involved at local level. In its memorandum to the Government, the ANC attached a document dealing with the problem of the KwaMadala hostel and in which many allegations were made against a number of individuals and organisations. It is clear that factual disputes will arise. As the Goldstone Commission is currently investigating the Boipatong incident, it is suggested that any findings concerning these allegations be left to the Commission.

Re the issue of dangerous weapons. The carrying of dangerous weapons has already been dealt with but can be further discussed. The Government would also want to discuss the application of measures to counter the illegal possession of all dangerous weapons, including fire-arms and explosives, and ways and means of stopping the introduction of such weapons into South Africa and of ensuring that such weapons are not used in the perpetration of political and criminal violence. Contrary to the ANC's allegations, these are mainly the weapons used to kill political opponents and to perpetrate criminal violence.

Re the issues of international involvement, 'political prisoners' and 'repressive' legislation. Although grouped together by the ANC, these demands concern three separate issues, two of which, namely 'political prisoners' and 'repressive' legislation, have already been the subject of extensive agreements. These two can nevertheless be further discussed and so can the third issue, namely ways and means of arriving at the truth about the Boipatong massacre and other acts of violence: and ways and means of preventing such occurrences in future together with the role the international community can play in this regard. With regard to these issues the Government would like to elaborate as follows:

International involvement

The Goldstone commission charged with investigating the Boipatong case involved international assistance to assess and evaluate. The Government wishes to reiterate its abhorrence of all the events surrounding the Boipatong incident and trusts that justice will prevail in the shortest possible time. At the same time the Government wishes to express its grave concern over newspaper reports to the effect that witnesses were instructed not to co-operate with the SAP in its investigation.

Political prisoners

The Government has fulfilled its obligations under the various agreements resulting in the release of a very large number of prisoners. What is now disputed is the release of a number of prisoners who have committed common law crimes such as murder and whom the Government maintains fall outside the ambit of the agreed definition on guidelines for identification of political prisoners. Yet the Government (and the ANC) have agreed at Codesa working Group 1 that a task group consider the identification of such prisoners, and the definition of 'political prisoners'.

Apart from the above, the Government and the ANC have been involved over a long period in bilateral talks on a number of issues identified as far back as the Pretoria Minute, which should and could be finalised in one single agreement with a multilateral effect, including the disputed prisoners; the lack of indemnity for MK and senior officials of the ANC; the future of MK; and the arms caches. Ancillary issues such as the question of treatment of former detainees in ANC camps abroad and whether such camps still exist will possibly have to be addressed.

'Repressive legislation'

Working Group 1 has made extensive unanimous recommendations in regard to security and emergency affairs at Codesa 2. The ANC's inexplicable delaying tactics are keeping these issues alive. The Government can not possibly abrogate its duty to govern and to take steps to reduce the level of violence, intimidation and crime. In this regard reference is made to legislation passed recently in Parliament, pertaining inter alia to illicit trafficking in arms and ammunition, usurping police and military powers, violence and intimidation, drugs and drug related crimes.

6. In conclusion, withdrawing from negotiations, especially from Codesa, cannot contribute to the resolution of any of these issues. The Government is only one of nineteen parties in Codesa. How can the ANC justify the deliberate wrecking of Codesa by putting demands to the Government? What better forum is there for

putting its demands, if this is what it really wants to do, than Codesa itself.

Annexure F

Government proposals regarding a transitional constitution for South Africa

PRINCIPLES GOVERNING A TRANSITIONAL DISPENSATION

- The Transitional Constitution must be a complete constitution.
- The Transitional Constitution must effect the fundamental replacement of the principles of the current Westminster system with those of a Constitutional State.
- The diversity of interests existing in the South African community must be accommodated in the Transitional Constitution.
- The further restructuring of the second and third tiers of government must be facilitated by the Transitional Constitution.
- The Transitional Constitution must satisfactorily underpin the maintenance of order and stability.

MAIN FEATURES OF A TRANSITIONAL CONSTITUTION

The following are the main elements of the Transitional Constitution proposed by the government:

- A parliament consisting of a National Assembly and a Senate
- An executive Council directly elected by all the voters
- A Cabinet appointed by the Executive Council
- An independent judiciary, with judges being appointed by a non-political body
- A justiciable Charter of Fundamental Rights
- Autonomous regional government
- Autonomous local government

- Special provisions regarding the following functionaries and institutions in order to safeguard them against political manipulation:
  - The South African Defence Force
  - The South African Police
  - An independent Auditor General
  - An independent Ombudsman
  - An independent Commission for Administration
  - The entrenchment of constitution-related legislation (such as electoral laws, laws concerning the courts and laws applicable to the Public Service) and of other laws such as those relating to existing pension rights and laws regulating standards for public offices and professions.

REPLACEMENT OF THE TRANSITIONAL CONSTITUTION

- For the amendment or substitution of the Transitional Constitution a majority of 70% will be required and 75% for the Charter of Fundamental Rights.
- If the Transitional Constitution has not been replaced within three years, a general election will be held in terms of the Transitional Constitution.
- The Transitional Constitution will be amended or replaced only within the framework of general constitutional principles as agreed upon at CODESA, and the Constitutional Chamber of the Appellate Division must certify this to be the case.

The following must, inter alia, be enshrined as general constitutional principles:
- The autonomy of civil society, i.e. the exclusion or interference by the state in the affairs of civil society, such as sport, culture, professional life, religion, trade unionism and traditions.
- Democratic standards to which political parties must conform.

The Transitional Constitution must itself also be drafted within the framework of the agreed general constitutional principles, including the above.

PARLIAMENT

The National Assembly

- The Transitional Constitution will provide for a National Assembly vested, together with a Senate, with legislative powers as well as the power to amend and replace the Transitional Constitution by special majorities.
- The National Assembly shall be elected proportionally by universal adult suffrage according to the party list system.

Senate

- The Transitional Constitution will provide for a Senate. An equal number of members will be elected from each of the electoral regions that will be delimited for this purpose, using the development regions as the point of departure. Seats are allocated to a region in proportion to the party support in that region.
- Legislation may be initiated in the Senate and all laws must be approved by both Houses. The Transitional Constitution will provide for mechanisms for the resolution of differences between the Houses as well as for exceptions in regard to specific subjects in respect of which the powers of the Senate may be upgraded or downgraded (e.g. financial laws, laws relating to education or specific regional matters).
- When the Transitional Constitution is amended or replaced, the boundaries of each region and its functions, powers and form of government will also have to be approved by a majority of the representatives from each electoral region that will be affected in each case.

REGIONAL GOVERNMENT

- There will be regional governments in the transitional dispensation. Agreement must be reached regarding the powers, functions and boundaries of regions and regional governments prior to the coming into operation of the Transitional Constitution. Should the process of the full establishment of the regional dispensation delay the implementation of the Transitional Constitution, the finalisation of the boundaries and the implementation of aspects of the system of regional government may be left to the Transitional Parliament.

- If some of the present regional authorities still exist when the Transitional Constitution comes into effect, they will continue to exist for the time being; provided that a TBVC state may participate in the transitional dispensation by undergoing a transformation of status beforehand from independent state to self-governing territory.

- The autonomy of regions will consist in their powers, functions and boundaries being derived originally from the Transitional Constitution and will not be subject to amendment without the concurrence of the authorities of the regions concerned.

Document 25

Response by Nelson Mandela to De Klerk's 2 July 1992 memorandum
4 July 1992

1. I have received the response of Mr F. W. de Klerk to a memorandum which I addressed to him on the 26th June 1992. I enclosed the statement of the Emergency meeting of the National Executive Committee of the ANC adopted on the 23rd June, 1992.

2. In my Memorandum and the statement of the ANC we pointed out that South Africa is on the brink of disaster for which we hold the NP government entirely responsible. Specific and concrete demands were made to Mr F. W. de Klerk as a means of finding a way out of the impasse.

3. These demands related to two crucial aspects:

3.1 Firstly, the deadlock in the negotiating process because of the refusal by the NP government to move together with all of us in the process of truly democratising South Africa. Our fundamental position in this regard is that we cannot accept an undemocratic constitution aimed at addressing the fears of a minority party about its own future at the cost of democracy. This is at the root of the negotiations deadlock. It is for this reason that we focused attention on the Constituent Assembly. We are clear in our demands that the NP government abandon positions directed at subverting the sovereignty of the Constituent Assembly, which include subjecting it to a veto by a second house and ensuring that a minority in the Constituent Assembly shall be able to frustrate an overwhelming majority.

3.2 Secondly, with regards to the violence in our country our demands centred on three aspects:

3.2.1 Ensuring that the direct and indirect involvement of the NP government, its surrogates, the security forces and police are brought to an end forthwith.

3.2.2 Ensuring that the De Klerk government immediately implement agreements reached with the ANC more than a year ago on curbing violence.

3.2.3 The establishment of an international commission of inquiry into the Boipatong massacre and all acts of violence as well as the international monitoring of violence.

4. In communicating with Mr F. W. de Klerk we made it crystal clear that '(his) response and practical steps . . . to these demands will play a crucial role in determining the direction and speed with which bona fide negotiations can take place'.

5. He has chosen to ignore the gravity of these demands. He seeks to channel them into endless negotiations and discussions. In particular, the content of his reply seeks to elevate government to a legitimate and credible force standing above the crisis. This is part of the deliberate attempts to perpetuate the notion of 'black on black' violence rather than draw attention to the central role of the de Klerk government and its security forces.

   He tries to enhance this position by calling for a meeting between Dr. Buthelezi and myself at which Mr F. W. de Klerk and his government will participate 'in view of its (i.e. the de Klerk government's) responsibility for the maintenance of law and order'. He persists in shielding his regime behind the back of the government-supported IFP. Government covert and open support for the IFP has been confirmed in numerous instances. These include the Second Interim Report of the Goldstone Commission, the International Commission of Jurists fact finding mission and the Amnesty International report.

6. De Klerk's memorandum, and his state of the nation address on 2 July 1992 are characterised by a threatening mode and a propensity towards repression. He assumes the legitimacy of the existing order and his government. He appears also to believe that the military power that his government commands can be a

means of resolving the conflict. This was demonstrated when Mr de Klerk attempted to visit Boipatong, where the people in the township demonstrated their anger and revulsion. Shaken by this overwhelming rejection at a press conference held immediately thereafter, he threatened to return the country to the old style repression of the P. W. Botha regime by raising the possibility of the re-imposition of the state of emergency.

7. We have sought to ensure that the de Klerk regime responds to our demands positively and undertakes practical steps. We have done so with the clear knowledge that the longer it takes to find a way out of the current impasse the more difficult it will be to reach agreement and the more difficult it will be to ensure peace and stability in the future. If he shared this commitment, there is nothing in our demands that he could not have addressed practically and immediately. His response has failed to address the crucial issues. It is riddled with factual inaccuracies, distortions and blatant party political propaganda. It confirms the fundamental feature of our society that he and his government want to be both player and referee. By responding in the manner he has done, Mr F. W. de Klerk has chosen to drive South Africa into a collision course.

8. I accordingly see no reason to mislead the public and the international community about the gravity of the crisis facing our country. No good purpose will be served in my meeting him at this stage.

9. The National Executive Committee will look into the question of providing a detailed reply to the memorandum I have received from Mr F. W. de Klerk.

Document 26

Nelson Mandela's reply to F. W. De Klerk
9 July 1992

Dear Mr De Klerk

I acknowledge receipt of your reply dated 2nd July, 1992.

It is unfortunate that your reply has not addressed the issues I raised in my memorandum of the 26th June, 1992. Instead, you deliberately obscure matters.

It appears that we are all agreed that South Africa faces a serious crisis. When it comes to charting a way out of the crisis, however, it is clear that there are hardly any points of convergence.

This is particularly so because you have chosen to elevate a number of peripheral issues to the status of 'fundamental' ones, while relegating those of critical significance to a secondary place. The matter is made worse by the factual inaccuracies, distortions and blatant party political propaganda involved in the manner in which you raised these so-called fundamental issues.

To call for face-to-face talks in such a situation is entirely unacceptable. We would sit down to do no more than haggle about what should constitute the agenda of such talks, rather than the serious business of taking our country to democracy and developing firm foundations for curbing and eliminating violence.

Reaffirmation about your commitment to a negotiated resolution to the South African conflict needs to be supported by stating positions which offer the potential to break the deadlock.

1. Negotiations

1.1 You state that 'the fundamental difference between the approach of the ANC and that of the government regarding *the purpose of negotiations* lies, on the one hand, in our commitment to constitutionality and a transitional government as soon as possible; and on the other hand, on the ANC's insistence on a unstructured and immediate transfer of power before a proper transitional constitution is negotiated'. (Paragraph 3 Page 4)

1.2 This is indeed a novel description of the purpose of negotiations, to say nothing about its gross distortion and patent party political propaganda.

The characterisation of your own position as 'commitment to constitutionality and a transitional government as soon as possible' bears very little relationship to the purpose of negotiations, as set out in the Declaration of Intent we adopted together at CODESA 1, namely:

5. to set in motion the process of drawing up and establishing a constitution that will ensure, inter alia:

(a) that South Africa will be a united, democratic, non-racial and non-sexist state in which sovereign authority is exercised over the whole of its territory;

(b) that the Constitution will be the supreme law and that it will be guarded over by an independent, non-racial and impartial judiciary;

(c) that there will be a multi-party democracy with the right to form and join political parties and with regular elections on the basis of universal adult suffrage on a common voters' roll; in general the basic electoral system shall be that of proportional representation;

(d) that there shall be a separation of powers between the legislature, executive and judiciary with appropriate checks and balances;

(e) that the diversity of languages, culture and religions of the people of South Africa shall be acknowledged;

(f) that all shall enjoy universally accepted human rights, freedoms and civil liberties including freedom of religion, speech and assembly protected by an entrenched and justiciable Bill of Rights and a legal system that guarantees equality of all before the law.

Working Group 2 was specifically charged with determining the set of general constitutional principles consistent with and including those in the Declaration, as well as the form and content of the constitution making body / processes.

1.3 The question of a transitional government was the subject matter of one of the five working groups created at CODESA 1. Unless the question of the constitution making body is dealt with as the primary focus of negotiations, issues relating to transitional arrangements are deprived of their proper relevance. Your insistence on elevating this to the central focus of negotiations betrays the positions your government has been taking and which lie at the heart of the crisis.

1.4 If there is to be a way out of this impasse then it is imperative that we isolate the question of transitional arrangements from that of the constitution making body. With regard to the constitution making body (Constituent Assembly), it is necessary that you pronounce yourselves in keeping with basic democratic principles. A democratic constitution will be fatally flawed if the body charged with drafting and adopting it is itself undemocratic – be it in its composition or the way in which it is to function. Your response to our positions is therefore critical. It is the authority of the people, through their elected representatives, that gives a constitution its fundamental legitimacy. Our position is founded on the basic features of any democratic structure charged with the task of constitution making:

1.4.1 The constitution making body shall be sovereign;

1.4.2 The constitution making body shall be bound by the general constitutional principles agreed upon at Codesa, with the necessary checks to ensure that these are adhered to;

1.4.3 It shall be democratically elected on the basis of one-person-one-vote in the context of multi-party democracy where each party would be represented in proportion to the votes gained;

1.4.4 It shall be single chambered and shall not be subjected to the veto or overseeing powers of any other body;

1.4.5 In the South African context there is the additional requirement that such a constitution making body constitute a unifying and legitimising process which must however not thwart the will of the overwhelming majority. Therefore, the constitution making body shall arrive at decisions by a two-thirds majority;

1.4.6 In order to ensure that regional differences, irrespective of whether they arise from ethnic factors or vested interests nurtured by the apartheid fragmentation of our country are fully accommodated, the Constituent Assembly shall:

- be composed of 50% delegates elected by means of a national list, and 50% elected on the basis of a regional list, both on proportional representation and one person one vote;

- In deciding on those aspects of the Constitution which deal with regional structures, their powers and duties, the Constituent Assembly would take decisions first by means of two-thirds majority of the entire Assembly and further that such a decision would require the endorsement of a two thirds majority of that half of the Constituent Assembly delegates who have been elected through the regional list;

1.4.7 So as to ensure that the transition is as expeditious as possible, there should be effective and timeous deadlock breaking mechanisms in the functioning of the constitution making body. The depth of the crisis facing our country is such that it is essential that there is a speedy transition to democracy. We cannot accept three years as a time frame for the Constituent Assembly to discharge its duties.

1.5 Your reply evades these questions. To the extent that it deals with any of them, what emerges is your opposition to such a sovereign and democratically elected constitution making body. The composition and function of this sovereign body is the acid test of your commitment to democracy.

You deliberately distort our proposals to constitute 'simple majoritarianism'. You falsely accuse us of wanting the Constituent Assembly to function in a constitutional void. At the same time you seek to pre-empt the work of the Constituent Assembly by the Codesa process.

Besides subjecting the work of the Constituent Assembly to the veto of a regionally elected Senate you seek to entrench federalism by subterfuge. This becomes clear by your requirement that the boundaries, powers, function and form of regional government will have to be approved by the majority of the representatives from *each electoral region* that will be affected in *each* case.

It is necessary that there should be a clear understanding that all interim arrangements relating to the administration and governance of regions shall be such as not to pre-empt the decisions of the constitution making body. The question of the form of government, be it federal or unitary or whatever, is a matter that should be left to a democratically elected constitution making body.

1.6 The manner in which you have elevated the transitional arrangements to the central focus of negotiations betrays your pre-occupation with obtaining guarantees of a constitutionally entrenched role for the National Party, which you recognise will remain a minority party in the event of a democratic constitution.

1.7 You are more than aware that your allegation that the ANC insists on 'an unstructured and an immediate transfer of power' bears no relation to the truth. Long before Codesa was established, the ANC proposed that there should be an interim Government of National Unity so as to ensure that no party occupies the position of player and referee. This demand was first put in the Harare Declaration of 1989. It was not put forward as an end in itself. It was proposed as a means by which a democratically elected and sovereign Constituent Assembly would be brought into being for the purposes of drafting and adopting a democratic constitution for a united non-racial and non-sexist South Africa.

1.8 In the agreements reached at Codesa with regards to transitional arrangements it is clearly stated in Paragraph 1.12 of the Report of Working Group 3 that 'the following agreements were reached with regard to the first stage of the transition. These agreements and their implementation are dependent upon agreement being reached by Codesa in respect of the second stage of the transition, including an Interim Constitution, and general constitutional principles'.

1.9 Indeed we were all parties to the insertion of this clause. That is to say, there appears to be agreement that none of us could walk blindfolded into the first stage of the transition if we could not define for ourselves and for the citizens of our country the central question as to the nature and functioning of a constitution making body. At the same time it is evidenced in the records of Working Group 3 that the ANC fully supports constitutional and legislative measures to ensure that there is no constitutional void.

1.10 And yet at the same time you have sought, by one means or another, to get an unconditional commitment from us to transitional arrangements without a clear agreement on the constitution making body. That is why we insist that the deadlock with regard to the constitution making body needs to be addressed by you.

1.11 It is a matter of public record that with regards to the Interim Government arrangements, it is the ANC which insisted on the idea of an Interim Government of National Unity in order to stress the need for an interim period that would be broadly inclusive. In pursuance of such inclusivity we proposed that all parties elected would be represented in the Interim Executive in proportion to their proven electoral support.

1.12 In the light of these proposals we cannot understand why your party persists in seeking to impose undemocratic solutions. All parties, including yours, are assured of a place in the future on the basis of proven electoral support.

All parties have been offered a place in the Executive in the interim period. To carry such interim arrangements into a future constitution to be adopted by the Constituent Assembly is to deny the principle of majority rule and vest minority political parties with veto powers. Furthermore this would place minority parties in a conflictual situation with the majority and undermine the security minority parties seek.

2. Violence

2.1 Your reply dismisses our charges against your government for involvement in the violence by a bland denial and the assurance that where 'elements in the state structures err' you will not hesitate to take appropriate measures. To say the least this is most unhelpful in resolving the crisis. (See Annexure 1; Government complicity in violence.)

In the statement of the emergency session of the National Executive Committee of the ANC we drew attention to the fact that your control of state power allows you the space to deny and cover up the role of the NP government, its surrogates, the state security forces and the police role in fostering and fomenting violence. Attached hereto are two further annexures setting out the evidence of numerous instances which unmistakably point in this direction (Annexure 2: Involvement of Security Forces in the fomenting and escalation of violence; and Annexure 3: South African Government support for the IFP.) The evidence relates to both acts of omission and commission.

2.2 In this context you do yourself a disservice by questioning the integrity of the ANC when you yourself have not carried out the agreements reached more than a year ago with regard to measures aimed at curbing the violence. Your remarks in relation to hostels and dangerous weapons are disingenuous. You are unable to cite even one tangible act you have taken regarding the upgrading of hostels. You provocatively put razor wire around Phola Park, yet you have not fenced-in a single hostel.

2.3 No one can be expected to go along with your protestations of clean hands and individual errors as a basis for resolving the problem of violence. The possibilities of finding a solution are made even more difficult by your insistence on making the rivalry between the ANC and IFP the primary factor. Government and the IFP have always acted together. We have yet to see a single condemnation by you of the IFP even though there are numerous cases of leading members of the IFP planning, directing and instigating violence on a mass scale. On the contrary there are persistent reports of government protection of IFP warlords by your security forces and police.

We can only conclude that the manner in which you called for a meeting between the IFP, ANC and the Government is aimed at blocking rather than resolving the problem of violence. Unless and until you take concrete steps against your state agencies and surrogates, the NP will remain part of the problem rather than the solution. Annexure 3 briefly sets out the nature of the relationship between the IFP, and the NP government.

2.4 There are several categories of demands with regard to violence requiring immediate action by your government.

2.4.1. It is completely unacceptable that you should dismiss our demand for specific steps relating to covert operations and state security forces by denying such actions. Despite the recommendations of the Goldstone Commission, Battalion 32 has not been withdrawn from internal deployment. Former Koevoet members are deployed as units of the South African Police.

Special Forces remain in existence. In case after case investigations concerning the involvement of members of the security forces have been found to be inadequate and tardy. Repression and harassment are extant in some of the self-governing states and so-called independent States.

Unless you act publicly on these issues the crisis will deepen. In the light of your total denial we suggest as a first and immediate step that you personally take over responsibility for the portfolios relating to the security forces and the police.

2.4.2   The agreements reached with the ANC more than a year ago and aimed at measures which will remove the hostels from being used as fortresses of violence have not been implemented.

2.4.3   To justify inaction even at this stage on whatever grounds is to turn a blind eye to the hundreds of deaths and thousands of injuries attributable to attacks by hostel inmates during the period in which you have failed to take practical steps. The fact that none of your answers explains why you have failed to repeal the law which you brought into being legalising the carrying of dangerous weapons can only be understood in terms of your special relationship with the IFP.

2.4.4   The measures that you have taken enabling the Goldstone Commission to incorporate an international assessor and to attach an evaluator to the police investigation team into the Boipatong massacre have not addressed our demand for an international commission of inquiry and the international monitoring of violence. It is unacceptable that your police force, which is an alleged party to the violence, should be charged with the investigations.

2.4.5   None of your explanations with regard to the release of political prisoners are sufficient to explain the reality that there are still hundreds of political prisoners in your jails.

2.4.6   With regard to repressive legislation your government refuses to countenance the repeal of legislation currently on your statute books and which has been universally condemned as repressive, illiberal and not conducive to free political activity. No claims regarding the duty to govern can justify their continued existence on your statute books. Our demands specifically drew attention to additional laws passed during the last week of the recent session of your parliament, that drastically restrict the rights of citizens and restructure the criminal law, and that are already being implemented.

2.4.7   Furthermore, your government persists in its course in unilaterally restructuring the affairs of our country at a time when you are supposed to be negotiating a transition to a democratic order.

These efforts actually amount to preempting and foreclosing on the rights and duties of a democratic order.

3. Other issues raised in your letter

3.1 In the face of the two critical issues which stand in the way of the transition to democracy, you have chosen to raise other issues as matters requiring urgent negotiations. Instead of addressing the critical issues with the statesmanship they require your entire letter takes the form of a party political reply. Perhaps this confusion on your side is understandable in the context of your persistent claims based on the right to govern and your position as State President.

3.2 Your charges against the ANC and its Allies are part of the baggage of apartheid ideology. We reject with contempt your propagandistic version of what is supposed to be happening inside the ANC and the Alliance. It has been the tradition of successive National Party regimes to try to discredit our Movement on the basis that you know black people better than black people know themselves.

3.3 With the right to peaceful demonstration goes our inherent right to determine its nature and aims. The dangers of further violence must be laid at the doors of those who are resisting change. Successive NP regimes have always sought to crush our mass campaigns by raising the spectre of violence and disruption as being inherent in our campaigns. This was so in the case of the Defiance Campaign of 1952, the numerous national stay aways, etc., including those of the recent period.

But the record is clear; wherever and whenever violence raised its head, it has been initiated and provoked by the government side. And in the more recent cases they include your surrogates.

4. Conclusion

4.1 Given the party political nature of your reply, we would urge you
to desist from this course in addressing our demands. Find a way
within yourself to recognise the gravity of the crisis. The starting
point for this is that you stop deluding yourself that it is the ANC
and its Allies' programme of mass action which is the cause of the
crisis. It would be a grave mistake if your government thinks that
resorting to repression and the use of the military and police
power that it commands can be a means of resolving the conflict.
Find a way to address the demands we have placed before you
with regard to the negotiations deadlock and those relating to the
violence so that negotiations can become meaningful and be
vested with the urgency that the situation requires. Failure to
respond in this way can only exacerbate the crisis. You may
succeed in delaying, but never in preventing, the transition of
South Africa to a democracy.

NELSON R. MANDELA

Document 27

1. The attached Record of Understanding was agreed to.
2. On the way forward –
   - The two delegations agreed that this summit has laid a basis for the resumption of the negotiation process.
   - To this end the ANC delegation advised the South African Government that it would recommend to its National Executive Committee that the process of negotiation be resumed, whereafter extensive bilateral discussions will be held.
   - It was agreed that the practicalities with regard to bilateral discussions will be dealt with through the existing channel.

Record of Understanding

1. Since 21 August 1992 a series of meetings was held between Mr Roelf Meyer, Minister of Constitutional Development and Mr Cyril Ramaphosa, Secretary General of the African National Congress.

   These meetings entailed discussions with a view to remove obstacles towards the resumption of negotiations and focused on the identification of steps to be taken to address issues raised in earlier memoranda. The discussions took note of various opposing viewpoints on the relevant issues and obstacles. It was decided that these issues should not be dealt with exhaustively in the understanding. This document reflects the understanding reached at the conclusion of the discussions regarding these obstacles and issues.

2. The understandings on issues and obstacles included the following, although it was observed that there are still other important matters that will receive attention during the process of negotiation:

    (a) The Government and the ANC agreed that there is a need for a democratic constitution assembly / constitution-making body and that for such a body to be democratic it must:

    - be democratically elected;
    - draft and adopt the new constitution, implying that it should sit as a single chamber;
    - be bound only by agreed constitutional principles;
    - have a fixed time frame;
    - have adequate deadlock breaking mechanisms;
    - function democratically i.e. arrive at its decisions democratically with certain agreed to majorities; and
    - be elected within an agreed predetermined time period.

Within the framework of these principles, detail would have to be worked out in the negotiation process.

    (b) The Government and the ANC agreed that during the interim / transitional period there shall be constitutional continuity and no constitutional hiatus. In consideration of this principle, it was further agreed that:

    - the constitution-making body / constituent assembly shall also act as the interim / transitional Parliament;
    - There shall be an interim / transitional government of national unity;
    - the constitution-making body / constituent assembly cum interim / transitional Parliament and the interim / transitional government of national unity shall function within a constitutional framework / transitional constitution which shall provide for national and regional government during the period of transition and shall incorporate guaranteed justiciable fundamental rights and freedoms. The interim /

transitional Parliament may function as a one or two-chambered body.

(c) The two parties are agreed that all prisoners whose imprisonment is related to political conflict of the past and whose release can make a contribution to reconciliation should be released. The government and the ANC agreed that the release of prisoners, namely, those who according to the ANC fall within the guidelines defining political offences, but according to the government do not, and who have committed offences with a political motive on or before 8 October 1990 shall be carried out in stages (as reflected in a separate document; 'Implementation Programme: Release of Prisoners') and be completed before 15 November 1992. To this end the parties have commenced a process of identification. It is the Government's position that all who have committed similar offences but who have not been charged and sentenced should be dealt with on the same basis. On this question no understanding could be reached as yet and it was agreed that the matter will receive further attention.

As the process of identification proceeds, release shall be effected in the above-mentioned staged manner. Should it be found that the current executive powers of the State do not enable it to give effect to specific releases arising from the above identification the necessary legislation shall be enacted.

(d) The Goldstone Commission has given further attention to hostels and brought out an urgent report on certain matters and developments in this regard. The Commission indicated that the problem is one of criminality and that it will have to investigate which localities are affected.

In the meantime some problematic hostels have been identified and the Government has undertaken as a matter of urgency to address and deal with the problem in relation to those hostels that have been associated with violence.

Further measures will be taken, including fencing and policing to prevent criminality by hostel dwellers and to protect hostel dwellers against external aggression. A separate document ('Implementation Programme: Hostels') records the identification of such hostels and the security measures to be taken in these instances.

Progress will be reported to the Goldstone Commission and the National Peace Secretariat. United Nations observers may witness the progress in co-operation with the Goldstone Commission and the National Peace Secretariat.

(e) In the present volatile atmosphere of violence, the public display and carrying of dangerous weapons provokes further tension and should be prohibited. The Government has informed the ANC that it will issue a proclamation within weeks to prohibit countrywide the carrying and display of dangerous weapons at all public occasions subject to exemptions based on guidelines being prepared by the Goldstone Commission. The granting of exemptions shall be entrusted to one or more retired judges. On this basis, the terms of the proclamation and mechanism for exemption shall be prepared with the assistance of the Goldstone Commission.

(f) The Government acknowledges the right of all parties and organisations to participate in peaceful mass action in accordance with the provisions of the National Peace Accord and the Goldstone Commission's recommendations. The ANC for its part reaffirms its commitment to the provisions of the Code of Conduct for Political Parties arrived at under the National Peace Accord and the agreement reached on 16 July 1992 under the auspices of the Goldstone Commission as important instruments to ensure democratic political activity in a climate of free political participation. The two parties also commit themselves to the strengthening of the Peace Accord process, to do everything in their power to calm down tension and to finding ways and means of promoting reconciliation in South Africa.

In view of the progress made in this summit and the progress we are likely to make when negotiations are resumed, the ANC expresses its intention to consult its constituency on a basis of urgency with a view to examine the current programme of mass action.

3. The two parties agreed to hold further meetings in order to address and finalise the following matters which were not completed at the summit:
   - climate of free political activity;
   - repressive/security legislation;
   - covert operations and special forces;
   - violence.

Agreed to at Johannesburg on 26 September 1992:

F W DE KLERK	N R MANDELA
State President	President: ANC

Implementation programme: hostels

(In terms of the Record of Understanding)

1. The hostels presently identified as problematic and have either had a history or present propensity to violence are listed in annexure 'H1'.[*]

2.2.1 The Government and the ANC endorse the recommendations by Justice Goldstone in his report to the State President dated the 18 September 1992 that certain hostels are associated with criminality and must be addressed and dealt with by the Government which has the primary responsibility for maintaining law and order.

---

[*] *The annexures to this document, H1, H2, and H3, contain logistical details for plans to end violence in hostels; their contents are not of direct concern to this volume and have not been included – H. E.*

2.2 The Government, having accepted the Goldstone Commission Report, will fence the following hostels in terms of the definition set out in paragraph 1.1 in annexure 'H2' in order to prevent criminality by hostel-dwellers and to protect the hostel residents from external aggression:

(a) Mzimhlope, Dube Nancefield, Dobsonville and Merafe (all situated in the greater Soweto area)

(b) Madala (situated in Kagiso)

(c) Sebokeng complex (situated in the Vaal area)

3. The following two hostels in KwaZulu, being Umlazi Section T Unit 17 and Kwa Mashu, have been identified by the ANC as being associated with violence. The Government has undertaken to consult with the Kwa Zulu Government in this regard.

4. The measures required to curtail and prevent violence and provide greater security to both the hostel dwellers and township dwellers alike have been identified and defined in annexure 'H2'.

5. The agreed implementation of these measures (annexure 'H2') in respect of each hostel is detailed in annexure 'H3'.

6. General conditions

6.1 Ownership of hostels

Ownership of hostels shall not be alienated without consultation.

6.2 Communication

6.2.1 A written report detailing all policing work carried out in respect of the identified hostels including a narration of violence occurring, confiscation of weapons, charges brought and all violence related crimes and activities, shall be submitted every two weeks by the police authorities responsible for the security of all hostels to the Minister of Law and Order.

6.2.2 A written report detailing the progress in respect of the implementation of this agreement, including the question of fencing and access control, shall be submitted to the Minister of Local Government and Lands and National Housing every two weeks.

6.2.3 Copies of the above reports shall be made available to the Goldstone Commission for dissemination to all interested parties.

  6.3 Review meetings

Meetings between the ANC and the Government to review the present agreement and reports including review of the list of hostels would take place as often as may be necessary.

  6.4 Time frames

6.4.1 Government shall present a detailed programme by no later than the 15th October, 1992 and to commence construction of the first fence(s) on or before the 22nd October, 1992 and to proceed thereafter with all due diligence and the process completed by 15th November 1992. Should a longer period be required for completion of this task, then urgent and more speedy temporary measures regarding fencing together with urgent policing action shall be undertaken immediately.

6.4.2 Government undertakes to commence with the repair work and maintenance in the terms set out in the paragraph above.

  6.5 Communication strategy

6.5.1 Liaison with the hostel communities will be undertaken by Government about the fencing programme paying particular attention to the temporary and stabilising features.

6.5.2 Government will further utilise the appropriate media to publicly convey the rationale for the fencing programme in such a manner that tensions are reduced.

  6.6 Ownership of private hostels

6.6.1 Government undertakes to meet with the private owners of hostels included in annexure 'H1' to solicit their co-operation and assistance in the compliance of this agreement. Progress reports in this regard shall be made available.

Document **28**

Negotiations: a strategic perspective
25 November 1992

As adopted by the National Executive Committee of the African National Congress – 25 November 1992.

The strategic perspective of the ANC is the transfer of power from the white minority regime to the people as a whole. This will usher in a new era characterised by the complete eradication of the system of apartheid, fundamental socio-economic transformation, peace and stability for all our people. The basic principle underpinning this new order is democratic majority rule.

1. Balance of forces

By the end of the eighties, the strategic balance of forces was characterised by:

1.1 The liberation movement enjoyed many advantages over the regime, both internally and internationally. All the pillars of the struggle had grown from strength to strength:

- a very high level of mass mobilisation and mass defiance had rendered apartheid unworkable;
- the building of the underground had laid a basis for exercising political leadership and was laying a basis for the intensification of the armed struggle;
- the world was united against apartheid.

1.2 At the same time the liberation movement faced certain objective weaknesses:

- changes in Southern Africa were making it increasingly difficult for the ANC in the conduct of struggle;
- there was no longer a visible intensification of the armed struggle;
- the international community was making renewed attempts to impose a settlement plan.

1.3 The crisis in Eastern Europe, and the resultant change in the relations between world powers brought the issue of a negotiated resolution of regional conflicts to the fore.

In this context, South Africa was not going to be treated as an exception. Importantly, these changes also exerted new pressures on the regime to fall in line with the emerging international 'culture' of multi-party democracy.

1.4 The apartheid power bloc was no longer able to rule in the old way. Its policies of repression and reform had failed dismally; and it faced an ever-deepening socio-economic crisis. At the same time the liberation movement did not have the immediate capacity to overthrow the regime.

1.5 All these factors set the stage for a negotiated resolution of the South African conflict. The regime was forced to unban the ANC and other organisations, release Nelson Mandela and other political prisoners, acknowledge the defeat of the apartheid ideology and seek negotiations with the liberation movement. This constituted a major strategic retreat for the regime and a victory for the democratic forces.

2. Shift in the balance of forces

2.1 The balance of forces is not static. In this phase of the negotiations:

- The regime strives to undermine and weaken the liberation movement through its strategy of Low Intensity Conflict and the beginning of counter-revolutionary war;
- The liberation movement seeks to weaken the capacity of the regime to act against the people and broaden the space for free

political activity through a combination of mass mobilisation, international pressure and self-defence.

2.2 In the recent period:

- The de Klerk regime has suffered a renewed crisis of legitimacy. It continues to fail to win the allegiance of the majority;
- The regime's camp stands more divided than it ever was since the unbanning of the ANC; its unpatriotic front with some bantustans has collapsed: it is increasingly losing the loyalty of the civil service and important elements in the security forces, many of whom are drifting to the extreme right-wing camp; in the October special session of the tricameral parliament, it failed to secure the support of a single other party outside itself: leading members of the party and government continue to jump ship for reasons of 'fatigue', 'depression' and 'disillusionment':
- The regime has lost all ability to arrest the unprecedented socio-economic decline, growing unemployment among both black and white, the general social disintegration and spiralling crime. However:
- the regime still commands vast state and other military resources:
- it continues to enjoy the support of powerful economic forces:
- objectively, the counter-revolutionary violence and the growing potential of long-term counter-revolutionary instability acts as a resource for the regime.

2.3 Also in the recent period:

- the ANC has established itself as a legal national political organi-sation:
- it commands the support of the majority of South Africa:
- the liberation movement enjoys the capacity to mobilise large-scale mass action:
- it is able to influence and mobilise the international community. However:
- the liberation movement suffers many organisational weaknesses;
- it does not command significant military and financial resources;
- it is unable to militarily defeat the counter-revolutionary movement or adequately defend the people.

2.4 As a result of mass action and negotiations some progress has been made in the recent period. Some examples of these are: the CODESA Declaration of Intent (which establishes national consensus on the broad direction in which the political process should unfold); the Record of Understanding; and broad consensus on the need for an Interim Government and Constituent Assembly. Though the regime has succeeded in delaying the transition, there remains a groundswell of support within society as a whole for a speedy resolution of the political and socio-economic problems.

2.5 In this context, the liberation movement is faced with various options:

(a) resumption of the armed struggle and the perspective of revolutionary seizure of power;

(b) mass action and international pressure, within the broad context of negotiations, until the balance of forces is shifted to such an extent that we secure a negotiated surrender from the regime;

(c) a negotiations process combined with mass action and international pressure which takes into account the need to combat counter-revolutionary forces and at the same time uses phases in the transition to qualitatively change the balance of forces in order to secure a thorough-going democratic transformation.

2.6 These options should be weighed against the following background:

2.6.1 The ANC's National Conference resolved, after weighing various factors – including the possibility of a negotiated resolution of the South African conflict and the objective situation outlined in Section 1 above – that the option of armed seizure of power was neither preferable nor viable at that juncture. The current situation does not warrant a review of this decision of National Conference.

2.6.2 An approach that aims to secure a negotiated surrender from the regime will entail a protracted process with tremendous cost to the people and the country.

2.7 Taking into account:

- the capacity of the liberation movement;
- the capacity of the regime to endlessly delay while consolidating its hold onto power and restructuring in order to undermine future democratic transformation;
- the cost to the people and the country of a protracted negotiations process;
- the need to as urgently as possible address the dire socio-economic needs of the people;
- the need to prevent a further consolidation of the counter-revolutionary forces:

    the third option, (c), is the most viable and preferable.

2.8 The liberation movement, however, should guard against being captive to a given approach. A combination of factors, including the conduct of the regime, may dictate a need to revisit our approach. Apart from the first two options, this may also include a much more enhanced role for the international community in the negotiations process.

3. Negotiations: the preferred option of the liberation movement

3.1 A peaceful political settlement has always been the first option of the liberation movement. It was only when the prospect of any peaceful settlement vanished that we adopted the perspective of an armed revolutionary seizure of power. On the other hand, for the regime, it was a failure of arms that imposed the obligation to concede the need for a political settlement.

3.2 Negotiations therefore represent a victory for the democratic movement and a defeat for the forces of apartheid.

3.3 Consequently, it must remain one of our strategic tasks to continue to draw the regime onto the terrain of free political activity, peaceful democratic action and genuine negotiations.

3.4 Delays in the process of peaceful transformation are not in the interests of the masses, who seek liberation now, and do not enhance our possibilities to effect the transformation to genuine democracy as effectively and as speedily as we should.

4. Phases of the democratic revolution

4.1 Our strategic perspective should take into account that the Democratic Revolution – for the attainment of majority rule – will proceed in various phases. Our possibilities relevant to each phase should not be pursued in a manner that produces defeats later because of a failure to recognise the dialectical inter-connection between various phases.

4.2 This strategic perspective should recognise the following phases, each one of which has its regularities and objective and subjective demands:

PHASE 1: The period prior to the establishment of the Transitional Executive Council. (In this phase we should aim to: secure an agreement on free and fair elections; Interim Government and Constituent Assembly; stop unilateral restructuring; broaden the space for free political activity; and address the issue of violence.)

PHASE 2: The period from the establishment of the Transitional Executive Council leading up to the election of the Constituent Assembly and the establishment of an Interim Government of National Unity. (In this phase we should aim to: consolidate peace through joint control over all armed forces; ensure free and fair elections; and mobilise for a decisive victory in the elections.)

PHASE 3: The period of the drafting and adoption of the new constitution by the Constituent Assembly. (In this phase we should aim to: establish an Interim Government in which the ANC would be a major player; adopt a new democratic constitution; and start addressing the socio-economic problems facing the country.)

PHASE 4: The period of the phasing in of the new constitution, which will include the restructuring of the state machinery and the general dismantling of the system of apartheid.

PHASE 5: The period of the consolidation of the process of democratic transformation and reconstruction.

4.3 At all stages, we should consider carefully the balance of forces, how to change that balance, and therefore place ourselves in a position in which we can determine the correct path to follow to further the process of democratic change. In this context, the broad masses should play a decisive role. The process must be mass-driven.

4.4 The balance of forces, our specific objectives and our long-term goals would at each stage dictate the need to: enter into specific, and perhaps changing, alliances; and, make certain compromises in order to protect and advance this process.

5. Goals of the national liberation struggle and our immediate objectives

5.1 The fundamental goal of the National Liberation Struggle is the transfer of power to the people as a whole and the establishment of a united, non-racial, non-sexist and democratic society. This should not be confused with the immediate objectives we set for ourselves in each phase of the transition. At the same time, we should ensure that the immediate objectives we pursue do not have the effect of blocking our longer-term goals.

5.2 The objectives we set and can attain in each phase, will depend on the balance of forces.

5.3 We must ensure that in entering a new phase (e.g. the establishment of an Interim Government) the balance of forces is transformed qualitatively in favour of the Democratic Movement. Negotiations can therefore result in the possibility of bringing about a radically transformed political framework (i.e. changing the conjuncture) in which the struggle for the achievement of the strategic perspectives of the National

Democratic Revolution will be advanced in more favourable conditions.

5.4   In setting objectives for the present round of negotiations, we must bear in mind that in the main one would not achieve at the table that which one cannot achieve on the ground. Depending on the balance of forces, we might not gain everything we set out to achieve. However, positions we adopt should be informed by our longer-term objectives. Our correct assessment of the balance of forces, the support of the masses and good negotiating tactics should ensure that our gains constitute a decisive leap forward.

5.5   In setting objectives today, our strategy should not focus narrowly on only the initial establishment of democracy, but also (and perhaps more importantly) on how to nurture, develop and consolidate that democracy. Our strategy must at once also focus on ensuring that the new democracy is not undermined.

5.6   Our broad objectives for the first two phases (as distinct from longer term goals) should therefore be:

5.6.1 the establishment of a democratic constitution-making process;

5.6.2 ending the National Party's monopoly of political power;

5.6.3 ensuring a continuing link between democracy and socio-economic empowerment; and

5.6.4 minimising the threat to stability and the democratic process.

6. Engaging the National Party regime

6.1   The objective reality imposes a central role for the ANC and the NP in the transition. The ANC is the custodian of the peace process – while the NP is the party in power. Using various forms of struggle, we ensure that the regime accepts movement forward in the process.

6.2   This means that the balance of forces has forced onto the South African political situation a relationship between the ANC and the NP characterised by:

- in the first place conflict, in so far as the regime attempts to block the transition: and
- secondly, constructive interaction in pursuit of agreements the regime has been forced to enter into.

6.3 How to manage this contradiction is one of our challenges of leadership.

7. The need for a government of national unity

7.1 We have already won the demand for an Interim Government of National Unity.

7.2 However, we also need to accept the fact that even after the adoption of a new constitution, the balance of forces and the interests of the country as a whole may still require of us to consider the establishment of a Government of National Unity – provided that it does not delay or obstruct the process of orderly transition to majority rule and that the parties that have lost the elections will not be able to paralyse the functioning of government.

This is fundamentally different from an approach to power-sharing which entrenches veto powers for minority parties.

7.3 Some objectives of a Government of National Unity:

7.3.1 Stability during the period of transition to full democracy: the enemies of democracy will try to destabilise the new government and make democracy unworkable.

7.3.2 Commitment to and responsibility for the process: we should seek, especially in the early stages, to commit all parties to actively take part in the process of dismantling apartheid, building democracy and promoting development in the interest of all.

8. Laying the basis to minimise the threat to stability and democracy

8.1   The new democratic government would need to adopt a wide range of measures in order to minimise the potential threat to the new democracy. However, some of these measures may have to be part and parcel of a negotiated settlement. The new government will also need to take into account the need to employ the talents and capacities of all South Africans, as well as the time it will take to implement an urgent programme of advancing the skills of those who have all along been deprived.

8.2   Strategic forces we need to consider right now are the SADF, SAP, all the other armed formations and the civil service in general. If the transition to democracy affects all the individuals in these institutions wholly and purely negatively, then they would serve as fertile ground from which the destabilisers would recruit.

8.3   Not only do these forces have vast potential to destabilise a fledgling democracy in the future, but as importantly, they have the potential to delay the transition for a lengthy period of time or even make serious attempts to subvert the transition.

8.4   A democratic government will need to restructure the civil service and the security forces in order to ensure that:

- they are professional, competent and accountable;
- they are representative of society as a whole (including through the application of the principle of affirmative action);
- they serve the interests of democracy; and
- the size of these institutions is determined by the objective needs of the country.

   In this process it may be necessary to address the question of job security, retrenchment packages and a general amnesty based on disclosure and justice, at some stage, as part of a negotiated settlement. These measures will need to apply to all armed formations and sections of the civil service.

However, the availability of resources and experiences of other countries need to be taken into account.

8.5 It is also necessary to consider other potential counter-revolutionary forces and find ways of engaging them and their mass base in the national effort to build a democratic society.

8.6 One of the basic guarantees to stability will be the implementation of development programmes to meet the legitimate needs and aspirations of the majority of South Africans. This places a serious responsibility on the ANC to determine priorities and possibilities for democratic socio-economic transformation.

9. Reaching the negotiated settlement

9.1 Elements of the final negotiated settlement would take the form of multi-lateral (CODESA-type) agreements. Other elements of the settlement package would take the form of bilateral agreements between the ANC and the NP – such agreements would bind the two parties.

9.2 The thorny question of the powers, functions and boundaries of regions in a new South Africa may be an issue on which we would enter into bilateral discussion with the NP and other parties, and seek to reach an understanding which the parties would pursue in the Constituent Assembly.

9.3 The question of a Government of National Unity after the adoption of a new constitution, and the future of members of the security forces and the civil service could be dealt with through direct engagement with these forces, as part of a bilateral agreement or in multi-lateral agreements.

25 November 1992

Document 29

Resolution on the need for the resumption of multi-party negotiations
5 March 1993

WE, THE PARTIES, organisations and administrations assembled in this Multi-party Planning Conference:

BEING FULLY CONSCIOUS of the responsibility we individually and collectively bear for the well-being of our country;

BEING DESIROUS that the problems of our country should be resolved peacefully through a process of negotiation;

REALISING that the economic upliftment of the country depends on the peaceful resolution of the country's problems, particularly the constitutional crisis (impasse);

ACCEPTING that all the people of this country and the whole community of nations throughout the world look to us to move the country forward towards a non-racial, non-sexist and fully democratic future;

NOW RESOLVE TO:

1. commit ourselves, individually and collectively to the resumption of multi-party negotiations in order to move as speedily as possible towards the attainment of our primary objective, which is the drafting and adoption of the new Constitution for South Africa by democratically elected representatives of all the people of this country and also ensuring that neither the present government nor any single party/organisation presides over the process alone.

AND FURTHER RESOLVE THAT:

2. The multi-party forum shall be reconvened as a matter of national urgency, not later than 5 April 1993;

3. Each participating organisation will send two delegates and two advisers.

4. The first meeting will determine, inter alia:

4.1 mechanisms and procedures (including Chairpersonship);

4.2 how to accommodate the views of those participants who were not in CODESA in relation to the agreements reached in CODESA;

4.3 how these agreements can serve as a constructive foundation for the resumed/commenced negotiations process to build on;

4.4 how this forum shall be structured and named;

4.5 the role of the international community.

5. The Facilitating Committee of this conference will have the responsibility of deciding upon and implementing the steps that are necessary to give effect to this resolution.

6. All participants are required to make an unqualified commitment to this process as a pre-requisite for their participation.

Document 30

The Negotiating Forum: resolution on violence
1 April 1993

We, the participants at the Negotiating Forum meeting at the World Trade Centre on 1 and 2 April 1993:

NOTING With revulsion the unacceptable escalation of violence that is engulfing our country;

OUTRAGED At the killings particularly of women and children;

CONCERNED About the damage violence is inflicting on all aspects of the economy, on relations among people and organisations and the consequent deepening of divisions;

AWARE That violence poses a threat to the negotiating process which if it continues could wreck the process and plunge our economy into an era of unprecedented conflict.

DO HEREBY UNEQUIVOCALLY

CONDEMN Without reservation the killing and maiming of the citizens of our country;

EXPRESS Our sympathy and condolences to all those who are suffering in consequence;

COMMIT OURSELVES To effective joint action by all of us leading to the eradication of violence and to the attainment of peace in our country as soon as possible; to peaceful negotiations as the only way to resolve differences.

AND THEREFORE RESOLVE TO

1. Identify those issues that cause violence and which threaten the negotiating process and the undermining of the effective implementation of the National Peace Accord.
2. Mandate the Negotiating Council to establish what urgent steps

and mechanisms are required to resolve the above issues as a matter of national priority. The Negotiating Council shall report to the next meeting of the Negotiating Forum.

Document 31

The Negotiating Forum: resolution on the transition process
1 April 1993

1. We, the participants at the Negotiating Forum meeting at the World Trade Centre, Johannesburg on 1st and 2nd April 1993, having,

1.1 Received a report from the Negotiating Council on the transition process;

1.2 Identified some of the issues concerning constitutional matters which the Negotiating Council must consider.

2. Resolve to instruct the Negotiating Council to consider and report on all matters arising from the consolidated Report, including the following and other Constitutional issues:

- Form of State and Constitutional Principles
- Constitution-Making Body / Constituent Assembly
- Transitional / Interim Constitution
- Transitional Regional / Local Government
- Fundamental Human Rights during the Transition
- Transitional Executive Council, its Sub-Councils, the Independent Elections Committee and the Independent Media Committee
- Future of the TBVC States
- Self-determination

3. The Negotiating Council shall present reports on progress made on the above issues to the Negotiating Forum.

Document 32

**The Negotiating Council: resolution on violence
3 June 1993**

THIS MEETING of the Negotiating Council:

Notes that the Technical Committee on Violence has submitted its report on the conditions that should be created to eliminate violence in accordance with the 'Declaration of Intent on the Negotiating Process' adopted on 7 May 1993;

Commends the Technical Committee for the comprehensive manner in which it has sought to address this question and the concrete proposals contained in its recommendations;

And hereby resolves that:

1. The National Peace Committee finalise proposed amendments to the Peace Accord as a matter of urgency so as to strengthen the Accord and increase its effectiveness;

2. The signatories to the Peace Accord meet as a matter of urgency to reaffirm their commitment to the Accord and to approve the proposed amendments to it;

3. Non-signatories sign the Peace Accord immediately;

4. Appropriate compulsory sanctions be developed by the Technical Committee on the Independent Election Commission for dealing with parties/administrations/organisations which transgress the Code of Conduct for Political Parties, but refuse to sign the Peace Accord;

5. Any party organising a public demonstration or any other form of mass action must comply with the guidelines set out in paragraph 2.6 of the Fourth Report of the Technical Committee on Violence;

6. The National Peace Committee submit proposed amendments to the Regulation of Gatherings Bill as a matter of urgency;

7. A series of phased confidence-building measures be adopted leading to the creation of impartial, legitimate and effective security forces. A distinction be drawn between statutory and non-statutory armies on the one hand and police forces on the other hand. The Technical Committee of the TEC and its Sub-Councils propose the precise mechanisms to be adopted;

8. Parties between whom conflicts exist, which have contributed to violence, in addition to participating in the MPNP [Multi-Party Negotiating Process], meet bilaterally to seek joint solutions to the conflicts between them;

9. An independent peacekeeping force with a multi-party composition be established and placed under the control of the Independent Electoral Commission or under multi-party executive control;

10. Every party to the MPNP commit itself without reservation to the holding of a free and fair election and to do everything possible to ensure that the electorate and the leaders and candidates of political parties are able to conduct their election campaigns and other political activities freely without being intimidated or obstructed and without fear of being killed;

11. The Technical Committee on Violence prepare detailed proposals on the desirability, financing, establishment and composition of a Peace/Youth Services Corps.

Document 33

Accord on Afrikaner self-determination
23 April 1994

BETWEEN THE FREEDOM FRONT, THE AFRICAN NATIONAL CONGRESS AND THE SOUTH AFRICAN GOVERNMENT/NATIONAL PARTY TAKING NOTE of the Constitution of the Republic of South Africa, Act 200 of 1993 as amended; and

TAKING NOTE of the unsigned Memorandum of Agreement between the African National Congress (ANC) and the Afrikaner Volksfront (AVF), dated December 21, 1993; and

TAKING NOTE of Constitutional Principle XXXIV, dealing with the issue of self-determination; and

SUBSEQUENT to the discussions between the delegations of the ANC, the AVF, the South African Government and eventually the Freedom Front (FF) –

The parties represented by these delegations record the following agreement:

1. The parties agree to address, through a process of negotiations, the idea of Afrikaner self-determination, including the concept of a Volkstaat.

2. The parties further agree that in the consideration of these matters, they shall not exclude the possibility of local and/or regional and other forms of expression of such self-determination.

3. They agree that their negotiations shall be guided by the need to be consistent with and shall be governed by the requirement to pay due consideration to Constitutional Principle XXXIV, other provisions of the Constitution of the Republic of South Africa, Act 200 of 1993 as amended, and that the parties take note of the Memorandum of Agreement, as referred to above.

3.1 Such consideration shall therefore include matters such as:

3.1.1 substantial proven support for the idea of self-determination including the concept of a Volkstaat;

3.1.2 the principles of democracy, non-racialism and fundamental rights; and

3.1.3 the promotion of peace and national reconciliation.

4. The parties further agree that in pursuit of 3.1.1 above, the support for the idea of self-determination in a Volkstaat will be indicated by the electoral support which parties with a specific mandate to pursue the realisation of a Volkstaat, will gain in the forthcoming election.

4.1 The parties also agree that, to facilitate the consideration of the idea of a Volkstaat after the elections, such electoral support should be measured not only nationally, but also by counting the provincial votes at the level of:

4.1.1 the electoral district, and

4.1.2 wherever practical the polling stations as indicated by the parties to, and agreed to by, the Independent Electoral Commission.

5. The parties agree that the task of the Volkstaatraad shall be to investigate and report to the Constitutional Assembly and the Commission on the Provincial Government on measures which can give effect to the idea of Afrikaner self-determination, including the concept of the Volkstaat.

6. The parties further agree that the Volkstaatraad shall form such advisory bodies as it may determine.

7. In addition to the issue of self-determination, the parties also undertake to discuss among themselves and reach agreement on matters relating to matters affecting stability in the agricultural sector and the impact of the process of transition on this sector, and also matters of stability including the issue of indemnity inasmuch as the matter has not been resolved.

8. The parties further agree that they will address all matters of concern to them through negotiations and that this shall not exclude the possibility of international mediation to help resolve such matters as may be in dispute and/or difficult to conclude.

8.1 The parties also agree that paragraph 8.0 shall not be read to mean that any of the deliberations of the Constitutional Assembly are subject to international mediation, unless the Constitutional Assembly duly amends the Constitution to enable this to happen.

8.2 The parties also affirm that, where this Accord refers to the South African Government, it refers to the South African Government which will rule South Africa until the April 1994-elections.

SIGNED BY: GEN. CONSTAND VILJOEN, LEADER:
FREEDOM FRONT
MR THABO MBEKI, NATIONAL CHAIRMAN:
AFRICAN NATIONAL CONGRESS
MR ROELF MEYER, MINISTER OF CONSTITUTIONAL
DEVELOPMENT AND OF COMMUNICATION ON BEHALF OF THE
GOVERNMENT AND THE NATIONAL PARTY
WITNESSED BY:
PROF. ABRAHAM VILJOEN & MR JURGEN KÖGL

April 23, 1994

Document 34

WE, THE UNDERSIGNED, pledge ourselves to Peace and Reconciliation in South African and agree to commit ourselves to the following:

1. The Inkatha Freedom Party agrees to participate in the April 26–28, 1994 elections for both the National Assembly and Provincial Legislatures.

2. All the undersigned parties reject violence and will therefore do everything in their power to ensure free and fair elections throughout the Republic of South Africa.

3. The undersigned parties agree to recognise and protect the institution, status and role of the constitutional position of the King of the Zulus and the Kingdom of KwaZulu, which institutions shall be provided for in the Provincial Constitution of KwaZulu/Natal immediately after the holding of the said elections. The 1993 Constitution shall for this purpose be amended before 27 April in accordance with Addendum A.

4. Any outstanding issues in respect of the King of the Zulus and the 1993 Constitution as amended will be addressed by way of international mediation which will commence as soon as possible after the said elections.

5. The South African Government undertakes to place the necessary facilities at the disposal of the Independent Electoral Commission (IEC) as it may require in order to facilitate the full participation of the IFP in the April 26–28, 1994 election.

6. The undersigned parties will facilitate proper provision for:

i)   Registration of the IFP
ii) The IFP Candidates lists
iii) Marking by voters of ballot papers.

The undersigned parties hereby undertake to abide by the technical arrangements to be made by the Independent Electoral Commission to implement the matters referred to in subparagraphs (i), (ii) and (iii) above in accordance with the details set out in Addendum B.*

This agreement shall be implemented with immediate effect.

SIGNED BY MANGOSUTHU G. BUTHELEZI President: Inkatha Freedom Party and Chief Minister of the KwaZulu Government
STATE PRESIDENT F. W. DE KLERK, South African Government/ National Party
PRESIDENT N. MANDELA, African National Congress
WITNESSED BY: PROF. W. A. J. OKUMU
19 April 1994

Addendum A

Amendment of section 160 of Act 200 of 1993.

  1. Section 160 of the Constitution is hereby amended by the substitution for the proviso to subsection (3) of the following proviso: 'Provided that a provincial constitution may –
     (a) provide for legislative and executive structures and procedures different from those provided for in this Constitution in respect of a province; and
     (b) where applicable, provide for the institution, role, authority and status of a traditional monarch in the prov-

---

* *The details contained in Addendum B are not directly relevant to this volume and have not been included here – H. E.*

vince, and shall make such provision for the Zulu Monarch in the case of the province of KwaZulu/Natal'. Amendment of Schedule 4 of Act 200 of 1993. Schedule 4 to the Constitution is hereby amended by the addition of the following paragraph to constitutional principle XIII: 'Provisions in a provincial constitution relating to the institution, role, authority and status of a traditional monarch shall be recognised and protected in the Constitution'.

Document 35

Constitutional principles
Schedule 4 of the Interim Constitution
Act 200 of 1993

I

The Constitution of South Africa shall provide for the establishment of one sovereign state, a common South African citizenship and a democratic system of government committed to achieving equality between men and women and people of all races.

II

Everyone shall enjoy all universally accepted fundamental rights, freedoms and civil liberties, which shall be provided for and protected by entrenched and justiciable provisions in the Constitution, which shall be drafted after having given due consideration to inter alia the fundamental rights contained in Chapter 3 of this Constitution.

III

The Constitution shall prohibit racial, gender and all other forms of discrimination and shall promote racial and gender equality and national unity.

IV

The Constitution shall be the supreme law of the land. It shall be binding on all organs of state at all levels of government.

V

The legal system shall ensure the equality of all before the law and an equitable legal process. Equality before the law includes laws, programmes or activities that have as their object the amelioration of the conditions of the disadvantaged, including those disadvantaged on the grounds of race, colour or gender.

VI

There shall be a separation of powers between the legislature, executive and judiciary, with appropriate checks and balances to ensure accountability, responsiveness and openness.

VII

The judiciary shall be appropriately qualified, independent and impartial and shall have the power and jurisdiction to safeguard and enforce the Constitution and all fundamental rights.

VIII

There shall be representative government embracing multi-party democracy, regular elections, universal adult suffrage, a common voters' roll, and, in general, proportional representation.

IX

Provision shall be made for freedom of information so that there can be open and accountable administration at all levels of government.

X

Formal legislative procedures shall be adhered to by legislative organs at all levels of government.

XI

The diversity of language and culture shall be acknowledged and protected, and conditions for their promotion shall be encouraged.

XII

Collective rights of self-determination in forming, joining and maintaining organs of civil society, including linguistic, cultural and religious associations, shall, on the basis of non-discrimination and free association, be recognised and protected.

XIII

1. The institution, status and role of traditional leadership, according to indigenous law, shall be recognised and protected in the Constitution. Indigenous law, like common law, shall be recognised and applied by the courts, subject to the fundamental rights contained in the Constitution and to legislation dealing specifically therewith.

2. Provisions in a provincial constitution relating to the institution, role, authority and status of a traditional monarch shall be recognised and protected in the Constitution.

   [Principle XIII substituted by sec 2 of Act 3 of 1994.]

XIV

Provision shall be made for participation of minority political parties in the legislative process in a manner consistent with democracy.

XV

Amendments to the Constitution shall require special procedures involving special majorities.

XVI

Government shall be structured at national, provincial and local levels.

XVII

At each level of government there shall be democratic representation. This principle shall not derogate from the provisions of Principle XIII.

XVIII

1. The powers and functions of the national government and provincial governments and the boundaries of the provinces shall be defined in the Constitution.

2. The powers and functions of the provinces defined in the Constitution, including the competence of a provincial legislature to adopt a constitution for its province, shall not be substantially less than or substantially inferior to those provided for in this Constitution.

3. The boundaries of the provinces shall be the same as those established in terms of this Constitution.

4. Amendments to the Constitution which alter the powers, boundaries, functions or institutions of provinces shall in addition to any other procedures specified in the Constitution for constitutional amendments, require the approval of a special majority of the legislatures of the provinces, alternatively, if there is such a chamber, a two-thirds majority of a chamber of Parliament composed of provincial representatives, and if the amendment concerns specific provinces only, the approval of the legislatures of such provinces will also be needed.

5. Provision shall be made for obtaining the views of a provincial legislature concerning all constitutional amendments regarding its powers, boundaries and functions.

[Principle XVIII substituted by sec 13(a) of Act 2 of 1994.]

XIX

The powers and functions at the national and provincial levels of government shall include exclusive and concurrent powers as well as the power to perform functions for other levels of government on an agency or delegation basis.

XX

Each level of government shall have appropriate and adequate legislative and executive powers and functions that will enable each level to function effectively. The allocation of powers between different levels of government shall be made on a basis which is conducive to financial viability at each level of government and to effective public administration, and which recognises the need for and promotes national unity and legitimate provincial autonomy and acknowledges cultural diversity.

XXI

The following criteria shall be applied in the allocation of powers to the national government and the provincial governments:

1. The level at which decisions can be taken most effectively in respect of the quality and rendering of services, shall be the level responsible and accountable for the quality and the rendering of the services, and such level shall accordingly be empowered by the Constitution to do so.

2. Where it is necessary for the maintenance of essential national standards, for the establishment of minimum standards required for the rendering of services, the maintenance of economic unity, the maintenance of national security or the prevention of unreasonable action taken by one province which is prejudicial to the interests of another province or the country as a whole, the Constitution shall empower the national government to intervene through legislation or such other steps as may be defined in the Constitution.

3. Where there is necessity for South Africa to speak with one voice, or to act as a single entity – in particular in relation to other states – powers should be allocated to the national government.

4. Where uniformity across the nation is required for a particular

function, the legislative power over that function should be allocated predominantly, if not wholly, to the national government.

5. The determination of national economic policies, and the power to promote inter-provincial commerce and to protect the common market in respect of the mobility of goods, services, capital and labour, should be allocated to the national government.

6. Provincial governments shall have powers, either exclusively or concurrently with the national government, inter alia -
   (a) for the purposes of provincial planning and development and the rendering of services; and
   (b) in respect of aspects of government dealing with specific socio-economic and cultural needs and the general well-being of the inhabitants of the province.

7. Where mutual co-operation is essential or desirable or where it is required to guarantee equality of opportunity or access to a government service, the powers should be allocated concurrently to the national government and the provincial governments.

8. The Constitution shall specify how powers which are not specifically allocated in the Constitution to the national government or to a provincial government, shall be dealt with as necessary ancillary powers pertaining to the powers and functions allocated either to the national government or provincial governments.

XXII

The national government shall not exercise its powers (exclusive or concurrent) so as to encroach upon the geographical, functional or institutional integrity of the provinces.

XXIII

In the event of a dispute concerning the legislative powers allocated by the Constitution concurrently to the national government and provincial governments which cannot be resolved by a court on a construction of the Constitution, precedence shall be given to the legislative powers of the national government.

XXIV

A framework for local government powers, functions and structures shall be set out in the Constitution. The comprehensive powers, functions and other features of local government shall be set out in parliamentary statutes or in provincial legislation or in both.

XXV

The national government and provincial governments shall have fiscal powers and functions which will be defined in the Constitution. The framework for local government referred to in Principle XXIV shall make provision for appropriate fiscal powers and functions for different categories of local government.

XXVI

Each level of government shall have a constitutional right to an equitable share of revenue collected nationally so as to ensure that provinces and local governments are able to provide basic services and execute the functions allocated to them.

XXVII

A Financial and Fiscal Commission, in which each province shall be represented, shall recommend equitable fiscal and financial allocations to the provincial and local governments from revenue collected nationally, after taking into account the national interest, economic disparities between the provinces as well as the population and developmental needs, administrative responsibilities and other legitimate interests of each of the provinces.

XXVIII

Notwithstanding the provisions of Principle XII, the right of employers and employees to join and form employer organisations and trade unions and to engage in collective bargaining shall be recognised and protected. Provision shall be made that every person shall have the right to fair labour practices.

XXIX

The independence and impartiality of a Public Service Commission, a Reserve Bank, an Auditor-General and a Public Protector shall be provided for and safeguarded by the Constitution in the interests of the maintenance of effective public finance and administration and a high standard of professional ethics in the public service.

XXX

1. There shall be an efficient, non-partisan, career-orientated public service broadly representative of the South African community, functioning on a basis of fairness and which shall serve all members of the public in an unbiased and impartial manner, and shall, in the exercise of its powers and in compliance with its duties, loyally execute the lawful policies of the government of the day in the performance of its administrative functions. The structures and functioning of the public service, as well as the terms and conditions of service of its members, shall be regulated by law.

2. Every member of the public service shall be entitled to a fair pension.

XXXI

Every member of the security forces (police, military and intelligence), and the security forces as a whole, shall be required to perform their functions and exercise their powers in the national interest and shall be prohibited from furthering or prejudicing party political interest.

XXXII

The Constitution shall provide that until 30 April 1999 the national executive shall be composed and shall function substantially in the manner provided for in Chapter 6 of this Constitution.

XXXIII

The Constitution shall provide that, unless Parliament is dissolved on account of its passing a vote of no-confidence in the Cabinet, no national election shall be held before 30 April 1999.

XXXIV

1. This Schedule and the recognition therein of the right of the South African people as a whole to self-determination, shall not be construed as precluding, within the framework of the said right, constitutional provision for a notion of the right to self-determination by any community sharing a common cultural and language heritage, whether in a territorial entity within the Republic or in any other recognised way.

2. The Constitution may give expression to any particular form of

self-determination provided there is substantial proven support within the community concerned for such a form of self-determination

3. If a territorial entity referred to in paragraph 1 is established in terms of this Constitution before the new constitutional text is adopted, the new Constitution shall entrench the continuation of such territorial entity, including its structures, powers and functions.

[Principle XXXIV inserted by sec 13(b) of Act 2 of 1994.]

Document 36

Certification of the Constitution of the Republic of South Africa 1996

CCT 23/1996
Constitutional Court
6 September 1996

Since 27 April 1994 South Africa has functioned under an interim constitution, the Constitution of the Republic of South Africa, 1993. The negotiating parties designed the Interim Constitution as a bridge between the old order and the new, to regulate the governance of the country under a government of national unity while a popularly mandated Constitutional Assembly (CA) drafted a new constitution. The Interim Constitution also served to mark out the further transitional steps to be taken.

One of these steps was that the CA had to adopt the new draft constitution within a period of two years and by a majority of at least two-thirds of the CA's members. A second requirement was that the constitutional text had to comply with a set of Constitutional Principles [CPs] agreed to by the negotiating parties and set out in Schedule 4 to the Interim Constitution. A third requirement of the Interim Constitution was that the constitutional text has no legal force unless the Constitutional Court certifies that all the provisions of the text comply with the Constitutional Principles. The Court must determine whether every requirement of the Principles has been satisfied by the provisions of the text and whether any provision in the text conflicts with the CPs. The Court's powers and functions in regard to certification of the text are confined to this determination.

The CA adopted the new constitutional text, the Constitution of the Republic of South Africa 1996, timeously and with the requisite majority. The Chairperson of the CA then transmitted the text to the Court for certification. The CA and all political parties represented in the CA were entitled to present oral argument to the Court. In addition the public at large was invited to submit representations relevant to the question of certification of the text. Many written submissions were received and over a period of nine days the CA, five political parties and certain other bodies and persons who had filed relevant submissions were afforded an opportunity to advance oral argument to the Court.

The Court's judgment is divided into eight chapters, each dealing with a particular main topic under various subheadings. Having sketched the background and context of the certification exercise, the judgment explains the Court's approach to its task and then deals with each identified issue bearing on the question of certification. In the main, these relate to the provisions in the Bill of Rights and their entrenchment; to the separation of powers between the executive, legislative and judicial branches of the state, including the independence of the judiciary; to the relationship between the legislative and executive tiers of government at the national, provincial and local levels, with special reference to the individual and collective powers and functions of the provinces; to the position of traditional leadership and customary law; and to the functions and independence of 'watchdog' institutions of state.

In Chapter III of the judgment the Court deals with a wide variety of questions relating to the Bill of Rights, ranging from 'horizontality', the position of juristic persons and the limitations clause, to labour relations, the property clause, socio-economic rights, language and education, access to information and marriage and family rights.

A major focus of the judgment is on provincial government issues, more specifically whether the constitutional text provides for 'legitimate provincial autonomy' and whether 'the powers and functions of the provinces' under the proposed constitution are 'substantially less than or substantially inferior' to those provinces enjoy under the Interim Constitution. Both issues are directly related to specific requirements of the Constitutional Principles. Chapters V and VII, comprising about half of the judgment, deal with these issues.

The Court's ultimate finding was that the constitutional text cannot be certified as complying fully with the Constitutional Principles. The following instances of non-compliance were identified:

Section 23, which fails to comply with the provisions of CP XXVIII in that the right of individual employers to engage in collective bargaining is not recognised and protected.

Section 241(1), which fails to comply with the provisions of CP IV and CP VII in that it impermissibly shields an ordinary statute from constitutional review.

Schedule 6 s 22(1)(b), which fails to comply with the provisions of CP IV and CP VII in that it impermissibly shields an ordinary statute from constitutional review.

Section 74, which fails to comply with –

CP XV in that amendments of the NT do not require 'special procedures involving special majorities'; and

CP II in that the fundamental rights, freedoms and civil liberties protected in the NT are not 'entrenched'.

Section 194, which fails in respect of the Public Protector and the Auditor-General to comply with CP XXIX in that it does not adequately provide for and safeguard the independence and impartiality of these institutions.

Section 196, which fails to comply with –

CP XXIX in that the independence and impartiality of the PSC [Public Service Commission] is not adequately provided for and safeguarded; and

CP XX in that the failure to specify the powers and functions of the Public Service Commission renders it impossible to certify that legitimate provincial autonomy has been recognised and promoted.

Chapter 7, which fails to comply with –

CP XXIV in that it does not provide a 'framework for the structures' of local government;

CP XXV in that it does not provide for appropriate fiscal powers and functions for local government; and

CP X in that it does not provide for formal legislative procedures to be adhered to by legislatures at local government level.

Section 229, which fails to comply with CP XXV in that it does not provide for 'appropriate fiscal powers and functions for dierent categories of local government'.

To the extent set out in the judgment the provisions relating to the powers and functions of the provinces were held to fail to comply with CP XVIII.2 in that 'such powers and functions are substantially less than and inferior to the powers and functions of the provinces in the IC [Interim Constitution].'

The Court emphasised that the constitutional text represents a monumental achievement. The basic structure of the proposed constitution is sound and the overwhelming majority of the requirements of the Constitutional Principles have been satisfied. The instances of non-compliance that have been identified should present no significant obstacle to the CA in formulating a text which complies fully with those requirements.

Judgment was delivered by the full Court.

Document 37

Rights

7.* (1)   This Bill of Rights is a cornerstone of democracy in South Africa. It enshrines the rights of all people in our country and affirms the democratic values of human dignity, equality and freedom.

   (2)   The state must respect, protect, promote and fulfil the rights in the Bill of Rights.

   (3)   The rights in the Bill of Rights are subject to the limitations contained or referred to in section 36, or elsewhere in the Bill.

Application

8. (1)   The Bill of Rights applies to all law, and binds the legislature, the executive, the judiciary and all organs of state.

   (2)   A provision of the Bill of Rights binds a natural or a juristic person if, and to the extent that, it is applicable, taking into account the nature of the right and the nature of any duty imposed by the right.

   (3)   When applying a provision of the Bill of Rights to a natural or juristic person in terms of subsection (2), a court –

      (a)   in order to give effect to a right in the Bill, must apply,

---

* *The original numbering as it appears in the South African Constitution has been retained here, hence the beginning at Article 7.*

or if necessary develop, the common law to the extent that legislation does not give effect to that right; and

(b)   may develop rules of the common law to limit the right, provided that the limitation is in accordance with section 36(1).

(4)   A juristic person is entitled to the rights in the Bill of Rights to the extent required by the nature of the rights and the nature of that juristic person.

Equality

9. (1)   Everyone is equal before the law and has the right to equal protection and benefit of the law.

(2)   Equality includes the full and equal enjoyment of all rights and freedoms. To promote the achievement of equality, legislative and other measures designed to protect or advance persons, or categories of persons, disadvantaged by unfair discrimination may be taken.

(3)   The state may not unfairly discriminate directly or indirectly against anyone on one or more grounds, including race, gender, sex, pregnancy, marital status, ethnic or social origin, colour, sexual orientation, age, disability, religion, conscience, belief, culture, language and birth.

(4)   No person may unfairly discriminate directly or indirectly against anyone on one or more grounds in terms of subsection (3). National legislation must be enacted to prevent or prohibit unfair discrimination.

(5)   Discrimination on one or more of the grounds listed in subsection (3) is unfair unless it is established that the discrimination is fair.

Human dignity

10. Everyone has inherent dignity and the right to have their dignity respected and protected.

Life

11. Everyone has the right to life.

Freedom and security of the person

12. (1) Everyone has the right to freedom and security of the person, which includes the right –
   (a) not to be deprived of freedom arbitrarily or without just cause;
   (b) not to be detained without trial;
   (c) to be free from all forms of violence from either public or private sources;
   (d) not to be tortured in any way; and
   (e) not to be treated or punished in a cruel, inhuman or degrading way.
   (2) Everyone has the right to bodily and psychological integrity, which includes the right –
   (a) to make decisions concerning reproduction;
   (b) to security in and control over their body; and
   (c) not to be subjected to medical or scientific experiments without their informed consent.

Slavery, servitude and forced labour

13. No one may be subjected to slavery, servitude or forced labour.

Privacy

14. Everyone has the right to privacy, which includes the right not to have –
    (a)   their person or home searched;
    (b)   their property searched;
    (c)   their possessions seized; or
    (d)   the privacy of their communications infringed.

Freedom of religion, belief and opinion

15. (1)   Everyone has the right to freedom of conscience, religion, thought, belief and opinion.
    (2)   Religious observances may be conducted at state or state-aided institutions, provided that –
        (a)   those observances follow rules made by the appropriate public authorities;
        (b)   they are conducted on an equitable basis; and
        (c)   attendance at them is free and voluntary.
    (3)   (a)   This section does not prevent legislation recognising –
            (i)   marriages concluded under any tradition, or a system of religious, personal or family law; or
            (ii)   systems of personal and family law under any tradition, or adhered to by persons professing a particular religion.
        (b)   Recognition in terms of paragraph (a) must be consistent with this section and the other provisions of the Constitution.

Freedom of expression

16. (1)   Everyone has the right to freedom of expression, which includes –

(a)   freedom of the press and other media;

(b)   freedom to receive or impart information or ideas;

(c)   freedom of artistic creativity; and

(d)   academic freedom and freedom of scientific research.

(2)   The right in subsection (1) does not extend to –

(a)   propaganda for war;

(b)   incitement of imminent violence; or

(c)   advocacy of hatred that is based on race, ethnicity, gender or religion, and that constitutes incitement to cause harm.

Assembly, demonstration, picket and petition

17.   Everyone has the right, peacefully and unarmed, to assemble, to demonstrate, to picket and to present petitions.

Freedom of association

18.   Everyone has the right to freedom of association.

Political rights

19.   (1)   Every citizen is free to make political choices, which includes the right –

(a)   to form a political party;

(b)   to participate in the activities of, or recruit members for, a political party; and

(c)   to campaign for a political party or cause.

(2)   Every citizen has the right to free, fair and regular elections for any legislative body established in terms of the Constitution.

(3)   Every adult citizen has the right –

(a)   to vote in elections for any legislative body established in terms of the Constitution, and to do so in secret; and

(b)   to stand for public office and, if elected, to hold office.

Citizenship

20.   No citizen may be deprived of citizenship.

Freedom of movement and residence

21.   (1)   Everyone has the right to freedom of movement.

(2)   Everyone has the right to leave the Republic.

(3)   Every citizen has the right to enter, to remain in and to reside anywhere in, the Republic.

(4)   Every citizen has the right to a passport.

Freedom of trade, occupation and profession

22.   Every citizen has the right to choose their trade, occupation or profession freely. The practice of a trade, occupation or profession may be regulated by law.

Labour relations

23.   (1)   Everyone has the right to fair labour practices.

(2)   Every worker has the right –

(a)   to form and join a trade union;

(b)   to participate in the activities and programmes of a trade union; and

(c)   to strike.

(3)   Every employer has the right –

(a)   to form and join an employers' organisation; and

(b)   to participate in the activities and programmes of an employers' organisation.

(4)   Every trade union and every employers' organisation has the right –

(a)   to determine its own administration, programmes and activities;

(b)   to organise; and

(c)   to form and join a federation.

(5)   Every trade union, employers' organisation and employer has the right to engage in collective bargaining. National legislation may be enacted to regulate collective bargaining. To the extent that the legislation may limit a right in this Chapter, the limitation must comply with section 36(1).

(6)   National legislation may recognise union security arrangements contained in collective agreements. To the extent that the legislation may limit a right in this Chapter, the limitation must comply with section 36(1).

Environment

24.   Everyone has the right –

(a)   to an environment that is not harmful to their health or well-being; and

(b)   to have the environment protected, for the benefit of present and future generations, through reasonable legislative and other measures that –

(i)   prevent pollution and ecological degradation;

(ii)   promote conservation; and

(iii) secure ecologically sustainable development and use of natural resources while promoting justifiable economic and social development.

Property

25. (1) No one may be deprived of property except in terms of law of general application, and no law may permit arbitrary deprivation of property.

    (2) Property may be expropriated only in terms of law of general application –
       (a) for a public purpose or in the public interest; and
       (b) subject to compensation, the amount of which and the time and manner of payment of which have either been agreed to by those affected or decided or approved by a court.

    (3) The amount of the compensation and the time and manner of payment must be just and equitable, reflecting an equitable balance between the public interest and the interests of those affected, having regard to all relevant circumstances, including –
       (a) the current use of the property;
       (b) the history of the acquisition and use of the property;
       (c) the market value of the property;
       (d) the extent of direct state investment and subsidy in the acquisition and beneficial capital improvement of the property; and
       (e) the purpose of the expropriation.

    (4) For the purposes of this section –
       (a) the public interest includes the nation's commitment to land reform, and to reforms to bring about equitable access to all South Africa's natural resources; and
       (b) property is not limited to land.

    (5) The state must take reasonable legislative and other measures, within its available resources, to foster conditions which enable citizens to gain access to land on an equitable basis.

    (6) A person or community whose tenure of land is legally insecure as a result of past racially discriminatory laws or

practices is entitled, to the extent provided by an Act of Parliament, either to tenure which is legally secure or to comparable redress.

(7)   A person or community dispossessed of property after 19 June 1913 as a result of past racially discriminatory laws or practices is entitled, to the extent provided by an Act of Parliament, either to restitution of that property or to equitable redress.

(8)   No provision of this section may impede the state from taking legislative and other measures to achieve land, water and related reform, in order to redress the results of past racial discrimination, provided that any departure from the provisions of this section is in accordance with the provisions of section 36(1).

(9)   Parliament must enact the legislation referred to in subsection (6).

Housing

26. (1)   Everyone has the right to have access to adequate housing.

(2)   The state must take reasonable legislative and other measures, within its available resources, to achieve the progressive realisation of this right.

(3)   No one may be evicted from their home, or have their home demolished, without an order of court made after considering all the relevant circumstances. No legislation may permit arbitrary evictions.

Health care, food, water and social security

27. (1)   Everyone has the right to have access to –

(a)   health care services, including reproductive health care;

      (b)   sufficient food and water; and

      (c)   social security, including, if they are unable to support themselves and their dependants, appropriate social assistance.

  (2)   The state must take reasonable legislative and other measures, within its available resources, to achieve the progressive realisation of each of these rights.

  (3)   No one may be refused emergency medical treatment.

Children

28. (1)   Every child has the right –

      (a)   to a name and a nationality from birth;

      (b)   to family care or parental care, or to appropriate alternative care when removed from the family environment;

      (c)   to basic nutrition, shelter, basic health care services and social services;

      (d)   to be protected from maltreatment, neglect, abuse or degradation;

      (e)   to be protected from exploitative labour practices;

      (f)   not to be required or permitted to perform work or provide services that –

          (i)   are inappropriate for a person of that child's age; or

         (ii)   place at risk the child's well-being, education, physical or mental health or spiritual, moral or social development;

      (g)   not to be detained except as a measure of last resort, in which case, in addition to the rights a child enjoys under sections 12 and 35, the child may be detained only for the shortest appropriate period of time, and has the right to be –

          (i)   kept separately from detained persons over the age of 18 years; and

          (ii)   treated in a manner, and kept in conditions, that take account of the child's age;

    (h)   to have a legal practitioner assigned to the child by the state, and at state expense, in civil proceedings affecting the child, if substantial injustice would otherwise result; and

          (i)   not to be used directly in armed conflict, and to be protected in times of armed conflict.

(2)   A child's best interests are of paramount importance in every matter concerning the child.

(3)   In this section "child" means a person under the age of 18 years.

Education

29. (1) Everyone has the right –

    (a)   to a basic education, including adult basic education; and

    (b)   to further education, which the state, through reasonable measures, must make progressively available and accessible.

(2)   Everyone has the right to receive education in the official language or languages of their choice in public educational institutions where that education is reasonably practicable. In order to ensure the effective access to, and implementation of, this right, the state must consider all reasonable educational alternatives, including single medium institutions, taking into account –

    (a)   equity;

    (b)   practicability; and

    (c)   the need to redress the results of past racially discriminatory laws and practices.

(3)   Everyone has the right to establish and maintain, at their own expense, independent educational institutions that –

(a)   do not discriminate on the basis of race;
(b)   are registered with the state; and
(c)   maintain standards that are not inferior to standards at comparable public educational institutions.
(4)   Subsection (3) does not preclude state subsidies for independent educational institutions.

Language and culture

30.   Everyone has the right to use the language and to participate in the cultural life of their choice, but no one exercising these rights may do so in a manner inconsistent with any provision of the Bill of Rights.

Cultural, religious and linguistic communities

31.   (1)   Persons belonging to a cultural, religious or linguistic community may not be denied the right, with other members of that community –
      (a)   to enjoy their culture, practise their religion and use their language; and
      (b)   to form, join and maintain cultural, religious and linguistic associations and other organs of civil society.
      (2)   The rights in subsection (1) may not be exercised in a manner inconsistent with any provision of the Bill of Rights.

Access to information

32.   (1)   Everyone has the right of access to –
      (a)   any information held by the state; and
      (b)   any information that is held by another person and that is required for the exercise or protection of any rights.

(2)   National legislation must be enacted to give effect to this right, and may provide for reasonable measures to alleviate the administrative and financial burden on the state.

Just administrative action

33. (1)   Everyone has the right to administrative action that is lawful, reasonable and procedurally fair.
    (2)   Everyone whose rights have been adversely affected by administrative action has the right to be given written reasons.
    (3)   National legislation must be enacted to give effect to these rights, and must –
        (a)   provide for the review of administrative action by a court or, where appropriate, an independent and impartial tribunal;
        (b)   impose a duty on the state to give effect to the rights in subsections (1) and (2); and
        (c)   promote an efficient administration.

Access to courts

34.   Everyone has the right to have any dispute that can be resolved by the application of law decided in a fair public hearing before a court or, where appropriate, another independent and impartial tribunal or forum.

Arrested, detained and accused persons

35. (1)   Everyone who is arrested for allegedly committing an offence has the right –
        (a)   to remain silent;
        (b)   to be informed promptly –

        (i)   of the right to remain silent; and

        (ii) of the consequences of not remaining silent;

    (c)   not to be compelled to make any confession or admission that could be used in evidence against that person;

    (d)   to be brought before a court as soon as reasonably possible, but not later than –

        (i)   48 hours after the arrest; or

        (ii) the end of the first court day after the expiry of the 48 hours, if the 48 hours expire outside ordinary court hours or on a day which is not an ordinary court day;

    (e)   at the first court appearance after being arrested, to be charged or to be informed of the reason for the detention to continue, or to be released; and

    (f)   to be released from detention if the interests of justice permit, subject to reasonable conditions.

(2) Everyone who is detained, including every sentenced prisoner, has the right –

    (a)   to be informed promptly of the reason for being detained;

    (b)   to choose, and to consult with, a legal practitioner, and to be informed of this right promptly;

    (c)   to have a legal practitioner assigned to the detained person by the state and at state expense, if substantial injustice would otherwise result, and to be informed of this right promptly;

    (d)   to challenge the lawfulness of the detention in person before a court and, if the detention is unlawful, to be released;

    (e)   to conditions of detention that are consistent with human dignity, including at least exercise and the provision, at state expense, of adequate accommodation, nutrition, reading material and medical treatment; and

    (f)   to communicate with, and be visited by, that person's –

        (i) spouse or partner;

      (ii)   next of kin;

      (iii) chosen religious counsellor; and

      (iv) chosen medical practitioner.

(3)   Every accused person has a right to a fair trial, which includes the right –

     (a)   to be informed of the charge with sufficient detail to answer it;

     (b)   to have adequate time and facilities to prepare a defence;

     (c)   to a public trial before an ordinary court;

     (d)   to have their trial begin and conclude without unreasonable delay;

     (e)   to be present when being tried;

     (f)   to choose, and be represented by, a legal practitioner, and to be informed of this right promptly;

     (g)   to have a legal practitioner assigned to the accused person by the state and at state expense, if substantial injustice would otherwise result, and to be informed of this right promptly;

     (h)   to be presumed innocent, to remain silent, and not to testify during the proceedings;

     (i)   to adduce and challenge evidence;

     (j)   not to be compelled to give self-incriminating evidence;

     (k)   to be tried in a language that the accused person understands or, if that is not practicable, to have the proceedings interpreted in that language;

     (l)   not to be convicted for an act or omission that was not an offence under either national or international law at the time it was committed or omitted;

     (m) not to be tried for an offence in respect of an act or omission for which that person has previously been either acquitted or convicted;

     (n)   to the benefit of the least severe of the prescribed punishments if the prescribed punishment for the offence has been changed between the time that the offence was committed and the time of sentencing; and

  (o) of appeal to, or review by, a higher court.

(4) Whenever this section requires information to be given to a person, that information must be given in a language that the person understands.

(5) Evidence obtained in a manner that violates any right in the Bill of Rights must be excluded if the admission of that evidence would render the trial unfair or otherwise be detrimental to the administration of justice.

Limitation of rights

36. (1) The rights in the Bill of Rights may be limited only in terms of law of general application to the extent that the limitation is reasonable and justifiable in an open and democratic society based on human dignity, equality and freedom, taking into account all relevant factors, including –

  (a) the nature of the right;

  (b) the importance of the purpose of the limitation;

  (c) the nature and extent of the limitation;

  (d) the relation between the limitation and its purpose; and

  (e) less restrictive means to achieve the purpose.

(2) Except as provided in subsection (1) or in any other provision of the Constitution, no law may limit any right entrenched in the Bill of Rights.

States of emergency

37. (1) A state of emergency may be declared only in terms of an
    Act of Parliament, and only when –
    (a) the life of the nation is threatened by war, invasion,
        general insurrection, disorder, natural disaster or other
        public emergency; and
    (b) the declaration is necessary to restore peace and order.
    (2) A declaration of a state of emergency, and any legislation
    enacted or other action taken in consequence of that
    declaration, may be effective only –
    (a) prospectively; and
    (b) for no more than 21 days from the date of the de-
        claration, unless the National Assembly resolves to
        extend the declaration. The Assembly may extend a
        declaration of a state of emergency for no more than
        three months at a time. The first extension of the
        state of emergency must be by a resolution adopted
        with a supporting vote of a majority of the members
        of the Assembly. Any subsequent extension must be
        by a resolution adopted with a supporting vote of at
        least 60 per cent of the members of the Assembly. A
        resolution in terms of this paragraph may be
        adopted only following a public debate in the
        Assembly.
    (3) Any competent court may decide on the validity of –
    (a) a declaration of a state of emergency;
    (b) any extension of a declaration of a state of emergency; or
    (c) any legislation enacted, or other action taken, in
        consequence of a declaration of a state of emergency.
    (4) Any legislation enacted in consequence of a declaration of a
    state of emergency may derogate from the Bill of Rights only
    to the extent that –
    (a) the derogation is strictly required by the emergency;
        and

  (b) the legislation –
    (i) is consistent with the Republic's obligations under international law applicable to states of emergency;
    (ii) conforms to subsection (5); and
    (iii) is published in the national Government Gazette as soon as reasonably possible after being enacted.

 (5) No Act of Parliament that authorises a declaration of a state of emergency, and no legislation enacted or other action taken in consequence of a declaration, may permit or authorise –

  (a) indemnifying the state, or any person, in respect of any unlawful act;
  (b) any derogation from this section; or
  (c) any derogation from a section mentioned in column 1 of the Table of Non-Derogable Rights, to the extent indicated opposite that section in column 3 of the Table.

Table of Non-Derogable Rights

1 Section Number	2 Section Title	3 Extent to which the right is protected
9	Equality	With respect to *unfair discrimination solely on the grounds of* race, colour, ethnic or social origin, sex religion or language
10	Human Dignity	Entirely
11	Life	Entirely

12	Freedom and Security of the person	With respect to subsections (1)(d) and (e) and (2)(c).
13	Slavery, servitude and forced labour	With respect to slavery and servitude
28	Children	With respect to: – subsection (1)(d) and (e); – the rights in subparagraphs (i) and (ii) *of subsection (1)(g); and* – subsection 1(i) in respect of children of 15 years and younger
35	Arrested, detained and accused persons	With respect to: – subsections (1)(a), (b) and (c) and (2)(d); – *the rights in paragraphs (a) to (o) of subsection (3), excluding paragraph (d)* – *subsection (4); and* – *subsection (5) with respect to the exclusion of evidence if the admission of that evidence would render the trial unfair.*

(6) Whenever anyone is detained without trial in consequence of a derogation of rights resulting from a declaration of a state of emergency, the following conditions must be observed:

(a) An adult family member or friend of the detainee must be contacted as soon as reasonably possible, and informed that the person has been detained.

(b) A notice must be published in the national Government Gazette within five days of the person being detained, stating the detainee's name and place of detention and referring to the emergency measure in terms of which that person has been detained.

(c) The detainee must be allowed to choose, and be visited at any reasonable time by, a medical practitioner.

(d) The detainee must be allowed to choose, and be visited at any reasonable time by, a legal representative.

(e) A court must review the detention as soon as reasonably possible, but no later than 10 days after the date the person was detained, and the court must release the detainee unless it is necessary to continue the detention to restore peace and order.

(f) A detainee who is not released in terms of a review under paragraph (e), or who is not released in terms of a review under this paragraph, may apply to a court for a further review of the detention at any time after 10 days have passed since the previous review, and the court must release the detainee unless it is still necessary to continue the detention to restore peace and order.

(g) The detainee must be allowed to appear in person before any court considering the detention, to be represented by a legal practitioner at those hearings, and to make representations against continued detention.

(h) The state must present written reasons to the court to justify the continued detention of the detainee, and must give a copy of those reasons to the detainee at least two days before the court reviews the detention.

(7) If a court releases a detainee, that person may not be detained again on the same grounds unless the state first shows a court good cause for re-detaining that person.

(8) Subsections (6) and (7) do not apply to persons who are not South African citizens and who are detained in consequence of an international armed conflict. Instead, the state must comply with the standards binding on the Republic under international humanitarian law in respect of the detention of such persons.

Enforcement of rights

38. Anyone listed in this section has the right to approach a competent court, alleging that a right in the Bill of Rights has been infringed or threatened, and the court may grant appropriate relief, including a declaration of rights. The persons who may approach a court are:
     (a) Anyone acting in their own interest;
     (b) anyone acting on behalf of another person who cannot act in their own name;
     (c) anyone acting as a member of, or in the interest of, a group or class of persons;
     (d) anyone acting in the public interest; and
     (e) an association acting in the interest of its members.

Interpretation of Bill of Rights

39. (1) When interpreting the Bill of Rights, a court, tribunal or forum –
          (a) must promote the values that underlie an open and democratic society based on human dignity, equality and freedom;
          (b) must consider international law; and
          (c) may consider foreign law.
     (2) When interpreting any legislation, and when developing the common law or customary law, every court, tribunal or forum must promote the spirit, purport and objects of the Bill of Rights.
     (3) The Bill of Rights does not deny the existence of any other rights or freedoms that are recognised or conferred by common law, customary law or legislation, to the extent that they are consistent with the Bill.

Document 38

Certification of the Amended Text of the Constitution of the Republic of South Africa 1996

CCT 37/96
Constitutional Court
4 December 1996

In its earlier decision in Ex parte Chairperson of the Constitutional Assembly: in re Certification of the Constitution of the Republic of South Africa 1996 1996 (4) SA 744 (CC) the Court ruled that a new constitutional text adopted by the Constitutional Assembly in May 1996 could not be certified. The judgment explained the nature, purpose and scope of certification. In essence it is to establish whether a constitutional text complies with a list of Constitutional Principles (the CPs) set out in Schedule 4 of the interim Constitution. The Court identified the features of the new text that did not in its view comply with the CPs and gave its reasons for that view. The Constitutional Assembly then had to reconsider the text, taking the Court's reasons for non-certification into account.

The Constitutional Assembly reconvened and on 11 October 1996 adopted an amended constitutional text (the AT). It contains many changes from the previous text, some dealing with the Court's reasons for non-certification and others tightening up the text. The AT was then sent to the Constitutional Court for essentially the same certification exercise as before. Political parties, the general public and the Constitutional Assembly were again invited to make written representations to the Court. Objectors were free to raise issues not raised before, or to submit that the Court had erred in some or other finding in the previous judgment. Objections to certification were received from the Democratic Party, the Inkatha Freedom Party, the government of KwaZulu-Natal [KZN] and eighteen private individuals or interest groups. Oral argument on behalf of the two political parties, the government of KZN and the Constitutional Assembly was heard on 18 to 20 November 1996.

The Court held that most of the grounds for non-certification of the earlier constitutional text had clearly been eliminated in the AT. The judgment focuses on remaining areas of contention, namely:

The Bill of Rights
Amendments to the Constitution
Local Government
Transitional Provisions
Traditional Monarch
Intervention Permitted by AT 100
Public Protector, Auditor-General and the Public Service Commission
Compliance with CP XVIII.2

The judgment discusses each of these topics in turn and concludes with consideration of whether the powers and functions of the provinces under the AT are substantially less than or substantially inferior to those provided for in the interim constitution, a requirement contained in CP XVIII.2.

Four objections are discussed in relation to the Bill of Rights. First, the Court rejected a contention that the right to choose a trade, occupation or profession is a universally accepted fundamental right that cannot be afforded to citizens only. Second, the Court rejected a submission that the AT fails to recognise and protect collective rights of self-determination sufficiently. The institutional structures of the AT, the protection of associational rights and the procedural provisions for their enforcement are adequate. Third, the exclusion of certain rights from those made non-derogable under a state of emergency did not, according the Court, constitute grounds for non-certification. Fourth, the Court rejected the contention that AT 203 in effect provides for a declaration of martial law.

As regards amendments to the Constitution the Court concluded that the provisions of the AT dealing with special procedures and special majorities for amendments to the Constitution and for entrenchment of the Bill of Rights are adequate.

As regards Local Government the Court dismissed objections to new features of the AT, holding that the AT had remedied the shortcomings expressed in the Court's earlier finding that the NT failed to provide a framework for the structures of local government in accordance with CP XXIV.

The Court further dismissed objections to two provisions of AT Sch 6 in relation to transitional provisions.

On the issue of the traditional monarch, the Court rejected an objection that the AT failed to afford protection to provisions in a provincial constitution relating to the institution, role, authority and status of the traditional monarch.

In the chapter dealing with the intervention permitted by AT 100 the Court held that there was no substance in the contention that the provisions of AT 100(1)(b) violate the principle of separation of powers and held that the provision for intervention by the national government in provincial government complies with CP XX1.2.

The Court thereafter noted the enhancement of the independence of the Public Protector and Auditor-General wrought by the AT and confirmed the adequacy of these amendments. The analysis focuses on the AT provisions dealing with the Public Service Commission, which strengthen the protection of the Commission to an extent compatible with the demands of CP XXIX.

A substantial portion of the judgment is devoted to an assessment of the extent to which the AT complies with the requirements of CP XVIII.2. The conclusion is that although the powers and functions of the provinces under the AT are still less than or inferior to those accorded by the interim Constitution, the disparity is not substantial.

The order of the Court reads as follows:

'We certify that all provisions of the amended constitutional text, the Constitution of the Republic of South Africa, 1996, passed by the Constitutional Assembly on 11 October 1996, comply with the Constitutional Principles contained in schedule 4 to the Constitution of the Republic of South Africa, 1993'.

Judgment was delivered by the full Court.

Chronology

31 May 1902

THE PEACE TREATY OF VEREENIGING ends the Anglo-Boer War that began in 1899. The Treaty is signed between Boer and British leaders.

12 October 1908

The first NATIONAL CONVENTION representing the exclusive interests of whites sits to negotiate South Africa's first constitution.

19 August 1909

THE SOUTH AFRICA ACT, South Africa's first constitution, is passed by the British House of Commons despite petitions and protests from the African majority.

31 May 1910

THE UNION OF SOUTH AFRICA is inaugurated. This marks the political disenfranchisement of the African majority.

8 January 1912

The AFRICAN NATIONAL CONGRESS (ANC) is formed.

December 1928

THE 'NATIVE REPUBLIC': the seeds of the concept of black majority rule are sown with this rallying call by the South African Communist Party (SACP).

August 1941

The ATLANTIC CHARTER is signed by Franklin D. Roosevelt and Winston Churchill. This Charter laid the basis for a bill of rights in South Africa.

16 December 1943

AFRICAN CLAIMS: the ANC's model for a bill of rights fashioned on the Atlantic Charter. (Schedule of Documents, Document 6)

26 June 1955

The Congress of the People adopts the FREEDOM CHARTER. (Schedule of Documents, Document 7)

28 May 1957

ALBERT J. LUTHULI WRITES TO J. G. STRIJDOM, South Africa's Prime Minister, pleading for the establishment of a non-racial convention. (Schedule of Documents, Document 8)

16 December 1960

The CONSULTATIVE CONFERENCE OF AFRICAN LEADERS is held in Orlando, Soweto. This Conference makes a call to all African people to attend an All-In Conference, the purpose of which would be to demand a National Convention representing all the people of South Africa.

25–26 March 1961

The ALL-IN AFRICAN CONFERENCE is held in Pietermaritzburg, Natal. This Conference resolves:

'1. WE DECLARE that no constitution or form of government decided without the participation of the African people who form an absolute majority of the population can enjoy moral validity or merit support either within South Africa or beyond its borders. 2. WE DEMAND that a NATIONAL CONVENTION of elected representatives of all adult men and women on an equal basis irrespective of race, colour, creed or other limitation, be called by the Union government no later than 31 May 1961; that the convention shall have sovereign powers to determine, in any way the majority of the representatives decide, a new non-racial democratic constitution for South Africa.'

20 April 1961

NELSON MANDELA WRITES TO H. F. VERWOERD, referring to the rising tide of unrest in many parts of the country. In his letter Mandela states that he was directed to write that 'It was the earnest opinion of Conference that this dangerous situation could be averted only by the calling of a sovereign national convention representative of all South Africans, to draw up a new non-racial and democratic Constitution.' (Schedule of Documents, Document 9)

31 April 1961

South Africa is declared a REPUBLIC.

16 June 1976

Uprisings (known as the 16 JUNE UPRISINGS) by pupils protesting against the imposition of Afrikaans as a medium of teaching in schools.

November 1985

MANDELA WRITES TO HIS PRISON WARDEN. His request for a meeting with the government would be positively received.

1 April 1989

UNITED NATIONS RESOLUTION 435 OF 1978 is implemented, beginning Namibia's transition to independence.

5 July 1989

NELSON MANDELA MEETS WITH P. W. BOTHA. In a document prepared for this meeting (Schedule of Documents, Document 12), Mandela states that 'I now consider it necessary in the national interest for the African National Congress and the government to meet urgently to negotiate an effective political settlement.'

21 August 1989

The ANC's HARARE DECLARATION (Schedule of Documents, Document 13) is adopted by the Organization of African Unity (OAU).

September 1989

A DEFIANCE CAMPAIGN AND MARCHES are organized by structures of the Mass Democratic Movement in the United Democratic Front.

15 October 1989

Several ANC LEADERS ARE RELEASED from prison.

8 December 1989

The CONFERENCE FOR A DEMOCRATIC FUTURE takes place, a meeting of 6000 representatives of the Mass Democratic Movement, and passes a resolution in favour of negotiation. (Schedule of Documents, Document 14)

12 December 1989

NELSON MANDELA WRITES HIS FIRST LETTER TO F. W. DE KLERK after a meeting with Ministers Kobie Coetsee and Gerrit Viljoen. Once again, Mandela warns of an urgent need for negotiations to take place (Schedule of Documents, Document 15). The ANC's National Executive Committee (NEC) meets in Lusaka and resolves to consider the option of a negotiated settlement.

2 February 1990

F. W. DE KLERK delivers a speech at the opening of Parliament announcing the UNBANNING OF THE ANC, THE SACP, AND OTHER LIBERATION MOVEMENTS. (Schedule of Documents, Document 16)

12 February 1990

NELSON MANDELA IS RELEASED from prison.

27 April 1990

The first group of ANC LEADERS returns to South Africa from exile.

2–4 May 1990

THE GROOTE SCHUUR ACCORD (Schedule of Documents, Document 17): the NP and the ANC agree on a common commitment to the resolution of the existing climate of violence and intimidation as well as a commitment to a process of negotiations. Temporary immunity is granted to members of the NEC and other specific members of the ANC. The NP undertakes to review security legislation, to work towards lifting the state of emergency, and to establish channels of communication between themselves and the ANC.

6 August 1990

THE PRETORIA MINUTE (Schedule of Documents, Document 18): the NP and the ANC agree that further releases of political prisoners will start on 1 September 1990; indemnity will be granted to persons as of 1 October 1990. The ANC unilaterally agrees to suspend all armed actions 'In the interest of moving as speedily as possible towards a negotiated peaceful political settlement'. Finally, the two parties agree that 'the way is now open to proceed towards negotiations on a new constitution'.

12 February 1991

THE D. F. MALAN ACCORD (Schedule of Documents, Document 19): the ANC's undertaking to suspend all armed action is further defined to mean that there will be no armed attacks, or threats of attacks, infiltration of personnel and material, creation of underground structures, statements inciting violence, and training inside South Africa. It is further agreed that: membership to Umkhonto we Sizwe (MK), the ANC's military wing, will not be unlawful; individual weapons will be licensed in terms of existing legislation; and the right to peaceful demonstrations will be maintained.

June 1991

The 'Inkathagate Scandal' and revelations about SADF involvement in death squads and the ongoing violence emerge. In response, the ANC suspends all bilateral meetings with the regime.

31 July 1991

An ANC National Executive Committee meeting demands the installation of an Interim Government. The ANC's National Working Committee (NWC) is instructed to begin laying the basis for the convening of the All Party Congress (APC).

August 1991

The NWC establishes the NEGOTIATIONS COMMISSION as a sub-committee.

14 September 1991

THE NATIONAL PEACE ACCORD is signed. This is the first multi-party agreement.

25 September 1991

IDEAS ON INTERIM GOVERNMENT are developed. The ANC's Negotiations Commission holds a workshop to develop its position on an interim government.

October 1991

THE PROCESS OF MULTI-PARTY NEGOTIATIONS IS INITIATED: the NWC instructs the Negotiations Commission to arrange bilateral talks with all other parties about the convening of the APC. Bilateral discussions are then initiated with, *inter alia*, the National Party (NP), the Labour Party, the Inkatha Freedom Party (IFP), parties operating in the homelands, and the governments of Venda and the Transkei. Bilateral meetings take place between the ANC and the NP government on 17, 24, and 31 October.

25–27 October 1991

THE PATRIOTIC FRONT (PF), a loose alliance of parties which have held an anti-apartheid position, is launched. The PF Conference agrees on a joint programme for the negotiated transfer of power. It is agreed that: only a constituent assembly elected on the basis of one-person-one-vote in a united South Africa could draft and adopt a democratic constitution; a sovereign interim government will be established, which should at the very least control security forces and related matters, the electoral process, state media, and defined areas of budget and finance, as well as secure international participation; the APC should be held as soon as possible.

2–12 November 1991

The ANC prepares for the ALL-PARTY CONGRESS (APC). Towards this end, the ANC consults with the Pan-Africanist Congress (PAC), the Azanian Peoples Organization (AZAPO), the Democratic Party (DP), homeland leaders, Mass Democratic Movement (MDM) organizations, religious leaders, and the National Party government. Broad agreement is reached. The first meeting of the APC is scheduled for 29 and 30 November 1991; its agenda includes: a climate for free political participation; general constitutional principles; a constitution-making body; interim government; the future of TBVC (Transkei, Bophuthatswana, Venda, Ciskei) states; the role of the international community, if any; and time frames.

15 November 1991

The first SCHEDULED APC CANNOT TAKE PLACE: the preparatory meeting for the APC scheduled for 15 November does not go ahead. The IFP insists that this meeting only be attended by the NP, the IFP, and the ANC. The ANC proposes that all parties be allowed to attend. This meeting is postponed to 20 November.

20 November 1991

The scheduled APC PREPARATORY MEETING IS AGAIN POSTPONED, this time to 29 November. The IFP is opposed to the convenors of the APC including two religious leaders, Johan Heyns and Stanley Mogoba; the IFP wants the Chief Justice to convene this meeting on his own.

29–30 November 1991

The ALL-PARTY PREPARATORY MEETING takes place. Twenty organizations and parties attend. It is decided that the name of the APC be The Convention for a Democratic South Africa (CODESA). It is agreed that the first meeting of CODESA will take place on 20 and 21 December 1991. For instances in which consensus fails to emerge, the principle of 'sufficient consensus' as a decision-making mechanism is agreed to. The PAC walks out of CODESA ten minutes before the end of the meeting, accusing the ANC of 'selling out'.

20–21 December 1991

The first meeting of CODESA takes place. The meeting adopts a DECLARATION OF INTENT (Schedule of Documents, Document 22). All parties with the exception of the IFP and the Bophuthatswana government sign the Declaration. The NP apologizes officially for the policy of apartheid and confirms for the first time that the party is prepared to accept an elected constituent assembly provided that it also acts as an interim government. Nelson Mandela also launches his fiercest public attack on F. W. de Klerk.

February 1992
THE NP ACCEPTS THE ANC'S DEMAND FOR AN INTERIM GOVERNMENT and the principles that a new South Africa be non-racial, non-sexist, and democratic. Working Group 2 produces an initial agreement on general constitutional principles. The regime, however, remains insistent that Umkhonto we Sizwe (MK) be disbanded. The ANC's position is that only an interim government can decide the fate of MK.

17 March 1992
An ALL-WHITE REFERENDUM is held. The NP government receives overwhelming support for reform.

March 1992
The ANC SUBMITS PROPOSALS FOR A TWO-PHASED INTERIM GOVERNMENT. Phase 1 should see the appointment by CODESA of an Interim Government Council to oversee the activities of the present government. Multi-party committees should take control of key functions such as law and order, defence, finance, and foreign affairs. Phase 2 (after elections) would then see the establishment of the constituent assembly and the interim government.

23 March 1992
The ANC tables proposals for an INTERIM MEDIA STRUCTURE. The proposals argue that the media has a central role to play in levelling the political playing field. It is proposed, therefore, that an Independent Media Commission be established.

7 April 1992
INITIAL AGREEMENTS emerge. Negotiations produce initial agreement that interim government should take place in two stages: the first stage would consist of the formation of a Transitional Executive Council (TEC); the second stage would commence after the elections and consist of the interim government and constituent assembly. The TEC would be multi-party in form and would function alongside the existing tricameral parliament. Multi-party sub-committees of the TEC with executive powers would be established for key areas of government.

27 April 1992
A special sub-committee recommends special, but not equal, participation by TRADITIONAL LEADERS IN THE NEGOTIATIONS.

4 May 1992
On the question of reincorporation, the CODESA task group dealing with reincorporation recommends unanimously that the TBVC STATES SHOULD BE REINCORPORATED into

South Africa provided that the will of those states is tested in the up-coming non-racial elections.

May 1992 (first week)

PARTIES PREPARE FOR CODESA II (CODESA's second plenary session) to take place on 15 and 16 May. Many issues still remain unresolved. The ANC hopes to achieve agreement at CODESA II on a two-phased interim government.

15–16 May 1992

CODESA II DEADLOCKS on the question of a constitution-making body. Technically, the deadlock manifests itself around the question of the special majorities required to adopt a final constitution. After consultations with other members of the Patriotic Front, the ANC puts forward a compromise proposal .

26 May 1992

The ANC holds its NATIONAL NEGOTIATIONS CONSULTATIVE FORUM. This meeting confirms the withdrawal of the ANC compromise position.

28–31 May 1992

The ANC HOLDS ITS NATIONAL POLICY CONFERENCE. The Conference provides guidelines for the transfer of power to the majority leading to the transformation of society. The Conference insists on various conditions before an election and a single-chambered Constitutional Assembly

allowing for a two-thirds majority for decision-making. It also asks for the drafting of a 'Transition to Democracy Act' as the transitional constitution.

17 June 1992

A massacre of more than forty people occurs at BOIPATONG.

23 June 1992

BILATERAL AND MULTILATERAL NEGOTIATIONS ARE BROKEN OFF. The ANC's National Executive Committee holds an emergency meeting to discuss the implications of the massacre. While it reaffirms its commitment to a negotiated settlement, it also resolves to break off all negotiations (both bilateral, with the NP government, and multilateral), makes fourteen demands, and accuses the regime of complicity in the violence.

26 June 1992

The ANC sets out its demands in a memorandum to F. W. de Klerk. (Schedule of Documents, Document 23)

2 July 1992

DE KLERK RESPONDS to the ANC's memorandum (Schedule of Documents, Document 24), denying government complicity in the violence and refusing to commit the government to the principle of majority rule. Nevertheless, the NP disbands Battalions 31 and 32, and Koevoet; refers the future of hostels to the

Goldstone Commission; issues a proclamation banning dangerous weapons; and agrees to international monitoring of the violence.

15–16 July 1992

In the announcement of an UNPRE-CEDENTED MASS ACTION campaign, the Tripartite Alliance (the ANC, the SACP, and the Congress of South African Trade Unions) commits itself to a month of rolling mass action in support of its demands.

2 August 1992

The UNITED NATIONS SECURITY COUNCIL holds a special session to debate the violence in South Africa. The UN adopts special resolution 765 calling for a special representative of the Secretary General, Cyrus Vance, to visit South Africa.

August 1992

The UNITED NATIONS MONITORING COMMITTEE arrives in South Africa to monitor the ANC's Mass Action Campaign. They attend various marches and demonstrations. Vance meets Pik Botha and voices concern over political prisoners, asking for their release. Botha responds by linking this to the question of a general amnesty, the abandonment of armed struggle, MK arms caches and ANC underground units.

31 August–2 September 1992

Towards the ESTABLISHMENT OF A CHANNEL OF COMMUNICATION, the National Working Committee of the ANC chooses its Secretary General as a channel of communication between the ANC and the regime. This 'channel' of communication replaces the official bilateral meetings and is meant to enable necessary communication between the ANC and the NP to continue.

26 September 1992

At a summit between the regime and the ANC a RECORD OF UNDERSTAND-ING is agreed to. This Record of Understanding deals with agreements relating to the Constitutional Assembly, interim government, political prisoners, problematic hostels, dangerous weapons, and mass action. (Schedule of Documents, Document 27)

29 September 1992

MASSACRES OCCUR AT BISHO where many protesters opposing the government of Ciskei are killed when soldiers open fire.

23, 25 November 1992

The ANC and the NP come to an AGREEMENT TO RESUME BILATERAL NEGOTIATIONS. As part of the process of resuming negotiations, the ANC embarks on a series of meetings with various parties. The ANC meets with the members of the Tripartite Alliance, the Patriotic Front, the DP, and the Afrikaner Volksunie (AVU). The National Executive Committee of the ANC meets at a special session focusing on negotiations and the need to curb violence. This meeting adopts a position paper on strategic perspectives (Schedule of Documents, Document 28), signalling the ANC's willingness to make compromises.

5 December 1992

PARTIES HOLD 'BOSBERAADS' (secluded meetings). The first of a two-part bilateral is held between the ANC and the NP regime. The first part deals with matters relating to security and violence, and the second part to elections, media, regional and local government, TBVC states, and the transitional constitution. The second part of the bilateral with the NP takes place between 20 January and 4 February 1993. The discussions are divided into two parts. It is agreed to propose to each of the principals that a multi-party negotiation planning conference be held in March. The purpose of this conference would be to plan the resumption of multilateral negotiations.

16, 18 February 1993

The ANC's National Executive Committee (NEC) meets and adopts a RESOLUTION ON NEGOTIATIONS AND NATIONAL RECONSTRUCTION. The NEC also endorses proposals for the holding of a multi-party negotiation planning conference on 5 and 6 March with a view to the resumption of multi-party negotiations.

4–5 March 1993

The NEGOTIATIONS PLANNING CONFERENCE is held at the World Trade Centre in Kempton Park, Johannesburg. Twenty-six parties, administration, organizations, and traditional leaders attend. A resolution calling for the resumption of negotiations is adopted (Schedule of Documents, Document 29). It is agreed that a multi-party negotiating forum will take place on 1 and 2 April 1993. The purpose of this meeting is to chart the path of the multi-party negotiations.

27–28 March 1993

THE PATRIOTIC FRONT MEETS. This meeting serves to secure consultations with all structures of the Mass Democratic Movement in developing a common perspective on the way forward. A resolution is adopted accordingly. The PAC and AZAPO refuse to attend this meeting.

1 April 1993

THE MULTI-PARTY NEGOTIATING FORUM MEETS. Twenty-six participants meet including the PAC, the Conservative Party (CP), and the Afrikaner Volksunie (AVU). The success of this meeting is reflected in the fact that it is able to complete two days of scheduled work in one. The meeting defines the issues to be dealt with at the multi-party negotiations.

10 April 1993

CHRIS HANI is assassinated.

22 April 1993

The TRIPARTITE ALLIANCE meets and resolves to make the following demands: that there be an immediate announcement of a election date; that the Transitional Executive Council (TEC) be installed as a matter of urgency; and that all armed formations be placed under immediate joint multi-party control. The ANC also calls for the negotiations to be speeded up.

26 April 1993

The FIRST PLANNING COMMITTEE OF THE MULTI-PARTY NEGOTIATIONS PROCESS meets and prepares a report relating to all agreements and discussions of CODESA.

30 April 1993

TECHNICAL COMMITTEES are formed: the report of the Planning Committee contains proposals on violence, the Independent Electoral Commission, state and statutorily controlled media, repressive and discriminatory legislation, and the TEC and its sub-councils. The Negotiating Council resolves to establish six Technical Committees to consider the various issues. The Technical Committees are composed of six people each, none of whom are representative of any political organizations or parties. This marks a change from the style of negotiations adopted during the CODESA period.

18 May 1993

The NEGOTIATING COUNCIL considers a further report by the Planning Committee. The report proposes the establishment of two further Technical Committees. The Planning Committee also approves a draft resolution to be adopted noting an urgent need to inspire confidence in the negotiating process and the ability to resolve problems peacefully. Accordingly, the resolution commits parties to ensuring that the negotiating process makes progress such that an election date is set within the following five weeks; also, that the election should take place no later than the end of April 1994.

1 June 1993

The NEGOTIATING COUNCIL agrees that sufficient progress has been made to enable it to agree to 27 APRIL 1994 as the date for South Africa's first ever non-racial elections. The Council instructs the Technical Committee on Constitutional Matters to draft a transitional constitution that will lead to the drafting and adoption of a final, democratic constitution by an elected Constitutional Assembly.

15 June 1993

The entire CONCERNED SOUTH AFRICANS GROUP (COSAG) STAGES A WALKOUT from the Negotiating Council, only to return to the next meeting of the Negotiating Council. The IFP submits a resolution calling on the Council not to consider any of the constitutional principles recommended by the Technical Committee, and to consider proposals for a federal constitution. This is rejected in a vote. The PAC abstains from this vote. Parties have been given the opportunity until this day to secure greater consensus for the resolution calling for an election for 27 April 1994. The resolution is accordingly confirmed.

22 June 1993

The Negotiating Council unanimously adopts a resolution constituting a DECLARATION ON THE SUSPENSION OF HOSTILITIES, ARMED STRUGGLE, AND VIOLENCE.

The Negotiating Council accepts the recommendations made by the Technical Committee on Violence and passes a resolution in terms thereof. IN A RESOLUTION ON THE INDEPENDENT ELECTORAL COM-MISSION AND THE INDEPENDENT MEDIA COMMISSION, the Negotiating Council calls for the establishment of these Commissions.

23 June 1993

After several months of preparation a SUMMIT BETWEEN NELSON MANDELA AND MANGOSUTHU BUTHELEZI of the IFP takes place. A joint undertaking that would pave the way for free political activity, joint rallies, agreement on the strengthening of the Peace Accord, and greater liaison between the ANC and the IFP in negotiations arises from this meeting.

2 July 1993

THE NEGOTIATING FORUM MEETS at last, vindicating the calls made in the Harare Declaration. Agreement is reached at this meeting on the following steps towards a new constitution: (1) the Multi-Party Negotiating Process (MPNP) shall adopt constitutional principles providing for both strong regional government and strong national government; (2) these constitutional principles shall be binding on the constituent assembly and shall be justiciable by a constitutional court; (3) a Commission on Delimitation/Demarcation will make recommendations on regional boundaries for the purposes of elections and regional government during the transitional period; (4) the MPNP shall agree on legislation to make provision for the levelling of the playing field and promoting conditions conducive to the holding of free and fair elections; (5) the MPNP shall agree on details of discriminatory legislation to be repealed; (6) the MPNP shall agree on a transitional constitution (i.e., a Transition to Democracy Act).

26 July 1993

The Technical Committee on Constitutional Matters produces its DRAFT OUTLINE OF A TRANSITIONAL CONSTITUTION for discussion by the

Negotiating Council.

31 July 1993

The COMMISSION FOR DELIMITATION OF REGIONS tables its report for discussion in the Negotiating Council on 2 August 1993. This report contains various criteria on the basis of which it recommends nine regions: Northern Transvaal, PWV (Pretoria, Witwatersrand, Vereeniging), Eastern Transvaal, KwaZulu/Natal, Orange Free State, Northwest Transvaal, Northern Cape, Western Cape, and Eastern Cape/Kei.

25 August 1993

The Technical Committee dealing with the TEC DRAFT BILL tables its eleventh working draft for discussion in the Negotiating Council.

25–28 October 1993

In a BILATERAL BETWEEN THE ANC AND THE NP to finalize agreements on the interim constitution, agreement is reached on a Government of National Unity, a provision agreeing to two deputy presidents, the required percentage to elect a deputy president, and the right to membership in the cabinet. The NP abandons its claim to a veto over decisions of cabinet.

16 November 1993

In a last-minute bilateral between Nelson Mandela and F. W. de Klerk, agreement is reached on the final issues required to complete the interim constitution. The agreements reached come to be known as the 'SIX-PACK' AGREEMENT.

18 November 1993

The ratification of the Interim Constitution by the plenary of the MPNP comes in the early hours of the morning of 18 November 1993.

January 1994

The TRANSITIONAL EXECUTIVE COUNCIL is established.

1 March 1994

The ANC AGREES TO INTERNATIONAL MEDIATION. This agreement is reached with Nelson Mandela and Mangosuthu Buthelezi on condition that the latter agrees to provisionally register the Inkatha Freedom Party for the elections. Before the international mediators can begin, however, disagreement wrecks the initiative.

March 1994

CISKEI AND BOPHUTHATSWANA COLLAPSE under the pressure of internal discontent and are reincorporated into South Africa.

27–18 April 1994

South Africa's first ever non-racial, democratic election takes place.

9 May 1994

The CONSTITUTIONAL ASSEMBLY is established, made up of 490 elected members.

August 1994

CONSTITUTIONAL ASSEMBLY ADMINIS-
TRATION is established to support and
facilitate the process of negotiation.

June 1994

The CONSTITUTIONAL COMMITTEE is
established. This becomes the premier multi-party negotiating body in
the Constitutional Assembly.

September 1994

Six THEME COMMITTEES are established to receive and collate the views of
all parties on the substance of the
constitution.

January 1995

An ADVERTISING CAMPAIGN inviting
public views on the constitution is
launched.

19 September 1995

The first consolidated DRAFT OF THE
CONSTITUTION is produced.

November 1995

The first REFINED WORKING DRAFT
of the constitution is published. This
provides the public with its first
glimpse of what the complete text
will look like.

15 February 1996

SIXTY-EIGHT OUTSTANDING ISSUES
require settlement before the constitution is complete.

14 March 1996

FIVE DEADLOCK ISSUES require agreement: the death penalty, the lockout
clause, the clause on education, the
appointment of judges, and the Attorney General.

20 March 1996

CONCERN ABOUT COMPLETING THE
CONSTITUTION in time is mounting.
The fourth edition of the working
draft is produced, and many issues
remain unresolved. It is uncertain
whether the Constitutional Assembly
will be able to complete its work by
8 May 1996, its deadline.

1–3 April 1996

The ARNISTON MULTILATERAL is
held. This multilateral turns out to
be vital in ensuring that parties
resolve their differences without the
glare of the media. It is extremely
successful.

16 April 1996

The CHANNEL BILATERAL between
Cyril Ramaphosa and Roelf Meyer is
reinstated to find solutions to differences between the ANC and the NP.

22 April 1996

SEVERAL ISSUES REMAIN DEAD-
LOCKED and require agreement: the
death penalty, the lockout clause, the
property clause, the appointment of
judges and the Attorney General,
language, local government, the
question of proportional representation, and the bar against members
of parliament crossing the floor.

23 April 1996

THE DRAFT CONSTITUTION IS TABLED.

The plenary debate to finalize the constitution begins without key outstanding issues being resolved.

25 April 1996

Negotiators table 298 amendments to the final draft text. However, most amendments are of a technical rather than substantial nature.

8 May 1996

THE FINAL TEXT OF THE CONSTITUTION IS ADOPTED.

1 July 1996

THE CONSTITUTIONAL COURT'S HEARING ON CERTIFICATION begins.

6 September 1996

THE CONSTITUTIONAL COURT REFUSES TO CERTIFY THE TEXT. The Court finds that the text does not comply with the required constitutional principles in eight respects. (Schedule of Documents, Document 36)

11 October 1996

The AMENDED TEXT OF THE CONSTITUTION IS ADOPTED by the Constitutional Assembly and tabled with the Constitutional Court.

18 November 1996

THE CONSTITUTIONAL COURT'S SECOND HEARING on certification begins.

4 December 1996

THE CONSTITUTIONAL COURT CERTIFIES THE FINAL TEXT of the constitution. (Schedule of Documents, Document 38)

10 December 1996

THE PRESIDENT, NELSON MANDELA, SIGNS THE FINAL CONSTITUTION INTO LAW in Sharpeville, Vereeniging. This date also marks International Human Rights Day. The Constitution is to come into effect on 4 February 1997.

17–21 March 1997

This week is named NATIONAL CONSTITUTION WEEK. More than seven million copies of the Constitution are distributed in all eleven languages in a national campaign. This campaign culminates in activities on 21 March 1997, South Africa's national Human Rights Day.

30 April 1997

The CONSTITUTIONAL ASSEMBLY CLOSES ITS ADMINISTRATION after accounting for all moneys spent.

Index

Every effort has been made to check the spelling of names of members of committees within the Constitutional Assembly. However, many of the names listed in the notes to chapters nine and ten (pp. 322–343) have been taken directly from the Assembly's registers, where the spelling of entries may have varied from time to time. In such cases all given versions have been included in the index.

Numbers in italics refer to photographs.

South African Defence Force (*continued*)
  Cuito Caunavale defeat, 20
  involvement in political violence accusation, 79
South African Indian Congress, 16
South African Native Congress (1907), 7
South African Native Convention (24 March 1909), resolution, 264
South African Property Owners' Association, 197
South African Youth Congress, 281
Soviet Union, 101, 305
Spaarwater, Maritz, 63
Sparg, Marion, 351
Stals, Chris, 153
state of emergency clause, 228, 647–50
Steenkamp, P. J., 335, 337
Stephen, Sir Ninian, 304
Steyn, Justice, 71
Steytler, N., 337
stock limitation laws, 14
street committees, 19, 67
Streicher, D. M., 337
Strydom, Barend, 291
'sufficient consensus' principle, 98, 303
Sulliman, M. A., 338
'sunset clauses,' 116–17, 142
Suppression of Communism Act, 14
Surty, M. E., 335, 339
Suttner, R. S., 335
Suzman, Helen, 103
Swanepoel, L. J., 335, 337

T

Taft, Noël, 340, *6*
'talks about talks,' 34, 83
Tambo, Oliver, 31–2, 269–70
  alleged crimes, 319
  communication lines with Mandela, 34
  Operation Vula, 59
  seizes negotiation initiative, 34
Tanzania
  communiqué to PAC, 99
  public administration experts, 341
Tarr, Mike, 109
Taunyane, D. P., 337
TBVC states (Transkei, Bophuthatswana, Venda, Ciskei), reincorporation, 72, 147
TEC. *See* Transitional Executive Council (TEC)
Technical Committee on Constitutional Matters, 156, 159, 328
Technical Committees, 182
Ten Proposed Regions for a United South Africa, 121
tensions in negotiation final stages, 203, 206, 212, 215, 349, *34*
Terre'Blanche, Eugene, 52
Thabethe, E., 339
Thatcher, Margaret, 24
  opposition to international sanctions, 30
Theme Committees, 182–3, 185–6, 336, 338–43, *6*
'third force' violence, 63–4, 69, 73, 75, 144, 284
Thobeka, V. M., 339
Thomas, Beverline, 338, 340
Thompson, B., 339
Tickell, Sir Crispin, 36
Titus, M., 323
Titus, Zamindlela, 307, 323–4
Tolo, L. J., 337
trade union movement, 383–4
traditional leaders
  concerns about constitution draft, 198, 338
  representation at CODESA meetings, 105, 110
'Transition to Democracy Act' proposal, 137